"Timely, fascinating and important."

—Evaggelos Vallianatos, *Huffington Post*

"One of my few heroes. As long as people like Varoufakis are around, there still is hope."

—Slavoj Žižek

"Varoufakis has written one of the greatest political memoirs of all time . . . It is the inside story of high politics told by an outsider . . . Varoufakis gives one of the most accurate and detailed descriptions of modern power ever written."

—Paul Mason, *The Guardian*

"A stylish memoir . . . Deeply personal and very well written, with an impressive array of literary allusions . . . [Varoufakis] outlines a cogent case against the austerity heaped on Greece."

—Kevin Featherstone, *Financial Times*

"Riveting . . . An extraordinary account of low cunning at the heart of Greece's 2015 financial bailout . . . [Varoufakis is] a motorcycling, leather-jacketed former academic and self-styled rebel who took pleasure in winding up the besuited political class . . . An admirably believable depiction of a Greek and European tragedy."

—John Kampfner, *The Guardian*

"*Adults in the Room* is a book that anyone interested in modern European politics should read. To say it is the best memoir of the Eurozone crisis is an understatement. It is a devastating indictment of [the] current state of Europe and a fascinating inside account of the logic of reformist politics and its limits and why it keeps going anyway . . . Varoufakis's account of the operations of EU 'decision-making' is truly shocking. He delivers a truly shocking anatomy of an apparatus bent on perpetuating its own bad logic and excluding alternatives."

—Adam Tooze, Kathryn and Shelby Cullom Davis Professor of History and Director of the European Institute at Columbia University, and author of *The Deluge*

"A very, very clever person, and in the basic argument about what's been going on in Europe, I think he's right."   —Martin Wolf

"An outstanding economist and political analyst."
                                                    —Noam Chomsky

"The most interesting man in the world."   —*Business Insider*

"The Thucydides of our time."   —Jeffrey Sachs

MATTHEW LLOYD / BLOOMBERG VIA GETTY IMAGES

YANIS VAROUFAKIS

ADULTS IN THE ROOM

Yanis Varoufakis is a former finance minister of Greece and a cofounder of an international grassroots movement, DiEM25, that is campaigning for the revival of democracy in Europe. He is the author of *Talking to My Daughter About the Economy*, *And the Weak Suffer What They Must?*, and *The Global Minotaur*. After teaching for many years in the United States, Great Britain, and Australia, he is currently a professor of economics at the University of Athens.

ALSO BY YANIS VAROUFAKIS

And the Weak Suffer What They Must?:
Europe's Crisis and America's Economic Future

The Global Minotaur: America, Europe and the Future
of the Global Economy

Talking to My Daughter About the Economy;
or, How Capitalism Works—and How It Fails

ADULTS IN THE ROOM

*My Battle with the European and
American Deep Establishment*

YANIS VAROUFAKIS

Farrar, Straus and Giroux
New York

*For all who eagerly seek compromise but would rather be
crushed than end up compromised*

Farrar, Straus and Giroux
175 Varick Street, New York 10014

Copyright © 2017 by Yanis Varoufakis
All rights reserved
Printed in the United States of America
Originally published in 2017 by The Bodley Head, an imprint of Vintage, Great Britain
Published in the United States in 2017 by Farrar, Straus and Giroux
First American paperback edition, 2018

Grateful acknowledgment is made for permission to reprint an excerpt from *Nineteen
Eighty-Four* by George Orwell, copyright © the Estate of the late Sonia Brownell Orwell.

Library of Congress Control Number: 2017947268
Paperback ISBN: 978-0-374-53805-7

Our books may be purchased in bulk for promotional, educational, or business
use. Please contact your local bookseller or the Macmillan Corporate and
Premium Sales Department at 1-800-221-7945, extension 5442, or by
e-mail at MacmillanSpecialMarkets@macmillan.com.

www.fsgbooks.com
www.twitter.com/fsgbooks • www.facebook.com/fsgbooks

1 3 5 7 9 10 8 6 4 2

CONTENTS

A Note on Quoted Speech

In a book of this nature, in which so much depends on who said what to whom, I have made every effort to ensure the accuracy of quoted speech. To this end, I have been able to draw on audio recordings that I made on my phone, as well as on notes I made at the time, of many of the official meetings and conversations that appear in this book. Where my own recordings or notes are unavailable, I have relied on memory and, where possible, the corroboration of other witnesses.

The reader should note that many of the discussions reported in this book took place in Greek. This includes all conversations that occurred with my staff at the finance ministry, in parliament, on the streets of Athens, with the prime minister, in cabinet, and between my partner Danae and me. Necessarily, I have translated those conversations into English.

The only discussions I report that took place in neither Greek nor English were those I had with Michel Sapin, the French finance minister. Indeed, Mr Sapin was the only member of the Eurogroup not to address the meetings in English. Either we communicated through translators or, quite often, he would address me in French and I would reply in English, our grasp of the other's language being good enough to carry on those conversations.

In every instance I have confined my account strictly to exchanges that are in the public interest and have therefore included only those that shed important light on events that affected the lives of millions.

Preface

When Donald Trump began to look like a possible winner towards the end of 2016, the liberal and centrist establishment in the United States went into an understandable paroxysm. It assailed the fake news spread by the alt-right and the deeply disconcerting prospect of illiberalism gone mad: the vilification of political opponents via character assassination, the adoption of loony economic policies and, last but not least, the campaigns to bring back torture and to hand over environmental protection to climate change deniers.

And yet the establishment's protestations did not entirely ring true to me, and to many others who agreed that Trump's rise deserved an outraged response. Why? Because for years before the arrival of Trump, Brexit and other populist disruptions, the West's establishment had itself practiced character assassination, truth reversal, loony economics and downright illiberalism.

This book tells a story that highlights the Western establishment's atrocious violation of its own principles as I experienced it personally. During my stint as Greece's finance minister in 2015, I struggled to extricate my country from the great depression to which the same establishment had condemned it five years before.

The book could be described as a memoir of my dealings with Barack Obama, Jack Lew, Larry Summers, Bernie Sanders, the US ambassador in Athens, Angela Merkel, Wolfgang Schäuble, Emmanuel Macron, Mario Draghi, et al. Or simply as the tale of a small, bankrupt country taking on the Goliaths of Europe and America in order to escape from debtors' prison before suffering a crushing if fairly honorable defeat. However, such a 'spin' would sacrifice the book's deeper significance for Americans and Europeans alike.

That significance goes well beyond kiss-and-tell revelations. The story it tells is not only symbolic of what Europe, Britain and the United States are becoming. It also provides insight into how and why our polity has fractured. As the establishment protests against Trump's authoritarian populism, it is salutary to be reminded that in 2015 this same establishment launched a ferociously effective campaign against the pro-European, democratically elected government of a small country in Europe.

Shortly after the ruthless suppression of our rebellion, the opposition lost its momentum in Spain; no doubt many voters feared they would suffer a fate similar to ours. Having observed the leaders of the European Union and its allies callously disregard democracy in Greece and scare off the Spanish, many supporters of the Labour Party in Britain went on to vote to leave the European Union in June 2016. Brexit boosted Donald Trump. Donald Trump's triumph blew fresh wind into the sails of xenophobic nationalists throughout Europe and the world. Vladimir Putin was suddenly rubbing his eyes in disbelief at the way the West was undermining itself so fabulously.

And then, a little like the parricide who throws himself at the court's mercy, demanding lenience because he is now an orphan, the establishment began to sulk and to protest. Alas, it had already lost the moral high ground. Once upon a time, the democratic project was about the readiness to 'pay any price, bear any burden, meet any hardship, support any friend, oppose any foe, to assure the survival and the success of liberty', to use JFK's stirring words. Alas, those ideals had been expunged from the practices of the West's leading powers a long, long time ago— and the story of Greece in 2015 offers a grandstand view of this loss.

The powerlessness of establishment power

But as useful as I hope the insights offered by this book into the establishment's troubles may be, my motivation for writing it goes deeper. Beneath the specific events that I experienced, I recognized a universal story—the story of what happens when human beings find themselves at the mercy of cruel circumstances that have been generated by an inhuman, mostly unseen network of power relations. This is why there are no 'goodies' or 'baddies' in this book. Instead, it is populated by people doing their best, as they understand it, under conditions not of their choosing. Barack Obama, Germany's leadership, Christine Lagarde, indeed each of the persons I encountered and write about in these pages, believed they were acting appropriately but, taken together, their acts produced misfortune on a continental scale. Is this not the stuff of authentic tragedy? Is this not what makes the tragedies of Sophocles and Shakespeare resonate with us today, so long after the events they relate became old news?

At one point, Christine Lagarde, the managing director of the International Monetary Fund, remarked in a state of exasperation that to resolve the drama we needed 'adults in the room'. She was right. There was a dearth of adults in many of the rooms where this drama unfolded. As characters, though, the people in the room fell into two categories: the banal and the fascinating. The banal went about their business ticking boxes on sheets of instructions handed down to them by their masters. In many cases, though, their masters – politicians such as Wolfgang Schäuble and functionaries such as Christine Lagarde and Mario Draghi – were different. They had the ability to reflect on themselves and their role in the drama, and this ability to enter into dialogues with themselves made them fascinatingly susceptible to the trap of self-fulfilling prophecy.

Indeed, watching Greece's creditors at work was like watching a version of *Macbeth* unfold in the land of Oedipus. Just as the father of Oedipus, King Laius of Thebes, unwittingly brought about his own murder because he believed the prophecy that he would be killed by his son, so too did the smartest and most powerful players in this drama bring about their own doom because they feared the prophecy that foretold it. Keenly aware of how easily power could slip through their fingers, Greece's creditors were frequently overpowered by insecurity. Fearing that Greece's undeclared bankruptcy might cause them to lose political control over the West, they imposed policies on Greece that gradually undermined their political control, not just over Greece but over . . . the West.

At some point, like Macbeth, sensing their power mutate into insufferable powerlessness, they felt compelled to do their worst. There were moments I could almost hear them say

> I am in blood
> Stepp'd in so far that, should I wade no more,
> Returning were as tedious as go o'er:
> Strange things I have in head, that will to hand;
> Which must be acted ere they may be scann'd.
>
> *Macbeth*, act 3, scene 4

An account by any one of the protagonists in a cutthroat drama such as this cannot escape bias nor the desire for vindication. So, in order to be as fair and impartial as possible, I have tried to see their actions and my own through the lens of an authentic ancient Greek or Shakespearean tragedy in which characters, neither good nor bad, are overtaken by the unintended consequences of their conception of what they ought to do. I suspect that I have come closer to succeeding in this task in the case of those people whom I found fascinating and rather less so in the case of those whose banality numbed my senses. For this I find it hard to apologize, not least because to present them otherwise would be to diminish the historical accuracy of this account.

PART ONE
Winters of our discontent

1

Introduction

The only colour piercing the dimness of the hotel bar was the amber liquid flickering in the glass before him. As I approached, he raised his eyes to greet me with a nod before staring back down into his tumbler of whiskey. I sank onto the plush sofa, exhausted.

On cue, his familiar voice sounded imposingly morose. 'Yanis,' he said, 'you made a big mistake.'

In the deep of a spring night a gentleness descends on Washington, DC that is unimaginable during the day. As the politicos, the lobbyists and the hangers-on melt away, the air empties of tension and the bars are abandoned to the few with no reason to be up at dawn and to the even fewer whose burdens trump sleep. That night, as on the previous eighty-one nights, or indeed the eighty-one nights that were to follow, I was one of the latter.

It had taken me fifteen minutes to walk, shrouded in darkness, from 700 19th Street NW, the International Monetary Fund's building, to the hotel bar where I was to meet him. I had never imagined that a short solitary stroll in nondescript DC could be so restorative. The prospect of meeting the great man added to my sense of relief: after fifteen hours across the table from powerful people too banal or too frightened to speak their minds, I was about to meet a figure of great influence in Washington and beyond, a man no one can accuse of either banality or timidity.

All that changed with his acerbic opening statement, made more chilling by the dim light and shifting shadows.

Faking steeliness, I replied, 'And what mistake was that, Larry?'

'You won the election!' came his answer.

It was 16 April 2015, the very middle of my brief tenure as finance minister of Greece. Less than six months earlier I had been living the life of an academic, teaching at the Lyndon B. Johnson School of

Public Affairs at the University of Texas at Austin while on leave from the University of Athens. But in January my life had changed utterly when I was elected a member of the Greek parliament. I had made only one campaign promise: that I would do everything I could to rescue my country from the debt bondage and crushing austerity being imposed on it by its European neighbours and the IMF. It was that promise that had brought me to this city and – with the assistance of my close team member Elena Paraniti, who had brokered the meeting and accompanied me that night – to this bar.

Smiling at his dry humour and to hide my trepidation, my immediate thought was, *Is this how he intends to stiffen my resolve against an empire of foes?* I took solace from the recollection that the seventy-first secretary of the United States Treasury and twenty-seventh president of Harvard is not known for his soothing style.

Determined to delay the serious business ahead of us a few moments more, I signalled to the bartender for a whiskey of my own and said, 'Before you tell me about my "mistake", let me say, Larry, how important your messages of support and advice have been in the past weeks. I am truly grateful. Especially as for years I have been referring to you as the Prince of Darkness.'

Unperturbed, Larry Summers replied, 'At least you called me a prince. I have been called worse.'

For the next couple of hours the conversation turned serious. We talked about technical issues: debt swaps, fiscal policy, market reforms, 'bad' banks. On the political front he warned me that I was losing the propaganda war and that the 'Europeans', as he called Europe's powers that be, were out to get me. He suggested, and I agreed, that any new deal for my long-suffering country should be one that Germany's chancellor could present to her voters as *her* idea, her *personal* legacy.

Things were proceeding better than I had hoped, with broad agreement on everything that mattered. It was no mean feat to secure the support of the formidable Larry Summers in the struggle against the powerful institutions, governments and media conglomerates demanding my government's surrender and my head on a silver platter. Finally, after agreeing our next steps, and before the combined effects of fatigue and alcohol forced us to call it a night, Summers looked at me intensely and asked a question so well rehearsed that I suspected he had used it to test others before me.[1]

'There are two kinds of politicians,' he said: 'insiders and outsiders. The outsiders prioritize their freedom to speak their version of the truth. The price of their freedom is that they are ignored by the insiders, who make the important decisions. The insiders, for their part, follow a sacrosanct rule: never turn against other insiders and never talk to outsiders about what insiders say or do. Their reward? Access to inside information and a chance, though no guarantee, of influencing powerful people and outcomes.' With that Summers arrived at his question. 'So, Yanis,' he said, 'which of the two are you?'

Instinct urged me to respond with a single word; instead I used quite a few.

'By character I am a natural outsider,' I began, 'but,' I hastened to add, 'I am prepared to strangle my character if it would help strike a new deal for Greece that gets our people out of debt prison. Have no doubt about this, Larry: I shall behave like a natural insider for as long as it takes to get a viable agreement on the table – for Greece, indeed for Europe. But if the insiders I am dealing with prove unwilling to release Greece from its eternal debt bondage, I will not hesitate to turn whistle-blower on them – to return to the outside, which is my natural habitat anyway.'

'Fair enough,' he said after a thoughtful pause.

We stood up to leave. The heavens had opened while we were talking. As I saw him to a taxi, the downpour soaked my spring clothes in seconds. With his taxi speeding away, I had the opportunity to realize a wild dream of mine, one that had kept me going during the interminable meetings of the previous days and weeks: to walk alone, unnoticed, in the rain.

Powering through the watery curtain in pristine solitude, I took stock of the encounter. Summers was an ally, albeit a reluctant one. He had no time for my government's left-wing politics, but he understood that our defeat was not in America's interest. He knew that the eurozone's economic policies were not just atrocious for Greece but terrible for Europe and, by extension, for the United States too. And he knew that Greece was merely the laboratory where these failed policies were being tested and developed before their imple-mentation everywhere across Europe. This is why Summers offered a helping hand. We spoke the same economic language, despite different political ideologies, and had no difficulty reaching a quick agreement on what our aims and tactics ought to be. Nevertheless, my answer had clearly bothered him, even if he did not show it. He would have got into his taxi a much happier man, I felt, had I demonstrated some interest in *becoming* an insider. As this book's publication confirms, that was never likely to happen.

Back at my hotel, getting dry and with two hours to go before the alarm clock would summon me back to the front line, I pondered a great anxiety: how would my comrades back home, the inner circle of our government, answer Summers's question in their hearts? On that night I was determined to believe that they would answer it as I had done.

Less than two weeks later I began to have my first real doubts.

Super black boxes

Yiorgos Chatzis went missing on 29 August 2012. He was last sighted at the social security office in the small northern Greek town of Siatista, where he was told that his monthly disability allowance of €280 had been suspended. Eyewitnesses reported that he did not utter a word of complaint. 'He seemed stunned and remained speechless,' a newspaper said. Soon after, he used his mobile phone for the last time to call his wife. No one was at home, so he left a message: 'I feel useless. I have nothing to offer you any more. Look after the children.' A few days later his body was found in a remote wooded area, suspended by the neck over a cliff, his mobile phone lying on the ground nearby.

The wave of suicides triggered by the great Greek depression had caught the attention of the international press a few months earlier after Dimitris Christoulas, a seventy-seven-year-old retired pharmacist, shot himself dead by a tree in the middle of Athens's Syntagma Square, leaving behind a heart-wrenching political manifesto against austerity. Once upon a time the silent, dignified grief of Christoulas's and Chatzis's loved ones would have shamed into silence even the most hardened bailiff, except that in Bailoutistan, my satirical term for post-2010 Greece, our bailiffs keep their distance from their victims, barricading themselves in five-star hotels, whizzing around in motorcades and steadying their occasionally flagging nerves with baseless statistical projections of economic recovery.

During that same year, 2012, three long years before Larry Summers was to lecture me on insiders and outsiders, my partner Danae Stratou presented an art installation at a downtown Athens gallery. She called it, *It is time to open the black boxes!* The work comprised one hundred black metal boxes laid out geometrically on the floor. Each contained a word selected by Danae from the thousands that Athenians had contributed through social media in response to her question, 'In a single word, what are you most afraid of, or what is the one thing you want to preserve?'

Danae's idea was that unlike, say, the black box of a downed aircraft, these boxes would be opened before it was too late. The word that Athenians had chosen more than any other was not *jobs*, *pensions* or *savings*. What they feared losing most was *dignity*. The island of Crete, whose inhabitants are renowned for their pride, experienced the highest number of suicides once the crisis hit. When a depression deepens and the grapes of wrath grow 'heavy for the vintage', it is the loss of dignity that brings on the greatest despair.

In the catalogue entry I wrote for the exhibition I drew a comparison with another kind of black box. In engineering terms, I wrote, a black box is a device or system whose inner workings are opaque to us but whose capacity to turn inputs into outputs we understand and use fluently. A mobile phone, for instance, reliably converts finger movements into a telephone call or the arrival of a taxi, but to most of us, though not to electrical engineers, what goes on within a smartphone is a mystery. As philosophers have noted, other people's minds are the quintessential black boxes: ultimately we can have no idea of precisely what goes on inside another's head. (During the 162 days that this book chronicles I often caught myself wishing that the people around me, my comrades-in-arms in particular, were less like black boxes in this regard.)

But then there are what I called 'super black boxes', whose size and import is so great that even those who created and control them cannot fully understand their inner workings: for example, financial derivatives whose effects are not truly understood even by the financial engineers who designed them, global banks and multinational corporations whose activities are seldom grasped by their CEOs, and of course governments and supranational institutions like the International Monetary Fund, led by politicians and influential bureaucrats who may be in office but are rarely in power. They too convert inputs – money, debt, taxes, votes – into outputs – profit, more complicated forms of debt, reductions in welfare payments, health and education policies. The difference between these super black boxes and the humble smartphone – or even other humans – is that while most of us have barely any control over their inputs, their outputs shape all our lives.

This difference is encapsulated in a single word: power. Not the type of power associated with electricity or the crushing force of the ocean's waves, but another, subtler, more sinister power: the power held by the 'insiders' that Larry Summers referred to but which he feared I would not have the disposition to embrace, the power of hidden information.

During and after my ministry days people constantly asked me, 'What did the IMF want from Greece? Did those who resisted debt relief do so because of some illicit hidden agenda? Were they working on behalf of corporations interested in plundering Greece's infrastructure – its airports, seaside resorts, telephone companies and so on?' If only matters were that straightforward.

When a large-scale crisis hits, it is tempting to attribute it to a conspiracy between the powerful. Images spring to mind of smoke-filled rooms with cunning men (and the occasional woman) plotting how to profit at the expense of the common good and the weak. These images are, however, delusions. If our sharply diminished circumstances can be blamed on a conspiracy, then it is one whose members do not even know that they are part of it. That which feels to many like a conspiracy of the powerful is simply the emergent property of any network of super black boxes.

The keys to such power networks are exclusion and opacity. Recall the 'Greed is great' ethos of Wall Street and the City of London in the years before the 2008 implosion. Many decent bank employees were worried sick by what they were observing and doing. But when they got their hands on evidence or information foreshadowing terrible developments, they faced Summers's dilemma: leak it to outsiders and become irrelevant; keep it to themselves and become complicit; or embrace their power by exchanging it for other information held by someone else in the know, resulting in an impromptu two-person alliance that turbocharges both individuals' power within the broader network of insiders. As further sensitive information is exchanged, this two-person alliance forges links with other such alliances. The result is a network of power within other pre-existing networks, involving participants who conspire de facto without being conscious conspirators.

Whenever a politician in the know gives a journalist an exclusive in exchange for a particular spin that is in the politician's interest, the journalist is appended, however unconsciously, to a network of insiders. Whenever a journalist refuses to slant their story in the politician's favour, they risk losing a valuable source and being excluded from that network. This is how networks of power control the flow of information: through co-opting outsiders and excluding those who refuse to play ball. They evolve organically and are guided by a supra-intentional drive that no individual can control, not even the president of the United States, the CEO of Barclays or those manning the pivotal nodes in the IMF or national governments.

Once caught in this web of power it takes an heroic disposition to turn whistle-blower, especially when one cannot hear oneself think amid the cacophony of so much money-making. And those few who do break ranks end up like shooting stars, quickly forgotten by a distracted world.

Fascinatingly, many insiders, especially those only loosely attached to the network, are oblivious to the web that they reinforce, courtesy of having relatively few contacts with it. Similarly, those embedded in the very heart of the network are usually too far inside to notice that there is an outside at all. Rare are those astute enough to notice the black box when they live and work inside one. Larry Summers is one such rare insider. His question to me was in fact an invocation to reject the lure of the outside. Underpinning his belief system was the conviction that the world can only be made better from within the black box.

But this was where, I thought, he was very wrong.

Theseus before the labyrinth

Before 2008, while the super black boxes functioned stably, we lived in a world that *seemed* balanced and self-healing. Those were the times when the British chancellor Gordon Brown was celebrating the end of 'boom and bust' and the soon-to-be-chairman of the Federal Reserve

Ben Bernanke was heralding the Great Moderation. Of course it was all an illusion generated by the super black boxes whose function no one understood, especially not the insiders running them. And then, in 2008, they broke down spectacularly, generating our generation's 1929, not to mention little Greece's fall.

It is my view that the 2008 financial crisis, which is still with us almost a decade later, is due to the *terminal* breakdown of the world's super black boxes – of the networks of power, the conspiracies without conspirators, that fashion our lives. Summers's blind faith that the remedies to this crisis will spring from those same broken down networks, through the normal operations of insiders, struck me even at the time as touchingly naive. Perhaps that is not surprising. After all, three years earlier I had written in Danae's catalogue that 'opening these super black boxes has now become a prerequisite to the survival of decency, of whole strata of our fellow humans, of our planet even. Put simply, we have run out of excuses. It is, therefore, time to open the black boxes!' But in real terms, what would this entail?

> *First*, we need to acquire a readiness to recognize that we may very well, each one of us, already be a node in the network; an ignorant de facto conspirator. *Secondly*, and this is the genius of Wikileaks, if we can get inside the network, like Theseus entering the labyrinth, and disrupt the information flow; if we can put the fear of uncontrollable information leaking in the mind of as many of its members as possible, then the unaccountable, malfunctioning networks of power will collapse under their own weight and irrelevance. *Thirdly*, by resisting any tendency to substitute old closed networks with new ones.

By the time I entered that Washington bar three years later I had tempered my stance. My priority was not to leak information to outsiders but to do whatever it took to get Greece out of debtors' prison. If that meant pretending to be an insider, so be it. But the instant the price of admission to the insiders' circle became acceptance of Greece's permanent incarceration, I would leave. Laying down an Ariadne's thread inside the insiders' labyrinth and being ready to follow it to the exit is, I believe, a prerequisite for the dignity on which the Greek people's happiness relies.

The day after my meeting with Larry Summers I met Jack Lew, the incumbent US Treasury secretary. After our meeting at the Treasury, an official seeing me out startled me with a friendly aside: 'Minister, I feel the urge to warn you that within a week you will face a character assassination campaign emanating from Brussels.' Larry's pep talk about the importance of staying inside the proverbial tent, along with his warning that we were losing the media war, suddenly came into sharp focus.

Of course, it was no great surprise. Insiders, I had written in 2012, would react aggressively to anyone who dared open up their super black box to the outsiders' gaze: 'None of this will be easy. The networks will respond violently, as they are already doing. They will turn more authoritarian, more closed, more fragmented. They will become increasingly preoccupied with their own "security" and monopoly of information, less trusting of common people.'[2]

The following chapters relate the networks' violent reaction to my stubborn refusal to trade Greece's emancipation for a privileged spot inside one of their black boxes.

Sign here!

It all boiled down to one small doodle on a piece of paper – whether I was prepared to sign on the dotted line of a fresh bailout loan agreement that would push Greece further into its labyrinthine jail of debt.

The reason why my signature mattered so much was that, curiously, it is not presidents or prime ministers of fallen countries that sign bailout loan agreements with the IMF or with the European Union. That poisoned privilege falls to the hapless finance minister. It is why it was crucial to Greece's creditors that I be bent to their will, that I should be co-opted or, failing that, crushed and replaced by a more pliant successor. Had I signed, another outsider would have turned insider and praise would have been heaped upon me. The torrent of foul adjectives directed at me by the international press, arriving right on cue only a little more than a week after that Washington visit, just as the US official had warned me it would, would never have descended onto my head. I would have been 'responsible', a 'trustworthy partner', a 'reformed maverick' who had put his nation's interests above his 'narcissism'.

Judging by his expression as we walked out of the hotel and into the pouring rain, Larry Summers seemed to understand. He understood that the 'Europeans' were not interested in an honourable deal with me or with the Greek government. He understood that, in the end, I would be pressurized inordinately to sign a surrender document as the price of becoming a bona fide insider. He understood that I was not willing to do this. And he believed that this would be a pity, for me at least.

For my part I understood that he wanted to help me secure a viable deal. I understood too that he would do what he could to help us, provided it did not violate his golden rule: insiders never turn against other insiders and never talk to outsiders about what insiders do or say. What I was not sure about was whether he would ever understand why there was no chance in heaven – or hell for that matter – that I would sign a non-viable new bailout loan agreement. It would have taken too long to explain my reasons, but even if there had been time I feared that our backgrounds were too different for my explanation to make any sense to him.

My explanation, had I offered it, would have come in the form of a story or two.

The first would have probably begun inside an Athenian police station in the autumn of 1946, when Greece was on the brink of a communist insurgency and the second phase of its catastrophic civil war. A twenty-year-old chemistry student at Athens University named Yiorgos had been arrested by the secret police, roughed up and left in a cold cell for a few hours until a higher-ranking officer took him to his office ostensibly to apologize. I am sorry for the rough treatment, he said. You are a good boy and did not deserve this. But you know these are treacherous times and my men are on edge. Forgive them. Just sign this and off you go. With my apologies.

The police officer seemed sincere and Yiorgos was relieved that his earlier ordeal at the hands of the thugs was at an end. But then, as he read the typewritten statement the officer was asking him to sign, a cold chill ran down his spine. The page read, I hereby denounce, truly and in all sincerity, communism, those who promote it, and their various fellow travellers.

Trembling with fear, he put the pen down, summoned all the gentleness that his mother Anna had instilled in him over the years, and said, Sir, I am no Buddhist but I would never sign a state document denouncing Buddhism. I am not a Muslim but I do not think the state has the right to ask me to denounce Islam. Similarly, I am not a communist but I see no reason why I should be asked to denounce communism.

Yiorgos's civil liberty argument stood no chance. Sign or look forward to systematic torture and indefinite detention – the choice is yours! shouted the enraged officer. The officer's ire was based on perfectly reasonable expectations. Yiorgos had all the makings of a good boy, a natural insider. He had been born in Cairo to a middle-class family within the large Greek community, itself embedded in a cosmopolitan European enclave of French, Italian and British expats, and raised alongside sophisticated Armenians, Jews and Arabs. French was spoken at home, courtesy of his mother, Greek at school, English at work, Arabic on the street and Italian at the opera.

At the age of twenty, determined to connect with his roots, Yiorgos had given up a cushy job in a Cairo bank and moved to Greece to study chemistry. He had arrived in Athens in January 1945 on the ship *Corinthia* only a month after the conclusion of the first phase of Greece's civil war, the first episode of the Cold War. A fragile détente was in the air, and so it had seemed reasonable to Yiorgos when student activists of both the Left and the Right had approached him as a compromise candidate for president of his school's students' association.

Shortly after his election, however, the university authorities had increased tuition fees at a time when students wallowed in absolute poverty. Yiorgos had paid the dean a visit, arguing as best as he could against the fee hike. As he left, secret policemen had manhandled him down the school's marble steps and into a waiting van. and he had ended up with a choice that makes Summers's dilemma seem like a walk in the park.

Given the young man's bourgeois background, the police had every expectation that Yiorgos would either sign gladly or break quickly once torture began. However, with every beating Yiorgos felt less able to sign, end the pain and go home. As a result, he ended up in a variety of cells and prison camps that he could have escaped at any point simply by putting his signature on a single sheet of paper. Four years later, a shadow of his former self, Yiorgos emerged from prison into a grim society that neither knew of his peculiar choice nor really cared.

Meanwhile, during the period of Yiorgos's incarceration, a young woman four years his junior had become the first female student to gain admittance to the University of Athens Chemistry School, despite their best efforts to keep her out. Eleni, for that was her name, began university as a rebellious proto-feminist but nevertheless felt a powerful dislike for the Left: during the years of the Nazi occupation she had been abducted as a very young girl by left-wing partisans who mistook her for a relative of a Nazi collaborator. Upon enrolling at the University of Athens, a fascist organization called X recruited her on the strength of her anti-communist feelings. Her first – and, as it would turn out, her last – mission for them was to follow a fellow chemistry student who had just been released from the prison camps.

This, in a nutshell, is the story of how I came about. For Yiorgos is my father, and Eleni, who ended up a leading member of the 1970s feminist movement, was my mother. Blessed with this history, signing on the dotted line in return for the mercy shown to insiders was never on the cards for me. Would Larry Summers have understood? I don't think so.

Not for me

The other story is as follows. I met Lambros in the Athens apartment I share with Danae a week or so before the January 2015 election that brought me to office. It was a mild winter's day, the campaign was in full swing, and I had agreed to give an interview to Irene, a Spanish journalist. She came to the apartment accompanied by a photographer and by Lambros, an Athens-based Greek–Spanish translator. On that occasion Lambros's services were unnecessary as Irene and I talked in English. But he stayed, watching and listening intensely.

After the interview, as Irene and the photographer were packing up their gear and heading for the door, Lambros approached me. He shook my hand, refusing to let go while addressing me with the concentration of a man whose life depends on getting his message across: 'I hope you did not notice it from my appearance. I do my best to cover it up, but in fact I am a homeless person.' He then told me his story as briefly as he could.

Lambros used to have a flat, a job teaching foreign languages and a family. In 2010, when the Greek economy tanked, he lost his job, and when they were evicted from their flat he lost his family. For the past year he had lived on the street. His only income came from providing translation services to visiting foreign journalists drawn to Athens by yet another demonstration in Syntagma Square which turned ugly and thus newsworthy. His greatest concern was finding a few euros to recharge his cheap mobile phone so that the foreign news crews could contact him.

Feeling he needed to wrap up his soliloquy, he rushed to the one thing he wanted from me:

> I want to implore you to promise me something. I know you will win the election. I talk to people on the street and there is no doubt that you will. Please, when you win, when you are in office, remember those people. Do something for them. Not for me! I am finished. Those of us whom the crisis felled, we cannot come back. It is too late for us. But, please, please do something for those who are still on the verge. Who are clinging by their fingernails. Who have not fallen yet. Do it for them. Don't let them fall. Don't turn your back to them. Don't sign what they give you like the previous ones did. Swear that you won't. Do you swear?

'I swear,' was my two-word answer to him.

A week later I was taking my oath of office as the country's finance minister. During the months that followed, every time my resolve weakened I had only to think back to that moment. Lambros will never know of his influence during the bleakest hours of those 162 days.

2

Bailoutistan

By early 2010, some five years before I took office, the Greek state was bankrupt. A few months later the European Union, the International Monetary Fund and the Greek government organized the world's greatest bankruptcy cover-up. How do you cover up a bankruptcy? By throwing good money after bad. And who financed this cover-up? Common people, 'outsiders' from all over the globe.

The rescue deal, as the cover-up was euphemistically known, was signed and sealed in early May 2010. The European Union and the IMF extended to the broke Greek government around €110 billion, the largest loan in history.[1] Simultaneously a group of enforcers known as the troika – so called because they represent three institutions: the European Commission (EC), which is the EU's executive body, the European Central Bank (ECB) and the International Monetary Fund (IMF) – was dispatched to Athens to impose measures guaranteed to reduce Greece's national income and place most of the burden of the debt upon the weakest Greeks. A bright eight-year-old would have known that this couldn't end well.

Forcing new loans upon the bankrupt on condition that they shrink their income is nothing short of cruel and unusual punishment. Greece was never bailed out. With their 'rescue' loan and their troika of bailiffs enthusiastically slashing incomes, the EU and IMF effectively condemned Greece to a modern version of the Dickensian debtors' prison and then threw away the key.

Debtors' prisons were ultimately abandoned because, despite their cruelty, they neither deterred the accumulation of new bad debts nor helped creditors get their money back. For capitalism to advance in the nineteenth century, the absurd notion that all debts are sacred had to be ditched and replaced with the notion of limited liability. After all, if all debts are guaranteed, why should lenders lend responsibly?

And why should some debts carry a higher interest rate than other debts, reflecting the higher risk of going bad? Bankruptcy and debt write-downs became for capitalism what hell had always been for Christian dogma – unpleasant yet essential – but curiously bankruptcy-denial was revived in the twenty-first century to deal with the Greek state's insolvency. Why? Did the EU and the IMF not realize what they were doing?

They knew *exactly* what they were doing. Despite their meticulous propaganda, in which they insisted that they were trying to save Greece, to grant the Greek people a second chance, to help reform Greece's chronically crooked state and so on, the world's most powerful institutions and governments were under no illusions. They appreciated that you could squeeze blood out of a stone more easily than make a bankrupt entity repay its loans by lending it more money, especially if you shrink its income as part of the deal. They could see that the troika, even if it managed to confiscate the fallen state's silverware, would fail to recoup the money used to refinance Greece's public debt. They knew that the celebrated 'rescue' or 'bailout' package was nothing more than a one-way ticket to debtors' prison.

How do I know that they knew? Because they told me.

Prisoners of their own device

As finance minister five years later, I heard it straight from the horse's mouth. From top IMF officials, from Germany's finance minister, from leading figures in the ECB and the European Commission – they all admitted, each in their own way, that it was true: they had dealt Greece an impossible hand. But having done so, they could see no way back.

Less than a month after my election, on 11 February 2015, in one of those spirit-numbing, windowless, neon-lit meeting rooms that litter the EU's Brussels buildings, I found myself sitting opposite Christine Lagarde, the IMF's managing director, France's ex-finance minister and a former Washington-based high-flying lawyer. She had waltzed into the building earlier that day in a glamorous leather jacket, making me look drab and conventionally attired. This being our first encounter, we chatted amicably in the corridor before moving into the meeting room for the serious discussion.

Behind closed doors, with a couple of aides on each side, the conversation turned serious but remained just as friendly. She afforded me the opportunity to present my basic analysis of the causes and nature of the Greek situation as well as my proposals for dealing with it, and nodded in agreement for much of the time. We seemed to share a common language and were both keen to establish a good rapport. At the meeting's end, walking towards the door, we got a chance for a short, relaxed but telling tête-à-tête. Taking her cue from the points I had made, Christine seconded my appeals for debt relief and lower tax rates as prerequisites for a Greek recovery. Then she addressed me with calm and gentle honesty: You are of course right, Yanis. These targets that they insist on *can't* work. But, you must understand that we have put too much into this programme. We cannot go back on it. Your credibility depends on accepting and working within this programme.[2]

So, there I had it. The head of the IMF was telling the finance minister of a bankrupt government that the policies imposed upon his country *couldn't* work. Not that it would be hard to make them work. Not that the probability of them working was low. No, she was acknowledging that, come hell or high water, they couldn't work.

With every meeting, especially with the troika's smarter and less insecure officials, the impression grew on me that this was not a simple tale of us versus them, good versus bad. Rather, an authentic drama was afoot reminiscent of a play by Aeschylus or Shakespeare in which powerful schemers end up caught in a trap of their own making. In the real-life drama I was witnessing, Summers's sacred rule of insiders kicked in the moment they recognized their powerlessness. The hatches were battened down, official denial prevailed, and the consequences of the tragic impasse they'd created were left to unfold on autopilot, imprisoning them yet further in a situation they detested for weakening their hold over events.

Because they – the heads of the IMF, of the EU, of the German and French governments – had invested inordinate political capital in a programme that deepened Greece's bankruptcy, spread untold misery and led our young to emigrate in droves, there was no alternative: the people of Greece would simply have to continue to suffer. As for me, the political upstart, my credibility depended on accepting these policies, which insiders knew would fail, and helping to sell them to the outsiders who had elected me on the precise basis that I would break with those same failed policies.

It's hard to explain, but not once did I feel animosity towards Christine Lagarde. I found her intelligent, cordial, respectful. My view of humanity would not be thrown into turmoil were it to be shown that she actually had a strong preference for a humane Greek deal. But that is not relevant. As a leading insider, her top priority was the preservation of the insiders' political capital and the minimization of any challenge to their collective authority.

Yet credibility, like spending, comes with trade-offs. Every purchase means an alternative opportunity lost. Boosting my standing with Christine and the other figures of power meant sacrificing my credibility with Lambros, the homeless interpreter who had sworn me to the cause of those people who, unlike him, had not yet been drowned in the torrent of bankruptcy ravaging our land. This trade-off never came close to becoming a personal dilemma. And the powers that be realized this early on, making my removal from the scene essential.

A little more than a year later, in the run-up to the UK referendum on 23 June 2016, I was travelling across Britain giving speeches in support of a radical remain platform – the argument that the UK ought to stay within the EU to oppose *this* EU, to save it from collapse and to reform it. It was a tough sell. Convincing Britain's outsiders to vote remain was proving an uphill struggle, especially in England's north, because even my own supporters in Britain, women and men closer in spirit and position to Lambros than to Christine, were telling me they felt compelled to deliver a drubbing to the global establishment. One evening I heard on the BBC that Christine Lagarde had joined the heads of the world's other top financial institutions (the World Bank, the OECD, the ECB, the Bank of England and so on) to warn Britain's outsiders against the lure of Brexit. I immediately texted Danae from Leeds, where I was speaking that night, 'With such allies, who needs Brexiteers?'

Brexit won because the insiders went beyond the pale. After decades of treating people like me as credible in proportion to our readiness to betray the outsiders who had voted for us, they still confused outsiders with people who gave a damn about their counsel. Up and down America, in Britain, in France and in Germany – everywhere – the insiders are feeling their authority slip away. Prisoners of their own device, slaves to the Summers dilemma, they are condemned, like Macbeth, to add error upon error until they realize that their crown no longer symbolizes the power they have but the power that has slipped away. In the few months I spent dealing with them, I caught glimpses of that tragic realization.

It was the (French and German) banks, stupid!

Friends and journalists often ask me to describe the worst aspect of my negotiations with Greece's creditors. Not being able to shout from the rooftops what the high and mighty were telling me in private was certainly frustrating, but worse was dealing with creditors who did not really want their money back. Negotiating with them, trying to reason with them, was like negotiating a peace treaty with generals hell-bent on continuing a war safe in the knowledge that they, their sons and their daughters are out of harm's way.

What was the nature of that war? Why did Greece's creditors behave as if they did not want their money back? What led them to devise the trap in which they now found themselves? The riddle can be answered in seconds if one takes a look at the state of France's and Germany's banks after 2008.

Greece's endemic underdevelopment, mismanagement and corruption explain its permanent economic weakness. But its recent insolvency is due to the fundamental design faults of the EU and its monetary union, the euro. The EU began as a cartel of big business limiting competition between central European heavy industries and securing export markets for them in peripheral countries such as Italy and, later, Greece. The deficits of countries like Greece were the reflection of the surpluses of countries like Germany. While the drachma devalued, these deficits were kept in check. But when it was replaced by the euro, loans from German and French banks propelled Greek deficits into the stratosphere.

The Credit Crunch of 2008 that followed Wall Street's collapse bankrupted Europe's bankers who ceased all lending by 2009. Unable to roll over its debts, Greece fell into its insolvency hole later that year. Suddenly three French banks faced losses from peripheral debt at least twice the size of the French economy. Numbers provided by the Bank of International Settlements reveal a truly scary picture: for every thirty euros they were exposed to, they had access to only one. This meant that if only 3 per cent of that exposure went bad – that is, if €106 billion of the loans they had given to the periphery's governments, households and firms could not be repaid – then France's top three banks would need a French government bailout.

The same three French banks' loans to the Italian, Spanish and Portuguese governments alone came to 34 per cent of France's total economy – €627 billion to be exact. For good measure, these banks had in previous years also lent up to €102 billion to the Greek state. If the Greek government could not meet its repayments, money men around the globe would get spooked and stop lending to the Portuguese, possibly to the Italian and Spanish states as well, fearing that they would be the next to go into arrears. Unable to refinance their combined debt of nearly €1.76 trillion at affordable interest rates, the Italian, Spanish and Portuguese governments would be hard pressed to service their loans to France's top three banks, leaving a black hole in their books. Overnight, France's main banks would be facing a loss of 19 per cent of their 'assets' when a mere 3 per cent loss would make them insolvent.

To plug that gap the French government would need a cool €562 billion overnight. But unlike the United States federal government, which can shift such losses to its central bank (the Fed), France had dismantled its central bank in 2000 when it joined the common currency and had to rely instead on the kindness of Europe's shared central bank, the European Central Bank. Alas, the ECB was created with an express prohibition: no shifting of Graeco-Latin bad debts, private or public, onto the ECB's books. Full stop. That had been Germany's condition for sharing its cherished Deutschmark with Europe's riff-raff, renaming it the euro.

It's not hard to imagine the panic enveloping President Sarkozy of France and his finance minister, Christine Lagarde, as they realized that they might have to conjure up €562 billion from thin air. And it's not difficult to picture the angst of one of Lagarde's predecessors in France's finance ministry, the notorious Dominic Strauss-Kahn, who was then managing director of the IMF and intent on using that position to launch his campaign for France's presidency in two years' time. France's top officials knew that Greece's bankruptcy would force the French state to borrow six times its total annual tax revenues just to hand it over to three idiotic banks.

It was simply impossible. Had the markets caught a whiff that this was on the cards, interest rates on France's own public debt would have been propelled into the stratosphere, and in seconds €1.29 trillion of French government debt would have gone bad. In a country which had given up its capacity to print banknotes – the only remaining means of generating money from nothing – that would mean destitution, which in turn would bring down the whole of the European Union, its common currency, everything.

In Germany, meanwhile, the chancellor's predicament was no less taxing. In 2008, as banks in Wall Street and the City of London crumbled, Angela Merkel was still fostering her image as the tight-fisted, financially prudent Iron Chancellor. Pointing a moralizing finger at the Anglosphere's profligate bankers, she made headlines in a speech she gave in Stuttgart when she suggested that America's bankers should have consulted a Swabian housewife, who would have taught them a thing or two about managing their finances. Imagine her horror when, shortly afterwards, she received a barrage of anxious phone calls from her finance ministry, her central bank, her own economic advisers, all of them conveying an unfathomable message: Chancellor, our banks are bust too! To keep the ATMs going, we need an injection of €406 billion of those Swabian housewives' money – by yesterday!

It was the definition of political poison. How could she appear in front of those same members of parliament whom she had for years lectured on the virtues of penny-pinching when it came to hospitals, schools, infrastructure, social security, the environment, to implore them to write such a colossal cheque to bankers who until seconds before had been swimming in rivers of cash? Necessity being the mother of enforced humbleness, Chancellor Merkel took a deep breath, entered the splendid Norman Foster-designed federal parliament in Berlin known as the Bundestag, conveyed to her dumbfounded parliamentarians the bad news and left with the requested cheque. At least it's done, she must have thought. Except that it wasn't. A few months later another barrage of phone calls demanded a similar number of billions for the same banks.

Why did Deutsche Bank, Finanzbank and the other Frankfurt-based towers of financial incompetence need more? Because the €406 billion cheque they had received from Mrs Merkel in 2009 was barely enough to cover their trades in US-based toxic derivatives. It was certainly not enough to cover what they had lent to the governments of Italy,

Ireland, Portugal, Spain and Greece – a total of €477 billion, of which a hefty €102 billion had been lent to Athens. If Greece lost its capacity to meet its repayments,[3] German banks faced another loss that would require of Mrs Merkel another cheque for anything between €340 billion and €406 billion, but consummate politician that she is, the chancellor knew she would be committing political suicide were she to return to the Bundestag to request such an amount.

Between them, the leaders of France and Germany had a stake of around €1 trillion in not allowing the Greek government to tell the truth; that is, to confess to its bankruptcy. Yet they still had to find a way to bail out their bankers a second time without telling their parliaments that this was what they were doing. As Jean-Claude Juncker, then prime minister of Luxembourg and later president of the European Commission, once said, 'When it becomes serious, you have to lie.'[4]

After a few weeks they figured out their fib: they would portray the second bailout of their banks as an act of solidarity with the profligate and lazy Greeks, who while unworthy and intolerable were still members of the European family and would therefore have to be rescued. Conveniently, this necessitated providing them with a further gargantuan loan with which to pay off their French and German creditors, the failing banks. There was, however, a technical hitch that would have to be overcome first: the clause in the eurozone's founding treaty that banned the financing of government debt by the EU. How could they get round it? The conundrum was solved by a typical Brussels fudge, that unappetizing dish that the Europeans, especially the British, have learned to loathe.

First, the new loans would not be European but international, courtesy of cutting the IMF into the deal. To do this would require the IMF to bend its most sacred rule: never lend to a bankrupt government before its debt has had a 'haircut' – been restructured. But the IMF's then managing director, Dominic Strauss-Kahn, desperate to save the banks of the nation he planned to lead two years down the track, was on hand to persuade the IMF's internal bureaucracy to turn a blind eye. With the IMF on board, Europeans could be told that it was the international community, not just the EU, lending to the Greeks for the higher purpose of underpinning the global financial system. Perish the thought that this was an EU bailout for an EU member state, let alone for German and French banks!

Second, the largest portion of the loans, to be sourced in Europe, would not come from the EU per se; they would be packaged as a series of bilateral loans – that is to say, from Germany to Greece, from Ireland to Greece, from Slovenia to Greece, and so on – with each bilateral loan of a size reflecting the lender's relative economic strength, a curious application of Karl Marx's maxim 'from each according to his capacity to each according to his need'. So, of every €1000 handed over to Athens to be passed on to the French and German banks, Germany would guarantee €270, France €200, with the remaining €530 guaranteed by the smaller and poorer countries.[5] This was the beauty of the Greek bailout, at least for France and Germany: it dumped most of the burden of bailing out the French and German banks onto taxpayers from nations even poorer than Greece, such as Portugal and Slovakia. They, together with unsuspecting taxpayers from the IMF's co-funders such as Brazil and Indonesia, would be forced to wire money to the Paris and Frankfurt banks.

Unaware of the fact that they were actually paying for the mistakes of French and German bankers, the Slovaks and the Finns, like the Germans and the French, believed they were having to shoulder another country's debts. Thus, in the name of solidarity with the insufferable Greeks, the Franco-German axis planted the seeds of loathing between proud peoples.

From Operation Offload to bankruptocracy

As soon as the bailout loans gushed into the Greek finance ministry, 'Operation Offload' began: the process of immediately siphoning the money off back to the French and German banks. By October 2011, the German banks' exposure to Greek public debt had been reduced by a whopping €27.8 billion to €91.4 billion. Five months later, by March 2012, it was down to less than €795 million. Meanwhile the French banks were offloading even faster: by September 2011 they had unburdened themselves of €63.6 billion of Greek government bonds, before totally eliminating them from their books in December 2012. The operation was thus completed within less than two years. *This* was what the Greek bailout had been all about.

Were Christine Lagarde, Nicolas Sarkozy and Angela Merkel naive enough to expect the bankrupt Greek state to return this money with

interest? Of course not. They saw it precisely as it was: a cynical
transfer of losses from the books of the Franco-German banks to the
shoulders of Europe's weakest taxpayers. And therein lies the rub: the
EU creditors I negotiated with did not prioritize getting their money
back because, in reality, it wasn't their money.[6]

Socialists, Margaret Thatcher liked to say, are bound to make a
mess of finance because at some point they run out of other people's
money.[7] How would the Iron Lady have felt if she'd known that her
dictum would prove so fitting a description of her own self-proclaimed
disciples, the neoliberal apparatchiks managing Greece's bankruptcy?
Did their Greek bailout amount to anything other than the socialization of the French and German banks' losses, paid for with other
people's money?

In my book *The Global Minotaur*, which I was writing in 2010 while
Greece was imploding, I argued that free-market capitalist ideology
expired in 2008, seventeen years after communism kicked the bucket.
Before 2008 free-market enthusiasts portrayed capitalism as a Darwinian
jungle that selects for success among heroic entrepreneurs. But in the
aftermath of the 2008 financial collapse, the Darwinian natural selection process was stood on its head: the more insolvent a banker was,
especially in Europe, the greater his chances of appropriating large
chunks of income from everyone else: from the hard-working, the
innovative, the poor and of course the politically powerless.
Bankruptocracy is the name I gave to this novel regime.

Most Europeans like to think that American bankruptocracy is
worse than its European cousin, thanks to the power of Wall Street
and the infamous revolving door between the US banks and the US
government. They are very, very wrong. Europe's banks were managed
so atrociously in the years preceding 2008 that the inane bankers of
Wall Street almost look good by comparison. When the crisis hit, the
banks of France, Germany, the Netherlands and the UK had exposure
in excess of $30 trillion, more than twice the United States national
income, eight times the national income of Germany, and almost
three times the national incomes of Britain, Germany, France and
Holland put together.[8] A Greek bankruptcy in 2010 would have immediately necessitated a bank bailout by the German, French, Dutch and
British governments amounting to approximately $10,000 per child,
woman and man living in those four countries. By comparison, a
similar market turn against Wall Street would have required a relatively

tiny bailout of no more than $258 per US citizen. If Wall Street deserved the wrath of the American public, Europe's banks deserved 38.8 times that wrath.

But that's not all. Washington could park Wall Street's bad assets on the Federal Reserve's books and leave them there until either they started performing again or were eventually forgotten, to be discovered by the archaeologists of the future. Put simply, Americans did not need to pay even that relatively measly $258 per head out of their taxes. But in Europe, where countries like France and Greece had given up their central banks in 2000 and the ECB was banned from absorbing bad debts, the cash needed to bail out the banks had to be taken from the citizenry. If you have ever wondered why Europe's establishment is so much keener on austerity than America's or Japan's, this is why. It is because the ECB is not allowed to bury the banks' sins in its own books, meaning European governments have no choice but to fund bank bailouts through benefits cuts and tax hikes.

Was Greek's unholy treatment a conspiracy? If so, it was one without conscious conspirators, at least at the outset. Christine Lagarde and her ilk never set out to found Europe's bankruptocracy. When the French banks faced certain death, what choice did she have as France's finance minister, alongside her European counterparts and the IMF, but to do whatever it took to save them – even if this entailed lying to nineteen European parliaments at once about the purpose of the Greek loans? But having lied once and on such a grand scale, they were soon forced to compound the deceit in an attempt to hide it beneath fresh layers of subterfuge. Coming clean would have been professional suicide. Before they knew it, bankruptocracy had enveloped them too, just as surely as it had enveloped Europe's outsiders.

This is what Christine was signalling to me when she confided that 'they' had invested too much in the failed Greek programme to go back on it. She might as well have used Lady Macbeth's more graceful words: 'What's done cannot be undone.'

'National traitor' – the origins of a quaint charge

My career as 'national traitor' has its roots in December 2006. In a public debate organized by a former prime minister's think tank I was asked to comment on the 2007 Greek national budget. Looking at the figures, something compelled me to dismiss them as the pathetic window-dressing exercise that they were:

> Today . . . we are threatened by the bubble in American real estate and in the derivatives market . . . If this bubble bursts, and it is certain it will, no reduction in interest rates is going to energize investment in this country to take up the slack, and so none of this budget's figures will have a leg to stand on . . . The question is not whether this will happen but how quickly it will result in our next Great Depression.

My fellow panellists, who included two former finance ministers, looked at me the way one looks at an inconvenient fool.[9] Over the next two years I would encounter that look time and again. Even after Lehman Brothers went belly up, Wall Street crumpled, the credit crunch hit and a great recession engulfed the West, Greece's elites were living in a bubble of self-deluded bliss. At dinner parties, in academic seminars, at art galleries they would harp on about Greece's invulnerability to the 'Anglo disease', secure in the conviction that our banks were sufficiently conservative and the Greek economy fully insulated from the storm. In pointing out that nothing could have been further from the truth I sounded a jarring dissonance, but it would only get worse.

In reality, states never repay their debt. They roll it over, meaning they defer repayment endlessly, paying only the interest on the loans. As long as they can keep doing this, they remain solvent.[10] It helps to think of public debt as a hole in the ground next to a mountain representing the nation's total income. Day by day the hole gets steadily deeper as interest accrues on the debt, even if the state does not borrow more. But during the good times, as the economy grows, the income mountain is steadily getting taller. As long as the mountain rises faster than the debt hole deepens, the extra income added to the mountain's summit can be shovelled into the adjacent hole, keeping its depth stable and the state solvent. Insolvency beckons when the economy stops growing or starts to contract: recession then eats into a country's income mountain, doing nothing to slow the pace at which the debt hole continues to grow. At this point alarmed money men will demand higher interest rates on their loans as the price for continuing to refinance the state, but increased rates operate like overzealous excavators, digging yet faster and making the debt hole even deeper.

Before the 2008 crisis Greece had, relative to the height of its income mountain, the deepest debt hole in the European Union. But at least the income mountain was rising faster than the hole was getting deeper, creating a semblance of sustainability.[11] All that changed menacingly in early 2009 once the bottom fell out of the French and German banks as a result of having stuffed their boots with toxic American derivatives rendered worthless by Wall Street's cave-in. Greece's double misfortune was that income growth in the country had hitherto been fuelled by further debt provided to corporations (often via the Greek state) by the same French and German banks that were lending to the state.[12] The moment these banks panicked and stopped lending to Greece's public and private sector simultaneously, the game would be up. Greece's income mountain would collapse at the same time as the state's debt hole became an abyss.[13] This was what I told anyone who would listen.

In the autumn of 2009 a new Greek government was elected on the promise of higher spending as a means of helping the nation's income mountain recover, but the new prime minister and his finance minister, from the PASOK social democratic party, did not get it. The state was irretrievably bankrupt even before they were sworn in. The global credit crunch, which had nothing to do with Greece, was about to stop European banks lending to us. For a country with debt-driven growth – debt denominated in what is essentially a foreign currency, monetary policy over the euro being wholly out of Greece's control – surrounded by European economies in deep recession and unable to devalue, Greece's income mountain was bound to dwindle at such a rate that the debt hole would consume the nation.

In January 2010 in a radio interview I warned the prime minister, whom I knew personally and with whom I was on rather friendly terms, 'Whatever you do, do not seek state loans from our European partners in a futile bid to avert our bankruptcy.' At the time the Greek state was making a superhuman effort to do precisely that. Within seconds government sources were chastising me as a traitor – a fool who failed to understand that such prognoses are self-confirming: retaining market confidence in the state's financial health was the only way to keep the loans coming, Convinced that our bankruptcy was assured whatever calming noises we emitted, I ploughed on. The fact that I had once written speeches for Prime Minister Papandreou caught the eye of the BBC and other foreign news outlets. Headlines such as FORMER GREEK PM ADVISER SAYS GREECE IS BANKRUPT titillated the media and cemented my reputation as the worst enemy of the Greek establishment.

Upton Sinclair once said, 'It is difficult to get a man to understand something when his salary depends upon his not understanding it.' In this case, the income and wealth of the Greek ruling class depended on their not being convinced of Greece's bankruptcy. If every man, woman and child in this generation and the next had to take on unsustainable loans in order to keep the Greek oligarchs' relationship with foreign bankers and governments sweet, so be it. No argument appealing to the interest of the remaining 99 per cent of Greeks and their descendants could have swayed them. But the more they plugged their ears against the dissonant facts, the greater the duty I felt to warn our people that the loans the establishment were seeking on their behalf would, in the name of avoiding it, worsen the bankruptcy and, as a result, consign the Greeks to a debtors' prison. Friends and colleagues warned me that my thinking might be correct but that it was bad politics to speak of bankruptcy. Not being a natural-born politician, I would respond with a line by John Kenneth Galbraith: 'There are times in politics when you must be on the right side and lose.' Little did I know how prophetic that would prove.

And so I continued my solitary struggle to convince a nation to embrace bankruptcy in order to avoid the workhouse that was being prepared for it if it did not. In February 2010 on national television I suggested that the problem with all extend-and-pretend loans is that, as in a game of musical chairs, the music has to stop at some point. In this case that would be the point at which the weakest Europeans, whose taxes and benefits would finance the loans, cried, 'Enough!' But by then we would be much poorer, much more indebted, as well as hated by our fellow Europeans. In April 2010, a month before the bailout, I published three articles in quick succession. In the first of them, on 9 April, under the title ARE WE BANKRUPT? I argued that if the state pretended it was not bankrupt, through bailout extend-and-pretend loans, Greeks would face the 'most spectacular bankruptcy among families and businesses in our postwar history'. But if the state confessed its bankruptcy and entered into immediate negotiations with its creditors, much of the burden would be shared with those responsible for the debt: the banks that indulged in predatory lending before 2008.

The establishment's response was simple and to the point: if our government were to demand debt restructuring, Europe would jettison us from the eurozone. My rejoinder was also simple and to the point: doing so would destroy France and Germany's banking systems and with them the eurozone itself. They would never do it. But even if they did, what was the point of being in a monetary union that crushes its constituent economies? So, unlike those opponents of the euro who saw the crisis as an opportunity to press their case for Grexit, my position was that the only way of staying sustainably within the eurozone was to disobey its institutions's directives.

Fewer than ten days before the bailout agreement was signed I fired another two shots across the government's bows. On 26 April, in an article headed EUROPE'S LAST TANGO I likened our government's efforts to secure a bailout to those of successive Argentinian governments which strove to preserve, through large dollar loans from the IMF, the peso's one-to-one link with the US dollar just long enough for the rich and the corporations to liquidate their Argentinian properties, convert the proceeds into dollars and wire them to Wall Street – before leaving the economy and currency to collapse and the accumulated dollar debt to crush the hapless Argentinian masses. Two days later I went all out with an article whose title says it all: LOOKING ON BANKRUPTCY'S BRIGHTER SIDE.

Five days later the bailout loan was signed. The prime minister, choosing an idyllic island as the backdrop for his address to the nation, hailed it as Greece's second chance, proof of European solidarity, the foundation of our recovery, blah blah blah. It was to be his undoing and the nation's one-way ticket to the workhouse.

Champion of austerity

In September 2015, after my ministry days were over, I made my first appearance on the BBC's *Question Time*, recorded in front of an audience in Cambridge. Its host David Dimbleby introduced me as Europe's anti-austerity champion, an open invitation to a laddish member of the audience to confront me with his pro-austerity philosophy: 'Economics is really simple. I've got ten pounds in my pocket. If I go out and buy three pints of beer in Cambridge, I'm probably borrowing money. If I carry on doing that, then I'm going to run out of money and I'm going to go bust. It's not difficult.'

One of the great mysteries of life, at least of my life, is how susceptible good people are to this awful logic. In fact, personal finances are a terrible basis for understanding public finance, as I explained in response: 'In your life you have a wonderful independence between your expenses and your income. So when you cut down on your expenses, your income is not cut. But if the country as a whole goes [on] a major savings spree, then its total income is going to come down.'

The reason for this is that at a national level total expenditure and total income are precisely equal because whatever is earned has been spent by someone else. So if every person and business in the country is cutting back, the one thing the state must not do is cut back as well. If it does so, the abrupt fall in total expenditure means an equally abrupt fall in national income, which in turn leads to lower taxes for the Treasury and to austerity's spectacular own goal: an ever-shrinking national income that makes the existing national debt unpayable. This is why austerity is absolutely the wrong solution.

If proof of this were ever needed, Greece has provided it. Our 2010 bailout had two pillars: gigantic loans to fund the French and German banks, and swingeing austerity. To put Greek austerity into perspective: in the two years that followed Greece's 'rescue', Spain, another eurozone country caught up in the same mess, was treated to austerity which amounted to a 3.5 per cent reduction in government expenditure. During the same two-year period, 2010 to 2012, Greece experienced a stupendous 15 per cent reduction in government spending. To what effect? Spain's national income declined by 6.4 per cent while Greece's by fell by 16 per cent. In Britain, meanwhile, the newly appointed chancellor George Osborne was championing mild austerity as a means of achieving his dream: a balanced government budget by 2020.[14] Osborne was among the first finance ministers I met after my election. The most startling aspect of that encounter – at least to those in the press who expected a frosty or outright acrimonious meeting – was that we found very little to disagree on. In the first few minutes of our discussion I suggested to him that 'While we may disagree on the merits of austerity, you are not really doing much of it, George, are you?'[15]

He agreed smilingly. How could he not? If an Austerity Olympics had been staged, Greece would have swept the board while Osborne's

Britain would have been an also-ran at the bottom of the medals table. Osborne also seemed appreciative of the help he was getting from the Bank of England, which from the moment the City went through its 2008 credit convulsion had printed billions to refloat the banks and keep the economy 'liquid'. Osborne referred to this Bank of England largesse combined with government spending cutbacks as 'expansionary contraction'.

'They are behind me every step of the way,' he told me, evidently relieved not to be in my situation, hostage to a European Central Bank that was doing precisely the opposite.

'I envy you, George,' I lamented. 'Unlike you, I have a central bank stabbing me in the back every step of the way. Can you imagine what it would be like, here in Britain,' I asked, 'if instead of your "expansionary contraction" you were forced, like I am, into a "contractionary contraction"?'

He nodded with a smile, signalling if not solidarity at least sympathy.

That a meeting between a Tory chancellor and a finance minister representing the radical Left in Greece went swimmingly is not actually as puzzling as the press would have everyone believe. Three years previously, with the euro crisis at full blast, a chartered accountants' chamber based in Australia decided to entertain the attendees at their annual conference in Melbourne by staging a debate between a left- and a right-winger from Europe. So they invited Lord (Norman) Lamont, former chancellor in John Major's government, and me to debate, convinced of the fireworks that would ensue. Unfortunately for them, they chose the wrong theme: the eurozone crisis. Having taken the stage in front of a large audience anticipating a cockfight, we quickly discovered that we agreed on almost everything.

The discussion was so amicable, in fact, that after we had left the stage together, we met Danae outside and the three of us proceeded to have lunch together at a riverside restaurant. Bathed in brilliant sunshine, the friendship blossomed – with the help of some delightful Aussie wine, as Norman keeps reminding me. After that we remained in touch, exchanging views in a manner that confirmed we had more in common than even we could have imagined. It was December 2014 when I shocked Norman with the news that I would be taking over Greece's finance ministry within a month. Since that day, and throughout my tumultuous months in office but also beyond, Norman has proved a pillar of strength, a safe friend and a constant supporter. In fact, before I stepped into 11 Downing Street to meet George Osborne in 2015, Norman had called him on the telephone to pave the way for our meeting with a few warm words about me.

While my friendship with Lord Lamont seemed odd to many, especially to my left-wing comrades in government, it fitted well within a broader pattern. Throughout the bleak years, from 2010 to this day, I have been continually stunned by the support that I, a proud leftie, have received from a variety of right-wingers – Wall Street and City of London bankers, right-wing German economists, even US libertarians. To give an example of how weird things got, on a single day in late 2011 I addressed three rather different crowds in New York City – one at Occupy Wall Street, another at the New York Federal Reserve and a third consisting of hedge fund managers and bank reps – and when I told all three audiences the same story about Europe's crisis, I received from each of these three camps of sworn enemies the same warm response.

What authentic libertarians, Wall Street's recovering bankers and Anglo-Celtic right-wingers liked about my otherwise left-wing position was precisely that which the Greek and European establishment loathed: a clear opposition to unsustainable, extend-and-pretend loans that repackage bankruptcy as an illiquidity problem. True-blue free marketeers are allergic to taxpayer-funded benevolence. They reject wholeheartedly my views on the desirability of substantial public investment in recessionary times and of tax-mediated income distribution at all times. But we agree that extending a bankruptcy into the future through taxpayer-funded loans is a horrific waste of resources and a gateway to mass misery. Above all else, libertarians understand debt. As a result, we saw eye to eye on the misanthropic fallacy behind the programme that Christine Lagarde was pushing me, four years later, to embrace.

The official explanation of how the establishment's programme was supposed to help Greece recover in 2015 might be termed 'Operation Restore Competitiveness'. The basic idea was this: Greece has the euro and therefore cannot attract investment from overseas by devaluing its currency, which is the usual strategy for regaining international competitiveness. Instead, it can achieve the same result through what is known as internal devaluation, brought about via massive austerity. How? Swingeing government expenditure cuts will bear down on prices and wages. Greek olive oil, hotel services on Mykonos and Greek shipping fees will therefore become much cheaper for German, French and Chinese customers. With Greece's competitiveness thus restored, exports and tourism will pick up, and with this miraculous transformation investors will rush in, thus stabilizing the economy. In time growth returns and incomes pick up. Job done.

It might have been a convincing argument if it were not for the elephant in the room – an elephant that libertarians recognize: no sane investor is attracted to a country whose government, banks, companies and households are *all* insolvent at once. As prices, wages and incomes decline, the debt that underlies their insolvency will not fall, it will rise. Cutting one's income and adding new debt can only hasten the process. This is of course what had happened in Greece from 2010 onwards.

In 2010, for every $100 of income a Greek made, the state owed €146 to foreign banks. A year later, every €100 of income earned in 2010 had shrunk to €91 before shrinking again to €79 by 2012. Meanwhile, as the official loans from European taxpayers came in before being funnelled to France and Germany's banks, the equivalent government debt rose from €146 in 2010 to €156 in 2011. Even if God and all the angels were to invade the soul of every Greek tax evader, turning us into a nation of parsimonious Presbyterian Scots, our incomes were too low and our debts too high to reverse the bankruptcy. Investors understood this and wouldn't touch a Greek investment project with a bargepole. The corollary was a humanitarian crisis that ended up bringing people like me into government.

Once I was there, with the international Left in permanent disarray, US libertarians and UK free marketeers were among my most effective supporters. Interestingly, their ideological, quasi-Darwinian commitment to letting the market's losers perish was pushing them towards my side. Mindful of the dangers of too much credit, their dictum that 'To every irresponsible borrower there corresponds an irresponsible lender' led them to the conclusion that bad loans should burden irresponsible lenders, not taxpayers. As for irresponsible borrowers, they should also pay the price of their irresponsibility, mainly through being denied credit until they proved their trustworthiness again.

Blacklisted

Throughout 2010 and 2011 almost every other day it seemed I appeared on radio and television imploring the government to confront reality and enter the phase of grim acceptance that Greek public debt had to be restructured. There was nothing radical or particularly left wing in this proposition. Banks restructure the debt of stressed corporations every day, not out of philanthropy but out of enlightened self-interest. But the problem was that, now that we had accepted the EU–IMF bailout, we were no longer dealing with banks but with politicians who had lied to their parliaments to convince them to relieve the banks of Greece's debt and take it on themselves. A debt restructuring would require them to go back to their parliaments and confess their earlier sin, something they would never do voluntarily, fearful of the repercussions. The only alternative was to continue the pretence by giving the Greek government another wad of money with which to pretend to meet its debt repayments to the EU and the IMF: a second bailout.

I was determined to spoil their party: to shout from any rooftop I could scale that our worst option would be to accept more loans. I tried various metaphors: 'It's like accepting a credit card,' I once said on television, 'in order to repay mortgage instalments that you cannot make because of a drop in your wages. It's a crime against logic. Just say no. A home repossession is a terrible thing, but eternal debt bondage is even worse.'

One evening, on returning to our flat after yet another session at ERT, the Greek state radio and TV network, the landline rang. I picked the phone up to hear a familiar voice. It belonged to Antonis Samaras, then leader of the conservative New Democracy party, at the time Greece's official opposition and the man I helped defeat four years later, in the January 2015 general election.

'We have never met, Mr Varoufakis,' he said, 'but having just watched you on ERT I felt an urge to call. For I cannot remember the last time I was so touched by something so profound I heard someone say on television. Thank you for your stance.'

He was not the only member of the Greek establishment to approach me. Indeed, my campaign had led to many secret discussions with socialist ministers, opposition conservative members of parliament, trade union bosses and the like who felt I was on to something.

Once I outlined my basic analysis, not one of them contested it. The socialists spoke like petty officers who know that the ship is heading for the rocks but are too scared to confront a captain in deep denial. The conservatives, at least up until November 2011, were a happier lot: with their leader Antonis Samaras adopting an anti-austerity, anti-bailout position, they felt freer to endorse my musings.

A few days later I was at ERT's studios preparing for yet another appearance on the main news bulletin. The network's CEO had previously approached me with an intriguing offer: to present a short programme almost daily that would follow the main news, offering my commentary on the unfolding economic drama. 'The government will not like it but your views are important and deserve an airing,' he had said decisively. Flattered, but also pleased by the head of state television's commitment to pluralism despite the government's fierce opposition to my views, I had agreed to think about it.

That night, ten minutes before show time, the CEO summoned me to his office for a chat. Sitting opposite him was the station's main anchor, a journalist who for two decades had been the darling of the PASOK establishment, well known for her dyed blonde hair, blue eyes, captivating voice and flirtatiousness. The CEO reminded me of his offer of a regular slot for me, to which the anchor added her enthusiastic approval. Just before we headed for the studio, under his watchful eyes, she came up with her caveat: 'I know that this is your thing, but please do not mention debt restructuring tonight. It makes it hard to keep you on air. The government go ballistic when they hear these words.'

I smiled and proceeded to the set. Once settled in, and after she had read the headlines, she turned to me with her usual au fait manner to ask, 'Mr Varoufakis, the government is telling us that the programme is going to succeed. But we hear other views also. What say you?'

Immediately I replied, 'Without debt restructuring, no programme, not just this one, stands a chance.' I thought I detected an almost imperceptible twitch under her heavy make-up.

Once the show was over, I headed straight for the car park, got on my motorcycle and rode home, certain that I would never be invited onto ERT's programmes again. Indeed, on the orders of the press minister (whose mere title fills any liberal heart with unease) I was unofficially blacklisted.[16] Four years later, exactly the same sin – insisting on debt restructuring – would lead Europe's top dogs to demand my removal from Greece's finance ministry and the Eurogroup. Who says Europe's establishment is not consistent?

The 2011 ERT ban was my first whiff of the incompetent authoritarianism that characterized the European Union's approach to the eurozone crisis. For their attitude to the crisis was essentially a moralistic one. Austerity is an awful economic policy that, as explained previously, is guaranteed to fail in bad times. But austerity is not really an economic policy at all. Austerity is a morality play pressed into the service of legitimizing cynical wealth transfers from the have-nots to the haves during times of crisis, in which debtors are sinners who must be made to pay for their misdeeds. Not satisfied with the Greeks', the Spaniards', their own people's submission to their authority, the troika demanded also that the other weaklings of Europe, including the many Germans struggling against poverty, take the guilt and the blame for the crisis too.

The German finance minister Dr Wolfgang Schäuble once told me that my opposition to austerity placed me in a minority of Europeans, citing opinion polls that showed support for government expenditure cuts. I replied that, even if that were true, a majority can be wrong about the cause of their malaise. During the Black Death of the fourteenth century, I reminded him, most Europeans believed the plague was caused by sinful living and could be exorcized by bloodletting and self-flagellation. And when bloodletting and self-flagellation did not work, this was taken as evidence that people's repentance was not sincere enough, that not enough blood had been let, that the flagellation was insufficiently enthusiastic – exactly as now, when austerity's abysmal failure is cited as proof that it has been applied too half-heartedly.

If he was amused, Wolfgang did not show it. But this is the point: stripped of its moral weight, austerity emerges as what it is: a failed economic policy founded on unethical moralizing. The reason the establishment found me infuriating was that I had a degree of success in applying cold logic to the problem and thus de-moralizing the debate on Greek debt, utilizing arguments that transcended the divisions between Left and Right and resonated powerfully with segments of both.

This is why, if they had been able, they would have blacklisted me not just from ERT but from every public forum on the continent.

Square of hope

At the same time as Greek state television was blacklisting me for continuing to campaign for a debt restructuring, the IMF was beginning to work towards . . . a debt restructuring. The German government wanted none of this, but the IMF, increasingly embarrassed at the mess the Europeans had dragged it into, was pushing hard. To appease the IMF, the Greek finance minister lukewarmly consulted debt restructuring experts in Washington, despite his determination to toe Berlin's line.[17] Meanwhile, Berlin and Paris were coming to the conclusion that Greece needed a new bailout loan, a haircut of some of its debt and a new government.

Their thinking was uncomplicated: the first bailout loan had almost all been spent on shoring up the French and German banks. The Greek state would soon need more money – a great deal more – to continue its pretence of solvency. But just as when you use a credit card to repay a mortgage, your overall debt only rises, so the size of the headline sum to be loaned to Athens as part of the second bailout in 2012 would have given the already fuming parliamentarians throughout Europe a collective stroke if it weren't accompanied by some kind of haircut. President Sarkozy and Chancellor Merkel resigned themselves to the idea of Greek debt restructuring on condition that it would burn only those creditors who were incapable of harming them much. By the summer of 2011, it was decided: the haircut would mainly hit Greek pension funds, Greek semi-public institutions and Greek savers who had bought government bonds, while the loans provided by the IMF and the European institutions in 2010 would of course remain inviolable.[18]

That this would spell the end of the wretched Papandreou government, which had pushed the first bailout through parliament, was considered an acceptable price to pay. After all, Prime Minister Papandreou, his finance minister, the whole Greek establishment, had only managed to get parliament to approve the first bailout by repeatedly asserting that it would save Greece's bacon, that debt restructuring was neither necessary nor desirable, and that anyone who said otherwise deserved to be tarred and feathered – or at least ostracized in the ancient Athenian way. Less than two years later, how could that same government push through the same exhausted and humiliated parliament debt restructuring plus a loan even larger than the first? They were doomed.

The impotence of the Papandreou government was evident not only in Parliament House but even more so just outside it, on Syntagma Square. *Syntagma* means 'constitution', and the square's name harks back to an uprising in 1843 against the Bavarian-born King Otto, in which the rebels imposed upon their foreign overlord a written constitution. The square is sandwiched between the Parliament House on one side, formerly King Otto's palace, and the ugly 1970s block that is the Ministry of Finance on the other. From certain parts of the square one can catch glimpses of the Acropolis, a reminder of bygone glories but also of the idea that the *demos* – 'people' – ought to matter. Since 1843, when King Otto was forced to back down, almost every demonstration or rally in Athens has begun, passed through or ended up at Syntagma Square, in front of Parliament House. Indeed, it is the site where I, along with millions of other Greeks of my generation, joined my first demonstration in the early 1970s, tasted the delights of CS gas and cut my political teeth.

During the spring of 2011, with the country already in savage recession, the spontaneous occupation of Syntagma Square began, possibly in emulation of similar occupations of public spaces in Spain by the so-called *indignados* – 'indignants' – protesting against austerity and demanding back their dignity. At first, one or two thousand people would gather after nightfall. But night after night the people would return, and every night thousands more gathered than the night before. This went on for three whole months. At its peak one hundred thousand people congregated in the square. Despite the occasional brief flare-up of low-level violence caused by fascists, riot police and hooded anarchists, what made these rallies special were the impeccably structured debates. No one could speak for more than three minutes; the speakers were drawn by lot; and every few hours the theme under discussion changed. (I recall thinking to myself how splendid it would be to emulate such orderly discussions in our universities.) It might not have been democracy at work, since no binding decisions were possible, but at least it was a huge *agora* vibrating with possibility, in sharp contrast to what went on in Parliament House nearby, site of our national humiliation and submission to a great depression.

Danae and I would take the ten-minute walk from our flat to Syntagma Square to breathe in the oxygen of hope. Twice I was asked to address the crowd. Just before stepping onto the makeshift podium,

I remember recalling that the last time I addressed a demonstration was somewhere in Nottinghamshire, at a picket line during the 1984 miners' strike. At least at Syntagma the weather was warm, the crowd much larger and I was no longer a 'meddling foreigner', which is what a British policeman had once called me. Yet the exhilaration was exactly the same. As I left the podium, visibly chuffed, Danae leaned close to my ear to ask, 'Are you sure you don't want to run for parliament?' I said I was. Whatever my personal feelings, I explained, the best contribution I could make to the cause would be to maintain the lines of communication I had established with politicians from different parties and try to work across party divides. But deep inside I wondered how much longer that would remain possible. The mists of discord were thickening.

In June 2011 the faltering Greek government was being forced by the troika to push through parliament one corrosive bill after another, including the effective termination of trade union rights. These were effectively the rites of Papandreou's departure, a last humiliation before the rug was finally pulled from under his feet by the second bailout. Sensing a crisis, the crowds at Syntagma Square were getting denser and meaner and soon were occupying the square around the clock. Ominously, divisions began to open up. In the upper square nationalists and fascists began to make their ugly presence felt, their slogans reflecting their hatred of all politicians, indeed of parliamentary democracy itself – the visible makings of Golden Dawn's ascent. In the lower square the much more numerous progressives would gather, striving to oppose both the establishment and the crude anti-establishment agitators of the upper square by honouring the tradition of well-organized pluralist debates.

Members of parliament, especially of the governing socialist party, would tell me on the phone or confess bitterly over a cup of coffee behind closed doors that they couldn't take it any more. Walking past the screaming, enraged, humiliated masses to enter the chamber in order to vote for bills that they detested was taking a heavy toll. They repeatedly told me they were on the verge of voting down their own government's troika-dictated bills, but time and again, with only one or two exceptions, they would be beaten back into the government's pen. Within a year, the socialist party that for three decades had commanded around 40 per cent of the vote saw its support collapse to a pitiful 5 per cent.

One day in late June five thousand police encircled Syntagma Square in a well-orchestrated operation to end its occupation. Using quantities of CS gas never seen before in a relatively confined urban space, along with stun and smoke grenades, water cannon and good old-fashioned police violence, they turned the square and surrounding areas into a wasteland. Hardened war correspondents of my acquaintance tell me they never imagined they would witness such state violence in a city like Athens. Walls and pavements were blackened by the smoke, and the whole city reeked of chemicals for weeks. On that day the last remnants of the government's legitimacy were well and truly expunged.

Bailoutistan 2.0

The technical details of how Prime Minister Papandreou was ousted are too sad to recount here. Suffice to say that, as in all good drama, the troika brought him down by means of political machinations involving the courtiers that surrounded his shaky throne. It is typical of the troika's cruel indifference towards those who serve it loyally that before they discarded George Papandreou they subjected him to the ultimate ignominy: in October 2011 he was obliged to travel one last time to Brussels to place his signature on the draft of the second bailout and the very debt restructuring he had been denouncing for so long on the troika's behalf as 'unnecessary and undesirable'.

Setting up a successor government capable of shepherding the second bailout through the Greek parliament was not a simple operation. Papandreou's demise and the weariness of the ruling socialists' parliamentarians pointed to new elections. But the ballot box is unpredictable and elections require at least a month, time that the EU, the IMF and the Greek elite did not feel they could spare. An interim coalition government would be formed instead, and only after it had pushed through the second bailout would an election be risked in the spring of 2012. To form that grand coalition, Antonis Samaras, the leader of the opposition conservative party, would have to be co-opted into the logic of the bailouts, which he had hitherto resisted.

It took one meeting – on 23 June 2011 in Berlin with Mrs Merkel – to break Mr Samaras's emotional attachment to my fierce condemnation of Bailoutistan that he had expressed in our phone conversation following my appearance on ERT. The lure of an eventual move into Maximos, the Greek prime minister's official residence, proved irresistible. He would not be the last leader to trade a principled opposition to Bailoutistan for that office. The plan was as follows: following Papandreou's resignation, a 'technocrat' prime minister would be installed, with the centre Left (PASOK) and the centre Right (New Democracy) providing ministers for the government and the necessary votes in parliament. Once they had seen the troika's second bailout through the legislature, this government would call for fresh elections, which Mr Samaras's New Democracy was bound to win given PASOK's implosion – the result of having borne the moral and political cost of the first bailout. As long as Antonis Samaras could find it within himself to jettison his anti-bailout narrative, endorse the second bailout and support the interim government from the wings, he need only wait six to eight months for his turn as prime minister. Which is precisely what happened.[19]

To underline the depth of the cynicism involved, the gentleman chosen to lead the coalition government was none other than the recently retired vice president of the European Central Bank. A former economics professor in my department at the University of Athens, Lucas Papademos would be obliged to forget some unfortunate utterances before moving into Maximos. Until three days before his swearing-in, Papademos was still parroting the troika's line that a restructuring of Greece's debt was 'neither necessary nor desirable'. But once he was standing on the threshold of Maximos, surrounded by journalists keen to have his first official statement, he pronounced with a perfectly straight face that his main duty as prime minister would be to oversee the restructuring of Greece's debt.

And so we come to the delightful moment in our history when the people who denounced as treacherous fools those of us who dared call for a debt restructuring found themselves to be the very same people called upon by the troika to implement it. By itself that would have been an amusing footnote if the point of the debt restructuring were indeed to render Greece solvent again. But that was never the intention.

To default on your creditors, to declare bankruptcy formally, is a terrible thing, but it has an upside: your debt shrinks and you get the chance to work hard again, pull yourself up by your bootstraps and regain the trust of potential investors. This is, for example, how General Motors recovered after 2009, indeed how Germany returned to the land of the living in the 1950s by means of substantial debt relief. But no, Greece was destined to make history. Under the terms of its second bailout in 2012 the new government would declare the largest non-payment in world history while simultaneously remaining in debtors' prison courtesy of the largest loan in world history.

The world-beating €100 billion debt default haircut hit Greece's powerless pensioners, its professional associations and small-time bondholders – who would be forced to kiss goodbye to the money the state owed them – while a world-record extend-and-pretend loan of €130 billion was pushed down the nation's throat, almost none of which would go to the Greek state per se. Instead, a large chunk of that money went to Greek bankers (to overcompensate them for money they had lost on the haircut government bonds), a second chunk went to Greece's foreign private lenders (as an incitement to make them accept the haircut), and the third chunk went to service the EU's and the IMF's loans from the first bailout agreement.[20]

What made Bailoutistan 2.0 a regime more sinister than its previous incarnation were three new institutions that, by sidelining parliament, damaged democratic sovereignty. These were a mechanism for bailing out the bankers, a new form of governance for the state's revenues and customs, and a department to organize, in the creditors' interests, fire sales of the family silver – in other words, privatization Greek-programme style. A quick look at these offers a valuable beginner's guide to Bailoutistan 2.0.

Possibly the vilest of these institutions was the first of them, the mechanism for bailing out the bankers. When money is injected into a private firm, the entity that provides it must receive shares in the firm in proportion to the injected value and an equivalent degree of control over its management. The second bailout stipulated that €41–50 billion was to be given to the bankers, new public debt that burdened the taxpayers. But rather than securing some degree of public control over the bankrupt banks in return for this money, an ingenious scheme was devised to circumvent this altogether. A new fund was created, wholly owned by the Greek state, called the Hellenic Financial Stability Fund (HFSF), into which €50 billion of the total €130 billion of the second bailout was channelled with the express order that it be passed on to the banks. Legally, the bankers would be required to pass shares to the HFSF that amounted to around 80 per cent of their banks' equity in return, but two devices ensured that parliament would still have no say in their management. First, parliament voted to agree that the shares held by the HFSF would carry no voting rights. Second, the HFSF's board of directors was to comprise foreign directors appointed directly by the troika and Greek nationals (including the CEO and the board's chair) whose appointment required the troika's approval. Moreover, none of the directors could be fired by the government or parliament without the troika's say-so. By passing this bill, parliament's last meaningful action with regard to banks kept alive by its citizens' indebtedness was to give up its oversight of them.

Turning to the Greek state's revenues and customs department, parliament again swallowed an abomination: the department head would now need to be endorsed by the troika and could not be fired without the troika's consent. In many countries the tax office (HMRC in Britain, the IRS in the United States) is independent of the Ministry of Finance or Treasury but answerable directly to the legislature. In Bailoutistan 2.0 the tax and customs office would be answerable to neither.[21]

To complete the triad of affronts, privatizations were assigned to an independent authority led by yet another troika-endorsed chairperson, whose motto might best be summarized as 'Everything must go!' Glossy prospectuses, featuring everything from the nation's ports and railways to pristine beaches and small islands, invited potential buyers to make an offer. The family silver was for sale, and the proceeds were to be collected by Greece's foreign creditors through local appointees.[22] Nothing captured better the people's frustration and resentment than the expressions on their faces while perusing these brochures.

How were parliamentarians persuaded to vote for legislation that denied them jurisdiction over three such crucial pillars of governance? They were blackmailed with the threat of Greece's expulsion from the eurozone. It was a vote that no system of jurisprudence should permit, and only an agonizingly wearied parliament could have acquiesced.

Who do I have to be?

'You have no right to do this. Just vote no!'

A young woman shouted these words at a member of parliament as he struggled past the Syntagma Square occupiers into Parliament House to vote for one of the Bailoutistan 2.0 bills.

'Who are you to judge what I should or shouldn't vote for?' he barked back at her as he elbowed his way in, sweat running down his face.

Her devastating answer came effortlessly: 'Who do I have to be?'

Bailoutistan is an ugly word, but it reflects an obnoxious reality: the turning of Greece into a debtors' prison on behalf of Northern Europe's banks. Those Syntagma Square nights framed the country's further transition from prison into institutionalized debt colony, but they also marked Europe's legitimacy crunch in the aftermath of its credit crunch. That a European country embedded in the continent's great common currency experiment would end up being pushed around like a banana republic is a devastating indictment of a union supposedly founded on the promise of shared prosperity and mutual respect.

Of course Europe's establishment had willed none of this. Before 2008 the elites in Berlin, Brussels, Paris and Frankfurt had believed their own rhetoric, as had those in the United States and the City of London: capitalism had delivered the Great Moderation; boom and bust was a thing of the past; banks had found a magical way to produce 'riskless risk' and were self-regulating marvellously. Those in authority believed that history had ended, and their job was one of micro-management, of nudging a magnificent self-guided, self-managing system in a broadly predetermined, rational direction.

But when Europe's financial system hit the rocks put in its way by Wall Street's self-destruction, Europe's elites panicked. The sight of French and German banks sinking without a trace made them reach into history's dustbin to retrieve the spirit of gunboat diplomacy and the inept economics that came with it. Greece just happened to be the place were these would again be applied, and Bailoutistan was the result.

When inordinate weight is loaded onto a flimsily constructed bridge, the weakest beam will break first. Greece was that beam. The reason it was has nothing to do with the European Union and everything to do with the sorry history of the modern Greek state and the oligarchy that ruled over it, but the cause of the disaster was the bridge's poor design. Even if Greece had been removed from the structure and replaced by a stronger beam, the bridge would have still collapsed.

It is true that in 2010 Greece's public and private sectors were incompetent, corrupt, bloated and indebted. That is why the euro crisis began there. We Greeks managed to acquire an unsustainable debt even before our state was formally created in 1827, and since then tax evasion has been something between an Olympic sport and a patriotic duty. Railing against this disgrace and the Greek oligarchy's excruciating ineptitude, which often translated into despotism, we progressives learned our politics in the 1960s and 1970s, demonstrating on the streets and in particular in Syntagma Square. And yet none of this explains the depth of Greece's post-2010 crisis or the subsequent establishment of Bailoutistan, a sad debtors' colony on the Mediterranean.

If Greece had stayed out of the euro in 2000, what would have happened? In the common currency's first eight years our state and private sector would have borrowed a tiny amount from the French and German banks, who would have been coy about lending to a deficit country whose currency was on a permanent slide. As a result, between 2000 and 2008 Greece would have grown at the pace of a tortoise compared to the debt-fuelled boom we actually experienced. And when the credit crunch hit in 2008 Greece would have faced a small, short, insignificant recession, like Romania's or Bulgaria's. Just as corrupt and inefficient as ever, Greece would have plodded along much as it did in the 1950s and 1960s without the humanitarian crisis in which it is now immersed. Progressives, sick of our society's ills, would have continued to demonstrate in Syntagma Square, unseen and unheard by the rest of humanity, and the world's headlines would have been free of any reference to the NEW GREEK TRAGEDY, GREECE'S THREAT TO GLOBAL FINANCE and the like. And, of course, this book would never have been written.

To err is human, as they say, but to fail spectacularly and with stunning human cost, it seems we needed Europe's grandest economic design, the euro. Greece was the canary in the eurozone's coal mine, whose death should have been a warning of the deadly financial fumes leaking through the continent's monetary system. Instead, in 2010 small, fragile, wasteful Greece became the scapegoat for Europe and its banks. Not only were the Greeks made to shoulder impossible loans on behalf of the French and German banks, not only were they made to submit to a life in a postmodern workhouse so that foreign parliaments could be kept in the dark, but they were also expected to internalize the blame. However, during those long glorious nights in Syntagma Square, Europe's establishment lost control of the blame game. The young woman who stood tall, proclaiming her right to question authority with that glorious 'Who do I have to be?' symbolized the turning point. Yes, our society was shot through with a multitude of malignancies, but no, our cruel and unusual punishment was not justified. And we would not take it lying down.

Catherine the Great once said that if you cannot be a good example, then you will just have to be a horrible warning. Greece's warning to the rest of Europe's laggards was indeed horrible: an iron cage forged by debt and austerity awaited those who fell foul of financial rules that the crisis made impossible to obey. But the young woman at Syntagma Square, Lambros the homeless interpreter, millions of others willing to make sacrifices but not to see them thrown into the bottomless pit of Greece's debt were determined to show the rest of Europe that there were humane alternatives, that Europe's plight while dreadful need not be tragic, that our fate was still in our hands.

After the brutal eviction of the Syntagma Square occupiers, the Greek summer heat took its toll and the occupiers never returned. Instead they filtered out into Greek society, where they spread the word, biding their time until the next conflagration. Then the spirit of Syntagma would become an unstoppable political movement which used the ballot box to establish a new government whose simple task was to dismantle Bailoutistan and knock down the prison walls. But to get there four years of arduous groundwork would be needed first.

3

They bend their tongues like their bows

He came home in the early hours of Sunday morning. Exhausted, Danae and I had already turned in but had been listening for the front door's reassuring thud before going to sleep. Danae's seventeen-year-old son had recently spread his wings and was observing the customary rites of an Athenian teenager on a Saturday evening: going out with friends to discuss the meaning of everything until late in the night, usually at cafés at Psyrri, a neighbourhood a stone's throw from the ancient *agora*. Athens is the safest of cities, and Psyrri even more so, but like any parent we welcomed the sound of the front door.

On that night, moments it seemed after sleep had taken me, the landline rang. Conditioned to associate calls after midnight with family illness, I jumped out of bed and rushed to the living room to pick up.

An eerily suave male voice asked, 'Mr Varoufakis?'

Hazily I said, 'Yes, who is this?'

'We are very glad to see that your boy has returned,' continued the voice. 'He had a great time, it seemed to us, in Psyrri. He then made his way back along Metropolis Street, taking a detour along Hadrian's Road, arriving home via Byron Street.'

With a chill running down my spine I shouted into the phone, 'Who the hell are you? What do you want?'

His answer was icy cool. 'Mr Varoufakis, you were misguided to put certain banks in your sights and in your articles. If you want your boy to continue to return home every day, every Saturday, you will cease and desist. There are better topics for you to meddle in. Pleasant dreams.'

My greatest fear had materialized.

It was November 2011 and already the second bailout was having an effect. Whereas the first bailout had been an exercise in making weaker Europeans (primarily Greece's pensioners and low-income workers) pay for foreign bankers (primarily French and German), the second bailout was aimed at Greece's own bankers: while the haircut sheared them of up to €32.8 billion, they would receive an injection of more than €41 billion as compensation, borrowed by Greek taxpayers from the rest of Europe's taxpayers. Greece's bankers had everything at stake in seeing this most peculiar transfer through.

Their concern was twofold. First, with the Greek parliament so degraded and its members so shattered, the bankers feared that the political process would stall before they got their money. Second, the European Central Bank, increasingly embarrassed by financiers' shenanigans and keen to be seen to be clamping down on them, was demanding that before they received more public money the banks raise some of their own. But how could Greece's bankers attract new capital given that, like the state, they were well and truly bankrupt? No sane investor would put money in a defunct bank.

Two men and a barrel of whiskey

To grasp the ingenuity with which two Greek bankers solved the problem it helps to know a joke I was once told in a Dublin pub involving two entrepreneurial drunkards.

Art and Conn, goes the tale, decide that they have to do something to lift themselves out of poverty, so they persuade Olcán, a local publican, to lend them a barrel of whiskey. Their plan is to roll it down the road to the next town where a fete is to be held, where they will sell its contents by the cup. Rolling the barrel along the road, they stop for a rest under a great oak. While they are sitting under the tree, Art finds a shilling in his pocket, rejoices and asks, 'Hey, Conn, if I give you a shilling can I have a cup of our whiskey?'

'Aye, go on,' replies he, pocketing the shilling.

A minute later Conn realizes he now has a shilling to spend, turns to his companion and asks, 'Art, what do you say? If I give you a shilling can I also have a cup?'

'Aye, Conn,' Art agrees, taking back his shilling.

And so they proceed, the shilling changing hands, until hours later Art and Conn are fast asleep under the oak tree with great grins on their faces, the barrel empty.

I have no idea whether Greece's bankers had ever heard this joke but their solution to the problem of raising capital for their banks was uncannily similar to Art and Conn's, with the difference that they would not be the ones to suffer the resulting hangover. Here is how our two bankers – let's call them Aris and Zorba – did it.

Aris's family founded offshore companies, to which Zorba agreed secretly to lend without collateral or guarantees the millions that Aris's bank needed. Why such generosity towards a competitor? Because Zorba and Aris were sitting under the same proverbial oak. Desperate to raise money for his own bank, Zorba agreed to the loan on condition that Aris's bank lent a similar amount to Zorba's family's offshore outfits. Aris's and Zorba's families then used the monies from their offshore accounts to buy new shares in their own banks, thus fulfilling the regulators' requirement that new capital be raised and thereby qualifying for the real money that the poor taxpayer was borrowing from the troika.

Where Aris and Zorba went one better than Art and Conn – whose hangover was compounded by the thought of their debt to Olcán – was the means by which they ended up owing nothing to anyone. Both sets of loans – from Zorba's bank to the Aris family offshores, and from Aris's bank to the Zorba family offshores – were written off soon after being granted and transferred to the banks's long list of non-performing loans.[1]

Of course Aris and Zorba were not being especially innovative. They were, in fact, standing on the shoulders of con men grander than themselves, such as the perpetrators of the Savings and Loans scam in the United States during the 1980s whose techniques they had copied. Where Aris and Zorba proved unique in the history of capitalism was in succeeding in getting away with their con with the active help of three of the most renowned global financial institutions: the International Monetary Fund, the European Union's Commission and the European Central Bank. These grand institutions committed the following three sins. First, they forced Greece's ruined taxpayers to borrow money from other European countries that they could never repay in order to pass it on to Aris and Zorba in the form of 'recapitalizations'. Second, they deprived Greece's taxpayers of any control over the banks that they now legally owned (being majority shareholders) and ensured that Aris and Zorba would remain in charge of them. Last, they condemned Greek taxpayers to a banking system that, despite the public monies ploughed into it, remained fully bankrupt, courtesy of the non-performing loans the bankers had generated.

Throughout 2011 I had made it my personal crusade, in parallel with a couple of investigative reporters, to expose the connections between Greece's bailout loans, the international institutions that granted them, Greek bankers' remarkable 'innovations' and the Greek political system. Evidently, this was the kind of meddling that could provoke interesting telephone conversations in the early hours of the morning.

Of tongues and bows

When foreign journalists interview me, they usually try to get me to acknowledge Greece's endemic corruption in an attempt to make me admit that I exaggerate the role of the EU, the IMF and the troika in engendering our great depression. Curiously, they are never interested in discussing the central role that the media has played in the process.

During my time as finance minister one of the many interviews I gave on Greek television was marked by a fascinating confession. It was a long interview that spanned almost every conceivable topic. During the first segment the interviewer came out all guns blazing, each question laced with pernicious allegations, giving me time to utter no more than four or five words before I was hit with the next. During the commercial break he approached me to whisper into my ear, 'Minister, I'm very sorry about this but you know our dire situation these days. Aris's bank is our only source of advertising.' I told him I understood. After that the interview proceeded at a more relaxed pace that allowed me a chance to be heard. It seemed that enough had been done, on that occasion at least, to secure the station its daily bread.

In fairness, this was only to be expected. Greek television stations had been in the red even before 2008. Indeed, none of them had ever declared a profit. Nor had Greek newspapers or radio stations. Had they been stand-alone enterprises, they would have filed for bankruptcy long ago. Except they were not. During the years of unsustainable, debt-fuelled growth Greece's media provided an important means of leverage for the developers that owned them. Government ministers could either award their owners lucrative state contracts or expect to be torn to shreds on air or in print. This is one of the many reasons why Greece ended up with motorways costing three times what they would in Germany, overpriced drugs in its hospitals, submarines that leaned like the Tower of Pisa, rivers of cash stowed away in offshore bank accounts and media outlets that always lost money but never shut down.

The silver lining of Greece's bankruptcy in 2010 was that the trough the developers used to feed from dried up, while their mouthpieces were suddenly left to fend for themselves, an impossible task given disappearing advertising revenue and a business model that was never meant to be viable. And yet only one network closed down during the crisis years, the rest continuing to function despite multiplying losses. How could that be? Aris and one or two other bankers provide the answer.

Quite simply, the bankers now took over the funding of the media in order to manipulate public opinion and thus control the political game that kept them in charge of their bankrupt banks. But, unlike the developers, the bankers were clever enough to eschew ownership of the insolvent television stations and newspapers. Instead, they kept the media alive by paying them ludicrous sums to advertise their services and more importantly granted them large extend-and-pretend loans just like the loans they were granting one another and just like the loans the EU and the IMF were granting the Greek state.

The triangle of sin was complete: the insolvent media were kept in a zombified condition by the zombie banks, which were maintained in their undead condition by a bankrupt government, itself preserved in a condition of permanent bankruptcy by the EU and the IMF's bailout loans. Is it any wonder that the Bailoutistan media extolled the benefits of the bailout and portrayed its bankers as victims of an unreliable state, while demonizing anyone who dared reveal what was really going on?

While I was in the thick of the struggle, Bill Black, an American colleague who had played a leading role in exposing similar shenanigans in the United States, the savings and loans scandal of the 1980s and 1990s in particular, made me laugh one day by sending me an email that contained only a short quote, which I interpreted as a gesture of solidarity: 'And they bend their tongues like their bow[s] for lies: but they are not valiant for the truth upon the earth; for they proceed from evil to evil.' (Jeremiah 9:3)

The young prince

Psyrri, a neighbourhood in Athens taken over by bustling youngsters at night, is a different place by day. Tiny workshops continue to struggle for existence, manufacturing nuts, bolts, buttons, tools and other stuff whose value is plummeting in the globalized economy. The air is thick with a cacophony of industrious noises alongside the delectable smells of bakeries and the odd jasmine shrub, and punctuated by the melancholy singing of Roma musicians, who wander the narrow streets with their accordions, horns and violins, collecting the odd coin from nostalgic passers-by.

I know Psyrri well, since my university office at the time was only a few hundred metres up the road from the neighbourhood while Danae's studio is located at its heart. Close by, at the edge of Psyrri, are the shabby offices of the Alliance of the Radical Left, universally known as Syriza. So when in early 2011 Nikos Pappas, the closest associate of Syriza's young leader, called me to arrange a meeting and suggested that the three of us meet in Psyrri, it made perfect sense.

We met at a discreet boutique hotel, one of those investments in the area that now epitomize the false dawn of the gentrification cut short in 2010. It would become our usual meeting place, its pastel-coloured walls witnessing exchanges that began on that day at a relaxed, almost academic pace but turned serious and purposeful by early 2012. Nevertheless, during that first meeting and for some time afterwards, I had no reason to believe we would be meeting again.

I had first laid eyes on Alexis Tsipras on a poster plastered all over Athens promoting his candidature for mayor in the local government elections of 2008. Danae, a long-time supporter of that particular strand of Greece's Left, was enthusiastic about a thirty-four-year-old running for a post usually held by dreary older politicians using it as a springboard into Maximos.[2] In the event Alexis doubled Syriza's vote in central Athens, and before long the party's old guard had organized an internal putsch which installed him as leader, shoving aside the man who had anointed Alexis as his eventual successor. In the general election the following year, though, when Alexis led the party for the first time, the headlines were dominated by the victorious surge of George Papandreou's ill-fated socialists, with Syriza[3] coming in fifth, collecting a miserable 4.6 per cent of the vote, half a per cent less than in 2007.

When I walked into the hotel, he and Pappas were already at a table, ordering lunch. Alexis's voice was warm, his smile unaffected, his handshake that of a potential friend. Pappas had wilder eyes, a high-pitched voice. He joked incessantly, whether the matter was funny or tragic; and tried to exude authority while being everyman to everyone. From the outset it was evident that Pappas had the young prince's ear, guiding, restraining and spurring him on, and this initial impression survived throughout the turbulent times that followed: these two young men, of similar age but different temperaments, were acting and thinking as one.

'I've been following your work for years, ever since I read your *Foundations*,' Pappas said, breaking the ice, referring to an economics textbook I had published in 1998.[4] Apparently he had been a postgraduate economics student in Scotland when he came across the book, and since then he had read the *Modest Proposal for Resolving the Euro Crisis*, which I had co-authored with Stuart Holland, a British Labour former MP and professor of economics at Sussex University. Stuart and I had been working on the *Modest Proposal* since 2005, motivated by the conviction that the euro would cause an almighty crisis which Europe might not survive.[5] After the euro crisis erupted, Stuart and I did our utmost to refine and promote the *Modest Proposal*, convinced that it was Europe's best chance of avoiding its demise. 'Tell Alexis what you are advancing in the *Modest Proposal*,' said Pappas.

I explained its basic logic, and then the conversation turned to a general assessment of the political economy of Bailoutistan and the strategies available to progressives intent on offering the country an escape from its prison of debt.

It soon became clear that, for political reasons, Alexis was vacillating over a basic issue: whether Greece should retain the euro. Even in 2011 Syriza was torn by internal disagreements over whether the party should or shouldn't make Grexit (departure from the eurozone, though not necessarily from the EU) its official policy. As we talked, Alexis's attitude to the question struck me as cavalier and immature. His focus was more on keeping control of the feuding wings of his party than on clarifying in his own mind what the right policy was. Judging by the meaningful looks coming from Pappas, it was clear that he thought so too and was hoping I would help shift his leader away from casual experimentation with the idea of Grexit.

In the hour or so that followed I did my best to impress upon Alexis that turning Grexit into an objective would be as large a mistake as failing to prepare for it. I also criticized Syriza for making silly promises such as that, if elected, the bailout agreement with the EU and the IMF would be unilaterally torn up.

'Why can't we tell them that if they do not accept our unilateral rejection of their programme, we will exit the euro?' Alexis asked.

I explained that there were three possible outcomes of a confrontation with the troika. The best outcome would be a new deal for Greece – involving serious debt restructuring, the end of self-defeating austerity and a series of reforms targeting the oligarchy – which kept us in the euro. The worst possible outcome would be to stay in the euro in the same position: in debtors' prison and with shrinking incomes, prospects and hopes. Grexit would be in between: far, far worse than a viable deal within the eurozone but better, in the medium and long term, than a continuation of the vicious circle of bailouts, austerity and depression for another five years or more.

I told him there was no way Berlin, Frankfurt, Brussels or the IMF would accept a take-it-or-leave-it offer from him; they would simply leave it. So to issue such an ultimatum would be to ensure the third outcome – expulsion from the eurozone – and to remove even the possibility of the first. To leave the door open to the best possible outcome, he needed to force a negotiation. On the one hand this meant rejecting Grexit as a threat (let alone an objective) while on the other signalling to the world that his worst fear was not enforced Grexit but the continuation of the current situation. However, I was unsure whether he was much interested in the nuances of this argument.

'But Yanis, many people, like Paul Krugman, say that we would be better off outside the euro anyway,' Alexis retorted.

I agreed that we would be better off if we had never entered the eurozone but hastened to add that it was one thing to have stayed out of the euro and quite another to leave it. Exiting would not get us to where we would have been had we not entered!

To try to shake him out of his lazy thinking, I outlined what I expected to happen immediately if Grexit were announced. Unlike Argentina, a country that had severed its currency's ties to the dollar, Greece did not have its own notes and coins in circulation. Grexit would involve more than severing the one-to-one exchange rate between the drachma and the euro. The result of such a severance in Argentina had been a drastic devaluation in the national currency, leading to a major surge in exports. This in turn led to a major reduction in the trade deficit, and so, eventually, to the restoration of economic health. Unlike the Argentinians, however, Greece would have to create a new drachma before then severing it from the euro.[6] But creating a currency takes months. In other words, Grexit would be like announcing a currency devaluation months before it happens, a strategy that comes with dire consequences: an exodus of euros and an absence of a local currency to facilitate daily transactions.

Would he be prepared, I asked Alexis, to stand in front of voters during an election campaign and tell them that this was what he was proposing? That this should be Plan A? Or would it not be better to tell voters this: we shall demand a renegotiation that yields a new deal for Greece rendering our social economy sustainable within the eurozone, but if the EU and the IMF refuse to negotiate meaningfully, then we shall not accept any more extend-and-pretend loans from Europe's taxpayers. And if they want to retaliate by pushing us out of the euro, at immense cost to both themselves and us, then let them do their worst.

Pappas was nodding enthusiastically, but Alexis seemed elsewhere. When I pushed him to explain his silence, his reply confirmed that he was preoccupied with the goings-on within Syriza rather than engaging properly with the issue at hand. I was unimpressed. As the meeting drew to a close, and at the risk of sounding condescending, I offered him some well-meant but unsolicited advice on a separate matter, which he may have found offensive: 'Alexis, if you want to be prime minister, you need to learn English. Get a tutor, it is imperative.'

Back home Danae asked me how the meeting had gone. 'He is a very agreeable person but I do not think he has what it takes,' I replied.

Those first meetings with Alexis and Pappas proved a turning point in more ways than one. Over the previous two years I had become used to meeting worried politicians from across the political spectrum – with the exception of communist party cadres, who live in a permanent bubble of self-confirming belief. But as 2011 drew to a close and the second bailout approached, there were fewer opportunities for genuine dialogue with anyone from the political centre, whether the shrinking PASOK socialists, many of whom simply recoiled into a private purgatory, or the New Democracy conservatives, many of whom had once shared my forebodings but who now co-opted

PASOK's stragglers into an alliance designed to see the second bailout through and their party into power. Quite suddenly the opportunities for cross-party dialogue had disappeared, like a fast-ebbing tide. In parliament only Syriza remained to fight against the establishment of Bailoutistan 2.0. This is why, when Pappas called back after the second bailout was first canvassed to propose another meeting, I did not think twice: whatever my misgivings, I accepted his invitation.

At our second meeting and in the meetings that followed I was pleasantly surprised: Alexis seemed transformed. Gone was the complacency, the fixation on Syriza's internal affairs and the casual attitude towards Grexit. He had clearly done his homework, even on the *Modest Proposal*.[7] He also told me proudly that he had engaged an English language tutor and was making good progress. (A few years later, when serving in his first government, I was listening in to a teleconference involving Alexis, Chancellor Merkel of Germany and President Hollande of France and recalled this moment: Alexis had the best English of the three.)

The best thing about our meetings was the emergent clarity and unity of purpose. I invested much energy in impressing upon Alexis and Pappas that in any negotiations with the EU and the IMF Alexis's success would depend as much as anything else on his ability to control Greece's banks. Alexis meanwhile seemed fully to embrace my recommendation of a three-pronged policy of *constructive disobedience*, which comprised firstly saying no to further extend-and-pretend loans and the austerity they came with; secondly putting forward moderate proposals for debt restructuring, lower tax rates and reforms that attacked the triangle of sin; and finally always keeping in mind that at some point, in a desperate bid to kill off demands for a debt restructuring and to avoid Mrs Merkel having to tell her parliamentarians the truth about what she had done in 2010, Berlin would threaten him with expulsion from the eurozone.

Archimedean point

At first I delayed telling Danae about the phone call threatening her son. Before worrying her maybe unnecessarily I wanted somehow to assess the risk. Surely it was just an empty threat meant to scare me into silence? But I realized I had no right to pass judgment alone.

As the second bailout approached, the media, the banks and the government were preparing feverishly for a last stand. There was no telling what they were capable of. So I plucked up the courage and told her.

Danae looked at me disapprovingly and issued a laconic, matter-of-fact ultimatum: 'Either you enter politics to protect us, or we're leaving the country.'

Without hesitation I replied, 'Then we're leaving.'

A few days later I was due to tour the United States to promote my new book on the global crisis.[8] While I was there, two job offers presented themselves, allowing me fortuitously to fulfil my bargain with Danae. By early 2012 our move to the United States was under way.[9]

On the day we boarded the plane Bloomberg screens beamed around the world of finance two newsflashes from the eurozone. The first read: 'Merkel Open to Debt-Sharing Compromise as Monti Sees Way to Persuade Her'.[10] The second was closer to home: 'Greeks Run University Professor Out of the Country for Telling Economic Truths'. If only the first newsflash had been right – it wasn't – maybe the second might have been wrong!

Thus Danae and I landed in Seattle, where I worked for a few months as economist in residence at the Valve Corporation[11] before moving on to Austin, where my great friend and colleague Jamie Galbraith had arranged for me to join the University of Texas's Lyndon B. Johnson School of Public Affairs, at which I was to teach courses that included one entitled Europe's Financial Crisis. Despite his considerable powers of prescience, I doubt he knew quite what he was getting embroiled in when he found me the post: three years later Jamie would end up joining me at the Greek Ministry of Finance to lead work on a vital top-secret project.

For more than two years Austin provided an Archimedean vantage point, the ideal place from which to observe but also to act. While it was heart-wrenching to watch from afar as the troika and its domestic minions formally turned Greece into Bailoutistan 2.0, the view from Austin offered clarity.

It also offered an opportunity to build a bridge between Washington and my new Syriza friends, not the most natural of allies. It seemed safe to assume that a future Syriza government would precipitate an almighty clash with Germany, the European Commission and the

European Central Bank. The last thing Alexis and Pappas needed was a hostile administration in the United States. So, from 2012 to 2015, with Jamie Galbraith's assistance and connections, I would do all I could to explain to American opinion makers and the Obama administration that the United States had nothing to fear from a Syriza government, whose priority would be first and foremost to liberate Greece from its crushing debt.

Austin is weird in the nicest possible way: paradise for live-music aficionados and an excellent place to forget the rest of the world's tribulations. But none of that was available to me. During the day, while Greece was asleep, I would prepare my lectures and work on my book about the deeper causes of 'Europe's inane handling of its inevitable crisis'.[12] At night, taking advantage of the time difference, I would appear over Skype on Greek television, follow the ongoing debates and write articles to continue my campaign.

The Greek winter and spring of 2012 were marked by quiet anguish and muffled indignation. Syntagma Square saw almost none of the mass action of 2011. As the recession bit harder, the people privatized their pain, staying at home to lick their wounds and look after their needy. The troika's technocratic coalition government led by the former vice president of the European Central Bank and supported by PASOK and New Democracy, was completing the construction of Bailoutistan 2.0.[13] The time was fast approaching when that government's work would be done and Antonis Samaras, the New Democracy leader, would trigger a general election that he hoped to win and move triumphantly into Maximos. In the event, the general election was called for May 2012.

Before the May election my exchanges with Alexis and Pappas were few and far between. With Papandreou's PASOK socialists staring oblivion in the face, the main protagonists were Samaras's New Democracy and Tsipras's Syriza, but neither I nor they imagined that a party which had won only 4.6 per cent of the vote in the previous election would have a fighting chance at forming a government, however grave the shift in the political tectonic plates.

My preference was for Syriza to present voters with a basic, progressive, Europeanist, logically coherent, non-populist programme as a foundation on which to build an image of a credible future government, one capable of negotiating the country's escape plan with the EU and the IMF. Alexis and Pappas were inclined to a different political programme, one that maximized short-term electoral gains at the expense (in my view) of long-term logical coherence. When I read the economic policy segment of Syriza's 2012 electoral manifesto, my irritation was such that I stopped after a few pages. The next day I was asked to comment on it by a Greek television reporter. I said I was inclined to support Syriza but that my resolve to vote for the party was conditional on my capacity to resist reading its economic programme.

The May election produced a hung parliament. The political centre, comprising PASOK and New Democracy, parties that together had previously commanded up to 80 per cent of popular support, were deserted by more than half of their voters. It was the price the two establishment parties paid for having ushered in Bailoutistan.[14] To call this a political earthquake would be an understatement. As often happens when debt deflation causes the political middle ground to implode, Nazism reared its ugly face, with Golden Dawn securing 7 per cent of the vote to become the fourth-largest party. Meanwhile, tiny Syriza quadrupled its previously puny vote to just 2 per cent short of Antonis Samaras's New Democracy. It was the first time since 1958 that the Left would rise to the lofty heights of the official opposition. Alexis and Pappas had cause to feel vindicated, ignoring the scorn I had poured over Syriza's economic programme.

But a parliament in which the largest party commands less than 19 per cent of the vote cannot produce a viable government. Its unavoidable dissolution paved the way for new elections a month later, in June 2012. It was to be an interesting month. In the absence of either a government or a functioning parliament, the EU and the IMF were forced to conjure up some breathtaking new illusions to maintain the pretence that the Greek state was meeting its debt repayments. Meanwhile, the only parties with any electoral momentum were Syriza and New Democracy, with Syriza rising faster albeit from a slightly lower base. If the trends of the previous weeks were to continue, Alexis had a shot at forming the next government. This realization shook up the oligarchy, the troika, Germany's political establishment and not least Alexis and Pappas, who were understandably panicking at the possibility that the cruel gods were conspiring to grant them their greatest wish.

Alarm bell

I had returned to Athens to vote in the May election when Pappas phoned to organize a meeting. Tsipras, he and I met in the same hotel in Psyrri in a state of considerable excitement: they were no longer on the fringes of the political game but were now riding a wave of popular support capable of producing real change within weeks, not years. But it was at that meeting that an alarm bell began to ring loudly in my head.

'Do you realize that, if we win, you will be handling our negotiations with the EU and the IMF?' asked Pappas with his trademark simper.

My stomach lurched. Pappas's eagerness to get me involved in the negotiations with the EU and the IMF was at odds with the fact that Syriza's economic policy portfolio belonged to Yannis Dragasakis – the party's shadow finance minister, a veteran politician of the Left who had played a central role in Alexis's elevation to the leadership and indeed in the creation of Syriza. While Alexis and Pappas evidently did not consider Dragasakis the man to do battle with the EU and the IMF, he was nonetheless responsible for scripting the party's economic agenda and was a party heavy whose toes they would avoid treading on. I inferred that Alexis and Pappas's understandable reluctance to do so was what lay behind their ill-thought-through enthusiasm for splitting the roles of chief negotiator and finance minister.

I took a moment before replying to Pappas's question. Training my eyes on Alexis, I told them I was honoured by their offer but that I did not see how splitting the roles could work. All negotiations would take place within the Eurogroup, where each government is represented by its finance minister: to have any credibility and negotiating power, that minister must have the full backing not only of their prime minister but also of the cabinet, parliament and electorate. Sending an unelected technocrat to negotiate with its creditors the country's economic liberation while someone else ran the domestic economy would be a disaster in the making.

Seeing that Alexis agreed with me, Pappas tried to salvage the discussion with a request that I prepare a briefing document that outlined the optimal negotiating stance of the government were Syriza to win on 14 June, three short weeks later. That night I sat down to complete the first of many, many versions of that strategy paper.

At its heart I set down two proposals to be presented to the EU and IMF for the restructuring of Greece's debt. First, the state's bankruptcy, the public debt, should be uncoupled from the bankruptcy of the country's banks and their private losses. This way the bankrupt state could not be held responsible for European taxpayers' money it had not received. More importantly, the banks' revival would not be held back by the state's indebtedness: after all, how could the Greek state back the banks when it too was bankrupt? Without such uncoupling, the Greek state and the banks operating in Greece would continue to drag each other down like a pair of weak swimmers caught in stormy waters, hugging one another as they sank towards the bottom of the sea. How could this be achieved? By turning Europe's taxpayers into the owners of the Greek banks so that they were no longer the de facto liability of the Greek state but were backed instead by the European people, and by having the EU institutions run them on their behalf.[15] This was the only way confidence in the banks could be restored.

Second, any repayments of the Greek state's debt to the EU and the IMF arising from its two bailouts should be conditional on the country's recovery first reaching a certain momentum.[16] This was the only way the national economy could be given a chance to revive.

Taken together, these two debt restructuring exercises would signal a new era: the EU and the IMF would no longer operate like a pre-Christmas Ebenezer Scrooge. Rather, they would become Greece's partners in promoting its economic recovery, without which their bailout loans would be haircut savagely anyway.

My briefing paper, written for Alexis and Pappas's eyes only, ended with a section on what reaction to expect from the good folk at the EU–IMF as well as Greece's domestic oligarchy: venomous hostility. Although ideal for helping Greece to recover and thus repay as much of its otherwise unpayable debts as possible, the two proposals were politically toxic for our opponents both within and outside Greece. My advice was as follows:

> What should Athens do if Europe's officials reject these two proposals outright, insisting instead on fresh extend-and-pretend loans?
>
> Unless a Syriza government is prepared to turn down *any* new loans until the debt has been effectively restructured,

there is no sense in winning the election in the first place. Saying no to new loans will of course come at a cost. The troika will threaten to shut down the banks, and the state will have to pay public-sector wages and pensions out of its taxes. This means that your government must brace itself for a tough negotiating period during which the state lives strictly within its means (reducing if need be the highest salaries and pensions until the primary deficit is eliminated) and paper money transactions are replaced by debit cards, web banking and some form of IOUs issued by the state. It won't be pretty, but extraordinary struggles for recovering sovereignty call for extraordinary measures. But here is the good news: if you are prepared to issue moderate, sensible demands and at the same time say no to their extending-and-pretending (and mean it!), the EU and the IMF will most certainly come to the table – it would cost them too much not to, both financially and politically.

I knew perfectly well that from 2010 the troika's reaction to any proposal involving a debt restructuring had been ferocious, for this would have required Chancellor Merkel to come clean on the ulterior motives behind the Greek bailout. The same reaction would now occur domestically, in Greece. In the minds of Greece's skittish bankers my campaign for debt restructuring boiled down to their liquidation, as control over the banks would be transferred to EU institutions and their ownership to the European taxpayers. Moreover, backing the banks was an entire political class used to receiving massive loans from their banker mates without collateral, guarantees or scrutiny. I cannot recall to what extent Alexis grasped the implications of this strategy, but I do recall telling him in detail what he should expect if he were to adopt my recommendation: nothing short of war. No wonder he was reluctant to embrace it.

'Are you advising me to call for the Greek banks to be given to foreigners? How can I sell this idea to Syriza?' Alexis asked me at a later meeting at party HQ.

'Yes, this is precisely what you must do,' I answered.

If he wanted a negotiated agreement within the eurozone, I explained, then he had to accept a basic truth: the Greek state did not have the money to prop up the Greek banks. Ergo, the only alternative to either Grexit, where all bets were off, or continued debt bondage, the worst of all scenarios, was European ownership of the banks. In fact, I said, this was something that should be happening anyway: just as it is nonsense to speak of Californian or Texan banking systems within the dollar zone, it was ridiculous to imagine that we could have separate, nation-based banking systems within the eurozone.

Alexis got it. But that did not mean he liked it. Particularly as Syriza's central committee was naturally drawn to the idea of nationalizing the banks. While the Greek media would shriek ALEXIS TO GIVE OUR BANKS TO FOREIGNERS! Syriza's leftists would denounce him for abandoning their long-term crusade to bring finance under the control of the state. Seeing his horror at the thought of the inevitable backlash, I warned him that liberating Greece would mean making powerful enemies, not just those who had a political imperative to keep the country a debt colony, but those within Syriza who wanted him to build a socialist paradise within the eurozone. But this was impossible anyway. The only thing possible within the eurozone was to liberate Greece from its debtors' prison. To achieve this, his only hope was to convince a majority of Germans to see themselves as partners in our recovery rather than serial funders of our black hole. They were about to pour their money into Greek banks, so he must offer them shares in those banks. Only then would they feel they had a stake in Greece's recovery. With that one stroke he would break the triangle of sin.

Alexis smiled. He told me he didn't mind confronting the bankers, but without any influence over the commercial banks operating in Greece, he argued, it would be impossible for a government to implement an industry policy or a development and reconstruction plan. He just couldn't see the Syriza central committee swallowing it. He had a point.

Put it to them this way, I suggested. As true internationalists, as progressive Europeanists, we would be taking bankrupt banks away from corrupt Greek privateers and handing them over to Europe's common people, to the same European citizenry injecting their money into those banks. At present the banks cannot provide the investment capital needed for Greece's recovery and growth, so we only stand to gain by handing them, and their liabilities, over. Meanwhile, I suggested, we could set up from scratch a new public development bank into which we would place Greece's remaining public assets. These could then be used as collateral to generate an influx of new

investment funding for development purposes, possibly in collaboration with the European Investment Bank.

Alexis liked the internationalist, progressive sound of this, but did he
like it enough to take it to Syriza's central committee and get Dragasakis
to accept it? The young party leader's dilemma was shot through with
many of the ills that ultimately undermined our battle plan in the spring
of 2015. I could see it in his face on that afternoon at Syriza's HQ. On
the one hand, he could see that what I was proposing was the only
escape route within the eurozone. But at the same time he could not
bring himself to break with the internal Syriza establishment.

Personally, I was convinced that my proposals would be rejected,
a perfect excuse for keeping my distance from Syriza. As long as Alexis
remained hostage to Syriza's internal delusions, I was resolute in my
decision to remain on the sidelines, offering critical advice if and when
asked, and relieved not to be involved. Three days later, on 24 May,
this relief grew when I read Alexis's speech detailing Syriza's economic
policies. The chasm between what they were proposing and what
could actually be achieved within the eurozone was immense. Within
an hour I had dispatched a long scathing email to both Alexis and
Pappas which highlighted the numerous logical flaws in what they
had just promised voters as well as my assessment of Dragasakis's
capacity to put together a convincing economic programme.[17]

Alexis's confused public pronouncements, the Greek oligarchy's
anti-Syriza hysteria, plus Chancellor Merkel's naked threats against a
Syriza-led Greece, combined to produce an election result that kept
Alexis in opposition.[18] I was at once relieved and saddened: relieved
that he would have another parliamentary term to get his act together,
and saddened that Bailoutistan 2.0 would now probably be cast in
stone by a new coalition government dancing to the troika's tune.[19]

A friendship's last gasp

Yannis Stournaras and I became close soon after I moved back to
Greece from Australia. This was in 2000, when I left the University
of Sydney for a professorship at the University of Athens, where
Stournaras was already an economics professor.[20] We made up an
informal quartet of academic economists with Georgos Krimpas, a
senior professor, and Nicholas Theocarakis, an astounding scholar

and dear friend. Krimpas had been Stournaras and Theocarakis's professor and mentor, making me the new kid on the block. I succeeded Krimpas as director of political economy, the discipline to which all four of us belonged.

Stournaras taught part time because of his government role under the PASOK administration that brought Greece into the eurozone. Indeed, during the accession negotiations in the 1990s, when Berlin was keen to keep Greece out, Stournaras served as chair of the Council of Economic Advisers, an important organ of the Ministry of Finance which he used to convince Berlin and Brussels to let Greece into the euro.[21] Once Greece was securely inside the euro, in 2000 the PASOK prime minister rewarded Stournaras with the Commercial Bank of Greece, where he became chair and CEO.[22] It was during this last phase of his career that we first met.

Despite his busy schedule, Stournaras was always on hand to do his share of teaching, and to do it happily and devotedly. While our economic perspectives differed considerably, as did our politics, his commitment to the university and the good chemistry between us provided the foundation for a developing friendship. When I set up an international doctoral programme, Stournaras was there to support it, enjoying the higher calibre of students we attracted. More improvements to the curricula followed, drawing indignation from corrupt student politicians and vigorous animosity from colleagues whose petty interests were threatened.[23] But the quartet stood firm, aided by many other colleagues. Soon we were socializing outside work, even spending weekends together.

On the night of the September 2009 general election, which brought George Papandreou to government, Danae and I were at Stournaras's north Athens apartment watching the count on television along with Yannis, his wife and another couple. Of the eight people in the room, Stournaras and I were the only ones who had not voted for PASOK that day – possibly because, like sausages, if you know what's in them . . .[24] A few months later Greece was bankrupt and the first bailout was on its way.

During that momentous year for Greece, 2010, Stournaras made a career move that raised eyebrows, becoming director of an economics think tank originally set up by Greece's National Confederation of Industries, the largest and most established bosses' guild in the land, traditionally affiliated to the conservatives of New Democracy. Soon after taking the helm, Stournaras began endorsing standard free-market solutions that were at odds with the social democratic principles he had long espoused under PASOK. But his move was less an apostasy from PASOK's socialists, his former crowd, and more a sign of what was to follow once the second bailout demanded a grand coalition government. Stournaras was a pioneer of the collapse of the centre Left and the centre Right into one, indivisible, pro-establishment, troika-friendly government – one that would take its ultimate shape after the June 2012 election.

A month before the May 2012 election I was passing through Athens on my way back to the USA from Berlin, where I had addressed a conference on the euro crisis. Upon arriving in Athens, I called Stournaras. We met the next day at a café in the lobby of a hotel at the foot of the Acropolis; we hugged, kissed and exchanged news of our daughters and partners. Turning to business, I briefed him on the discussions I had just had in Berlin with officials from the European Central Bank and the German government, with financial journalists and the like. I also mentioned a conversation I had had with financier George Soros. I told Stournaras that Soros agreed with my assessment of the Greek situation as well as with the gist of my economic policy proposals for Europe as a whole.

Stournaras and I then proceeded to discuss the troika's Greek programme. It was clear that Greece's bankruptcy had created a gulf between us, turning pre-existing differences of opinion into a theoretical, empirical and political crevasse. Stournaras insisted that the troika's programme was viable provided it was implemented vigorously. I asked him to explain. He did so with his usual ebullience.

'It's simple,' he said. 'It can be done on the basis of the three fours principle: 4 per cent growth rate, 4 per cent government budget primary surplus, and 4 per cent interest paid out on our bailout loans.'[25]

'Sure, that would nail it,' I replied. 'Except that it is *impossible* for the Greek economy to achieve a 4 per cent growth rate and a 4 per cent budget primary surplus at once.' I argued that if the government stated it intended to achieve a 4 per cent budget surplus, this would translate in the mind of any investor into even higher tax rates and was bound to deter them.

The conversation was going nowhere. But I still believed our friendship, one of the few remaining bridges between opposing camps, was an asset that could be harnessed for the greater good. Just before we parted, I said that the two of us had a responsibility to remain friends. He seemed to be heading towards some lofty government position whereas my ideas were taking me in the other direction, towards the opposition. But above all else we should not allow ourselves to be turned against one another at a human level. He nodded in agreement and we parted ways with a hug that, thinking back, was on the luke-warm side.

Two months later, just before the June 2012 election, the University of Athens Economics Faculty was considering my application for leave without pay, so I could return to Austin and continue to teach there. Such a request was perfectly normal and the faculty's vote to accept it little more than a formality, but this application occasioned a tumultuous debate. The reason was that Stournaras had presented the faculty with the following question: why should the University of Athens grant me leave to return to the United States when my purpose there was to collaborate with George Soros in the shorting of Greek bonds?

To short a government bond means to make a bet that its value will fall, effectively speculating that the country's public debt will become unattractive to investors. If enough people spend enough money shorting a bond, confidence in the bond falls, it loses value and the short becomes self-fulfilling. Stournaras's bizarre accusation was that I was speculating on the New York money markets in cahoots with George Soros in order to profit from a downgrade of the Greek state's creditworthiness.

Allegations such as this – that I was a self-serving opportunist working towards bankrupting the Greek state – were a favourite of my opponents. Anti-Semitic rightist conspiracy theorists had attacked Soros as a Jew for leading a campaign to bring Orthodox Christian Greece down. From 2010 onwards, when I started arguing that the Greek state was bankrupt and advocated embracing our bankruptcy, these circles insinuated, and later proclaimed, that I was his stooge. The first time I heard the accusation, in 2011, I was merely amused. Now Stournaras had added a whole new twist to these ludicrous charges, presumably based on my account of my discussion with George Soros in Berlin.

The simple facts are that I have never bought or sold – let alone shorted – a bond or a share in my life, and I had never before met or communicated with Soros except at our shared panel event in Berlin in the spring of 2012.

Upon hearing of his outrageous allegation I picked up the phone, seething with anger, and called Stournaras to ask, as calmly as I could, why he had made it. He apologized immediately, citing 'stress' and the 'bad influence' of media reports that I was working for Soros. I said I accepted his apology, but in my heart I knew Stournaras had crossed the Rubicon to a terrain incapable of supporting any bridge between us.

A few days later, after the June 2012 election ushered in Antonis Samaras's coalition government, I heard on the news that Stournaras was to be the country's next technocratic – unelected – minister of finance. He stayed in the job for two years, using his tenure to implement the loan conditions of the second bailout as faithfully as he could – so much so that the swingeing austerity introduced in wave after wave of cutbacks and tax hikes accelerated the recession, terminally destabilizing the Samaras government. Less than two years after its election victory, in the May 2014 European parliamentary election, Samaras's New Democracy received fewer votes than Syriza and subsequently fell well behind in the opinion polls. A month later the term of the governor of Greece's central bank expired, and Samaras used the opportunity to appoint Stournaras. Were the establishment parties to lose the next general election, at least they would leave behind someone at the central bank who was willing and able to undermine the incoming Syriza government. Which is precisely what Stournaras did.

The hotel café where we met in April 2012 had, as things turned out, witnessed our friendship's last gasp.

Success story

While Stournaras was taking over at the finance ministry during the hot summer of 2012, the folks at the EU and IMF were trying to solve a little conundrum of their own. The loans for the second bailout had been delayed by the twin Greek elections and would not start arriving before the autumn. Unfortunately, Athens was meant to send just under €3.5 billion to the ECB, one of its many unpayable debt repayments, on 20 August. How could that happen given that the coffers were empty?

When the troika has a will it discovers a way. Here is the wizardry they used to conjure up the necessary illusion, narrated in slow motion so that the reader can fully appreciate the magic.

- The ECB granted Greece's bankrupt banks the right to issue new IOUs with a face value of €5.2 billion – worthless pieces of paper, given that the banks' coffers were empty.
- As no sane person would pay money to buy these IOUs, the bankers took them to the finance minister, Stournaras, who stamped on them the bankrupt state's copper-bottomed guarantee – in reality a useless gesture since no bankrupt entity (the state) can meaningfully guarantee the IOUs of another bankrupt entity (the banks).
- The bankers then took their worthless IOUs to the Central Bank of Greece, which is of course a branch of the ECB, posting them as collateral for new loans.
- The Eurogroup gave the green light to the ECB to allow its Greek branch to accept these IOUs as collateral and, in exchange, give the banks real cash equivalent to 70 per cent of the IOUs' face value (a little more than €3.5 billion).
- Meanwhile, the ECB and the Eurogroup gave Stournaras's finance ministry the green light to issue new Treasury bills with a face value of €3.5 billion – IOUs issued by the state, which of course no investor would touch in their right mind given the emptiness of the state's own coffers.
- The bankers then spent the €3.5 billion they had received from the Central Bank of Greece – in fact from the ECB itself – when they pawned their own worthless IOUs in order to buy the state's worthless IOUs.
- Lastly, the Greek government took this €3.5 billion and used it to pay off . . . the ECB!

Such ingenuity propels Art and Conn's logic to stunning new heights. It eclipses many of the shenanigans that made Wall Street bankers the object of worldwide opprobrium. It adds a whole new dimension to Walter Scott's famous lines 'Oh, what a tangled web we weave: / When first we practise to deceive!' Then again, without such tangled webs, how could the world be deceived that Greece was solvent and on the mend, now that the right government had been voted in? But as soon as one such web had been woven another became necessary.

Around the same time as this was going on, Christine Lagarde was being put under pressure by non-European IMF member states – countries such as Brazil, India, Japan and Malaysia – to stop the charade and tell Berlin in particular that unless Greece's debt was restructured the IMF would walk away from the whole mess. In the autumn of 2012, as the second bailout was being finalized, Lagarde made a remarkable move revealing quite how intense this pressure had become: she approached Stournaras suggesting that they walk together into the Eurogroup and demand from Wolfgang Schäuble, Germany's finance minister, a drastic haircut of Greece's debt.

But instead of jumping at this unique opportunity to forge an alliance with the IMF, Stournaras informed Schäuble of Lagarde's proposal to band together against him and asked the German finance minister's permission to accept it. Naturally, Schäuble instructed Stournaras to 'forget it'. Which Stournaras proceeded to do.[26]

At that time I happened to be attending a banking conference in the United States. There I bumped into one of the IMF's bigwigs. 'What was he [Stournaras] thinking?' he asked angrily. 'Do these guys have a better idea of how to make ends meet? Is there a plan? I just don't get it.'

They did have a plan, I informed him. Except that it was a plan for staying in government under the pretence that the country was on the mend. Its code name was (I like to think) Greek Success Story.

The Greek Success Story plan had four sequential elements: the Merkel Boost, the Speculative Bubble, the ECB Put, and the Pretend Debt Restructuring. The first of these, the Merkel Boost, was already in place. In September 2012 Chancellor Merkel, egged on by Mario Draghi, the ECB's president, and probably Beijing, stopped over in Athens on her way from China to Berlin.[27] In the few hours of her stay she patted Prime Minister Samaras on the back, signalling to the world media that Grexit was off the table and that Greece, having chosen the right government, would be allowed to stay in the eurozone.

This brief piece of theatre was sufficient to create a minor rally in Greek property values, which had gone through the floor during May and June 2012 when the world was abuzz with talk of Grexit in the face of Syriza's rise and the hung parliament in Athens. As previously explained, if Greece were bundled out of the eurozone, all prices would be redenominated in new drachmas, whose exchange rate would instantly plummet, shaving considerable value from shares, villas and yachts. But markets have a tendency to overreact. When they fall they fall inordinately, and when a good news story arrives they rebound unreasonably. The Merkel Boost was just such an event: a market that had almost died suddenly rallied with irrational exuberance.

The plan's second element, sanctioned of course by the troika, was to turbocharge this exuberance by creating a Speculative Bubble around the Greek banks. The idea was simple. As financiers began to look at Greece as an underpriced investment opportunity thanks to the Merkel Boost, the government would offer them a deal they could not refuse: buy shares in Greece's bankrupt banks now, and if their price rises in the future you will be guaranteed more shares at the original low price, while if they fall your losses will be generously absorbed by the Greek taxpayer. What financier could resist?

The idea here was to create a flow of speculative money into Greece's dilapidated banking system and to present it as evidence of recovery, thus attracting other speculators in real estate, the natural ally of any financial bubble. Having demonstrated to Berlin and to the ECB that the new troika-driven government was turning the ailing ship around, Athens would then hit the ECB with its request: back our debt just as you are backing Ireland's, Portugal's, Spain's and Italy's.[28] If Prime Minister Samaras and Finance Minister Stournaras could secure this backing, there would be nothing to stop them from selling new Greek debt to private investors: even if Greece were sinking further into the quicksand, investors' bonds would be guaranteed by the ECB. Greek voters could then be told that their country was once again trusted by international investors and ergo no longer bankrupt. This was their plan's third element, the ECB Put.

The fourth and last element of their plan was a wholly inadequate yet symbolically important Pretend Debt Restructuring. In a Eurogroup meeting that took place in November 2012, around the time Stournaras was giving Lagarde the cold shoulder, Schäuble rewarded Stournaras with the promise of a possible, albeit superficial, debt restructuring by the end of December 2014. The condition was that Athens would remain loyal to the troika programme, complete it as agreed and balance its books.[29]

The hope was that these four elements of the Greek Success Story would produce and maintain a feeling of recovery that would reach its climax by late 2014, just in time for a new election in early 2015.[30] But after a strong start, with the financial variables reflecting a robust Merkel Boost and a promising Speculative Bubble, the government's plans got stuck in the mire of an unforgiving reality. For while the variables that affect the bottom line of Wall Street speculators such as the infamous John Paulson – who rushed in right on cue to profit from the bubble around Greek bank shares – were flourishing, the variables of daily life for normal Greeks were becoming even more unbearable.

The government began beating the drum for the Greek Success Story in early 2013. That year Greeks' total income fell by a heart-wrenching margin of more than 5.6 per cent, a figure that would have caused a revolution in countries such as Britain, Germany or the United States. In Greece it was the fifth successive year of precipitous falls. It wasn't just the poor who were unconvinced by the government's story, though. In a bid to produce the primary surplus it had promised Schäuble in return for its debt restructuring the following year, the government introduced a land tax that lost it the support of the upper echelons of the middle class, who might have remained asset rich but whom the recession had rendered income poor like everyone else. A new joke did the rounds in which parents threatened to bequeath to their offspring all their property if they didn't behave.

The government presumably then realized that its story was falling on deaf ears because around this time influential conservatives in Prime Minister Samaras's inner circle considered approaching the Golden Dawn party to bolster its support, even seeking an electoral pact with the Nazis, albeit in a rebranded incarnation.

In April 2014, with the opinion polls firmly against it and the European parliament elections looming, the Samaras government launched the ECB Put. With the behind-the-scenes assistance of the ECB, which hinted at its willingness to back the government's new bonds, the finance ministry proudly celebrated its return to the private debt market and the end of bankruptcy, borrowing a few billion from institutional investors who had agreed in advance to participate in the charade. It fooled no one. Investors and voters could see that incomes were continuing to shrink and debts to rise. A month later, in the elections to the European parliament, Syriza topped the poll. For the first time the Greek Left had won a nationwide election, albeit a European poll but paving the way for the real thing in early 2015.

In one of my meetings with Germany's finance minister, after the Greek Success Story had collapsed in January 2015 and Syriza were in government, I asked him out of curiosity and without expecting an answer, 'Wolfgang, when did you decide to cease supporting [the] Samaras [government]?'

'In June 2014' was his unhesitating and disarmingly honest response.

It made sense. Samaras had lost the European parliamentary election of May 2014 despite the boost he had received in April from the ECB-mediated bond sale. In Schäuble's eyes Samaras was a lame duck. Schäuble must have been sick and tired of worrying that every time a bill went to the Greek parliament Samaras's paper-thin majority would evaporate. Moreover, after his defeat in the European elections, Samaras lost some of his zeal and began to drag his feet when it came to implementing the troika's directives. Schäuble was no doubt mightily displeased. No wonder he gave up on the Samaras government that month.

It was no accident that June 2014 also witnessed Stournaras's move from the Ministry of Finance to the newly vacated governorship of the Central Bank of Greece. He too was abandoning a sinking ship.

A five-pronged strategy

Throughout 2013, ensconced in my Austin sanctuary, I was doing all I could to help Alexis develop a credible strategy while steering clear of Syriza's internal struggles. The year began with an opportunity to help him win friends in Washington, DC, where he was due to address the prestigious Brookings Institution. Pappas asked me to write the speech, which I was glad to do, using it to convey to American policymakers two now familiar but fundamental points. First, that Syriza was a pro-European party which would do its utmost to keep Greece in the eurozone, but that that did not mean accepting failed, self-defeating policies; to stay in the eurozone, indeed for the eurozone to survive, a new programme was needed that placed debt restructuring first and foremost, followed by reforms that undermined the Greek oligarchy's stranglehold on the economy.[31] Second, the United States had nothing to fear from a Syriza government's economic or foreign policy, a point that I reinforced a little later in a *New York Times* op-ed jointly written with Jamie Galbraith.[32] As previously mentioned, my thinking was that when we were about to open a front against Brussels, Frankfurt, Berlin and Paris, a second front against Washington was pointless, but of course many in Greece, including in Syriza, took the opportunity to portray me as an American stooge.

Two months later, in March 2013, news reached me from Cyprus that stopped me dead. Immediately I sat down to write a long angst-ridden email to Pappas, for his and Alexis's eyes. 'I implore you to take seriously what is happening in Cyprus,' I wrote. 'Think of it as a dress rehearsal of what the troika will do to you the day after you win power.' A new government had just been elected in Cyprus. The following day the troika closed down the island's banks, dictating terms to the new president for their reopening. Incredulous but unprepared, the new president had signed on the dotted line.

'They are trying this tactic out today in Nicosia,' I explained, 'not because Cyprus is that important but rather because of its relative unimportance, which makes it the perfect shooting range to test their new bazooka on before using it against you, against our comrades in Spain, Italy, etc. They are doing this for its demonstration effect, so that you know that the troika is willing and able to shut down a country's banks to impose its will upon the government – especially a newly elected one that demands some sovereignty back. Watch and learn!'

The next day Alexis and I spoke on the phone, his voice conveying considerable trepidation.

'Is there anything we can do to deter them?' he asked.

'Yes, but you will need not only the right deterrence strategy but also a tightly knit team to work on making it operational,' I replied.

'Send me a proposal' were his last words.

I promised to deliver it in person.

In Athens that May, in his spacious office in Parliament House, I met Alexis's economic team for the first time. As well as Pappas and Dragasakis, the shadow finance minister, it included two other Syriza members of parliament whom I knew and liked well: Euclid Tsakalotos, a dear colleague at the University of Athens, and George Stathakis, an economics professor from the University of Crete. At that meeting I presented the proposal Alexis had requested, which was an enhanced version of the strategy paper I had provided in June 2012: *A Five-Pronged Strategy for a Sustainable Greece in a Sustainable Eurozone.*

The mood in the room was ebullient, which confirmed that my earlier efforts to dissuade Alexis from turning Grexit into an objective, or from using it as a threat, had not been wasted. While I lost a great many friends on the broader Left and within Syriza, who never forgave me for my role in expunging Grexit from Syriza's policy objectives, Alexis's inner economic sanctum was evidently keen to pursue a viable solution within the eurozone. The purpose of the *Five-Pronged Strategy* was to persuade them that this was not just desirable but actually possible, that a Cyprus-like coup could be avoided and to propose how it might be done. First came the deterrence strategy.

I. KEEPING THE ECB AT BAY AND THE BANKS OPEN

From late 2012 onwards, Mario Draghi, the ECB's wily president, managed to hold the creaking euro together by promising to buy mountains of debt from Europe's failing economies – Italy, Spain, Ireland and the rest – in the form of government bonds.[33] Despite securing Angela Merkel's green light for his plans, Draghi's greatest foe was the German central bank, the Bundesbank, whose president challenged Draghi's right and authority to buy potentially bad Graeco-Roman debts – indeed, doing so directly was in violation of the ECB's charter and Draghi had had to come up with some ingenious methods to circumvent it. The Bundesbank took Draghi to court over the matter.[34] If Draghi's promise to buy such debt were consequently to vanish in the face of this formidable legal challenge, then the only thing keeping the euro alive would be gone. The Bundesbank's argument against Draghi was that he had no legal basis for accepting losses from government bond purchases. This gave any Greek government significant leverage because tens of billions of Greek government bonds remained on the ECB's books: these had been purchased by the ECB under its previous President as part of the Securities Market Programme (SMP) between 2010 and 2011. My advice to Syriza was that if the ECB threatened to close Greece's banks their government's response should be unilaterally to haircut the so-called SMP bonds – thus strengthening the Bundesbank's legal challenge to Draghi's plan to buy French, Italian, Spanish, Irish and Portuguese bonds in order to save the Eurozone – and they should make this intention clear to him. This would make Draghi very reluctant to do to Greece what had been done to Cyprus.

2. DEFANGING THE BANKRUPT BANKERS

As Pappas, Alexis and I had previously discussed, dismantling Bailoutistan 2.0 required the handing over of the banks to their new owners, Europe's taxpayers, and the uncoupling of their losses from the Greek state's debt. A Syriza government should therefore negotiate with the troika for the banks' shares and management to be transferred to European institutions, whose job would be to nurse them back to health on behalf of all Europeans. To do this Syriza needed to unite left-wingers, who believe in the socialization of banks, with libertarians, who loathe the idea of propping up bankrupt bankers with capital taken from powerless taxpayers.

3. SENSIBLE FISCAL POLICY AND DEBT RESTRUCTURING PROPOSALS

Shout from the rooftops that a Syriza government would be committed to a state that lives within its means in good times and bad. In technical terms that would mean a small primary budget surplus not exceeding 1.5 per cent of national income – not enough to repay the unrepayable public debt but sufficient to keep the state solvent while giving the private sector a chance to breathe again. As a prerequisite for this, Syriza would need to propose debt restructuring of sufficient scale that further debt repayments could be accommodated by a 1.5 per cent primary surplus. During the period of negotiation with the Eurogroup and its troika over this final point a Syriza government should be prepared to survive any shortage of cash by squeezing the highest salaries and most generous pensions as much as is necessary to make ends meet.

4. EMERGENCY PLAN TO COMBAT THE HUMANITARIAN CRISIS

In the meantime a Syriza government should immediately provide food, energy and shelter to the hundreds of thousands of families who are suffering most. Lambros and those about to fall through the cracks should be the government's top priority. Existing identity documents could be replaced with a smart card equipped with debit payment capabilities at a low cost. These capabilities would be activated for families below the absolute poverty line, for use in supermarkets and for essentials such as electricity and housing.

5. MODEST PROPOSAL FOR RENDERING THE EUROZONE VIABLE

As a progressive Europeanist force, a Syriza government should negotiate not just on behalf of the Greeks but also go to Brussels with
comprehensive proposals for Europe's public debt, banks, investment
policies and poverty-fighting capacities – proposals without which the
eurozone is unsustainable. To this end, my recommendation to the
Syriza economic team was that they adopt the *Modest Proposal for
Resolving the Euro Crisis* that Stuart Holland, Jamie Galbraith and I had
been working on for years.

In order to succeed in these aims, I told the meeting, your government must go to Brussels with a comprehensive proposal that is good
not just for Greece but for every other European country too. You
must give a clear signal that Athens will no longer be bullied into
accepting further extend-and-pretend loans. You must make the people
at the EU and the IMF realize that you have arrived on the scene with
a commitment to staying in the eurozone and of compromising. But
they must realize that, if need be, you are prepared to walk out of
the negotiations, whatever their threats, for if you are not, there is no
point in entering the negotiating room in the first place.

Alexis and Pappas looked satisfied. Euclid and Stathakis also indicated their broad agreement. It fell to Dragasakis to ask the pertinent
question: 'How can we convince the Eurogroup, the ECB and the
troika that we are not bluffing?' The question was supremely apt; the
whole strategy relied on this one point.

My response was that Syriza's preferences and priorities had to
become common knowledge. It had to become commonly known
that a Syriza government wanted above all else a viable agreement
within the eurozone but that it preferred Grexit, a terrible outcome,
to capitulation, the worst outcome. If this order of preferences was
widely known, then the blame for Grexit, with all the costs and legal
issues that it would entail, could only fall on the EU and the IMF. The
choice would then be entirely theirs and known to be theirs.

Of course even if Syriza's true preferences were known, the EU
and IMF officials would no doubt test Alexis's resolve to its utmost.
It was possible too that the EU and IMF would ultimately prefer to
throw Greece out of the euro than deal consensually with a Syriza
government, or that in pushing Alexis to the brink they might effect
Grexit by accident. A long constructive discussion followed in which

we considered these possible scenarios, but the key point I made was this: whether or not they could convince the Eurogroup, the ECB and the troika that they were sincere in these preferences, there was no point in any of it if they weren't. This is what they needed to work out among themselves, I told them:

> Do you truly believe in your bones that 'doing a Samaras', capitulating to the troika like him, is worse than being thrown out of the euro? If you are not sure, let Samaras stay in Maximos. For what is the point of winning power to clash with the creditors only to fold the moment the troika calls and then take the blame for their inhumanity? Win power only if you are not intending to bluff because you are convinced that capitulation is even worse than a terrible Grexit. Only then will Greece get a chance to stay sustainably in the eurozone and to put Grexit behind it once and for all.

As he was showing me out, Pappas put his arm around my left shoulder and said, 'That was brilliant. It will be our line from now on.'

Gathering qualms

It was the night of 11 June 2013, an hour before midnight, when the television screens froze. For two hours they broadcast nothing but a still of a journalist cut off in mid-sentence as he explained that the government had decided to close down the three state television channels, all the regional and national radio stations, and the satellite service that provided the Greek diaspora with Greek programming. It was the equivalent of all BBC television channels suddenly going dark at the same time as every BBC radio station went silent.

Unable to believe my eyes and ears, my mind raced back to the time of Greece's fascist dictators, whose first move in their coup was to take control of the state television channels. They at least had bothered to broadcast a picture of the Greek flag, although accompanied by military music. In Bailoutistan the troika-subservient government just froze the picture for two hours. Then Greece's TV screens turned black. That blackness was an apt metaphor for the new government's authoritarian turn as the dismal failure of its success story became apparent.

Within minutes of the blackout, demonstrators invaded the ERT building – from which I had been banned in 2011 – beginning a months-long occupation that rekindled the spirit of Syntagma Square. The next morning Danae, Jamie Galbraith and I flew to Thessaloniki to offer our support to the local ERT staff. While there I gave a speech, followed by Jamie and Alexis, to a large packed hall. My return to ERT, as one of the thousands of demonstrators and a guest on the unofficial programmes that the staff broadcast over the Internet, could not have been more bittersweet.

Prompted by these events and following my meeting with Syriza's economic team, something of a coherent agenda began to take shape over the course of that summer. In November 2013 Jamie and I organized a two-day conference at the University of Texas on the theme 'Can the eurozone be saved?' with Alexis, Pappas and Stathakis attending and giving well-received speeches. The idea was to introduce the three Syriza leaders to establishment figures from Europe and the United States, trade union leaders, academics and journalists.

It was also a good opportunity to test Alexis's commitment to the logic behind the *Five-Pronged Strategy*. During the conference he and Pappas were present at a heated debate between me and Heiner Flassbeck, a left-wing German economist and former junior finance minister in the Schroeder administration, who argued that Greece's liberation from debtors' prison was impossible within the eurozone. He maintained that Grexit was the correct objective for a Syriza government, or at least the best threat to use against its creditors – the same position as that of the Left Platform, an official faction within Syriza that numbered among its supporters one-third of Syriza's central committee.[36] It was in Austin that I became convinced of Alexis's rejection of this position and his belief that if anyone were to threaten Grexit, it must be the troika, not Syriza.

The winter passed with Samaras's government struggling to sell its 'success story' and Greek society sinking further into the economic mire. April 2014 marked Samaras's last hooray with Stournaras selling government bonds to investors who were reassured by the ECB's tacit backing. In May 2014, however, Syriza topped the polls in the European parliamentary elections, confirming that no one was fooled. A month later Wolfgang Schäuble gave up on the Samaras government. Change was in the air.

That June, back in Greece once more for the summer, I met Alexis and his economics team to warn them about a new threat. In the fine print of an otherwise innocuous press release the ECB had just announced that in the near future it would stop accepting the IOUs issued by banks and backed by the governments of bailed-out countries as collateral for further loans. In other words, a vital component of the smoke-and-mirrors machinery used by Greece's four largest banks to ensure their day-to-day liquidity would be removed. The date on which the new policy became effective set alarm bells ringing in my head: March 2015 – the month the president of Greece's term expired, when new elections were likely to be held and when in all probability Syriza would form a government.

'Do you see where I am going with this?' I asked Alexis, Pappas, Dragasakis, Euclid and Stathakis, having passed on the ECB's bomb-shell. The day after they won power, I warned them, Mario Draghi would call them with the news that, as previously announced, the ECB must deny Greece's banks liquidity, effective immediately. The ECB was creating the conditions necessary to close down the banks without any warning or reason just as Syriza was taking over.

Dragasakis's face sank. 'And what happens then?'

The only way the banks could continue to function, I said, was at the discretion of the Central Bank of Greece, which could continue to lend to them through a scheme known as emergency liquidity assistance (ELA). The Central Bank of Greece is in effect a branch of the European Central Bank, so even then the cash would be coming from the ECB, albeit indirectly and at a higher rate of interest, and could ultimately be switched off.[37] But there was a more immediate obstacle to contend with before all this happened.

'Is it a coincidence that three days from today Prime Minister Samaras will transfer Stournaras from the finance ministry to the governorship of the central bank?' I asked. 'It's obviously a stratagem in anticipation of your electoral victory.'

At that point Alexis grew angry. 'The first thing I shall do as prime minister is demand Stournaras's resignation. I will drag him from the central bank kicking and screaming if need be.' Pappas offered a number of even more drastic solutions to this problem.

I pointed out that it hardly mattered who sat in the governor's office; a Syriza government's priority was to deter Draghi from closing down the banks in the first place. As per the first part of the *Five-Pronged Strategy* I had presented the previous year, they would need to make clear to Draghi that bank closures by the ECB would trigger a move from Athens that might well bring down the eurozone. The question was: were they committed enough to do so and to take on all those on Draghi's side, not just Stournaras but local bankers such as our Aris and Zorba as well?

Alexis and Pappas responded with enthusiasm: they would not hesitate to do this. Euclid, reputedly the most militantly left wing in the team, agreed. Stathakis nodded. Dragasakis, on the other hand, replied in a manner that I would learn to expect: 'Let's proceed on the basis of the good scenario,' he said, adding, 'If forced, we will have to respond.'

A week later, in the majestic gardens of the Athens Byzantine and Christian Museum, Alexis and I appeared in front of another large audience to present the Greek translation of the *Modest Proposal for Resolving the Euro Crisis*. Alexis's whole team was in the audience, with Dragasakis in the front row, an impressive show of support for the strategy.

A couple of days afterwards, Alexis, Pappas and I met again.

'Do you realize,' asked Pappas, 'that no one else but you can oversee the implementation of the negotiating strategy you are proposing? Are you ready to do this?'

I replied that my commitment to the fight was a given, but that I didn't believe in technocrats being parachuted into a political process. In truth I still had fundamental concerns. Negotiating on a country's behalf requires a democratic mandate. The *Modest Proposal* represented my personal convictions, and I had no desire to legitimize the de-politicization of economic policy, that most political of realms. Besides, Dragasakis, Euclid and Stathakis had built Syriza up from scratch over decades. They commanded the respect of the party. By comparison, I could never be more than a proxy for them, and this would undermine my ability to run the negotiations with the authority required. Lastly, my qualms regarding the incongruity between Syriza's internal priorities and a credible government agenda had not disappeared.

A week later, Wassily Kafouros, a dear friend from my undergraduate years in England, added to my misgivings. He asked me if

I was the only person not to know that Dragasakis was extremely close to the bankers. I said I didn't believe him. 'Where is your evidence, Wassily?' I demanded.

'Evidence I do not have,' he admitted, 'but it is commonly known that he has made it his business, even back in his communist party days, to keep the bankers close.'

I assumed the accusation was false, and although doubts still slithered through my mind like restless serpents I decided I could not afford to worry about problems that lay beyond my capacity to solve. Those who had earned an electoral mandate had to unbend the evil bows. For now all I could do was point out the traps and suggest ways to avoid them.

4

Treading water

The Ship of Stone, the Stoneship for short, is what sailors call them: three large rocks protruding from the open sea in the mouth of the Saronic Gulf. Seen from an approaching boat a mile or so away they do indeed look like a ghost ship heading slowly towards Cape Sounion, home of Poseidon's enchanting temple. Swimming in the unnervingly deep blue waters in the Stoneship's shadow so close to shipping lanes has something of an edge to it.

In August 2014 Alexis and I were treading water fifty metres or so from the Stoneship, as far from prying ears as it was possible to be. Our conversation turned to trust. Did Alexis trust his team to lead the charge against the bankers such as Aris and Zorba? Did he trust them to negotiate with the troika without fear of – or a desire for – Grexit? Would they stand tall against a troika willing and ready to asphyxiate them via the banks while Greece's oligarchs went berserk?

Alexis was skilfully evasive, striking a consistently optimistic tone. Restraining myself so as not to overwhelm him with my doubts, I nonetheless had to ask the question that had been burning in my mind from the moment Wassily planted it there.

'Alexi,' I said, trying to sound as nonchalant as I could, 'I hear Dragasakis is too close to bankers. And, generally, that he may be going along with our escape plans while in reality he is working to maintain the status quo.'

He did not answer right away. Instead he looked towards the Peloponnese in the distance, before turning back to me. 'No, I do not think so. He is OK.'

I did not know what to make of his brevity. Did he harbour doubts too but on balance trusted in his senior comrade's probity or was he dismissing my question? To this day I do not know the answer. What

I do know is that he kept insisting I had no choice: when the moment came, I had to play a leading role in the negotiations.

Loath to list my reservations once more, I replied spontaneously, 'OK, Alexi, you can count on my help. But on one condition.'

'Which one?' he asked with a smile.

'That I have a major say in Syriza's economic agenda prior to the election. We cannot have a repeat of 2012.'

Alexis promised he would have Pappas keep me in the loop and consult with me before they put anything out on economic policy. It was time to swim back to Alexis's partner Betty and Danae, who were waiting on a small inflatable tenuously anchored to the seabed.

Blood, sweat and tears

A month later, back in Austin, I heard on the news that Alexis had delivered a major speech in Thessaloniki outlining Syriza's economic platform. Gobsmacked, I got hold of the text and read it. A wave of nausea and indignation permeated my gut. Straight away I went to work. The article that emerged less than half an hour later was used soon after its publication by Prime Minister Samaras to lambast Syriza in parliament: 'Even Varoufakis, your economic guru, says that your promises are fake.' And so they were.

The Thessaloniki Programme, as Alexis's speech was labelled, was well meaning but incoherent and definitely inconsistent with the *Five-Pronged Strategy*, which Alexis and Pappas had supposedly endorsed. It promised wage rises, subsidies, benefits and investment paid for with sources of funding which were either imaginary or illegal. There were also promises we should not have wanted to fulfil. Above all, it was at odds with any reasonable negotiating strategy that kept Greece within the eurozone, despite advocating that it should remain there. It was in fact such a ramshackle programme that I did not even bother to criticize it point by point. Instead I wrote:

> How I would have loved a different speech from Alexis Tsipras, one beginning with the question 'Why vote for us?' before proceeding to answer it with 'Because we are promising you only three things: blood, sweat and tears!'

Blood, sweat and tears, which Winston Churchill promised the British people in 1940 as he was assuming the helm of government, in return for their support and help to win the war.

Blood, sweat and tears, which will earn all Europeans, not just us Greeks, the right to hope for an end to the muted but ruthless war against dignity and truth.

Blood, sweat and tears, which we should be ready to shed to put the country back on track, something that today is impossible if we continue to behave like model prisoners hoping for early release from debtors' prison and to borrow more while cutting the incomes from which we must meet our repayments.

Indeed, if you want to vote for us, you must do so only because you agree that the blood, sweat and tears that we are promising you are a fair price to pay to hear the truth from the lips of government ministers and to have representatives in Europe who will neither beg nor bluff but instead adopt a strategy no government has hitherto adopted, the strategy of speaking

Truth to power.

Truth to our partners.

Truth to the citizens of Europe.

Truth regarding the sorry state of our banks.

Truth about our 'surpluses'.

Truth about non-existent investment.

And finally, the most painful, Truth about the zero prospects for recovery while the death embrace continues between a bankrupt state, bankrupt banks, bankrupt firms and bankrupt institutions.

Lastly, before you vote for us, know that we dread an electoral victory more than we fear defeat, that we are scared stiff at the thought we may win. But if *you* decide to vote us in to deliver the blood, sweat and tears we are promising in exchange for truth and dignity, if *you* overcome *your* fear, then we promise to overcome *our* fear to govern this country and to steer it to emancipation from hopelessness.[1]

On its publication, friends and foes alike thought this marked the end of my brief affair with Syriza's leadership. I thought so too until

Pappas called a few days later, sounding chipper and as if nothing had happened. I put it to him that my article changed everything.

'It changes nothing,' he retorted light-heartedly. 'You will get to shape the *actual* economic programme. The Thessaloniki Programme was a rallying call for our troops. That's all.'

Exasperated, I gave him a piece of my mind, stressing that the support of our troops was essential and lying to them was hardly the way to ensure it. Unabashed, he assured me ominously, 'There is party policy and there is government policy. You will author the latter and leave the former to us.'

I asked who was behind the Thessaloniki Programme. Pappas said Dragasakis had overseen it, assisted by Euclid. Dragasakis's hand did not surprise me but Euclid's involvement was disappointing. I expected more from my friend. 'Whoever wrote that monstrosity,' I said, 'it throws a spanner into any sensible negotiating strategy.'

I put the phone down with a mouth so dry and bitter I had to drink several glasses of water before talking things over with Danae. The leadership were telling each other one story while the party faithful were being served a completely different one. It was a recipe for confusion, division and defeat against adversaries who were united, mighty and determined. The narrative we gave our people and the troika officials, the EU and IMF leadership, Berlin and Washington, indeed the international press and the markets, should be one, indivisible, credible, unbending message. Upon hearing my view that Pappas and Alexis's tactics were bound to wreck any future negotiation, Danae reacted sharply: 'You cannot be part of this.'

I agreed.

The decision to keep my distance brought instant relief, but my peace of mind lasted only a couple of months. In late November 2014, as I was preparing to fly to Florence to address a conference, the call came once again. It was Pappas. When he discovered I was on my way to Italy he implored me to make a side trip to Athens before returning to Austin. 'It is urgent that you come,' he said. Reluctantly I changed my ticket.

In Florence I addressed a gathering of worried Italian officials, bankers and academics, presenting a newer version of the *Modest Proposal*, a set of policies that could be implemented instantly within Europe's existing rules to stop the euro crisis in its tracks everywhere, not just in Italy or Greece.[2] The next morning I caught the train to

Rome and from there the short flight to Athens, wondering along the way what Alexis and Pappas had in store for me. The newspapers at the airport were abuzz with rumours of an early election. Had my Syriza friends absorbed the message in my article?

The taxi dropped me off at our empty flat. I dumped my suitcase and was pleasantly surprised at my motorcycle's willingness to start despite three months of idleness. A quarter of an hour later I was parking it under Alexis's apartment block, where I was greeted by two sentries at street level. The lift took me to the top floor, where Alexis, Betty and their two delightful young boys live. Pappas and Dragasakis were there too. It was early in the evening.

It wasn't until the early hours of the following morning that I finally emerged, drove back to our flat to collect my suitcase and caught a taxi to the airport for my flight to Austin.

'What happened?' asked Danae on the phone.

'I'll tell you when I see you,' I replied. Holding my tongue on the phone for fear of eavesdroppers had begun.

A full and frank exchange

The mood in Alexis and Betty's apartment had been cheerful. Samaras's government had plummeted in the polls, elections now looked imminent, and they wanted to discuss strategy in the event of Syriza's now probable victory.

I was not in the mood to share their excitement. The Thessaloniki Programme had heightened my fears that Alexis was about to waste what might well be our generation's last chance to get Greece out of its prison of debt, so I made a point of emphasizing the hardships and risks ahead, reiterating the points I had tried to impress upon them at our meeting in June. It was all well and good to pray for the 'good scenario' that Dragasakis liked to invoke, but we urgently needed to prepare for a more probable, and far nastier, one.

'Let me tell you what I think you will face on day one of your administration,' I began once we had all settled down in the living room. 'Expect a bank run to begin the Monday after your election.'[3]

Rumours that the ECB might close the banks would cause depositors to withdraw their euros to store under their mattresses or wire abroad, I explained, just as had happened in 2012 and in Cyprus the

following year. EU and IMF officials would be in no hurry to negotiate
with a government they wanted to undermine. They would sit on their
hands, bide their time and wait for Alexis and his team to come face
to face with the first of the impossible repayments to the IMF and the
ECB due from March 2015 onwards.[4] As we had discussed in June, a
Syriza government therefore had to be prepared to signal from the
very beginning that if the EU and IMF refused to negotiate in good
faith it would simply not make those repayments. If that happened,
the EU and IMF would undoubtedly respond that the ECB was no
longer able to provide liquidity to the Greek banks, as their IOUs were
backed by a government in default, a threat tantamount to switching
off their emergency liquidity assistance, thus shutting them down.

The mood in the room darkened.

'I hope none of this transpires. Maybe it won't. But it would be
foolish not to prepare for it,' I said. 'If they choose this belligerent
path, their purpose will be to work out what you are made of, whether
you are bluffing and what your true priorities are.'

'What do you think Merkel wants?' said Alexis. 'I cannot believe
she thinks it's in her interests to stir up another crisis.'

'Berlin will not dare upset the markets by closing Greece's banks
down,' interjected Pappas. 'Greece is not Cyprus. They cannot push
us around like that without consequences.'

I begged to differ. In my view Merkel and Schäuble had no intention of going to their parliament to support debt relief for Greece, a
move tantamount to confessing that the first two bailouts had been
given under false pretences. The only way Berlin could avoid such a
confession was to arrange a third bailout loan, keeping Greece in
debtors' prison but officially not in default. But as each bailout required
the sacrifice of a Greek prime minister (Papandreou for the first,
Samaras for the second) and a fresh government to push it through
parliament, they would try either to win Alexis over to their side or
to create such chaos that his government fell, allowing for its replacement with a compliant technocratic administration, just as they had
had in 2012.

Alexis looked grim. 'But what about Pappas's point?' he said. 'Are
they not scared of tumult in the markets?'

'They are,' I explained, 'but just when you might be moving into
Maximos, the ECB will be unleashing a torrent of money with which
to stabilize the eurozone.' Such a 'quantitative easing' programme

involved the mass purchase of government bonds using the digital printing presses of the ECB. This would push down interest rates in key states such as Italy, Spain and France. Two years in the planning, it was Mario Draghi's strategy to buy time for the euro.

'It would be idiotic to think of this as a coincidence,' I said. 'Merkel may well feel that the moment the markets are flooded by ECB money, an ECB-led enforced Greek bank holiday will go reasonably smoothly for her and Europe's financiers.'

'How do we upset their plan then?' asked Alexis.

'To extract from them a half-decent agreement,' I said, 'you must give the ECB good cause to hesitate before shutting down the banks.'

Key deterrent: the ECB's remaining Greek debt

The strategy for deterring a bank shutdown that we had discussed in June – based on the *Five-Pronged Strategy* I had presented at my first meeting with Alexis's economic team in May 2013, itself based on the initial paper I had presented in June 2012 – hinged on the legal battle between Mario Draghi at the ECB and the Bundesbank under Jens Weidmann. Draghi had promised to buy vast amounts of government bonds from Europe's shaky economies in order to prop up the euro-zone. The Bundesbank had taken him to court over this, claiming it violated the constitution of the ECB. In February 2014 the German courts had referred the matter to the European Court of Justice, which ruled in favour of Draghi, but their judgment included caveats – caveats that in my analysis gave a future Syriza government considerable leverage. My reading of them was that Draghi's power to continue buying government debt was conditional on protecting the ECB from any write-down of government debt the ECB already owned. This included the so-called SMP bonds: Greek government bonds it had acquired from private investors as part of what it had branded the Securities Market Programme.

The sum that the Greek state still owed the ECB in the form of these outstanding bonds came to $33 billion. From Greece's perspective it was a lot of money, especially given that repayments of $6.6 billion were coming up in July and August 2015. But from the ECB's perspective it was financially insignificant when compared to the one trillion euros and more that the ECB was planning to release. Nonetheless, those few billions of Greek debt to the ECB were legally momentous: any haircut of that sum or delay in its repayment would open Draghi and the ECB up to legal challenges from the Bundesbank and the German Constitutional Court, undermining the credibility of its overall debt-purchasing programme and causing a rift with Chancellor Merkel, who would never take on both the Bundesbank and the German Constitutional Court at the same time. Facing their combined might, Draghi was sure to find his freedom drastically curtailed, thus undermining the markets' faith in his hitherto magical promise to do 'whatever it takes' to save the euro – the only thing preventing the currency's collapse.

'Mario Draghi is about to unleash a major debt purchasing programme in March 2015, without which the euro is toast,' I said. 'The last thing he needs is anything that will impede this.'[5] A Syriza government had therefore to signal to Draghi that it wanted a mutually advantageous deal with the EU, the ECB and the IMF and was willing to compromise to get this. But it must also signal, discreetly but firmly, that if Draghi were to shut down Greece's banks in response to a Syriza victory, it would consider this a *casus belli* and would immediately legislate to postpone redemption of the Greek government bonds owned by the ECB by, say, two decades. I had no doubt that if a Syriza government signalled early on its intention to retaliate by haircutting the Greek SMP bonds held by the ECB in this way, it would deter the ECB from closing down the banks.

'Draghi is too wise a central banker to risk this simply in order to allow Berlin to steamroller you,' I told Alexis. 'Of course, on the other hand, if you fail to convince him that you are serious about haircutting those SMP bonds, he will have no reason to antagonize Berlin by refusing its request that he crush you with an enforced bank holiday.'

As in 2012, so again in Alexis's apartment that night, I was at pains to stress one simple thing: in this and in every aspect of the negotiation they faced, Syriza could not afford to bluff. Even if Draghi did shut down the banks, Alexis's government had to be ready to keep the economy ticking over for several weeks. If he continued to stand his ground even then – signalling to Berlin and to Frankfurt that, while his government's aim was an honourable agreement, it nonetheless preferred a costly and unwanted Grexit to the nightmare of capitulation to debt bondage – then the real negotiations would begin.

Was this a battle they were prepared to see through to the end?

Pappas seemed offended that I should ask. Alexis, more restrained, said with an air of resignation, 'We have no alternative.' Dragasakis said nothing.

It was imperative then that they had a plan for buying time, I told them; a way of getting through several weeks so that they would not have to choose between Grexit and surrender the very moment the ATMs closed. This would also give Merkel and Draghi the chance to step back from a terminal rupture once it became clear that Syriza meant business. To do this, they would need a payments system ready to kick in the moment the banks closed.

A parallel payments system

The scheme I outlined, alluded to in June 2012 and in the *Five-Pronged Strategy* of May 2013, was based on theoretical work I had done previously on how fiscally stressed eurozone governments could gain some room for manoeuvre through a novel utilization of their tax office websites. The gist of it was simple.

Suppose that the state owes Company A €1 million but is delaying payment owing to the state's liquidity squeeze. Suppose also that Company A owes €30,000 to Jill, one of its employees, plus another €500,000 to Company B, which supplied it with raw materials. Meanwhile, Jill and Company B also owe, respectively, €10,000 and €200,000 in taxes to the state. Now imagine that the tax office creates a reserve account for each taxpayer (per tax file number, to be precise), including for Companies A and B and Jill. The state can then just 'deposit' €1 million into Company A's reserve account simply by typing it in and provide each taxpayer with a PIN to be used to transfer 'funds' from one taxpayer's reserve account to another. Company A could then transfer €30,000 to Jill's reserve account and €500,000 to Company B's reserve account, which Jill and Company B could then use to repay the €10,000 and €200,000 they respectively owe the state in tax arrears. The immediate cancellation of many arrears would have been thus effected.

Such a system would be great to have in Portugal, in Italy, indeed in France even during the best of times, but it would be critical in Greece during the emergency of an ECB-enforced bank holiday, allowing all sorts of transactions to continue, not just those with the state. For example, pensions could be partly paid into a pensioner's tax office reserve account, and the pensioner could then transfer a part of that sum to, say, her landlord, who would also have tax to pay. Even though these credits could not be withdrawn from the system as cash, the scheme would continue to work for as long as the state continued to accept the credits in lieu of tax. And it could work remarkably well if it were developed further in two ways.

Every Greek citizen already has an identity card. Imagine if this were reissued as a smart card featuring a microchip similar to those in modern debit and credit cards. The ID cards of pensioners, public-sector workers, people on benefits, government suppliers – anyone who has financial dealings with the state – could be linked to their tax office reserve accounts and used to pay for goods and services at supermarkets, petrol stations and the like. In other words, even if the banks were to close down, even if the state was rendered illiquid, the government could still meet its obligations simply by assigning tax credits to people's ID cards – as long as the total value credited did not run the government into a fiscal deficit, of course.

Second, the same system could be used to allow the government to borrow from Greek citizens, thus bypassing the commercial banks, the hostile and suspicious money markets and, of course, the troika. As well as receiving tax credits from the state, citizens could be given the option to buy credits from the tax office online, using web banking linked to their normal bank accounts. Why would they want to do this? Because the government would offer them a discount of, say, 10 per cent, if they later used those credits to pay their taxes, say, a year down the line. The state would in effect be borrowing from its citizens at an interest rate (10 per cent) that no European can get from any bank these days. As long as the total level of tax credits sold by the government was capped and fully transparent, the result would be a fiscally responsible increase in government liquidity, greater freedom from the troika and thus a shorter path to the ultimate goal of a viable new agreement with the EU and the IMF.

Seemingly impressed, Dragasakis asked me to produce a written blueprint for this scheme, while Alexis and Pappas appeared soothed by the thought of the precious time it would buy them after a rupture with the creditors. Within forty-eight hours of my return to Austin I had sent a ten-page technical blueprint to Pappas to pass on to Alexis and Dragasakis.

Let's briefly fast-forward four months to March 2015 and to a cabinet meeting of the Syriza government with Alexis, as prime minister, in the chair. After an assessment of the confrontation with the troika that had begun with a vengeance on day one, just as anticipated, I outlined a bill my ministry had tabled in parliament to combat the humanitarian crisis: debit cards would be issued to three hundred thousand families living below the poverty line, with a credit of a few hundred euros per month to cover their basic needs.

'But these cards are just the beginning,' I said. 'Soon they could replace ID cards and provide the basis of a payments system that functions in parallel with the banks.'

After I explained how the system would work, I outlined its many advantages: it would give the government more fiscal space, support the poor without subjecting them to the stigma of using coupons and, above all, signal to the troika that Greece had a payments system that would allow our economy to function even if they closed down our banks. Lastly, I pointed out that if the troika decided to push Greece out of the eurozone, as the German finance minister had been wanting to do for years,[6] this same payment system could be redenominated to a new currency at the press of a button.

When the cabinet meeting was adjourned, most of the ministers present approached me to express their enthusiasm, some patting me on the back, others embracing me, one telling me that she was moved and inspired.

Five months later, after my resignation, the press lambasted me for having entered into a tough negotiation without a back-up plan. For days I was mocked in the media not just by opposition politicians but also by many Syriza MPs for walking into the lion's den without a strategy for what to do if the banks were shut down. I waited to see if Alexis or anyone else in the cabinet came forward to put the record straight. None did. So, during a teleconference conducted by David Marsh of the Official Monetary and Financial Institutions Forum in which I was replying to questions on what had gone wrong with the Greek government's negotiations with the EU and the IMF I made known my plans for a parallel payments system.

The discussion was supposedly being held under the Chatham House Rule, allowing participants to quote what is said but not to attribute it to the speaker, but this convention was ignored. Recordings of my entire presentation were soon made public. Immediately those same journalists and politicians who had been ridiculing me for not having a Plan B suddenly accused me of the direct opposite: VAROU-FAKIS'S SECRET GREXIT PLAN was a typical headline, suggesting that I had gone behind Alexis's back to engineer a devilish plot for getting Greece out of the euro. Calls to indict me on criminal charges began to mount. Indeed, while these lines are being written a charge of high treason is hanging over me in Greece's parliament for undermining Prime Minister Tsipras by means of a 'secret plot'.

It is a source of personal pride and joy to me that the troika's cheerleaders within Greece use every opportunity they can to undermine me. I consider their attacks a badge of honour, conferred for having dared to say no to their demands in the Eurogroup. But to have former cabinet colleagues, those very same people who filed past me to praise my proposed payments system, either pretend they have never heard of it or join in with the denunciations fills me only with sadness.

The offer

The offer caught me completely unawares. Around midnight in Alexis's flat the discussion moved from deterrence and parallel payments systems to practical politics. Alexis briefed me on the high probability of an early election. The government's term had more than two years left to run, but it was doubtful it could survive beyond March 2015, when the five-year term of the president of the republic expired. Unless Prime Minister Samaras could muster a reinforced parliamentary majority around his chosen presidential candidate, parliament would be automatically dissolved and elections called.[7] Alexis then delivered his offer, unassumingly and under Dragasakis's watchful eye.

'If we win, and there is no doubt we shall, we want you to become finance minister.'

Throughout my journey from Austin to Athens I had been reciting the precise wording in which I would turn his offer down – except that I had been anticipating a completely different offer from the one he had made, that of chief negotiator under Finance Minister

Dragasakis. But now Alexis was proposing to unify the two roles and make me responsible for both.

To buy time, and in genuine puzzlement, I turned to Dragasakis. 'But I thought that you would assume the finance ministry.'

Alexis stepped in to explain: 'Dragasakis will be deputy prime minister overseeing the three economic ministries,' meaning the Ministry of Finance, the Ministry of the Economy and a new Ministry of Productive Reconstruction.[8]

This changed everything. The proposed cabinet structure was sensible. The only reason for turning down Alexis's offer now would have been doubt regarding his and Dragasakis's true intentions, calibre or character. It would have been awkward, to say the least, to bring up such fundamental doubts with them directly. I raised another issue of principle instead.

'As you know,' I said, 'I have serious reservations about the Thessaloniki Programme. Indeed I have very little respect for it and, given that it has been presented as your pledge to the Greek people on economic matters, I cannot see how I can, in all honesty, assume the responsibility of implementing it as finance minister.'

Predictably, Pappas jumped in at this point to restate his insistence that the Thessaloniki Programme was not binding for me. 'You are not even a member of Syriza,' he pointed out.

'But would I not be expected to join if I am to become your finance minister?' I asked.

Alexis interjected with a studied response: 'No, under no circumstances. I *don't want* you to become a member of Syriza. You need to remain unburdened by our party's tortuous collective decision-making.'

My head was ringing with alarm bells. Alexis's point was reasonable but pregnant with immense risks. One the one hand, remaining semi-detached from Syriza, a party whose flimsy economic policies I had criticized for years, would afford me a precious degree of freedom and allow Alexis to blame those of my decisions that contradicted party policy on the fact that I was not bound to it. At the same time, this blame could snowball into condemnation of me at the drop of Alexis's or Dragasakis's hat, leaving me exposed to animosity from the party whose backing I would need so badly when struggling against the troika and the Greek oligarchy. Again, this was hardly a concern I could have shared with them.

The pressure to decide was mounting, but I needed to know for sure: were we truly in agreement over both aims and means? If not, my life would have remained blissfully uncomplicated.

'Let's see if we can agree on fundamentals before we discuss my role in a Syriza government,' I said.

My intention was to try out on them an up-to-date, firm, clear-cut version of the *Five-Pronged Strategy* I had proposed to Alexis in 2012, before it was so ingloriously discarded.[9]

The covenant

First and foremost, I began, came meaningful debt restructuring.[10] We had to agree that this was the be-all and end-all of a Syriza government. Getting Greece out of debtors' prison was more important than preventing privatizations or any other objective on Syriza's agenda. They agreed.

With debt restructuring, I continued, we could finally put an end to the austerity–deflation spiral and aim at a small government surplus – I specified a target of at most 1.5 per cent of national income. This would require sharp reductions in VAT and the corporate tax rate in order to re-energize the private sector.

'Why should business pay less?' Alexis protested.

I explained that I thought the private sector should pay more in total tax revenue, but the only way to achieve an overall increase in their contribution at a time of next to no sales and with bankrupt banks unable to provide credit even to profitable firms was to reduce the corporate tax rate. Dragasakis stepped in to say he agreed, apparently allaying Alexis and Pappas's initial consternation.

When it came to privatizations, I continued, we would have to make compromises if we wanted an agreement with the EU and the IMF. Syriza's blanket rejection of privatization would have to be replaced with a policy of considering them case by case. Fire sales of public holdings had to end, but there would be some assets, such as ports and railways, that we should make available conditional on a minimum level of investment, on the buyer's commitment to granting workers proper contracts and the right to union representation, and on the state retaining a large, even if minority, shareholding, the dividends from which would be used to assist pension funds. Meanwhile, those assets that were to remain under public ownership should be handed over to a new public development bank, which would use them as collateral in the raising of funds to be invested in these same public assets so as to boost their value, create jobs and enhance future revenues. They agreed on this too.

Now came the delicate issue of Aris, Zorba and their fellow bankers. Remembering the awkward conversation with Alexis in the Stoneship's shadow, I chose my words carefully in Dragasakis's presence. I asked them to what extent they were prepared to take on bankers with Aris's and Zorba's background and force them to surrender control of their banks, which were essentially the property of the taxpayers. I reminded them of the curious alliance between our bankers and the European Central Bank, which was keeping their banks alive via government-backed IOUs. Either institution was capable of asphyxiating a Syriza government.

Pappas brimmed with revolutionary zeal, decreeing that all the bankers would be sent packing. More cautious but nonetheless positive, Alexis added that this was why it was important to have a senior person as deputy prime minister, meaning Dragasakis, to rein in the bankers.

But were they prepared, I asked, to adopt my proposal that these bankrupt banks be placed under the management and ownership of the EU? I knew this was an extraordinarily challenging proposal for a left-wing party that tended if anything towards nationalizing the banking sector. A perilous silence followed.

Alexis broke it by asking the inevitable question: 'But why can't *we* nationalize the banks? The state owns majority stakes in them anyway. Can't we just pass a law that converts our non-voting to voting shares?'

I replied that unless we were prepared to turn the banks over to the European Union, we would not be able to unburden the Greek state of the liabilities incurred by their fake recapitalization. Bank nationalization would only make sense in the event of Grexit. 'But we are committed to refusing to think of Grexit as an objective, correct?'

'Correct,' came Alexis's immediate reply.

'In which case, can we agree that our negotiating position on the banks should be that their shares, along with the liabilities for their recapitalization, should be transferred to the European Union, with new boards of directors no longer in the pocket of Greece's bankers?'

Alexis and Pappas agreed, but I noticed that Dragasakis chose not to respond directly, remarking only that it was important to stay within the limits of legality – a point that ought to have been self-evident. His avoidance of the question reinforced my suspicions. So far though, all three seemed happy with the agenda. Nevertheless, I felt the need to recapitulate one more time what we had agreed our aims to be.

'Debt restructuring comes first. Second, a primary surplus of no more than 1.5 per cent of national income and no new austerity measures. Third, wide-ranging reductions in sales and business tax rates. Fourth, strategic privatizations under conditions that preserve labour rights and boost investment. Fifth, the creation of a development bank that would use remaining public assets as collateral to generate a domestic investment drive, and whose dividends would be channelled into public pension funds. Sixth, a policy of transferring bank shares and management to the European Union while creating a public "bad bank" to deal with the banks' non-performing loans, so as to prevent evictions and the mass expropriation of small business by vulture funds.'

Again they agreed, this time with greater conviction.

But I was not finished yet. Their agreement had to extend also to my proposed negotiating strategy, complete with its key deterrent, the threat to haircut our SMP bonds, and the parallel payments system with which to buy time in the event of an impasse that would bring on bank closures. I went through these points and they agreed once more.

Then came my final and most pressing point: 'Key to having a shot at a decent agreement is that we share a common understanding that we are not going to bluff against the troika. Are we clear on that?' I enquired anxiously.

Dragasakis asked what I meant. Was this a genuine question or tactical amnesia? Regardless, I was happy to make the key point once again, the same point I had been making since our very first meeting: 'It is not a bluff to issue a statement of intent if you are intending to carry it out *regardless of what the other side does*.'

Alexis understood: 'We heard. You're saying that we will not sign even if threatened with Grexit. Correct?'

I confirmed that that was exactly my point: there was no point entering into a tough negotiation with the world's most powerful credit institutions unless we were after a viable agreement within the euro, did nothing to jeopardize such an agreement, but were also clear in our minds that between surrender to a renewed sentence in debtors' prison and Grexit we preferred the latter.

'Are we clear on this?' I repeated.

'It goes without saying,' was Alexis's response, accompanied by another passionate confirmation from Pappas. Dragasakis remained conspicuously silent, offering only a friendly and tired smile. It was the closest we could have come to a covenant.

It was now my turn to decide.

Yes or no?

The moment of truth had arrived. In front of me there lay an offer I *could* refuse. The risks of accepting were clear and mountainous. While I liked Alexis and was willing to believe in him, the events of 2012 and, more recently, his casual disregard of our Stoneship agreement to involve me in the shaping of Syriza's Thessaloniki Programme had given me more than sufficient cause for scepticism. And as Danae said after my subsequent return to Austin, I was exploitable because I was expendable: 'If you bring back a decent deal, they will claim the credit. If not, you will get the blame.'

An outsider in relation both to Syriza and to the establishment, I was the ideal target to attract the slings and arrows of the troika, of the domestic establishment, of Syriza's loyalists and party members, and to deflect them from Alexis and his caucus. I did not mind playing the role of target; it is what finance ministers do on behalf of their prime ministers and cabinets. It would be worth it, but only as long as our covenant was intact and everyone understood that this was a fight not worth entering unless we were prepared to take it to the wire. I was. Were they? It was a question I did not have enough evidence to answer.

At the same time I faced an ethical dilemma. Did I have the *right* to turn Alexis's offer down? Here was the prime minister-in-waiting presenting me with an opportunity to put my money where my mouth was – to implement the negotiating strategy and the economic reform programme I had been advocating from the sidelines ever since Greece was confined in its peculiar prison. Socrates' definition of a good life is one that you do not regret on your deathbed. How would I feel when, in my old age, I recounted the moment I turned my back on that opportunity?

If only I could talk it through with Danae, I thought. But with thousands of miles separating us, and after such a long seance at Alexis's apartment, nothing less than a decision there and then would do. And so I reached it. But before accepting I had one last condition: that I first succeed in getting myself elected to parliament. I was not prepared to be another extra-parliamentary finance minister like Stournaras and his successor.[11]

'But Yanis, you have never contested an election before,' Alexis objected. 'You don't have the infrastructure in place, and the elections are coming up soon, with you living in Texas!'

Pappas intervened with a compromise: I could be on the list for one of the places in parliament allocated by the party leader.[12] Alexis then suggested it might be appropriate if I were placed low down on the party list in an 'honorary' position, which would not bring a seat in parliament but which would signal the high esteem in which I was held by Syriza.

I was adamant. 'That will not do. Either I get a direct mandate from the electorate, unmediated by the leadership, or I shall stay away.' It was not a question of honour. 'If I am to face up to Wolfgang Schäuble in the Eurogroup, a seasoned politician who has received his people's backing for decades, I need to go in there with thousands of votes backing me too. Otherwise, I would lack the necessary legitimacy.'

'But what happens if you do not get elected?' Alexis insisted.

'Then the people will have said that they do not want me to represent them in the Eurogroup. Simple! The idea of technocrats negotiating economic treaties on behalf of the ignorant masses is repugnant to me and deserves to be buried.'

'Which constituency do you want to contest?' asked Dragasakis.

'Greater Athens is the one that I have been voting in all my life, so Greater Athens it is.' This seemed the obvious answer to me.

'Greater Athens is brutal, Yanis. Are you sure?' Alexis asked.

'So be it,' I replied.

Most constituencies in Greece elect more than one member of parliament each. Greater Athens is the largest constituency in the country, with more than 1.5 million registered voters, electing 44 of the parliament's 300 members. I was fully aware that it was also Pappas and Dragasakis's constituency.[13]

Seeing my determination, Pappas weighed in positively: 'He will get elected easily,' he said, ending the discussion but not my disquiet.

Not wanting me to join Syriza as a member made some sense. Resisting my election to parliament was altogether more disconcerting as it heightened the disturbing possibility that my utility to Alexis was inversely proportional to my autonomous political legitimacy. Still, it could equally have been that Alexis was simply concerned that I would not do well enough with the voters on polling day. This thought plus the covenant we had just agreed upon made it impossible to turn the offer down, despite my sea of doubts.

As we were walking to the front door, a thoughtful Alexis said to me, 'You will need to put together a team to prepare in case they push us out of the eurozone. Start working on this soon.'

'I will, Alexi,' I replied. This was the birth of what became known as Plan X – to be activated only if and after Berlin and the ECB activated their own Plan Z for pushing Greece over the cliff of Grexit.[14] 'But know this, Alexi,' I added. 'The best and only way of securing our place, long term, in the eurozone is to shower the creditors with moderation while simultaneously signalling to them our unwavering determination to activate our deterrence strategy if they try to crush us.'

Alexis nodded in agreement. Dragasakis, looking very tired, smiled faintly and asked me to keep him in the loop. I promised him I would.

Chronicle of an ambush foretold

Time went into overdrive after that late-November morning in 2014. Danae and I immediately began to plan our move back to Athens by the end of January, in good time for a possible election in March. However, Prime Minister Samaras had a different plan.

On 8 December he announced that he was bringing the presidential election forward, with the first – essentially ritual – vote to be held nine days later, on 17 December, the second ritual vote on 22 December, and the third – decisive – vote on 27 December.[15] On hearing the news, I assumed that he must somehow have found the numbers he needed to secure another two years in government. Why else would he bring forward a vote that could shorten his government by two whole months?

The following day I began to question my theory. On 9 December the Greek finance minister applied to the Eurogroup for a two-month extension of the second bailout agreement, which was due to expire on 31 December 2014. Why only two months when the troika had proposed a six-month extension? If Samaras had the numbers and could hold on to office for another two years, he should have wanted at least six months before pushing through parliament the third bailout loan agreement that the troika's policies necessitated. Why cut himself such a short rope? The only explanation I could come up with was that he was not cutting it for himself – he was cutting it for us.

Speaking to Pappas and Alexis from Austin, I gathered that this was indeed the case. Samaras knew he did not have the numbers, was resigned to a late-January election that he knew he would lose, but was counting on the troika to close down Greece's banks on expiry of the bailout agreement, which would now fall on 28 February 2015, thus snuffing out a four-week-old Syriza government. This would clear the way for a technocratic administration, just as had taken office in 2012, to pass the third bailout loan agreement, followed by his triumphant return to Maximos. Among ourselves we began to refer to this as Mr Samaras's 'left intermission' ploy.

Our theory was confirmed by two developments. First, in response to the opinion polls, which were predicting a Syriza victory, Samaras and his ministers began to brief that their fall would be followed the next morning by bank closures. This was tantamount to a sitting government inciting a bank run. Then, on 15 December, Stournaras, until the previous June Samaras's finance minister but now in charge of the country's central bank, included in an official speech a phrase unique in the annals of central banking.

> In the context of my duties as governor of the Bank of Greece, and in my capacity as a member of the Governing Board of the European Central Bank, I must note that the crisis of the last days is becoming serious, that *liquidity in markets is diminishing at a high rate* and that the risk not only of the reduction in economic growth that recently restarted but also of an irreversible impairment of the Greek economy is large.[16]

Never before had a central banker violated so blatantly his mandate to maintain financial stability. Central banks were created in order to prevent bank runs at times of shrinking liquidity by reassuring the markets that liquidity would remain plentiful. With his statement Stournaras had done the opposite, accelerating the bank run that the sitting government had begun in order to undermine a future Syriza government.

On 20 December the Samaras government pushed through parliament the two-month extension to the second bailout loan agreement, casting 28 February in stone as the date on which the banks would close if no new agreement with the EU–IMF were reached. A week later, Prime Minister Samaras's candidate for the presidency failed to secure the necessary majority. An election was called for 25 January 2015. The die had been cast. I would have to rush back to Athens with only days to contest my first ever election in a country I had not lived in for three years.

Watching all this unfold from Austin, I saw quite clearly the ambush that awaited me. Nor did it come as a surprise. And yet there are times in life when, however expected the malice may be, observing it transpire fills one's heart with sadness. I recalled an old joke: two golfers exchange their life stories as they move from one hole to the next. The first one confesses that he made his fortune when his ailing factory burned down and he was able to claim the insurance. The second golfer then confesses that he also made it big when his own business was destroyed by a flood, netting him a nice cheque from the insurance company. The first golfer looks puzzled. 'But how did you start the flood?' he asks.

Prime Minister Samaras and Governor Stournaras had started a fire on our home front, in the form of a bank run, that we would need to put out while at the same time negotiating with powerful foreign creditors who did not really want their money back. Meanwhile, our own central bank, Europe's central bank, Greece's oligarchy and indeed the media would be pouring fuel onto that fire. Our only ally against such an alliance would be a battered, fed up but hopefully determined *demos*.

Truth without fear

Ever since Greece had been imprisoned within its cage of unpayable debt, I had been portrayed as a fool. The establishment called me one because I refused to acknowledge that saying no to their bailout meant ejection from the euro. In a show of touching bipartisanship, many leftists also called me a fool for precisely the same reason: they saw my aim of emancipating Greece within the eurozone as a pipe dream.

This unlikely right–left consensus told Greeks they faced a simple choice: suffer in silence in your debtors' prison to keep the few euros left in your pocket, or get out of the euro, possibly of the European Union. While disagreeing over which of the two options was preferable, the troika and its Greek cheerleaders, the Greek communist party and the members of Syriza's Left Platform all agreed: Varoufakis is at best a useful idiot, leading Greece's rebellious populace into a horrid defeat (the intransigent Left's allegation), and at worst a dangerous narcissist, possibly an agent of satanic forces, wishing to destabilize Europe in association with George Soros and other American–Jewish foes of the euro (the establishment's insinuation). These two schools of thought managed the impossible: simultaneously to portray the same person as an enemy of Greece's place in Europe *and* as an agent of Brussels.

Mindful of the real dangers posed by this powerful consensus, in early 2014 I sat down and wrote a book, published in Greek only and entitled *The Genesis of Bailout Greece*. In it I restated the argument I had been making for years: Greece should never seek Grexit but should demand a viable agreement within the eurozone. Such an agreement was feasible, though far from certain, provided we were not intimidated by the threat of enforced Grexit.

A week before the general election of 25 January 2015 I launched the book at the Athens Megaron Music Hall in front of hundreds of attendees and another two hundred thousand viewers via a live video stream. This was to be my one and only pre-election campaign event, so I used it to present to the voters my negotiation aims and strategy, just as I had done to Alexis, Pappas and Dragasakis, concluding as follows.

> The only conclusion that can be drawn here is that, unless we disdain surrender more than Grexit, there is no sense in negotiating with the EU–IMF. If Syriza, deep down, thinks that Grexit is worse than another bailout, it might as well surrender at the beginning – or even better avoid winning the election. This does not mean that we should want Grexit or that we should be working towards it. It

means that the only way of securing a viable agreement within the eurozone is to table moderate proposals to our creditors regarding a compromise new deal while being determined not to capitulate at the threat of Grexit.

Turning to our creditors' likely preferences, I truly believe that Grexit is an empty threat, as it will cost the EU around one trillion euros in written-off public and private debt as well as a chain reaction of bankruptcies within Europe's financial labyrinth. Interestingly, the very same people who in 2010 were admonishing me for daring to say that the Papandreou government had the leverage to say no to Berlin and Brussels because Grexit in 2010 would have blown up France and Germany's banks, are now scolding me for proposing today, in 2015, a strategy that could have worked in 2010. Well, I have news for them: I was right then, as they now acknowledge, and I may very well be right today: Grexit will still, despite all the things they have done to ring-fence themselves from its shock waves, cost them an arm and a leg – and this is why I still believe it is an empty threat.

Of course I may be wrong. They may fear a compromise with us more than they fear Grexit. But even if I am wrong, ask yourselves: despite the undoubtedly sharp cost of Grexit, is continued membership of the euro under permanent debt bondage and the eternal recession it brings better?

Ladies and gentlemen, just like a peace-loving people do not want war but will not surrender their freedom because they are threatened with war, it is perfectly rational to disdain Grexit, as I do, but not be prepared to live in a state of permanent great depression because we are threatened by it.[17]

As the election approached and the rumour spread that I might be the next minister of finance, I was walking a tightrope. Traditionally, finance ministers are economical with the truth. Indeed, it is considered their duty to deny planned changes, such as to interest or exchange rates, even while they are preparing them, in order to prevent any damaging pre-emptive reaction in the markets which will undermine the changes' desired effect. In my case I had to tell the Greek people the truth about our creditors' forthcoming financial aggression without encouraging the bank run that undermined my capacity to negotiate a decent deal on their behalf.

I chose a strategy of telling it as it was, peppered with optimism for the good outcomes that would follow if only we remained committed to our covenant. Interviewed on commercial television one morning, I said, 'If Syriza is not determined to respond to Mario Draghi's threats to close banks and ATMs by putting the phone down on him after reminding him that his aggression violates the European Union's treaties and spirit, there is no purpose in our being elected. Our people must be ready for such threats coming from an ECB that behaved that way towards the Irish and the Cypriots.'

Not exactly soothing words from someone rumoured to be heading for the Ministry of Finance, but as the people were our only ally, I could not afford to keep them in the dark. They had to be prepared for the worst. At the same time I had to keep their spirits up. Asked in another television interview if the ECB would close down our banks, I replied tactically: 'If we play our cards right, there is just as much of a chance that this will happen as there is that the sun will not rise from the east tomorrow morning.'

In an article I published the day after that television interview I was more candid, warning that during our negotiations the stock exchange, share values and all financial variables would go into spasm, while trying to balance frankness with optimism: 'While these negotiations last, apoplexy will consume markets and speculators. But when the negotiations conclude, with Greece emerging as a solvent country, then the markets will start dancing harmoniously to our tune.'[18]

Striking the right balance – how to inform without alarming, how to warn without fuelling fear – was an agonizing dilemma.

Some others were much simpler.

Rejecting the enemy's weapons

Many of my economist friends – who suspected that I was about to land the worst job in the universe – wrote to me, emailed and phoned to lend support. Some suggested that on my first day in office I should introduce capital controls. That is, rather than wait for the ECB to close down our banks and ATMs on the grounds of halting the very bank run that they had begun, why not pre-empt them by slapping restrictions on how much cash depositors could withdraw from their accounts or wire abroad? The idea was that by slowing the bank run we could buy more time *before* the banks were closed in which to negotiate under calmer circumstances. There were three reasons for rejecting this counsel.

The first was that imposing capital controls would have been the obvious first step of a party that intended to return to the national currency in order to devalue it and thus gain competitiveness: in that case, introducing capital controls would be essential to prevent the outflow of money caused by the expected devaluation. In other words, introducing capital controls would have been the right move only if we were intending to leave the eurozone – to opt for Grexit – and would therefore have contradicted both my negotiating aims and my strategy for signalling credibly what these aims were. Moreover, even if we managed to convince Brussels of our sincere desire to remain within the euro, capital controls would signal a willingness to become second-rate citizens of the eurozone, as stragglers who had euros but who could not do as they pleased with them. My intention was to signal the precise opposite.

The second reason was that the time available for negotiations was fixed by our debt repayment schedule, so capital controls would not actually buy us any time. These repayments were due to begin in April 2015 and continue until August, which demanded a new agreement by June 2015 at the very latest. Even if I could have waved a magic wand to stop the bank run dead, the negotiations would still have to be completed within four to five months at the very most. Capital controls would not change this one iota.

The third reason was that capital controls are inconsistent with monetary union, whose spirit and reality they violate. The whole point of the eurozone or any common currency area is that money is free to move unimpeded. If I were to introduce capital controls on day one of our administration, how could I censure the ECB for threatening us with them? The moment I did so, all the accusations against me and the Syriza government – of being anti-European, of preparing Greece for Grexit, of undermining the indivisibility of the eurozone – would be vindicated. Moreover, our own people would be puzzled: why is a government that is pressing for a good agreement within a common currency area stopping us from getting our money out of our own bank accounts and from sending it to other countries in the same monetary union? The blame game would have been lost before the negotiations even started.

Another suggestion for helping a Syriza government buy time during the negotiations came from, among others, Thomas Mayer, formerly chief economist at Deutsche Bank. His idea was to introduce a second currency parallel to the euro within Greece in order to create more liquidity and space for us to manoeuvre. It was an interesting idea but one I had actually considered and rejected in 2010 as a solution to the euro crisis.[19] Its gist was that wage rises, aimed at reversing austerity, be awarded in a new currency backed by government debt. The new currency would of course devalue immediately in relation to the euro. Thus, while Greek workers' pay packets and pensions would increase a little, Greek labour, as measured in euros, would devalue in relation to German, French or Portuguese labour, making Greece more competitive.

I gave Thomas Mayer two reasons why I could not endorse a parallel currency. First, 'Parties and interests opposed to us are already creating an atmosphere of terror by claiming that we have a hidden agenda to bring Greece out of the euro, plunder people's savings and put Greece on the road to becoming a new Argentina. Your proposal's propaganda value to our opponents would tend to infinity.' Second, there was no need for it because the parallel payments system that I was working on provided us with the flexibility we required.

Months later it struck me that these two measures – capital controls and a parallel currency – would be wielded by Germany's finance minister, Dr Wolfgang Schäuble, against me. The early decision to reject the enemy's own weapons was thus vindicated, and yet, soon after I resigned the finance ministry I was accused of devising diabolical plans to introduce them both.

C'est la vie in Bailoutistan.

Moderate single-mindedness

As the election approached, it was imperative to send two signals to Mario Draghi and the rest of the EU–IMF officialdom, one of moderation, the other of single-mindedness: you can trust me to propose a debt restructuring that combines substance with finesse, that does the job of giving Greece a chance but does not clash with the ECB's rules and, importantly, can be sold to fidgety Bundestag politicians by Angela Merkel as her own *wunderbar* idea. But make no mistake: we shall not be beaten back into our pen even if you close down Greece's banks.

On 17 January 2015, a week before the election, I issued a press release in my now official capacity of parliamentary candidate for Greater Athens, in which I outlined my proposals for restructuring Greece's public debt. First, we should split it into its four main constituent slices:

1. Money owed to the ECB in the form of the bonds it had purchased in 2010/11 (the so-called SMP bonds that would have been haircut by 90 per cent in 2012 had they not done so).[20]
2. The largest slice (60 per cent of our total debt), owed to the rest of Europe from the two bailouts.
3. A smaller slice owed to the IMF (about 10 per cent of our debt mountain).
4. Money still owed to private investors after the 2012 haircut (around 15 per cent of total debt).

This is what I proposed we do with each of these slices. Our debts to the IMF (3) and to private investors (4) would be honoured in full. The latter was too small for it to be worth opening a front against hedge funds, which might lead to an Argentina-style international dispute with few potential benefits. Besides, they had already swallowed a haircut of 90 per cent of what they were owed in 2012. As for the IMF, despite its complicity in enabling Brussels and Berlin to impose debt bondage upon Greece by peddling economic forecasts they knew to be false, we would not want to antagonize the United States (which considers the IMF one of its own) in addition to Berlin. Moreover, a haircut of the IMF loans would also hit non-European countries such as Malaysia and Japan that had nothing to do with Europe's internal squabbles and which might otherwise lend a sympathetic ear to our government.

The money we owed the ECB (1), the Trichet Legacy as I called it after the then president of the ECB who bought the SMP bonds, was an absurd debt. We only owed it because of the ECB's error in buying

Greek bonds after Greece had become insolvent at around 70 per cent of their face value when their market value was not much more than 10 per cent of face value. Since then we had been engaged in the pathetic ritual described fully in Chapter 3 (see 'Success story') of borrowing from the ECB in order pay the ECB to redeem these bonds while pretending not to do so. This shenanigan had to end.

In a rational Europe this absurd debt would simply be written off. Alas, the ECB's charter does not allow for this. To accommodate the ECB's charter, I took a leaf from the British Treasury's book. The British government had long practised the issue of open-ended, or perpetual, bonds. These yield interest, but the government may repay the principal at a time of its choosing, if ever. Indeed, perpetual bonds issued at the time of the South Sea Bubble in the 1720s and by Neville Chamberlain and Winston Churchill during and just after the Great War were only repaid by the British Treasury in late 2014 and early 2015. I proposed the following: our government would issue new perpetual bonds, with the same face value as the bonds the ECB owned, bearing a small interest rate but with no expiry or redemption date. These bonds would then be swapped for the ECB's ones, to be parked neatly and for ever on the ECB's assets books, bearing a trickle of interest in perpetuity, thus allowing Mario Draghi to respect his charter, since at no point would the Greek debt be written off or even down.

Finally, regarding the largest slice of debt (2), accrued in the two bailouts and owed to Europe's taxpayers, I proposed another type of swap. Existing debt obligations to Europe's bailout fund would be swapped with new Greek government thirty-year bonds, again of the same value as the existing debt (so no formal haircut) but with two provisions: first, annual payments were to be suspended until the country's income recovered to beyond a certain threshold; second, the rate of interest would be linked to the rate of growth of the Greek economy.[21] That way, our creditors would become partners in Greece's recovery and have an incentive to see the pie from which they would get their money back grow.

These debt-swap proposals, tabled before the election, would be the basis of my actual proposals to Greece's creditors once I was in office. They were moderate and politically palatable to the creditors, as they included no outright haircut. They signalled to the public and to potential investors that the EU was accepting a new role: no longer the harsh creditor of an insolvent state, it would become a partner in Greece's growth, as its own returns would be proportional to Greek nominal income growth. They would have been enough to cause an influx of investment into an investment-starved Greece. They would have ended the Greek recession with winners all round, the only exceptions being the cockroaches that flourish in the filth caused by prolonged misery.

Not once did any official of the EU or the IMF articulate a criticism of the logic behind these proposals. How could they? As the CEO of one of America's largest investment banks remarked after hearing them, 'You are offering them a deal that a Wall Street bankruptcy lawyer could have come up with.' Quite. It took the election of a radical Left government in Greece for Athens to bring to Brussels, Frankfurt and Berlin moderate debt proposals – an indication of the organized folly that the European Union had descended into after the euro crisis hit it.

However, not for a moment did I believe, back then in January 2015, that the unquestionable logic and obvious moderation of my proposals would win our creditors over. As I had been telling Alexis since 2012, *any* proposal from us that contradicted the troika's Greek programme would be met with naked aggression and the threat of shuttered banks. Logic hardly mattered. Mutual economic advantage was irrelevant. The creditors did not want their money back. What mattered to them was their authority, and that was being challenged by a leftist government whose success at negotiating a new deal for its country was the creditors' greatest nightmare, as it might give ideas to other Europeans labouring under the same crisis and the same irrational policies.

Modest, reasonable, technically competent debt-swap proposals were important, but they were not enough. It was imperative that, before crossing the threshold of the finance ministry, I should signal to the other side that their aggression would cost them; that the moment they moved to close down the banks, I would activate our key deterrent and the parallel payments system, as per my informal covenant with the Syriza leadership. My signal took the form of a statement made in January 2015 during a BBC interview.

My advice to the next finance minister [of Greece] is this: if the ECB threatens to close down the nation's banks, you should respond instantly by haircutting the Greek government bonds that the ECB still owns. They are still ruled by Greek law, so the ECB would have to sue Greece in the Greek courts, not in London or Luxembourg. Simultaneously, he or she should put in place a payments system that can function in parallel to the banks so as to create euro-denominated, homegrown liquidity and, importantly, allow the economy to function if the ECB do decide to close down the banks.

As I was to establish later, the message was received. The battle lines had been drawn.[22]

5

Raging against the dying of the light

As the election approached, a strange mix of togetherness and loneliness overcame me. On the streets, at public meetings, in taxis and at Syriza's headquarters, where I would meet Alexis and the rest of the team, I experienced solidarity, warmth, sympathy and immense support. But deep inside I knew I was institutionally isolated, resource-poor, entirely on my own. Not having been a member of parliament before, not even a party member, and having lived in Austin for the previous three years, I had no support network, as Alexis had remarked.

My colleagues aspiring to enter government had secretaries, drivers, private offices, important connections. In contrast, I had Danae's moral support, my motorcycle and our apartment at the foot of the Acropolis, where I gave interviews, held meetings, composed my blog posts and conducted all the business of the campaign. At one point I received a call from Syriza HQ telling me that as a parliamentary candidate the law required me to open a special bank account in which to deposit all contributions to my campaign and from which to draw all campaign-related expenses. I opened the account, since it was mandatory, but deposited precisely nothing in it as I neither sought nor received any contributions, had no staff and spent precisely zero on promotional material. My only campaigning device was a Greek-language blog I created myself, using a free blogging platform, as an addendum to my existing English-language blog. That was it.

But while I did not need any of the trappings of conventional political campaigning to get elected, I was troubled by the prospect of walking into the finance ministry without a team, relying entirely on civil servants who had until then been faithful servants of Bailoutistan, with additional staff provided exclusively by Dragasakis and Syriza HQ. So I used the few weeks I had in the run-up to the election to gather the best team around me that I could.

To help me identify a deputy finance minister for the key position of overseeing the Treasury, I had coffee with Alekos Papadopoulos, a 1990s-era former PASOK finance minister whom I had known for years, trusted for his probity and considered the only finance minister to have had his finger on the state's financial pulse during his tenure. While Alekos remained an opponent of Syriza, he was personally supportive and promised to come up with a name. The same night he texted me the name of Dimitris Mardas, whom I had never heard of but who my experienced friend insisted was capable and above board. Next morning I called Mardas with an offer he had never imagined.[1]

Even more crucial was the post of president of the Council of Economic Advisers. In the eurozone heads of government cannot achieve anything without the close collaboration and loyalty of the finance minister who represents them in the Eurogroup. Likewise, finance ministers cannot succeed without a similarly close relationship with the president of their ministry's Council of Economic Advisers, who represents them in the so-called Eurogroup Working Group. Supposedly this is where preparations are made for Eurogroup meetings, but in reality it operates as the shadowy crucible in which the troika forges its plans and policies.

However, this position had been filled on my behalf by Dragasakis even before I set foot on Greek soil. Dragasakis had selected George Chouliarakis, a thirty-something economist who had taught at Manchester University before being seconded to the Central Bank of Greece. 'He is a good lad and has been preparing the ground for us, working informally with people inside the Council of Economic Advisers,' Dragasakis told me when we first met after my arrival in Greece, a few weeks before the election. While my close friend Wassily was appalled, always sceptical of Dragasakis's intentions and choices, I was happy that someone was already on the ground, preparing it.

Upon meeting Chouliarakis I took a liking to him, despite evidence of a severely circumscribed capacity to engage and an excessive tendency to keep his cards close to his chest. My concerns were allayed though when he told me that as an undergraduate at the University of Athens his mentors had been two progressive, highly intellectual economics professors very dear to my heart, one of whom was my dear friend and colleague Nicholas Theocarakis, a member of the academic quartet that had formed immediately after my arrival at the university in 2000 which also included Stournaras.[2] This news was also a boost in view of my plan to appoint Nicholas general secretary for fiscal policy.

In putting together my team, I was troubled by the thought that none of us had any experience of actually dealing with the troika – with the technocrats who were used to coming to Athens on behalf of the EU, the ECB and the IMF, entering its ministries, interrogating its ministers of state and imposing their will on them like bailiffs – although this was to be expected of a group of people who had never served Bailoutistan and whom civil servants and troika officials alike treated like mortal enemies. Fortunately, one day I came across Elena Panariti, someone who knew the troika's language and their modus operandi.

Elena had worked for years in Washington, primarily at the World Bank, where she forged excellent connections with powerful people associated with the institutions behind the so-called Washington Consensus (the package of reforms that the US prescribed for economies in crisis), including former Treasury Secretary Larry Summers, to whom she would later introduce me (recall Chapter 1), and David Lipton, second-in-command at the IMF. Her work in Peru on behalf of the World Bank in collaboration with the despotic regime of President Fujimori had made her a figure of hatred among the Left in Greece and elsewhere. Her defence was that, whoever it was for or with, the work itself was important and progressive, getting people living in shanty towns title deeds to their shacks, allowing them to invest in these dwellings, to live within them with peace of mind and to use them as an asset that gave them access to the formal marketplace.

As a member of parliament under George Papandreou, who had appointed her via the party list, it was true that Elena had voted in favour of the first bailout, but she never bought the lie that the bailout was going to work financially and Greece would soon be out of the woods. As she told me at the time, she voted in favour because of the immense psychological pressure that Papandreou and his people had exerted upon her. And to her credit, Elena subsequently turned into one of the bailout's strongest critics. In a remarkable moment of parliamentary theatre she stood up during a crucial select committee meeting in 2011 and in her trademark Greek, which is not her first language, her voice breaking with emotion, she slated her own ministers and their acquiescence in Greece's conversion into a debt colony.[3] So when I met her again a few days before the election I did not hesitate for a moment to ask her to join my team, for there is no better person to fight the devil than one who has served him and, through that experience, become his sworn enemy.

The same applied to Natasha Arvaniti, a former student in the economics PhD programme that Nicholas Theocarakis and I had set up in 2003 at the University of Athens. Natasha had since joined the civil service before being seconded to Brussels, where she worked for the troika. As a European Commission technocrat, she had been sent to Nicosia to enforce the Cyprus bailout. Having seen first hand the devastation that the troika leaves in its wake wherever it goes, Natasha was a very welcome member of my team. With the help of people like her and Elena, I would be able to decipher the troika's mood and signals more accurately and plan our negotiating tactics accordingly.

The downside of such recruits was that within Syriza and Alexis's inner circle those keen to pull the rug from under me had plenty of ammunition with which to argue that I was preparing our surrender.

'We're going to have problems within the party, Yanis,' Alexis warned me one day. 'Do you really need people like Elena and Natasha? They're tainted by their association with the bailouts. Our people are livid.'

'Alexi,' I replied, 'do you realize how fierce our confrontation with the troika is going to be? They take no prisoners, these people. I need to have staff on my team who know them, who know what's in their box of tricks, whom they will recognize as worthy opponents.' There was something else too, I explained: I trusted Elena and Natasha because, unlike our own people, they had guilty consciences. They had experienced the indignity of the troika's activities for themselves; they had been toughened by them, and for that reason I was certain they were less likely to be co-opted by their opponents than some of our wet-behind-the-ears troika-slayers.

Unperturbed by Alexis's discomfort, I went on to enlist the help of other troika defectors, some of them from abroad. One was Glenn Kim, who came on the recommendation of an ally in the media. Glenn was a banker, had been involved in many of the big bond deals between Greece, the eurozone and Germany, and was now working independently on contract for various European governments. He was 'quite an expert', I was told, on the GDP-linked bonds that I intended to propose as part of Greece's debt swap. I contacted Glenn right away.

A few days later, ten days before the election, Glenn and I were sipping coffee at a café very close to Stournaras's Bank of Greece. He came clean, confessing to having played a leading role in designing not just the Greek bailout but the eurozone's bailout-funding institutions on a retainer from, among others, the German finance ministry.[4]

'What we did to Greece in 2011 and 2012 was appalling,' he admitted.

I asked him what he was up to currently. He told me he was working for the government of Iceland, helping to restructure its public debt and work towards lifting the capital controls that had been imposed in the wake of its own financial collapse in 2008.

'Your idea of GDP-indexed bonds is good,' he told me, 'and I think I can help you refine it. It will be my way of making amends for the long-term damage that we, and people like me, did to Greece.'

Never one to look a gift horse in the mouth, I agreed and asked him to be ready to come to Athens on 26 January, if we won the election of the previous day.

A cynic might say that professionals like Glenn were in it for the money and for their own career purposes. Possibly. But having people such as Glenn on my side, who knew where all the skeletons were buried, was a priceless weapon. (When the troika's apparatchiks saw him among my team, they almost had a stroke.) But I also suspected that in Glenn's case I could rely not only on his professionalism but on something beyond enlightened selfishness. Two days before the election, Glenn seemed to confirm this in an email to me in which he wrote, 'Yanis, if all goes to plan, the good folks of Greece (and in fact Europe as a whole) will have charted a new course for their future . . . in thinking about this weekend, I am reminded of Homer's words: "Εἷς οἰωνὸς ἄριστος, ἀμύνεσθαι περὶ πάτρης."' This is from Homer's *Iliad* and means, 'There is no better omen than fighting for our country.'

Another foreign powerhouse also offered its services to our cause: the French investment bank Lazard, led by Daniel Cohen and Matthieu Pigasse. Like Glenn, Lazard had acted as a consultant and facilitator of the second second bailout, charging the struggling Greek state tens of millions of euros for its services. So, when Daniel and Matthieu asked to see me, I was puzzled, guarded and sceptical. But they won me over with a frank account of their complicity, an equally frank apology and an offer to help get Greece back on its feet by providing their considerable services pro bono.

With these illustrious defectors on our side, our technical strength was bolstered no end. No one in Syriza or known to the party had access to such expertise. They would be my heavy artillery. Of course, my association with them was used to suggest a variety of sins. It was no coincidence that on the very same day Glenn shocked the troika with his presence in Brussels, an opposition member tabled a question in parliament asking why the Greek government needed to have a 'Korean' on its team and what his links with me were, implying some sordid relationship with American, Asian or other dark forces.[5] Meanwhile, Syriza people, often well meaning and genuine in their concerns, warned the party faithful that I was preparing to make a Faustian bargain with the troika.

In fact, Elena, Natasha, Glenn and the good people of Lazard stood tall against the troika even after Syriza's young zealots fell. Together with some other former students and graduates of the University of Athens doctoral economics programme, these troika defectors backed our cause selflessly, producing splendid economic modelling, putting indefatigable legwork into the negotiations and giving me mammoth moral support before each meeting with the Eurogroup, in Maximos or any of the other rooms where adults behaved very, very badly.

While building a team of experts, I was also engaging friends and potential allies outside Greece. One of my missives for help went to Lord (Norman) Lamont. 'Dear Norman,' it read,

> As you may have gathered from press reports, Greeks are going to the polls this coming Sunday. For better or for worse I am standing for a seat in the Greater Athens constituency and, according to pollsters, I seem 'condemned' to win it. Even worse, if my party forms the government (which is not unlikely) I stand to inherit the Ministry of Finance – replete with empty coffers and outrageous pressure from Brussels and Frankfurt. Might I count on you as a prospective counsel in the turbulent times ahead?
> Trusting that you are well.
>
>   Yanis

Norman responded immediately. Yes, he was willing and ready to offer counsel. When I told him that the issue ran a lot deeper than debt and bonds, that it pertained to our parliament's sovereignty and raised the question of whether democracy was a luxury to be denied citizens of an indebted state, he replied,

> I entirely agree with what you say of course about democracy and the sovereignty of parliament. I keep trying to remind Cameron and Osborne that if they get the chance to renegotiate our relationship with the EU, as they hope, it should be about restoring sovereignty and not just economics and competitiveness. You and I are at one on that. I also agree with you there has been too much emphasis in the eurozone on austerity alone . . . Assuming you become finance minister I will be very happy to do what I can to help . . . I have some ideas. Good luck personally. Yours ever.
>
> Norman

My friendship with true-blue Tory and Eurosceptic Lord Lamont of Lerwick, the chancellor who had ensured that Britain dropped out of the European Monetary System, thus guaranteeing that the UK would not join the euro, was at odds with my image as a loony-left extremist. It was also taken as further proof by some that, guided and prodded by Lamont, I was hell-bent on getting Greece out of the euro.

Of course, precisely the opposite was true. When a few months later things came to a head and Wolfgang Schäuble was pushing us towards Grexit, Norman's advice to me was to think twice before even considering it, such were the costs and perils of returning to a national currency. Throughout my 162 days in office Norman proved a pillar of strength, advising me on the final draft of my reform, debt and fiscal proposals to the EU and the IMF. If only more left-leaning politicians had stood as firm, the outcome might have been altogether different.

Besides Norman, my overseas supporters included Columbia University economist Jeff Sachs, who played a central role as adviser and advocate, the aforementioned Thomas Mayer of Deutsche Bank fame, Larry Summers and Jamie Galbraith, who had worked for years with me on refining the *Modest Proposal for Resolving the Euro Crisis*, helping reduce the antipathy towards Alexis and Syriza in Washington, writing speeches for Alexis and organizing conferences to prepare the Anglosphere for the new Syriza administration.

On 20 November I dispatched a cheerful email to Jamie:

> Jamie,
> Yesterday Alexis told me that he had received a phone call from a prominent bank owner, who threatened that the bank's ATMs will not function the day after our election if Alexis appoints me minister of finance. Alexis responded by asking him how old he is. The banker replied: sixty-five. Alexis then said: If you overthrow me, I am young enough to rise again. You are not!

It was one of those moments of sheer pride in my friends, old and new, and joy at having acquired vicious foes.

Wasteland

Without the skills of a T.S. Eliot or a John Steinbeck, it is difficult to convey the scale of Greece's devastation in January 2015. A numerical comparison will have to suffice.

Britain in the early 1980s suffered a major convulsion when unemployment quadrupled. The damage was done by a recession lasting a single year, 1980–1, when national income fell by 1.26 per cent. The next recession to hit Britain came a decade later, lasting also a single year (1990–1), with national income shrinking by 1.78 per cent. More recently, following the Credit Crunch, another single-year recession (2008–9) left the country reeling, with a drop in national income of a substantial 5.15 per cent. Compare and contrast these three traumas with what befell the Greeks.

By 2010, the year of the first bailout, national income had fallen by a whopping 7.5 per cent since the previous year. Did things improve as a consequence of the bailout? On the contrary, during 2010–11 incomes fell by a further 8.9 per cent. By comparison, 2011–12 was a good year, the economy shrinking further by a trifling 1.1 per cent. To what did we owe the relative lull? Ironically, to the political crisis caused by the depression, which meant that we either had no government or too weak a government to legislate further austerity!

But as soon as Prime Minister Samaras came to office in June 2012 with a small but solid parliamentary majority, the troika ensured he made up for lost time by cranking up the austerity machine with a vengeance. The result? The cruellest year yet, with national income plunging a further 14 per cent by the end of 2013 and another 3.3 per cent during 2014.

When British friends remark sympathetically that Greece is today where Britain was during the Great Depression, I thank them for their kindly intended comparison but am forced to correct them. Between 1929 and 1932 Britain's economy shrank by 4.9 per cent and unemployment rose from 8 to 17 per cent. (At this point I imagine a Greek version of John Cleese's character in *Monty Python*'s 'Four Yorkshiremen' sketch crying out, 'You were lucky!' 'Luxury!') By comparison, Greece has endured six consecutive years of recession, the loss of 28 per cent of its national income, more than one in five workers losing their job, and an unemployment rate propelled from 7 to 27 per cent, with youth unemployment at more than 65 per cent.

And yet today, as these lines are being written, there are still those who believe that by the end of 2014 Greece's economy was returning to health and would have been out of the woods by the end of 2015 had it not been for the idiocy of those Greek voters who jeopardized the recovery by voting in people like me on 25 January 2015. Like unruly children screaming, 'Are we nearly there yet?' from the back seat and distracting the driver, the Greek electorate caused their country to swerve off the road to recovery just as it was entering the final straight. And had it not been for the actions of the insufferable finance minister of the populist government they elected, a third bailout would never have been necessary. Do they have a point?

The jagged grey line in Figure 1 shows Greece's total income, undiluted by statistical tricks and given in raw euros. The black line superimposed upon it is a four-month average, providing a clearer sense of the overall trend. The shaded oval highlights the period in 2014 when the alleged recovery began. Can you spot it? The Greek voters could not.

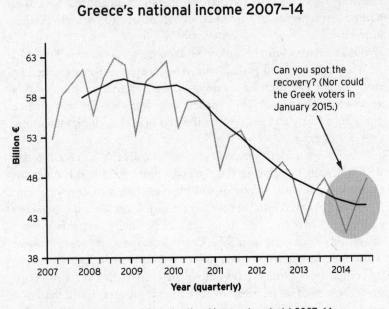

Figure 1: Greece's unadjusted national income (quarterly) 2007–14, with a four-month moving average superimposed.

Soon after it became clear that I might become Greece's finance minister in this economic environment, I gave a speech attended by members of the European parliament, journalists and other so-called opinion makers. Asked whether a new government might jeopardize the 'recent recovery', I had no alternative but to expose them to the wretched facts that almost never appeared in the press.

> There are 10 million Greeks living in Greece (falling fast due to emigration), organized in around 2.8 million households with a 'relationship' with the tax authorities.
>
> Of those 2.8 million households, 2.3 million (and 3.5 million tax file numbers) have a debt to the tax authorities that they cannot service.

One million households cannot pay their electricity bill in full, forcing the electricity company to 'extend and pretend', thus ensuring that a million homes live in fear of darkness at night and the electricity company is insolvent. Indeed, the Public Power Corporation is disconnecting around 30,000 homes and businesses a month due to unpaid bills.

For 48.6 per cent of families, pensions are the main source of income. Meanwhile the troika demands that pensions be cut even further. What was the €700 old age pension has been reduced by about 25 per cent since 2010 and is due to be halved over the next few years.

The minimum wage has shrunk (on the troika's orders) by 40 per cent.

Other benefits have been cut by more than 18 per cent.

Some 40 per cent of the population say they will not be able to meet their financial commitments this year.

Unemployment has risen 160 per cent so that 3.5 million employed people now support 4.7 million unemployed or inactive Greeks.

Of the 3 million people constituting Greece's labour force, 1.4 million are jobless.

Of the 1.4 million jobless only 10 per cent receive unemployment benefit and only 15 per cent any benefits at all. The rest must fend for themselves.

Of those employed in the private sector 500,000 have not been paid for more than three months.

Contractors who work for the public sector are paid up to 24 months after they provide the service and pre-pay the sales tax to the tax office.

Between 2008 and 2014 small and medium-sized companies reduced their workforce by 29.3 per cent and their output (in value added terms) by 40.2 per cent.

Half the businesses still in operation throughout the country are seriously in arrears with their compulsory contributions to their employees' pension and social security funds.

In 2013 36 per cent of the population officially lived at risk of poverty or social exclusion. That percentage is on the rise.

Household disposable income has contracted 30 per cent since 2010.

Healthcare expenditure was cut by 11.1 per cent between 2009 and 2011 alone, with significant rises in HIV infections, tuberculosis and stillbirths.

Could any of these bleak statistics, which documented our nation's conversion into a wasteland, be seen as a sign of improvement? Or do they perhaps explain the Greek voters' inability to spot their country's supposed economic recovery?

Greek-covery?

Nonetheless, in December 2014 the government and the troika were adamant: their success story was true and the economy was showing clear signs of green shoots. They even coined a neologism: Greek-covery. But manufacturing output, which in 2011 had fallen by 4 per cent and in 2012 by another 15 per cent (equal to the entire loss of manufacturing output during Britain's Great Depression), had registered a small upturn in 2013 but in 2014 had started shrinking again. Meanwhile, industrial production during 2014 was down by 3 per cent and net investment was negative.[6] As for employment, although the minimum wage had fallen by a world-beating 40 per cent, making Greece the land of dreams for the world's neoliberals, full-time employment continued to decline, precarious employment rose by a smidgeon and overall hours worked fell.[7] So what evidence could there possibly have been to make this claim?

Partly, it relied on a peculiar set of statistics. Technically, real income – economists' jargon for income adjusted to take into account the changing price of goods – was up. But this was a mirage created by a dramatic decline in prices, which made purchasing power appear much stronger but took no account of the countervailing and over-riding costs of massive debt. Appendix 1 provides a full debunking of this nonsense.

Mainly, it relied on the fact that by 2013 Greece had become a surplus nation, meaning essentially that its exports exceeded its imports, suggesting an overall improvement. Since 2010 the troika had been promising the Greeks that the silver lining to the cloud of wage cuts would be a growth in exports, as the reduction in the costs to business within Greece would increase its competitiveness. By the end of 2014 the troika and the government were on an I-told-you-so spree, along with the foreign media, financial newspapers, government and EU economists. 'Greece posts first current-account surplus for many decades,' they trumpeted.

Had they considered the last time Greece posted a trade surplus, they might have understood that the situation was actually awful. This was in 1943, under the Nazi occupation, when Greeks could not afford to eat, let alone import goods from abroad, but still managed to export a few oranges, a few apples and the like. In 2014 the economic collapse had produced a similar state of affairs. The sorry reason for our current account surplus was that the deepening recession had crippled imports, while exports of goods were flat despite the massive reduction in labour costs.[8] A cause for mourning had been spun as a reason to celebrate.

The reality was evident everywhere. Even when the government put Greece's remaining family jewels up for sale, there were either no takers or only those of the shady variety. When, for example, the national lottery was put on the market, the highest bid came from a consortium whose ways I would come to know all too well after assuming the finance ministry: having paid a pittance for the state's only cash cow, they then demonstrated its remarkable capacity to prey on hopelessness to the full. Even worse was the sale of the state gas monopoly, in which only Mr Putin's favourite conglomerate, Russian giant Gazprom, showed an interest. Hours before the sale's announcement, Gazprom decided not to meet the tiny asking price after all, with their spokesperson citing the deflationary spiral ravaging the Greek economy as the reason for withdrawal. How could they pay even today's price when it might be worth only half that tomorrow? they asked.

Real estate, a fairly safe investment in normal times, fared just as badly. The site of the old Athens airport at Hellinikon is a prime plot: more than twice the area of London's Hyde Park, it is located next to the most upmarket suburbs of Athens on the coast of the Saronic Gulf with its turquoise waters. And yet only one bidder appeared – and demanded as a condition of their bid that the state invest almost as much money in the site's development as they were offering.

Meanwhile, the Samaras government and the international financial press were waxing lyrical over the success of the great recapitalization of the Greek banks effected by the second bailout. And yet in February 2014, months after the money had been received from the troika, asset management company Blackrock reported that the banks were so full of non-performing loans that they required yet more cash. By June 2014, with Schäuble running out of patience with the Samaras government, the IMF was leaking that an extra €15 billion was needed for the banks, a significantly larger sum than the roughly €11 billion left in the kitty from the second bailout loan. By the end of 2014, with Greece's second bailout running out of time and cash, and the government facing another €22 billion of unfunded debt repayments the following year, the troika could have been in no doubt that a third loan was necessary. In other words, the IMF and Dr Schäuble knew full well that a third bailout loan would be required at the same time as the Samaras government was insisting that, were it to be returned in the next general election, there would be no such loan.

The fairy tale of an emergent recovery – or the promise that one was around the corner – was the perfect definition of one of my favourite English phrases: adding insult to injury. But why add insult? Was the injury not enough? There is an answer, and it is not pretty.

On 21 January 2015, four days before election day, I was on the phone to Jamie Galbraith sharing my deepest fears. Initially, the Greek-covery nonsense had been a strategy to win the election, but now Samaras and his ministers were resigned to losing it, they were redeploying the recovery fairy tale to prepare the ground for winning the blame game instead. By pretending that the third bailout loan was *not* necessary, when the truth became apparent that it was they could argue that it had only become so as a result of our government's negotiating stance. Indeed, from the troika's perspective having a Syriza government introduce the third bailout was politically perfect as it would absolve them of the devastation they had been causing since 2010. All pain thereafter, including the rolling-over of unsustainable debt and new austerity measures, could then be blamed on

Syriza's reckless attempt to confront them – and on one person in particular.

Jamie agreed that if our nerve wavered during the negotiations I would be in trouble, but he was certain that Alexis would remain steadfast till the end. Having been caught up in the electrifying moments at Thessaloniki in June 2013, when the three of us had addressed enthusiastic crowds together, Jamie did not share my doubts in this area, and, with only a few days before the polls opened, we needed all the confidence and enthusiasm we could muster.

Moreover, it was my belief that for years Wolfgang Schäuble, Germany's finance minister, had favoured Grexit but had been repeatedly frustrated in this ambition by Chancellor Merkel's opposition. I would not have been surprised if Wolfgang saw a Syriza government determined to clash with the troika as providing him with the ideal opportunity to convince Merkel that it was time to throw the Greeks out of the eurozone. The risk for him was that Syriza might fight to the end, with Mario Draghi and Merkel ultimately relenting and giving Alexis a fair deal. To Wolfgang Schäuble that was *the* nightmare scenario, as it would open the way for the Spaniards, the Portuguese, the Italians and any other European people to re-establish some control over their economic lives.

The buck would stop with me. But what was the alternative? An historical accident had given us a rare chance to do right, speak truth to power, and work to bring a genuine recovery to our wasteland. It would have been unforgivable to turn it down.

Gree-sterity

While our troubles were legion, the troika had its fair share too. The IMF had been uneasy from the very beginning, dragged into the mire of Bailoutistan by a European leadership for whom the French banks and their personal ties to Germany's leadership mattered more than the fund's internal rules and cohesion. Since 2011 the IMF had been making noises that debt relief was essential, had unsuccessfully sought a common front with Athens against Berlin in 2012, had let the cat out of the bag in June 2013 by stating that the Greek banks' 2012 recapitalization had been grossly inadequate and inept, and as late as May 2014 had issued a report that 'debt sustain-ability remains a serious concern' – polite language for saying that it was at catastrophic levels.[9] After years of spectacular analytical and predictive errors, the IMF's analysts – indeed all the troika's officials with some economics training – had finally realized that the very basis of their Greek programme was flawed, making it impossible to implement.

Appendix 2 provides a full explanation of the IMF's flawed analysis, but for a simple demonstration of the self-defeating nature of austerity, take a look at Figure 2.

The horizontal axis depicts the extent of practised (cumulative) austerity over the five years that followed the credit crunch up until just before Syriza's victory.[10] Germany's total austerity amounted to 2 per cent, Italy's 3 per cent, Portugal's 5.4 per cent, the UK's 6.3 per cent, Spain's 6.8 per cent, Ireland's 9 per cent, and Greece's 18 per cent. The vertical axis, meanwhile, shows the cumulative growth in national income during the same period. Very clearly, the greater the austerity the lower

Austerity versus national income growth 2009–14

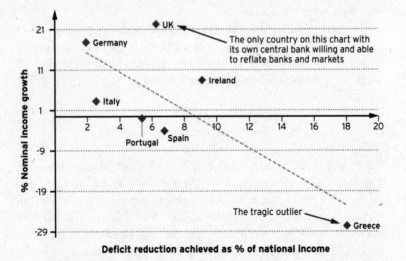

Figure 2: The degree of austerity is measured on the horizontal axis as the reduction in the government's structural deficit as a percentage of national income. The vertical axis is nominal national income growth over the same period.

the growth in national income.[11] Greece's position at the bottom right-hand side of the graph is enough to tell its heartbreaking story.

As Christine Lagarde would later tell me in person, the conundrum the troika faced was that there was now too much political capital at stake to admit their error.[12] The day before the election, a financial journalist told me during a break from our interview that he thought it took a determined disregard for the truth to argue that Greece was recovering. I disagreed: 'It is not so much that they do not want to tell the truth. They are panicking and making it up as they go along, keen to avoid treading on the toes of bankers first, Mrs Merkel later. Now they fear for their jobs if they tell the truth.'

And yet, as we were about to win that election, the troika, the media and the Greek government were debating not how to end this loop of doom but what level of austerity would suit their political agendas best: too little austerity would make a mockery of the troika's inco-herent arithmetic, too much would undermine the Greek-covery narra-tive and anyway be impossible to get through a sceptical parliament.[13]

This is why the people of Greece voted for Syriza, an acronym for the Alliance of the Radical Left. They had not suddenly fallen in love with the radical left, which had hitherto languished on the margins of power. They had no interest in jeopardizing any nascent recovery. They had no ambition to confront Brussels, Berlin, Paris, Frankfurt and Washington. They did not even mind making more sacrifices or tight-ening their belts further if this would work. No, they voted for us because they had had enough of making sacrifices that achieved nothing, enough of measures that sank them deeper in indignity, insolvency and despair while others celebrated their recovery. That is why we received the votes not just of radicals and factory workers, taxi drivers and farmers, but of decent conservatives, struggling business people, right-wing patriots and monks – from everyone in fact concerned, like Lambros the homeless man who had made such an impression on me, for those people who had not yet fallen into the hole waiting to consume them.

First contact

It was while I was running for election that Germany's ambassador to Greece invited me to the ugly fortified embassy of the Federal Republic, a stone's throw from Britain's equally ugly mission and not far from the graceful neoclassical mansions serving as the embassies of Italy, France and Egypt. A tall, lanky man, the German diplomat treated me to a long and exciting afternoon. Pappas warned me that the ambassador had signalled to Alexis his clear dissatisfaction with the news that I might be appointed finance minister. If he had, it did not show. What did show was his eagerness to take my measure.

I found him intelligent and pleasant to talk to, though intense and bristling with ideas on what we should, and should not, do were we to win the election. Over the course of more than two hours, he inducted me into my forthcoming job with a simulated but comprehensive negotiation involving everything on Greece's economic agenda: debt, taxation, banks, market reforms, privatization, labour markets. He clearly knew his stuff and did not hide his government's attitude: in Berlin's eyes, Greece had forfeited its sovereignty long ago, and its government would be treated as petitioners. But he also showed some understanding of Berlin's complicity in the Greek disaster, with hints at a readiness to compromise that revealed his sympathy for the SPD (Germany's Social Democratic Party).

The same day Pappas passed on to me a missive with some advice on what to do after we won office from Jörg Asmussen, a youngish man of some significance in the SPD. Asmussen had started his political career at the finance ministry under Wolfgang Schäuble during the turmoil of 2008, at which time a coalition of Merkel's Christian Democrats and the SPD was in power. He had been the ministry's point man in helping to save the German banks, a role that had given him kudos but also a front seat to witness the process by which Greece was incarcerated in its debtors' prison. His services to the finance ministry were rewarded with a seat on the European Central Bank's executive board, a position of immense authority for a young man with few banking credentials. In 2013, when his ECB stint ended, Asmussen returned to Berlin as a junior labour minister with a key remit: to introduce a minimum wage for the first time in Germany, a major reform that Chancellor Merkel had agreed with her SPD coalition partners, inciting the wrath of her own party.

The moment I heard that Asmussen had written to us, I pricked up my ears. He punched well above his official weight and was the man I had expected the troika to use as a feeler, a first contact between them and us. He was ideally suited to the role. This was a Social Democrat who had worked closely with arch economic conservative

Wolfgang Schäuble as the German banks were collapsing, a man who had been at the helm of the ECB in 2012 when Grexit was on the cards before Mario Draghi put his foot down, signalling to Chancellor Merkel to take it off the table, and one of the very few people to have worked on the ECB's Plan Z – the scheme by which Greece might be detached from the eurozone at minimum cost to the other member states. What I had not anticipated was that Asmussen would not be coming to us alone. Rather, he had written with the express purpose of introducing us to another functionary of even greater significance, Thomas Wieser.

I knew of Wieser's official role within the EU bureaucracy. As president of the Eurogroup Working Group, he led the cabinet of deputies whose job it is to prepare the Eurogroup meetings, the forum at which their respective finance ministers make all their key decisions. In theory then Thomas Wieser was the deputy of Jeroen Dijsselbloem, Dutch finance minister and president of the Eurogroup. What I did not know then but came to understand later was that in reality he was the most powerful man in Brussels, far more so than Jean-Claude Juncker, president of the European Commission, or Pierre Moscovici, commissioner for economic and finance affairs (the commission's finance minister), or even, on occasion, Dijsselbloem himself. At such times he seemed to run the whole show.

In his email Asmussen adopted the posture of a left-leaning potential ally of our new government who wanted to see us succeed. To that end, he asked us to trust and work with Wieser, an Austrian Social Democrat, describing him as a 'friend', 'reliable', 'trustworthy' and 'a key one in the Brussels machinery'. In addition, Asmussen suggested Wieser would help us carve out the time we needed in which to conduct our negotiations. According to Asmussen, Wieser was proposing a 'programme extension' as a 'good way forward, to have a kind of protection for Greece while deeper renegotiations are undertaken. It might be worthwhile that your economic team gets in contact with him quickly after the elections.' Asmussen ended with 'if I can be of any help, just let me know'.

It sounded hopeful. The previous Athens government had negotiated an extension with the troika that would end a month after our election, more a guillotine to cut our heads off than a platform on which to build a new agreement, so yes, we wanted a further extension.

And if Wieser and Asmussen wanted to help construct one, that would be splendid. But did they?

Attached to Asmussen's email was an unsigned 'non-paper' – jargon for an unofficial document circulated for negotiation purposes which is wholly unbinding – written by Wieser that began by stating the completely obvious, namely that our government 'will face a very tight liquidity situation'.[14] This was followed by a dry announcement that we should not expect to receive any of the money the ECB owed us (around €1.9 billion profit on those SMP bonds of ours that it held and had agreed to return to us), nor any of the loans agreed under the previous government that Greece needed in order to (pretend to) repay its debts.[15] But, Wieser made clear, the troika still expected us to honour Greece's debt obligations to them.[16] The asphyxiation of the Greek government that would be caused by this would lead to 'liquidity concerns' and, inevitably, to 'market tension'. In short, we shall squeeze you so much and so publicly that investors will pull out of Greece, depositors will accelerate their bank run, and your government will suffocate. This was the stick.

After the stick came Wieser's carrot: the troika might give us an extension to the existing second bailout loan agreement, granting us a reprieve beyond the guillotine deadline of 28 February 2015, and might increase the maximum value, set by the ECB, of short-term Treasury bills (T-bills) we were allowed to issue for the purpose of quick cash loans – essentially our credit card limit – so that we could withdraw some extra cash with which to pay the IMF in March, but this would be conditional on our taking a 'cooperative approach' to the troika.[17]

The message could not have been clearer: we were to be fiscally waterboarded until we agreed to participate in the sick ritual of extending and pretending that we had been elected to put an end to.[18] After reading the email I briefed Alexis and Pappas on the situation: as we had expected, they were activating a plan to throttle us. I took the opportunity to reiterate our covenant: we should look to secure the extension beyond 28 February that Wieser was offering in order to give the negotiations a chance, but only if we remained committed among ourselves to defaulting if they refused to negotiate in good faith a different type of agreement. Both reconfirmed their commitment.

I then sat down to pen our response to Wieser. Exuding moderation and a willingness to work with him, I made two crucial points.

The first concerned the profit owed to us on our SMP bonds, which Wieser had said we should not expect back from the troika. 'Not handing back Greece's own money unconditionally,' I wrote, 'is difficult to justify even if previous Greek governments have consented to some such legalism. It is our express view that these funds should be released immediately by the ECB. This way, funding is secured, using Greece's own rightful assets, through the end of March.'

My second point addressed Wieser's thinly veiled threat of 'market tension', which echoed Stournaras's incendiary statement of 15 December.[19]

> The expectation of a potential impasse does yield uncertainty which, in turn, may cause liquidity problems. But what causes this expectation of impasse in the first place? It is the insistence of EU and ECB officials that, within days of being elected, the new Greek government must sign on the dotted line of an agreement that it campaigned in favour of renegotiating.
>
> Democratic Europe must give Greece fiscal space to allow its new government to table proposals that will constitute the foundation of a viable agreement. Denying the new Greek government this fiscal space causes the liquidity problems. To then portray these liquidity problems as exogenous constraints is to be in denial of the ECB's and the EU's responsibility for having caused them.

After I'd sent the email, just before Danae and I left to attend a pre-election meeting, she asked me what I had been working on.

'A beautiful new friendship,' I replied.

Democracy at gunpoint

Two nights before the polls opened on 25 January 2015 my Syriza friends were agonizing only over the extent of our impending victory and whether it would suffice to secure an outright majority in parliament. But my mind was elsewhere.

Three days earlier Glenn had emailed confirmation that the noose was tightening. Since 15 December, when Stournaras accelerated the bank run that Prime Minister Samaras had begun, depositors had withdrawn €9.3 billion from Greek banks, and the rate of withdrawals had hit €1 billion daily. By the time of the election, €11 billion would have found its way abroad or under mattresses.[20] To be able to pay out so much money, the banks had had to increase their dependence on the ECB to the tune of more than €60 billion. The threat of Mario Draghi to close down the banks was providing precisely the conditions he needed to justify doing so.[21]

In the run-up to polling day the only future government colleague with whom I managed to share my fears was Spyros Sagias. Danae and I met him in his apartment in the Athenian coastal suburb where I had grown up. Surprised by the security men stationed under his apartment block, we took the lift to his airy penthouse decorated with a few well-chosen pieces of contemporary Greek art overlooking the marina. Sagias was a pudgy middle-aged man with a reassuringly deep voice who excused himself for being under the weather. He was nursing a heart condition, which did not seem to dull his intelligence or prevent him from demonstrating a perceptive eye.

Sagias was not a politician but, as he introduced himself half-jokingly, a systemic lawyer. ('Systemic' is post-2008 jargon for banks that are deemed too big to fail.) There was hardly a large-scale business deal involving private interests and the public sector that Sagias and his successful practice had not been involved in: privatizations, large-scale construction projects, mergers, all were within his ambit. Until recently he had even provided legal counsel to Cosco, the Chinese conglomerate that had acquired part of the port of Piraeus and was eager to take over the whole of it, a privatization that Syriza vehemently opposed. When Pappas informed me that Sagias was destined to become our cabinet secretary, I was surprised but also pleased: at least we would have a legal eagle on the team, a counsellor who knew how to author legislation and moreover where all the skeletons of the *ancien régime* were buried.

Sagias went straight to the subject that was foremost on my mind, asking how exactly the ECB would try to asphyxiate us. First, I explained, Draghi would cut off the direct flow of liquidity from the ECB to our banks, referring them to Stournaras's Central Bank of Greece for more expensive short-term loans instead (the so-called emergency liquidity assistance or ELA mechanism, funded indirectly by the ECB). Then, the second stage, the ECB Governing Council would prohibit Stournaras from providing any further ELA to the banks, at which point tellers would run out of cash, depositors would riot and the banks would close down. Already by 21 January 2015, I told Sagias, two of Greece's four systemic banks had applied to Stournaras's ELA for liquidity. 'The scene is set,' I concluded. 'They are just waiting for us to come on stage.'[22]

I then outlined our key deterrence strategy and the essence of the covenant with Alexis, Pappas and Dragasakis that was the basis of my accepting the finance ministry. He agreed with the plan.

'So, what brings you to this government?' I asked. 'Your background doesn't immediately suggest a reason.'

'I am only doing it because I believe in Alexis,' he replied. As a young man he had inclined to the Left, he explained. Even after he shifted to the very heart of the establishment, oiling the cogs of the system, deep inside he always maintained a romantic link with the Left. 'So when I met Alexis, it struck me that I wanted to put my experience at his disposal. I am not here for Syriza. I am here to protect Alexis. He will need a great deal of protection. And so will you. Make no mistake, Yanis: they will all try to undermine you, from the worst of the bankers to Dragasakis to everyone in Syriza. It's going to be nasty.' It turned out I was not the only one ridden with angst as we were about to take over the reins of government.

I decided I liked Sagias. He knew that he was tainted by decades of consorting with the oligarchy and did not care to hide it, but I was more inclined to trust people who had known and worked for the establishment than young zealots, who are prone to becoming its born-again servants. His honesty, the way he personalized his reasons for coming on board, his warnings about Dragasakis and the Syriza evangelists, along with the art on his apartment walls, made me feel at ease with him.

Nevertheless, as we were leaving he confessed that he was having second thoughts. 'I am still not 100 per cent sure I shall accept the position,' he told me.

'You must!' I urged him. 'This is a 28 October moment,' I said, referring to the day the Greek government rejected Mussolini's ultimatum to surrender in 1940. 'We cannot duck this.'

'I will think about it,' he said in such a way that led me to believe he would accept.

Back at our apartment, an email arrived from Jamie asking, 'What's the exact agenda, so far as you know?'

'Not to be throttled at birth by the troika and local bankers . . .' I replied.

Doing my sums with Glenn's help, it turned out that for 2015 alone the Greek state needed €42.4 billion just to roll over its debts, the equivalent of 24 per cent of national income. Even if the troika were to disburse all the money specified by the second bailout loan agreement, we would still be €12 billion short. For a country with no capacity to borrow from private investors, empty coffers and a devastated population, meeting these debt repayments meant only one thing: the plunder of what was left in the reserves of pensions funds, municipalities, hospitals and public utilities, while going to the troika cap in hand to borrow huge amounts more, pledging to squeeze our pensioners, municipalities, hospitals and public utilities yet further, all in order to give the money back to the troika. Only a lobotomy could have convinced me that doing this was in our people's interest.

On polling day people would walk up to me in the street, pat me on the back and make me promise I would not go back on my word. We support you, but don't you dare do a U-turn, because if you do we shall round on you, was the unanimous message.

Partners beyond the pale

While Alexis was drawing up plans for the composition of his cabinet, I was trying to whittle down the number of our potential enemies. Glenn suggested I should bring some private financiers on side. There were two reasons for doing this: very little of Greece's debt was owed to them as they had been repaid in full from the bailout loans (in fact, only 15 per cent of the total debt was now owed to private bodies), and they understood arithmetic; they could see that my basic argument was right. Why not have such rich, powerful and well-connected people with us, rather than antagonize them? Glenn's suggestion was that I make overtures in the form of a statement: 'We do not foresee a need to seek any further restructuring of Greek Government-related debt in the hands of private-sector investors.' In the event, I went further, stating not only that we foresaw no need but were 'opposed to the notion' of it.

Meanwhile, in the little thinking time I had to spare, I joined the discussions about the government's composition. If we did not win a working majority, a coalition was on the cards. But who would be our partners? Excluding the parties that had governed until this point and brought us the bailouts, the communist party, which was simply not interested, and of course the Nazis of the Golden Dawn, there were two possibilities.

One was the River (To Potami), a socially liberal centrist party led by a journalist with whom Danae and I had been friendly and for whose news site I had written hundreds of articles. On a personal level, this was the party that I would have preferred to get into bed with. Its key figures were people whom I knew and got on well with. But there was a major snag: they had adopted a strongly pro-troika position.

Negotiate with the troika as toughly as you want but under no circumstances contemplate a rupture, they would tell me. There is no point in entering a negotiating room if you are not prepared to contemplate walking out, I would retort. No, a coalition with the River would have been strategic suicide and actually pointless. The troika would know that the moment they pressed the button to close down the banks the River would pull the plug on us, censuring me in parliament for having caused a rupture with the creditors.

In any case, Syriza's leadership, and Alexis in particular, had already made their minds up. But while I understood their choice, the very idea of it was nauseating. Alexis had struck a deal with Panos Kammenos, leader of the Independent Greeks. Kammenos, the party's founder, had been a junior minister in previous New Democracy governments, but in 2011, to his credit, he voted against the techno-cratic coalition headed by the former vice president of the ECB, whose mission was to pass the second bailout through parliament. Expelled by New Democracy for doing so, he had set up the Independent Greeks with several other New Democracy defectors. The party they created could only have been born in the sad madness of Bailoutistan. In its fierce opposition to the bailouts, it was located to the left of the PASOK socialists, the River and the New Democracy conservatives, but on social issues and foreign relations it took extreme right-wing positions, exuding ultra-nationalism, thinly veiled racism, intense sexism and homophobia.

As if that were not enough, Kammenos was prone to making allegations about politicians he disliked that had no basis in fact – reminiscent of those anti-Semitic conspiracy theories that bundle together small truths to create huge lies – and I doubt I had endeared myself to him when, in response to allegations he had made about George Papandreou and his family, I provided a deposition in their successful suit against him for defamation.[23] The idea of serving in the same cabinet as Kammenos did not fill me with pleasure.

Alexis explained his decision to enter into a coalition with Kammenos simply and concisely. We had a choice, he told me. One option was to form quickly and painlessly a coalition government with the Independent Greeks, with Kammenos appointed minister of defence on condition that he did not interfere with any decisions pertaining to the negotiations or to social issues, where the Syriza progressive agenda would prevail. The second option was to enter into prolonged negotiations with the River in order to form a government that the troika could topple at any time. 'It's a no-brainer,' he concluded.

As the following months revealed, Alexis was right. Kammenos and his colleagues kept their word and were fully supportive of our negotiating stance. Indeed, the first time we met Kammenos showed no animosity towards me. Quite the opposite, in fact. He hugged me and addressed me respectfully, promising his complete support for my strategy. Nonetheless, the sound pragmatic reasons for this partnership did not dampen my abhorrence for our partners' blend of nationalism, xenophobia and commitment to a pre-modern link between church, army and state. Of all the difficult questions foreign journalists put to me in the ensuing weeks, the most painful were the ones about that uneasy alliance.

'If you can dream – and not make dreams your master'[24]

Around 8 p.m. on 25 January 2015 we knew we had won handsomely. A few hours later we discovered that we were a mere two seats short of an absolute majority.[25] The streets were thronged with celebrating crowds.

Before joining them, I sat down to write two blog posts, one message of thanks (in Greek) to my voters and one message of hope (in English) to the wider world. In the first I wrote of my recent meeting with

Lambros. 'As I enter the gates of the Ministry of Finance,' I wrote, 'I shall be thinking of his words. Not our interest rate spreads, not the Treasury bill yields, not the *Memorandum of Understanding* with the troika. Only his words will be on my mind.' For non-Greek speakers puzzled by our victory, I borrowed from Dylan Thomas to post the following.

> Today, the people of Greece gave a vote of confidence to hope. They used the ballot box, in this splendid celebration of democracy, to put an end to a self-reinforcing crisis that produces indignity in Greece and feeds Europe's darkest forces.
>
> The people of Greece today sent a message of solidarity to the north, to the south, to the east and to the west of our continent. The simple message is that the time for crisis-denial, retribution and finger-pointing is over. That the time for the reinvigoration of the ideals of freedom, rationality, democratic process and justice has come to the continent that invented them.
>
> Greek democracy today chose to stop going gently into the night. Greek democracy resolved to rage against the dying of the light.
>
> Fresh from receiving our democratic mandate, we call upon the people of Europe and, indeed, the world over, to join us in a realm of shared, sustainable prosperity.

I am often asked how I dealt with the overwhelming stress of the days and months that followed. My answer is that on 9 January, the day I announced my candidature for a Greater Athens parliamentary seat, I had written a signed but undated letter of resignation. On my blog I wrote,

> It was never my intention to enter the electoral game. Ever since the crisis began, I entertained hopes of maintaining an open dialogue with reasonable politicians from different political parties. Alas, the bailouts made such an open dialogue impossible . . . My greatest fear, now that I have tossed my hat in the ring, is that I may turn into a politician. As an antidote to that virus I intend to write my

resignation letter and keep it in my inside pocket, ready to submit it the moment I sense signs of losing the commitment to speak truth to power.

On 25 January, before Danae and I left our apartment to join the celebrating crowds and make our way to Syriza HQ, I made sure that I had that letter in my inside pocket. From that Sunday night onwards I carried it with me everywhere I went, from meetings at Maximos or the finance ministry to the Eurogroup and Wolfgang Schäuble's office. Its presence gave me solace and a sense of freedom. But like all freedoms, it came at a price: the more astute of my adversaries recognized this freedom in me and detested me for it.

At 6 a.m. on Monday, with the count completed, I received a text message from my friend Wassily: 'Unbelievable! You got 142,000 votes.' But satisfaction at having won my seat with a comfortable majority quickly gave way to apprehension when I checked the full results: no Syriza candidate, indeed no candidate of any party, had received more votes in the whole of Greece. It was a success I knew I would eventually be punished for.

That morning Alexis was sworn in at the outgoing president's residence before making his way to Maximos, where the departing prime minister would normally have been waiting for the handover ceremony. But as Antonis Samaras was not there, Alexis just walked in and got down to work; the cabinet had not yet been finalized, and the government was due to be sworn in the very next day.

Having resigned myself days before to the alliance with Kammenos and his Independent Greeks, my only intervention on cabinet appointments was insisting that the other two ministries covering key economic areas should be given to Euclid and Stathakis. While the main burden of negotiations in the Eurogroup would fall upon me, I was keen to have Euclid in the cabinet and in a ministry linked to economic policy so the two of us could back each other up in Berlin, Paris, Brussels and Frankfurt.

Towards that evening, Sagias, who in the end accepted the position of secretary to the cabinet, called to discuss procedural matters. During our conversation he dropped a bombshell: Alexis had left Euclid out of the cabinet.

'Why on earth . . . ?' I asked.

To preserve Syriza's inner equilibrium, he explained, Alexis had appointed Panayiotis Lafazanis to the ministry instead. This was terrible. Like Dragasakis, Lafazanis had been an activist in the Communist Party of Greece for many years, but while Dragasakis had since shifted to the Right, Lafazanis remained wedded to a Soviet mindset and led the Left Platform, which controlled one-third of Syriza's central committee. Crucially, Lafazanis and his supporters believed that Grexit should be party policy. Over and over again he had stated his view that if we did not threaten to leave the eurozone we would never achieve a decent deal. With Lafazanis in one of the key ministries, and with Euclid – who agreed with our covenant – outside the cabinet, my negotiation strategy was in jeopardy.

As soon as Sagias had put down the phone, I called Alexis to say that Lafazanis's appointment was a mistake and that I could not accept Euclid's exclusion from the cabinet. Alexis replied that he had offered Euclid a position as my deputy in charge of the tax office, but that he had turned it down angrily on the basis that he did not have the relevant expertise.

'He spoke badly to me, Yanis. Sod him! Let him languish for a while in the house as Syriza's parliamentary spokesperson.'

'First, Euclid is right,' I told Alexis. 'Taxation policy is not his strong point. But in any case the reason for giving him the ministry now being run by Lafazanis was so that he could be at my side during the negotiations.' If Euclid had responsibility for the tax office, he would be stuck in Athens while I travelled alone. 'The two of us together, both ministers, will make a powerful team. This is a grave loss, Alexi,' I said.

'It is too late now,' Alexis replied. 'I need Lafazanis inside the cabinet and in an economic ministry to prevent him from pissing in from the outside. If I strip him of it now, on the night before our swearing-in, he will turn even more against me than he already is. The Left Platform will be up in arms.'

He had a point. I had to think of another way to get Euclid into cabinet.

'There is an alternative,' I said. Within the Ministry of Foreign Affairs there was the post of general secretary of foreign economic relations. I suggested that we upgrade the post to alternate minister of foreign affairs responsible for foreign economic relations. Euclid could then come with me everywhere as a full minister with a portfolio closely related to the negotiations with Germany, the EU and the IMF. 'What do you say?' I asked.

'Sounds OK. But will Euclid accept? When we spoke a few hours ago he swore at me and I responded in kind.'

'Do I have your word that you will create such a position and appoint him to it if I secure his agreement?' He gave me his word. 'Leave it to me, Alexi.'

I immediately called Euclid. His voice conveyed sadness and anger. When I explained my solution he perked up but said, 'But Yani, Alexis's behaviour was atrocious. The way he took back his commitment, and for what? To put Lafazanis, a man who wants to blow up the negotiations before they start at the head of a critical economic ministry? I want nothing to do with him.'

I calmed him down somewhat by reminding him of the historic moment we were facing and with a kind word for Alexis, who after all had a difficult balancing act to perform.

'I'm livid with him too,' I continued, 'but it's time to find a solution.' I explained that the new role being offered was perfect for a two-man ministerial caucus to run the negotiations. 'Please accept it,' I begged him.

'But I can't trust Alexis to appoint me to the position,' he retorted.

'Well then, trust me. Do you?'

'I do,' he said.

Minutes later I called Sagias, and Euclid's name was added to the cabinet to be sworn in the following morning.

The swearing-in ceremony took place at the presidential residence. Ministers, deputy ministers and junior ministers filed past the president and then divided into two groups, one large one small. The reason for such an early split in our ranks? We were the first Greek government in which most ministers declined to swear an oath on the Bible and opted instead for a secular affirmation of allegiance to the constitution. But since the Independent Greeks were determined to swear on the holy book, we took our oaths in two separate groups.

The ceremony lasted no more than an hour, the new ministers keen to go to their ministries for the handover ceremonies, but as my predecessor had requested a few more hours to clear his desk, I was in no hurry. When the president had retired to his quarters, Alexis suggested I drop into Maximos, located next to the presidential residence, for a chat before I made my way over to the Ministry of Finance building on Syntagma Square. To give Alexis time to get settled, I immersed myself in discussions with a couple of other ministers whose handovers had also been delayed and then walked across to the prime minister's official residence. As I went in, the police stationed outside saluted as if I were General Patton. It was something I never, ever got used to.

Once inside, I took a moment to look around. For a building synonymous in Greece with power, it was smaller than I had imagined but tasteful in an Italianesque way. Making my way to the inner sanctum I walked past the prime minister's secretaries' office, where it was amusing to find our party workers, more used to the dingy surroundings of Syriza's HQ and now looking decidedly out of place amid the splendour of Maximos.

'You'll get used to it, Eleni,' I said to one of them.

'Yes, Minister,' she replied mockingly.

Upon entering Alexis's new office, I looked at him and, taking my cue from Eleni, bowed my head with a mock-humble 'Prime Minister . . .' We both burst out laughing. He rose from his chair and we embraced. 'What the hell have we done?' I asked, still laughing. 'What next?' I added more as a lament than a question.

He did not reply but grinned and shook his head. 'We asked for it.'

My wandering eyes alighted on a huge and hideous painting of the Greek flag hanging over the prime minister's desk. It succeeded in making a flag that I am actually very fond of look ugly and domineering, suggesting the very opposite of the nuanced patriotism it is meant to symbolize.

'Either that goes or I go,' I told Alexis.

'Don't worry. It goes. It's awful,' he replied.

When our eyes met again, Alexis had acquired a serious look, which he followed up with serious words: 'Listen! Don't get comfortable in here. Don't learn to love the trappings of office. These offices, these chairs, are not for us. Our place is out there, on the streets, in the squares, with the people. We got in to get a job done on their behalf. Never forget that this is why we are here. For no other reason. And be ready. If the bastards find a way to stop us from delivering what we promised, you and I must be ready to hand back the keys and get out on the streets again, to plan the next demonstration.'

The earth could have stopped turning and I would not have noticed. It was a moment to savour. I felt ashamed at the qualms I had had about Alexis. Fear and anxiety evaporated. I did not care if the light died, as it inevitably would. Here we were, together, raging against its dying.

It was time to get down to work.

PART TWO
Invincible spring

6

It begins . . .

The sentry outside Maximos was aghast. 'Are you going out alone, Minister?' he asked.

I nodded as the electric gate opened, mindful of the waiting photographers camped outside but determined to arrive at the Ministry of Finance on foot and in solitude. They were just as taken aback as the sentry and scrambled to follow me, laden with equipment, falling over their cables and each other. By the time I had turned left onto Queen Sophia Avenue at the corner of the National Gardens, which separate Maximos from Parliament House and Syntagma Square, they had given up.

Walking past the side entrance to Parliament House I was reminded of the exchange I had witnessed between the aggressive parliamentarian and the demonstrator – his 'Who are you to judge what I should or shouldn't vote for?' and her magnificent 'Who do I have to be?' Every step towards Syntagma Square brought back a face, a slogan, a memory from those long nights in 2011 when Athens had come alive in opposition to our collective indignity. Crossing Amalia Avenue, right in front of parliament, onto Syntagma Square itself was to cross onto sacred ground.

The sun had set and a cool January breeze was rattling the remaining leaves on the trees, sending pedestrians hurrying on their way. The street lights had not yet come on, and in the dusk it took a few moments to locate the tree, enshrined with flowers and handwritten messages, next to which Dimitris Christoulas, the retired pharmacist, had shot himself. With almost no one around, I took a moment to build a mental bridge between that tree and the brightly lit offices of the Ministry of Finance that I could see opposite. A moment later I had crossed Philhellenes Street to enter the ministry that would be my crucible for the next 162 days. As I entered the building, a cheer rose from the fifty or so women camped outside: some of the ministry's legendary cleaners, who had been dismissed overnight and without compensation two years before by the previous government. 'Don't betray us!' they shouted.

'I won't,' I replied firmly as I headed for the lift.

The lift door opened onto the sixth floor, and a secretary led me to the ministerial suite where my predecessor awaited. He was alone and greeted me graciously. His desk was strikingly bare. None of the gadgets that fill a modern office was in sight, not even a computer. Its only visible weapon against the sea of troubles that besieged it was an icon of the Madonna on the shelf behind the minister's desk. The large high-backed desk chair, which was no doubt intended to project authority, looked as uncomfortable as it was ugly. The array of old-fashioned phones on a side desk were straight out of a 1970s movie, and the books on the shelf were clearly gifts that no previous minister had cared enough to read or take away. The oil paintings on the wall were on loan from the National Gallery. It would have taken only a word to have them replaced, but I felt no urge to get comfortable in that office.

The rest of the furniture had an air of decadence, especially the fading red velvet couch – perfect, I thought, for the finance ministry of a bankrupt state. The only exception was a large rectangular wooden meeting table, which I immediately decided would become my workstation, a long way from the ministerial desk, which I made a point of never using. The table made me feel as at home as it was possible or desirable to feel in that spacious but sad office with such a sorry recent past. The office had one outstanding redeeming feature: a wide, tall window offering a magnificent view of Syntagma Square and Parliament House beyond. One look through it is enough to stiffen the resolve of anyone who has ever harboured an ounce of pride in modern Greece's long struggle for democracy.

My predecessor was gentle, pleasant and visibly relieved that his ordeal was over. He had two dossiers for me, one medium-sized blue one and a bulging red file. The blue dossier contained ministerial decrees that he had not had the opportunity to sign and which he encouraged me to consider. The red dossier was labelled 'FACTA' and pertained to a deal that the United States was ultra-keen to foist onto every country, which would allow the US Treasury to keep tabs on American citizens' foreign financial transactions.[1] Intriguingly, he had no documents to hand over regarding Greece's loan agreement with the EU and the IMF, though he offered to brief me on our repayment schedule, which of course I could already recite, chapter and verse. Days later, when I asked for a copy of the original second bailout loan agreement, I received the astounding reply: 'Minister, your predecessor seems to have taken the only copy with him, along with his private archive.' Curious as this may sound, it was not the most stupefying discovery of those early days.

While I would have enjoyed the chance to discuss with him his failed last-ditch attempt to conclude the second bailout programme, which was meant to have ended three weeks before, the discussion would have been of academic interest only – concluding the bailout was impossible for the simple reason that it had been designed at the outset to fail.[2] Meanwhile, most of the country's news journalists, a forest of cameras, foreign correspondents and various curious officials had assembled in the ministry's press room, awaiting the traditional press conference held jointly by the outgoing and incoming ministers, and were becoming increasingly restless. We had to move on.

Before we did, my predecessor asked me to give some thought to keeping three of his non-permanent staff, especially a single mother who would have faced intolerable hardship were I to let her go. Naturally, I agreed. At the same time I suddenly realized that the three secretaries in the minister's office whom I had just met were not civil servants but his private employees. As such, they would be leaving too. After the press conference I would return to an empty sixth floor to engage in battle with the world's most powerful creditors without secretaries, staff or indeed a computer. Thankfully, I had my trusty laptop in my ruck-sack. But who would furnish me with the Wi-Fi password?

Parsimony versus austerity

After a dignified speech by the outgoing minister, it was my chance to set the scene. 'The state must have continuity,' I said after thanking my predecessor for his efforts. 'But there will be no continuity of the motivated error that began to devastate our society in 2010 and which has been repeated continuously ever since: treating our state's insolvency as a shortage of liquidity.'

Once I had outlined my analysis of how Greece's impossible debt and unacknowledged bankruptcy had caused the depression, I turned to a distinction of great importance, one that left-wingers and Keynesians often fail to highlight: that between parsimony and austerity. 'We are in favour of parsimony,' I said, surprising many in the audience.

> Greeks did splendidly when we lived austere lives, when we spent less than we earned, when we channelled our savings to the education of our children, when we were proud that we were not in debt . . . But an austere life is one thing and Ponzi austerity is quite another. Over the past years we have had a phoney austerity that cuts the low incomes of the weak while adding mountains of new debt to existing mountain ranges of unpayable debt. We shall end this practice, beginning at home, within this ministry, where parsimony will edge austerity out.

With huge reductions in private expenditure and massive cuts in public spending, families and companies were unable make ends meet. In other words, the government's attempt to create an unfeasible public surplus had made it impossible for people to live within their means. Put simply, public austerity had to end because it was killing private parsimony. We would begin with the Ministry of Finance's own accounts. To demonstrate the principle, I announced a symbolic move: the immediate sale of the two BMW 7 series armour-plated limousines that a previous minister had ordered for himself, costing a scandalous €750,000, I was informed. My motorcycle would do nicely, especially in the infuriating Athens traffic. I also announced that I and my two deputy ministers would desist from hiring the hordes of expensive advisers which had invaded the ministry with each previous administration, not to mention the multinational consultancy companies that charged tens of millions to deliver catastrophic advice. Parsimony would thus return to the Ministry of Finance under a new administration whose main aim was to put an end to austerity.

When a few days later I travelled to Brussels and Berlin to begin talks with officials, one of the first things they took issue with was another of the announcements I had made in that first press conference: the rehiring of the three hundred cleaners who had been sacked by the previous government, some of whom had cheered me as I entered the ministry. 'Backtracking on reforms' was the expression used to criticize me. Some even suggested that rehiring the cleaners was a *casus belli*. The fact that I had saved many times their wages through genuine parsimony did not matter to them, nor did the perverse morality of casually paying tens of millions of euros for a few days' worth of calamitous advice while dismissing the people who cleaned up after the consultants for no more than €400 a month. (The fact that standards of hygiene had declined was apparently also considered immaterial.) If the country's bankruptcy was to be blamed on its victims, then the ministry's cleaners were ideal scapegoats.

But the cleaners' gender and class, their demonstrable powerlessness, their dependence on the state for a minimally safe job, their defiance and determination to camp outside the Ministry of Finance for months on end were to my mind symbolic of something else. They reminded me of the British women who had set up a peace camp in 1981 at Greenham Common to protest against the deployment of new medium-range US nuclear missiles. Those women drew upon themselves the ire, eventually the hatred, of an establishment that recognized in them a challenge to its patriarchal authority. So it was with the ministry's cleaning women: not only did they symbolize the groundswell of public feeling against austerity, they threatened to feminize the struggle, just as women partisans had against the Nazi occupation of the 1940s.

At any rate, their dismissal, literal and metaphorical, exemplified the policy of victimizing the depression's victims in order to teach the Greek citizenry that it was to blame for the nation's implosion. By sacking them, the previous government was demonstrating the cleaners' guilt. By rehiring them I was committing a sin worse even than championing parsimony at the expense of austerity.

Moderation versus subservience

As I saw it, my task as the finance minister of a bankrupt country was not to offer false hope through fake optimism, but rather to promote moderate policies and realistic expectations. So I was pleased to be able to conclude that first press conference with a genuinely good piece of news with regard to our impending negotiations.

'TV evangelists of subservience have been calling upon us for weeks now to issue a declaration of allegiance to the troika and its programme, for otherwise Europe will not even talk to us,' I said. 'Anyone calling for this must have a poor opinion of Europe.' I then went on to describe a telephone conversation I had had on election day with Jeroen Dijsselbloem, president of the Eurogroup and finance minister of the Netherlands.

Jeroen had called to congratulate me on our victory and lost no time before asking the obvious question: what were our intentions regarding the ongoing Greek programme? I replied as accommodatingly as possible while making the point that had to be made: our new government, I said, recognized that it had inherited certain commitments to the Eurogroup while hoping and trusting that its partners would also recognize that we had been elected to renegotiate key elements of our loan agreement and its associated programme. Thus it was incumbent upon us all to find common ground – a bridge I called it – between the existing programme and the new government's priorities and views. Jeroen agreed immediately with a plain, 'This is very good,' proposing to pay me a visit on the following Friday, 30 January 2015. Out of courtesy I offered to visit him in Brussels instead if that suited him better, but he insisted that he and his entourage should honour their new Greek colleagues with a visit.

Encouraged by Jeroen's acceptance of our common task – to throw a solid bridge over the chasm between their programme and our mandate – and with an eye to the unfolding bank run that the previous regime and the Bank of Greece had fuelled weeks before, I emphasized my determination to establish common ground. As for the narrative of confrontation that the media were perpetuating, I went to some lengths to dispel it at the press conference:

> Journalists like to report on conflict. They see *High Noon* shootouts everywhere. I was listening to the BBC portray my impending meeting with Jeroen Dijsselbloem as a shootout, as a game of chicken to see who will blink first. I understand the appeal of such depictions to ratings-hungry journalism. But Jeroen and I agreed that we shall deconstruct the foundation upon which predictions of belligerent clashes are based. There will be no threats. It is not a matter

of who will yield first. The euro crisis only has victims. The only winners are the bigots, the racists, those who invest in fear and division and in the serpent's egg, as Ingmar Bergman might have said.[3] With Jeroen Dijsselbloem on Friday we shall build on a relationship that annuls Europe's deconstruction.

I meant every single word.

After the press conference I returned to the offices on the sixth floor to find them eerily empty. My predecessor had left, along with his staff, leaving behind two young women almost trembling in expectation of being instantly dismissed by their new 'radical Left' boss. I reassured them that the last thing I had time for was a purge of the previous regime's staff, closed the door behind me and pulled up a chair at the large table. I took my laptop out of my rucksack, plugged it into the mains and, while waiting for it to boot up, looked out of the window that framed Parliament House, my mind racing to compile a list of the day's most pressing priorities.

When I looked back to my laptop screen, I remembered that I did not have the Wi-Fi password. I got up, opened the door to the secretaries' office and called out, 'Anyone here?'

Soon one of the two visibly relieved and somewhat embarrassed secretaries appeared from some distant room. Half an hour later we located someone who knew someone else who knew the password. And thus the new minister acquired a very, very slow connection to the Internet – not the most auspicious beginning to a long, lonely campaign against the most highly weaponized and best prepared creditors in the history of capitalism.

American friends

The first phone call I received that evening from overseas came from an unrecognized number in the United States. It was Danae, who had arrived in Austin and was calling to see how I was coping. As soon as we hung up, the phone rang again. Once again the unknown number on the screen began with the US dialling code. I picked up to hear a distant, gentle male voice with what sounded like a New England accent.

'You do not know me, Mr Varoufakis, but I felt the urge to call you to congratulate you on your election and to lend all the support I can give. My name is Bernie Sanders, and I am a senator from Vermont. Mutual friends have given me your number and I hope you do not mind the intrusion.'

Mind the intrusion? We needed as much support as we could muster. After thanking him, I explained that of course I knew who he was – Jamie Galbraith had told me all about Vermont politics.[4] Bernie went on to say that he was about to write to Christine Lagarde to state in no uncertain terms that he would be watching the IMF's behaviour towards Greece. Was there anything in particular that I would like him to mention?

Yes, there was. First, I asked that he state clearly that the Greek programme that the IMF had been policing since 2010 had failed dismally as a result of the ridiculous levels of austerity the IMF had helped impose. Second, I asked that he point out that the resulting great depression had bred the monsters of the Nazi Golden Dawn and that if our democratic pro-European government were to be squashed by its creditors, it was highly likely that democracy itself would be strangled in its birthplace, just as it had been during the Second World War. Bernie promised he would make both these points, and added that he would make another, one that the International Monetary Fund would take seriously: if the IMF continued its abysmal behaviour towards Greece, he would press in the US Senate to reduce its funding.

Since 2012 Jamie Galbraith and I had worked hard to win American progressives over to the cause of dismantling Bailoutistan. When I called Alexis to relate Bernie's offer of help, Alexis provided further evidence that those efforts had not been wasted. President Obama had called him with the customary congratulations but also with a suggestion that a meeting be organized soon between Jack Lew, the US Treasury Secretary, and myself. I asked Alexis to convey my readiness to meet Lew at his earliest convenience. Soon after, Obama made an extraordinarily helpful public statement: 'You cannot keep on squeezing countries that are in the midst of depression,' he told CNN's Fareed Zakaria, adding, 'At some point there has to be a growth strategy in order for them to pay off their debts to eliminate some of their deficits.'

An hour or so later, my mobile phone rang again with yet another US number. It was Jeff Sachs, a Columbia University economics professor and head of the Earth Institute. He was calling to offer his services in our 'worthy struggle', as he put it, to convince the creditors to proceed with large-scale meaningful debt relief and a sustainable fiscal policy. Jeff was one of those American economists who aged well, turning increasingly progressive with experience. Always close to the IMF in spirit but also in practice, he had participated in IMF 'rescue' programmes in the 1990s, most of which had gone badly wrong (for example Yeltsin's Russia) with some exceptions like Poland. Like the economist Joe Stiglitz, who became a staunch critic of the Washington Consensus after witnessing the horrors perpetrated by the IMF and its programmes during the 1998 South East Asian crisis, Jeff had been shaped by the experience of seeing from the inside the bad behaviour of international creditors and the IMF towards bankrupted states such as Argentina. Both men had been transformed as economists and public intellectuals by these hands-on experiences and were to prove remarkably generous and dedicated supporters of our cause.

My last American phone conversation of the day was with Jamie Galbraith. I told him about the auspicious messages from Bernie, Jeff and Obama before discussing his arrival in Athens, where I wanted him to begin urgent work on our Plan X – the contingency plan that Alexis had first asked me to prepare at the end of our long late-night meeting at his flat in November 2014 and which was to be deployed only if Grexit was forced upon us. Given that the ECB had a plan for Grexit, devised by among others Thomas Wieser and Jörg Asmussen,[5] as did every major European bank, we had a duty to develop our own. Indeed, I was under express orders from the prime minister to ready one. The reason I picked Jamie to lead the team was that the plan needed to be developed in total secrecy, since public knowledge of its existence would undoubtedly accelerate the bank run in anticipation of the devaluation of the currency that would inevitably result from its redenomination, which would in turn provide the ECB with the perfect excuse to close our banks, thereby forcing Grexit upon us: Plan X would become self-fulfilling. If I had asked a civil servant from within the finance ministry to head the team, a fatal leak would have been inevitable. In fact, finding anyone within Greece with Jamie's expertise and capacity for discretion would have been impossible. In the event, he worked for several months on Plan X literally next to me – in a room within my ministerial inner sanctum.

A couple of hours later, the letter that Bernie Sanders had sent to Christine Lagarde arrived in my in-box. It was an absolute gem. The following extract captures its marvellous essence.

This week, the Greek people elected a new government and invested that government with a mandate to reverse the failed austerity policies of the last six years. Austerity has not only impoverished the Greek people, leading to an unemployment rate of upwards of 25 per cent, it has created a political vacuum so dangerous that the neo-Nazi party Golden Dawn has gained seats in parliament . . . The people of Spain, Italy, and Portugal are watching, and if this situation is not addressed with sufficient consideration for the broad swath of workers and citizens involved, the results of continued austerity could lead to more severe political consequences and a worldwide financial crisis. Fortunately, this is not inevitable.

The International Monetary Fund, as a multi-lateral institution and one member of the troika . . . has an important role to play in this episode. As ranking member of the Budget Committee, I am concerned about the IMF using United States government resources to impose austerity on a people that cannot take any more of it and risking severe financial contagion in doing so . . . There is substantial debate over whether the American government should increase the amount of US resources available to the IMF for lending to foreign countries, including questions over how to score the cost of such commitments. Without wading into this debate, I would like to understand how our commitments are being used in this case, and whether those commitments are being used to induce financial contagion and right-wing political extremism through excessive austerity or to aid in helping Greece achieve a manageable debt load and a sustainable economy.

By the time I had finished admiring the letter, it was 3 a.m. Time to put friendly Americans out of my mind and convert my mental list of domestic priorities into the following day's concrete agenda: meet officials to be briefed on the state's official funding situation; appoint secretarial staff and a press officer; convene meetings with the tax office to implement our strategy to tackle tax evasion; establish close partnerships with my deputies in charge of tax policy and budget management; liberate the ministry's macroeconomists and statisticians from the imperatives of the troika and set them to the task not of obfuscating reality but of getting its measure as accurately as possible. Lastly, there was the sensitive task of putting together a small team to begin work on the parallel payments system.

Over the next forty-eight hours the sixth-floor office that until so recently had attracted our people's wrath, would become my home. With Danae having flown back to Austin the day before to close down our apartment and ship everything back to Greece, at least I had no reason to leave the office. The fading red couch would be ideal for the three hours' sleep available before the ministry woke up every morning. Adrenalin would do the rest. A few hours later a bright sun rose above Parliament House bathing the office in a luminous yellow. The new day dawned hopefully.

Define 'not too bad'

It began with a meeting involving officials from the Treasury and the ministry's public debt management agency. I welcomed them into my office, mindful of the need to dispel any fear that I would turf them out or marginalize them in favour of Syriza loyalists. In a short opening speech I told them that their party political allegiance or past collaboration with the troika, however enthusiastic it might have been, was irrelevant as far as I was concerned.[6] I emphasized my determination to be their greatest champion as long as they worked diligently and loyally; equally, I made clear that I would be their worst nightmare if they chose to serve other interests instead. Relief flooded the room, and a conversation began in a spirit of mutual respect and cooperation.

Spreadsheets were laid on the large table, graphs and diagrams were shared, lists of repayments and obligations were drawn up, timelines were presented (with the colour red dominating the charts from mid-February onwards). After every qualification had been made and uncertain assumptions stated, I asked the one and only question that mattered: 'How long?'

It was 28 January 2015. What I was asking was how many days did we have before the state's coffers would be so bare as to necessitate a choice between defaulting to our main creditor, the IMF, or failing to pay fortnightly pensions and civil servants' salaries. My question was followed by a few seconds' silence. When my eyes met those of a senior Treasury official, he put on a brave face and said, 'Things are not too bad, Minister.'

'Define "not too bad",' I said.

'Anything between eleven days and five weeks,' he replied, his eyes turning to his notes to avoid mine. 'It depends on the rate of our tax revenue inflows and some operations we can perform to repo [sell temporarily] various reserves,' he concluded.

So much for the Greek-covery and the substantial surplus the outgoing Samaras government had been celebrating in a bid to convince themselves that the Greek people had been wrong to dismiss them at the polls. Not that I had expected anything different, but it is one thing to know the numbers, it is quite another to have them recited to you in the electric chair.

Keep me out of jail!

A phone call to a friend and colleague who had been a minister in previous governments solved my secretarial problem. Summoned by their former boss, Fotini Bakadima and Anna Kalogeropoulou turned up to take the reins. Their experience was evident immediately: it was as if they had always worked there. In the months that followed they would prove their loyalty and dependability too.

The other key appointment for the team, a chief of staff, was taken care of before I had even had the chance to look for one myself. The deputy PM's office dispatched a Syriza member and lawyer by training, George Koutsoukos, who had been working as a civil servant in the finance ministry, to fill this role. While I was suspicious of his connections to Dragasakis, George won me over – not least because he was a published novelist. *No one who publishes novels while serving in Greece's finance ministry deserves to be mistrusted*, I thought.

Still, while I was determined to work well with my parachuted-in chief of staff – and in fact ended up working very well with him indeed – I felt the urgent need for a minder whose loyalties would not be shared with any of my new Syriza comrades, let alone the deputy PM. So I picked up the phone to summon Wassily, the dear friend who had warned me of Dragasakis more than a year before.

I had met Wassily in 1978 as a first-year undergraduate at Essex University. Our first encounter was on a basketball court. Playing for opposite sides, we clashed for the ball, exchanged words that are reproducible neither in print nor in polite society, and had to be restrained by fellow players. For months afterwards my feelings for Wassily were those of intense dislike – as were his for me, apparently. But after the long Winter of Discontent had come and gone, with Mrs Thatcher having moved to 10 Downing Street in April and the June exams approaching, the general gloom that descended upon us took the edge off our mutual loathing. One evening in the student union bar we agreed to collaborate on an economics assignment. By the early morning, with the assignment completed, the antipathy had metamorphosed into an intense friendship that grew over the years.[7]

'What do you want from me?' Wassily asked once we were in my office alone, visibly unimpressed by the surroundings or the fact that his friend was now minister of finance.

'To keep me out of jail, Wassily,' I replied. He understood. Ministers of finance are at the mercy of their minders. They sign dozens of documents, decrees, contracts and appointments daily. It is humanly impossible to examine closely everything they sign. All it takes is a hostile or absent-minded aide, and suddenly the minister faces the wrath of the public or a summons to court.

Wassily accepted without a second thought and, as soon as I had signed his secondment from the government's Centre for Economic and Planning Research, got down to work. As the day's meetings unfolded, Wassily roamed the corridors to work out who did what to whom, as Lenin might have said, and how they impeded or aided my work.

Swiss cheese

Famously Norman Lamont once quipped that John Major's government, from which he had recently been removed, remained 'in office but not in power'. As I would explain to him years later, his remark's pertinence reached its apogee in the case of the Greek government in general and my ministry in particular. It was not just that, like any other government, we were at the whim of the markets' violent reactions. It was far, far worse than that.

As described in 'Bailoutistan 2.0' in Chapter 2, the conditionalities of the second bailout loan, which had been implemented in stages between 2012 and 2014, included momentous attacks not just on social spending but on the very sovereignty of the Greek state, specifically on its control over essential departments within the Ministry of Finance. As well as creating the Hellenic Financial Stability Facility (HFSF), which after 2012 held the banks' majority shareholdings on behalf of the state, and a privatization unit whose job was to conduct fire sales of Greece's public assets, both of which answered not to the Greek people but to the troika, the jurisdiction of the tax office had also been co-opted by our creditors – specifically, to the Eurogroup Working Group, presided over by Thomas Wieser. By scooping out these three crucial chunks of the Ministry of Finance and placing them beyond the reach of Greece's democratic process, they had effectively turned the ministry into something resembling a Swiss cheese.

Greece's tax office provides one of the most fascinating examples of neocolonial rule in modern times. As Greece's finance minister, the tax department was under my jurisdiction and nominal control, so if a tax evasion scandal broke I would be held responsible for it in parliament and in the eyes of the public. Yet I had zero authority over the activities of the department. I lacked the right to censure, fire or replace its head, and I was not even consulted on how the department was run – all this in a country world famous for tax evasion and for the tax immunity of its oligarchs. In addition, the statistical authority whose computations of the government's budget and balance were used to determine whether the fiscal targets agreed with its creditors had been met or not also answered not to me but to the troika. In a nutshell, I was responsible for, but not equipped to administer, the nation's taxes, banks, property and statistics.

During those first forty-eight hours in the ministry, with my thoughts trained on the impending visit of the Eurogroup president, I was deeply conscious of the fact that a large number of civil servants within my ministry understood that their careers depended a great deal more on serving Brussels than their minister or parliament's will. In the ensuing months many of those civil servants would prove themselves to be diligent, honest and patriotic by working inordinately long hours with conspicuous selflessness and in defiance of exorbitant pressure from the troika. Nonetheless, reclaiming national sovereignty and democratic control on our parliament's behalf over their ministries – and their allegiance – had to be as high a priority as restructuring the source of that bondage, our public debt. To that end, I made an appointment with the head of Greece's intelligence service.[8]

Yannis Roubatis is a striking yet diminutive man. Softly but exceptionally well spoken, he impresses by weighing each of his words so carefully. Originally a journalist, in the 1980s he served as the official spokesperson of Andreas Papandreou's socialist government before becoming a socialist member of the European parliament in the 1990s.[9] On paper Roubatis seemed well qualified to head an intelligence service better known for US-sponsored subversion of Greek democrats and leftists than for defending Greece from foreign foes: as a young man he had written a doctoral thesis at Johns Hopkins University that exposed the infiltration of the Greek government by the CIA, and the government he served in the 1980s did a great deal to sever the link between foreign agencies and Greek spooks.

From the word go I felt comfortable with Roubatis, or at least as comfortable as one can feel with a spy chief. His analysis of the situation our new government was facing was in sync with mine. His declaration of loyalty to the government and stated resolve to be our non-intrusive helper were welcome. His advice on simple measures that could be taken to deter the dirty tricks that our opponents might employ during the negotiations was well taken. But most of all I appreciated his confirmation that the loyalty of whole departments within my ministry lay elsewhere and his making me privy to how cosy the relationship between the heads of these departments and troika officials had become.

After that first meeting I would bump into Roubatis regularly at Maximos in an office next to the prime minister's where he often waited to meet Alexis before or after one of the regular meetings of our 'war cabinet' – which was how we referred, only partially in jest, to our core negotiating team.[10] Roubatis would brief me on the latest intelligence and advise me on how to keep my communications with the prime minister secure. But as I would soon discover, the head of one's intelligence service can imperceptibly turn from a useful friend into a lethal foe.

Ultimatum

On Friday, 30 January, three days after I had assumed the ministry, the president of the Eurogroup, Dutch finance minister Jeroen Dijsselbloem, dropped in. He came with a large entourage that included Thomas Wieser, president of the Eurogroup Working Group and the true power broker within the eurozone. I waited for them by the sixth-floor lift. We met, shook hands warmly and proceeded to my office for some refreshments before moving to an adjacent conference room, the two teams facing each other across a large rectangular table.

On my side of the table I had my two alternate ministers plus Chouliarakis, chair of my Council of Economic Advisers, Stathakis, economy minister, whose office was one floor above mine, and Euclid. Among the heavyweight troika officials on Dijsselbloem and Wieser's side was Declan Costello, an Irishman famous even in Ireland for his hardline policy towards indebted nations, now the European Commission's mission chief for Greece, plus the Dutch ambassador to Greece. Dragasakis made a short welcoming speech then left the room immediately. I followed up with a welcoming speech of my own before Jeroen Dijsselbloem said a few words on behalf of the Eurogroup. Niceties were exchanged and good intentions were aired in what can only be described as a tense encounter. Then the moment of truth arrived when I invited Jeroen into my office for a tête-à-tête.

With the door closed behind us, I attempted to melt the ice by sharing the words of optimism with which I had closed my inaugural press conference a few days earlier. Let's defy the prophets of confrontation, I proposed. Let's prove wrong the media who imagine this to be some *High Noon* encounter. I assured him that our new government was only interested in compromises on a path leading to a mutually advantageous agreement. But to assist the birth of this new partnership, we would need to work out a better negotiation process, one that was not injurious to the Greeks' sense of pride. The troika's methods in Greece over the past five years had been counterproductive.

'Yes,' he agreed. 'The troika has not left the best impression here.'

'That's a major understatement, Jeroen,' I said with a smile. I urged him to see it from the perspective of the people on the ground. For years now groups of technocrats dispatched by the IMF, the European Commission and the European Central Bank had arrived at Athens airport, from which they had been driven at high speed under police escort in a convoy of Mercedes-Benzes to the various ministries, where they had proceeded to interrogate elected ministers and dictate to them policies that affected the lives of millions. Even if these policies had been wonderful, they would have been resented. 'We must find another way to work together,' I said, one that would allow our people to embrace whatever policies he and I agree upon. At the very least, Greece's elected ministers should not be expected to conduct their business with anyone other than their elected equals; technocrats could prepare the ground, establish the facts and the figures, but should not conduct the ministerial negotiations.

I was happy to hear him say that, yes, he agreed that the process would have to be reconsidered, although in hindsight I suspect his accommodating attitude was less to do with an appreciation of what I had been saying and more to do with his evident eagerness to change the subject and return to the same question he had posed on the telephone a few days earlier: 'What are your intentions for the Greek programme? Are you planning to complete it?' he asked.

I repeated the answer I had given him over the phone: our new government, I replied, recognized that it had inherited certain commitments to the Eurogroup while at the same trusted that its partners would recognize in return that it had been elected only a few days before in order to renegotiate key elements of this programme. His response was abrupt and aggressive. 'This will not work!' he declared.

I reminded him that when I had given the same answer to the same question three days earlier, he had replied, 'This is very good.' Jeroen brushed my reminder aside. The Greek programme, he mused, was like a horse. It was either alive or it was dead. If it was alive, we had to climb on it and ride it to its destination. If it was dead, then it was dead. Not knowing what to make of his metaphor and unwilling to adopt it, I tried to reason with him.

There was a reason, I explained, why the previous government had fallen on its sword and called elections so early in its term. And there was a reason why Antonis Samaras had been sent to the opposition benches by the voters who had elected us instead. And the reason was simple: it was simply impossible to complete the second Greek programme, and the voters understood that. 'If it could have been, Jeroen, you and the previous government would have completed it,' I remarked.

For a moment he seemed lost for words, so I continued: the troika's own numbers showed that even if the programme was completed and Greece received the few billions left in the second bailout kitty, we would still be €12 billion short. Where would I find a missing €12 billion? Think of the effect this unanswered question is having on private investors, I urged him: it reinforces their resolve not to lend to the Greek state again until a serious restructuring of our debt has been effected. And think of the broader picture too, I implored him: the government's debt repayments in 2015 alone amounted to 45 per cent of all the taxes it hoped to collect; meanwhile, national income, measured in euros, continued to fall, and everyone was anticipating an increase in taxes to meet the repayments. No investor in their right mind invests in an economy where demand is shrinking and taxes are rising.

There were only three options available to us, I said. One was a third bailout to cover up the failure of the second, whose purpose was to cover up the failure of the first. Another was the new deal for Greece I was proposing: a new type of agreement between the EU, the IMF and Greece, based on debt restructuring, that diminished our reliance on new debt and replaced an ineffective reform agenda with one that the people of Greece could own. The third option was a mutually disadvantageous impasse.

You do not understand, Jeroen told me, his voice dripping with condescension. 'The current programme must be completed or there is nothing else!'

It was an astonishing statement. The head of the eurozone's finance ministers was refusing to engage with a simple funding issue. He was making it impossible for me not to ask, 'But where will the missing €12 billion come from, Jeroen? Am I wrong that the second programme can only be completed if a third one is first negotiated? Can you see any way that would render its completion financially feasible without a new programme that can only be agreed to after exhaustive negotiations between all nineteen finance ministers [in the Eurogroup]? Is there any doubt that I will not be able to complete this programme even if I were willing to violate the mandate that the Greek voters gave me to renegotiate it?'

Jeroen refused to engage with my questions and the underlying facts. Apparently he had not come to Athens to discuss numbers or financing. One could only assume that he had come instead in the expectation that I would perform an instant U-turn – a quick victory allowing him to board his jet at Athens airport with my oath of allegiance to the programme, to the Eurogroup and to the creditors in his briefcase.

The fact that the president of the Eurogroup was so deluded as to think this was a possibility is a fascinating comment on the recent history of the European Union. It reveals how experience has taught functionaries operating on behalf of Europe's deep establishment to expect newly elected government ministers, prime ministers, even the president of France, to buckle at the first whiff of an ultimatum backed by the ECB's big guns.[11] Since 2008, when the only thing keeping most eurozone member states' commercial banks open was the Eurogroup's goodwill – which Mario Draghi's ECB needed in order to issue the official waiver that allowed him to accept the banks' junk collateral in return for cash – several governments had succumbed to policies they detested: the Baltic states, Ireland, Cyprus, Spain, Portugal, all had been beaten into submission.[12] In fact, Dijsselbloem had boasted that the way Cyprus had been treated in 2013, soon after he had taken over the Eurogroup presidency, was the 'template' for future crises. It was the threat of bank closures that had done it – this was the ace he carried in his sleeve on the day of his visit to me – and now he played it.

There was an alternative to committing to completing the programme, he told me. I was glad to hear it, I replied hopefully. Turning his eyes to meet mine, he said purposefully, 'You and I hold a joint conference where we announce that the programme has crashed.'

I replied that the word 'crash' was not exactly soothing for markets and citizens. What do we replace it with? I enquired.

A shrug of his shoulders and a look of faux puzzlement was his response.

'Are you threatening me with Grexit, Jeroen?' I asked calmly.

'No, I have not said this,' he protested.

'Can we please be frank here?' I said. 'There is too much at stake to pussyfoot around. You did say that if I insist on renegotiating the programme, the programme crashes. This means one thing and one thing only. And we both know what that is.'

It was of course that the ECB, either centrally or through the Central Bank of Greece, withdrew its waiver and refused to accept the collateral of Greek banks any more, forcing them to close. At that point our government would have no option but to issue its own liquidity. And if the impasse continued our nominally euro-denominated liquidity would, at some point, turn into a new currency. This was Grexit.

'So, you *are* giving me an ultimatum,' I continued. 'You are in effect telling me: commit to a programme that cannot work or you crash out of the eurozone. Is there any other reading to what you just said?'

The president of the Eurogroup shrugged his shoulders again and grinned.

'It is a sad day for Europe when the Eurogroup president presents a freshly elected finance minister with an impossible ultimatum,' I said. 'We were not elected to clash with the Eurogroup, and I am not interested in clashing with you. But nor were we elected to abdicate during our first week in office by espousing an impossible programme that we came in with a mandate to renegotiate.'

Our eyes met in mutual recognition of the impasse. The only thing left to do was to agree on what each of us would say during the press conference scheduled to follow our meeting, so as to conceal the deadlock and thus prevent it affecting the financial markets. He proposed a first draft; I made a couple of corrections; we agreed. I suggested that, after the speeches, it would be best to take no questions. He countered that we had better take a couple. Answering journalists' pointed questions would give him the opportunity to jangle the markets' nerves just a little – enough to accelerate by a notch or two the bank run that the troika had kick-started weeks before. Loath to be portrayed as muzzling the press, I agreed.

The press room was packed. Once the TV feeds had been established and the noise subsided, I began with predictable niceties consistent with my narrative of a new beginning in Greece's relationship with its creditors and the Eurogroup. Every word had been agreed before-hand. He too respected our agreement and did not stray from the script as we laid a veneer of boring normality over the meeting. Then came the questions.

The first was addressed to Jeroen. Would he be agreeable to the convening of an international conference on Greece's debt, similar to that in London in 1953, which had resulted in substantial debt relief for Germany?[13] He responded flippantly that Europe already had a permanent debt conference – the Eurogroup! I smiled at his answer, making a mental note to use it myself if an opportune moment presented itself.

The second question was addressed to me. Would I cooperate with the troika? My answer was fully in line with what I had told Jeroen in my office: 'We must be clear in our minds about the great difference between the properly instituted institutions of the European Union, such as the European Commission and the European Central Bank, as well as international institutions such as the IMF – organizations and institutions to which Greece proudly belongs – and a tripartite committee that is associated with the imposition of a programme that our government was elected to challenge and to dispute. Our government will proceed under the principle of maximum cooperation with the well-constituted legal institutions of the European Union, and of course the IMF. But with a tripartite committee whose objective is the enforcement of a programme whose logic we consider to be anti-European, with that committee, which even the European parliament considers to be flimsily constructed, we have no intention to cooperate.'

It was the same point that I had just made to Jeroen in my office and with which he had reluctantly agreed: yes to working closely and well with the institutions, but no to the humiliating troika process. As he listened in his earpiece to the translation of my response, an expression of increasing disapproval appeared on his face. When the translation finished, he angrily removed his earpiece and leaned over to whisper in my ear, 'You just killed the troika!'

'Wow!' I answered. 'This is an unearned compliment.'

Turning away, Jeroen jumped to his feet to storm out. But I had managed to stand up at the same time and offer him my hand. Somewhat thrown by my gesture, and as he had to walk past me to reach the exit, he awkwardly took my hand in his without stopping. The photographers pounced. Their pictures showed an ill-mannered Eurogroup president rudely brushing past me before the customary handshake had been completed.

The streets of Athens would never be the same for me after that press conference. Taxi drivers, suited gentlemen, old women, schoolchildren, policemen, conservative family men, nationalists and far-Left recalcitrants alike – a whole society whose sense of pride and dignity had been offended by the previous governments' servitude to the troika and its political bosses – would stop me in the street to offer thanks for that brief moment. A bus driver even stopped his bus in the middle of the road to get out and shake my hand.

Like all good things, it came at a price. The media, the establishment and the oligarchy now considered me Public Enemy Number One. One member of parliament posted a message of support for the Eurogroup president on Facebook, reading, 'Hang on, Jeroen!' This was an echo of a famous expression Greek black marketeers had used in support of Rommel's North African campaign, fearful that an Allied victory there would bring the end to Greece's occupation and consequently their business.[14] Accusations of narcissism, boorishness and sociopathy were thrown at me in direct proportion to the rising tide of warmth and appreciation on the streets.

Besides earning me the undying hatred of Greece's triangle of sin, Jeroen's press-room antics had a more tangible effect, boosting the expectation (and thereby the fact) of an escalating liquidity squeeze. The Athens stock exchange fell to new lows; the banks' shares declined even faster, and withdrawals accelerated. Leaving the press conference, I realized there was not a moment to lose. It was time to pack my bag and go on the tour of northern Europe I had been planning. Its two purposes were to steady the nerves of the world's financiers and to work out the extent to which Jeroen's ultimatum had the backing of the IMF and the rest of the Eurogroup, France's government in particular.[15]

As I made my way back to my office, my secretary informed me that the French finance minister was keen to receive me in Paris. This would be the first stop on my journey, where as well as formal meetings with my French counterparts, four secret meetings had been planned: with Poul Thomsen, the IMF's European chief, with Pierre Moscovici, the European commissioner responsible for the EU's economic and finance portfolio, with Benoît Cœuré, the ECB's second-in-command, and with President Hollande's chief of staff. Next would be London, where the financial world's heart beats. Over the previous few days I had been in touch with Norman Lamont, who had organized meetings for me with people in the City, Martin Wolf at the *Financial Times* and George Osborne at 11 Downing Street. Additionally, and very importantly as it turned out, the London branch of Deutsche Bank convened a meeting of more than two hundred financiers keen to talk to me. After London, I would travel to Rome to see Pier Carlo Padoan, Italy's finance minister. Finally, a visit to Frankfurt would be required, for talks with Mario Draghi and the rest of the ECB's executive council in their brand new office tower.

As I walked, I called Euclid to break the news: we would be off the day after tomorrow, I told him. Euclid protested that he needed to get his ministry in some order first. I cut him short: the whole point of clashing with Alexis and getting Euclid into his post had been in order to take him with me around Europe. 'At least I get to keep your right-wing tendencies in check, especially around your Tory mates,' Euclid replied only half-jokingly.

Alone in my office, I sat down to catch my breath. My mobile rang. It was Danae calling from Austin. How was I? Couldn't be better, I joked. I gave her a sketch of the day's events plus my travel plans. She countered with an account of her own clashes with the petty tyrants who ran our building in Austin and the bureaucracy of vacating the flat. And then she asked me if I felt overwhelmed. I replied that it was the enemy near at hand that scared me the most, the domestic establishment with its tentacles deep inside my ministry. Danae's only concern was our unity: 'If Alexis and you stick together, you can do it.' To this day I think she was right.

Home front

I had twenty-four hours before flying off to Paris, but waging war against the domestic establishment could not wait until my return. At around 8 p.m. I was joined by my chief of staff Koutsoukos and Wassily. The declaration of war against the oligarchy had been made before the election. In an interview with Paul Mason on the UK's *Channel 4 News* I had declared, 'We are going to destroy the basis upon which they have built for decade after decade a system, a network that viciously sucks the energy and the economic power from everybody else in society.' With Koutsoukos and Wassily taking notes, I set out the agenda: catching hundreds of thousands of tax cheats and shocking Greek society out of its tax-evading ways; breaking down the collusion between the supermarket chains that exploited consumers and their suppliers; protecting a financially desperate population from the invasion of gambling machines that the previous government had committed me to; empowering the government's own anti-corruption ombudsman; lastly, planning the assault on the towers of sleaze that were Greece's four systemic banks.

'What about the media?' asked Wassily.

Pappas was responsible for that kettle of rotting fish, I told him.

'Your good mate, yeah?' my friend asked with a meaningful grimace.

'Do I detect sarcasm here, Wassily?' I asked.

'The question is whether you can detect the opprobrium that your mate is spreading left, right and centre against you,' was his retort.

It was not something I wanted to hear, not least because I very much feared it might be the truth.

One by one the battlefields were discussed and our strategy was decided. To combat tax cheats, Koutsoukos suggested that I appoint Panayiotis Danis special secretary of the ministry's financial and economic crime-fighting unit. This was the only part of the state's tax office that the troika had not taken under its tutelage. Stripped of many of its powers and personnel, it was a shadow of its former self, but its formal survival and the fact that it remained under my full control made it an ideal foundation on which to build a team of untouchables led by Danis.[16]

Chasing tax cheats using normal procedures was not an option. It would take decades just to identify anything like the majority of them and centuries to prosecute them successfully; the more we caught, the more clogged up the judicial system would become. We needed a different approach. Once Danis was on board a couple of days later, together we thought of one: we would extract historical and real-time data from the banks on all transfers taking place within Greece as well as in and out of the country and commission software to compare the money flows associated with each tax file number with the tax returns of that same file number. The algorithm would be designed to flag up any instance where declared income seemed to be substantially lower than actual income. Having identified the most likely offenders in this way, we would make them an offer they could not refuse.

The plan was to convene a press conference at which I would make it clear that anyone caught by the new system would be subject to 45 per cent tax, large penalties on 100 per cent of their undeclared income and criminal prosecution. But as our government sought to establish a new relationship of trust between state and citizenry, there would be an opportunity to make amends anonymously and at minimum cost. I would announce that for the next fortnight a new portal would be open on the ministry's website on which anyone could register any previously undeclared income for the period 2000–14. Only 15 per cent of this sum would be required in tax arrears, payable via web banking or debit card. In return for payment, the taxpayer would receive an electronic receipt guaranteeing immunity from prosecution for previous non-disclosure.[17]

Alongside this I resolved to propose a simple deal to the finance minister of Switzerland, where so many of Greece's tax cheats kept their untaxed money.[18] In a rare example of the raw power of the European Union being used as a force for good, Switzerland had recently been forced to disclose all banking information pertaining to EU citizens by 2017. Naturally, the Swiss feared that large EU-domiciled depositors who did not want their bank balances to be reported to their country's tax authorities might shift their money before the revelation deadline to some other jurisdiction, such as the Cayman Islands, Singapore or Panama. My proposals were thus very much in the Swiss finance minister's interests: a 15 per cent tax rate was a relatively small price to pay for legalizing a stash and allowing it to remain in safe, conveniently located Switzerland. I would pass a law through Greece's parliament that would allow for the taxation of money in Swiss bank accounts at this exceptionally low rate, and in return the Swiss finance minister would require all his country's banks to send their Greek customers a friendly letter informing them that, unless they produced the electronic receipt and immunity certificate provided by my ministry's web page, their bank account would be closed within weeks. To my great surprise and delight, my Swiss counterpart agreed to the proposal.[19]

The merit of the scheme was its simplicity. We would not be asking people to repatriate money from foreign banks or even to declare where they were keeping it, whether in Switzerland or under the mattress. By offering instead a low tax rate with zero penalties or bureaucracy, I expected to replenish the empty state coffers with a great deal of money, buying my ministry time and freedom.

It was already midnight when we wrapped up our discussion of this plan, but we were nowhere near finished for the night. Next we discussed the great plague that was about to be unleashed upon our weakest citizens: the approximately 16,000 video lottery terminals that the privatized national lottery company OPAP had secured a licence to introduce throughout Greece. A population devastated by poverty and loss of income, in the midst of a great psychological and economic depression, was to be milked of the last remaining cash in its pockets through the mass installation of gambling machines. I could scarcely imagine a viler policy endorsed by a civilized state.

Initially I toyed with the idea of rescinding the licence. The problem was that OPAP would litigate and probably win, costing the state money it did not have. But there was another way. The finance ministry was responsible for the gambling regulator, the quaintly named Hellenic Gaming Commission.[20] Since we could not eliminate the virus, we would have to regulate it instead. Two restrictions came to mind: one was a maximum loss per person per day (a limit of €60 seemed reasonable); the other the obligation to type into the machine one's tax file number, which would act as a disincentive to anyone who might not want there to be an official record of their gambling, exclude underage players and ensure that winnings could be taxed as per the existing legislation. Koutsoukos liked the idea and suggested someone to chair the Gaming Commission. Two months later, after many trials and tribulations, Antonis Stergiotis's appointment was approved by parliament at my recommendation.[21]

Next on the agenda were the corrupt practices of powerful companies. The good people of the Confederation of North Greek Industries had alerted me to the restrictive, cartel-like practices of certain supermarket chains, oil companies and the like, which were undermining the economy. For example, supermarkets would require small-scale producers to pay them for stocking their goods – for 'advertising' them in their stores – in effect forcing them to reduce their prices. Yet the producers would still pay tax on the higher declared price, with the supermarket pocketing the difference. Similarly, I had it on good authority that an oil cartel bigwig was exporting €300 million worth of refined petrol to Bulgaria, but Bulgaria was reporting imports of no more than €100 million. 'What is happening to the remaining €200 million?' I asked my informant. 'It is poured into some ditch in no-man's land between Greece and Bulgaria,' was his sarcastic answer. By that he meant that tanker trucks left Greece with fully documented exported petrol but then re-entered via some illicit dirt road without crossing the Bulgarian border. The petrol was then sold in Greece *sans* VAT and fuel tax.

Corruption within our ministries was what allowed these big businesses to function with impunity. There was a lone anti-corruption warrior, Wassily told me, a Mr Rakintzis, the official state ombudsman, whose job it was to coordinate the fight against graft. I would make a point of meeting him, increase the resources available to his depleted office and do something that had not been done before: stage a joint press conference that would announce the finance ministry's full support of him and his office.

The last item on our agenda that night was Greece's banks. I asked for ideas on how to approach the impending confrontation when I put my proposal for 'europeanizing' them to the EU. Wassily interrupted me in typical fashion: 'The horses have bolted, Yani,' he said, showing me a decree that had arrived that evening from the deputy prime minister's office, fully authorized by the cabinet secretary. It stipulated that jurisdiction over all matters pertaining to the banks had been moved from the Ministry of Finance to the office of the deputy prime minister. 'Don't tell me I didn't tell you so,' said Wassily. 'Dragasakis has taken his banker friends under his wing to protect them from the likes of you.' Fearing that Wassily might be right, I still had no choice but to give Dragasakis the benefit of the doubt.

Before calling it a night, I asked Chouliarakis, chair of the ministry's Council of Economic Advisers, to come to my office. He arrived a quarter of an hour later, clearly unhappy to have been summoned from his own office just down the corridor. As I would be meeting secretly with well-armed troika officials, I told him it would be useful to have in my briefcase a rough and ready first stab at a debt sustainability analysis (DSA) with which to make the initial case for debt restructuring being our government's top priority. Chouliarakis left the room and returned a short while later with a two-page document: it was the DSA drawn up by the IMF. Given that we had only taken over three days earlier, it was perfectly understandable that Chouliarakis had not yet produced a DSA of our own. What was not acceptable was that he began to defend its accuracy and value when I knew that even the IMF knew it to be wrong. In the nicest possible way I asked him to go back to the drawing board and do it again. Without expressly agreeing to do so, he made his excuses and left.

With the long day finally at an end, I collapsed on the red couch, where Wassily was already sprawled. It was 3 a.m. on Saturday, 31 January.

'I think we did well today, Wassily,' I ventured.

He looked at me. 'Yes, you did well, but I am prepared to wager good money that in six months Dragasakis will be prime minister and Chouliarakis will have replaced you.'

'Maybe –' I smiled '– but at least we will know that we did our best and they their worst.'

That night I went home for the first time in seventy-two hours. I walked, alone. It took no more than twenty minutes, past Melina Merkouri's oversize bust opposite Hadrian's Gate, taking a right towards the Herod Theatre, then a sharp left at the New Acropolis Museum, and I was home. A few pedestrians and a taxi driver noticed me and gave me the thumbs up. Those solitary walks from the ministry to our flat, or between Maximos and Syntagma Square, were to become my source of hope and courage.

Mulling over the previous day, thinking ahead to my trip abroad, T.S. Eliot's line came to mind: 'If you aren't in over your head, how do you know how tall you are?'

Lull

A knock on my door at around 11 a.m. woke me up. It was Esmeralda, Danae's daughter, checking on me. Where had I been for the past three days? Was I in one piece? I reassured her that all was well. She pointed out that sightseers had been gathering outside our first-floor flat trying to get a glimpse of the interior, the more daring of them photographing one another astride my motorcycle. She warned me in a motherly fashion to put some clothes on before going into the kitchen area to make coffee.

Paris-bound in the early evening, my plan was to stay in during the day to prepare a one-page technical non-paper on debt restructuring. I knew that the officials I was about to meet laboured under the carefully cultivated impression that my government was about to demand a debt write-off that was politically unfeasible. With my non-paper I sought to demonstrate that mutual gains were possible. For years I had recited to my students Adam Smith's famous lines 'It is not from the benevolence of the butcher, the brewer, or the baker that we expect our dinner, but from their regard to their own interest. We address ourselves, not to their humanity but to their self-love, and never talk to them of our own necessities but of their advantages.'[22]

Similarly, it would be a waste of breath to appeal to the creditors' humanity, to claim that Greece had been unfairly treated or to invoke some moral right to debt relief. These people knew perfectly well how the Greeks had been treated and they cared not one bit. My task was to win a war not a debating society argument. To do so I had to address myself to the creditors' own advantages.

So, in the non-paper (reproduced in Appendix 4) I illustrated how not signing up to further extend-and-pretend loans could serve the creditors' interests. It contained simple debt-swap ideas which would cost them, politically and financially, far less than the continuation of the vicious cycle that had begun in 2010 or the throttling of our government that Jeroen had hinted at the day before.

When I finished it, I called Xenia, my eleven-year-old daughter who lives in Sydney. 'Dad,' she said before I even got the chance to say hi, 'do you realize that you have ruined my life?' Apparently paparazzi had camped outside her school waiting to snap a shot of the Greek finance minister's daughter. I did my best to soothe her, to no avail. 'Why can't you just resign? Life is unbearable,' she insisted. I told her that she should not worry; plenty of people were working hard to bring about my resignation. She was not reassured in the slightest.

When Xenia had ended our chat, a lingering worry resurfaced in the silence of the apartment. Would Alexis, Pappas and Dragasakis back my debt-restructuring proposals? Yes, they had agreed to its basic logic as part of our covenant and had given me carte blanche to propose such debt swaps. Nevertheless, prior to my enlistment Syriza's position on public debt had been nothing more than a crude demand for an unqualified write-down. With half the party still demanding a unilateral haircut of most of the debt, most not even privy to the idea of a debt swap, and with only a tenuous, verbal covenant binding the leadership trio to my strategy, I could easily imagine having the rug pulled from under me at home while in the thick of the battle abroad.

The only colleague that I trusted to understand fully and support my debt-restructuring proposals was Euclid. As a Syriza insider, he could present my proposals to the party faithful for what they were: a shrewd strategy for getting Greece the debt relief it needed without putting Chancellor Merkel in a politically impossible situation. I spent another hour preparing a briefing for Alexis, copied to Pappas and Dragasakis, hoping to bring them into the fold as well by demystifying my proposals and providing the arguments and motivation they would need to back them within Syriza's central committee and in cabinet against those who might accuse me of insufficient revolutionary fervour or of backpedalling.

It was afternoon by the time the non-paper, the briefing to Alexis and several urgent phone calls were behind me. I looked at my watch and realized I had an hour and a half before I had to be back at the ministry, where a car (a small ten-year-old Hyundai, now that the BMWs were gone) would pick me up to take me to the airport. My sister had texted me earlier to say that our ninety-year-old father was visiting her; if I could spare the time, a quick visit might be a good idea, as I could see them all at once: my dad and sister, her husband and my eight-year-old niece. I jumped on the motorcycle and within five minutes had carved my way through the thin Saturday-afternoon traffic.

Arriving at my sister's flat was to step out of my life as a minister and into a vibrantly comforting, other world. Seeing my relatives gathered together, doing mundane family things, I realized how painful several lacunae had been: Danae's absence in Austin, the loneliness of my political position and, underlying them both, the loss of my mother, which I had dared not acknowledge these past seven years except at the odd moment when my guard was down.

7

Auspicious February

Back at the flat, I prepared a small suitcase, slipped my laptop into my rucksack and stepped outside to hail a taxi. Uncharacteristically for Athens, the driver who pulled over got out of his cab to greet me and place my suitcase in the boot. Ten minutes later we were at Syntagma Square, in front of the ministry. Lovely as the driver was, his good wishes for an overseas trip which the media were reporting as 'pivotal' for the nation were so lengthy that I was eventually in danger of missing my flight. When I finally managed to bid him farewell, I was so anxious that I rushed from the taxi clutching only my rucksack. It wasn't until I reached the doorway of the ministry that I realized I had left my suitcase in the cab, containing not just my change of clothes but my overcoat. All I had with me was the black jacket, white shirt and black trousers I was wearing. *Too late*, I thought. I would have to do some shopping in Paris. It was a mistake that would leave a small mark on cultural politics, at least in the UK.

On the plane Euclid was rereading a Jane Austen novel. Restless, I took out a notebook and scribbled down my thoughts

> Our message to our partners is it cannot be business as usual. The Greek social economy is subject to a persistent doom-loop between public debt, private losses, negative investment and a vicious deflationary dynamic . . .
>
> Our message to ourselves is it cannot be business as usual. We need to reform. Reforms are not a necessary evil – it is our dream to live in a Greece that reforms itself on the basis of a reform programme that we own, not one that appears to us symbolic of national humiliation. No one owes us a living. But no one has the right either to

hold us in debtors' prison in perpetuity, preventing us from earning our keep.

The troika's reform agenda, against the backdrop of the nation's pauperization, was like McKinsey implementing a plan to restructure a corporation without support from shareholders and in opposition to the Board . . .

Greece has been gazing too long into the abyss. And the abyss has begun to gaze back at us. Time to turn our gaze to hope . . .

In 1967 it was the tanks that toppled Greek democracy. Yesterday I was threatened, by no less a figure than the president of the Eurogroup, with a closure of the banks. Democratic Europe should not tolerate this.

Upon landing, I was met by our ambassador in Paris. It was after ten at night on Saturday. My secretary had already informed him that I would be arriving without any coat or change of clothes, so he dutifully rushed me to the Champs-Elysées in search of a shop that wasn't closed. Only Zara was still open. The ambassador and I rushed upstairs to the men's department to find they sold no coats and that the only vaguely suitable shirts they had were two ultra-tight ones, both blue. Lacking alternatives, I bought them. But what of a coat? The shops would be closed on Sunday, and my meetings in London began at 8 a.m on Monday. More importantly, the temperature was below freezing. I was anxious enough at the prospect of confronting some rather powerful people; the prospect of trembling with cold as I did so was too much.

'Not to worry, Minister,' said the ambassador as he was dropping me off at my hotel. 'I shall run home and fetch a coat that I think will fit you.' Half an hour later he returned bearing a longish leather overcoat. Even I could see that it was not exactly ministerial, but I must admit I thought it rather swanky and offbeat (and it certainly enhanced my opinion of Greece's ambassador to the French Republic). Moreover it had two major advantages: it fitted me and it was warm. Little realizing that two days later the coat would become famous, I gratefully accepted it.

At 7 a.m. on Sunday I was up and ready to go. Before my official meetings with Michel Sapin, France's finance minister, and Emmanuel Macron, the country's economy minister, my schedule began with a series of secret meetings to be held in quick succession in a private room in the basement of our hotel, out of sight of prying journalistic eyes. First up was Pierre Moscovici, the European commissioner for economics and finance, who apparently lived not too far away.

Promising liaisons: 1. The commissioner

Before he became a commissioner at the EU, Moscovici was France's finance minister. When the European Commission's top economic post became vacant, the French president François Hollande insisted that a Frenchman be given the role. But there was a catch. Berlin was (and remained) eager to see Brussels clamp down on France's budget deficit, so the last thing they wanted was to hand this job to a Frenchman, far less a former finance minister of France. On the other hand, Berlin had to reward President Hollande for the major U-turn he had performed on their behalf in accepting their austerity agenda immediately after winning the election on the back of a campaign promise to resist it. This conundrum was solved in a manner that anyone in Pierre Moscovici's place would have found demeaning: Moscovici was given the job, but a new position, vice president of the European Commission, was invented to oversee him. To add insult to injury, Berlin gave this new post to the former prime minister of Latvia, whose greatest claim to fame was the imposition of austerity measures so harsh that they 'solved' his country's economic crisis by causing half the population to emigrate.

From the outset Pierre approached me as a friend, a comrade even. He told me he understood my arguments entirely. At some point he confessed that in his youth he had been a Marxist. Though no longer a radical, he wanted me to understand that there was enough of a left-winger left in him to appreciate my government's position. No wonder Berlin did not trust him. When I described my recent encounter with Jeroen Dijsselbloem, he winced with distaste at his behaviour and advised me to pay no attention to his threats.

Taking heart at Pierre's warmth, I tested my agenda on him: it was essential that a different type of agreement should govern Greece's relationship with the EU, but to get a chance to hammer out what that should be we needed time and fiscal space; we needed, in other words, a six-month bridge between the previous programme

and a new contract between the EU and Greece. I used the word
'contract' in the spirit of Jean-Jacques Rousseau, I explained: a mutually beneficial relationship between equals. This new long-term
contract must include proper debt restructuring, a realistic fiscal policy
and a reform agenda that targeted the oligarchy. Lastly, we needed
to replace the troika's current attitude to Greece with a process that
respected Greek sensibilities and the rule of law, both European and
domestic.

When Pierre responded, I could hardly believe my ears: he offered
nothing less than a paean to the agenda I had just outlined. The
troika's methods had been very bad for the EU's image, he admitted.
'It has to end' were his specific words. To my joy and amazement, he
also agreed with my point about separating the European Commission,
the ECB and the IMF from the troika that they had assembled –
precisely what had caused Dijsselbloem's outrage two days previously.
'Technocrats must talk with technocrats and ministers with ministers,'
he acknowledged. I added that it was absurd that the officials charged
with representing Greece's central bank were acting as bailiffs and
imposing fire sales upon the government they were meant to serve.
Pierre agreed wholeheartedly. It was unacceptable, he reiterated,
adding that he thought it important not only for Greece but also for
Europe that the troika be replaced with direct political negotiations
over economic matters in Brussels between me and him.

There was hardly anything left for me to say. He had done my job
for me. So we shook hands warmly and agreed to remain in touch in
order to plan for the first Eurogroup meeting, scheduled for 11
February, when this new chapter in our relationship would commence.

'I hope that this is indeed a new beginning, Pierre,' I said as I walked
him upstairs to the lobby.

'It is, it is,' he replied smiling warmly.

Euclid, who had been present throughout, seemed amused. 'Let's
see what goodies our friend from the IMF has in store for us,' he said.

Promising liaisons: 2. The troika man

Poul Thomsen, my next guest in the hotel's dungeon, is probably the
most despised foreigner in Greece. The tall Dane's surname is synonymous with the troika and Bailoutistan. In 2010, when the troika

was being assembled, he was appointed by the IMF to head its Greek mission.

Unlike the ECB or the European Commission, the IMF had decades of mission experience. In the 1970s its technocrats had made a name for themselves by visiting failing states in Africa and Latin America to impose austerity, privatizations, school and hospital closures, liberalization of food and fuel prices and the like in exchange for IMF loans. When the troika was put together by Berlin to do the same on Europe's periphery, beginning with Greece, IMF technocrats were deployed to lead the way. Unlike previous IMF mission chiefs though, Thomsen was being entrusted with the fortunes of a First World country.[1]

As a reward for his unmitigated failure in Greece, Thomsen was promoted to head the IMF's entire European department. Negotiating with Thomsen therefore presented a special difficulty: he had a vested interest in resisting any acknowledgement that the Greek programme had failed. It was a little like negotiating the dismantling of Bernie Madoff's Ponzi scheme with Bernie Madoff.

To my intense surprise, Poul Thomsen needed no persuasion. Having listened to my analysis of Greece's predicament and my agenda, he offered a response that makes me smile even to this day: 'Look, we know that we cannot expect a left-wing government to do things that even your right-wing predecessors wouldn't do. I understand that you need to bring back collective bargaining and cannot expect you to consent to privatizing everything.[2] But the one thing that we would expect of you, in accordance with your own pronouncements, is that you go after the oligarchs, targeting tax evasion in particular.'

Was I dreaming? I told him he had my cast-iron guarantee that we would not leave any stone unturned in pursuit of them. We would also sell to the private sector assets whose privatization would benefit our social economy, as long as the new owners committed themselves to high levels of direct investment and proper protection for workers and the environment. But, I added, for any reform agenda to work, we would need a get-out-of-debtors'-prison card. At that point I took from my folder the one-page non-paper outlining my debt swaps proposals and gave it to him. Thomsen looked at it, smiled and dumbfounded me once more.

'This is fine. But it is not enough. We need an immediate annulment of part of your debt. No swaps, no delays. Just take €53 billion and erase it.'

That's it, I concluded: I *am* dreaming! He was talking about eliminating at a stroke the entire debt that Greece still owed the EU member states from the first bailout of 2010. Had some member of Syriza's Left Platform infiltrated Thomsen's mind? Was he possessed by some radical spirit?

Suddenly I found myself on the defensive. I could not have agreed more, I told him, but how could Berlin be persuaded to agree to such a proposal? And what about all the other EU governments? Was it politically feasible for them to get this through their parliaments?

Thomsen's reply turned on a technical point: the monies given to Athens under the first bailout agreement were exceptional in that they were all bilateral loans from other eurozone capitals; by contrast, the second bailout loans came from Europe's bailout fund, the EFSF, which had also lent money to Ireland, Portugal, Spain and Cyprus. If we restructured Greece's debt to the EFSF, then Dublin, Lisbon, Madrid and Nicosia would seek similar relief, whereas Greece's first bailout could be annulled without giving the other bailed-out countries any grounds for protest.

As desirable as his proposal was, I told him, I still did not see how Berlin would agree to it, nor how he would avoid the accusation that he was advocating the annulment of debt owed to Europe but not to the IMF.

'I'm just telling you what the IMF position is,' he said, shrugging his shoulders.

Not wishing to spoil a wonderful first meeting, I turned the conversation to the subject of Greece's primary surplus targets and stressed the importance of their being sensible, at around 1.5 per cent of national income.

'I agree,' Thomsen replied laconically.

My Sunday in Paris could not have begun better. Would my next guest spoil it?

Promising liaisons: 3. France's ECB man

Third on the list was Benoît Cœuré, widely regarded as France's man on the ECB Executive Board, a description that he detests but which he can hardly escape given that, prior to moving to Frankfurt, he had spent his entire career in the French Treasury. A mild and agreeable man, Cœuré seemed to me to have a good grasp of the challenge the ECB faced given the eurozone's terrible economic and financial architecture.

I was pleased at the urgency of the first question he raised: was I really intending to restructure unilaterally the Greek government (SMP) bonds that the ECB owned? It was a matter of great concern in Frankfurt, he told me.

I was happy to settle this matter right away. From my point of view, these bonds were both a blessing and a curse, I explained. They were a curse because their purchase had done absolutely nothing to help Greece in 2010, and had the ECB *not* bought them that part of Greece's debt would have been written down by around 90 per cent in 2012. 'Having to borrow now from EU taxpayers to pay the ECB for bonds that it should not have purchased in the first place is ridiculous to say the least,' I said. At the same time, they were a blessing because they gave the ECB and Greece common cause – and leverage – against Dijsselbloem and the Eurogroup. If the ECB threatened to close down our banks at Dijsselbloem's behest, we would reply with a counter-threat to write down the SMP bonds unilaterally; neither the ECB nor Greece wanted this. My simple proposal was: let's not threaten one another. If Benoît told Jeroen that the ECB would not be part of a coup against the Athens government, then we, the Athens government, would not even consider any unilateral moves in relation to these bonds. 'Can we agree on this?' I asked.

He smiled. Of course there should be no threats, he agreed.

We moved on to the debt swaps I was proposing. I gave him my non-paper and briefly talked through it. He thanked me for it, though it was evident he had studied my proposals already. He thought they were sound, but the main concern of the ECB Executive Board was that they should not be seen to violate their own rulebook. I claimed that swapping SMP bonds for a new perpetual bond or equivalent debt instrument was perfectly consistent with the ECB charter. He thought about it for a moment and, while he remained concerned, came to the conclusion that, 'Yes, this might work.'

Last we discussed the burning issue of liquidity. Our government would need a few months of breathing space in which to conduct negotiations, which meant some way of meeting the repayments to the IMF that were imminent without having to scrape the bottom of the barrel of the Greek public sector, endangering pensions and civil service salaries. I reminded Benoît of what the ECB had done in the summer of 2012 to help the then freshly elected Samaras government during a similar period of negotiations: it had raised their credit card limit (in Treasury bills) from €15 billion to €18.3 billion in order to enable them to make the repayment then due to the ECB.[3]

Benoît remembered. And he agreed that something of the sort would have to be done.

'Except that, instead of doing this you have been tightening the noose around our necks even before we were elected,' I said to him.

Benoît pretended not to understand. So I reminded him of Stournaras's remarkable statement on 15 December 2014, which had begun the bank run. 'This was an act of war against the next government, a uniquely offensive dereliction of duty in the annals of central banking,' I said.

Benoît lowered his head and told me that he too thought that Stournaras's statement had been 'inappropriate' and 'inexplicable'.

'And I do not think that Stournaras acted without the OK from Frankfurt, Benoît. No one believes this in Athens,' I added.

Benoît said nothing.

Filling the silence, I continued: if the ECB didn't do what was necessary to end a bank run of its own making, if it didn't extend to us the helping hand we needed in order to conduct our negotiations, many would see it as political intervention by the ECB – one set of standards for the Samaras government, another for ours. Benoît smiled again, this time more widely, as if in acknowledgement of Frankfurt's curious position: officially apolitical but in reality playing a key role in European politics.

Who are you and what have you done with my Michel?

After my last informal meeting of that long morning – what turned out to be a pointless conversation with one of President Hollande's aides who apparently lacked the authority to say anything of substance – it was time to switch from unofficial to official mode. The Greek embassy's German car arrived outside the hotel to take us to meetings with France's finance and economy ministers. The three of us, Euclid, the ambassador and myself, rode quietly to Bercy, the large complex where both ministries are housed on the banks of the River Seine.

At the entrance I was met by an effusive Michel Sapin. A jovial man in his early sixties, Sapin was the only finance minister in the Eurogroup who did not speak English. But he made up for it with a warm character. Typically Latin in his hand gestures and body language, he made me feel genuinely welcome as we walked to his office.

Once we were sat down with our aides and translator, I was asked to make an opening statement, which I used to outline the main items on our economic agenda, my debt-restructuring ideas, including the non-paper, which Sapin seemed keen to see, prefaced with an expression of allegiance to Europeanism and my contention that the Greek crisis, and its perpetuation, was wounding Europe unnecessarily. I explained that I was proposing a new relationship between Greece and the EU based on Jean-Jacques Rousseau's concept of a contract between equals.

Michel's response was that of a brother-in-arms: 'Your government's success will be our success. It is important that we change Europe together; that we replace this fixation with austerity with a pro-growth agenda. Greece needs it. France needs it. Europe needs it.'

It was the cue I needed to put forward the basic elements of the *Modest Proposal*, which Stuart Holland, Jamie Galbraith and I had been working on for years. I explained how the ECB could partially restructure the whole of the eurozone's public debt without haircuts and without asking Germany to pay for everyone else or guarantee the periphery's public debt. I outlined how investment-led recovery could produce a new deal for Europe by channelling the ECB's quantitative easing programme into infrastructure projects or green energy bonds issued by the European Investment Bank. Michel listened intently and, when I had finished, declared that such proposals were the way forward for Europe. We had delayed the implementation of such policies for too long, he said. Together we must restart Europe, he thundered. The only thing that Michel did not do was suggest we join hands and rush out to storm the Bastille singing the Marseillaise!

Our discussion, lengthened as it was by the need for translation, lasted around an hour and a half. It was pleasant and free of any disagreement, and coming as it did after such encouraging conversations earlier that morning, I began to put the confrontation with Jeroen Dijsselbloem behind me and consider a decent compromise agreement as a real possibility.

As Michel and I were making our way from his office to the obligatory press conference – he speaking in French, which I understand,
and I responding in English, which he grasped sufficiently – he
informed me that Berlin had been in contact. They were very upset
that I had come to Paris without also offering to go to Berlin, he told
me in a low voice. I was more than happy to go to Berlin too, I told
him. The reason I was in Paris and not there was that he had invited
me and they had not. My intention was to ask Wolfgang Schäuble to
Athens, since he had not invited me to Berlin. Michel smiled. 'You
should go to Berlin immediately after Frankfurt. They asked me to
convey this to you.'

'Sure, happy to oblige. Is this an invitation or a summons?' I asked
only half-jokingly.

'Just go,' he replied, patting me on the back.

In the press room two lecterns stood side by side in front of the
French, Greek and EU flags. Michel spoke first and began by welcoming
me and saying a few words about the great sacrifices the Greek people
had made during the past few years. But then, quite suddenly, his tone
changed. The joviality and comradeship disappeared and were replaced
with a harshness more familiar from the other side of the River Rhine:
Greece had obligations to its creditors, and the new government would
have to honour them; discipline must be maintained and any flexibility
contained within the current arrangements. Nothing about the new
Rousseau-inspired social contract that we had agreed upon. Not a
word about ending austerity or adopting public-investment-led pro-
growth policies for the good of all of Europe.

When my turn came, I stuck to my prepared statement which
included the following.

> France is for us Greeks not just a partner but also one of
> our spiritual homes. The very existence of the Greek state
> owes a great deal to the French Enlightenment that
> sparked off our own Enlightenment and equipped the
> Greek national liberation movement with its philosophy
> and elan. Today, I had an opportunity to outline to Mr
> Sapin our government's plans for reforming Greece within
> a changing Europe that puts an end to the self-reinforcing
> debt-deflationary cycle damaging everyone in Europe as
> we speak. It is our view that to accomplish this we must

deliberate in the spirit of the great Europeans who, beginning with Jean Monnet, found practical means to forge mutually beneficial unity out of seemingly implacable discord. We shall suggest to our partners across Europe that we resurrect together one of Jean Monnet's operating principles. Namely, that if parties sit down at opposite sides of a negotiating table and proceed from long-established positions, there will be little chance of success. But if we sit on the same side of the table and place the problem on the opposite side, success is certain in a Europe with so much room for mutual prosperity. Today we sat on the same side of the proverbial table. It is our government's intention to do the same in every European capital, each time placing the problem on the table's opposite side. Today, starting here in Paris, let me say that I am guided by a single objective: to promote the interests not of the average Greek but the interests of the average European. To ensure that our economic and monetary union succeeds by succeeding everywhere.

Although I managed to finish my prepared speech lauding solidarity and French idealism, I felt as if I had been punched in the stomach.

As soon as we left the press room, Michel instantly switched back to his amicable joviality, holding my hand as if I were his favourite long-lost cousin. Determined to maintain my exterior poise, I turned to look at him and, faking puzzlement, asked, 'Who are you and what have you done to my Michel?'

To my great astonishment, not only did he clearly understand what I was saying, he did not seem angered by it in the slightest either. Instead he stopped, held my arm a little more tightly, adopted a sombre expression and, switching to English almost as if he had practised the line, shared an opinion of historic importance and sadness: 'Yanis, you must understand this. France is not what it used to be.'

Indeed, France is not what it used to be. In the months that followed, the French government and the country's entire elite proved their inability, as well as reluctance, to deter attacks on our government that were, in the long term, aimed at Paris. While I never expected them to go out of their way to assist us against their interests, I was ill prepared for the French establishment's abandonment of its own interests, which were not served by reinforcing the surplus countries' domination of fiscally stressed ones.[4] Michel Sapin's performance that day is an excellent allegory for what is wrong in the French Republic.

In the lift on our way to see Emmanuel Macron, also based at Bercy, Michel confessed that he was not an economist by training and asked me if I knew what his postgraduate thesis had been on. I said I did not. 'The numismatic history of Aegina,' he informed me with a smile even broader than the one with which he had first greeted me. My jaw dropped. France's minister of finance, having just unleashed a surprise public assault on me on Berlin's behalf, was now trying to bond with me by confessing that he did not know much about economics but was an expert on the ancient coins of the little island off the coast of Attica that Danae and I call home.[5] Irony does not even begin to convey what I felt.

France's minister for the economy was the opposite of its minister of finance. Where Michel Sapin ducked, deferred and simulated, Emmanuel Macron listened actively and engaged directly, his eyes radiant and ready to display his approval or disagreement. The fact that he had good English and a grasp of macroeconomics as well meant we were soon on the same page regarding Europe's need for a genuine investment programme that would put its trillions of idle savings to work for the collective good. From my first meeting with him, I regretted dearly that it was Sapin who represented France in the Eurogroup and not Macron. Had they swapped roles, things might have ended up differently.

Finally, after a long day, Euclid and I were ready to leave Bercy. As we were walking out, Michel came down to say farewell. It was there that he taught us one thing that we shall always remember and thank him for: how to tie a scarf the French way.

Downing Street

The Eurostar was on time. London beckoned. Not a moment too soon. Before I had even taken over the ministry, €11 billion – amounting to 7 per cent of bank deposits in Greece – had been withdrawn thanks to the Stournaras–ECB bank run. Greek banks were already applying for the ECB's emergency liquidity assistance.[6] The noose was tightening. The purpose of this, the next leg of my journey, was to change the financial climate and buy us time.

Early on Monday, 2 February 2015 I breakfasted with Martin Wolf, economics editor of the *Financial Times*. Within minutes he had agreed with my broader macroeconomic objectives and debt restructuring proposals, expressing concern only about Europe's political will to embrace them. Afterwards I met Norman Lamont and several key economists and financiers, an event put together by Norman's friend David Marsh, head of the Official Monetary and Financial Institutions Forum, a central banking think tank. The purpose was the same: to brief them and win them over to my proposals. It seemed straight-forward, given their moderation and common sense.

My appointment with George Osborne was for 11 a.m. Greece's ambassador to London, a seriously clever man who had served as head of Greek intelligence before Roubatis, accompanied me and Euclid. Downing Street's iron gate was opened by smiling coppers, and the embassy's ageing Jaguar pulled up thirty metres or so from the door of Number 11. It was a bright but bitterly cold Monday morning. Should I wear the rather striking leather coat our ambassador in France had lent me, or should I take it off and, wearing only my light black jacket, risk shaking with cold in front of the massed photographers? Preoccupied with more substantive matters, I got out of the car as I was. For days thereafter images circulated throughout the media of a leather-clad finance minister arriving to meet George Osborne.

Before I arrived in London, Norman Lamont, who had acted as something of a go-between, had signalled that Osborne would be grateful if I refrained from criticizing his economic policies in public. 'We are in a pre-election period and the atmosphere is very sensitive,' Norman had told me.

'Given that I'm seeking George's support, I have no interest in criticizing his policies,' I replied.

In advance of our meeting, Osborne's office had explained to the press why he had good cause to hold talks with me: it was the chan-cellor's view that Greece's debt crisis posed the 'greatest risk to the global economy'.

Thanks to these preparations, the visit went perfectly smoothly. Inside 11 Downing Street the conversation was friendly and to the point. Things got interesting when Osborne began to offer a mildly critical assessment of his own handling of the British economy. I had not expected there to be any expression of self-doubt in front of a left-wing finance minister, and this facility for self-reflection warmed me to him. He acknowledged how important it had been to have the support of the Bank of England 'every step of the way', and smiled sympathetically at my predicament, which could not have been more different in that respect. He agreed that the policies imposed on Greece by the troika had given austerity a terrible name. I was tempted to share my view that his own version of austerity would backfire on him too, but good manners and determination not to push my luck stopped me. We turned instead to what we thought should be done with the euro.

Here George Osborne was in a bind. His fellow Tories despised the common currency, even those who wanted Britain to remain in the EU. Osborne had little positive to say about the euro either, but when I ventured to suggest that the disintegration of the euro would be bad for the British economy, he was not slow to agree. I shared my own sense of the dilemma: 'I find myself in the peculiar situation of constantly proposing policies for shoring up a currency whose design and creation I had opposed. But I do believe that even those of us most critical of the euro have a moral and a political duty to try to fix it, simply because its disintegration will cause so much human pain.'

Osborne's position on the euro was also something of a paradox. Despite being a Eurosceptic and an opponent of the euro he could also see that its breakdown would cause instability and unleash powerful deflationary forces upon the British economy. The only way of shielding Britain was for the euro to be saved. And the only way of saving the euro was greater integration of the eurozone, which was precisely the kind of thing that the majority of Tories doggedly opposed. By proposing radical steps to fix a currency that neither of us liked, Osborne was losing friends among Britain's Eurosceptic Right and I was losing friends among my left-wing comrades. Despite the ideological chasm that separated us, the crisis caused by Europe's ridiculous monetary architecture had put us in the same boat.

With most of the serious stuff out of the way, George, myself and Euclid sipping English breakfast tea, the discussion moved on to more light-hearted topics. Osborne saw fit to compliment me on my English.

'Thank you, George, but save your compliments until you've heard Euclid speak.' Having been raised in London, Euclid's English was that of a native. But what truly impressed George was that Euclid was an alumnus of St Paul's, the public school on the bank of the Thames that George had also attended. Once they got going it sounded like a posh school reunion. Afterwards, whenever Euclid mocked me for my Tory mates, I would remind him of his public school connections.

On our way out, I left my host with a parting thought: it would be splendid if I could have his support in Ecofin, the EU's Economic and Financial Affairs Council, in my efforts to resist the perpetuation of policies for Greece that we had agreed were absurd. Osborne nodded but when the time came did not help even once, choosing instead the Little Englander approach, never saying anything in Brussels unless it affected narrow British interests, the City's in particular. Such is its power, the City was where we were heading next, for a series of meetings with London's financiers organized by my acquaintances at Deutsche Bank. Whether I could win them over or not would be apparent the following morning on Bloomberg screens around the world. In the meantime, as Euclid and I made our way from the door of Number 11 to the Jaguar, the mass of photographers, TV cameras and journalists erupted again.

Back at the hotel for half an hour's rest before the next leg of the marathon, my mobile phone rang. 'Where on earth did you pick up that coat?' asked Danae. She was calling from Austin, where she had been alerted to my fashion statement by friends watching early-morning television.

'What's wrong with it?' I asked. 'I thought it was rather fetching, wasn't it?'

Her censure was emphatic and follows me to this day. 'I need to finish up here in Austin and return immediately,' she said.

Yes, I thought to myself. *I do need her to return as soon as possible, but for reasons that have nothing to do with style.*

Wooing the financial genie

More than two hundred representatives of all sorts of financial outfits had assembled in the large room. The Deutsche Bank functionary of Greek origin who had kindly organized the event made a brief introduction. Rather than stand at the lectern on stage, I chose to roam with a hand-held microphone. As I began, I was painfully aware of the challenge expressed so brilliantly by Ambrose Evans-Pritchard, the *Daily Telegraph's* economics editor, in one of his columns: 'Greece's plight, while terrible, is not tragic in the ancient Athenian sense: its fate is still in its own hands. With a skilful strategy, it can still all end in smiles, not tears.'

My strategy, at least in that room, was simple: tell it as it is, unembellished, complete with an admission of our own government's weaknesses. Nothing impresses financiers more than a combination of honesty and smart financial engineering.

Honesty meant that I would not beat about the bush on two issues. First, I told them, the Greek state had gone bankrupt in 2010, and no amount of austerity or new loans could change that. I could see from their faces that they were relieved to encounter a Greek finance minister who would not attempt, like all his predecessors, to present the Greek state as illiquid but on the right track towards solvency. These people knew the truth and were encouraged to hear me acknowledge it.

Second, I admitted that we had a divided cabinet; that, yes, there were those who wanted Grexit, who were not interested in negotiating with the EU and the IMF, convinced that nothing good would come of it, and who just wanted out. And then there were those of us around the prime minister whose objective was a negotiated solution within the eurozone. But, I added on a positive note, this division would not affect the negotiations, which would be conducted by my core team. Our Grexiteer colleagues would not get in the way but would be patient and give us a chance to demonstrate that a viable agreement was possible. As long as Greece's official creditors, the EU and the IMF, were willing to strike a mutually advantageous agreement, the world of finance had nothing to fear from my Left Platform colleagues in government.

Then came the financial engineering proposals summarized in my non-paper. Given the financial expertise of my audience, I spoke about them in far greater technical detail than I had done elsewhere so that they could have been in no doubt that I knew precisely what I was talking about – and that these were the kind of proposals they would have made themselves given the opportunity.

Finally, I turned to a topic close to the heart of neoliberal-minded financiers: privatization. I began by acknowledging the likelihood that many in the room, occupying the opposite end of the political spectrum to me, would disagree with my views on the merits or otherwise of privatization. But what I was sure we would agree on, I said, was that it is silly to sell assets off when prices have fallen through the floor; that fire sales to buyers who had no plans to invest but were only interested in asset-stripping were a terrible idea. Given the dire circumstances in which we found ourselves, I assured them that our government was not going to be ideological about this: if I was asked whether I was in favour of or against privatization, my answer would be, 'It depends on the asset in question – a port, a railway, a beach, an electricity company?' Beaches I would never sell, I told them, just as I would never sell the Parthenon. And the privatization of electricity grids reliably leads to environmentally and socially suboptimal outcomes. But when it came to ports and airports, I would form a view based on four criteria: how much the buyer was committing to invest in the asset; the buyer's commitment to workers' rights to union representation and decent wages and conditions; environmental standards; and the extent to which the buyer would be obliged to leave room for and encourage the benefit of small and medium local businesses. If these four criteria were met, then I would be more than happy not only to consent to privatization but also to promote it energetically.

A sea of hands was raised when I invited questions. For more than two hours I made my way around the room, answering each and every one of them. Some were hostile, others friendlier. I made a point of dealing exhaustively with them all. Judging by the warm applause at the end of the session, I felt that the job had been done.

As our hosts accompanied Euclid and me on our way out, three or four of the most influential City players in the room approached to say they were impressed. 'You will see this reflected in the markets tomorrow,' one of them assured me while shaking my hand cordially.

'In other circumstances, I would be compiling my report to the Central Committee with a recommendation that you are dispatched to the Gulag,' joked Euclid.

'Comrade, I'm happy to be sent to the Gulag for right-wing tendencies as long as the job is done – and if you promise to visit me occasionally so that I can be reminded of the expression of horror on your face just now!' I retorted.

Later that evening we were treated to dinner at the residence of our London ambassador. Norman Lamont and David Marsh were there, as was my great American supporter and adviser, Jeff Sachs, who arrived straight from Heathrow. I was pleased to have him at my side. Another of the guests was Reza Moghadam. Reza was with Morgan Stanley but, like Jeff Sachs, had previously worked at the IMF. More significantly, he had held Poul Thomsen's job there until only a year before. My conversation with him was fascinating. He confirmed everything that I had been saying about the Greek programme since 2010 – the IMF's gross error in participating in the Greek bailouts, the troika's callousness and, in particular, the sole reason that the IMF and the EU were asphyxiating us: because they did not have what it took to confess the error of their ways. As I remarked to Euclid, who had been listening with incredulity, it was one thing for us lefties to be saying all this, it was quite another to be hearing it from the horse's mouth – from the guy who had actually been implementing the Greek programme until only a few months ago.

Over coffee and after-dinner drinks I wondered if maybe my proposals had done the trick. London-based financiers, Tory politicians, influential journalists and former members of the IMF all appeared to see my point. Yes, we were a left-wing government, but all we were asking was for some basic common sense to prevail at the centre of European power.

That night the mainstream press coverage of my visits to Paris and London seemed positive. The BBC reported: 'The economist-turned-finance-minister seeking to renegotiate Greece's huge debt obligations says his priority is the well-being of all Europeans and has ruled out accepting more bailout cash . . . He said, "We have resembled drug addicts craving the next dose. What this government is all about is ending the addiction."'[7]

The message was getting through at last. But as I turned out the lights for a few hours' sleep in advance of my flight to Rome, I was anxious what the next morning would bring. Would the Athens stock exchange rebound? I desperately needed a boost in the money markets to provide a signal to investors and other EU governments that we had what it took to create a wave of optimism; to plant the idea in the minds of the EU and IMF that they would benefit from a deal with us.

An inconvenient achievement

At 8 a.m., after the first cup of coffee of the day, I received a phone call with a most peculiar message: my menu of debt-swap proposals

had received the enthusiastic approval of the Adam Smith Institute
(ASI), the think tank founded in 1977 that paved the way for Margaret
Thatcher's neoliberal project and which to my mind represented every-
thing I had opposed during my years in the UK. The statement by
ASI fellow Lars Christensen read:

> The European Central Bank's job is to ensure nominal
> stability in the eurozone economy. The ECB should not
> bail out governments and banks. Unfortunately again and
> again over the past six years the ECB has been forced to
> bail out eurozone states. Hence, the ECB has repeatedly
> conducted credit policy (rather than monetary policy) to
> avoid eurozone countries defaulting . . . By linking Greece's
> EU and ECB debts to Greek nominal GDP, as Varoufakis
> has suggested, Greece's public finances would be less
> vulnerable to monetary policy failure in the eurozone. The
> chancellor George Osborne should be an enthusiastic
> supporter of Varoufakis's debt plan as it would cut the cost
> of the ECB's tight money policies and reduce the danger
> of another major eurozone crisis.[8]

Of course it made perfect sense: swapping outstanding debt for
growth-linked bonds accompanied by a crackdown on tax evasion and
moderate budget surpluses was more a libertarian's cup of tea than
a left-winger's. As I had remarked to the City's financiers the previous
day, it was a measure of the depth of the euro crisis that it took a
radical left-wing government to table mainstream liberal proposals for
its solution.

The ASI was all well and good, but how would the markets respond?
The answer was magnificently! Bloomberg's headline could not have
been more gratifying: GREEK STOCKS GOING NUTS.

> Greek stocks are soaring Tuesday on hopes of a resolution
> to the debt standoff between Greece's new radical govern-
> ment and its creditors. As of 3.12 p.m. GMT (10.12 a.m. ET),
> the Athens Stock Exchange General Index is up 11.2 per
> cent. The news comes after Greece's new finance minister
> Yanis Varoufakis told the *Financial Times* that instead of
> requesting a write-off of its €315 billion (£237 billion; $357

billion) foreign debt, the government would ask to swap Greek debt for two new types of bonds linked to growth.

A quick phone call back to Athens confirmed the good news. Not only had the stock exchange gone up by 11.2 per cent but, more importantly, shares in Greece's banks had risen by more than 20 per cent and thousands of depositors were returning the cash under their mattresses to the bank. It was a short-term achievement but an important one: it demonstrated that our narrative of real reforms and sensible debt restructuring had the potential to win over markets and citizens.

It was time to fly to Rome.

Italian tip

I was escorted from Rome's Fiumicino airport to the finance ministry by two police cars and two motorcycles, sirens blaring. But stuck as we were in Rome's thick traffic, all our escort managed to achieve was noise pollution, irritating other road users and my own embarrassment. Creating more noise than substance, they brought Mateo Renzi's government to mind.

Pier Carlo Padoan, Italy's finance minister and formerly the OECD's chief economist, is in many ways a typical European social democrat: sympathetic to the Left but not prepared to rock the boat. He knows that the EU in its current configuration is heading in precisely the wrong direction but is only willing to push for inconsequential adjustments in its course. He has the capacity to understand the fundamental illness afflicting the eurozone but is loath to clash with Europe's chief physicians, who insist there is nothing to treat. In short, Pier Carlo Padoan is a convinced insider.

Our discussion was friendly and efficient. I explained my proposals, and he signalled that he understood what I was getting at, expressing not an iota of criticism but no support. To his credit, he explained why: when he had been appointed finance minister a few months earlier, Wolfgang Schäuble had made a point of having a go at him at every available opportunity – mostly in the Eurogroup. By the time we met, Padoan had managed to strike a modus vivendi with

Schäuble and was evidently not prepared to jeopardize it for Greece's sake.

I enquired how he had managed to curb Schäuble's hostility. Pier Carlo said that he had asked Schäuble to tell him the one thing he could do to win his confidence. That turned out to be 'labour market reform' – code for weakening workers' rights, allowing companies to fire them more easily with little or no compensation and to hire people on lower pay with fewer protections. Once Pier Carlo had passed appropriate legislation through Italy's parliament, at significant political cost to the Renzi government, the German finance minister went easy on him. 'Why don't you try something similar?' he suggested.

'I'll think about it,' I replied. 'But thanks for the tip.'

Central bank sabotage

The next morning, Wednesday, 4 February, I had set the alarm on my phone for 4 a.m. Shortly afterwards I was on a plane to Frankfurt, where my first meeting was with another Italian, Mario Draghi, president of the European Central Bank.

Frankfurt's streets were covered in black ice, and the leaden sky seemed to hover just above the car's roof. It was still morning. The surroundings of the ECB's new tower still resembled a building site, so the final approach took us along dirt roads. Euclid and I were greeted at the door by several functionaries and whisked to the top floor in an express lift. The newness was potent, the views from large glass windows a relief from the smell of paint.

In the boardroom the ECB's top guns had gathered. Benoît Cœuré, whom I had met in Paris a few days earlier, was the only one sporting a friendly smile. Mario Draghi looked tense, while the two Germans on the ECB Executive Board, Peter Praet and Sabine Lautenschläger, were reserved in their greeting. They all sat down one side of a long table opposite me – Euclid to my left, the view over Frankfurt behind them – and I was invited to open proceedings with a statement of intent.

Mindful of the importance of brevity, I began by introducing my government's priorities and intentions vis-à-vis the Greek programme, and then, in no more than ten minutes, outlined our sequence of proposals: debt restructuring based on debt swaps that financiers the world over considered sensible and proper, a primary budget surplus of 1.5 per cent in perpetuity, a development bank to replace fire sales, a public 'bad bank' to deal with the banks' non-performing loans, deep reforms in various markets and so on. As I concluded, I handed Mario Draghi the non-paper summarizing my debt-swap proposal.

Draghi began his reply with a brief speech on the ECB's independence and his determination to play no role in the politics of the negotiations between my government and other eurozone states, emphasizing the prohibition that prevents the ECB from 'monetary financing' via the commercial banks. 'And I must tell you that recent developments in Greece are putting us in a difficult position,' he informed me ominously. 'Later today our governing board is meeting and it is very likely that your waiver will be withdrawn.'

The waiver was what allowed the ECB to provide our banks with liquidity in return for junk collateral.[9] It could be provided only if the Eurogroup consented – a purely political decision and one that amounted to 'monetary financing' despite Draghi's protestations to the contrary. Withdrawing the waiver was the first of the two steps required to close down Greece's banks; the second would be switching off emergency liquidity assistance. Draghi pointedly refrained from revealing whether he agreed with the withdrawal or not; he was merely warning me that he would not be surprised if a majority of board members supported it.

So there I had it: within a few sentences of his welcoming remarks, Mario Draghi was signalling a commitment to escalating the asphyxiation that the ECB and Greece's central bank governor had begun before we were elected. It was an explicit, calculated act of aggression.

I began my reply by expressing my great and genuine respect for the manner in which Draghi had striven from the first day of his presidency to do whatever it took to save the euro while adhering as far as possible to his bank's charter and rules. This skilful balancing act was what had bought Europe's politicians the time they needed to get their act together, address the crisis properly, and thus alleviate the impossible circumstances in which the ECB had found itself: responsible for saving the eurozone's failing economies while being prohibited from using the essential means – ones available to any normal central bank – of doing so.

'Alas, the politicians did not use the time you bought for us wisely, did they?' I said. The expression on Mario's face conveyed embarrassed agreement. I continued:

You have done a fantastic job in keeping the eurozone together as well as in keeping Greece in the euro, especially in the summer of 2012. What I am here to put to you today is that you continue to do this during the next few months, granting us politicians the time and monetary space necessary to strike a workable deal between Greece and the Eurogroup; one that ends the Greek crisis once and for all, thus enabling you fully to respect your independence and your rulebook vis-à-vis Greece, while we politicians get down to the business of healing our country's wounds through policies that bring a sustainable, real recovery. But none of this will happen unless we have your support.

Two days ago I went to London to soothe the nerves of the City, to create trust and to reverse the negative 'recent developments' that you mentioned. It was a great success. As you know, Mario, yesterday the banks' shares and the Athens Stock Exchange rose sharply. I would have thought that it is a central bank's duty to help a finance minister reinforce such a boost in market confidence, rather than to reverse it. If the ECB today removes the waiver it will be tantamount to destroying the market optimism that I worked so hard in London to create.

I sensed Mario was put out by the charge against him – that he was about to undo an improvement in market sentiment by resorting to legalisms. A prerequisite for the waiver was an ongoing programme, he said, triggering a bitter exchange.

'Your government is not committing to the existing programme,' he told me, echoing Jeroen Dijsselbloem.

'All we are doing is seeking to renegotiate the programme to make it viable,' I retorted.

'It will be expiring in any case on 28 February.'

'Fine. Why don't you wait until after the next Eurogroup meeting [scheduled for Wednesday, 11 February] before you pull the waiver and undo the good work I did in London? Mario, we won government with only four weeks in which to renegotiate the programme. This deadline is so short as to be ridiculous. But to have it curtailed today by three weeks [by] our central bank is unacceptable.'

'It does not matter much, Yanis, *when* we pull the waiver since the Greek banks have run out of most eligible collateral.' He spoke as if the waiver decision was inevitable, beyond his control, an act of God.

If it did not matter when they pulled the waiver, I argued, then there was no need to do it that very afternoon. 'Why not wait for the Eurogroup meeting only a few days away? Why snuff out the gains I just made in London?'

His only comeback was to insist that it was not he who was proposing the waiver be removed, implying again that it was out of his hands.

At this point I could have lambasted the president of Europe's central bank for washing his hands of a major decision taken by his own board that would destroy precisely the thing that central banks were created to shore up: market confidence. But I did not, partly because there was a slim chance that he did oppose the waiver's removal but was unable to stop it. Instead I told him that I trusted he would be able to prevail upon the ECB Governing Council to keep the waiver and thus not jeopardize yesterday's Athens stock exchange revival, just as I trusted that he would support my debt restructuring proposals. 'I am saying this here, at the ECB, because it is in this building not in Brussels that Europe has the experts capable of understanding and supporting them.'

The first item in my non-paper was the proposal to swap the SMP bonds held by the ECB for a new Greek government perpetual bond. This was sensitive ground. The SMP bonds were, as we both knew, the backbone of my deterrence strategy and his Achilles heel. If Greece unilaterally wrote them down, we would in all probability wreck his quantitative easing programme. I wondered what he would have to say about them.

His tactic was to skirt around the issue, dismissing the idea of a swap as a form of 'monetary financing' and therefore impossible. I begged to differ: a write-down might, I conceded, be interpreted strictly as an indirect form of monetary financing, but my proposal was for swapping one kind of debt (short term) for another (infinitely long dated). The Greek government would continue to owe the ECB €27 billion, but instead of repaying that capital within a few years it would undertake to make regular if small interest payments to the ECB ad infinitum. No write-down, no monetary financing. 'This is something that the authors of the ECB rules could not have banned simply because they had never considered it,' I concluded.

Unexpected help came from Benoît Cœuré. He turned to Draghi
to say that my proposal had merit and should not be dismissed. Even
if the ECB was reluctant to accept a new Greek perpetual bond in
return for its remaining SMP bonds, maybe we could 'triangulate':
the European Stability Mechanism (ESM), the EU's bailout fund, could
give €27 billion in cash to the ECB in order to redeem the SMP bonds,
while Greece could issue its perpetual bond, with a face value of €27
billion, and give it to the ESM. I immediately recognized a further
merit of Benoît's idea, which was that by leaving no Greek bonds on
the ECB's books (perpetual or SMP), Greece would qualify for Draghi's
forthcoming round of quantitative easing.[10]

Quickly changing the subject, Draghi complained that my public
comments about the insolvency of the Greek banks were making it
hard for him to keep them open, given that his rulebook banned him
from keeping insolvent banks afloat. I responded by pointing out that
the waiver the Greek banks had been granted was itself a clear admission that they were insolvent; why grant it otherwise? The problem
was that this temporary fix had become permanent as a result of our
collective failure to deal with the underlying insolvency. 'Surely our
task now is to end the death embrace, the doom loop, between insolvent banks – that the ECB is forced to keep afloat against its rules –
and an insolvent state at which Europe's taxpayers keep throwing
good money after bad?'

Peter Praet and Sabine Lautenschläger, sitting on Mario's left, looked
aghast, not because what I was saying was preposterous but – I am
convinced – because it was very close to their own criticism of the Greek
bailouts and the ECB's role in them. Praet began to question me on
privatizations. I gave the same answers as I had in London when addressing
my City friends. They seemed satisfied with the argument but unhappy
with the reality on the ground in Greece – my feelings entirely! After a
few more questions and a short statement from Euclid, which was a little
more combative than mine, the meeting drew to a close.

As we were leaving, Mario approached me and together we left the
boardroom. Walking along a corridor, away from others' ears, he
attempted to mollify me on the issue of the possible withdrawal of
our waiver by the ECB's Governing Council that afternoon. I would
have none of it.

'Mario, I shall hold you personally responsible if the waiver is
removed on the day after I pushed the banks' shares up by 20 per

cent. If you do this it will be a first in the history of central banking –
a central bank working to undermine a finance minister's success at
improving market sentiment.'

Draghi looked coy. Again, he protested that it was really not up to
him; that he did not control the ECB Governing Council. Once more
he argued that I was not helping him keep the waiver by continuing
to speak of his Achilles heel, the possibility of a unilateral haircut of
the SMP bonds.

All I wanted was for us to work together, I reassured him. 'Not
only will I not haircut those bonds unilaterally, I will not even think
of it – as long as you do not close down our banks,' I promised.

'I will do my best,' he replied. 'But it is not always up to me.'

Time and again since the euro crisis began, I have had to correct
the fundamental misconception that it is a tussle between Germans
and Greeks, north and south, between a stingy Berlin and a profligate
European periphery. On the contrary, the enemies of European solidarity, rationality and enlightenment reside in Greece, in Germany, in
Italy – everywhere. And the same is true of their defenders.

After the ECB meeting a couple of media engagements kept me
in Frankfurt for a few hours. During that time I was accompanied by
four German secret service bodyguards, two walking ahead, two
trailing a few steps behind. Whenever we took cars, they would get
in last and alight first to size up the surroundings. Unsmiling and
intense, with their crew cuts, earpieces, microphone cufflinks, rubber
boots and subtle uniforms, they were impervious to my objections to
their constant presence.

When my interviews were done, they took me to the airport, where
they continued to do their thing, silently, efficiently, as I made my way
through to catch my flight to Berlin. Before boarding the plane I asked
for permission to go to the loo. One of them, obviously the team
leader, followed me inside, standing too close for comfort. But I knew
he was just following orders so I relaxed, and soon I was washing my
hands and on my way out.

Before we reached the other three bodyguards, who were waiting
by the gate, he spoke for the first time. In very good English he asked
permission to address me. 'Of course,' I said.

'Minister,' he said, 'I want you to know that what you are doing is
very important – not only for your country but also for us. You are
giving us hope that there is a chance that we shall be liberated too.'

Whenever I hear people, including friends and supporters, tell me that Europe is finished, that there can be no common path for Germans, Brits, Italians and Greeks, I reach into my memory to retrieve the words of that German secret service officer.

It's for you!

Soon after landing in Berlin I was scheduled to have a secret dinner with Jörg Asmussen and Jeromin Zettelmeyer. Asmussen was the junior minister for labour affairs, but a key figure in the German political system with close contacts at the ECB, where he had been a member of the Executive Board until a year before, and a power broker within the Social Democrats (SPD), the federal government's junior coalition partners. Zettelmeyer worked directly for Sigmar Gabriel, the vice chancellor of the federal government, economy minister and SPD leader. The purpose of the dinner was ostensibly to build bridges between the Syriza government and the section of the German government controlled by the Social Democrats. They presented themselves as our allies and supporters within the Berlin administration, offering me advice and protection from the 'big bad wolf', as one of them jokingly referred to Wolfgang Schäuble.

The agreement was that I would go to the restaurant alone, incognito and by cab, and that I would not tell anyone we were meeting. The implication was that it would backfire on all of us if word leaked. 'Let's keep this just among ourselves,' Jeromin had said to me on the phone. Of course the fact that he called my mobile meant that it was already quasi-public knowledge – as Yannis Roubatis, our government's head spook, had explained to me. Just as I was ready to leave my hotel room, I received an email from Jeromin telling me that they had changed the restaurant booking because the original choice was 'too public', confirming once more the importance of discretion. Partly because of this emphasis on secrecy, and partly because I was exhausted and looking forward to disconnecting for a couple of hours, I left my mobile phone in my room.

I found a taxi in a cold dark street nearby and gave the driver the address of the out-of-the-way pizzeria where we were now meeting. On arrival, as per my instructions, I walked upstairs to the first floor, which had been reserved just for us. Over pizza and red wine a friendly discussion developed.

Jörg and Jeromin spoke to me like friends, comrades even. It was becoming a pattern among social democrats, I thought, recalling my encounter with Michel Sapin. The objective, as they put it, was to create a common Syriza–SPD agenda sophisticated and sensible enough to make it hard for Angela Merkel and Wolfgang Schäuble – their Christian Democrat colleagues in government but political opponents in general – to oppose. It sounded good to me. Too good, to be honest. Then again, if a decent agreement could be hammered out with Jörg's and Jeromin's help, fine. If not, what did I have to lose?

As our discussion drifted from one topic to another, the basic plan I was proposing seemed to satisfy them. The question that preoccupied them was what objections the Christian Democrats would make and how these could be addressed. The more we talked the more I felt as if I was having dinner with a pair of consultants working for my government. Until, that is, Jörg's phone rang. He answered it, put the phone to his ear, then looked at me seriously and, without speaking a single word into the phone, said, 'It's for you. Mario wants to speak to you.'

So much for the secrecy of our meeting. *These people don't even try to keep up the pretence*, I thought to myself. I got up, took Jörg's phone and walked out into the dark corridor above the pizzeria's kitchen, immersed in pleasant smells and noises.

'Hello, Mario, what can I do for you?'

'I wanted to let you know, Yanis,' Draghi said in a steady voice, 'before you learn it from the media, that as I foreshadowed this morning, the Governing Council voted to withdraw your banks' waiver. But this does not mean much since your banks will continue to be supported by your central bank via emergency liquidity assistance.'

'I appreciate you going through all sorts of interesting channels to find me and inform me in person, Mario,' I said. 'Since you are giving me the opportunity to respond in person on the telephone, allow me to say that this decision – the withdrawal of the waiver a day after I single-handedly lifted the banks' shares and reversed the bank run, a week after our election, indeed a week *before* my first Eurogroup meeting, and three whole weeks before the expiry of the programme extension – can only be interpreted as a hostile, deeply political move by the ECB against my government.'

Draghi made a faint attempt to deny that there was anything political about this move but I would have none of it. It was a decision, I told him, that would be interpreted in Athens as an unwarranted, over-hasty and aggressive move concerted with the Eurogroup president's ultimatum.

When I returned to the table I found Jörg and Jeromin in a different mood. I put on a brave face, pretending that nothing much had happened, but of course they knew better. Gone was the atmosphere of comradeship, of sharing in a joint project to rejig the Greek programme against Schäuble and Merkel's designs. So I stopped pretending and let them have my assessment of the ECB's decision. Asmussen replied as if he was still on the ECB's Executive Board, whispering unconvincing excuses. All the heroic talk of a Syriza–SPD collaboration had evaporated with a single phone call that exposed the whole dinner for what it was: a clumsy set-up.

They were not bad people either

I returned to my hotel at around midnight, switched on my phone and called Alexis to tell him Draghi had pulled the waiver.

'Be uncompromising but see if Gabriel can be of any help,' he advised me sounding unperturbed.

'Judging by his two messengers last night, Alexi, I am not hopeful,' I said. We needed to signal persistently our determination to activate our deterrent the moment they pulled the ELA on our banks, I told him.

'Get some sleep now. You have to be fresh for Schäuble,' Alexis replied light-heartedly.

First I had to write a press release to soften the blow of the waiver withdrawal. The happy task of the finance minister, I ruminated: packaging a shock as a non-event.

Meanwhile, upon hearing the news, the ever-vigilant and helpful Glenn Kim sent me an email with his analysis of its immediate financial effects. It confirmed that even before the stock exchange opened or depositors had a chance to make fresh withdrawals, the banks would take a major hit.[11] My task was to pen a statement that on the one hand hinted at my intense disapproval of the ECB's aggression while at the same time it steadied nerves, minimized the inevitable sharp turn in market sentiment and preserved some of the gains I had made in London.

Anticipating that when I went to see Schäuble the following day I would be accosted outside the federal finance ministry by journalists demanding a reaction to the ECB move, I prepared the following statement.

> The ECB is basically trying to abide by its own rules, motivating both us and our partners to reach a political and technical agreement quickly, while keeping the Greek banks liquid. I trust that Greek depositors understand that day-to-day stability is guaranteed and that we are negotiating new terms that will bring recovery and a permanent solution. To us, the timing of the ECB decision was particularly surprising as it risks creating an unnecessary sense of urgency, given that we had until 28 February before the current Greek programme expires. I trust that the hasty decision was due to the timing of the ECB Governing Council's regular 'non monetary policy' meeting yesterday. From their point of view, it was probably the right timing.

It was all I could do. Of course, in the event the stock exchange fell, the banks' shares dropped and the deposit outflows resumed. Some of the previous day's gains were preserved but it was only a matter of a day or two before the withdrawal wiped those out as well. The only silver lining was that none of this would matter in the medium term. The real issue was whether Berlin could be persuaded to compromise, or would an all-out confrontation be necessary, as I had been expecting since 2012.

On the way to the federal finance ministry I noticed two emails had arrived on my phone. One was from Jamie Galbraith informing me that Bernie Sanders was about to write to Janet Yellen, the US Federal Reserve chair, to ask her to indicate to the ECB that its behaviour had been appalling and ultimately globally destabilizing. The second email was from Glenn. This was a brief on Wolfgang Schäuble, for whose office Glenn had consulted in his previous life. Typically for a financier's brief, it came in bullet points:

He is a lawyer through and through.

His command of economics is quite weak. I can recall on more than one occasion him mixing up yields and prices and making references to financials without understanding what they mean.

Absolutely hates the markets. Thinks that markets should be controlled by technocrats.

He practically relishes being the bad cop.

But:

He is also an ardent Europeanist.

He believes in the destiny of a German-like Europe (though unable to grasp the contradiction in such a term).

He is someone that can be debated with.

Hostility was in evidence even before I met the great man. I was met on the ground floor of the Federal Ministry of Finance by a junior minister. Before getting into the lift, he asked me playfully, but with enough of a hint of aggression to establish that he was not actually joking, 'When am I getting my money back?' I was tempted to reply, 'When you persuade Deutsche Bank to return it to you.' I said nothing, smiling widely, my mind on the main game.

The lift door opened onto a long cold corridor at the end of which Wolfgang Schäuble was waiting in his wheelchair. This was a man whose speeches and articles I had been reading and following for two and a half decades. I fully understood that to him I was a damned nuisance, but the smile on my face and the hand I extended towards him were meant with genuine respect and in the secret hope that we might establish a decent, civilized modus vivendi. Strangely, that wish was granted in the end, despite the awfulness of what happened next: refusing my offer of a handshake, Germany's federal minister of finance performed a swift U-turn in his wheelchair and propelled himself at impressive speed towards his office, commanding me to follow with a wave of his hand – which of course I did, Euclid rushing behind me to keep up.

Once inside his office, my host relaxed, his expression turning kinder. We sat around the customary conference table, he with two junior ministers at his side opposite Euclid, our Berlin ambassador and myself. As always, I was invited to make an opening statement. I gave a variant of the same speech I had given in my meetings with Sapin, Osborne, Padoan and Draghi. The difference was an emphasis on two points that I knew resonated powerfully in Berlin. First, I was not asking for a debt write-down, and I made clear that the overall utility of my debt-swap proposals would benefit Germany as well as Greece. Second, I stressed the importance I placed on catching tax cheats and effecting reforms that would encourage entrepreneurship, creativity and probity across Greek society.

Schäuble's opening line was friendly enough, insisting that we address each other by first name. But immediately thereafter he proceeded to make clear that he had no interest in anything I had just said. Instead, unable to resist the opportunity to suggest German probity and Greek delinquency, he offered to send five hundred German tax officials to Greece to help catch the evaders. I told him that I very much appreciated his generosity but expressed concern that, finding themselves unable to read Greek tax returns or the associated documentation and therefore incapable of auditing our taxpayers, his officials might become disheartened. I had a better idea: why didn't he appoint the general secretary of my ministry's tax office?

My suggestion startled him visibly. So I continued. Thanks to the troika, I explained, I was responsible for the tax office but had no control over it; the person in charge of it was neither appointed by nor answerable to me or my parliament, even though I was accountable for her actions. My proposal was as follows: he would choose a German tax administrator of unimpeachable credentials and spotless reputation to be appointed immediately and to be fully accountable to the both of us, and if she or he required additional support from his ministry, that was fine by me. 'I know you don't like dealing with me or with my government,' I told him. 'But, be that as it may, you can rest assured that in me you have a genuine ally in the fight against tax evasion.' Finally, I informed him of the plan I had put in place to create an algorithmic method of identifying tax evaders between 2000 and 2014.

It was not what Dr Schäuble had expected. But two things showed his determination to avoid any serious engagement with this proposal either. First, he proceeded to change the subject, away from this potentially fruitful discussion, before we had a chance to strike an impressive deal on fighting tax evasion in Greece, never to return to it. Second was the topic he chose to turn to instead: his theory that the 'overgenerous' European social model was no longer sustainable and had to be ditched. Comparing the costs to Europe of maintaining welfare states with the situation in places like India and China, where no social safety net exists at all, he argued that Europe was losing competitiveness and would stagnate unless social benefits were curtailed en masse. It was as if he was telling me that a start had to be made somewhere and that that somewhere might as well be Greece.

My rejoinder was that the obvious solution was the globalization of welfare benefits and living wages, rather than the globalization of insecure working poverty. In response, he reminisced at length about a secret mission he had undertaken in the 1970s and 1980s, to liaise with the East German authorities on behalf of his Christian Democrat party. 'The DDR people were not bad,' he told me. 'They had good intentions for a social welfare system that was not economically possible.' The insinuation was perfectly clear.

'Are you comparing me with a well-meaning DDR minister trying to sustain an unsustainable political and economic system?' I asked. 'Let me reassure you, Wolfgang, that despite what your friends in Greece may have told you, I am a committed democrat, a determined pluralist and an unwavering Europeanist. And so are my Syriza party colleagues. We have as much in common with the DDR's ways and means as the CDU has with Pinochet's regime: nothing whatsoever![12] As for our proposals regarding pensions and welfare benefits, they are part and parcel of a broader fiscal policy yielding small but *positive* budget primary surpluses. Fiscal and economic sustainability is our number-one priority. Greeks have had enough of living on deficits.'

In response he backpedalled, protesting that he had not intended to make such a comparison at all.

Go to the institutions!

With this unfortunate misunderstanding behind us, I channelled the conversation back to debt restructuring and my debt-swap proposals. Schäuble did not even glance at my non-paper. He passed it to his junior minister with an air of scorn saying that it was a matter for the 'institutions' – the very word I had used at my joint press conference with Jeroen Dijsselbloem in Athens, suggesting that even the German finance minister now felt uncomfortable with the term 'troika'. This would be Berlin's standard tactic throughout. Whenever we put a proposal to Chancellor Merkel or Minister Schäuble – on debt, privatizations, pensions, tax evasion and so on – they would simply refer us to the 'institutions'. The implication was that there would be no negotiation between Berlin and Athens; it was simply not their job.[13]

At this point Euclid made an excellent intervention. On the German side, no one other than Wolfgang had spoken. In elegantly structured sentences Euclid pointed out the irresponsibility of leaving matters of great political importance to technocrats with a proven record of mishandling the Greek fiscal, debt and social crisis, revealing the absurdity of Schäuble's response. It was wonderful to have Euclid on my side, upping the ante and allowing me to make a placatory suggestion. If I were to go to the 'institutions' with my proposals, to have any chance of hammering out a workable deal it would be in everyone's interest to allow for a period of 'peace and quiet', of financial stability. Wolfgang nodded as if in agreement.

This was in contrast to the Eurogroup president's attitude. I described how he had threatened me with bank closures, in my office, a mere three days after I had moved into it. 'Not exactly a convivial move,' I said dryly.

Wolfgang reacted angrily. 'He had no reason to go to Greece. He had no mandate.'

Not a man to fake emotion, Schäuble convinced me that Dijsselbloem must have acted alone. If he had done so in the hope of an easy win on his master's behalf, it was fair to say that he had failed: his master was evidently not pleased.

Stunned by the reproach, aghast at the praise

At the customary press conference afterwards Wolfgang adopted his stern public persona, telling the gathered media that we had had a cordial meeting during which he had 'explained' that Greece had 'obligations' that must be respected regardless of which party was in government.

'We agreed to disagree,' Schäuble said, dispelling any notion that our discussion had reached any common ground.

'We did not even agree on that,' I interjected.

I wanted to make clear that my host had been unwilling to debate anything, but also that things had changed: Greece now had a minister of finance who would not be pushed around just because the Greek state was insolvent. Having established this, I made a statement aimed at healing the rift that was developing between ordinary Germans and Greeks. 'Some are tempted to imagine that the solution lies in the separation of our peoples,' I said.

> Thankfully, today I did not just visit the finance minister of Europe's powerhouse economy. Above all else, I visited a European statesman for whom European unity is a lifelong project and whose work and efforts to unify Europe I have been following with great interest since the 1980s. Today, my message to Minister Schäuble was that in this government he has a potential partner in the search for European solutions to a variety of problems afflicting not only Greece but the union more broadly.

Turning to my host, I said,

> From our government you can expect a frenzy of reasonableness. You can expect proposals that are aimed not at the interest of the average Greek but at the interest of the average European – the average German, Slovak, Finn, Spaniard, Italian. You can expect from us an unwavering commitment to telling it as it is, without tactical stratagems or subterfuge. These are our commitments. What we request is perhaps the most precious of commodities: time. A short space of time during which our government can present to our partners, to the IMF, to the ECB, to the European Commission, comprehensive proposals and a road map for the very short term, for the medium term, and for the long term.

On the challenges facing the EU more generally, I suggested that we respect established treaties and processes without crushing the delicate bud of democracy. When I visited Paris, I said, I had told the French minister of finance that it had felt like a homecoming, that I was returning to one of Greece's spiritual homes. In Berlin I expressed the same feeling and described how for almost two centuries the land of Goethe, Beethoven, Hegel and Kant had been a source of inspiration to Greeks across the political spectrum. But there was something more that bound Greece and Germany together, I continued.

> As finance minister in a government facing emergency circumstances caused by a savage debt-deflationary crisis, I feel that the German nation is the one that can understand us better than anyone else. No one understands better than the people of this land how a severely depressed economy combined with ritual national humiliation and unending hopelessness can hatch the serpent's egg within one's society. When I return to Athens tonight, I shall find myself in a parliament in which the third-largest party is a Nazi one. When our prime minister laid a wreath at an iconic memorial site in Athens immediately after his swearing-in, that was an act of defiance against the resurgence of Nazism.[14] Germany can be proud of the way Nazism has been eradicated here. But it is one of history's cruel ironies that Nazism is rearing its ugly head in Greece, a country which put up such a fine struggle against it in the 1940s. We need the people of Germany to help us in the struggle against misanthropy. We need our friends in this country to remain steadfast in Europe's postwar project; that is, never again to allow a 1930s-like depression to divide proud European nations. We shall do our duty in this regard. And I am convinced that so will our European partners.

The next day the German press lambasted me for having dared to mention the Nazis in front of the German finance minister in Göring's old Air Ministry building. Meanwhile Greek nationalists were praising me for having called Schäuble a Nazi. I was not sure whether I should be more appalled by the praise or by the reproach.

Siemens

After our statements Wolfgang and I took questions. One of them concerned Siemens, the German conglomerate, and a man called Michael Christoforakos who used to head their operations in Greece. Some years earlier a scandal had occurred when an investigation initiated in the United States suggested that Christoforakos had been bribing Greek politicians to secure government contracts on behalf of Siemens. Soon after the Greek authorities began investigating the matter, Christoforakos absconded to Germany, where he was arrested. But the German courts were preventing his extradition to Athens.

'Did you, Minister,' asked a journalist, 'impress upon your German colleague the German state's obligation to help the Greek government snuff out corruption by extraditing Mr Christoforakos to Greece?'

I tried to provide a balanced and reasonable answer: 'I am sure that the German authorities will understand the importance of assisting our troubled state in its struggle against corruption in Greece. I trust that my colleagues in Germany understand the importance of not being seen to have double standards anywhere in Europe.'

And what did Dr Schäuble say in reply? Looking put out, he mumbled that this was not a matter for his finance ministry. Maybe it was not. But the Siemens case and Schäuble's willingness to wash his hands of the problem illuminate the underlying challenge that Greece and all Europe faces.

As I have frequently observed, there is a widespread belief in Europe's north that the continent is populated by hard-working law-abiding ants on the one hand and lazy tax-avoiding grasshoppers on the other, and that all the ants live in the north while mysteriously the grasshoppers congregate in the south. The reality is much more muddled and sinister. Corruption takes place across borders, in both north and south. It involves multinational corporations whose connections to the deep establishment are not contained by national boundaries either. Part of what prevents us from tackling this mighty network is a refusal on the part of the establishment to acknowledge its true nature. When Christoforakos was indicted for stuffing bribes into politicians' pockets, I was not surprised: by a remarkable coincidence, my own uncle resigned from the same post at Siemens in the late 1970s when he found himself being pressurized to do precisely the same thing. Along with millions of Greeks, I was outraged that the German authorities refused to extradite Christoforakos so that he could face charges in Greece. I was even more horrified that in Athens Stournaras, my former friend who was then minister of finance, tabled in Parliament on 28 August 2012 an out-of-court settlement with Siemens that ended all prosecution of the company and paved the ground for not just Christoforakos but also the Greek politicians whose pockets he had been accused of lining to escape trial.

My press conference with Schäuble turned out to be the beginning of a hostile media campaign. Especially in Germany, I was portrayed as an anti-German, reform-denying, narcissistic defender of Greek graft and inefficiency. Eventually, through sheer repetition, the mud stuck. Months later, after my resignation, Euclid would be portrayed as the sensible, responsible, understated minister who put the negotiations back on the rails and saved Greece from my amateurish recalcitrance. But Euclid and Alexis were actually being rewarded for the end of any serious challenge not only to Bailoutistan but also to the network that binds companies like Siemens to banks and politicians in both Greece and Germany.

As these lines are being written, Michael Christoforakos continues to live freely in Germany, Stournaras continues as governor of Greece's central bank, the Siemens scandal has still not resulted in a single politician facing charges, Dr Schäuble and Euclid continue the non-negotiations that confine Greece ever more securely in its debtors' prison and, amazingly, a charge of high treason is pending in Greece's parliament – against me.

Social democracy's Waterloo

After Wolfgang Schäuble it was the turn of Sigmar Gabriel to host me at his Economy Ministry. Almost everyone expected this to be my soft landing, the agreeable social democratic vice chancellor and leader of the SPD consoling me after what was always going to be a bloody affair at the Ministry of Finance. But I harboured no such expectations, and not just because of the previous night's set-up involving Gabriel's envoys, Jörg and Jeromin.

The meeting at Gabriel's office, with Jörg, Jeromin, Euclid and our Berlin ambassador also present, went splendidly. It was almost a carbon copy of my meeting with Michel Sapin a few days earlier in Paris. The same platitudes were aired, the same vows of undying solidarity. 'Your success will be our success,' Sigmar told me early on in the meeting. He added, without my prompting, that what had been done to Greece was sinful and would stigmatize Europe for a long time, blaming it on the Christian Democrats' domination of EU politics at the time of the 2010 euro crisis. When I suggested that our government's election was an opportunity for Europe to get its act together, not just in the context of the Greek drama but by redeploying existing institutions to procure the macroeconomic stability necessary to fend off the rise of nationalism, right-wing populism and xenophobia, Gabriel looked positively overjoyed. He even listened intently while I explained the basic elements of our *Modest Proposal*, promising to look into them in detail.

Then the conversation moved to matters specifically Greek. I made my pitch for debt-swap operations, handing over my non-paper. He seemed well disposed and even went so far as to say that a debt restructuring was long overdue. But his preference was to focus on tax evasion and industrial development. That was fine by me, as it gave me the opportunity to explain what I was trying to do with my team of untouchables and their algorithmic pursuit of tax cheats, as well as my plans for a development bank that would use Greece's remaining public assets to elicit homegrown investment as part of an industrial policy targeting Greece's most promising sectors.

Gabriel seemed satisfied with the direction of the conversation but wanted to raise a practical point. While yachting in Greece the previous summer he had been appalled at how difficult it was upon mooring his yacht in almost any of the island harbours to pay his mooring fees. He would approach the coastguard officer in charge only to be told, 'It's OK. There's no hurry – give me whatever you wish,' with no receipt for payment or indeed any sign of due process.

I agreed that informality used to cover up petty corruption, which cumulatively affects the economy and society as a whole, was a major problem that my ministry simply had no resources to address. I also related to Gabriel how in the summer of 2014 the number of people arriving in Mykonos and Santorini, the two Cycladic islands most popular with tourists, had doubled, and yet during the same period VAT receipts had declined by 40 per cent. When I put this scandalous situation to the man heading my ministry's Economic Crime Fighting Unit, I was told that as a result of years of austerity cuts and attempts by the troika to sideline the ECFU, his staff had been reduced to no more than one hundred people for the whole of Greece. When he dispatched officers to Mykonos or Santorini, the culprits would get word that they were heading their way even before their ferry boat had left Piraeus harbour.

To get to the bottom of these corrupt practices, I told Gabriel, we needed innovative methods that put the fear of God into tax cheats. He agreed and suggested that probity would return only if proprietors were worried their next customer might be working for the tax office. I told him that I was already considering authorizing the tax office to employ outside personnel whose job would be to pose as regular customers at bars, restaurants, petrol stations, doctors' surgeries and the like. Lacking enforcement authority, their job would simply be to record transactions electronically so that the authorities could then work out if there were grounds for investigation or prosecution. Once the word spread that the tax office had eyes that saw and ears that heard, a gigantic amount of petty tax evasion would end, with tremendous benefits to the state's finances. Gabriel was keen on the idea, and as we were walking to the press room for yet another joint press conference put his arm around me and encouraged me to implement it.

Once at our respective lecterns in front of the cameras, the microphones and assorted journalists, it was déjà vu. More specifically, it was Paris all over again. Gabriel was a changed man. Once again a European social democrat attempted to out-Schäuble Schäuble in public. All the talk about a joint social democratic project for Greece and Europe vanished. The common ground we had established on industrial policy, ending austerity and debt restructuring gave way beneath my feet. The meeting of minds regarding strategies for tackling tax evasion evaporated. All was replaced with aggression towards my government and a harsh lecture on my obligations to our creditors, which were paramount and beyond negotiation. To add insult to injury, he added a reference to the troika's 'flexibility'.

With my by-now outstandingly low expectations of Europe's social democrats further downgraded by my previous night's experience with Jörg and Jeromin, I continued unperturbed and gave my standard spiel about our government's quest for sustainability by means of moderate proposals to recalibrate radically the troika's failed Greek programme. But as we were leaving the press room, I asked Sigmar how easy it was for him to say one thing in private and quite another in public. 'It is something that I'm finding very hard,' I added.

He claimed not to understand what I was referring to but did say that being in coalition with the Christian Democrats was constraining. I responded that he should learn the lesson of PASOK, the Greek social democratic party, which had had a similar habit of adapting their narrative to suit their coalition with the New Democracy conservatives. 'They crashed from 40 per cent to 4 per cent. I would not want to see the party of Willy Brandt go the same way' were my last words to him.[5]

A month later I proposed to the 'institutions' the idea of Greece's tax department employing outside personnel in an attempt to shift Greek social norms away from habitual petty tax evasion – just as I had discussed with Sigmar Gabriel that day. This was just one of many reforms to the tax office that I put forward, the most important being enforced digitization of transactions and a limit of fifty euros on cash dealings. Troika officials leaked the proposal to the press, which went to town. Instead of the serious reforms demanded by the troika (such as raising VAT rates in a broken economy where people evaded VAT), I was portrayed as putting forward foolish proposals involving wired-up tourists and housewives encouraging Greeks to snitch on their neighbours.

Did Sigmar Gabriel or any in his circle defend the proposal that he had seemed so keen to see me implement? The answer may not surprise you. If anything, his office helped spread the propaganda. If anyone wonders about the nature and causes of the general Waterloo now facing European social democracy, this story may provide some clues. Of course, compared to the way Sigmar Gabriel was to behave four months later, during the last week of June 2015, this change of heart does not even register on the Richter scale of cowardice.

8

The frenzy before the storm

I returned to Athens late on Thursday night. My first Eurogroup meeting was scheduled for the following Wednesday (11 February). We had a long weekend in which to prepare.

For three days and nights the sixth floor of the ministry teemed with a group of people sent by Lazard and my own close associates, which included Glenn Kim, Elena Panariti, former PhD students and other technical experts who had volunteered to help. At the top of the agenda were three crucial documents that had to be tabled at the Eurogroup: an up-to-date debt sustainability analysis (DSA) demonstrating how the debt swaps I was proposing were not only consistent with recovery but indispensable for returning Greece to sustainable growth; a list of proper, progressive reforms to replace the troika's programme; and a proposal for a more rational and efficient process for monitoring Greece's progress. At the same time Jamie Galbraith arrived from the United States and took up residence in a small office hidden within the ministerial suite. I greeted him with a hug and the words, 'Welcome to the poisoned chalice.'[1, 2]

The quality and volume of everyone's work was impressive and the source of great optimism. But to put together a comprehensive policy document for nationwide reform, the team required input from the other ministries too. Early on Friday morning I had put a call out to each of my cabinet colleagues, asking them to send through a complete set of the reforms they were planning to implement. Once they had arrived on the sixth floor, the team assessed these contributions and came to see me in my office. It was not looking good. Most were simply slightly edited versions of Syriza's pre-election policy proposals, half-baked and badly written up. We would need to put a great deal of work into them before they were presentable in Brussels. Of course that was as it should be: we were a new government and needed what most new governments need – a honeymoon period in which pre-election plans could be developed with the help of experienced civil servants into implementable policies. We did not have that privilege, perhaps because ours was less a government and more a committee planning a mass escape from Bailoutistan.

While sifting through the material that would go into my submission to the Eurogroup I received an email from Willem Buiter, Citigroup's global chief economist, offering to help in any way he could and expressing his amazement and anger at the ECB's move to withdraw the waiver 'so early'. Hours later Paul Krugman addressed the same issue in his *New York Times* column: 'Maybe the Germans imagine that they can replay the events of 2010, when the central bank coerced Ireland into accepting an austerity programme by threatening to cut off its banking system. But that's unlikely to work against a government that has seen the damage wrought by austerity, and was elected on a promise to reverse that damage.'

This was precisely what I was hoping: that our government stayed steadfast against Berlin's attempt to deploy the ECB against us. My only objection to the article was its title, A GAME OF CHICKEN. For years I had been arguing that our interactions with Greece's creditors, and Berlin in particular, were *nothing* like a game of chicken: if the one who blinks first loses, it only makes sense to hold your ground if you think that in the end your opponent will back down. In our case, however, as Krugman himself admitted, we had every reason to stay unswerving even if we thought Chancellor Merkel and President Draghi would do the same. This was the essence of my covenant with Alexis.

In the meantime, the *High Noon* narrative was particularly damaging to our cause because it distracted public opinion worldwide from what was really at stake: the common interests of all Europeans. To address this I authored an op-ed for the *New York Times* entitled NO TIME FOR GAMES IN EUROPE.[3] In it I made three points: first, as finance minister of a bankrupt small nation I lacked the moral right to bluff. All I could do was honestly present the economic facts, table proposals for re-growing Greece, explain why these were in Europe's interest and reveal the red lines beyond which logic and duty prevented us from going. Second, as I used to tell my students, game theory only applies when you can take the players' motives for granted. In poker or blackjack this assumption is unproblematic, but in the current deliberations, I wrote, 'the whole point is to forge new motives. To fashion a fresh mindset that transcends national divides, dissolves the creditor–debtor distinction in favour of a pan-European perspective, and places the common European good above petty politics, dogma that proves toxic if universalized, and an us-versus-them mindset.' But what if refusing to back down brought the Greek people much pain? My third point was simply that there are 'circumstances when we must do what is right not as a strategy but simply because it is . . . right . . . One may think that this retreat from game theory is motivated by some radical-left agenda. Not so. The major influence here is Immanuel Kant, the German philosopher who taught us that the rational and the free escape the empire of expediency by doing what is right.'

In addition to writing this article and the frenzy of preparation for the Eurogroup, I had two other distractions to contend with. One was my first appearance in parliament, on the occasion of the election of the new speaker and my and Euclid's belated swearing-in (delayed because of our travels). The second was a visit from the US ambassador, who would be accompanied by a delegation from the US Treasury.

At midday on Friday, 6 February, I walked to parliament alone, stopping briefly to speak with well-wishers as I crossed Syntagma Square. Entering the house as an elected MP filled me with pride. A tall policewoman realized I was a novice and gave me directions through the building's unfamiliar corridors to the ministers' entrance to the chamber. Walking through that door, I found myself suddenly amid the ministerial benches, with the podium to my left and the speaker's bench towering above. In front of me, arranged like an amphitheatre, were three hundred seats, one for each member, the same number as there were Spartans at the famous battle of Thermopylae. On the far right (appropriately) I couldn't help but recognize the seventeen MPs of the Golden Dawn, so keen were they to dress and look like Nazis.

The decision to appoint Zoe Konstantopoulou speaker was rich in symbolism. Over the previous two parliamentary terms this impressively tall and uncompromising Syriza MP had single-handedly exposed the gross violations of procedure employed by previous governments to pass the legislation dictated by the troika. Voting her in as the speaker was a joy and a statement that never again would parliament be reduced to rubber-stamping its own servitude. And when a few moments later Zoe called upon me to affirm my allegiance to the constitution and thus become formally an MP, I felt impervious to the slings and arrows already being aimed at me from Brussels, Berlin and Frankfurt.

It was in this mood that I walked back across Syntagma Square to the ministry to receive the US ambassador and the delegation that Jack Lew, the US Treasury secretary, had dispatched from Washington, DC. Jeff Sachs and Jamie Galbraith had been hard at work lobbying key US officials such as Janet Yellen at the Fed, Samantha Power at the UN and David Lipton at the IMF to help secure us a ninety-day breathing space free of threats to our banking system or deadlines for impossible repayments in which to conduct our negotiations. Given President Obama's helpful public statement shortly after our election, not to mention Bernie Sanders's exquisite letter to Christine Lagarde, I felt confident that the United States would be an important source of support. Alas, my meeting with the ambassador put paid to that particular expectation.

Nothing of what the ambassador said was in sync with Barack Obama's publicly stated view that 'you cannot keep on squeezing countries that are in the midst of depression'. On the contrary, he went to some lengths to lecture me on how important it was to accept the parameters of the programme and to go along with the IMF. I did not see how I could do both, I informed him, since the IMF had been saying for a while now that the Greek programme could not work without serious debt restructuring and the relaxation of current levels of austerity. Indeed, the IMF's European chief, Poul Thomsen, had told me explicitly at our meeting in Paris that we needed to erase €53 billion of Greece's public debt immediately and recalibrate the programme to minimize austerity and rewrite the reform agenda. With the ambassador looking uncomfortable, I turned to the US Treasury delegation and asked them for their opinion on the matter. Their response seemed much more in tune with Obama's line, but within minutes the ambassador was interjecting to restate his uncompromising message.

There was no doubt that, for whatever reason, America's ambassador to Athens was following a line different to that of the White House and possibly of the US Treasury. But as time went by, I would discover that Jack Lew's Treasury was also edging closer to the views of the ambassador than those of the president. The fact that Lew did not invite me to Washington during those first weeks, contrary to President Obama's suggestion to Alexis, should have alerted me to this rift. At that moment though only one thing mattered. When Jeroen Dijsselbloem tried to bully me into submission a few days before, I had stood up to him. Not to do the same now would have been an indefensible and anti-European double standard.

Looking out of the window on that clear winter's day to where the inimitable Attic sun bathed Parliament House in vibrant colours, I began by confessing to the ambassador that I had never aspired to be a minister. Yes, I was happy to be doing the job, I told him, but only out of my sense of duty to a nation in debt bondage, a duty whose sole purpose was to rewrite the terms of our contract with the EU and the IMF, so as to turn it from a predatory relationship into a workable and equitable one. So accepting the current parameters of that contract was simply not an option. Here again the ambassador interjected, this time with a vague, implicit but perfectly recognizable threat. Out of respect for the people who had appointed me to my office, I felt obliged to cut him short.

'Ever since I assumed this ministry, this room has become the focal point of the hopes and expectations of millions. But it is *not* my natural habitat. My natural habitat is out there,' I said, pointing to Syntagma Square. 'I am happier there demonstrating against this office, as I have been doing since I was thirteen. If I am pushed to pledge allegiance to the failed programme that condemns my people to a continuation of our present indignity, rest assured that I will jump at the opportunity to return there as one of thousands of demonstrators. It would in fact make my day.'

The ambassador got the message and was soon on his way. I would not have been surprised to learn that, upon returning to his embassy, he had dispatched a wire: 'Varoufakis is not for turning. If the present programme is to continue, his removal is imperative.' What I did not know was who the recipient of such a message might be. The State Department? The White House? The Treasury? By mid-April I had a fairly good idea.

Pre-positioning: the 70 per cent gesture

On Saturday morning, 7 February, I attended our first cabinet meeting. Oscar Wilde's quip about democracy was at the back of my mind: 'It is impractical, and it goes against human nature. This is why it is worth carrying out.'[4] Having wasted a few precious hours on a largely ceremonial occasion at which too many of us spoke for too long to say too little, I rushed back to the office, where the Lazard team and my people were working on the three non-papers I would be taking to Brussels.

I felt they were coming along satisfactorily. Our debt sustainability analysis, helped also from afar by Jeff Sachs, was irrefutable in its empirical findings and projections and lent clear support to the debt swaps and the fiscal policy I was proposing. The reform agenda was comprehensive, especially our proposals for the management of public assets and the banks' non-performing loans, even if the contribution of key ministries (labour, energy, health, the environment) was thin. Lastly, the proposed replacement for the troika's process was undeniably sensible: our plan was to unbundle the troika into its component parts, with the ECB concentrating on its primary mission, namely to keep the banks liquid and the financial markets stable, the IMF offering technical assistance on a number of areas, and the European Commission undertaking all political negotiations with the Greek government.

By Sunday night the three papers were complete, allowing me to concentrate on preparations for my first big moment in parliament, the delivery of my programmatic statement, the finance minister's outline of economic policy for the parliament's full term, which would take place the following morning. With my first Eurogroup due within twenty-four hours, this was also an opportunity to set out the proposals I would be making there and the spirit in which they would be conveyed. With this in mind, I focused my statement on four themes: transparency, analysis, commitment to uncompromising moderation and, finally, a major gesture of goodwill to our creditors.

'I have this idea, ladies and gentlemen,' I began my speech on Monday, 'of trying out an innovative policy: of coming to the house to address members truthfully about the economic situation facing the country.' Unlike previous finance ministers, who had presented our economy's terrible free fall as a success story of recovery, I promised I would continue to refer to our state as bankrupt until we achieved solvency. This was what I meant by transparency.

I then suggested that the failure of previous governments to rescue Greece from its plight was due to their acceptance 'of impossible conditions they could never carry out, even if they had intended to – an acceptance which made successive Greek governments almost as guilty in accepting what they could not fulfil as the creditors were in imposing what they were not entitled to exact'.[5]

This was what I meant by analysis: 'If the troika's programme was a very bitter medicine that cured our disease, I would recommend taking it. But it is not. Their programme is poisonous and only worsens the Greek patient's condition,' I concluded. The best strategy was to stop taking it. Otherwise, it threatened to poison the whole of the European Union with its deflationary effects, as it had been doing since 2010, the only beneficiaries being the ultra Right and the enemies of liberal democracy.

On the theme of uncompromising moderation, I had this to say:

> Tomorrow I shall be telling my Eurogroup colleagues that we accept the principle of continuity between previous government undertakings and our new government's mandate . . . Ours is not the only democratic government in the eurozone. We have a mandate but so do the other eighteen finance ministers sitting in the Eurogroup . . . But this means establishing common ground, throwing a bridge over our differences . . . It will take goodwill to do so and a period of calm, free of the type of threats that have unfortunately been issued . . . I commit to not passing any legislation during the negotiations that derails our target for a small budget primary surplus. At the same time I expect our partners to take our proposals and our analysis seriously . . . This is what a negotiation ought to mean.

From the opposition benches several New Democracy and PASOK MPs interjected boisterously. 'Negotiate as hard as you want,' they shouted, 'but rule out falling out with the troika. Rule out any rupture!' I gave the only logical response I could:

> If you cannot imagine walking out of a negotiation, you should never enter it. If you cannot fathom the idea of an impasse you might as well confine yourself to the role of a supplicant who implores the despot to grant him several privileges but who accepts in the final analysis whatever

the despot grants. This was not our mandate on 25 January. Our mandate was to negotiate. Which means to work towards avoiding a rupture while refusing to rule out a rupture. This is what I promised voters and this is what we are delivering. You had your chance of getting the country out of debtors' prison through your model prisoner strategy. Now it is our turn to try to liberate Greece through a genuine negotiation.

A heated debate ensued, though I had not even reached the most controversial part of my speech, the gesture of goodwill to our creditors: 'As reasonable partners we shall include in our reform agenda up to 70 per cent of the measures in the existing programme and augment them with a plan to combat the humanitarian crisis that has afflicted our people after years of politically motivated denial of the crisis's causes and nature.'

The official document describing Greece's programme, known as the *Memorandum of Understanding (MoU)*, was a list of reforms (austerity targets, the institutional elimination of social benefits, privatization targets, administrative and judicial changes and so on) that the previous government had agreed to as the conditions (conditionalities in troika-speak) for receiving the second bailout loan. There was no way we would implement these conditions in full, since doing so would involve accepting massive pain for absolutely no gain, especially as more than 90 per cent of the bailout loan had been disbursed before we were even elected. However, careful study of the *MoU* list in 2012 had made clear to me that many of its measures could be implemented without too much social damage. Accepting these elements, which comprised about 70 per cent of the *MoU*, in return for our demands, while rejecting the genuinely toxic measures of the remaining 30 per cent, was a strategic move. As I had argued in my op-ed in the *New York Times*, when one finds oneself bargaining from a position of relative weakness, as we did, it is sensible to make all the compromises upfront and then stick to one's guns without bluffs or stratagems.

This gesture provoked a great furore: the establishment parties accused me of not having yielded enough to the troika, while leftists lambasted me for having given away too much. The following morning I had the opportunity, as finance minister, to wrap up the debate that preceded parliament's vote of confidence in the incoming government. In my speech I tried to put the matter to rest.

> For us the bailout that we reject means one thing: the combination of new loans piled on existing non-payable private and public debt which come under conditions that reduce the incomes from which old and new debts must be repaid . . . What percentage of the twisted bailout logic do we accept? Precisely zero per cent. We shall not accept a single measure that reinforces the doom loop boosting the debt-to-income ratio or the tax rates imposed on those who are already exhausted by punitive taxation. We shall not accept even one of the *MoU* lines that sacrifices a single Greek citizen on the altar of reality denial.

But, I concluded, an agreement requires compromise on both sides. Many of the measures in the *MoU* list were unproblematic and could be implemented without any of the sacrifices that we rejected as unacceptable. Indeed, some of the measures, such as the idea of a minimum guaranteed income, were to be desired.

In normal circumstances this position would surely have been considered sensible and moderate. After all, it was those at the extremes – committed Grexit-supporters on the one hand and die-hard troika loyalists on the other – who were angered by it. But Greece is not living in normal circumstances.

Enlisting the OECD

Before I headed off to Brussels for the Eurogroup meeting I had arranged to receive a delegation from the Organization of Economic Cooperation and Development (OECD). Created by Washington in 1950 to administer the Marshall Plan in postwar Europe, the OECD was one of the three major institutions designed by the United States to keep another Great Depression (and thus the Soviet bear) at bay, the others being the IMF and the World Bank.

It so happened that I had a good personal relationship with the OECD's secretary general, Ángel Gurría. Our good chemistry was born out of a common appreciation of the need to restructure unsustainable debt. Ángel had made his name as the finance minister of Mexico who had negotiated a major haircut of its unpayable public debt in the 1980s. Before I even imagined that I would become Greece's finance minister, Ángel had invited me to the OECD's offices in Paris to give a lecture on the European crisis and to meet him and his team as part of the regular briefings they organized to keep abreast of the latest thinking about global capitalism. After the fateful late-night meeting with Alexis in November 2014 when I accepted his offer of a role in the government, I reconnected with Ángel and his people. Syriza did not have the expertise to come up with a bespoke fully fledged reform agenda on its own. Having such a prestigious global institution not only contribute to that agenda but then vouch for it once it was finalized would be a powerful means of pre-empting the inevitable criticism.

The OECD delegation had arrived the day before on Tuesday, 10 February. I met them in the roof garden of the Grande Bretagne, an historic hotel also on Syntagma Square. Over dinner we discussed Greece's situation and found ourselves in complete agreement over our new collaboration. My single request was that they publicly ditch their so-called toolkits – a set of reforms that the OECD had put together at the behest of the troika and previous Greek governments aimed at ordinary people. Ángel promised that we would start afresh, conceding that the toolkits had not been the OECD's finest hour.

The dinner lasted until after midnight. Early next morning we met again, this time at Maximos, in front of the cameras and with considerable pomp and ceremony. The prime minister welcomed the OECD's secretary general, with myself, Deputy Prime Minister Dragasakis and Economy Minister Stathakis also present, thus formally making it known that the new Syriza government would be working closely with the rich countries' club to develop a new pro-growth reform agenda. In his response to Alexis's welcoming speech, Ángel Gurría expressed his enthusiasm at the partnership and, as agreed, his disavowal of the OECD's toolkits, which would be replaced with better and more appropriate market reforms.

My appreciation and respect for the former Mexican finance minister grew that morning. He knew that the troika would be displeased and that the OECD would suffer the consequences of their displeasure. But hearing him speak those words confirmed that it was possible to join forces with globally credible institutions – that it was possible to have them as partners, not antagonists, in our efforts to bring fresh air to Greece to drive away the stench of stagnation and hopelessness.

Minutes after the official ceremony ended, I was in a car heading for the airport and Brussels. The first Eurogroup beckoned.

At the Eurogroup

A prison is not newsworthy when the inmates suffer quietly. But when they stage a revolt, and the authorities crack down, then the satellite trucks appear. Even before my plane landed in Brussels, the press was reporting Alexis's recent speech in parliament as evidence we were rolling back reforms and digging our own graves.[6] When I actually arrived at the European Commission's building, where the Eurogroup was scheduled to take place, the din of the assembled press corps was impressive.

Before the Eurogroup meeting itself, I met Christine Lagarde, head of the IMF. Her positive attitude and openness to the proposals in our non-papers were a psychological boost. (It was at the end of this meeting that Christine made her plea that I work within the programme, despite her remarkable acknowledgement that it was destined to fail, as described in Chapter 2.) Afterwards, her message to the gathered journalists was: 'They are competent, intelligent, they have thought about their issues. We have to listen to them. We are starting to work together, and it is a process that is starting and is going to last a certain time.'

A short way down the corridor, as we made our way to the meeting itself, we came across Jeroen Dijsselbloem. Seeing Christine and me engaged in friendly conversation, Jeroen looked decisively sullen. Perhaps the unhappy memory of his luckless visit to see me in Athens had sprung to mind. We entered and took our places.

The Eurogroup is an interesting beast. It has no legal standing in any of the EU treaties and yet it is the body that makes Europe's most vital decisions. At the same time most Europeans, including most politicians, know almost nothing about it. It convenes around a huge rectangular table. Finance ministers are seated along its two longer sides, each accompanied by a single aide who also represents them in the Eurogroup Working Group. However, real power sits at either end of the table.

At one end, to my left, sat the Eurogroup president, Jeroen Dijsselbloem. On his right was Thomas Wieser, the Eurogroup Working Group president and the real power at that end of the table; on his left were the IMF representatives, Christine Lagarde and Poul Thomsen. At the other end of the table was Valdis Dombrovskis, commissioner for the euro and social dialogue, whose real job was to supervise (on behalf of Wolfgang Schäuble) Pierre Moscovici, the economic and financial affairs commissioner, who sat on the Latvian's left. On Dombrovskis's right, meanwhile, sat Benoît Cœuré and beyond him Mario Draghi representing the ECB.

At the same corner of the table as Draghi, but on the longer side and at right angles to him, sat Wolfgang Schäuble. Their proximity would on occasion give rise to intense heat, though never any actual light. Along the same side as Schäuble were what I came to see as his cheerleaders: the Finnish, Slovakian, Austrian, Portuguese, Slovenian, Latvian, Lithuanian and Maltese finance ministers. My seat was almost diagonally opposite Schäuble's, alongside the other profligates, nicely lined up together: to my left was Ireland's Michael Noonan, to my right Spain's Luis de Guindos, and next to de Guindos was Italy's Pier Carlo Padoan. France's Michel Sapin also sat on our side, next to Padoan.

In normal Eurogroup meetings a fascinating ritual illustrated the manner in which the troika and its processes had taken over the governance of continental Europe – one reason why Greece's appalling drama, which gave rise to the troika, is so significant. Every time an item was tabled for discussion – for example, the French national budget or developments in Cyprus's banks – Dijsselbloem would announce the topic and then invite the representatives of the institutions to present their views in turn: first, Moscovici on behalf of the European Commission, then Christine Lagarde (or Poul Thomsen in her absence) on behalf of the IMF, and finally Mario Draghi on behalf of the ECB (with Benoît Cœuré stepping in on the rare occasions that Mario was absent).[7] Only after these unelected officials had given their assessment and set the tone and terms of the debate did the elected ministers get a chance to speak. Moreover, for almost all the meetings at which I was present the ministers received no substantial briefing on *any* of the topics under discussion. A reasonable and impartial spectator might easily have concluded that the purpose of the Eurogroup is for the ministers to approve and legitimize decisions that have already been taken by the three institutions.

However, the Eurogroup meeting of 11 February 2015 was not a normal one. For the first time a country was being represented by a finance minister who had been elected on a platform of confronting the troika, the Eurogroup's backbone. The air was filled with tension. Before the meeting Dijsselbloem had contacted Alexis with an offer to bend the Eurogroup rules that limit each member state to two representatives. Given this was our government's first meeting and one of such vital importance, Jeroen was keen to allow the deputy prime minister to attend as well. And so, in addition to having George Chouliarakis, Dragasakis's appointee, at my side, I had Dragasakis as well. Wassily believed this was an attempt by Dijsselbloem, in cahoots with Alexis, to dilute my impact. I did not mind at all. The more the merrier, I thought.

Continuity versus democracy

Finance ministers attending their first Eurogroup get the chance to present their policy priorities in a maiden speech. I began mine by appealing to my colleagues' weariness.

> I understand your fatigue with the Greek drama. But believe me, the Greek people have had much more than enough of it too . . . Our government faces the task of earning a precious currency without depleting an important capital good: we must earn your trust without losing the trust of our people. For their support is an important capital good in Europe's struggle to sort Greece out and to render it stable and, indeed, normal.

Next I committed our government to sound finances, deep reforms and a wholesale assault on vested interests. 'Why should you expect us to deliver that which other Greek governments have not?' I asked. 'Simply because we are not tied to any interest groups . . . We will not only commit to reforms, we shall deliver them.'

But to succeed in this we would need to have the people on our side. And this would require them to feel justly treated. This, I explained, was why we had rehired cleaners and school janitors whom the courts had judged to have been illegally dismissed by the previous government on the troika's orders. This was why we had promised to reverse cuts to pensions for old people living beneath the (extremely low) Greek poverty line. This was why we were looking into ways of gradually restoring the minimum wage in the private sector. Those assembled in the Eurogroup had my commitment, I told them, that none of these small-scale measures would have a measurable fiscal impact. The price tag on these minor interventions in return for a renewed sense of justice was tiny. To think of the illegal firing of a cleaner as a reform, and her rehiring as evidence that reforms were being rolled back was unhelpful if not absurd.

To demonstrate our openness to the involvement of international organizations, I mentioned our new collaboration with the OECD and proposed to work closely with the IMF and the ECB in its areas of expertise, while calling upon the European Commission to play its role as political mediator between Athens and the other capitals. On the question of privatizations and the development of public assets, I declared our government to be

> undogmatic . . . ready and willing to evaluate each and every one project on its merits alone. Quick fire sales of public property, when asset prices are deeply depressed, is not a smart policy. Instead the government will create a development bank, which will incorporate state assets, enhance their equity value through reforming property rights and use them as collateral for the purposes of providing, in association with European investment institutions such as the European Investment Bank, funding to the private sector . . . In association with the ECB we shall set up a public bank to clean up non-performing loans to render the banks able to support small business and families.

What happens, I asked, in a democracy when two principles clash? Democracies find a compromise that reflects the common will. That day we were facing such a clash, I suggested. There was the principle of continuity: our government, whether we liked it or not, had been committed by previous Greek governments to a programme. But there was also the principle of democratically mandated change: their governments, whether they liked it or not, were obliged to respect the fact that the Greek voters had given us a mandate to challenge that programme. What was our duty in this European forum? To establish a new partnership that found common ground between the previously agreed Greek programme and our government's fresh mandate. To that end, I invited the IMF to state clearly its views on our debt's sustainability and my debt-swap proposals.

Jeroen Dijsselbloem had joked in Athens that the EU already had a permanent debt reduction conference – the Eurogroup. I turned this into a proposal: 'We welcome Mr Dijsselbloem's recent statement in our joint press conference in Athens that the Eurogroup is the proper forum to act as a permanent European debt conference, addressing debt problems in euro-area member states. We therefore propose to create a specific Eurogroup working group gathering member states' representatives and experts.' (While speaking, I noticed the angry look that Schäuble gave a seemingly apoplectic Dijsselbloem and could not help but smile.)

I then moved from the essential business of restructuring our massive debt to the need for short-term financial stability. The troika was demanding that the bankrupt Greek state pay just under €5 billion to the IMF by July 2015 and then, during July and August, a further €6.7 billion to its own central bank. I proposed that we begin with a modest agreement that the ECB would pay back the €1.9 billion it owed Greece from its past years' profits on our SMP bonds.[8] This was Greece's own money. If the creditors wanted us to keep up our repayments to them, the least they could do was give us access to our own money. Anything less would surely be an invitation to default.

> Moreover, we propose to work urgently on a bridge financing mechanism to ensure Greece's liquidity position over the coming months . . . Let me be very clear on this: the government asks for this . . . on the condition that it is the starting point for genuine negotiations in good faith for forging a different contract between us, based on a realistic primary surplus effort and efficient as well as socially just structural policies – including of course many elements of the previous programme that we accept. We need assurances on this point. Such an extension cannot be taken as acquiescence to the logic of the former agenda that has been rejected by our people.

After delving into some of the technicalities involved, I made my final plea:

> Europe is whole and indivisible, and the government of Greece considers that Greece is a permanent and inseparable member of the European Union and our monetary union . . . Some of you, I know, were displeased by the victory of a radical left-wing party. To you I have this to say: it would be a lost opportunity to see us as adversaries. We are dedicated Europeanists. We care about our people deeply but we are not populists promising all things to all Greeks. Moreover, we can carry the Greek people along with an agreement that is genuinely beneficial to the average European. In us you will find trustworthy partners who do not see these meetings as a means of extracting something out of nothing, of gaining at anyone's expense.

Elections versus economic policy

Dragasakis and Chouliarakis were nodding approvingly as I wrapped up. Luis de Guindos, the Spaniard on my right, looked concerned.[9] As soon as I had finished, Michel Sapin, the French finance minister, stood his nameplate on its side, the standard way of asking for the floor. Jeroen obliged him.

Shortly after announcing my willingness to accept 70 per cent of the *MoU* measures in the context of a new partnership, I had received a message from Paris that this gesture appealed to the French government greatly. Michel now proceeded to wax lyrical about my suggestion that a bridge be built between the Greek programme and our new government's plans, paving the way for a new type of contract between Greece and the Eurogroup. But before Michel concluded, Wolfgang placed his own nameplate in an ominously vertical position. Later I would realize that this was probably the first and last time Michel Sapin dared express unequivocal support in the Eurogroup for anything I said. The chain of command within the Franco-German axis was about to be established, even within the first hour of my first Eurogroup.

As he spoke, Schäuble directed a piercing look at Sapin. 'Elections cannot be allowed to change economic policy,' he began. Greece had obligations that could not be reconsidered until the Greek programme had been completed, as per the agreements between my predecessors and the troika. The fact that the Greek programme *could* not be completed was apparently of no concern to him.

What startled me more than Wolfgang Schäuble's belief that elections are irrelevant was his total lack of compunction in admitting to this view. His reasoning was simple: if every time one of the nineteen member states changed government the Eurogroup was forced to go back to the drawing board, then its overall economic policies would be derailed. Of course he had a point: democracy had indeed died the moment the Eurogroup acquired the authority to dictate economic policy to member states without anything resembling federal democratic sovereignty.

After Dr Schäuble's speech several of his cheerleaders took to the floor to back him – as also did the Spanish, Irish, even the Belgian and the Austrian ministers, whose premiers had shown support for our government in private meetings.[10] While some, including the Lithuanian, Slovakian and Slovenian finance ministers, clearly believed Schäuble's pronouncements on economic policy to be sound and self-evident, it became apparent that even those who disagreed with the economics of austerity would support him – in the case of Italy, Spain and Ireland out of fear that upstart Greece might escape having to do what they had been forced to do already, in which case their own people might demand to know why they had not resisted austerity too – and in the case of a small but significant group, with France at its centre, out of fear that Schäuble would force austerity upon them in the future if they undermined him.

When my turn came to reply, I tried to make light of Wolfgang's Platonic contempt for democracy.

The notion that elections cannot be allowed to change economic policy, indeed any policy, is a gift to [founder and leader of Singapore] Lee Kuan Yew supporters or indeed the Chinese communist party, who also believe this to be true. There is of course a long tradition of doubting the efficacy of the democratic process. But I would like to think that this tradition has been expelled long ago from the heart of democratic Europe. It now seems that the euro crisis has brought it back. I urge you all to band together in a collective bid to resist it. Democracy is not a luxury to be afforded to the creditors and denied to the debtors. Indeed, it is the lack of due democratic process in the heart of our monetary union that is perpetuating the euro crisis. Then again, I might be wrong. Colleagues, if you think that I am wrong, if you agree with Wolfgang, then I invite you to say so explicitly by proposing that elections should be suspended in countries like Greece until the country's programme is completed. What is the point of spending money on elections and asking our people to get all fired up to elect governments that will have no capacity to change anything?

Dragasakis leaned over and congratulated me. Whatever our differences, he had enjoyed hearing me make that point. But as no one else had anything to say on the matter, Dijsselbloem announced, 'We shall now adjourn for ten minutes and then resume to draft the communiqué.' The time was 6 p.m., one and a half hours since the meeting began, but our work was just beginning: the communiqué was clearly all that really mattered.

Communiqué sans communication

Previously I had asked the secretariat to circulate my three non-papers so that all the Eurogroup ministers would be able to consider my proposals on paper and in some detail. The secretariat now alerted me to a difficulty, and Jeroen Dijsselbloem and Thomas Wieser approached me to explain that it was 'not possible'. Incredulous, I asked, 'Are you telling me that you will prevent me from communicating to my colleagues a few pages with the gist of our proposals on key issues concerning the Greek programme that is today's sole topic of conversation?' Yes, this was precisely what they were telling me. But why? What was the reason? Could there be any rationale for such a refusal?

The answer came once we had reconvened – from Wolfgang. If he were to receive my proposals, he claimed, he would be legally obliged to table them in the Bundestag, Germany's federal parliament in Berlin. And then all hell would break loose as the various factions within his party and the opposition raised concerns about them. My proposals would be dead even before the institutions had had a chance to consider them. 'So, take your proposals to the institutions,' he suggested once more. (Indeed, whenever I sought to share my proposals with other ministers in various Eurogroup meetings, I would be rebuffed. On one occasion Jeroen informed me that were I to email my proposals to the other finance ministries I would be in breach of protocol, which would mean the proposals could never be considered.) Not wishing to clash over everything at once and with the draft communiqué about to be distributed, I held my tongue.

Eventually the draft was handed out. One glance was enough to know it was unacceptable as it explicitly committed Greece to completing the second bailout programme via the implementation of the entire *MoU* 'with maximum flexibility within the programme to accommodate the new Greek authorities' priorities'.

'Maximum flexibility' is the troika's equivalent of Henry Ford's sales pitch for the Model T: you can have it in any colour you wish as long as it is black. It meant that the overall level of fiscal cuts was non-negotiable, although Athens could propose an alternative distribution of the pain within the population. It was the fiscal equivalent of Sophie's Choice.

Taking the floor I pointed out that Jeroen's draft constituted a wholesale rejection of the bridge we had proposed, supported by France, between the programme of the *MoU* and our fresh mandate. To demonstrate good faith, I said I would accept it nonetheless if we could agree to the insertion of one adjective which would make an important difference. 'Could you add "amended" in front of "programme"?' I asked Jeroen.

He was pleasantly surprised by my suggestion. In fact I was making a huge concession by allowing the word "programme" to remain.

'Would you be happy to commit to the completion of the amended programme?' he replied.

I consulted briefly with Dragasakis and Chouliarakis. While the agreement would be opposed by many of our cabinet colleagues and MPs, who would rightly react angrily to any commitment to the programme, in the end it all hinged on the interpretation of the word 'amended'. They agreed.

'Yes, Jeroen, we are prepared to commit to an *amended* programme that is financially sound, fiscally sustainable, socially just and contains reforms that our people can embrace,' I said.

'We shall adjourn briefly,' the Eurogroup president announced.

While waiting, I struck up a jovial conversation with my Spanish neighbour, Luis de Guindos. Despite my representing a government that constituted a deadly threat to his own, the chemistry between us was good. 'You should have seen what I went through when I first landed this job and our banks were collapsing. It was terrible!' he said, pointing in Wolfgang's direction. It was not the beginning of a wonderful friendship between the two of us, although it would ultimately yield a fascinating exchange a few months later in his office in Madrid, but there were a few officials with whom it was easy to communicate without nastiness, pettiness or incomprehension getting in the way. We did not agree politically or ideologically but shared a common language and the desire to get to the bottom of whatever problem was staring at us. One day I realized what they all had in common: they were all Goldman Sachs alumni!

When the meeting reconvened, Jeroen looked downcast. Wolfgang could not accept the insertion of 'amended' in front of 'programme', he announced. Wolfgang switched his microphone on to explain that the insertion would oblige him to take the matter to the Bundestag for approval. The Greek programme as prescribed in the *MoU* had been voted in by the German parliament, he reminded us. Any amendment would need to be voted on too. But since the programme was due to expire in exactly seventeen days, there was no time to agree to detailed amendments, table them at the Bundestag and pass them. Thus, the Greek government had no alternative but to commit to the existing programme or accept that its banks should close on 28 February. The clash over Greece's economic policy and reform agenda was turning into a tale of two parliaments. But while Wolfgang Schäuble invoked the German parliament in order to force the Greek parliament to relinquish its authority, I was not to grant him that concession. Judging by his body language, he knew it.

When Wolfgang had finished, Jeroen looked at me with open hostility. 'Yanis, I hope you realize that you cannot afford to leave this room without an agreed communiqué. You are facing a hard deadline. Any extension of the programme needs at least two weeks to be passed through the four parliaments that must vote for it to satisfy constitutional imperatives.[11] Our Finnish colleague tells me that their parliamentary calendar is extremely tight and they need to start the process of approving any application to give you an extension by tomorrow morning. If there is no agreed communiqué tonight, the Finnish parliament will not have the time to approve the extension and the ECB will be forced, on 28 February, to pull the plug. So there is no room left. Accept this communiqué now or the train will leave the station.'

Looking at him and Wolfgang, I replied, 'It is a sad day for Europe's democracy when, on his first visit to the Eurogroup, a freshly elected finance minister is being told that his arguments and proposals never really mattered, that his mandate is entirely irrelevant. For this is what you are telling me, Jeroen. You are telling me that, owing to technical constraints involving various parliamentary procedures and deadlines, even if I had tabled divine proposals that everyone in this room were ecstatic about, and which could save my people terrible indignity and hardship, the programme is the programme is the programme, and no deviation from it can be contemplated. It is my duty as a European democrat, my burden as the finance minister of a broken country, to say no to this ultimatum.'

Christine Lagarde intervened. She acknowledged the Greek government's right 'to be heard' and made some polite noises about our debt but without challenging Wolfgang.

Thanks to her intervention a new adjective emerged as a possible substitute for 'amended' 'Would you commit to an *adjusted* programme?' I was asked.

Thinking on my feet, I decided to be flexible. It was a poor alternative – 'adjustments' implied the programme was fundamentally sound, whereas it was because the programme had failed and was impossible to complete that it needed real amendment – but we could accept this new adjective in return for a specific addition to the communiqué. In the spirit of cooperation with the Eurogroup, I said I could recommend to the Greek prime minister that we commit to completing an 'adjusted programme' as long as the communiqué also committed the Eurogroup to working with our government to address the humanitarian crisis that was now afflicting our people as a result of the programme.

'I cannot accept this,' Jeroen said. 'The term "humanitarian crisis" is too political!'

'There is nothing more political, Jeroen,' I snapped back, 'than the attempt to overlook a humanitarian crisis because it would be too *political* to acknowledge it.'

It was clear that we were at an impasse. At around 10.30 p.m. another adjournment was called. Outside Christine Lagarde approached me and attempted to persuade me to accept the word 'adjusted' and withdraw my demand that the humanitarian crisis in Greece be acknowledged in the communiqué.

'Do you realize it is not just up to me?' I said. 'We have a parliamentary party that will be up in arms if I declare our mandate null and void at our first Eurogroup. I have a prime minister waiting nearby who would be appalled.' I then expressed my disappointment that she and Poul Thomsen had not put to the Eurogroup what they had conceded in our private discussions. Christine replied that such matters should be left till later. For now, she insisted, it was important to endorse the communiqué and prevent us all from falling off the cliff. I told her I needed to consult with Alexis.

With Lagarde pushing me towards Wolfgang's embrace and Commissioner Moscovici and Finance Minister Sapin keeping their distance, only one Frenchman was lending moral support, Emmanuel Macron, the French economy minister. Having no seat in the Eurogroup himself, he had called to wish me well just as I was stepping into the meeting. During the negotiations over the communiqué he sent me regular requests for updates. What was my feeling? How was the meeting going? I replied that I was prepared to bend over backwards to make a decent communiqué possible. 'The first draft was appalling, let's hope that they will not prove ridiculously stubborn,' I texted him. At 10.43 Emmanuel responded, advising me to keep cool and seek a compromise but only if they moved in our direction. At 11.02 I texted back, 'They are pushing us out of the door . . . They wanted to roll me into a communiqué that not even Samaras would have signed.'

It was time for another consultation with Dragasakis. I put it to him that we could either win ourselves some time by accepting 'adjusted', or we risked having our banks close down almost immediately, before we had had a chance to prepare the country for such a shock. Looking exhausted, he asked me for my opinion. I said that I was leaning towards compromise on the communiqué so that we had an opportunity to put all the plans we had agreed into operation while the banks were still open. He agreed and so did Chouliarakis. All this time Alexis and Pappas were holed up in their nearby hotel room, preparing for the EU summit about to take place. During the Eurogroup I had been keeping them up to date with text messages. Now it was time to talk directly to my prime minister.

We spoke for almost an hour, even though Jeroen approached to tell me that it was not normal for a minister to call their prime minister while in a Eurogroup meeting. I replied that it was not normal to force a minister to make an on-the-spot decision that could lead to the instant closure of his country's banking system. It was an animated conversation, but with all the other ministers in the room talking in small groups, looking on, I had to keep a poker face.

When I read Alexis the draft that featured the phrase 'adjusted programme' he was quick to tell me that we could not get it past the cabinet, let alone pass it through parliament. I conveyed Jeroen's threat, 'the train will leave the station'. Alexis asked me what Draghi's position was, given that the ECB would give that proverbial train the green light to do so. 'Draghi has said nothing. He just looks unhappy,' I said.

Over the course of our conversation, with my mobile phone growing hotter and my bile rising, I must have changed my mind three or four times, oscillating between 'Stuff them!' and 'Let's accept the damned communiqué and fight the troika when it comes to defining what an "adjusted programme" should look like.' Dragasakis, meanwhile, was signalling to me that I should persuade Alexis to yield. I confess that my will wavered and I needed Alexis's steadiness at the end of the phone to bolster me. After ten hours of continuous, confrontational deliberations in an exceedingly hostile environment I suddenly developed an urgent need to get out of that fluorescent-lit windowless room. I had never imagined that I would crave Brussels's cold, dark, empty streets in the middle of a February night, that I could feel such a desire to rush outside and soak up the rain and breathe in the air. But that is exactly how I felt. For a fleeting instant I understood how finance ministers before me had succumbed to the pressure to sign up to Bailoutistan. On a human level I sympathized with them. Once it was all over and I was back at my hotel, I phoned Danae to share the night's burdens, including this thought: 'If we did not have the millions of Greeks who had believed in us, who expected that in the Eurogroup I would refuse to sign up to the hated programme, I would most likely succumb too. How could Papakonstantinou, Venizelos, Stournaras resist such an irresistible pressure when all they had back home to shore them up was the oligarchs and the bankers?'

Alexis, on the other hand, at a distance from that cauldron of a room, was wavering a lot less, and in the end he was adamant. But with my resolve fully recovered and having received my instructions, I saw an unseemly game played out before my eyes: Schäuble and the Finnish minister were leaving the room. Almost immediately after they had gone, Jeroen approached me to explain: 'Our Finnish colleague has had to rush to the airport to catch his plane. Wolfgang has left too. There can be no further amendment to the communiqué now that they have gone. Either you accept it as is or it is all over.'

Not to worry, I told Jeroen. It was perhaps best that Wolfgang had left, as we could not possibly sign the communiqué. He shouldn't take it personally; we just did not have a mandate to do this. I was sure he would not have signed either if the Dutch parliament had denied him the mandate to do so, I said.

Somehow Jeroen managed to look even angrier.

I sat down again and explained what had happened to Dragasakis. He doubted the wisdom of Alexis's decision, but I told him that, even though I had wavered, the prime minister was right. It had been important to have Alexis in contact but outside the room, in which the heat and the tension had blunted our judgement.

'You just ran out of money!'

It was not clear what we were waiting for, but Jeroen and Thomas Wieser were now engaged in conversation, with Lagarde contributing occasionally and various functionaries providing assistance. Moscovici, on the other hand, had been excluded. He hovered around, occasionally sending a friendly smile towards me.

At one point Wolfgang came back into the room. 'They are toying with us,' I said to Chouliarakis. 'The more they do this, the more adamant I am becoming that it would be a mistake to compromise.'

Eventually Christine approached me one more time to say, calmly, that she thought we had made a mistake. Then Jeroen tried his luck one more time: would I take this last opportunity to agree to the draft communiqué? he asked. Would he accept my original proposal to insert 'amended' before 'programme', an idea that he had liked before Wolfgang shot it down? I replied.

We had confirmed that the impasse was final. Ministers were beginning to move towards the doors. I waved to Dragasakis and Chouliarakis that it was time to leave. As we were going, one of Schäuble's cheerleading team asked in a concerned voice, 'Is it your plan to leave the euro?'

'Not at all,' I replied. 'But this does not mean that we shall accept conditions that cannot be fulfilled under the threat of expulsion.'

Another minister from the former Soviet bloc opted for a more aggressive stance: 'You just ran out of money,' he said spitefully.

'Well, that's OK,' I replied with a grin. 'The Beatles taught me long ago that it can't buy me love anyway.'

In the corridor I noticed that Dragasakis was walking unsteadily. I rushed up behind him, took his left arm and helped him to the bathroom. His face was white and covered with sweat, his eyes unfocused, his breathing irregular. I waited outside and was relieved when he emerged much steadier on his feet and with a surer smile. As we made our way towards the Greek delegation's office I reflected that the human cost of the day's charade was out of all proportion to what had been achieved. The finance ministers of nineteen European countries, the leaders of the ECB, the IMF and the European Commission, not to mention deputies, countless translators and support staff had just wasted ten hours blackmailing one minister. What a waste of human potential, I thought.

Once in our office I briefly updated Alexis on the phone. 'Put on a brave face,' he said. 'People are celebrating in the streets and supporting us. Cheer up!' A secretary showed me a tweet from his account with a picture of a rally and the message: 'In the cities of Greece and Europe the people are fighting our negotiation battle. They are our strength.' Indeed, as I was to find out the next day, thousands of cheering people had gathered in Syntagma Square while I was holed up with the Eurogroup. They were dancing and waving banners proclaiming BANKRUPT BUT FREE and STOP AUSTERITY. Simultaneously, and even more touchingly, thousands of German demonstrators, led by the Blockupy movement, were encircling the ECB building in Frankfurt in solidarity with us. A German supporter of a completely different stripe came to mind: the secret service officer at Frankfurt airport.

The meeting might have ended but my work was far from done: hundreds of reporters were waiting in the press room. Jeroen was sure to use our refusal to agree to a communiqué as a means of accelerating our bank run by ensuring the news was broadcast around the globe. My task would be to perform with sufficient aplomb for the public and the markets not to despair at the misbehaviour of the 'adults in the room'. That was why Alexis had been trying to raise my spirits.

On my way to the press room the security staff helped me run the gauntlet of cameramen who took no prisoners in their pursuit of the revealing close-up shot. Once inside the small, packed room, it was down to me to drive a large wedge between the way I felt and the way I appeared. My insides felt crushed by the stress, and I feared the tension would cause my voice to break or, worse still, produce a tear or two. But when the moment came, I found to my astonishment that within me there lived a stranger, one who was capable of rising to the task of facing a media circus, even of drawing strength from it. This encounter with the stranger within was truly a surprise.

> This Eurogroup was never meant to settle any issues. I was invited because I am the new kid on the block, so to speak. I was given a wonderful opportunity and a very warm welcome to present our views, our analysis, our proposals, both regarding substance and regarding the road map. And since we are meeting again on Monday, I think it is perfectly normal and natural that we should simply move to the Monday meeting.

Friends and critics have censured me for deceiving the public. I have been asked many times: why did I not spill the beans about what actually happened in there? Why did I not expose their blackmail and contempt for democracy? The answer I give is: because the time had not yet come. Our mandate was to reject any oath of allegiance to the existing programme, to the previous governments' *MoU*, to any new loans or austerity measures. Our purpose was to go to the wire without any intention of backing down. I had accepted the finance ministry on the understanding that we would respond to behind-the-scenes threats with our own deterrence plan. Our mission, in other words, was neither to declare war nor to surrender at the secret threat of war. Moreover, it was imperative to call Jeroen's bluff – that the train would leave the station that very night – by waiting until the next morning.

A journalist asked me if it was true that the prime minister had called during the Eurogroup to back me and Dragasakis in our decision to scuttle a communiqué. I wanted to reply that both Dragasakis and I had been wavering in the direction of accepting and that I owed Alexis a debt of gratitude for supporting me during a moment of weakness, but of course I could not say anything of the sort. Instead, I said, 'No one scuttled anything. This meeting was about getting to know each other and to create a road map for the future.' Another journalist interjected to ask for my impression of my first Eurogroup experience. 'It was fascinating!' I replied. 'I particularly enjoyed the very different views I sampled tonight.'

The media reporting of the impasse did not go entirely the troika's way. The *New York Times* summed it up nicely: 'With Greece about to run out of money and in need of German support for emergency funds, Mr Varoufakis appeared to be outmanned and outgunned. Nonetheless, he was the one who delivered the ultimatum in the meeting: renegotiate Greece's €240 billion bailout deal or risk a mutually destructive disaster.'

It was 3 a.m. by the time the embassy car dropped me off at my hotel. The night was dark. Brussels looked bleak. The rain was falling hard on the hotel awning, making an almighty racket, a northerly wind driving it almost horizontal. But this was exactly what I had been dreaming of for hours. Instead of heading to my room, I walked out into the downpour, meandering through the empty streets. How the human mind forges vistas of pleasure out of pure bleakness is a fascinating mystery.

9

A moment to savour, darkly

Early next morning Pappas, Dragasakis and I met Alexis in his hotel suite. The European Council summit was beginning that night with all eyes on the Ukrainian crisis. Chancellor Merkel and President Hollande had been immersed in negotiations in Kiev and Moscow and would be arriving in Brussels exhausted, their minds full of the Crimea, Putin and war – pressing matters far removed from Greece's travails.

We faced a risk but also an opportunity. From 2011 I had been advising Alexis that Angela Merkel was the key to any resolution of the Greek drama. Since I had become a minister, journalists had repeatedly asked me who Greece's best allies were within the EU. My response was always a single word: Merkel. 'Not President Hollande or Prime Minister Renzi?' they would ask. 'No,' I would reply. 'Chancellor Merkel is the only politician who can recalibrate Europe's policies on Greece.' And so I advised Alexis to approach Merkel that very evening with a direct request to end the stalemate in the Eurogroup, where Wolfgang Schäuble ruled supreme.

The tension between Angela Merkel and Wolfgang Schäuble was well documented. Schäuble dominated the Eurogroup with his control over Dijsselbloem and his bloc of cheerleading finance ministers, mainly from Eastern Europe. Only Merkel had the authority to contain him. As I was to discover later, the person she relied on for this task was Thomas Wieser, probably the only deep establishment functionary equidistant from her and the German finance minister. But to get Merkel temporarily to break Schäuble's stranglehold over the Eurogroup and thus allow for the possibility of a negotiated settlement, which Wolfgang would not contemplate otherwise, she would need a powerful incentive. Being seen to be giving Greece a chance or being magnanimous to our people would not cut it. But what would?

The answer I had been peddling since 2012 was Mario Draghi. Angela Merkel would surely intervene if Draghi were to convince her that the stability of the eurozone depended on it. And what would make Mario do such a thing? Successfully convincing him of our determination to haircut his SMP bonds if he closed down our banks, putting his whole quantitative easing programme in jeopardy.

Alexis understood. He would approach Merkel during the summit. As a brief, I wrote down our minimum conditions for him on hotel stationery: first, end the liquidity squeeze to create the space for proper negotiations; second, replace the troika process with a new Brussels-based institution that would allow Greek ministers to talk directly to the European Commission; third, end the toxic language of 'extending' and 'successfully completing' the current Greek programme; fourth, end the escalating austerity with a deal for a small primary budget surplus not to exceed 1.5 per cent of national income in any year.

As we were discussing his approach, Alexis's phone rang. 'It is Dijsselbloem,' he whispered. Apparently Jeroen was offering to come over to our hotel for a chat. When he arrived, the rest of us retired to an adjacent room, leaving Alexis alone. After only ten minutes, Alexis came into the room where the rest of us awaited with a smile on his face. Jeroen wanted to make peace and had offered a new adjective: instead of 'amended' or 'adjusted' he was proposing that we commit to a 'modified' or 'updated' programme. I advised Alexis to insist on there being mention of the humanitarian crisis too.

Meanwhile, Jeroen was in the corridor speaking on his phone. He looked like a primary school pupil being reprimanded by a severe teacher. 'Wolfgang has shot him down once more,' I whispered to Pappas.

Before Alexis could get back to Jeroen with his further request, the clearly upset Dutchman confessed that 'modified' would not work either, made his excuses, promised to return with more suggestions and headed for the lift. As he passed me I asked him the question I had been aching to put to him ever since he had arrived at the hotel: 'What happened to that train, Jeroen? Have we not missed it after all? Has it reversed back into the station perhaps? Is it leaving again?'

Naturally he did not answer. How could he? The president of the Eurogroup had been caught out. The threats he had issued repeatedly during the previous night's shameful ambush had evaporated in the morning's faint Belgian sun.

That afternoon Jeroen was back. This time he proposed to Alexis that the two of them issue a joint statement saying that the Eurogroup and the Greek government would proceed to discuss the technical parameters for moving on from the current programme in accordance with the new government's plans. It was a complete climbdown. A few minutes later I emailed Jeff Sachs with the news: 'We scored a tiny triumph today – our refusal to budge under enormous pressure yesterday led them to retreat fully from the insistence that we submit an application for extending the current programme as is.'

How had this come about? We found out when Alexis shared some information he had received from a Greek foreign ministry source. On arrival in Brussels, exhausted from her Ukrainian odyssey, Merkel had called Jeroen hoping for good news on Greece. When she heard of the stalemate she had apparently got cross and instructed him, as Eurogroup president, to find an accommodation – forthwith! Which is what he had proceeded to do.

A tiny triumph indeed. But it also established a pattern that would in the end prove lethal: Alexis's over-reliance on Merkel's goodwill and Jeroen's practice of speaking directly to Alexis. There was of course nothing wrong with eliciting helpful interventions from the German chancellor or with direct exchanges between Jeroen and Alexis that unblocked negotiations. What would ultimately be calamitous was the combination of two side-effects of our success: one was the confidence which Alexis gained, against my expressed doubts, that Merkel would continue to mediate on our behalf regardless of whether we were prepared to deploy our deterrent; the other was the manner in which that initial meeting between Dijsselbloem and Alexis developed into a wedge that would eventually estrange the premier from the only minister who could, and would, trigger that deterrent.

Inside the troika's lair

It was the afternoon of Thursday, 12 February when Dijsselbloem returned to offer Alexis the joint statement. The next Eurogroup meeting, at which a breakthrough was needed, was scheduled for the following Monday. That left us with three days in which to build the bridge that we had been advocating.

The German chancellor wanted our technical team to meet the troika's in order to begin discussion of our government's proposals and priorities. It was agreed that they would meet over Friday and Saturday in Brussels, leaving only Sunday for the politicians to conduct their last-minute deliberations before the Eurogroup. That gave me less than an hour in which to decide on the composition of the team we would send to confront the troika's seasoned mercenaries, if they were to make it to Brussels for the commencement of negotiations the following day. Working the phone frantically from my hotel room, I ensured that our best people were contacted and the travel arrangements made.

Meanwhile the troika was able to draw on hundreds, if not thousands, of support staff working at some of the world's best-resourced institutions – the IMF, the ECB and the European Commission. Their point men – and they were all men, at least in that first meeting – had years of experience of pushing their 'special adjustment programmes' and 'bailout' agendas down the throats of weak governments, Greek ones included. By contrast, our small team comprised George Chouliarakis, chair of the ministry's Council of Economic Advisers, and four young experts that Dragasakis had also enlisted before the election. They had only recently been brought together and had next to no experience or support network behind them, so I asked two experienced negotiators to join them: Elena Panariti, the only person on our side with inside experience of the IMF, and Glenn Kim, who had of course been instrumental in the design of Europe's bailout fund. Despite the firepower that Glenn and Elena brought to bear, Dragasakis's team viewed them with suspicion. Moreover, we still lacked serious backroom support. To ameliorate this I arranged for a technical adviser from Lazard and Jamie Galbraith to sit in a room adjacent to the negotiations, where they could run calculations and draft proposals. Lastly, I called Euclid to ask him to come to Brussels with our team to provide political supervision. After a few protests he agreed to drop everything and come.

On Friday morning we all arrived at the European Commission building for the two-day 'consultation'. The security guards at the entrance gave us the third degree, delaying our entry by half an hour.

Once inside, we were taken to a seminar room, where the people from the troika awaited. Among them were some familiar faces: Declan Costello (an 'un-Irish Irishman', as an Irish ambassador once described him) and of course Klaus Masuch, the ECB representative who had done so much to turn the people of Ireland against that institution.[1] The troika's representatives recognized a familiar face – Glenn's – and immediately protested.

When I asked what the problem was, they were initially lost for words. Costello eventually said, 'But he is not Greek!'

'So?' I asked. 'Since when is the Greek government constrained to include in its negotiating team only Greeks? Isn't your side multinational?'

Their rejoinder was revealing. 'But we know him. He has been involved in debt-restructuring exercises. We cannot be seen to be negotiating with a debt-restructuring expert.'

'As I have no right to veto your team members, you will have to accept mine,' I replied.

Our greetings at an end, and as I was the only person of full ministerial rank in the room, I began proceedings with a statement of our joint purpose.[2] My closing remarks were:

> My message to you is that this is a government interested only in Greece's recovery within a policy framework that is therapeutic for the eurozone as a whole. This is not going to be another government that tries to fool you into believing that we shall adopt a certain reform programme just in order to get the next loan tranche. You may have gathered that we do not give a damn about the next loan tranche. We prefer to go down in flames than to keep extending this indignity. The one thing the people of Greece tell us time and again is: stop the practice of the past years of coming to you cap in hand for more money, pretending to be changing the country when the country was deforming, not reforming.

On that note I withdrew to leave the teams to their discussions under Euclid's supervision. It was the first time the troika's representatives had been ordered to negotiate with technical staff of their own rank in Brussels rather than cross-examining our ministers in

Athens. In the weeks to come they would make their feelings about this demotion abundantly clear.

Over the next two days Euclid and Jamie kept me continuously informed of progress. At first the troika appeared neither aggressive nor unfriendly. The IMF's representative expressed scepticism as to how much, and how quickly, we could claw money back from rich tax dodgers, was happier with our ideas for the management authority we proposed should handle the banks' non-performing loans, and reserved his outright hostility for anything to do with trade union rights. But while the meetings themselves began in a civilized fashion, foul play was taking place outside the room, with the troika leaking to the media that 'the Greek story doesn't bind together'. Maybe it didn't fully, I responded to journalists, but it did bind together a great deal more than the troika's spectacularly failed programme.[3]

On the second day, Euclid reported, the troika turned up the hostility dial. Unwilling to acknowledge the design faults in their cherished programme, they behaved instead as if their job was to assess our ability to implement that programme. Some of the points they raised were frankly ludicrous, their accusation that we had no plan for financing our debt repayments winning the medal for conspicuous hypocrisy. Euclid's assessment was that they were conducting an experiment in calculated aggression and that it would be disastrous to acquiesce. Jamie's view was that the time had come for official Europe to realize that keeping Greece out of default would require a bridge facility and a time frame for major amendments. To impress this essential fact upon them, his advice was 'Make your exit from this swamp Tuesday afternoon [the day after the Eurogroup] and let them come to you if they want to. Apologies if this is all teaching my grandmother how to suck eggs.'

Thirteen days to the threatened bank closures

Our team's two-day meeting with the troika was never going to produce a breakthrough. Our purpose was to show good faith to Chancellor Merkel, who had intervened to ensure that our proposal for a bridge was accepted. The troika's purpose was to defend its programme while leaking to the media that we were incompetent fools whose ideas were all over the place. The real battle would take place at the political level before and during Monday's Eurogroup – on 16 February, thirteen days, according to Jeroen's threat, before every bank branch and ATM in Greece would shut down if we failed to reach an agreement.

Meanwhile my team worked frantically on a new non-paper combining and improving on our proposals. Jeff Sachs produced excellent work on Greece's debt. The Lazard team worked diligently with Elena on fiscal policy, banks and the broader reform agenda. Jamie did wonders coordinating the work. And Euclid strove to prevent me from making too many concessions in my framing analysis.[4] The international press was pretty much united in its condemnation of our efforts, parroting the troika's accusation that we were backtracking on reforms and had arrived in Brussels without any coherent proposals. The one thing they disagreed on was what Greece should be doing to stem the bank run that their reports were doing so much to fuel: half reported that I was planning to introduce capital controls, the other half admonished me for *not* doing so.

In fact, this was a question we were considering among ourselves in case the Monday Eurogroup failed to reach an agreement. Participants in this internal and secret exchange, held partly in person and partly via email, were the Lazard team, Jeff Sachs, Willem Buiter of Citibank, Jamie Galbraith, Elena Panariti, Glenn Kim, Euclid Tsakalotos and myself. I started the discussion with this statement:

> A euro 'trapped' in a eurozone member state bank operating under capital controls (e.g. Cyprus) is worth less than a paper euro or a euro elsewhere. Indeed, one could buy a nominal sum of euros' worth of deposits in a Cypriot bank for fewer paper euros or euros deposited in a German or French bank account. This discount is, in effect, an exchange rate. Capital controls, thus, are a form of 'exit' – temporary and reversible to be sure but exit nevertheless. The name on the currency would not change, but in all other respects, the currency is devalued overnight upon the imposition of capital controls.[5]

The first responses I received came from Elena, Jamie and one of my advisers from Lazard. Their gist was that if I imposed capital controls the ECB would be absolved of responsibility for the bank run it had caused and would no longer have to make the agonizing decision to switch off liquidity (ELA) to Greece's banks. Meanwhile, capital controls would be a godsend to the German government. Imposed by Athens, they would be interpreted as our admission of the need to deny our profligate citizenry access to their deposits – all at zero cost to the creditors, since our debt would remain in normal (non-devalued) euros. It would be a terrible self-inflicted defeat. Not only would we have to live under what would be to all intents and purposes a restrictive twin currency system, but the troika would have every right to claim that it had been our own choice to do so. The only non-Greeks to be hurt by capital controls would be the Greek subsidiaries of European corporations, but most of them – such as Carrefour and Crédit Agricole – had already withdrawn from Greece since 2010.

Jeff Sachs was the most vociferous opponent of self-inflicted capital controls. He phoned me to say that in all his years of advising governments he had never seen a surer way of committing political suicide than a finance minister passing legislation that stopped citizens from withdrawing their bank deposits. Politically, it was imperative to avoid them. And if capital controls could not be avoided – if, for example, the ECB pulled the plug on ELA – it was crucial that the sitting government opposed them fiercely and blamed them, as would be right and proper, on the ECB that imposed them. Willem Buiter was of the same opinion: self-imposed capital controls would deplete our political capital while doing nothing to help reduce austerity at the level of fiscal policy. Their verdict was clear: we should never, ever embrace capital controls.

Something more obliged us to reject them: by effectively creating a dual currency, capital controls fundamentally damaged the integrity of the eurozone. The Syriza government believed in the importance of doing all it could to save the eurozone and make it work for every member state, not just Greece. As capital controls would be detrimental to the EU member states' common interests, for that reason alone we had to oppose them. And if the ECB forced capital controls upon us, as it had the power to, the whole cabinet should join the inevitable demonstrators outside the closed banks with banners castigating the ECB and the Central Bank of Greece for such a fundamental dereliction of duty. In that regrettable scenario we would be duty-bound to put emergency measures in place, which would mean inaugurating our own euro-denominated parallel payments system – as well as making good on our stated intention to haircut the ECB's SMP bonds.[6]

In the weeks and months that followed, this remained my consistent advice to Alexis and our war cabinet, a mantra that Alexis and especially Pappas endorsed fully.[7] In the meantime my public position on capital controls was consistently and repetitively the same: our government was striving for a rational, mutually beneficial agreement within the eurozone; capital controls made no sense in a functioning currency union and would damage its integrity, so we opposed them; if capital controls were introduced, it would not be because we wanted, sought or approved them.

That same weekend Jeff Sachs was hard at work on the other side of the Atlantic, trying to convince the Fed to weigh in on our behalf and persuade the ECB to abandon its ongoing asphyxiation strategy. His message to Janet Yellen was simple: the new Greek government's programme of reforms and fiscal targets was reasonable; they understood well that Grexit was an exceptionally dangerous path, one that would not be taken at their instigation but only under duress from the ECB; Yellen ought to tell the Europeans not to risk destabilizing the world economy over a few billion dollars and to advise Draghi to desist from introducing capital controls that would solve nothing.

Meanwhile the press was increasingly targeting me personally in its reports. In response to a BBC profile that labelled me 'Greece's Cassandra', Bill Black, the American economist who had campaigned so effectively against Wall Street, came to my defence.

> So why does the BBC treat Varoufakis as a sexy leftist and Dijsselbloem as the respected spokesperson for the troika even though Dijsselbloem is a fanatic ideologue who has caused massive human misery because of the intersection of his inflexible ideology and economic incompetence? Varoufakis's views on the self-destructive nature of austerity as a response to the Great Recession are mainstream economic views. He certainly is a leftist, but his policy views arise from different ideological traditions most people would find antagonistic [to left-wing thinking]. That makes him a non-ideologue as the term is defined. The troika, by

contrast, is led entirely by ideologues. The primary difference is that they are exceptionally bad economists and exceptionally indifferent to the human misery they inflict on the workers of the periphery that they despise and ridicule. The BBC, the *New York Times* and the *Wall Street Journal* will never write a 'profile' of the troika's leadership that makes any of these points. The BBC profile is another example of what I call revealed biases. Journalists and media organs routinely reveal and betray their biases – biases that they hotly deny but rarely escape.[8]

But the line that raised my spirits most before my second Eurogroup came not from a left-winger or political fellow traveller but from Citi's global chief economist, Willem Buiter. At the end of an email advising against capital controls, he wrote, '*Noli illegitimi carborundum!*' which he also helpfully translated for me: 'Don't let the bastards grind you down!'

Breakthrough?

The night before the Eurogroup Alexis called with good news. The president of the European Commission, Jean-Claude Juncker, had secretly sent us a draft communiqué: could I look at it? Was it what we wanted?

A quick look made clear it was a major breakthrough.

> Greece belongs and will stay in the euro. The . . . [previous] programme agreed between Greece and its European and international partners was necessary to correct macroeconomic imbalances and put Greece on a path to secure its financing and restore market access. *But the economic and social impact of the crisis on Greece and its citizens has been immense.* There is a need to move to a *new relationship based on a mutually beneficial agreement for Greece and for Europe as a whole.* The objective is to work together on a new growth-model for Greece based on social fairness, sound public finances, a competitive export-oriented and investment-based economy, a

stable and well-supervised financial system and a modern public administration.

Its re-evaluation of the troika was also excellent.

Greece wishes to end the undue intrusive approach of the troika, understood as technocrats who operate without political mandate. Pending the agreement of a new deal by June/July, it should be possible to organize the discussions with European and international partners in a more constructive format concerning both missions and dialogue, and to ensure that technical discussions are at every moment backed by a political mandate taking full account of the need for growth and the social fairness of all reforms.

Additionally, there were helpful provisions for ending our liquidity squeeze.

[T]emporary bridge financing could be made available from the release of SMP profits . . . Progress in agreeing this needs to be based on mutual trust and credibility [what counts are actions and not words]. To this end, Greece should rapidly adopt and implement a number of key reforms.[9]

This was nothing short of an endorsement of the proposals I had been putting to every official I had met since my original trip to Paris.

Alexis and the rest of our leadership were relieved – as was I – but deep down I remained sceptical. It looked too good to be true. When I voiced my concerns, Alexis said he understood but encouraged me to hope for the best. That night I had a little more sleep than usual.

The commissioner's humiliation

The following morning my secretary informed me that Pierre Moscovici, EU economics and finance commissioner working under Jean-Claude Juncker, wanted to see me in his office at 1.30, half an hour before the Eurogroup was meant to commence. I told her I could feel 'snakes slithering in my gut', a Greek expression for being filled with foreboding.

When I entered his office, Pierre stood up to greet me. We shook hands warmly and he invited me to sit down. Without a further word he passed me a document to read. It was a version of the draft communiqué I had read the previous night . . . only a touch better. He asked for my opinion.

'Where do I sign?' I replied.

'Really?' asked Pierre.

'Absolutely.'

Pierre looked tremendously satisfied. 'Well, in that case we shall have an easy Eurogroup. Can I get you a coffee?' I accepted his offer.

While sipping my EU standard-issue coffee, I asked if he was sure that his draft would pass through the Eurogroup. Would Jeroen accept it? How would Wolfgang respond?

'Not to worry. It is all agreed.'

'By whom? What about Christine and Mario?'

'They are on board too.'

'Are you sure, Pierre?'

'Yes, we just had lunch to discuss this: Jean-Claude, myself, Mario, Christine and Jeroen.'

'And what about Wolfgang?'

'No, Wolfgang was not part of it. He will not like it. But once he sees everyone else agrees, he will relent.'

'I'm finding it hard to picture Jeroen agreeing with this communiqué in opposition to a disaffected Wolfgang – especially after our last Eurogroup.'

'Just leave it to me. All I want from you is to leave it to me and to the others to push it through. Speak as little as possible so as not to antagonize Wolfgang.'

'I'm more than happy to stay silent, Pierre.'

'No, no, do speak, but say that you support the draft communiqué and leave it at that.'

A long silence followed. We had fifteen minutes until the Eurogroup began. I continued to drink my coffee in a state of relief. *An easy Eurogroup; who could have imagined it?* I thought. Eventually my incredulity overcame me. It seemed too good to be true, I told Pierre. I just could not picture Jeroen reading out and supporting this draft under Wolfgang's piercing gaze. Pierre smiled confidently, took the draft communiqué in his hands, stood up and said he would prove it to me. We would go and talk to Jeroen right away. And so we did, Pierre leading the way down the corridor to Jeroen's office. We had ten minutes until the Eurogroup was scheduled to commence.

Pierre knocked on Jeroen's door and entered without waiting. The Eurogroup president's office was twice the size of the commissioner's and filled with aides, some sitting on a couch, others on chairs, one of them on the floor, working busily on laptops, talking to one another, all preoccupied with last-minute preparations. A powerful smell of bodies and the steamed-up windows suggested they had been labouring for a while and with some intensity. As we entered, Jeroen was standing by a long conference table in the midst of his toiling aides, reading a sheet of A4. The moment the aides saw us, they picked up their gear and papers and left the room. The thick atmosphere and the speed of their retreat heightened my premonition that all was not well.

Jeroen nodded to us to come in and sit down. He sat at the head of the table, his back to the window. Pierre sat two chairs along to Jeroen's right with his draft communiqué in his right hand. I positioned myself two chairs to Pierre's right, facing Jeroen with Pierre's profile between us. Jeroen took the A4 sheet he had been reading and slid it towards me across the table. 'Read this and tell me what you think,' he said.

I read it. It was worse even than the draft we had rejected at the first Eurogroup. It committed the Greek government 'to complete the current programme', allowing us to pursue our mandate only within the 'existing built-in flexibility of the current programme'. All the concessions in the drafts presented by Juncker the previous night and by Pierre a few moments earlier had been expunged. Even the phrase 'adjusted programme' had been dropped. In this draft the programme, undiluted by any adjective, returned with a vengeance.

I told Jeroen what I thought: that the last Eurogroup had come to an impasse because he had insisted on a communiqué that was, if anything, a touch more fathomable than this one. Turning to Pierre, who was already looking downcast, I asked what was going on. 'You just showed me a draft communiqué that I was happy to sign on the spot. You are the EU's commissioner for economic affairs. I am the finance minister of a stricken EU member state. Can I please have some clarity from the only person in this room that has official status to represent the EU?'[10]

Without looking at me, Pierre turned to Jeroen and made his first and last attempt to salvage the European Commission's dignity. 'Can we combine some of the phrases in your draft and this?' he implored in a broken voice, pointing at the draft he was holding in his right hand.

'No!' Jeroen cut him down with what could only be described as controlled aggression. 'Everything that could be taken from that draft has been taken,' he stated categorically.

I turned to Pierre. Something important was at stake at that moment, I told him, something that went beyond Greece's plight or that day's Eurogroup meeting: it was the principle of compromise and of mutual respect and of the European Commission's authority to safeguard them. 'Pierre,' I asked, 'are you just going to submit to the enforcement of this totally one-sided communiqué against the commission's views and the draft that you prepared?'

Avoiding eye contact and in a voice that quavered with dejection, Pierre responded with a phrase that might one day feature on the European Union's tombstone: 'Whatever the Eurogroup president says.'

More relaxed now, Jeroen proposed that I cross out words or phrases I 'did not like' and replace them with alternatives. So I took out my pen and did exactly that. In the opening line of Jeroen's communiqué, after 'the remarkable adjustment efforts undertaken by Greece and the Greek people of the last years' I added, 'which unfortunately failed to deliver recovery due to the existing programme's design faults'. Further down, I crossed out the commitment 'to complete the current programme' and replaced it with a commitment 'to work with Greece's European and international partners towards the design and implementation of a reform and recovery programme that the Greek people can embrace and own'. Once I was done, I slid the draft back to Jeroen.

The Eurogroup president lost his temper. Raising his voice, he accused me of time-wasting and of threatening to torpedo a second Eurogroup – accusations that were being tweeted and reported only minutes later by respected journalists, such is the efficiency of Brussels's propaganda machine.

I replied carefully but with increasing firmness, 'Jeroen, you are in no position to raise your voice at me. In the last Eurogroup you violated your obligation as Eurogroup president to offer guidance to a new finance minister. Instead, you misled me *intentionally* by repeatedly issuing a threat that the very next morning proved to be empty. I strongly advise you to refrain from raising your voice at me ever again. If not you will leave me with no option but to make your scandalous behaviour public.'

Jeroen immediately backed down. In times of tension he sometimes got overly animated, he admitted.

'Not to worry, it happens to all of us.'

With the animosity dissipating, Jeroen looked at his watch, which revealed that we were late for the Eurogroup meeting. 'Let's not delay further,' he said, as every minute that went by with the three of us absent from the floor would encourage unhelpful rumours. As we rose to leave, he suggested that as the meeting obviously could not produce an agreement we should keep it short in order to contain the damage. It occurred to me that damage of some kind was surely his intended outcome, but I held my tongue.

From the moment Jeroen shot down his suggestion of a compromise until the three of us walked into the Eurogroup, Pierre had remained silent. During the Eurogroup meeting, whenever I looked at him I imagined the horror Jacques Delors or any of the EU's founding fathers would have felt had they observed the scene in Jeroen's office. Listening to him express views in the meeting that were subservient to Schäuble and Dijsselbloem, views that I knew perfectly well he did not agree with, I was hearing the sound of the EU's descent into ignominy. His humiliation was emblematic to me of the complete subjugation of the European Commission to forces lacking legal standing or democratic legitimacy. In the months that followed, Pierre Moscovici and I remained on friendly terms and agreed on all matters of substance, but our agreement was as irrelevant as the draft communiqué he was still holding in his hand when we left Jeroen's office. Indeed, from that day onwards, every time he or Jean-Claude Juncker tried to help our side, I felt a sense of dread, for I knew that those with real power would strike us down pitilessly in order to teach Moscovici and Juncker a lesson and beat the European Commission back into its pen.

A few weeks later Pierre began to spread the story that at that meeting in Dijsselbloem's office on 16 February 2015 Jeroen and I had nearly come to blows and that he had had to step in to separate us. Later, in his memoirs, he claimed that it had been impossible to negotiate with me and welcomed my disappearance from the Eurogroup. I can only assume that these were attempts to deal with his own disgrace.

A crucial non-event

Those fifteen minutes in Jeroen's office felt much longer – and certainly more momentous – than the hours spent in the subsequent Eurogroup meeting, which began with a report from the institutions on the discussions between our two technical teams. Having made some polite noises about my team's presentation, the troika's representatives expressed their 'concerns' that our government's plans were not inspiring them with confidence that we could 'successfully complete the current programme'. Had they been trying to sound like a stuck record, they could not have done better.

So, once again, I did what I had to do.

> Our reluctance to accept the phrase 'extend the current programme and successfully complete it' stems from the determination of this government never to issue a promise that it cannot keep . . . I could, for instance, placate everyone by accepting for example the €5 billion privatization target, so as to reach agreement. But I know that I cannot deliver. Just like previous governments could not deliver in a market-place of collapsing asset prices . . . Our task is to carry out the deep reforms that my country needs and to maximize the net present value of our debt repayments to you. But if I accept the priorities, the matrix, of the current programme, I know that I shall be giving the debt-deflationary spiral another boost, I shall lose our people's support and, as a result, the country will become un-reformable . . . As the recently appointed finance minister of a country that has a credibility deficit in this room, I trust that you will understand my reluctance to promise that which I do not believe I can deliver.

As I was speaking I was thinking of the people of Greece, of Europeans everywhere, as well as of the infamous markets. How would they all respond to the news that a second Eurogroup had concluded with an impasse? How would they interpret it? I decided that the best path was one of truth and straight talking. In my press conference address I felt relaxed as I told the world as politely as possible what had really happened behind closed doors. ,

I am pleased to report that the negotiations were conducted in a collegial spirit, clearly revealing a unity of purpose . . . to establish common ground, so as to reach a meaningful, sustainable new long-term contract between Greece, official Europe and the IMF. Moreover, I have no doubt that they will continue tomorrow and the day after until there is an agreement. If this is so, why have we not managed to agree on a communiqué, a simple phrase, that will unlock imme-diately this period of deliberation?

The real reason concerns a substantial disagreement on whether the task ahead is to complete a programme that this government was elected to challenge the logic of, or to sit down with our partners with an open mind and rethink this programme, which in our estimation and in the estimation of most clear-thinking people has failed to stabilize Greece, has generated a major humanitarian crisis and has made reforming Greece, which is absolutely essen-tial, ever so hard. Remember, a debt-deflationary spiral does not lend itself to successful reforms of the form that Greece needs in order to stop being dependent on loans from its partners and from the institutions.

Last Wednesday, in the previous Eurogroup meeting, we turned down a pressing demand to subscribe to 'extending and successfully concluding the current programme'. As a result of that impasse, on the following afternoon (last Thursday, and prior to the summit) President Jeroen Dijsselbloem and Prime Minister Alexis Tsipras agreed on a joint communiqué to the effect that the two sides would explore common ground between the current programme and the plans of the new government for a new contract with Europe. This was a genuine breakthrough.

This afternoon there was another breakthrough. Prior to the Eurogroup meeting I met with Mr Moscovici, whom I want to thank for his highly positive role in this process, who presented me with a draft communiqué that I was happy to sign there and then, as it recognized the humanitarian crisis and spoke of an extension of the current loan agreement, which could take the form of a four-month intermediate programme as a transitional stage to a new contract for growth for Greece that will be deliberated and concluded during this period. It also stated that the commission would provide technical assistance to Greece to strengthen and accelerate the implementation of reforms. On the basis of that understanding between us and the commission, we were more than happy to apply for the loan agreement to be extended . . . Our only condition for the other side was that we should not be asked to commit to measures that are recessionary during the extension, such as pension cuts or VAT hikes.

Unfortunately, minutes before the Eurogroup meeting that splendid document was replaced by the Eurogroup president with another document that took us back not even to last Thursday, but indeed to last Wednesday, when we were pressurized to sign up to an extension not of the loan agreement but with the programme itself . . . Under those circumstances it proved impossible for the Greek government, despite our infinite goodwill, to sign the offered communiqué. And so the discussions continue.

We are ready and willing to do whatever it takes to reach an honourable agreement over the next two days. Our government will accept all the conditions that it can deliver upon and which do not reinforce our society's crisis. No one has the right to work towards an impasse, especially one that is mutually detrimental to the people of Europe.

This was the second time we had said no to the troika within five days. With twelve days left before the imposition of an indefinite and undesirable bank holiday, we had shown that we would not blink for the simple reason that we were not bluffing.

The war cabinet

In spite of all the evidence to the contrary, there is one abiding reason to remain confident that Europe is capable of creating good institutions: the European Investment Bank (EIB). The EIB is owned by all EU member states, whose finance ministers are its governors. The morning after my second Eurogroup meeting I had the privilege of participating in the EIB board of governors' meeting. In my inaugural presentation I expressed my enthusiasm about the EIB's potential and said a few words on how an EIB–ECB alliance might wrench Europe out of its deflationary spiral without any need for politically difficult treaty changes.[11]

Werner Hoyer, the German president of the EIB, expressed his strong interest in developing the idea, but my old mate George Osborne remained silent, preoccupied perhaps by the wave of Europhobia back home, as did Jeroen Dijsselbloem, who must also have had more important things than Europe's deflationary forces on his mind. It was time to return to Athens.

Arriving home, I was at last delivered from a state of loneliness that no amount of adrenalin can compensate for. Danae had returned from Austin, having completed our move in spite of the prize-worthy bureaucratic incompetence not just of Greece but of the United States. During the frenzied three days that followed the fact that we were still unable to spend any proper time together mattered little. It was enough to know she was near.

At Maximos, however, Alexis, Pappas and Dimitris Tzanakopoulos, Alexis's chief of Staff, were subject to fits of rage.[12] 'What did you expect of the troika?' I would ask. 'A quick capitulation?'

Dimitris would look at me with intense scepticism. 'If you want to sign the *MoU* you will have to do it over my dead body,' he would bellow at the top of his voice. Pappas would regularly shout too, though not at anyone in particular. As for Alexis, while calmer than the other two, he also lost his cool on occasion and threatened to blow up the negotiations. They were right to be outraged: we had just won an election fair and square, but official Europe was giving us absolutely no opportunity to develop our policies, run our ministries or even set our own priorities. I even understood why Dimitris was inclined to doubt me: as a non-Syriza adjunct with close ties to American insiders like Larry Summers and Jeff Sachs, I was by definition ideologically suspect, a possible stooge bent on dragging Alexis down.

In such a volatile atmosphere my best ally was Spyros Sagias, the burly secretary to the cabinet, for despite our many differences, we shared the view that any rupture with the creditors should be the result of cold calculation. In the meantime, to placate my agitated comrades and steady their nerves, I had to persuade them that I too was more than ready to withdraw from the negotiations, which looked very much like a charade, but that we should choose our moment well and calmly, avoiding any accidental breakdown in a process that was always going to be unforgiving. Until that point we should expend our efforts on making it as hard as possible for Draghi and Merkel to *justify* throttling us – first to themselves, then to the rest of the world.

While placating the agitated, I also had to energize the placid. In the five years since Bailoutistan had come into being my ministry's staff had learned to take the Greek state's subjugation to the troika for granted. It was imperative to stiffen their resolve and make them realize it was possible to operate once again as civil servants of a sovereign state. The same was true beyond the ministry as well: the whole country was in need of inspiration. With every press conference I had given in Brussels rejecting the creditors' demands, Greeks of all political colours and dispositions had stood taller with self-respect, but it was vitally important to explain that there was no place in our newfound dignity for nationalist or anti-German bigotry.

Even at the best of times, twenty-four hours often prove insufficient to deal with the tsunami of problems that rise through the bureaucracy each day to land in a finance minister's in-box. Imagine the difficulty of running the finance ministry of a bankrupt country in the midst of an all-consuming negotiation such as ours. During those three days back in Athens I did my utmost to manage the domestic projects we had set in motion, which were so important to striking a deal with our creditors – our tax evasion-busting efforts above all else.

On Wednesday, 18 February I also worked on two ministerial reports: one described my team's dealings with the troika in Brussels, summing up our proposals and making technical improvements on them; a second concentrated exclusively on reforming the tax authorities and, more broadly, public administration.

While writing them I conducted an email correspondence with Larry Summers, whose influential support could only help our cause. His pithy advice was deliciously in character: we should put forward a deal that looked like a win for Merkel and the EU but at the same time served justice and truth. *Easier said than done*, I thought, although I recognized the important point he was making. More specifically, Larry advised that I seek a six-month extension to the loan agreement that was due to expire with potentially calamitous consequences ten days later. I replied that there was a snag: six months would stretch into July and August, when €6.7 billion had to be paid to the ECB to redeem some of the SMP bonds, the very bonds I was proposing should be restructured or swapped for perpetuals or other long-dated instruments. I also related Moscovici's humiliation before my eyes, which elicited Larry's summary conclusion that the European Commission was dead in the water.

During our long and detailed exchange it became clear that before committing to help me Larry wanted to be sure that my position was pragmatic rather than inflexible. Once that was established, he wanted to know if Alexis could be trusted to agree to a sensible deal or if he was a loose cannon. I assured him that Alexis was as interested in a mutually beneficial agreement as I was, but that we would only make serious concessions in public when the other side demonstrated an intention to do the same. With these preliminaries out of the way, Larry looked to get a sense of the negotiations so far and a glimpse of how things looked from our perspective. At one point he recommended that we find a champion, someone sympathetic to our position and with the gravitas to take our case to the 'highest authorities'.

'This is why we are talking to you,' I replied. It was an answer that seemed to please him, judging by his agreement to help push our case with contacts at the IMF and the ECB.

That same day Jeff Sachs phoned me with a message from Wolfgang Schäuble's office. It proved to be an important one. Berlin was signalling that a breakthrough was possible. It appeared that they would grant us a stay of execution on condition I was willing to signal four things to the Eurogroup: interest in an extension of the loan agreement not of six months but of only seventy-five days, acceptance of 'the concept of debt sustainability', recognition of 'the need for structural reform to regain competitiveness' and agreement that the IMF must be part of the 'new parameters'.

Happy to oblige, I replied to Jeff point by point. Their request that the bridge be only seventy-five days long sat comfortably with my concern that a permanent outcome (either a good agreement or a final rupture) should be reached while our government still enjoyed incredible popularity (around 75 per cent approval ratings) and before the ECB's SMP bonds expired in July. In response to their request that I accept 'the concept of debt sustainability', I asked Jeff, 'Are our German friends acquiring a sense of humour? I go to bed every night and wake up every morning dreaming of what the troika's programme lacks – debt sustainability!' Jeff burst out laughing. Regarding the recitation of Berlin's favourite mantra – 'structural reforms' to increase 'competitiveness' – I said that I was happy to indulge them, exactly as I do on Good Friday when even atheists like me are expected to sing along to 'O My Sweet Spring'. Lastly, I saw no reason to expel the IMF from the 'new parameters' as long as I was not committing to the destruction of what was left of the trade unions or the pension system and while it continued to be the only creditor institution whose officials, Christine Lagarde and Poul Thomsen, were proclaiming that our public debt had to be haircut severely.

That afternoon the war cabinet met at Maximos, where Alexis had been receiving similarly conciliatory messages from the German Chancellery. The initial subject of debate was whether we should send a formal letter to Dijsselbloem requesting an official stay of execution from the Eurogroup. My view, with which Sagias and Dragasakis agreed, was that requesting an extension was part of our mandate as long as we did not commit to the programme in order to secure it. We then discussed the four conditions proposed by Berlin. The IMF's continued presence proved the hardest to swallow for some members of the war cabinet. Then a message came from Berlin that there was now a fifth commitment that we would need to make before being granted an extension: 'Recognize Greece's financial obligations to all its creditors.'

This seemed like a deal-breaker. The *raison d'être* of our government was debt restructuring, with a large segment of the party demanding swift and deep haircuts. 'How can we possibly recognize our debt to all our creditors?' asked an enraged Tzanakopoulos. I proposed we interpret their request in a nuanced way: a corporation can 'recognize' a debt to its bankers while still seeking deep debt restructuring to help it recover from a crisis that threatens to ruin both its shareholders and the bank. Similarly, we could 'recognize' Greece's public debt while at the same time insisting that it be immediately restructured *so that the creditors could get more of their money back*. The wing of Syriza demanding immediate and unilateral haircuts on the basis that the debt itself was illegal would of course be outraged, but ultimately this approach prevailed within the war cabinet. It was agreed that I would write to the Eurogroup with a formal extension request. By implication we would be agreeing to Berlin's condition that we 'recognize' the debt, while negotiating its restructuring.

While pleased with the decision, I was concerned that the pendulum might have swung too far in the direction of compromise. Before returning to my office to pen our request, I presented the cabinet with two possibilities. The better scenario was that Draghi and Merkel had seen enough by now to know that we would not budge, and for this reason were about to press Schäuble – and therefore the Eurogroup, which was almost fully under his control – to grant us a bridge with a view to negotiating a reasonable long-term agreement, including debt restructuring, that would settle the Greek question once and for all. The more likely scenario, however, was that the extension was a tactical ploy: by delaying any outcome they were simply waiting for the depletion of both our current popularity and our small liquidity reserves so that by the time the extension expired in June they could be sure of our exhausted government's total capitulation.

If the latter was indeed the case then, I argued, our best strategy would be to request the extension while at the same time signalling to the troika that any attempt to wear us down through a tightening of the liquidity noose would be met with a refusal to make the forthcoming repayments to the IMF; that any effort to push us back into the straitjacket of its failed programme or to deny us debt restructuring would be met with a cessation of negotiations; and that any threat of closing down our banks and imposing capital controls would be met with unilateral haircuts of the ECB's SMP bonds, with the activation of the parallel payments system and with changes to the law governing the Central Bank of Greece in a manner that restored parliament's sovereignty over it.

By the same token, the worst strategy would be to request an extension, get it, but then fail to signal our readiness to trigger these measures if our creditors were to stray from the spirit of the interim agreement. Were we to make that error, I argued, they would drag us through the mud over the period of the extension and then, at the moment of our greatest weakness, around the end of June, slaughter us.

They all agreed – Pappas and Alexis enthusiastically, Dragasakis with a noncommittal nod, Sagias with a helpful reminder that the ECB's SMP bonds were the last sliver of Greece's public debt still under the jurisdiction of Greek law, which meant that any challenge to our decision to haircut them unilaterally would be heard not in a hostile London or New York court but in the Greek courts.

Over the next four months, as the liquidity squeeze grew tighter and threats of bank closures and capital controls mounted, I would regularly remind Alexis and the war cabinet of this decision. Every time I did so, he and they would confirm their commitment to it.[13] Alas, as the weeks went by their enthusiasm waned and the confirmations began to sound ritualistic. Day by day, week by week, my worst-case scenario began to creep up on us.

Happy days and constructive ambiguity

Back at my office I put together the letter requesting the extension, had it read by my team, checked by Alexis and Sagias in his capacity as cabinet secretary and the government's top lawyer and then sent it on to the Eurogroup president. Its stated purpose was to allow Greece and the Eurogroup to begin work 'on the new contract for recovery and growth that the Greek authorities envisage between Greece, Europe and the International Monetary Fund, which will replace the current agreement'.

It was a letter in the spirit of compromise. Indeed, as I had told the French finance minister at our first meeting in Paris, I chose the word 'contract' to replace the IMF's 'programme' in order to reflect Rousseau's notion of an agreement between equals. As such, the letter contained phrases that the troika would despise, such as 'social fairness and mitigating the great social costs of the ongoing crisis' and 'the substantive, far-reaching reforms that are needed to restore the living standards of millions of Greek citizens through genuine economic growth, gainful employment and social cohesion', as well as phrases that would be hard for our side, especially the Syriza rank and file, to stomach. 'The Greek authorities recognize Greece's financial obligations to all its creditors,' I wrote, and intended 'to cooperate with our partners in order to avert technical impediments in the context of the Master Facility Agreement which we recognize as binding'. The letter represented the furthest we could go to satisfy Berlin.

That night, once the letter had been dispatched and while we waited for Brussels to reply, I allowed myself a rare indulgence: Danae and I attended the Greek National Theatre to see a performance of Samuel Beckett's *Happy Days*. As we left, the journalists waiting nearby expressed surprise at our choice of such a bleak play. Compared to the crude asphyxiation one experienced at the Eurogroup, I told them, Beckett's vision of a woman's gradual burial lifted the heart not just because great art is inherently uplifting but also because of his protagonist's remarkable capacity to meet her suffocation with inexhaustible defiance.

Next morning the answer came via back channels from Berlin and Brussels. My letter had been deemed 'helpful' and a 'good basis' for a Eurogroup agreement the following day. But what did that mean? After the false dawn a few days earlier when the European Commission's excellent draft communiqué had been torpedoed by the Eurogroup president, nothing could be taken for granted. So, on 20 February I flew to Brussels in hope but without a trace of its uncouth cousin optimism.

Before the Eurogroup assembled, I had a quick meeting with Christine Lagarde. She was confident that agreement was around the corner. 'But will Wolfgang give up on his crusade to commit me to the programme and the *MoU*?' I asked. The expression on Christine's face expressed confidence but also concern.

Then I met Jeroen. It was our first (and last) businesslike meeting. Jeroen wanted to break two pieces of bad news to me. First, the extension would be for four months rather than the six I had requested in my letter. As I had indicated to Jeff Sachs, I did not mind that at all. Second, the ECB was adamant that a 'credit card' facility of up to just under €11 billion (designed to be used on behalf of Greece's banks if they needed emergency capital) be transferred from the HFSF to its parent facility in Luxembourg, the EFSF. This was a little like your bank telling you that an overdraft facility you have been granted but have not yet used would be transferred to your bank's headquarters from your local branch.[14]

I told Jeroen I would grant these concessions, which were of little real consequence as far as I was concerned, in return for something I truly valued: policy space. Eurozone member states receiving money from Europe's bailout fund (the EFSF and later the European Stability Mechanism) have to be 'assessed' every few months. This was inescapable, and we had always been prepared to accept it as a condition of the interim agreement we were seeking. The multi-billion-euro question was: assessed by whose criteria? Wolfgang Schäuble's immediate answer would have been the criteria laid down in the *MoU* of the existing programme. My mandate, however, was to demand that the new Greek government regain the right to be the author, or at least co-author, of these criteria, and that in rewriting these criteria we put an end to the ridiculous levels of austerity that prevented Greece from recovering. In short, I demanded that the *MoU*, or at least the 30 per cent of its articles that were unacceptable, be replaced with a new list of reforms proposed by our government, while our primary surplus target be reduced from 4.5 per cent of national income to no more than 1.5 per cent.

To my great surprise, Jeroen agreed. As for the primary surplus, he suggested that we replace the target of 4.5 per cent with the words 'sizeable primary surpluses', leaving the question of whether 1.5 per cent was 'sizeable' enough to be negotiated. I counter-proposed that we replace 'sizeable' with 'appropriate'. Again he agreed, and soon the draft communiqué was complete.

> The Greek authorities will present a first list of reform measures, based on the current arrangement, by the end of Monday February 23. The institutions will provide a first view [of] whether this is sufficiently comprehensive to be a valid starting point for a successful conclusion of the review. This list will be further specified and then agreed with the institutions by the end of April.

If this paragraph made it through to the final communiqué, I thought, it would constitute a triumph for the eurozone's weaker countries. It would be the first time a government incarcerated within a bailout programme had been granted the right to replace the troika's *MoU* with an agenda for reform of its own composition. Of course it was only a preliminary victory since the institutions' approval would be required before the agenda was agreed, but it was a giant step in the direction of emancipation – the equivalent of a prisoner escaping from solitary confinement, jumping over the prison's perimeter fence and running through the woods.

The communiqué's major downside was that it offered Greece no respite from the liquidity squeeze. During a brief meeting within the Eurogroup I put it to Mario Draghi that, with this agreement in place, the ECB had no excuse not to reinstate the waiver, signalling an end to the threat of bank closures and a return to normality. As long as the ECB then allowed Greece's banks to buy Treasury bills at the rate

they had been doing prior to our election, then by my team's calculations, assuming some serious economizing as well, we could survive
until the end of June, giving us four months in which to build the
long-term agreement we were seeking. Some say I should have
demanded this commitment from Draghi in writing. Others have called
me a fool for not having done so.

They are probably the same people who would have called me an
idiot if I *had* demanded a written commitment from Mario, thus
yielding another impasse. After all, according to the ECB's rules, its
President is not at liberty to issue such written statements. The point
of the interim agreement was merely to carve out the time necessary
to see if common ground existed. Instead of specificity, we were
looking for language that was sufficiently ambiguous to satisfy both
parties without exposing the rifts that remained between us. At this
stage avoiding each side's red lines was essential if there was to be
any progress. Euclid reminded me of the term often credited to Henry
Kissinger for this diplomatic technique: 'constructive ambiguity'. This
was our immediate task.

White smoke: the 20 February agreement

The Eurogroup meeting of 20 February 2015, a mere eight days before
Greece's banks were due to be shut down, was the easiest one I sat
through. A monument to studied ambiguity, it also confirmed the
German chancellor's capacity to wrest command of the Eurogroup,
albeit momentarily, from the man who generally controls it – her own
finance minister. Emmanuel Macron, France's economy minister, sent
me a text just before the Eurogroup telling me that he had had lunch
with Angela Merkel and had pressurized her to help deliver a deal
acceptable to both sides. I was also informed that Merkel had given
Dijsselbloem direct instructions to end the Greek saga, at least for the
time being, by approving the communiqué.

In every other Eurogroup, once the floor was opened for statements
by the ministers, the same ritual occurred. First, Dr Schäuble's cheerleading team of Eastern European ministers would compete with one
another as to who could out-Schäuble Schäuble. Then ministers representing previously bailed-out countries such as Ireland, Spain, Portugal
and Cyprus – Schäuble's model prisoners – would add their Schäuble-

compatible twopenn'orth before, finally, Wolfgang himself would step
in to put the finishing touches to a narrative that had been under his
thumb throughout. Alas, on 20 February 2015 nothing worked for him
the way it should. Released from Wolfgang's spell by the German
chancellor's direct instructions, Jeroen read out the draft communiqué
and then gave me the floor to express my support for it – which I
readily did, hailing it as an important moment in Europe's history, a
moment when European leaders demonstrated that democracy is not
a luxury to be afforded to creditors and denied to debtors, a moment
when the logic of common ground and common endeavours prevailed
over dogma unsupported by economic reality.

After my short speech Jeroen opened the debate to the others. No
nameplates were stood on their side. None! Instead of the usual rush
of Schäuble cheerleaders, there was an awkward silence. Fearful of
Wolfgang, they would not speak in favour of the draft communiqué,
but they dared not speak against it either when it had the backing of
Angela Merkel. Caught between two masters, they lowered their heads
and kept their thoughts to themselves. Their dilemma was made no
easier when Mario Draghi and Christine Lagarde proceeded to offer
the draft communiqué their support, though with no enthusiasm.
Predictably outraged, Wolfgang repeatedly took to the floor to demand
that the communiqué reconfirm Greece's commitment to the MoU
and the existing programme, which he insisted was the only show in
town. But Jeroen would not budge.

That Wolfgang doggedly opposed the communiqué there is no
doubt, but every time he spoke against it, his voice grew shriller and
his arguments weaker. Eventually I lost count of how many times he
intervened – it must have been more than twenty. The only ministers
to back him were Portugal's, who spoke only twice, and my next-door
neighbour, the Spanish minister Luis de Guindos, who spoke up more
than ten times – surely a reflection of his government's fear that any
Syriza success would inspire support for its equivalent, Podemos, in
Spain's impending general election.

Confined to the role of observer in this clash between an absent
Merkel and an omnipresent Schäuble, I had time to look at my
phone and exchange messages with my comrades. The meeting had
begun at 3.30 p.m. At 8.30 Euclid texted me anxiously to find out
how things were progressing: 'Are we oscillating to a successful
conclusion?'

'So far Wolfgang is hopelessly isolated,' I replied.

'Has Draghi committed to releasing the noose?'

'Not formally. Will talk to him soon.'

Alexis also texted: 'The media is reporting that things are going well for us. Stay cool, patient and prevent any edits that worsen the communiqué for us.'

'So far so good,' I texted back. 'Wolfgang is failing to control the proceedings.'

At 8.39 I texted Euclid and Alexis to inform them of an extraordinary development: Wolfgang had left the room, clearly angry.

Alexis could not believe it. 'Can we leak this?' he asked.

But a few minutes later Wolfgang returned. I stood up and walked over to him to say that, while I understood his opposition, an interim agreement based on the communiqué on the table would be excellent for both our countries and could become the foundation of an end to this otherwise endless drama. He conveyed his appreciation of my gesture but seemed too annoyed to indulge me.

At 8.56 Alexis asked me for an update.

The Schäuble camp was not giving up, even though it had been reduced to just the Iberian contingent and mainly to Luis de Guindos. But Jeroen was managing to contain them. 'The Dutchman is handling it well,' I replied.

At 9.14 Alexis asked me if there was a chance that the German–Spanish alliance could scuttle the communiqué.

'They are trying their best,' I responded. A few minutes later I informed him that Lagarde had taken to the floor in support of the communiqué. 'She is salvaging it,' I texted. Alexis seemed pleased but, like Euclid, was preoccupied with the ECB. Would Draghi stop the asphyxiation? I replied that we should get this agreement in the bag first. Then I would put it to Draghi that he had a duty to end the hostilities, beginning with the return of the waiver. One step at a time.

At 9.28 Alexis texted again: was there a chance of failure? Had the communiqué been altered since Jeroen first read it out?

Nine minutes later I texted him back, 'We won this one. But let's not celebrate. The last thing we need is to upset Wolfgang further.'

A little later an anxious Emmanuel Macron texted me too. 'We had a good result,' I informed him. 'Now we need to get down to work. Thanks for the help.'

Emmanuel replied with a comradely 'Let's keep fighting.'

On my way out of the room, I walked over to Mario Draghi to have the chat that he wanted to avoid. I reminded him of what he had told me in his office sixteen days earlier as well as over the phone later that night, when he had pulled with suspicious haste the Greek banks' waiver, cutting them off from ECB liquidity: that once there was an agreement at the Eurogroup level, the ECB would no longer have a reason to deny Greek banks the waiver. Mario nodded and promised, now the Eurogroup had extended Greece's loan agreement, that the ECB Executive Board would discuss the matter soon. I pressed him for a date when Greek banks would be reconnected to ECB liquidity. As he was walking away he said it would be 'soon' but probably not before the following Wednesday, when the top echelons of the ECB were scheduled to meet. For now it was as much as I could do.

I headed for the press room, relieved that this time the waiting journalists would be able to report white smoke signalling an agreement. But I was also pleased that Alexis still had his eye on the ball: in his last text before the press conference he reminded me to emphasize in front of the cameras that the phrase 'appropriate surpluses' in the communiqué translated into no more than 1.5 per cent of national income and the 'end of 3.5 per cent'.

Two months later, as I was making my way back from Alexis's office to the finance ministry, I would reread that text, my spirit almost broken.

A moment to savour, darkly

It took three Eurogroup meetings for Greece and Europe to turn a page. In the end, as I told the gathered press, we showed that negotiation means compromise but also a readiness to say no to proposals, suggestions and offers that we do not have the moral right, the political right, the mandate to say yes to. We combined logic and ideology, respect for the rules and respect for democracy. We countered the view that a heavily indebted country cannot have elections that change anything. We stood firm under immense pressure. Our struggle was not a nationalist, populist attempt to improve our people's lot at the expense of other Europeans. From day one we said that we were not in the business of short-changing our partners but of recalibrating our policies with the interests of the whole of Europe in mind. We refused to see our negotiation as a zero-sum game where our gain would be someone else's loss.

Having thanked Jeroen for steering that evening's Eurogroup towards an interim agreement, I hailed it as an opportunity to get down to work. Over the weekend, I informed the press, my team and I would be working round the clock to prepare our government's list of reforms to be submitted in three days' time. 'It will be hard work,' I admitted, 'but we shall do it gladly now that we have moved on to a new relationship of equals,' for this was our opportunity to prove that partnership, not coercion, was the route to success.

The weekend ahead was going to be very long indeed. Yes, we had won the right to replace the most toxic part of the *MoU* with our own radically different reforms. But that right did not translate automatically into a reality. It was merely the first step towards a new deal for Greece. The agreed process involved three further steps. Once we had submitted our list of reforms via email – by late afternoon on Monday, 23 February, less than seventy-two hours later – the institutions would have until Tuesday morning to study the proposal in time for a Eurogroup teleconference on Tuesday afternoon. There, Draghi, Lagarde and Moscovici, representing the three creditor institutions, would pronounce on whether my list was 'sufficiently comprehensive' to be used as the benchmark by which my government would be assessed. The third step, the assessment, would be in mid-April, which if successful would lead to a release of funds with which to repay the IMF. Only then, with these three steps completed, could we enter the Promised Land of negotiations, to be concluded by the end of June (when the interim agreement expired), over the new contract for recovery and growth that we were demanding – our Holy Grail.

I am often asked whether I thought there was ever a serious probability of successfully navigating those treacherous waters to a new deal for Greece within the eurozone. I answer that the actual probability was neither computable nor important. We had to give our creditors the chance to come to the table with humane, logical ideas, and the opportunity to listen to ours. It was always going to be a long shot, but our mandate from the people of Greece was to do our utmost to secure a sustainable future within the eurozone.

To this day I receive ferocious criticism for having concluded the 20 February Eurogroup agreement. Greece's parliamentary opposition, tainted by their signatures on the two previous bailout programmes, were keen to claim that I had signed up to their *MoU* but, being the fool that I am, without receiving any of the money. Of course, they overlooked the fact that it had taken three Eurogroup meetings to remove any mention of the *MoU* or programme from the communiqué. Curiously, Syriza's Left Platform argued the same, ascribing the blame for our eventual surrender to the 20 February agreement rather than to any of the war cabinet's subsequent failures. There are also critics who argue that constructive ambiguity always favours the stronger party in a negotiation, neglecting to mention that Schäuble fought tooth and nail to block the agreement. And there are comrades, including Euclid, who criticized me after the fact for failing to insert into the communiqué a phrase that committed the ECB to ending our liquidity squeeze, forgetting that the ECB's sacred independence meant no such phrase could ever be included in a Eurogroup communiqué.

Nonetheless, what the hail of criticism for the 20 February agreement that followed our eventual defeat in July 2015 did confirm was my and Danae's prognosis after I had accepted the offer of the finance ministry in Alexis's apartment: no matter what its true causes might be, our government's failure would have a single parent – me.

What is interesting though is the absurd but widespread notion that our eventual defeat was hard-wired into that Eurogroup agreement. The interim agreement of 20 February was a necessary but insufficient first step towards escaping Bailoutistan. To make it sufficient and set us on the road to liberation, it had to be accompanied by an unwavering willingness on the part of the war cabinet to enact our pre-agreed battle plan during the window during the window of opportunity it provided. We needed constantly to be prepared to activate our deterrent the moment we were threatened with bank closures and capital controls. And to be prepared we had to believe that the worst possible outcome for Greece would be to sign up to an extension of Bailoutistan in order to keep the banks open. This use of the 20 February agreement would have definitely delivered us from Bailoutistan. One way or another, sustainability and dignity would have returned to Greece, either by means of a negotiated new deal within the eurozone or through a painful rupture that would at least restore Greece's capacity to make its way in the world.

On the flight from Brussels to Athens those Greeks who happened to be on the plane were ecstatic, even though most supported the opposition parties. We had stood up to the troika and were returning home with an honourable interim agreement that Germany's finance minister had tried his best to scupper. What was not to celebrate? But despite the fatigue and my eyelids growing heavy, one question haunted me: would the war cabinet do what was necessary to keep the troika in line? And would we activate our deterrent if the creditors tried any dirty tricks?

Back in Athens I received an email from Norman Lamont. 'I was amused that *The Economist* criticized you for saying Greece was bankrupt,' he wrote. Norman's amusement stemmed from the fact that, by saying this, I was implying that the ECB's executives had been breaking their own rules for years, for the European Central Bank's own statutes prohibited it from loaning money to bankrupt states. Clearly, the story originated with allies of the ECB who, unlike Norman, were not amused and were briefing against me. More worryingly, the fact that these leaks were coming from Frankfurt *after* the 20 February agreement suggested that the ECB was not about to loosen the noose. It confirmed in my mind that, unless we were truly prepared to default to the IMF, haircut the ECB's SMP bonds and prepare our parallel payments system, the creditors would not honour the spirit of the interim agreement.

In the same email Norman gave me his perspective on the events of the past few days:

> You seem to be facing a lot of headwinds (like Ulysses?) but nonetheless making some hard-earned progress against the tide. I guess the big prize is what you get after four months even if you have to yield a bit on the short term 'structural reforms' (a phrase everyone uses but no one knows what it means). Anyway for what it is worth I think you are ahead of the unlikeable Schäuble on points.

That Wolfgang was furious about this widespread impression, I had no doubt. That he would hit back, I knew. What I had no inkling of was that the knife would be wielded first from within my ministry and, a little later, from within our own war cabinet and in the same office in Maximos where Alexis had moved me to tears on the day of our swearing-in.

10

Unmasked

On my way from the airport to parliament, where a relieved cabinet was already discussing the Eurogroup agreement, my mobile phone brought acclaim and damnation in equal measure. Jeff Sachs emailed praise for achieving 'a 120-day period to think and brainstorm together . . . an historic breakthrough, breaking all of the rules of top-down management in the eurozone. All kudos!' But two left-wing heroes of my childhood whose views I cared about deeply – Manolis Glezos, hero of the anti-Nazi resistance and a member of the European parliament in February 2015, and the legendary composer Mikis Theodorakis – denounced the agreement.[1] They were all correct. It *was* an historic breakthrough but it *would* bring defeat and humiliation if we were not careful.

Later that Saturday, 21 February, I arrived back at the ministry to work on the list of reforms that we would propose as a substitute for the *MoU*. The padded door to my office shut behind me with a thud and I dived in. My mission was to excise the toxic commitments of the *MoU* – the 'miscellany of ugliness', as some of my team liked to refer to them – which amounted to some 30 per cent of the overall document and which pushed for greater austerity and an intensified class war against the weakest, and replace them with new policy intentions. These needed to be phrased in such a way that the troika would not object to them, but had to open the door to the genuinely therapeutic measures we had been arguing for, which it would most certainly oppose. In theory I had forty-eight hours to complete the document. In reality, with so much else pressing upon me, I had a lot fewer.

Once it was submitted on Monday evening, Mario Draghi, Christine Lagarde and Pierre Moscovici would have the following morning in which to review it before the Eurogroup teleconference scheduled for Tuesday afternoon. There would be no quibbling; three of them would simply pass judgment on the list of measures in turn, giving it either a green light or a red flag, with ministers having no say.

A red flag at the teleconference would be ruinous. The hard-won results of our efforts over the previous weeks would evaporate, the banks would shut down and we would look like spurned petitioners. It was essential to know whether this was going to happen in advance, well before Monday night. If an impasse was inevitable, then I would refuse to submit *any* reform list and instead hail the instincts of old warriors like Glezos and Theodorakis at a press conference where the failure of the negotiations would be announced and explained. At the same time, I was equally desperate to avoid a stalemate because of some minor difference that could have been smoothed over. To keep a line of communication open with the creditors, I had left my deputy and representative in the Eurogroup Working Group George Chouliarakis behind in Brussels. His brief was to elicit from key Brussels functionaries where the creditors would draw their red lines, test the creditors' sensitivity to our own and ultimately warn me prior to Monday night if a deadlock was on the cards.

All that Saturday night I was holed up alone in my office, sweating over the escape plan that my incarcerated nation would present to its jailors. I began with its fourth and final section, which I entitled 'Humanitarian Crisis'. I chose this title as a litmus test. Jeroen Dijsselbloem had dismissed the phrase as 'too political' for inclusion in the communiqué at my first Eurogroup. If Tuesday's teleconference rejected my list because of this section, I would know what to do: announce the end of negotiations at Eurogroup level, press the Off button on my teleconference device and call Alexis to deploy our deterrent. Throughout the document the challenge was to strike the right balance between ambiguity and specificity. But while I would remain intentionally ambiguous in many areas, the last entry in this final section was very clear. It expressed the ambition to commit the Greek government, and a kicking and screaming Eurogroup, to providing poor families with a stigma-free prepaid debit card to pay for food, shelter, medicine and electricity.

With the final section completed, I began to unpick those *MoU* entries that damaged basic rights. I wrote in a ban on evictions from a family's main home; a reassessment of the criteria for privatizations to include minimum investment levels, environmental standards, labour rights and a concern for local communities; the establishment of an investment bank to exploit public assets and share the profits with the suffering pension funds; the suspension of previously agreed reductions of pensions; an affirmation of our commitment to reinstate the right to trade union representation; a guarantee that minimum civil service wages would not be cut further; and so on. In exchange I let a large number of the MoU's 'prior actions' stand. Some were ugly, some bad, a few good. But that's what the spirit of compromise dictated. In the closing discussion of the 20 February Eurogroup Dijsselbloem had specified that my list should be 'wide but shallow', taking up no more than three pages. In the end I sent them five.

Working with the enemy

On Sunday George Chouliarakis returned from Brussels with news. He had been holding talks with the European Commission's key troika representative, Declan Costello, who apparently was positive and keen for us to pass Tuesday's test. I asked if he had shown Costello my draft. He had, and the response had been good, but Costello wanted us to reframe the list in the troika's preferred lingo and template. 'They are happy with the content but are keen to retain their own format. Let me go to my office, freshen up, and reformat our list in their language,' Chouliarakis suggested. It sounded good. Accepting their stale format but losing some of their terrible content was well within my red line.

When George returned, he brought with him a disappointing document. Its language was clearly that of the troika's MoU, but the insertions that were supposed to reflect my earlier draft were also either absent or unacceptably watered down. So I pulled out a chair and invited George to sit next to me while I edited his text. It was an uneasy collaboration. We tried hard to work together, with some success, but it was clear that we were on different wavelengths – analytically, politically, culturally. For George the document was an end in itself. For me it was a stepping stone to what came after the reform list was agreed: front-loaded debt restructuring. Without debt restructuring my reform list, indeed any reform agenda, would be rendered irrelevant by the process of extracting debt repayments. This would keep Greece trapped within a debt-deflation spiral – a state in which any society is impervious to reform and will eventually fail. At the analytical level our differences were also beginning to mount. The more we discussed fiscal policy the more I was struck by George's tolerance of the troika's ridiculous economic models, which I thought engendered a disconcertingly relaxed attitude to its usurious fiscal targets.

A finance minister should have complete confidence in the chair of their Council of Economic Advisers, who manages the team of economic analysts that do the minister's number-crunching and who represents the minister at crucial forums. I did not have that confidence, but that was not George's fault. It was mine for not having made it my top priority to find someone of my own for that key position and to insist on their appointment against the deputy prime minister's will. Still, there was a job to do and we had to do it. Over many hours, sitting next to each other, we did our best.

Using my laptop I reshaped Chouliarakis's Word document until we were both happy with it. Just after 9 p.m. we sent it to Costello for his response. The reply arrived a little more than three hours later. Happily, the litmus test had not been failed. To my surprise, Costello raised no objections to the 'Humanitarian Crisis' section. Indeed, he did not even mention it, choosing instead to confront me on 'two other areas where the text would cause major problems': evictions and privatizations.

Any moratorium on evicting families from their primary residence jarred terribly with the troika. It had promised bankers the freedom to repossess and auction off all residences, large and small, primary or secondary. It demanded the liquidation of businesses and households in arrears, compensating them with a few hundred euros each month with which to pick themselves up off the scrapheap on which Lambros and so many others were already languishing. Even though Costello could not have known of (or given a damn about) my oath to Lambros, he was smart enough to realize that I would not countenance accepting these measures. So he proposed some 'language', as he put it: how about saying that the government was committed to 'avoiding' evictions without mentioning a moratorium 'at this stage'? Chouliarakis thought it a reasonable concession in the grander scheme of things. I agreed.

On privatizations Costello pushed me on two fronts. First, he demanded that no privatization effected by the previous government was to be reversed and that privatizations be allowed to continue if the tender process had already commenced. On this I agreed to respect ongoing tenders while inserting a clause that left it to the courts to decide whether a privatization should be reversed, safe in the knowledge that Greece's judges were keen to have their constitutional powers restored to them so that, for the first time since 2010, they could keep a check on the looting of the country and undo the scandalous fire sales.[2] Second, the troika was dead against my proposal for a new public development bank that would use public assets as collateral to generate investment and share any profit with the haemorrhaging pension funds. Costello's diplomatic solution was to suggest I leave it out of my list altogether 'as it would take several months to develop the idea and is not something which needs to be discussed or settled in the immediate future'. It was another concession that I agreed to, making a mental note to place it at the top of my priorities from April onwards.

After a few hours' sleep on my office red couch, I embarked on a marathon of meetings to secure the consent of the prime minister, war cabinet colleagues and key ministers. Everyone had a strong view about one item or another on my list, while the strongest opposition came from colleagues belonging or close to the Left Platform. From their perspective, our negotiations with the creditors were fundamentally ill advised, and the couching of my list in troika-speak bordered on the treacherous. This reflected their view that Grexit ought to be our goal – a line that was not only strategically wrong, to my mind, but also at odds with the mandate we had been given by the electorate. Despite these and other objections, by the afternoon of Monday 23 February we had achieved a consensus.

Around the same time I received three separate emails from troika officials 'recommending' that I reintroduce parts of the *MoU* that I had excised. Each of them wrote, unlike Costello, in a private capacity, as 'friends' who wanted to avert a 'dead end'. I replied matter-of-factly to each that I was not prepared to resuscitate toxic measures that not even Costello had demanded. If they felt strongly enough, I suggested, they could advise their leaders (Lagarde, Moscovici and Draghi) to reject my reform list during the following day's teleconference.

They relented, informally agreeing to the list I had dispatched on Monday afternoon. But not without an injurious delay. Their reluctant green lights did not arrive until just after midnight. Was this a tactical delay? If not it was certainly serendipitous for their side. For, unwilling as I was to formally submit my list until I had had word that it would not be rejected, I had been forced to wait. Midnight had come. Nothing. Then, at ten minutes past, all three had responded with miraculous synchronicity. By thirteen minutes past midnight, my list had been sent to Costello and his counterparts in the ECB and the IMF.

One might imagine that a delay of thirteen minutes is neither here nor there. Not so when the dogs of the propaganda war are out to get you. On Tuesday morning the world's media used those thirteen minutes to portray me as incompetent, tardy, disorganized. VAROUFAKIS MISSES DEADLINE FOR SUBMITTING REFORM LIST was the typical headline. It was a charge I could not challenge without revealing that I had been negotiating secretly with Greece's creditors before formally submitting the list. Still, as charges against me went during that period, it was trifling. That Tuesday morning the Brussels propaganda machine was hard at work, and another charge, incomparably greater in its capacity to wound, was on its way.

Soon after leaking that I had been late in submitting my proposals, they went on to leak the list itself – hours before a meeting of the Greek cabinet convened to approve it formally. The majority of my fellow ministers had not yet seen the list and were understandably peeved that they should have first had sight of it while scanning the news on their tablets on the way to Parliament House. But what turned their legitimate annoyance into an immense political and personal blow were the headlines under which it appeared: COSTELLO'S LIST was a typical example from the Greek media sympathetic to the troika. VAROUFAKIS: THE TROIKA'S LATEST STOOGE was a left-wing site's interpretation. One of the ministers filing into the meeting gave me a look that combined pity and disappointment and told me that he had not imagined I would be taking orders from Costello.

Dazed by the preposterous accusation that Costello had authored my list, my initial reaction was to dismiss it as yet another fabrication, except that on this occasion the media had a hook on which to hang their charge. Apparently, one smart journalist (who later became a friend) discovered that by clicking on the 'Properties' tab of the leaked document, one could see its 'Author' – which the software defined as the registered user of the computer on which the document had first been created. Hearing this I grabbed my laptop, opened the document containing my reform list, clicked on 'File' and then on 'Properties' to see that next to 'Author' it read 'Costello Declan (ECFIN)' and just below, under 'Company', two words that completed my humiliation: 'European Commission'.

With the cabinet meeting about to commence, it took an immense effort to stifle my fury and concentrate on gaining the ministers' consent. But immediately after I had secured it, after a two-hour debate, I returned to the ministry and summoned Chouliarakis. Yes, he admitted, the document that he had presented to me in my office, which I had then proceeded to edit radically, had been created by Declan Costello in Brussels, not by him. 'And you did not see fit to tell me this? To inform your minister that *your* document, which I was clearly unhappy with, was composed by our chief enemy?' I asked. No answer. 'Let's say that it escaped you at first, or that you were embarrassed to admit it,' I continued. 'When you saw me labouring over it to amend its contents radically, struggling with a Word document created by the troika's sternest functionary, did it not occur to you *then* to warn me? Not even as I was about to email it to the troika?'

In a manner wholly typical of Chouliarakis, he shrugged off my questions with infuriating nonchalance and a face which hid thoughts no one could have deciphered.[3] Under normal conditions he would have been sacked there and then, but normality was a luxury that I never experienced during my time in office. The landline was already ringing. The Eurogroup teleconference was beginning. I took my place next to the receiver, clutching my notes, with Chouliarakis next to me. A greater battle demanded my full attention.

Schäuble's revenge

When negotiating from a weak position, a crackling telephone line only makes things worse. In face-to-face meetings one can at least use one's voice, eye contact and physical presence to gain greater control of the room. The teleconference format, by contrast, makes an already challenging meeting harder still. On this occasion, to level out the grossly uneven playing field I had succeeded in securing a commitment from Jeroen Dijsselbloem that the teleconference would only allow the leaders of the three institutions (European Commission, ECB and

IMF) to deliver a binary verdict: was my list 'sufficiently comprehensive to act as the basis for a successful conclusion of the final review' of Greece's second bailout agreement or was it not? That was the only question on the table that day. Indeed, at the end of the previous Eurogroup meeting on 20 February Jeroen had told everyone, much to Wolfgang Schäuble's particular disappointment, that there would be no debate during our teleconference on 24 February. Its limited remit was to allow the institutions to emit either white smoke or black. Nothing else.

With prior agreement to my list having been secured, albeit unofficially, it would have been exceedingly surprising if white smoke did not appear. But if it did not, I had enough ammunition to expose the troika's duplicity at a press conference and win the blame game. My main fear was that Wolfgang would somehow overturn the ban on a debate, initiate one over the sputtering phone line and somehow get the *MoU* back on the table. All my mental energy went into imagining how he would try to do this and how I would stop him. My best defence lay with Jeroen's prior and explicit commitment, but did I trust the Dutchman?

As it turned out, Wolfgang did not have to gatecrash the teleconference with a debate, nor did Jeroen have to go back on his promise to prevent one. The set-up was cleverer than I had imagined. It became apparent as soon as the institutions' leaders opened their mouths. The first to speak was Dobrovskis, the Latvian vice chair of the European Commission: 'In the view of the Commission this list is sufficiently comprehensive to act as the basis for a successful conclusion of the final review . . .' White smoke as expected, I thought with a sigh of relief. But then Dobrovskis continued: 'Let me stress, however, that . . . this list does not substitute the *MoU*, which constitutes the official legal basis for the programme.'

Confounded at first, I quickly recognized what was going on: Wolfgang Schäuble had risen from his humiliation three days before and was once more in full control. Over the weekend, while I had been struggling to produce a replacement for the *MoU*, the German finance minister had been successfully turning the tide back in his favour – so successfully that he did not have to interrupt, force a debate or even speak at all in order to resuscitate the *MoU*.[4] By stating clearly that my list did not 'substitute the *MoU*' Dobrovskis had done Schäuble's work for him. For if the list did not replace the *MoU*, then there was no point in the list at all. We were back at the impasse of the first Eurogroup.

Was Dobrovskis acting alone? Pierre Moscovici, Mario Draghi and Christine Lagarde spoke up to confirm that he was not.

'We understand, consistent with the Eurogroup decision of last Friday,' said Mario, 'that the list does not call into question the current arrangements and thus existing commitments in the context of the *MoU*, which are the basis of the review.'

'Consistent with the Eurogroup decision of last Friday'? A better example of Orwellian double-speak would be hard to imagine – spoken shamelessly by the president of the European Central Bank in the full knowledge that restoring the *MoU*'s primacy was in precise and direct violation of both the spirit and the letter of the 20 February agreement.

Mario Draghi's gigantic fib was hastily repeated by Christine Lagarde: 'I can literally endorse and adopt all the points made by Mario,' she began. '. . . [T]he discussion about completion of the review . . . cannot be confined to the list presented by the Greek government, and I think that Mario's mention of the *MoU* is particularly relevant . . . Finally it would be extremely helpful if Yanis could explain to us the government's liquidity condition so that the review can begin.' So there I had it. A carefully planned ambush that began with an outrageous U-turn and ended with a thinly veiled threat.

'Yanis must now answer a couple of points raised in the context of the necessity of agreeing all measures with the institutions,' came Jeroen's twopenn'orth. 'That's the basis on which we work.'

As I pressed the button that activated my microphone, my mind was racing. *What should my reaction to this shocking violation of our agreement be? How do I pick up the gauntlet?* To buy myself some thinking time, I began by addressing all the relatively minor points mentioned by Dobrovskis, Moscovici, Draghi and Lagarde. With every word, the agony grew.

Accepting the ridiculous proposition that the 20 February agreement did not commit us to replacing the *Memorandum of Understanding* with our reform list would have been tantamount to accepting the reinstatement of the *MoU* in full. It would annul everything we had fought for. It would have been to accept everything Wolfgang Schäuble had demanded in our very first Eurogroup meeting and everything that Jeroen Dijsselbloem had tried to push down my throat at our first encounter. Above all, it would have constituted an unforgivable betrayal of our people: those who had trusted us recently, as well as old warriors like Glezos and Theodorakis, who had already rushed to denounce me for the capitulation now staring me in the face.

While talking about privatizations and fiscal targets, two options were competing in my mind. One was to end the teleconference respectfully, stating that the Greek government was withdrawing from negotiations at the Eurogroup level because the institutions' leaders had rendered them irrelevant with their attempt to reintroduce the full-strength *MoU*. The second option was to remain in the process but to contest the institutions' interpretation of the 20 February Eurogroup agreement and to state for the record that the Greek government well and truly rejected the *MoU*'s reinstatement in accordance with that agreement's spirit and letter.

The moment of truth was approaching. It was a choice I had to make on the spot, with only Chouliarakis looking on. It was the hardest decision I have ever had to make.

Mea maxima culpa

It was clear in my mind that withdrawing from the process would trigger the closure of our banks the following morning, Wednesday, 25 February 2015, one month exactly after our election victory. With only four days left before Greece's loan agreement expired, the ECB would undoubtedly have pulled the plug on them. Immediately after ending the teleconference, therefore, I would have to rush to Maximos with the dismal news and with a firm recommendation to activate our deterrence plan immediately. This would mean announcing the date when the SMP bonds would be haircut, the establishment of electronic IOUs via the tax office's website and an amendment of the law governing the Bank of Greece. It was a tough call. But I should have made it.

Instead, disastrously, I opted for the softer alternative. When the critical moment arrived during my speech, this is what I said:

> I heard from all three institutions that [our] list is not a replacement for the *MoU* and that this list will simply be grafted upon the *MoU* . . . Now, as you know, we spent three

Eurogroup meetings discussing the imperative of combining the programme with our government's imperatives. And I was – this government was – under the impression that we are making a fresh start . . . We shall insist . . . that the review be completed on the understanding that this government's list of reforms is the starting point.

Looking back, this was appallingly timid. While I correctly stated that the 20 February agreement had suspended the *MoU* and replaced it with my reform list as the basis for the review, I should have made the continuation of the process conditional on a reaffirmation of this principle. Of course, had I insisted on such an affirmation I would most probably not have got it. And then I would have had to withdraw from the teleconference, thus triggering the rupture. But my thinking at the time – the reason why I refrained from doing so – rested on three conjectures.

First, the reaffirmation of the *MoU* was purely verbal. It had taken place in the context of a Eurogroup teleconference that was not about to issue a communiqué and whose remit was only to approve my list. The only agreement on paper remained that of the 20 February Eurogroup, which privileged my reform list, making no mention of the *MoU*, while also creating space for a negotiated end to austerity and also to debt restructuring.[5] By not withdrawing from the teleconference I was not actually endorsing the return of the *MoU* in any shape or form.

Second, our government was only twenty-seven days old. Setting up the parallel payments system necessary to deal with the closure of the banks and preparing for the hardship shuttered banks would bring simply required more time.

Third, any decision by me to end the process during that teleconference would have been taken without either the prime minister or the cabinet's consideration. My statement as finance minister that we rejected the institutions' attempt to reinstate the *MoU* sufficed for the time being. The government, united and steeled by the creditors' connivance, would, and should, take collective responsibility for the decision over the precise timing of our withdrawal from the negotiations.

The first two conjectures were valid. The third was not. Had it been, the decision I made during that teleconference would since have been vindicated. If our side had stood firm, as I assumed it would, and calmly chosen the right moment to retaliate, I would not be writing these lines overwhelmed by regret. Alas, we did *not* stand united against the troika's attempt on 24 February to reimpose the *MoU*. We were divided and ultimately we were ruled.

Did I have sufficient information at the time to predict this? I did not have a great deal, but with hindsight I think I had enough. The cosiness between Chouliarakis and Costello revealed by that Word document should have alerted me to the divisions among us. Blinded by my unwillingness to contemplate any alternative, I was unable to imagine that my deputy's actions were due to anything other than a failure of judgement. It suited me to ascribe that incident to his lethargy and introversion. However, there was something else motivating me – something more than a justifiable reluctance to be paranoid. Something like fear.

At the press conference on the night of 20 February I had celebrated the agreement as a major turning point. I was not wrong. Wolfgang Schäuble had been defeated, if only temporarily, in a straight fight in his own backyard. As Luis de Guindos and Jeff Sachs had noted, it was a game-changing success. Our government and people latched on to it as a godsend. We had won 120 days of something like normality and the right to negotiate a substantially new reform agenda, new fiscal targets and debt restructuring. It was a moment to savour. Had I come out of the teleconference on 24 February with the news that all bets were off, that the dream of an honourable compromise had evaporated and that the banks were closing down forthwith, the disappointment would have been unbearable. Psychologically I failed to rise to the challenge of accepting that burden.

The problem with errors is that, like crimes, they beget new ones. My failure to pull the plug on the 24 February Eurogroup teleconference was to be compounded with an even greater one a few days later.

Snookered

My first concern was to brief Alexis on the troika's reversal and the decision I had made. We met in the prime minister's office in parliament, where I put him in the picture. The creditors had duped us, I told him. They were trying to put the *MoU* back on the table and it would take a concerted effort to keep it off. 'Unless we remain ready to activate our deterrent and to default on the IMF and the ECB, they will drag us back into their process, defang us, exhaust us and, by the end of June, hang us out to dry,' I told him plainly.

Alexis listened carefully before telling me that I should not worry. If they wanted to go down that road, they would soon be made to think again. It was precisely what I wanted to hear. And so I continued with my efforts to keep the process on track.

Now that the Eurogroup teleconference had formally approved my reform list, our government was obliged to issue a formal request to its creditors for the extension of its loan agreement from 28 February to 30 June, as had been agreed. The onus was on me to send the creditors that formal request. The problem lay in the format that the request would take.

The following day, Wednesday, 25 February, George Koutsoukos, my chief of staff, presented me with a template of the letter I should send to the European Commission, the ECB and the IMF requesting the extension.

'Where did this come from?' I asked.

'From Dijsselbloem's office,' Koutsoukos replied.

I read it quickly. It was unacceptable. While I was happy to use certain key expressions required by the creditors, I was not prepared to sign on the dotted line of a letter written wholly by them. Our government's commitment to recovering Greek national sovereignty compelled me to insist that we should compose the letter and that it should reflect our purpose and rationale in requesting the extension to the loan agreement. Koutsoukos fully agreed but warned me that Brussels had made it clear they would not tolerate any amendment of their draft.

With the letter in my hand I dashed to Maximos for a meeting with Spyros Sagias, our cabinet secretary. He was as appalled and enraged by the creditors' stance as I was. We talked to Alexis, who concurred: my letter to our creditors could not be authored by the creditors. It was not a matter of symbolism but of essence and sovereignty. Over the next two hours Sagias and I sat in an office adjacent to the prime minister's drafting a new letter of our own. I then returned to the ministry to have it sent to Brussels for their response.

Thomas Wieser, president of the Eurogroup Working Group, would provide this feedback, so I asked my representative on the Working Group, George Chouliarakis, to pass it on to him. Afterwards I went home to freshen up, pick up Danae and head off for dinner at the Chinese ambassador's residence, the purpose of which was to calm the troubled waters of our government's relationship with Beijing.

Early next morning, Thursday, 26 February, a message from Thomas Wieser awaited me at the ministry: the deadline for amending the letter requesting the extension of the loan agreement had lapsed. Either I signed the letter as sent to me or it would not be considered.

'Lapsed?' I asked Koutsoukos angrily. 'When did it lapse?' Koutsoukos did not know. 'Find out before noon,' I told him.

While Koutsoukos made his enquiries, I made my way on foot to the Bank of Greece, where my former friend Governor Stournaras was giving a speech on the occasion of the annual meeting of the central bank's shareholders. Determined to respect the institution, I felt it was important to attend. Any hope that equivalent respect might be shown to the government I represented soon disappeared. Listening to Stournaras I realized it was the kind of speech that Antonis Samaras, the former prime minister, would have made had he defeated us on 25 January: a paean to the previous government's policies, a repetition of the lie that Greece had been recovering prior to our election, a total espousal of the troika's agenda and a series of veiled threats against the government. It was as if Stournaras was rehearsing for an interview in front of a panel made up of Schäuble, Dijsselbloem and Draghi. *A sad day for the notion of central bank independence*, I thought as I was leaving, regretting that I had wasted two precious hours.

Back at the ministry I called Koutsoukos and Wassily to my office to get to the bottom of Wieser's missive. After further enquiries I was told that the deadline for amending the letter had passed three days ago – on 23 February, the same day I had had to submit my list of reforms.

Within minutes I was back at Maximos with Alexis, Sagias and Pappas. 'They have gone too far,' I said. 'Telling me on 25 February that I could amend the letter's content but that the deadline to do so had lapsed two days earlier on the 23rd was a declaration of war. I cannot sign this letter after having been set up in this manner.' They all agreed. Alexis suggested that I contact Wieser to make it clear to him that, given their behaviour, I would not be signing the letter and would reveal their dirty tricks to the world.

From the ministry, I composed a suitable message for Wieser: 'You informed me on 25 February of an opportunity to amend the letter by which I shall request the loan agreement's extension, while ensuring that this opportunity expired two days earlier. Naturally, I cannot proceed on this basis.' Koutsoukos passed it on to Brussels. Two hours later he brought me Wieser's reply: a letter had been sent to me on 21 February informing me of the deadline of the 23rd.

'Did we ever receive that letter?' I asked Koutsoukos, Wassily and my secretaries. None of them had seen any evidence of it. 'Call Wieser's office now,' I told them. 'Let them know that we did not receive their letter of 21 February and consequently are demanding a copy showing who the recipients were in Athens.'

It was late in the afternoon when the reply came. Wieser's office informed mine that the email of 21 February with all relevant information regarding the extension request process had been sent to five Greek officials: Chouliarakis, in his capacity as my Eurogroup deputy and Eurogroup Working Group representative; Dragasakis (deputy prime minister); Stournaras, as governor of the Bank of Greece; the head of my ministry's public debt management authority; and the head of the banks' bailout fund, the HFSF. I asked to see the email. It was there in black and white: dated 21 February, it was indeed addressed to those five people. I was flabbergasted. My accusation that Brussels had set the deadline retrospectively had been conclusively refuted.

Of the five people on Wieser's mailing list, there were two I could not hold responsible: the chief of the public debt management authority and the chief of the HFSF, who were tangentially involved and simply being kept in the loop by Wieser. As for Governor Stournaras, he was the troika's local functionary in more ways than one. If I relied on him for information in my struggle against the creditors I deserved everything I got. This left me with two comrades who had both the constitutional duty and the political responsibility to pass the message on to me: Chouliarakis and Dragasakis.

First I called Dragasakis. Had he received the email? He could not recall. 'My office is copied to so many emails that we lose count,' was his reply. I was not convinced. His staff would have fully understood the significance of any email from Wieser, and this one especially.

'Did I not tell you weeks ago?' said Wassily. 'Dragasakis has been setting you up every step of the way. Only this morning his people were briefing journalists that you were in the clasp of the troika.'

Even if that were true, I lacked any evidence to accuse the deputy prime minister of intentional mischief.

With Chouliarakis things were very, very different. As my Eurogroup deputy, his job was to be my line of communication with Thomas Wieser and the rest of the troika. It was his precise remit to pass on to me even the most insignificant message from the creditors, let alone an email of such monumental importance. When I challenged him, he too claimed that the message had got 'lost' in his in-box.

'How can such an email get lost in your in-box, George?' I asked, barely able to believe what I had heard. Just as he had two days earlier when I had confronted him with Costello's creation of the Word file, Chouliarakis reacted as if he had nothing to be apologetic about, as if nothing much had happened.

'You have not heard the last of this, George,' I said with utmost self-restraint before rushing back to Maximos to deal with the crisis he had caused.

This thing of darkness I acknowledge mine

At Maximos, Sagias and Alexis were up in arms. They understood the political cost of the trap that Chouliarakis had landed us in. Accepting the creditors' words in full and without any emendation in a request of this nature was pure poison: it would suggest that we had not wrung the extension from them on our terms, but that the troika had chosen to impose it on theirs; it would vindicate those who were arguing that the troika was calling the shots and that our attempts to wrest back Greek sovereignty were pathetically misguided. (When I later told Sagias how Dragasakis and Chouliarakis had reacted when confronted by me, he smiled bitterly, touched the side of his head with his right index finger as if to say 'I told you so' and reminded me of his prediction, during our first days in office, that Dragasakis was aiming to undermine Alexis.) Sagias advised me in the strongest terms to sack Chouliarakis. 'Get rid of him immediately!' he said, adding a variety of unpublishable expletives. I was determined to, but first we had to deal with the situation at hand.

Alexis was highly reluctant for me sign the creditors' letter, and, with his lawyer's hat on, Sagias thought it extremely risky for me to do so without any formal political backing. The normal course of action would have been to put the letter to parliament. However, Alexis could not bring himself to do this. Asking parliament to approve a letter to the troika written in full-blown troika-speak would upset our own MPs, play into the hands of the Left Platform, who were already accusing us of capitulation to the creditors, disappoint our voters and enthuse the opposition, who would take great pleasure in crowing that we had joined them in yielding to the creditors. Either way, we were in a bind. If I did not sign the letter, either because I refused to or because parliament rejected our request to authorize it, the banks would close and the three-month extension would be lost. On the other hand, if I did sign the letter we would be playing straight into the hands of our enemies. Somehow we had to reach a decision, and we had to reach it before the sun rose over Mount Hymettus on Friday morning.

That Thursday night lasted an eternity. Ministers came and went, party functionaries ebbed and flowed through the prime ministerial offices, the surrounding hall and rooms, but none of the briefings and meetings and discussions threw any new light on our predicament. Throughout, Sagias and I sat in Alexis's office exchanging unpromising ideas, occasionally pacing up and down trying to square the circle.

Among those who visited us that night was Stathakis, the economy minister. He became so angry at Chouliarakis for having landed us in this mess that he took me to task first for hiring him – I reminded him that he had been appointed directly by Dragasakis, somewhat against my wishes – and then for not having fired him over the Word document involving Costello. Again, I had to remind him that even then I would have been too late as Chouliarakis's misdeeds had been contemporaneous: he had failed to pass Wieser's email on to me the same day the Costello document affair had been exposed. In any case, I told him, we had a serious problem to solve before firing Chouliarakis. Stathakis concurred and, nodding repeatedly, took his leave. Watching him head home, I felt horribly envious. Thankfully, adrenalin did its duty and within moments I regained my sense of purpose.

The night was growing heavy and Alexis seemed lost. 'I cannot take this letter to parliament. The Left Platform will slaughter me and the opposition will ridicule me,' he kept repeating. I suggested that we try an innovative solution: the truth! We should brief our MPs on exactly what had happened. 'We have nothing to be ashamed of,' I insisted. We would simply tell them that Wieser had sneakily informed only a few people of the deadline and that we had found out only after it had lapsed. We could use it as an opportunity to re-confirm with our MPs, including our Left Platform comrades, the government's collective commitment to our strategy: buy time to give the negotiations a chance but be ready to pull the plug at a time of *our* choosing if the creditors continued to impose the *MoU* and reject debt restructuring.

Alexis was unimpressed. This would divide the party and our MPs, he said. 'Briefing them on what happened would reveal that some on our side knew about the letter but failed to tell us.'

Sagias agreed. We could not afford a public display of disunity or accuse members of the government of incompetence – at least not without firing them too. 'Is this the time to begin turning against each other in public? When the creditors are encircling us from all directions?' He had a point. And so the night grew longer and our mood darker.

I could not let the black hole consume us. Someone had to fight against it. In a split second I made a decision: I would relieve Alexis of this burden and take the blame squarely on my shoulders. I was the ideal scapegoat for Syriza criticism and the perfect target for the opposition. Given Alexis's commitment to stay the course that we had been plotting together, national interest dictated that the extension be secured. Personal cost was irrelevant.

'Are you sure you cannot go to parliament, tell it as it is, secure a vote that authorizes me to sign the letter and turn the page?' I asked him.

He looked tired and depressed as he turned to Sagias, who, looking the same, advised him against it.

'In that case, Alexi,' I said as decisively as I could, 'I shall take sole responsibility. I'll sign the bloody letter without parliamentary approval, send it to the creditors and turn the page. And if this means I shall be exposed to our comrades' opprobrium, to a legal witch-hunt, it is a risk I must take. We cannot go on like this. Time's up!'

Alexis's eyes lit up. 'Would you do that?'

'If anyone's going to go down over this, let it be me,' I said. 'After all, that's why you chose me, isn't it? Remember you asked me not to join Syriza so that I could do things that party membership precluded? Well, if not now when? I'll do this, Alexi, but only on the understanding that the moment the troika try to confine us to the

MoU and put us permanently into debt bondage, we pull the plug – as we agreed. Right?'

Alexis did not answer me. Instead he turned to Sagias. 'Can he sign just like that?' he asked.

Sagias was sceptical. 'You'll be thrown to the wolves without a legal opinion covering your back,' he warned. 'At the very least we need to get the State Law Council president to give us a written legal opinion that it is within the minister of finance's remit.'

'Call him now,' Alexis said. It was four in the morning. Half an hour later the poor man was at Maximos, looking pale and diffident.

The State Law Council comprises conservative lawyers who provide ministers and other government bodies with legal opinions calibrated in such a way as to cover their collective backs. Caution is their mantra and avoiding controversy their religion. The said gentleman had been in the job only a few weeks, his appointment a parting gift from the outgoing prime minister, Antonis Samaras. Summoned by the new prime minister at that godforsaken hour, with me and Sagias staring at him intently, he looked petrified, so much so that I felt for him. Nonetheless, the circumstances were larger than any of us in the room. His legal opinion was necessary before I could sign a letter that would buy Greece three months in which to find out, once and for all, whether a decent agreement with its creditors was possible.

Legally, what we were asking him to do was entirely reasonable. Sagias had shown due diligence and, from a constitutional and jurisprudence perspective, the situation was crystal clear: as finance minister I was fully within my rights to sign a letter requesting an extension of our loan agreement on behalf of the government. The problem, at least according to the president of the State Law Council, was one of precedent. 'Prime Minister,' he mumbled, 'on every previous occasion, the letter that the finance minister sent to the creditors requesting a loan agreement was first approved by parliament.'

Alexis, Sagias and I responded to his protestations like a well-rehearsed trio. There was a huge difference, we argued, between signing a new loan agreement, which naturally requires parliamentary approval as it commits the nation to new liabilities and new obligations, and signing a letter that requests an extension of an existing loan agreement, which involves no new loans or obligations. Our point was perfectly valid, but he seemed paralysed by the notion of providing a legal opinion in support of something that had no precedent.

He remained in that state for some time, during which Alexis and I strove to shift him from it with a mixture of logic and firmness. In the end, our pressure bore fruit. The harried head of the government's legal service went back to his office, authored a legal opinion that the finance minister had the authority to sign this particular letter and sent it to my office by official courier. As soon as I had received the opinion, I signed the formal letter of request and, with revulsion in my stomach, had it sent to the creditors. It was a thing of darkness. And I had acknowledged it as mine.

Would Alexis honour our covenant in return? Was he happy to give the negotiations a chance but equally prepared to activate our deterrent if they went nowhere? In the early hours of Friday, 27 February I was confident, though not certain, that he was. The following day, crippling doubt set in.

Unmasked

Replacing Chouliarakis had become imperative. A country's Eurogroup Working Group representative and Eurogroup deputy must be the tip of its finance minister's spear. With a finance ministry resembling Swiss cheese, I desperately needed the chair of my ministry's Council of Economic Advisers to be someone in whom I had total faith, both as an economist and as a human being. I had neither. I considered Chouliarakis's analytical skills to be woolly, his academic credentials paltry, and his reliance on the troika's inane econometrics worrisome. As for his character, he was the opposite of a team player: opaque, almost always late for meetings and often remarkably difficult to locate. He rarely answered his phone when I called him, and even his secretary rarely knew exactly where he was. From what Euclid and Alexis told me, he rarely answered their calls either. The question 'Where is Chouliarakis?' became a running joke among the three of us. If asked, I would shrug my shoulders and say, 'How should I know? I am only his boss.' The joke had now worn thin, to say the least.

Nevertheless, far from savouring the prospect, I was reluctant to fire him. The last thing we needed was to give the hostile media any sign of internal strife. But the Costello document and the Wieser email had exposed the government to ridicule and the nation to a premature rupture with its creditors. If nothing else, it was now

impossible to keep him on as my link with that astute and menacing duo.

Later that morning, after we had all had a few hours' sleep, I was
back at Maximos to brief Alexis on my plan to replace Chouliarakis.
The idea was to promote him from chair of the Council of Economic
Advisers to general secretary for fiscal policy, a position of higher rank
in the ministry but one in which he could do relatively little damage
and which was currently unfilled. In his place I was proposing to
appoint my colleague at the University of Athens Nicholas Theocarakis,
whose appointment as general secretary for fiscal policy had been
delayed for bureaucratic reasons. As a top Cambridge-trained economist, politically close to Syriza even before Syriza was formed, and a
friend I could trust with my life, he was the ideal replacement.

Alexis was not happy. I had to remind him of the damage
Chouliarakis had inflicted because of his failure to do his job. Alexis
did not dispute my reasons but to my puzzlement remained unsup-
portive of my plan. It was only when I told him that Sagias and
Stathakis were also of the opinion that Chouliarakis had to go that
he relented. 'If that's what you want to do, go ahead,' he said looking
unhappy and deflated.

On my way back to the ministry I sought excuses for Alexis's reluctance. I supposed that he was being careful not to upset Dragasakis as
he had such a lot invested in his alliance with the deputy prime minister.
Still, what I could not understand was Alexis's failure to appreciate the
solution I had proposed, which involved promoting Chouliarakis,
thereby sparing both him and Dragasakis any embarrassment.

With this question lingering in my mind, I called Theocarakis.
'Nicholas, I have an offer for you that you cannot refuse. I need you
to accept the position of chair of the Council of Economic Advisers,'
I told him. Nicholas was torn. On the one hand, as a great friend and
a loyal Syriza supporter, he felt he should accept. On the other hand,
by leaving the University of Athens in 2012 for the United States I had
already burdened him with the task of keeping the Department of
Political Economy together, along with the progressive doctoral
programme in economics that we had both worked very hard to set
up since 2001. If he accepted my offer, he was concerned that everything he had been working for at the university would collapse.
However, when I explained the critical juncture the country faced and
the personnel problems I had been dealing with, he agreed.

It was time to summon Chouliarakis. Once he arrived in my office, I cut to the chase. I explained that the two recent incidents had made it impossible for me to have anything like the degree of trust in him that was essential for someone in his role. And it was not just those two incidents, I added. Even if they could be excused as temporary lapses, there was his lack of punctuality, his general unavailability and his continued use of the troika's demonstrably faulty macroeconomic models. And so I came to my proposal that he be promoted to general secretary for fiscal policy, with Nicholas Theocarakis replacing him as chair of the Council of Economic Advisers.

I knew that Chouliarakis would not like it. It was understandable; no one likes to be told that they are not trusted, that their economic models are faulty and that they are about to be moved up in order to be moved out of the way. But not in my worst nightmare had I expected the reply he gave me.

'It is your decision, Yanis. Just know that if you decide to take the Council of Economic Advisers away from me, I shall not accept the general secretariat for fiscal policy, nor any other position in the government. I shall instead go to the Bank of Greece, where Stournaras has a position ready for me.'

The mask was off. The cynicism was extraordinary. He had just told me, quite brazenly, that he was ready to work directly for the troika rather than sever his privileged links with the troika's functionaries in my ministry. Not only this, he had openly admitted that he was already in cahoots with the troika's primary ally, the governor of the Greek Central Bank, who had begun the bank run in the run-up to our election as part of their bid to keep us from office. I was aghast. To avoid an ugly exchange, I told him that I would consider his reply and that he could go. I left instantly for Maximos to warn Alexis that we had a fifth columnist in our midst.

For months before we had won the general election, Alexis and his team had considered Governor Stournaras an obstacle to a Syriza government. Rightly so. Former Prime Minister Samaras had shifted Stournaras from the finance ministry to the governorship of the central bank precisely in order to undermine a possible Syriza administration. Alexis had repeatedly told me and others that removing Stournaras was his top priority. Ironically, I had advised moderation and tempered his animosity towards Stournaras, pointing out that the government could not remove the governor of the Bank of

Greece without a major clash with the ECB's executive council. For as long as the ECB negotiated with us in good faith, I argued, we needed to show respect for its Greek branch – although if they closed down our banks and tried to overthrow our democratically elected government, then obviously all bets were off. But in trying to contain Alexis's fury towards Stournaras, I had created the impression among the Syriza leadership that I was soft on the troika's favourite son in Athens.

I was convinced that Alexis would blow his top when I told him that the chair of our Council of Economic Advisers was threatening to defect to Stournaras. He did no such thing. Instead, he looked at me with the same depressed expression he had worn hours earlier when I had announced my decision to fire Chouliarakis. With apparent sympathy towards the apostate and with a disconcerting dullness in his eyes, he said, 'I understand the lad – he has had this arrangement with Stournaras for a while now.'

It was as if the director of MI5 had revealed to Britain's prime minister that their top agent had threatened to work for Russia's FSB if he were shifted from his post, only to have the prime minister reply, 'I understand the lad – he has had this arrangement with the FSB for a while now.'

If my response to the troika's attempt to reinstate the *MoU* during the Eurogroup teleconference of 24 February had been regrettably tepid, my performance in the face of Alexis's astonishing insouciance bordered on the pathetic. Admittedly my glimpse into Alexis's inner world had been brief, but the ghastliness it revealed, however fleetingly, should have provoked me into an eruption. Anything less than rage at Chouliarakis for having dared to threaten us with defection should have alerted me to the troika's presence in that office, to the fact that its tentacles were not just confined to my ministry. To my shame, I looked the other way, allowing wishful thinking to airbrush what I had seen. A pattern was thus established. Again and again during the weeks and months that followed, instead of recognizing his evident duplicity, I would find excuses for Alexis's backtracking from our covenant. I would blame it on fear, depression and inexperience, relying eventually on sheer faith that the moment would come when he would bounce back, shake off the tentacles, reactivate his belief in our cause and honour the magnificent words with which he inspired me that first day at Maximos.

What could I have done differently? Hindsight blurs history and tortures the mind with sterile hypotheticals. I am certain of one thing, though: had I had that glimpse into the abyss before I entered the Eurogroup teleconference of 24 February, I would have most definitely pulled the plug on the troika there and then. The only reason I had not done so was my conviction that Alexis could be counted on to trigger the rupture at a later, commonly agreed, stage if need be. That conviction evaporated when he apologized for Chouliarakis's outrageous threat to work for the enemy.

My only enduring excuse for turning a blind eye to hard, unwelcome facts, for giving Alexis the benefit of the doubt, was what was happening on the streets of Athens, in the towns and villages of Greece. A whole nation had reclaimed its dignity on the basis that the two of us would hold our heads high in Brussels, Frankfurt and Berlin on their behalf. An overwhelming reluctance to undermine that dignity stopped me from doing what I now know was necessary to defend it. I should have confronted Alexis's backtracking – in public if necessary. Instead I carried on believing that we were as one, while the troika, having inserted the edge of its steely wedge between us, began the slow, tortuous process of pushing it right through.

11

Whittling our spring

Spring arrived early in Greece in 2015. Thanks to a wet winter, a mutiny of wild flowers was already in evidence during the first sunny days of March. It provided a marvellous backdrop to the people's rebellion against their creditors. The extension of our loan agreement had been granted, giving us until 30 June to forge a new contract. The grumblings of some Syriza MPs notwithstanding, the mood across the land was ebullient.[1]

For the troika's officials, sitting in their fluorescent-lit offices in Brussels, Frankfurt and Washington, it was a nightmare. Unable to fly to Greece and be driven through Athens in convoys of Mercedes-Benzes and BMWs, they had no way of demonstrating their authority and regaining psychological control over the Greek people. If they were not careful, dangerous ideas might infect the minds of other Europeans – Spaniards, Italians, possibly the French – such as the idea that it was possible, even within *this* Europe, to regain one's sovereignty and to restore a nation's dignity. For the troika, getting its money back would have been nice but, in the grander scheme of things, was of secondary importance. The creditors knew that more austerity and the rejection of my debt swaps would shrink Greek incomes, ultimately increasing their own long-term costs, but they did not mind. As the Slovak finance minister, Schäuble's keenest cheerleader in the Eurogroup, put it a few months later, 'We had to be tough on Greece because of their Greek Spring.'[2] Just as the Prague Spring had been smashed by Soviet tanks, in Athens hope would be crushed by the banks. The strategy for doing so was as follows.

First, by refusing to agree a road map to any specific destination – let alone our desired one – or any credible milestones along it, they cultivated and maintained a deep and corrosive uncertainty in Greece as to its future. Any financial planning, whether in the home, a small business or across a large corporation, short term or long term, was made impossible. Such 'permanent temporariness' is a tried and tested strategy for keeping an occupied land subdued.[3]

Second, they deployed what I have described elsewhere as fiscal waterboarding.[4] Like waterboarding a prisoner, the victim (in this case a eurozone government) is brought to the edge of asphyxiation. But just before an actual default, which would trigger the ECB's closure of the country's banks, the creditors provide just enough liquidity to keep the suffocating government alive. During this brief respite the government passes whatever austerity or privatization measures the creditors demand. In our case, fiscal waterboarding began with a carefully orchestrated bank run before we were even elected and was ramped up with the removal of our waiver on 4 February 2015.

With a minefield of debt repayments ahead of us, and in the midst of profound uncertainty that made Greeks reluctant to pay their taxes, the troika hoped that by early June at the latest we would be gasping for air and ready to capitulate. The only danger was that Alexis might honour our covenant: default on the creditors, inaugurate a parallel payments system and throw the ball into Mrs Merkel's court. To avert this, they deployed a third strategy, one that had allowed the British empire to rule the world for so long with so few military resources: divide and rule.

Since 2010 our creditors had succeeded in using Greece's ruling elite – the triangle of sin, as I called them – to carry out their occupation. As well as separating the elite from the population at large, institutions had also been made accountable directly or indirectly to the troika. As we have seen, the tax office, the bank bailout authority and the statistical office had all been removed from parliamentary scrutiny. Alongside this, a network of think tanks, media and marketing outfits had dispensed trickle-down legitimacy and propagated acquiescence. But our government's election had broken the triangle and wounded its machinery. The troika now had to divide our government in order to reassert its rule.

So much for the strategy. How was it to be implemented?

Picking opponents

Since my first Eurogroup, Jeroen Dijsselbloem had conducted an intensive campaign to bypass me altogether. He would phone Alexis directly, even visit him in his hotel room in Brussels. By hinting at a softer stance if Alexis agreed to spare him from having to deal with me, Dijsselbloem succeeded in weakening my position in the Eurogroup, and by extension Greece's too.

Perhaps more significantly, the troika was brilliant at choosing its opponent at the so-called technical level as well, which is to say in the Eurogroup Working Group. On 27 February, dazed by Alexis's reaction to Chouliarakis's threat to join the enemy camp and recalling that Wolfgang Schäuble's deputy in the Eurogroup Working Group was not the chair of his Council of Economic Advisers but an official within the Ministry of Finance, the idea came to me to keep Chouliarakis at the Council of Economic Advisers, thus avoiding a public firing that would have rocked an already shaky boat, but to replace him as my Eurogroup deputy and as Greek representative in the Eurogroup Working Group with Nicholas Theocarakis by appointing Nicholas to the formally senior position of general secretary for fiscal policy within the finance ministry.

It was a terrible, terrible idea. The first time the Eurogroup Working Group met after Nicholas's appointment was on 17 March in the form of a teleconference. Thomas Wieser, who was presiding, lost no time in stating his preference: 'It is a pity that George Chouliarakis cannot join today and instead Nicholas Theocarakis is on the line.' From then on, Wieser, Dijsselbloem and the rest of the troika campaigned unashamedly for Chouliarakis's reinstatement. It took them two months, but by the end of April they had their man back.

I understood perfectly why the troika wished to get me and Nicholas out of the way. In contrast to Chouliarakis, Nicholas understood the econometric models the troika used for its fiscal predictions better than Wieser and the others did, knew what their weak points were, and was determined to oppose the Eurogroup Working Group's lazy assumptions before they ended up as 'facts' at the Eurogroup. As for me, they knew I would never sign a third bailout agreement, and since it is only the finance minister who can sign a loan agreement on behalf of a eurozone member state, my removal was fundamental. Besides, it is plainly a huge advantage to be able to pick one's opponent. What litigant or general or business leader would decline the opportunity to do so? What I had not seen coming was Alexis's readiness to acquiesce. Divide and rule produced a farce featuring a troika appointee negotiating with the troika on behalf of a government elected to oppose it.

The eurozone runaround

Henry Kissinger famously quipped that when he wanted to consult Europe he did not know who to call. Our predicament was even worse. As we have seen, any attempt to enter into a meaningful discussion with Wolfgang Schäuble was blocked by his insistence that I 'go to the institutions' instead. Once there, I soon discovered that the institutions were also divided, and in more ways than one. Famously, the IMF was dead keen on debt restructuring while the ECB was dead against it. But the European Commission was even worse: in private talks Commissioner Moscovici would agree readily and enthusiastically with my arguments about a consistent fiscal policy and on issues like labour relations. But then the commission's representative in the Eurogroup Working Group, Declan Costello, would reject all these ideas out of hand.

The uninitiated may be excused for thinking that this eurozone runaround was the result of incompetence on the part of the creditors. While there is an element of truth in this, it would be the wrong conclusion. The runaround is a systemic means of control over governments of countries whose banking and/or public sectors are financially stressed. Indeed, to politicians like Wolfgang Schäuble it is a welcome feature of the eurozone. A finance minister who wants to table, say, debt-restructuring proposals is simply denied the name of any person to speak to or a telephone number to call so that she or he simply does not know who to talk to. As for apparatchiks like Wieser and Costello, the runaround is essential to their personal power.

The Swedish national anthem routine

On the assumption that good ideas encourage fruitful dialogue and can break an impasse, my team and I worked very hard to put forward proposals based on serious econometric work and sound economic analysis. Once these had been tested on some of the highest authorities in their fields, from Wall Street and the City to top-notch academics, I would take them to Greece's creditors. Then I would sit back and observe a landscape of blank stares. It was as if I had not spoken, as if there was no document in front of them. It was evident from their body language that they denied the very existence of the pieces of paper I had placed before them. Their responses, when they came, took no account of anything I had said. I might as well have been singing the Swedish national anthem. It would have made no difference.

Possibly because of my academic background, this was the Brussels experience I least expected and found most frustrating. In academia one gets used to having one's thesis torn apart, sometimes with little decorum; what one never experiences is dead silence, a refusal to engage, a pretence that no thesis has been put forward at all. At a party when you find yourself stuck with a self-centred bore who says what they want to say irrespective of your contribution to the conversation, you can take your glass and disappear to some distant corner of the room. But when your country's recovery depends on the ongoing conversation, when there is no other corner of the room to retreat to, irritation can turn into despair – or fury if you grasp what is really going on: a tactic whose purpose is to nullify anything that is inimical to the troika's power.

The Penelope ruse

Delaying tactics are always used by the side that considers the ticking clock its ally. The troika's approach was to give my proposals the Swedish national anthem treatment while refusing to make any proposals of their own beyond the non-viable programmme of their *MoU*, squeezing the last remnants of liquidity from the Greek state in the meantime. In addition, they deployed what I referred to as the Penelope ruse.

In the Homeric tale of Odysseus' faithful wife, Penelope fends off aggressive suitors in her husband's absence by telling them that she will announce whom among them she will marry only after she has completed weaving a burial shroud for Laertes, Odysseus' father. During the day she weaves incessantly but at night unravels her work. The troika's Penelope ruse had two elements. One was to threaten that if we dared make our proposals public, they would never be discussed – just as Penelope told her suitors that if they proposed to her before her weaving was finished, she would discount them from selection altogether. The other was to issue endless requests for data, for fact-finding missions to Athens, for information about every bank account held by every public organization or company. Like Penelope, they would spend all night undoing the spreadsheets of data that they had put together during the day.

Absurdly, they even demanded access to ministry departments that were entirely under their own control. It is a simple fact that parts of some Greek ministries – what I referred to as the holes in the Swiss cheese – sent their data and documents first to the troika for its approval and only later to us, their ministers. Nevertheless, the troika demanded the right to send people to Athens to visit those same ministries in order to gather the very data that they were sifting and approving before we had even laid eyes on it. The more data they mined, the worse the reality it purported to describe became, the greater our society's pain and the faster our state's liquidity evaporated.

Truth reversal and all or nothing

Meanwhile, Operation Truth Reversal was on. Through tweets, leaks and a campaign of disinformation involving key nodes in the Brussels media network, the troika spread the word that I was the one wasting time, arriving at meetings either with no proposals at all or with proposals that lacked quantification, consisting only of empty ideological rhetoric. In contrast, the troika succeeded in presenting itself as the champion of a wholly comprehensive solution that included reform of all aspects of Greece's social economy. How I longed for such a comprehensive solution! Except that the troika was advocating one in name to make it impossible in practice.

No comprehensive agreement was possible – or indeed viable – unless it included some form of debt restructuring and provision to deal with the banks' bankruptcy. Without this, no fiscal policy would add up in the long term, and no Greek would be willing to embrace the proposed reforms. But Berlin simply refused to discuss debt restructuring. Given how little time we had to strike a deal, a realistic approach would have been to identify four or five areas where agreement could be reached quickly, draft the necessary legislation, push it through Greece's parliament and thus establish a foundation for a longer-term agreement. By insisting on a comprehensive deal in which everything was agreed at once – with the sole exception of the single issue on which everything relied – they ensured that nothing could be agreed at all.

Causal confusion

Bullies blame their victims. Clever bullies make their victims' culpability seem self-evident. Of the three institutions I was dealing with, the ECB proved particularly adept at this. It all hinged on the vexed question of Treasury bills, or T-bills.

T-bills are short-term IOUs that a government issues to gain immediate access to liquidity. Usually T-bills are considered ultra-safe as they mature within, say, three months, and it is most unlikely that a government will go bankrupt in such a short time. So there is considerable demand for T-bills from institutional investors such as banks and insurance companies, who need to park their cash somewhere safe. Moreover, investors can post them as collateral with their central bank to get cash. In short, T-bills are almost as liquid as cash but they also bear interest. That's why they are in demand.

However, the ECB places restrictions on how much outstanding T-bill debt a government can have at any one time, as excessive issuing of new ones can undermine trust in the government's capacity to redeem its outstanding Treasury bills, rendering the T-bills themselves unsafe. In other words, T-bills provide a government with the equivalent of a credit card, with the borrowing limit set by the ECB. Greece's liquidity between the 20 February agreement and the 30 June deadline depended for the most part on Mario Draghi maintaining our credit card limit and on there being continued demand for our Treasury bills among Greece's banks. Previously, just after the Samaras government was elected, the ECB increased its T-bill limit from €15 billion to €18.3 billion – albeit for the purely self-serving purpose of funding the government's redemption of its bonds held by the ECB.

However, when our new government took office, with only a few days before the cash ran out, demand for Greek T-bills dried up. Mario Draghi used this as evidence that our T-bills were too risky and thus justified banning the Greek banks from buying them, ostensibly to shield them from the risk but effectively to suffocate our government. By reversing the direction of causality, he created a lethal weapon against us. The fact that X happens before Y does not always mean that X causes Y. For example, the fact that the demand for toys increases prior to Christmas every single year does not mean that Christmas is caused by a prior increase in the demand for toys.

And so it was with my ministry's T-bills. The reason demand dried up was the anticipation, fuelled by leaks from within the ECB, that the ECB would squeeze our government's liquidity, thus bringing Greece to the verge of bankruptcy. Just as the anticipation of Christmas causes an increase in the demand for toys, so the anticipation that the ECB would asphyxiate us caused a decrease in demand for my ministry's T-bills.[5]

Mario Draghi's claim that he was only following the ECB's rules in stopping Greek banks from buying new T-bills – thus preventing us from rolling over the debt from our outstanding T-bills into new ones as the existing ones matured – was ingenious. How can you blame a man for following the rules imposed on him by the charter of his institution? Surely there was nothing else he could do? Surely the fault was mine for imagining that I could convince him, through posturing and moralizing speeches, to do otherwise? It was simply prudent action on the part of an ECB that prioritized the health of our banks, the implication being that our government had brought its liquidity problems upon itself.

Or was it? In reality, after 2008 any attempt by the ECB to impose its charter rigorously and dispassionately would have ruled out any of the various waivers, reinterpretations and extraordinary shenanigans that have so far prevented the eurozone from collapsing altogether. Far from being apolitical, the ECB's huge discretionary power over when to enforce its rules and when to circumvent them – when to strangle a government and when not to – make it the most political central bank in the world. Like any tragic despot too powerful to remain idle but at the same time powerless to act decently, Draghi ended up making our government the exception by imposing upon us rules that had been waived for everyone else.

The dragon's teeth

While the ECB's shameful threat to choke the Greek government was responsible for the lack of interest in our T-bills, we were nonetheless falling into Draghi's trap by indulging an archaic leftist hostility to potentially advantageous foreign investment, enabling the troika to present us as boorish leftists who deserved the ECB's asphyxiation. I was determined to put an end to this by killing two birds with one stone: by attracting foreign investment into the real economy while demonstrating our capacity to attract buyers for our T-bills.

Syriza's instincts were right on one count: Greece did not need any more fire-sale privatizations. What we needed were patient investors willing to plough large sums of foreign money into our rusting infrastructure and breathe new life into our fading industry. If this required partial privatization, I was all for it. The best possible start I could make in this direction was to reverse Syriza's foolhardy commitment to getting rid of Cosco, a Chinese-government-owned conglomerate, from the port of Piraeus.

Since 2008 Cosco had been running two of the three container quays in Athens's main port. Moreover, after years of negotiations with previous governments, Cosco was close to securing a 67 per cent shareholding in a thirty-five-year lease of the third quay in a bid to control the port almost completely.[6] From 2008 to 2015 Syriza had campaigned not only to prevent this but also to eject Cosco altogether from Piraeus. In fact a couple of my fellow cabinet ministers owed their election to parliament to this campaign.

Naturally, news of Syriza's electoral success did not go down well in Beijing.

From a strategic perspective, it struck me as daft to antagonize Beijing at a time when the battle lines against Berlin, Frankfurt and Brussels were being drawn. Beyond strategy, however, I was also convinced that Syriza was wrong to target Cosco and the Chinese. Years before we came to power, while my Syriza colleagues railed against Cosco, I had published articles in which I not only backed Cosco's involvement in Piraeus but went on to recommend the sale of Greece's antiquated, dysfunctional and loss-making railway system to Chinese companies too. As I explained at the time, while I considered the privatization of British Rail a colossal blunder, Greece was in a league of its own. Our ports and railways were nineteenth-century museum pieces demanding massive investment that the Greek economy could not (and French and German companies would not) provide. China was the obvious solution. Chinese companies had access to billions in investment funding, remarkable engineering capacities and a long-term interest in completing their prized new Silk Road, linking China to Europe via the revamped Suez Canal and a railway from Piraeus to Central Europe, thus cutting freight delivery times to the heart of the continent by eight whole days as compared to sailing around Gibraltar to Rotterdam. All that was necessary was an honest, mutually beneficial agreement between the governments of our two ancient civilizations.

From my first day in office I had had it in mind to initiate this process. Glenn Kim had done his research and reported back with unsurprising news: yes, Beijing was disturbed by the anti-Cosco pronouncements of some of my cabinet colleagues, but there was a splendid opportunity to repair the damage by launching a charm offensive. Glenn summed up the tangible benefits of following his recommendations as follows.

> First priority is to secure short-term funding for [Greece], which may be vital in the coming days ahead. Secondly, secure long-term investment monies that will bring about significant capital improvements in parts of the nation's commercial infrastructure, as well as create potential new jobs. Thirdly, demonstrate to your European partners that the new government is able to attract key foreign investment monies in the earliest days of its administration.

Precisely what I had been thinking. To test the waters I had asked my secretary to accept a dinner invitation from the Chinese ambassador for the evening of 25 February. (Had I known as I was accepting the ambassador's invitation that it would coincide with the drama over the letter requesting the extension of our loan agreement, I might have thought twice. I had to decline invitations from almost every ambassador to Greece in the aftermath of my election and appointment for lack of time.) The fact that I chose to drop everything in order to keep this appointment was a measure of the importance I attached to mending fences with the Chinese and investing in a long-term relationship with them.

The night before, I had explained the significance of the dinner to Danae. On the 25th, having rushed from Maximos back to our flat, I was startled and pleased to see Danae wearing a fabulous Chinese silk dress that she had bought in 2006, when we had visited Shanghai on our travels – during a different lifetime, it seemed. The ambassador and his wife were clearly pleased by my acceptance of their invitation, not to mention Danae's dress, but at first hid behind a veil of reserved courtesy. However, by the end of the night the mood had turned positively upbeat, friendly, celebratory even.

During the entrées and main course I listened as the ambassador gave the Chinese side of the story. In a soliloquy that conveyed great frustration he beseeched me to avert any hostile actions against Cosco. Clearly mistaking me for one of the contingent within Syriza keen to evict the Chinese from Piraeus, he was aiming low, hoping only to convince me that it would be terrible to undo what Cosco had already built up. Thus when I stated my case during dessert, the ambassador could not contain his satisfaction. While acknowledging that there would be resistance within Syriza, I shared my vision with our host – a vision that not only involved an enhanced presence for Cosco in Piraeus, under specific conditions, but a lot more to boot.

'Greek shipyards are dying, and skills acquired over millennia are dying with them,' I told the ambassador. So I proposed, in a second phase of collaboration, that Cosco and other Chinese companies should invest in our three main shipyards, turning them into repair hubs for the container ships that Cosco would increasingly attract to our part of the Mediterranean. 'But what is the point of securing the port of Piraeus,' I continued, 'if the railway that will transport your containers to central Europe is derelict, slow and unsafe?' I argued that a similar investment in Greece's railways made sense as well. Lastly: 'Greece has a highly educated workforce, yet wages have fallen by 40 per cent. Why not get companies like Foxconn to build production or assembly facilities in a tech park, enjoying a special business tax regime in an area close to Piraeus?'

Stimulated by this catalogue of joint ventures, the ambassador changed gear. From petitioning for a stay of execution for Cosco, he began to speak with the self-assurance of a partner as we discussed the many benefits of embarking on this collaboration. But while suspicion abated, caution remained.

'Minister, you must understand that, from Beijing's perspective, Cosco is the dragon's jaw. First, we must ensure that its teeth bite hard so that the dragon gets in. Once it is in, have no concerns or doubt: the rest of the dragon will follow.'

The message was clear: let's complete the Cosco deal first; everything else will follow.

I agreed. 'Will you signal to Beijing that their worries about our government are misplaced?' I asked.

'The moment you and your wife sadden us by departing,' he answered. Then he added, 'Beijing would appreciate some public token of commitment to our new relationship, some gesture that will demonstrate to those sceptical in our government that we have a new situation.'

'How about visiting Cosco's Piraeus operations with you in the following days? Will this do?' I suggested.

'Would you do that, Minister? Really?' he asked with the smile of a child promised an enormous present.

'Yes, of course. What you see and hear is what you get from me,' I reassured him.

'Can we bring a Chinese camera crew along?' he asked incredulously.

'I insist that you do.'

The rest of the evening was like a reunion of old friends. The Piraeus visit was scheduled for two days later, to be followed by a meeting in my office, where we would agree initial terms.

When Cabinet Secretary Spyros Sagias found out about my agreement with the ambassador and my impending tour of Cosco's facilities, he could not contain his joy. Prior to the general election Sagias had provided legal advice to Cosco. As such he was constrained by an almighty conflict of interest from canvassing in favour of Cosco. Having done so myself, I had not only relieved him of his conflict of interest, I had redirected the wrath of anti-Cosco Syriza cabinet ministers firmly in my direction. It was a risky move on my part but, as I explained to him, I had taken it because it was important that someone should. 'You did very, very well,' Sagias said.

The visit to Piraeus accomplished all it was meant to. Despite the heavy rain that persisted throughout the morning and over lunch, Danae and I were treated to a full tour of the facilities. Captain Fong, Cosco's local manager, was rugged, fully on top of the entire operation and extremely smart. He allowed a Greek manager and the company's lawyer to act as our guides, while steering the event with gestures, an effusive smile and a few carefully chosen words. Without pointing it out, he made sure that we noticed the sharp contrast between Cosco's part of the container port, which was super-modern and running beautifully, and the adjacent quay, still under state control, which looked sad, rusty and almost abandoned.

As we were making our way to lunch, I spotted a canteen where some employees were taking a break and broke away from my hosts to speak to them. They shook my hand and smiled a lot, but when I asked them about working for Cosco they were coy. 'It's good,' was about as much as they were willing to say. The expressions on their faces were hard to read. Looking over my shoulder, I saw Captain Fong and his Greek white-collar entourage watching us. I made a mental note to insist on full union rights for all workers as a pre-requisite for any deal before saying my goodbyes.

From there my hosts whisked me up to the company restaurant, where a rare view awaited us: the ancient harbour immediately below, the island of Salamis in the background, and between them the straits where the famous naval battle between the Persians and Athenians took place in 480 BC. Now a third ancient people were making their mark in history here.

'Which do you want first, Minister, the good news or the bad?'

After lunch, which featured an odd but pleasant blend of Greek and Chinese recipes and a quick interview for a Chinese TV crew, we arranged a follow-up meeting with Cosco's Greek representative and Sagias in order to negotiate the terms of the deal. A few days later, on the evening of 2 March, we convened at my ministry. The meeting was short and efficient.

I repeated my commitment to speed up the privatization of the port of Piraeus, to be followed by even bigger and bolder joint ventures, and spelled out the same conditions that I had already explained to the Chinese ambassador: Cosco's shareholding in Piraeus would be reduced from 67 to 51 per cent, with the difference (16 per cent of the equity) to be retained by the Greek state with a view to passing it on to the suffering pension funds of naval, shipyard and municipal workers; Cosco would commit to an investment of up to

€300 million within eighteen months; all Cosco employees at Piraeus would be unionized, collective agreements on wages and conditions would apply and there would be no workers hired via subcontractors; and coastal shipping would be handled by the municipality of Piraeus, with the active participation of the local authorities of the islands served by the port, ensuring that communities in the area shared in the benefits.

Lastly, as a token of its desire to help Greece get back on its feet again, I required a commitment from the Chinese government to purchase immediately €1.5 billion of the T-bills that Mario Draghi's ECB had prohibited the Greek banks from buying. And once the impasse with our creditors had been brought, one way or another, to an end, I said, 'Athens would be tremendously grateful to the people of China if Beijing helped Greece launch its first new bond issue with a purchase of at least €10 billion.'

Cosco's representative seemed confident that my terms would be given a sympathetic hearing in Beijing, and further communications with the Chinese ambassador confirmed that my new friends were happy with the deal and that a positive response would be forthcoming from the land of the dragon, now that its teeth were in. Indeed, a tangible sign of good faith followed less than forty-eight hours later, on the morning of 4 March, when the head of my ministry's public debt management department called me with the news that China's treasury had, indirectly and secretly, bought €100 million worth of our T-bills – news that brought me to the brink of satisfaction.

But not quite there. Lest we forget, two days later I would have to find €301.8 million to hand over to the IMF. A week after that, on 13 March, I would have to do the same with another wad of €339.6 million. Three short days after that, on 16 March, I would have to come up with a whopping €565.9 million to wire to the IMF. Then, on 20 March, €339.6 million more would have to be extracted from our depleted coffers to be sent the same way. During March alone, then, we would haemorrhage to the IMF more than €1.5 billion. In that context, the €1.5 billion T-bill purchase promised by Beijing would have given me three weeks in which to catch my breath before the fiscal waterboarding recommenced on 13 April, when a further €452.7 million would have to be paid to the IMF. After that, between 12 May and 19 June, another six instalments were due to the IMF totalling €2.52 billion. But the hottest months were yet to come: in July we would have to pay almost €4 billion to the creditors with another €3.2 billion to follow in August.[7]

In other words China's liquidity injection of €1.5 billion would not have nearly sufficed. Indeed, however willing Beijing might have been, no injection of loans, however large, could have saved us from insolvency. As I had been saying for years, they could only have extended it. Nevertheless, €1.5 billion would have bought us at least two months to ascertain whether a new contract with our creditors was possible, while making it impossible for Mario Draghi to maintain his argument that no one other than the Greek banks cared to purchase our T-bills. At the same time, it would also have demonstrated our capacity to attract foreign investment, to be flexible and to turn a colonial fire sale into a mutually beneficial agreement with one of the world's superpowers.

Sagias and I briefed Alexis and began preparations. The intention was to restart the formal bidding process for the port of Piraeus under the new conditions that the Chinese had accepted, while behind the scenes the two governments agreed the Chinese loans to the Greek state. Soon the plan was finalized and ready for implementation. First, Beijing would inject the remaining €1.4 billion of the promised €1.5 billion into our T-bills. Almost simultaneously Deputy Prime Minister Dragasakis would make a formal trip to Beijing to strengthen relations between the two governments and informally seal the agreement. Lastly, Alexis would follow up with a full state visit in April or May to make public and sign the comprehensive agreement between Athens and Beijing.

It was a splendid opportunity for both countries. A lifeline for Greece and a giant leap forward for China's new Silk Road into the heart of Europe. Dragasakis left for Beijing on 25 March, accompanied by our foreign minister. Counting on the €1.4 billion that would pour into my ministry by the end of the month, I scraped the bottom of the barrel to find the €1.5 billion we were obliged to pay the IMF during March. The idea was to use that month to give the creditors one last chance to reach out to us with serious intent for a viable agreement. China now had a stake in our success, and our ability to attract Chinese investment would be a significant weapon in the negotiations. The cash itself would then buy us a further month in which to table our own fully fledged plan for Greece's recovery.

On 31 March, the day Beijing had promised the breakthrough purchase of €1.4 billion in T-bills, I was at my office waiting for the phone to ring. The auction was meant to end at around 11.00 a.m. At 10.30, unable to contain myself, I called the ministry's public debt manager. 'No news yet,' I was told, 'but don't worry. The Chinese make a habit of entering auctions at the very last moment.' So I waited.

At 11.02 my phone rang. I jumped to answer it. 'There's good news and there's bad news, Minister. Which do you want first?' asked the public debt manager.

'Begin with the good news,' I said.

'Well, the Chinese have entered the auction, but the bad news is that they only bought another €100 million.'

Before we had hung up, I was dialling the Chinese ambassador on my mobile. Once I had told him what had happened, he said, 'I cannot believe this. Can I come to your office right away?'

'Of course,' I replied.

Half an hour later, a frazzled Chinese ambassador was sitting on my red sofa. In what I believe to have been genuine anguish, he pleaded with me to believe that he had had no inkling that something like this would happen, that he was hugely embarrassed and that he would do all he could to get to the bottom of the shortfall. From within my office he tried to place calls to the Chinese ministry of finance but could not get through. So he went back to his office promising to get back to me as soon as he heard.

A few hours later he called, sounding far more relaxed. 'Minister, I can assure you it was a technical hitch. Beijing is very sorry about it. In two days' time, when you have another T-Bill auction, the purchase will go through.'

I felt a mixture of relief and incredulity. On the one hand it made no sense for Beijing to lie via its ambassador, who appeared genuinely keen to cement our deal. On the other, the idea that China's technocrats had simply made a mistake was equally unbelievable. Time would tell.

Two days later I was in my office awaiting the same call from our public debt manager. At 11.05 the phone rang. 'There's good news and there's bad news, Minister. Which do you want first?' *Not again*, I thought.

'Please don't tell me that they entered the market with another €100 million,' I implored him.

'Precisely what they did,' came his reply.

This time I did not bother to call the ambassador; I went straight to Maximos. There I told Alexis what had happened and suggested strongly that he contacted the Chinese prime minister.

The next day Alexis relayed the news from Beijing. Someone had apparently called Beijing from Berlin with a blunt message: stay out of any deals with the Greeks until we are finished with them.

When I spoke to the Chinese ambassador again, I tried to convey to him how our people felt when foreign powers, pretending to be our partners, steamrollered their hopes for recovery and dignity.

'I understand, I understand,' he replied. And I believed him.

So ended a dreadful episode in the long saga of the creditors who had no interest in getting their money back – with the scuttling of a marvellous agreement between two ancient countries.[8]

The tides of March

At the beginning of March it felt as if the tide had suddenly gone out, leaving the hopes I had carried back to Athens after the 20 February Eurogroup agreement exposed, bedraggled, stranded. The creditors' promises to allow us to co-author our own country's reform agenda and to negotiate a life-saving debt restructuring had been withdrawn even before February was over. But unlike February, whose cold breeze had braced my resolve, March's warmer touch made me freeze.

The difference was the narrow crack that had opened up across the bond linking me to Alexis – narrow but now impossible to ignore. However successfully I managed to put it out of sight, I could not put it entirely out of mind. With every concession we made that month and with each delay in Alexis's reactions to the troika's aggression, I sank deeper into doubt. Would he be prepared to activate our deterrent when the troika chose to put him to the test? By the end of March, and certainly by the beginning of April, the impartial spectator within was telling me that our opponents had succeeded in intimidating him. It took a little while longer for the rest of me to catch up.

There were two aspects to our talks with the creditors: the negotiation over our reform agenda, which was meant to be concluded by mid-April, and the negotiation over debt restructuring and ending austerity. To keep hope's flame alive, it was essential that these two strands not be separated: only with debt restructuring would a reform agenda make any sense. But despite the differences between them, the creditors were impressively united towards us and invested tremendous effort into prising the strands apart: only once we had accepted their reform priorities would they contemplate discussing debt restructuring. It was an increasingly lonely struggle. Alexis, Pappas, Dragasakis and even my friend Euclid seemed increasingly ready to accept a deal that included only vague promises on debt as long as some of Syriza's sacred cows – the reintroduction of collective bargaining agreements and the preservation of pensions, for example – were left alive. They were drifting into the mentality of the famous Brussels fudge.

The contrast between the troika's rigid will and my side's shrinking ambitions enhanced my sense of dread and loneliness. War cabinet meetings were turning into exercises in weighing up the utility of different forms of surrender based on Syriza survivability come the next election. At such moments I felt contemptuous of intra-party politics and glad that I kept out of them. Pappas would go on and on about preserving the administrative ban on large-scale dismissals that the IMF was keen to abolish. Alexis focused more on the pensions that Berlin had in their sights. Others banged on about privatization. I could not bear it. I too cared deeply about all these issues, but what was the point if we did not first and foremost end the doom loop? What was the point of preserving an administrative ban on mass dismissals if austerity were to be reinforced thus causing companies of all sizes to fail? What was the point of focusing on pensions when the state on which our pension systems depended was insolvent?

Every attempt I made to return our deliberations to what really mattered – debt restructuring, the end of austerity, investment and bad banks – was treated as a distraction from the main agenda. Were we still committed, I would ask, to start defaulting on the IMF and later the ECB by the end of March or at the latest the beginning of April if the troika refused to discuss debt restructuring seriously? Were we still determined to retaliate to their threats of capital controls and bank holidays with haircuts of the ECB's SMP bonds and the activation of our parallel payments system? In response they would humour me, ever less convincingly, with repetition of oaths of allegiance to our strategy.

Back at the ministry I would attempt to pick up my spirits and plough ahead. The fact that any agreement would require my signature, and mine alone, made me feel simultaneously pivotal and expendable. But until I was expended, I thought, I had some power to keep debt relief at the top of the list, to unify the two negotiations, to continue to hold Alexis to our covenant, to strive for international alliances, to push for the completion of our algorithmic cornering of major tax cheats, to develop our parallel payments system and, last but not least, to promote a bill to address the humanitarian crisis. It was the least I could do for Lambros and the millions of others who, to use an old Peloponnese expression favoured by my grandmother, had made us the object of 'all their devotions and [should we disappoint them] all their curses'.

The next Eurogroup meeting in Brussels, where we would take stock of the negotiations, was on 9 March. It was wholly in the troika's interests that there should be no progress to report, a shortcoming which they would blame on our recalcitrance, and when the IMF's Poul Thomsen called me on 1 March to announce that the troika was ready to fly to Athens, I knew they were going in for the kill.

Welcoming the troika's officials into our ministries would have triggered precisely the wrong kind of negotiation, in which technocrats from the European Commission, the ECB and the IMF would demand concessions from our ministers on the minutiae of the troika programme. If we were to respond by agreeing to talk about such matters only as long as we also talked about debt swaps and austerity too, they would simply refuse, telling us that negotiating our debt was above their pay grade, which of course it was. The only way to avoid being cornered in this way was to insist that there be no negotiations in Athens between the troika's middle managers and our elected ministers. In other words, our refusal was not just symbolic, it was critically strategic. Nonetheless, troika officials began reporting to the press that our refusal to welcome them to Athens was 'ideological', whereas they simply wanted to get the necessary work done.

On 3 March I briefed my team on the importance of keeping the two negotiations unified and insisting on a comprehensive agreement. I remember warning them that the troika would respond with threats of capital controls and informing the most trusted among them of the deterrent that a tiny team was working on: the parallel payments system and the SMP bond haircuts. Meanwhile, Jeff Sachs was hard at work in Washington meeting David Lipton, number two at the IMF, and Poul Thomsen in a desperate attempt to bridge our differences.

The media battled continued. A day or two later, Mario Draghi publicly described me and Alexis as 'loquacious'. Jamie Galbraith responded in typical style: 'Normally a central banker would deliver such a message in private, and the fact that he chose to do otherwise was evidence of loquacity.' When asked by Italian daily *La Repubblica* to comment on the accusation that I spoke to my Eurogroup colleagues with greater 'candour' than one would expect of a finance minister, Jamie replied, 'While it might be true that Varoufakis has departed from the customary standard of candour among finance ministers, since I support raising those standards anyway, it is not evident to me that there is a problem.'

On 5 March, in an attempt to upset troika strategy, I sent a letter to the Eurogroup president, Jeroen Dijsselbloem, demanding the commencement of negotiations, including a proposal to implement immediately seven of the reforms the institutions had approved in our teleconference of 24 February. Their response was to rubbish the seven proposed reforms accompanying my letter to Jeroen, targeting for greatest ridicule the idea that German Vice Chancellor Sigmar Gabriel had been so keen on in our meeting in February: clamping down on tax evasion by employing people from all walks of life to record transactions as they happened.[9] Ever since, our plans for the algorithmic capture of large-scale tax evasion had been entirely ignored, dismissed with derisive references to 'wired tourists'.

That same day my alternate finance minister Nadia Valavani and I were working to finalize our Humanitarian Crisis Bill. At its heart were two measures: the provision of a prepaid credit card for 300,000 families living without food, shelter and electricity, and a Herculean effort to bring the 40 per cent of the Greek population who had dropped out of the tax system because they were in arrears to the state back into the fold. How? By letting them pay back a small amount, even €20, each month. Although millions had been rendered so impecunious by the crisis that they would have difficulty paying even such a small amount, we were confident that they would do all they could to find it in return for the right to reactivate their tax file numbers and leave the purgatory of official bankruptcy. It was an act of mercy and economic common sense. Indeed, within a month of the system's subsequent introduction €700 million had been paid into the state coffers by those striving to return to the formal sector.[10]

With the Humanitarian Crisis Bill almost done, I had an important phone call to make. My secretary had informed me that US Treasury Secretary Jack Lew wanted to speak to me. Our conversation began well enough with his request that I update him on the negotiations. I told him that, despite our hope that the 120-day interim agreement of 20 February would lead to a new process that would break the deadlock, over the past week the institutions and some of their key partners had issued statements that apparently reversed the agreement, violated its spirit and demanded that we revert to the previous arrangements, something we could not and would not do. His response was more in keeping with the line taken by the US ambassador to Greece than that of President Obama's public statements: in essence, the US Treasury agreed with us on the issue of austerity but we still had to give in. I explained that I was not confident of raising the payment owed to the IMF on 18 March. Secretary Lew replied with a comment to the effect that we should place our trust in our creditors.

Kemal Dervish, a Turkish former finance minister who was working at Brookings in Washington and with whom I was corresponding, warned me not to heed such advice. In his view, Poul Thomsen's promotion from chief of the IMF's mission in Greece to European director was disastrous for us: the old Greek programme might be a dismal failure but it was his baby. 'There is nothing you or anybody can do about it, but [it's] all the more important to meet Christine Lagarde personally,' he said. 'I do have good relations with her, and she is fundamentally a very reasonable woman. But she has so many fires to fight, not least of course the Ukraine mess, which tends to swamp everything here.'[11] This was not too far off my estimation, but was there any way of coming to a sensible agreement with Christine that sidelined the programme that her European director was determined to defend?

A far more likely person to unlock the negotiations was Angela Merkel. She was the only reason we had found common ground at the 20 February Eurogroup. But the moment Merkel turned her back on Schäuble and Dijsselbloem, the *MoU* was brought back and the process collapsed. With the next Eurogroup meeting around the corner and the negotiations still stalled, I suggested to Alexis that he call Merkel: 'Surely, if she wants to prevent her good work from two weeks ago from going to waste, she must intervene again?'

That night Alexis spoke to the chancellor on the phone. She responded warmly and positively. She said she would send Thomas Wieser to Athens on a mission to find a way forward. We were encouraged. Thomas Wieser was exorbitantly dull, incredibly powerful and a man who knew how to walk the tightrope binding Angela Merkel and Wolfgang Schäuble together. He was ideal.

Emissary without a missive

The condition on which Chancellor Merkel sent Wieser to us was absolute confidentiality. Our ministries were not to be involved in planning his visit; there would be no government car to pick him up, and the meeting would have to be held at a secluded private residence. I decided that our flat was ideal. An unofficial car was sent to pick Thomas up from the airport and deliver him straight to us. The empty street outside our building, thanks to a cold grey day, put paid to any concern that tourists visiting the New Acropolis Museum opposite might recognize him.

It is fair to say that Thomas Wieser brought the weather with him into the flat. Our seven-person party – Dragasakis, Theocarakis, Chouliarakis, Euclid, Alexis's secretary, Danae and myself – was keen to welcome Wieser warmly. Wieser was equally keen to keep his distance. His first sentence was disheartening: 'I'm happy to be here even though I do not know why I'm here.' Surely the person who had asked him to visit us must have explained the reason, I asked. 'I have no idea who sent me,' he replied. 'I just found a note at my office instructing me to board a plane for Athens.'

Unwilling to beat about the bush, I spelled out the facts: we were at an impasse, one that only Chancellor Merkel's intervention could overcome. She had proved amenable to such an intervention and had offered to send him to us informally to discuss how to reboot the negotiations.

Incredibly, Wieser would have none of it, continuing to deny any knowledge of the chancellor's involvement in his trip. Instead, over the course of a lengthy meal, he laid down the law with the charisma of a bailiff and the sensitivity of a litigator. Outlining the coming weeks and months, he carefully avoided the substance of the negotiations, instead giving us chapter and verse on Eurogroup and Eurogroup Working Group rules and constraints. From his litany of troika-speak, one thing of interest emerged: we should expect no easing of the squeeze on our liquidity before 30 April – which was presented as a natural, apolitical consequence of bureaucratic constraints.

In response I told Wieser that unless we received a sign from the creditors that they were serious about a compromise on the reform agenda and a sensible fiscal policy made possible by meaningful debt restructuring, we would not reach 30 April without a default to the IMF. 'Independently of our preferences and political will,' I said, 'our liquidity will run out well before then.'

He replied that we could last much longer by plundering the reserves of non-governmental but publicly owned institutions such as pension funds, universities, utility companies and local authorities.

'And why would we want to do that?' I asked. If the creditors showed no interest in negotiating in good faith, why should we continue to extract yet more flesh from the scrawny body of our society in order to service a debt to the IMF that even it considered to be ultimately unpayable?

Faced with this question, Wieser's training kicked in. He recoiled behind the fact that he had no mandate to discuss debt restructuring and austerity.

Realizing that this line of conversation was a waste of time, I brought up the €1.2 billion that my legal and financial advisers informed me Greece could claim from the creditors as its own. Apparently, the previous government had spent that sum from the state's reserves on bailing out a few of Greece's smaller banks even though it had been agreed that this money should have come from the second bailout loan deposited with the HFSF. Given that I was not willing to plunder the remaining reserves as he had suggested, I asked Wieser whether we could use this credit to meet our IMF payments for March, buying us both extra time to negotiate. 'It sounds reasonable,' replied Wieser, advising me to send a formal request to Jeroen, his boss, for access to that €1.2 billion. (Days later, when I did so, Jeroen referred me to the president of the Eurogroup

Working Group . . . Thomas Wieser! And what was Wieser's verdict, now that he had been given the authority to decide? That what I was requesting was 'too complicated'.)

Seeing no glimpse of a potential breakthrough, the only useful thing that remained was to try to establish some form of human bond between us – to at least bring some humanity into the proceedings, if only for the sheer hell of it. Euclid, Nicholas Theocarakis, Danae and I took the lead, changing the subject to anything other than the negotiations: we spoke of art, music, literature, our own families. For six hours in all we ate simple but excellent Greek food and drank a considerable amount of wine followed by Cretan *raki*. Thomas Wieser's resistance was extraordinary. He ate and drank and smiled frequently, but the force field that he erected to prevent any camaraderie from developing between us proved impenetrable.

As the evening drew to a close, Nicholas asked Wieser if he was related to Friedrich von Wieser, the pioneering right-wing economist and Austrian finance minister whose thinking had shaped the minds of libertarians such as Ludwig von Mises and Friedrich von Hayek. Thomas answered that, yes, he was indeed the grandson of his cousin, but confessed that he did not know much about his works. Reaching into our bookshelves, I pulled out a thick volume that Nicholas and I had co-authored in 2011, in which we referred to von Wieser's influence in a chapter aptly titled 'Empires of Indifference'.[12] I offered it to Thomas for him to keep. He accepted.

As he was leaving, heading to a hotel before his flight back to Brussels the following morning, I longed for my academic days, when disagreements were resolved through the power of argument rather than brute force. Weeks later, as the troika's brute force was reaching its climax, I recalled one of von Wieser's most memorable lines, wondering whether he would be pleased or appalled by his descendant's part in the eurozone's travails: 'Freedom has to be superseded by a system of order.'

To the Eurogroup!

Wieser's visit brought home a stark reality: with twenty-four hours left until the next Eurogroup meeting, Merkel was not willing to intervene as she had done previously. Perhaps she was never serious about achieving common ground with us; perhaps she had lost tactical ground to Wolfgang Schäuble. It didn't matter. The choice facing us was the same: withhold all payments to the troika for as long as they continued to asphyxiate us, signal that there would be no negotiations on the basis of their *MoU*, insist that debt restructuring and an end to punitive austerity were strict prerequisites. Or prepare to surrender.

Before flying to Brussels, I briefed Alexis and the war cabinet on the demands we should expect to face at the Eurogroup: first, that we suck the life out of our non-governmental public institutions to keep repaying the IMF; second, that we allow the troika to return victoriously to Athens; third, that the talks be confined within the template of the *MoU*. I was alarmed that the second of these seemed to exercise them most and that their anger did not seem to extend to the third.

It transpired that I had good cause to be concerned. As I was preparing for my trip, I got scent of an interesting development: Chouliarakis had resurfaced in Maximos and was now heading an informal team of Syriza advisers working behind my back on a list of concessions to be gifted to the troika. Having a second team of economic advisers to shadow the finance ministry's is not necessarily a bad thing for a prime minister. Given the seriousness of the situation we faced, such checks and balances were prudent, but this particular team and the manner in which Alexis was using them posed a real danger. They combined the worst of Syriza's fixations with the most obnoxious of the troika's obsessions, advocating increases in corporation tax, for example – a perfectly good left-wing policy under normal circumstances but not when business was bleeding to death – in order to meet the troika's demands for a higher government surplus. This worst-of-both-worlds economic policy directly undermined my advocacy of reduced austerity as a prelude to lowering tax rates.

Meanwhile, Spyros Sagias was devising bills related to financial matters that were outside both his remit and his competence – for example, on transfer pricing, which relates to the exchange of goods between two separate subsidiaries of the same conglomerate – and trying to impose them on me. Even worse, the day before I was due to fly to Brussels to attend the Eurogroup, our defence minister, the right-wing conspiracy theorist we had had to tolerate in order to retain our parliamentary majority, made a statement straight from

Mephistopheles's notebook. The London *Daily Telegraph* headline summed it up: GREECE'S DEFENCE MINISTER THREATENS TO SEND MIGRANTS INCLUDING JIHADISTS TO WESTERN EUROPE.[13] It was exactly what we did not need. Gradually Maximos was writing the textbook on how *not* to run a negotiation.

I had one last meeting with Alexis before boarding my plane. I warned him that the troika would stall, blame us for the delay, demand that we legislate to plunder all our remaining reserves in order to keep paying the IMF, and then, once Greece was as dry as a Peloponnese sultana, close down the banks to turn the people against us. We had to stop the rot. If the forthcoming Eurogroup was the set-up I was expecting it to be, our only recourse was a hard default on the IMF and the parallel activation of our deterrent.

As I was handing him various non-papers that I was planning to present in Brussels, I told Alexis, 'I shall talk privately to all of them, the IMF, Schäuble, Draghi, Moscovici. I shall be conciliatory beyond belief, ready to compromise as much as it is possible without jeopardizing Greece's recovery chances. I shall speak only the language of cooperation and goodwill. But if, Alexi, they respond with their usual mix of aggression and truth reversal, leaving us no room to manoeuvre, upon my return we must act decisively. I trust that you agree.'

Alexis agreed. And so I set off for Brussels determined to be maximally compromising – to make sure beyond a shadow of a doubt that Greece's creditors were committed to denying us even a minimally rational agreement.

Soon I had my proof that this was so. And Jeff Sachs, who accompanied me in all the bilateral meetings I had, is my witness.[14]

12

Merkel's spell

At 11 a.m. on 9 March, the morning of the Eurogroup meeting, I met Poul Thomsen in the lobby of my hotel in Jeff's presence. Poul began the conversation by assuring me that the IMF were 'not dogmatic'. They had lost patience with the Greek programme well before our left-wing government was elected, he told me. Poul spoke angrily about the Samaras government. 'We lost patience with them. They failed to deliver on almost everything they had committed to,' he claimed. 'Samaras told the Germans what they wanted to hear, did nothing else, and then in view of the election used the money he got to pour tax waivers and other favours on his people.'

At that point I interjected to say that, in view of his experiences with previous Greek governments, surely he would appreciate our reluctance to make promises that we either did not intend to, or simply could not, keep. 'Poul,' I told him sincerely, 'just know that, if you and I come to a viable agreement, I shall move heaven and earth to implement my side of the deal. But we cannot do this while in the toxic fog of permanent bankruptcy. We need debt sustainability before anything else.'

'Greece needs debt relief before it can agree to any compromises,' Jeff added. 'First the creditors must allow it oxygen to breathe and then [they can] place further demands.'

Thomsen seemed in agreement, judging by his nodding and positive expression. 'I do not think that a reasonable debt sustainability analysis would be difficult or that your short-term liquidity issues would be difficult to surmount,' he said.

I replied by taking his point to its natural conclusion: 'Yes, Poul, I have no doubt that your good people in DC have excellent analyses of why our debt is ridiculously unsustainable. Nor do I doubt that our short-term liquidity difficulties can be sorted out with one wave of Mario Draghi's hand, or of the IMF's for that matter. But however helpful that would be, it is not the issue, is it? The elephant in the room is the question of debt restructuring, without which we shall remain insolvent and un-reformable. Neither your analysis that this is so nor a relaxation of our liquidity constraints can change that. We need to have upfront debt relief. And you, the IMF, are the only ones who can push for this. So the ball is in your court. Will you?'

Thomsen clearly understood but remained non-committal, mumbling something about 'the Europeans' being difficult to shift on the matter. I insisted: either they shifted or there would be no agreement, and a very expensive, very preventable accident would occur.

'The Europeans have their ways . . .' was Poul's cryptic final comment.

The next of our bilateral meetings was with the two leading lights of the central bank whose heavy boot was on our throats.

Jeff and I walked into a small office to meet Mario Draghi and Benoît Cœuré. Mario greeted Jeff like an old friend and was clearly impressed that he was by my side, but despite the warmth in his voice, his message was unchanged. In the spirit of maintaining its apolitical independence, the ECB was not going to lift a finger, let alone its boot, from our throat without a green light from the Eurogroup. I rehearsed my usual counter-argument: that there was nothing more political than reducing our liquidity during these negotiations, given that the ECB had increased it during its negotiations with the Samaras government in the summer of 2012. Draghi attempted to dismiss this point on a technicality. Jeff intervened to say that where there is goodwill there is a way to prevent an accident. Draghi was unmoved.

I then made the point that, at the very least, the ECB could release to us the almost €2 billion profit it had made on our SMP bonds, which was to have been paid to Greece in 2014. As I spoke I looked squarely at Benoît, who I knew agreed with this argument. 'If you want us to pay the IMF during the next weeks, and given that we lack the money to do it, this is a reasonable suggestion. It is *our* money after all,' I said.

Mario replied that releasing the profit on the SMP bonds to us was not within his gift. He was obliged to pass it on to the central banks of the eurozone member states, they to their governments and the governments to Greece after agreement at the Eurogroup.

'I know all this, Mario,' I said, 'but it is our money nevertheless.' Whatever arcane rules the Eurogroup had concocted – without the approval of the European parliament or any legitimate body of the EU – I was merely trying to find a practical way to avoid defaulting on the IMF in the next two weeks, I told him. 'The situation is simple: we owe one part of the troika, the IMF, a sum that we do not have. At the same time another part of the troika, the ECB, owes us a similar sum. Logic dictates that we cancel out these two sums.' I was not even asking the creditors to trust me with our money, simply to take the money the troika conceded it owed us and use it to pay itself. 'Have the money transferred, if need be, from the ECB to national central banks, to member-state governments and then directly to the IMF. This is a practical, logical, fair solution.'

'This is not up to me,' Draghi said. 'It is up to the Eurogroup.'

Jeff tried valiantly one more time. 'Mario,' he said, 'I have been listening to this discussion and I must tell you that I am concerned. Yanis has been trying to propose a practical solution to a simple-to-solve problem. You rejected that solution, which is fair enough if there are technical problems, but I have not heard from you any alternative solutions.'

Mario shrugged his shoulders. 'It is not for the central bank to offer such solutions. This is a matter for the politicians.'

'Just wait and see what the politicians do when I raise the subject with them,' I said to Jeff as we were leaving. 'They will refer me to back to the ECB, possibly to Poul Thomsen.' Jeff shook his head in disbelief.

I met Nicholas Theocarakis, who had replaced Chouliarakis as my Eurogoup deputy, at the entrance to the meeting. This would be his baptism of fire. But as we walked into the room who should I see at the chair next to mine but George Chouliarakis!

Nicholas and I greeted him, and the three of us sat down as the other ministers and their deputies filed in. Chouliarakis knew that each minister was allowed only a single deputy at the Eurogroup – leaving aside the exception made for our government's first Eurogroup, when Dragasakis was allowed to sit in – and to this day I cannot imagine what he was thinking. When I leaned over to ask politely that he wait for us with Jeff Sachs in the Greek delegation's office, he refused, explaining that he had neglected to inform Wieser formally that Nicholas had replaced him. 'Don't worry about that,' I told him. 'I will deal with Wieser.'

Meanwhile, Jeroen had declared the meeting open. Sitting next to him, Wieser had spotted the scene that Chouliarakis was making. Never one to miss an opportunity to criticize us, he walked over to tell us that one of my two associates had to leave. Huffing and puffing, Chouliarakis finally got up and left. Later I found out that, instead of waiting in our office, he simply went to the airport and boarded a flight back to Athens.

The Eurogroup of 9 March was a wholly predictable affair. One after the other, like arsonists watching a blaze that they had started and commenting on its progress, the troika's leaders blamed us for stalling the negotiations. When my turn came, I explained as moderately as I could the two causes of the stasis: the troika's refusal to enter into genuinely comprehensive negotiations that included my debt-swap proposals and the relaxation of austerity that these would enable, and their demand, the IMF's in particular, that their so-called missions return to Athens for direct 'consultations' with our ministers. I reminded my fellow finance ministers that I had written to Dijsselbloem demanding the commencement of negotiations and concluded with a plea to end the stonewalling and the asphyxiation of our government using the practical proposals that I had already presented to Mario Draghi and Benoît Cœuré.

Once more Draghi repeated his insistence that the ECB was operating strictly within its rules while avoiding decisions that would politicize its work. I decided to expose this lie gently but firmly.

> The present circumstances are similar to [those of] the summer of 2012, in the sense that there is a new Greek government, the programme is suspended, there are negotiations about negotiations, and the Greek state has pressing repayments coming up. But the ECB today is refusing to behave towards our government in a manner comparable to how it behaved in 2012 towards the previous government. Mario's claim that the ECB is above politics is not supported by the facts. Indeed, the only reasonable explanation of its behaviour today is that the ECB is biased against a government that its governing council members dislike for purely political reasons.

As I outlined the facts and figures that made this contention irrefutable, I could see in the corner of my eye that Mario Draghi was looking uncomfortable. Wolfgang Schäuble, on the other hand, looked anything but. Unwilling to let the ECB president off the hook, I continued:

> Before the 20 February agreement, the ECB president had told me that, once we strike an interim agreement with the Eurogroup, the waiver would be returned and liquidity restored to the Greek banks. This promise remains unfulfilled. And it is not the only one. When requesting the restoration of our T-bill limit, Mario had told me in no uncertain terms that it would happen once there was evidence of demand for our T-bills from customers other than the Greek banks. Well, I have it on good authority that five days ago a Chinese investor purchased €100 million of our T-bills. Alas, there has been no relaxation of the asphyxiating constraint. I am tiring you with these details for one reason only: because our hard work to get to the 20 February agreement is being undermined in ways that you may not be privy to and for which our government is not responsible.

Instead of engaging with my very serious accusation that the ECB was acting politically, Jeroen hastily attempted to end the discussion. He proposed that we issue a quick statement saying that the negotiations would begin in two days with the institutions coming to Athens. I immediately replied that I welcomed the commencement of negotiations but proposed they take place in Brussels instead. Jeroen retorted that the negotiators might need data that could only be found in our ministries. I said that we were happy to welcome technical personnel from the institutions to Athens in order to collect data to be brought to the two sides' negotiators in Brussels. At that point, in a rare helpful intervention, Pierre Moscovici suggested that he and I work this out over the next couple of days. We had successfully avoided falling into the trap of accepting the troika's return.

Judging by the exchange of text messages that followed the meeting, Alexis was happy. 'We are spinning it as a success: political negotiations to commence in Brussels along the lines of the 20 February agreement in order to end the impasse.' He also had a warning for me. Apparently Michael Noonan, the Irish finance minister, was reported to have said that I was about to be replaced. 'We have denied this,' Alexis texted me. In a separate message he added, 'I think that the Irishman is trying to facilitate the creditors' plan to undermine you because you are a tough negotiator.'

Separately, Alexis texted me to say that Jeroen had contacted him directly to push for the troika to come to Athens two days later on 11 March: 'He told us that you agreed to that. Pappas replied that he did not believe that Varoufakis would ever have agreed.'

I responded, 'He threatened that it will all be over if the troika does not return. I told him his threats will not work.'

Alexis fumed at Jeroen's cheap tactics: 'Jeroen threatened me with a cessation of the negotiations as he was "getting tired". Pappas told him to take a deep breath because we were only at the beginning of an historic process. Yani, end this today before it takes us under.'

I knew what he meant: ensure that the negotiations took place in Brussels; prevent at all costs the return of the troika to Athens. 'Not to worry, Alexi. I shall nip this in the bud,' I reassured him. To do so I needed to talk to Moscovici urgently. But first I had two appointments to keep.

Jeff's shock

After the obligatory post-Eurogroup press conference, at which Jeroen lamented a 'wasted two weeks', clearly implying that we were the ones responsible for the delay, I collected Jeff from our delegation office and headed down the corridor to the office of the Federal Republic of Germany.

To a Europeanist like me there is something beautiful about that corridor, off which every European country has an office. Admittedly it is on a nondescript floor in an ugly building, but the fact of its existence should be something to be seriously proud of. As it was, I headed for Wolfgang's office with Jeff and Nicholas Theocarakis, dreading what might occur but with a plan.

Thinking back to what transpired I am reminded of Mike Tyson's fantastic line at the height of his tumultuous boxing career: 'Everyone has a plan until they get punched in the mouth.' My plan had been inspired by a tip I received from Pier Carlo Padoan, the Italian finance minister, when I had met him in Rome a little more than a month earlier. Pier Carlo had managed to break the ice with the German finance minister by offering to push through Italy's parliament a reform bill Wolfgang was proposing. Its successful passage won him Wolfgang's trust. 'Offer him something similar,' had been Pier Carlo's advice.

Wolfgang began the meeting in top form. 'Your prime minister and your cabinet have managed to make us lose all confidence in your government,' was his opening line.

'But, Wolfgang,' I said genuinely bemused, 'we never had your confidence. We are, for goodness' sake, a government of Greece's radical Left party! How could *you* have confidence in *us*?' Wolfgang smiled at my frankness. 'But,' I hastened to add, 'believe me when I tell you that I want to *earn* your confidence and your trust.' I continued: 'The question is how? I will not lie to you, Wolfgang, like others before me with promises that I can neither fulfil nor intend to. That would accomplish the opposite. The only way I know to win your trust is by making a promise that is difficult to fulfil but which, firstly, I want to fulfil and, secondly, you want me to fulfil. So, here is my suggestion: why don't you tell me what are the three or four major reforms that you think we should implement in Greece? If we can agree on three or four major reform bills, that we both agree would be therapeutic for Greece and increase your chances of getting your money back, then all I ask you is for four weeks without the present liquidity squeeze. During those four weeks I shall endeavour to pass these bills through our parliament and begin implementing them. If I am successful, you will then have cause to begin to trust me. If not, proceed with your plan to throttle us.'

I had not briefed Jeff about my plan, but it seemed to go down well with him and he appeared eager to hear Wolfgang's response. I suspect Wolfgang's reply came as something of a surprise to him. 'I am not going to negotiate with you. As I have told you last time, you must go to the institutions!'

'But Wolfgang,' I replied, 'time is running out. In a week or two we will have to default to the IMF with untold consequences for all. You tell me to go to the institutions. But the institutions simply lack the mandate to do what it takes to avert a crash or to negotiate with us a viable agreement for Greece within the eurozone. I am telling you all this because there are forces at work trying to derail the process.'

Wolfgang's face went from apathy to engagement. Even though I had learned from past meetings that such changes in Wolfgang's expression were pregnant with disappointment, on that occasion I could never have predicted his extraordinary response. 'I don't think that *any* government can keep Greece in the eurozone,' he declared.

'Is this the chancellor's view too?' I asked.

'She has other ideas,' he replied dismissively.

If I had any remaining doubts that getting their money back was towards the bottom of our creditors' priorities, Wolfgang had just put paid to them. It appeared that Germany's finance minister had resigned himself to the idea that his country would not be getting any money back at all. For if a country like Greece were to leave the euro, its new currency would devalue substantially, and so an already unsustainable euro debt would become even more unpayable.

With that bombshell Wolfgang had killed our conversation. Anything I might say to him about finding a way for Greece to repay a sizeable portion of its debts was redundant in the face of his conviction that Greece could not survive in the euro, irrespective of how the country was run. But any discussion about Grexit was impossible too as Mrs Merkel had 'other ideas'. Stalemate!

As we left for our next meeting, Jeff was practically pulling his hair out. 'I cannot believe what my ears just heard,' he said, his face contorted. 'Does Wolfgang not realize that he is jeopardizing everything that we have been building for sixty years?'[1] He continued to voice his exasperation as we made our way back to the Greek office: 'Even if we assume that they don't care about people in need, are these guys not aware that, for a relatively small amount of money, they are running the risk of pissing off many very rich and powerful people?' His question was left hanging as we went in.

Klaus Regling, whom Wolfgang Schäuble had appointed head of the eurozone's bailout fund (initially the EFSF, later the ESM), was waiting for us. A functionary with next to no discretionary power, he lacked the authority to make any difference to our situation. Still he had asked to see me and, out of courtesy, I had agreed. I hoped to use the opportunity to put to him several ideas regarding the debt swaps I was proposing which fell within the remit of his fund. From the outset, however, he proved even more unwilling to discuss solutions than anyone else I had spoken to that long, long day. The only thing he seemed keen to say was that I owed him €142.6 billion.

As there was very little to reply to that, except perhaps to recite the title of Dario Fo's play *Can't Pay Won't Pay*, I presented him instead with a moral dilemma: 'Given that, as it seems, in a week or two we shall run out of money with which both to repay the IMF and to pay salaries and pensions, what do you advise me to do, Klaus? The choice is between defaulting on the old and the frail or defaulting to the IMF. Which is of course an unnecessary dilemma given that our central bank owes us a similar amount.'

For Klaus it was a no-brainer. 'You must never, ever default to the IMF. Suspend all pension payments instead. This is what you must do,' he said with striking conviction.

I chose not to point out that, even if we let every old age pensioner die of hunger, it would still be impossible to repay the IMF and the ECB over the next few months, but said, 'It is a sad day when the head of Europe's stability mechanism is advising me to do something that will violently destabilize our society and economy.'

At the end of a busy but arid day punctuated only by Wolfgang Schäuble's statement that Grexit was inevitable, Jeff rewarded me with what I took to be a massive compliment: 'Having sat in your meetings with Thomsen, Draghi, Schäuble and Regling, I must tell you that I have never seen anything like this in my decades of experience with meetings between debtor governments and creditors such as the IMF, the US government, the World Bank . . . In every meeting you were positive, bristling with ideas regarding practical solutions. And they kept knocking your ideas down, even though they were good ideas, without proposing a single one of their own. Unbelievable!'

Caging the troika

Alexis's directive had been crystal clear: the troika could not be allowed to return to Athens as if nothing had changed. So was Jeroen's threat that if the troika's return to Athens were impeded, he would end the process.

Smiling, I dismissed his threats. 'What matters now,' I said, 'is that the negotiations begin in a fashion maximizing the chances of an agreement. Try to be a little more positive about this. In any case, did we not agree that the precise location and process would be the subject of talks between Moscovici and me?'

'Fine,' he conceded sullenly, 'but I want this settled within twenty-four hours.'

Pierre Moscovici and I met that same morning in Brussels. He was entirely sympathetic to our rejection of the troika's return. In fact, he repeated his view that the troika process had been a humiliation not only for Greece but also for the European Commission, whose role the troika's behaviour undermined. And in less than a quarter of an hour we had agreed on a sensible process: the political negotiations over debt restructuring, fiscal policy and reform agenda would take place in Brussels. Ministers would talk to ministers and to Pierre (who as a commissioner is equivalent in rank to a minister), while our deputies deliberated in adjacent rooms. Meanwhile, the institutions would be free to dispatch 'technicians' to Athens for the purposes of on-the-spot data mining and fact finding. They would talk only to Greek 'technicians' about the facts and the data they sought and would refrain entirely from debating or negotiating political decisions. Instead, the facts and data they gathered would be passed back to those engaged in the political negotiations in Brussels. Pierre proposed the new process be called the Brussels Group – the Bee Gees, as Nicholas Theocarakis jokingly named it.

Once Pierre and I had agreed on the Bee Gees, we discussed how to prevent ill-intentioned members of the troika from undermining our agreement. Pierre thought it crucial that we keep the plan secret until Mario Draghi and Christine Lagarde were on board. He feared that if certain people got wind of it, they would find ways to kill it off before it even got going. (While he mentioned no names, I am sure his list of potential spoilers included Thomas Wieser, Declan Costello and of course Poul Thomsen.) So he asked me to maintain radio silence while he tried to convince Mario and Christine. I promised that I would tell only Alexis, and he promised to get back to me within twenty-four hours – before Jeroen's latest deadline expired.

A tense day followed, in which Pierre and I exchanged messages and drafted a joint communiqué describing the new process, but we succeeded well within the deadline. The Bee Gees were ready to roll. I called Nicholas Theocarakis and asked him to assemble our troops to arrive in Brussels the next morning, ready for battle. I also called

Spyros Sagias, who was to orchestrate the reception of the troika's technicians in Athens.

Sagias feared rightly that, once in Athens, the troika's storm troopers would attempt to revert to their usual ways, while Alexis was adamant that they should not be allowed the unconstrained access to our ministries they were accustomed to. So the government booked a whole floor at the Athens Hilton and reserved a conference area in its basement to house the troika's technical HQ. At the troika's request, ministry officials and technicians from our side would visit them at the Hilton, bearing the files, laptops and hard drives necessary to satisfy their entirely disingenuous hunger for data and facts – data and facts that they knew even before we did as they controlled our ministries' departments more than we did.

The first skirmish occurred less than twelve hours after our visitors settled in, when Christine Lagarde signalled to my office that her IMF team in Athens was dismayed at being incarcerated in the Hilton and feared for its safety. Allegedly, the Greek government had not provided any security personnel. I telephoned Roubatis, our chief spook, to get the lowdown, and then immediately called Christine. She repeated the story she had been told – that her people in Athens were distressed at their vulnerability. I told her that around three hundred plain-clothes police and secret service officers were guarding the Hilton, as Roubatis had just informed me. Never before, I said, had so much security been provided for the IMF's mission to Athens. Christine was taken aback and expressed a preference for uniformed police. 'Why?' I asked. I did not get an answer. Could the reason have been that the troika wanted to be visible? Without their motorcades escorted by police with sirens blaring, how would the Greek people know that they had arrived? Perhaps it was only to be expected that they needed to be seen to be in Athens and in control.

From day one the troika teams in Athens strove to violate the separation between the political and the technical that Pierre and I had agreed. Questions submitted to our ministries included: 'How do you intend to deal with the pension funds' chronic deficits in view of Greece's demographics?' While this was a perfectly good question, it pertained to political choices and not to the establishment of facts or the measurement of our situation. Meanwhile, their actual requests for data were so extensive and voluminous that it would have taken an army of civil servants weeks to fulfil them.

In the Brussels Group, meanwhile, the political negotiations were going nowhere thanks to a potent cocktail of the eurozone runaround, the Penelope ruse and the Swedish national anthem routine. To be fair, our side also contributed to the fiasco that these negotiations were turning into. Nicholas Theocarakis had the onerous task of managing an already disparate team that was fundamentally split in two: between my team of professionals, including Elena Panariti, Lazard personnel and Glenn Kim, and Chouliarakis and his younger Syriza cohort. Chouliarakis and company refused to coordinate with my team, arriving late for meetings, going for lunches and dinners at critical moments and generally behaving with the arrogance of those who believed they had the prime minister's ear. 'At times I felt like a childminder,' was how Nicholas expressed his frustration to me.

By contrast, although they had nothing of substance to propose and their only concern was how to avoid any discussion of debt restructuring, the troika were on time, in tune and on target. Nicholas reported to me that when Glenn Kim entered the room, Declan Costello protested again: 'We cannot have someone in the room who works on debt write-downs.' Naturally Nicholas asserted our right to have whoever we chose in our team, but Costello's tactic was telling: warm and fuzzy with Chouliarakis and his gang, cold and brazen with Glenn, Nicholas and Elena – classic divide and rule.

Our side's failings were apparent in Athens too. The troika's requests for non-existent facts and reams of data they already possessed may have been ridiculous, but it is also true that our ministries were less than competent in responding. Some, especially those under the control of the Left Platform, refused point-blank to cooperate on the grounds that the whole exercise was a charade. That was a fair point, but for better or worse our government's policy was to cooperate fully within the framework of my agreement with Pierre Moscovici and within the spirit of the 20 February Eurogroup agreement, which committed us to doing our utmost to establish common ground with the creditors. For as long as Alexis and the war cabinet were committed to negotiating in good faith, the fact that the creditors were violating their side of the bargain did not justify non-cooperation. Theocarakis, Sagias and I spent hours negotiating with some of our colleagues, sometimes pleading with them to reply to requests for data competently and on time. Often we failed to convince them to do so. Sometimes we had to get the data from alternative sources outside the ministry in question or call on the cooperative functionaries of one ministry to get answers that another ministry ought to have provided.

Despite our own side's failings, there is not a shadow of a doubt that they were not responsible for the impasse. Even if our Brussels Group team and the ministries at home had acted in exemplary fashion, the outcome would have been exactly the same. In the spring of 2015 Greece's creditors were in no mood to negotiate; they were resolved to re-establish their authority over a territory of their empire that had rebelled and to ensure that none of their other possessions got a similar idea. While commentaries in the *Wall Street Journal* and the *Financial Times* made out that Brussels and Athens were the scenes of a major disagreement over fiscal targets, tax rates and administrative reforms, in reality what was happening was the equivalent of the nineteenth-century gunboat diplomacy used by the British Empire.

Alexis, Sagias and Pappas seemed to understand this. Although, little by little and to my great distress, they were abandoning our objective of restructuring the debt and ending austerity, at this stage they were still prepared to take decisive action in order to prevent the troika's reoccupation of our ministries. Sagias worked tirelessly to keep their technical team confined to the Hilton, while Pappas was threatening to expel them altogether. And on 15 March, when a ridiculous list of questions related to pensions arrived from the troika's technical team, Alexis exclaimed, 'Enough is enough!'

He was right. The questions had nothing to do with data or facts; they were purely political. Indeed, they were questions that not even Wolfgang Schäuble could have answered had he been asked them. Germany's mature and well-funded state has not worked out how to render its pension system sustainable in the long run, given its country's difficult demographics. How could the Greek government be expected to answer such questions given its newness, the state's insolvency and a situation in which one in two families had no one in paid work and survived on a single pension? By putting such questions to the civil servants of our overwhelmed social security department, the troika's technical representatives were inciting them to an act of bad faith: either they would refuse to answer, in which case they could be accused of failing to cooperate, or they would be forced to go well beyond their remit.

With a Eurogroup Working Group teleconference approaching on 17 March, at which we were to 'take stock' of the negotiations, Alexis ordered me to instruct Nicholas to make it clear that the troika's

Athens team had crossed a red line. To make sure there would be no misunderstanding, I sat down in Alexis's office to write Nicholas's statement so that Alexis could read it first and approve it, which he did the moment he laid eyes on it.

The proceedings of what turned out to be an historic teleconference began in the usual fashion with the troika's representatives presenting their position. Declan Costello spoke first, then Benoît Cœuré, finally Poul Thomsen. All three read from the same predictable script.

> There will be no agreement in April unless the Greek side accelerates . . . we need a comprehensive approach . . . there is an urgency to step up the intensity of the work . . . the Greeks must understand the need not only to respect previous commitments but also the European provisions . . . it would be a pity if they violated the process of consultations to which they are committed . . . we are worried about Athens's temptation towards unilateral action . . . the humanitarian deal and new instalment law is a matter of concern to us . . . the process is highly unsatisfactory . . . they treat the mission as a nuisance . . .

Once they had finished, and Thomas Wieser as chair had expressed his regret that Greece was not being represented by George Chouliarakis, it was Nicholas's turn to read the script that Alexis had instructed me to write and which he had approved. In an initially unsteady voice, owing to the gravity of what he was about to do, Nicholas said the following:

> I am sorry to report that the behaviour of the institutions' technical teams in Athens, in the opinion of my government and the prime minister, has violated the agreement that the technical team in Athens would only collect facts and data. My prime minister has now elevated the negotiations at the highest political level. The solution now must be reached not at the technical level but at the political level, which is much above the Euro Working Group level. In this sense I do not think that this teleconference serves a useful purpose and I am clearly and unequivocally not authorized to say any more here.

For a few seconds there was silence. Weiser then tried to carry on as if Nicholas had not spoken. Others joined him in a bizarre effort to pretend that discussion of the negotiations with Greece could proceed. Instructed to do so by Alexis and myself, Nicholas reached for our teleconference device and pressed the Off button. We looked at each other. And smiled. It was a proud moment but one we knew we would pay for dearly. Within hours, leaks to the media from the usual sources were portraying Nicholas, one of the most congenial, cultivated, nuanced, moderate and brilliantly educated Europeans I know, as a brute, an imbecile and a spoiler.

That same day Declan Costello sent an email to Nicholas, to be passed on to me, warning us not to table our Humanitarian Crisis Bill in parliament. He 'strongly urged us' to consult with him, Thomas Wieser, Poul Thomsen et al. before proceeding. 'Doing otherwise would be proceeding unilaterally and in a piecemeal manner that is inconsistent with your commitments,' he wrote. It was a perfect gift – my cue to push the bill immediately through parliament while making Costello's email public, thus exposing the troika's opposition to our plan to extend urgent help to those Greek families suffering the most. The outcry in Greece and beyond was deafening. Costello must have kicked himself. But the troika learned their lesson well: from then on they never emailed or put in writing anything that revealed their intent or character – at least, not until one day in late June when they were ready for the kill.

The next morning the troika's technical team headed for the airport. For the first time in weeks I felt that there might still be a chance to unite our side behind a comprehensive plan to end the crisis written for the Greek people by their own government. But to succeed it would require a collective willingness to do to Mario Draghi, Angela Merkel and Christine Lagarde what Nicholas had done in his inaugural Eurogroup Working Group teleconference: press the Off button.

Merkel's spell

During his years in opposition Alexis had been publicly disparaging about the German chancellor. His sarcastic quips about 'Frau' or 'Madame' Merkel had been plastered all over the press, while Syriza had been promising that the moment they won office they would unilaterally tear up the *MoU*, write off the debt and perform other amazing feats inconsistent with their stated intention of negotiating a new deal for Greece within the eurozone and the EU. Alexis in particular had laboured under the illusion that forces beyond Europe, from Russia and China to the United States and Iran, would come to our assistance, while Europe's periphery would somehow help contain Berlin in general and Mrs Merkel in particular.

This was in direct contrast to my oft-stated opinion that of all Greece's potential allies in Europe or beyond, Mrs Merkel was our best hope. Naturally, this view startled those, including Alexis, who expected me to look instead towards countries such as France, Italy or Spain, for whom Merkel represented the common enemy. But I was convinced that no government of a deficit eurozone country would dare oppose Berlin, even if they wanted to in their heart of hearts. Instead, the key to our success lay in Angela Merkel's determination to keep the eurozone together, as a result of her small-'c' conservatism and her aversion to structural breaks.[2]

From 2010 to 2014 I had made it my business to convince Greek politicians that the only way to force Chancellor Merkel to step in to deliver debt relief and a reasonable agreement for Greece would be to present her with a simple choice: evict us from the eurozone at your own political cost or deliver us from the workhouse. I was and remain convinced that, unlike Wolfgang Schäuble, who would have jumped at the opportunity to chuck us out of the eurozone, Angela Merkel would shy away from this course, however reluctantly. And from the day I assumed the finance ministry I had kept my eye on the German leader, ensuring that nothing we did would prevent her, if she chose, from presenting our debt-swap proposals and revised reform agenda to the Bundestag as her own solution to the Greek crisis. Allowing her to portray these proposals as her own was a necessary condition for a decent agreement. But it was nowhere near sufficient. To motivate her to adopt our proposals at all we had to remain determined to stand our ground in the face of Wolfgang and his sidekicks' threats of Grexit. Only then would the chancellor step in.

And there lay the difference between Alexis and me. He had a very negative view of Merkel, seeing her as an enemy who would never yield unless Washington or Moscow or some other power forced her to. But I saw in her a pragmatic politician who would, once all other alternatives had been exhausted, do the right thing. Unlike many Greeks, I neither demonized Merkel but nor did I expect her to act on our behalf without due motivation. Thus, when she intervened helpfully before the 20 February Eurogroup, my expectations were confirmed: the chancellor *would* step in at the last moment and as a last resort *if she feared that we would not budge*. Equally, when a couple of weeks later she promised another positive intervention which Wieser's visit to our flat put paid to, my expectations were also fulfilled: the chancellor would *never* yield *until she had to*.

But Alexis saw Merkel's behaviour differently. When she intervened before 20 February, his negative expectations resulted in euphoric surprise. Then, with his expectations raised, Merkel was at liberty to dash them at will, causing Alexis to sink into the depths of misery. She used this capacity to toy with Alexis, lifting his spirits, depressing them and raising them again as it suited her. I did my best to weaken her influence over my prime minister with my own analysis of her behaviour, arguing that the only way to secure a decent agreement was to ensure she was constantly aware that we were not afraid to press the Off button. But it was not working. By April I sensed that Alexis had succumbed to the chancellor's spell.

The reader would be wrong to think that Alexis was easy prey for Mrs Merkel. He was not. It took the legacy of the Cold War to push our young prime minister towards her, and it took her astounding work ethic to subdue him fully once he was there.

The cataclysmic civil war of the 1940s had left Greeks bitterly divided and in awe of two hegemons: Russia and America. Rightists looked to the United States as their bulwark against the red bear, while leftists hoped the USSR would support them were they ever to win government. Of course by the time Syriza came to power, the USSR no longer existed, yet a section of Syriza continued to see Moscow as a potential friend in our struggle against the neoliberal troika. Quite a few even nursed fantasies of petrodollars sent by Vladimir Putin to support our cause.

While relatively unsusceptible to this delusion, Alexis seemed nevertheless convinced that some help would come from Russia. When he told me this I did my best to discourage him. 'Russia is not China,' I remember telling him. Even if Putin was prepared to provide money in exchange for some pipeline or state-owned company, I told Alexis we should turn it down for three reasons. First, Putin was an unsafe friend, and Russian business notoriously incapable of and disinclined towards proper long-term investment – unlike for instance the Chinese. Second, Russia was at sea financially, and any promise of substantial help would prove hollow. Third, Putin and his regime had an appalling human rights record: did we, whose only real backers were the progressives of Europe, want to be associated with such a state?

At the same time, our problematic coalition partners from the far Right had the opposite idea: that we throw ourselves at the feet of the United States so as to extricate ourselves from Merkel's grip. On one occasion, during a break from a cabinet meeting, Defence Minister Kammenos walked over to say that I should not allow the Germans to worry me. 'I can get you billions from the other side of the Atlantic and a swap deal with the Fed that will make it painless to get out of the euro,' he said.[3] I smiled and tried hard not to give him a piece of my mind. He continued, suggesting that I meet a friend of his, a Greek-American on Wall Street who had it all worked out. Alexis was listening and said that I should look into it. As the finance minister of a financially stressed country I had an obligation to leave no stone unturned, so although I was convinced it was a sham, I did my duty and met the said gentleman at my office and even asked Jamie Galbraith to visit his associates in New York. As I had guessed, the proposed dollar lifeline was a phantom.[4] By the time I had confirmed and reported to Alexis that the Fed swap and the American cavalry were a delusion, Putin had apparently also told him not to expect any money or indeed any help at all from Russia. 'You must strike a deal with the Germans,' he said.[5]

With no hope of support from either Cold War superpower, Alexis had little option but to turn to Merkel, which left him vulnerable to her psychological manipulation and remarkable diligence.

In the wake of the fruitless fiasco that was the Eurogroup of 9 March, Alexis spoke to Angela Merkel on the phone to ask for a second intervention. In response the chancellor requested that he have his people carefully annotate the *MoU* with their precise points of disagreement and what they proposed instead. Naturally, Alexis agreed and called me immediately afterwards with a request that I prepare the document. That night I stayed at the office alone, once more doing battle with the *MoU*'s fifteen paragraphs. Underneath each paragraph I wrote a colour-coded commentary: in green I explained which aspects of the paragraph we agreed with and why; in red I listed our objections and explained them; finally, in blue, I presented alternative policies with which to replace what we objected to. By the following morning, the original four-page document had grown to twenty-seven pages.

On 20 March, three days after the Eurogroup Working Group teleconference at which Theocarakis had pressed the Off button, Alexis was due in Brussels for an EU summit. Angela Merkel had suggested that after the formal dinner the two of them get together so that he could present the document and they could discuss it. In the event the formal dinner dragged on longer than expected, almost to midnight, and Alexis thought that the chance for their tête-à-tête had disappeared. Not so. The indefatigable Angela took him to an adjacent seminar room and proceed to spend hours with him, going over every sentence, every word, every nuance in the document. When at last they had finished, she congratulated him on the text he had brought – twice, in fact, as Alexis told me with a self-satisfied glow. Her congratulations, her diligence and her mastery of the Greek programme in incredible detail made quite an impression on Alexis.[6]

Merkel's influence over him had been growing steadily, and when the chancellor finally delivered her *coup de grâce*, it targeted the solidarity between Alexis and me. In essence, her proposal was this: given the deep dislike that most Greeks harboured for Wolfgang Schäuble, she suggested that they sideline their finance ministers – let Varoufakis 'cancel out' Schäuble, and Schäuble 'cancel out' Varoufakis, to use her words – while she and Alexis worked behind the scenes to reach a reasonable agreement. To do this, Angela Merkel suggested they establish a third level of negotiations, separate from the Brussels Group and the Eurogroup and free of me and Schäuble, at which Alexis was promised concessions impossible at the Eurogroup.

Alexis loved the idea. A secret meeting was thus arranged to take place in Frankfurt between their envoys, who would be known thereafter as the Frankfurt Group. Merkel chose Martin Selmayr, a German functionary in the European Commission, to represent her, while Alexis selected Nikos Pappas. They were joined by Benoît Cœuré, representing Mario Draghi, and the ubiquitous Poul Thomsen, representing Christine Lagarde. The Frankfurt Group was a microcosm of the Eurogroup except for three casualties: Wolfgang, myself and Pierre Moscovici, who was replaced as Juncker's representative by another Frenchman, Luc Tholoniat, who also worked for the commission.

The Frankfurt Group proved largely irrelevant, but it had its one major, intended effect: Alexis became convinced (or so he said) that I was making an enormous contribution to the cause by 'cancelling out' Wolfgang, but in reality Angela Merkel had succeeded in sidelining me. It was a brilliant ploy which succeeded in spreading discord in our ranks and offering Alexis hope that she fully intended to dash.

Within a month of the formation of the Frankfurt Group, bundling me and Schäuble together had had a sinister side-effect: in the collective consciousness of the war cabinet Wolfgang and I were now in the same mental box – two combatants that neutralized one another. But by the middle of May, what had begun as a compliment – that in sacrificing myself I had succeeded in taking out Schäuble – had metamorphosed into a charge against me: that I was in cahoots with Wolfgang Schäuble, plotting with him behind the back of the chancellor and my prime minister to introduce capital controls and bring Greece out of the euro.

Such an insinuation could never have been believed without generous assistance from within our War Cabinet. Imagine my horror when I discovered that not only was assistance being given but that it was based on, possibly initiated by, false reports from Greece's intelligence services.

To this day people still ask me, 'When was Alexis turned?' It is a question that I refuse to engage with since I know I shall never be able to answer it to my satisfaction. Nevertheless I listen to the answers others give with some interest. Of those, one fascinated me. In early 2016 Danae and I were having dinner with another couple, a film director and his wife. As our partners were debating the question, the film director and I kept silent, until suddenly he volunteered a laconic answer: 23 March 2015. Startled by his accuracy and certainty, I asked why that particular date. Being the visual artist that he is, he pulled out a tablet to show me two photographs by way of explanation: one was of Alexis entering the Chancellery on his first formal visit to Berlin, a couple of days after his late-night meeting with Merkel in Brussels.[7] In it he looked downtrodden. The second was of him leaving an hour or so later accompanied by Chancellor Merkel, with a military guard of honour paying its respects. He looked jubilant.

'Do you know what he's thinking as he's exiting the Chancellery?' my friend asked.

'I have no idea.'

'*What the hell am I going to do now with Varoufakis?* That's what he's thinking.'

13

The right stuff, foiled

'When has a revolution ever delivered anything other than disaster?'

A fellow lecturer at the University of East Anglia, where I was teaching in the mid-1980s, once put this question to me. For him, an Englishman influenced by the thinking of Edmund Burke, it was a rhetorical question rich with truth and wisdom. For a Greek it was nonsense. Our very country would not exist had it not been for the revolution of 1821 – an insurrection against the Ottoman empire that stood a tiny chance of success and was opposed at the time as reckless by a large part of the Greek elite.

Every year, on 25 March, every village, town and city in the country puts on a parade to celebrate that reckless utopian act of faith which, almost by accident, yielded modern Greece. I have to admit I have always found these parades a little too kitsch and militaristic, but in 2015 the spirit of the 1821 insurgency seemed to acquire new meaning for the majority of Greeks. This time the spring was brimming with something more than wildflowers and swallows; pride and dignity were blossoming again throughout the land, as well as among the Greek diaspora in the Americas and Australia. So when Alexis asked me to represent the government at one of the parades, I said yes and requested that it be the parade in Chania, the Cretan city where the largest parade on the island was scheduled for that year.

Apart from some ancestors on each of my parents' sides, I have little linking me to the island, and yet Crete is special to me. Danae is convinced that I have a Cretan character, whatever that means, and my Australian-born daughter, who has been to Crete only once, tells her mates in Sydney that she is Cretan. Whatever the background, I was excited that Danae and I would attend the Greek Revolution Day parade in Chania. When the day came, we walked around the centre of Chania with a large group of local officials, making our way slowly to a marquee, where I then stood next to the archbishop of Crete, the mayor and the chief of police to watch the procession of local school-children, police units, firefighters, ambulance staff, platoons of men and women dressed in revolution-era gear and, touchingly, five veterans from the Battle of Crete in wheelchairs pushed by their grandchildren.[1] As the parade passed, the participants turned towards me to salute their government's representative. It made me feel at once proud and ridiculous, but I confess I enjoyed every moment of it, despite the anarchist in me constantly taking the mickey. Afterwards, we laid a wreath at the war memorial and made our way slowly through a dense crowd towards the taverna where lunch had been laid out.

As we walked, men and women anxiously squeezed my hand, hugged me, spoke words of encouragement, all conveying one message: 'Don't give in! Do not dare surrender! No U-turn!' At one point I noticed a journalist filming us. When a middle-aged lady repeated the slogan 'Rupture now!' I stopped, took her hand and, with an eye to the reporter, said, 'I'm sure you understand that this is something that we must be united behind. It's not just for us to do. We must hang together.'

'We're with you!' she insisted.

'Yes, but you must be with us on the day after the rupture too!'

The footage was the main news item on all television stations that night, as I had hoped. Genuine negotiations with our creditors had still not begun, and the moment of either rupture or surrender was approaching. Millions were urging us towards the former. Alexis had already put the question in the war cabinet: 'Would those calling for rupture today be with us afterwards? Or will they then curse us for having brought the rupture about?' It was an important question and one that I wanted to address publicly.

After we arrived back in Athens that night, Alexis and I had a long telephone conversation. 'Did you really tell a granny that she had better be with us after a rupture?' he asked.

'Yes, Alexi, I did. We must prepare our people. It is inexcusable to behave as if there is nothing to worry about. We must gradually let them into the true picture if we want them by our sides in the event of a clash.'

Alexis agreed but cautioned that alarming people would worsen the bank run. It was a valid point, but I sensed that Alexis was grad-ually retreating towards delay at all costs.

Changing the subject, I relayed to Alexis a phone conversation I had just had with Larry Summers, who had called with information and solid advice: the IMF was planning to demand a wicked turn of the austerity screw. They would claim we were facing a huge primary budget deficit of between -2 per cent and -5 per cent of national income. It was an absurd projection, given that we were running a primary surplus at the time; indeed, even after the events of the summer of 2015, the financial year closed without a primary deficit.

Alexis was upset and expressed some animosity towards Summers. I explained that Larry was not condoning the IMF position; he was telling us that whatever else we conceded we must not accept more austerity. Obama, Lew, the IMF, every banker in Wall Street and the City all understood that it was a cruel, unusual and stupid punishment. 'Larry's message is simple,' I said. 'We should not yield on the one thing that the world's most powerful people agree with us on.'

Alexis accepted the point and seemed more relaxed. To defuse the tension we exchanged a joke or two before hanging up.

It was late, well after 2 a.m. Danae and I sat on the sofa for a moment's peace and togetherness before turning in. She asked me how I felt. As I began to answer, she got out her phone and started videoing. 'These are historic moments,' she explained. It was something that Danae would go on to do quite a few times thereafter. The experience of watching those videos has been painful enough to deter me from returning to them more than once. That night my spontaneous response was: 'I feel alone, Danae. I sit in my ministerial office, supposedly the head of fourteen thousand civil servants. But in reality I am on my own, confronting a large, fully weaponized army without even a small shield for protection . . . hell, without even a proper press office to let the world know of the solid policy work that my tiny team is doing; let alone protect me from lies and distortions that would make Joseph Goebbels proud.'

That feeling – and evidence that it was justified – would only get stronger.

From gloom to the sublime to the absurd

By the end of March all the Greek state's spare liquidity had been spent on our IMF repayments. According to the second bailout loan agreement, these repayments, amounting to around €1.5 billion, were meant to have been covered by means of disbursements from Europe's bailout fund and the IMF, but these had of course been withheld as part of the strategy to force us to capitulate. The €1.9 billion the ECB owed us had also been withheld and the €1.5 billion that Beijing had offered us had been blocked. It was a miracle that my ministry managed to find that €1.5 billion for the IMF while also meeting our obligations to civil servants and pensioners. It proved that, despite the deep crisis, the Greek state was living well within its means and that all the talk of my demanding loans from other European countries to pay for extravagant pensions and salaries was nonsense.

Nonetheless, we had come to the end of the road. We had given the creditors a whole month to test their willingness to meet us halfway, to come to the table in good faith and discuss a proper plan for ending the Greek crisis. They had failed that test purposely. The Brussels Group was stalled as the troika dismissed every one of our proposals while putting forward no ideas of their own. Not once had we received even a single page from them containing any practical solution or policy. And yet the mainstream media even in Greece were reporting that the Greek government was failing to submit costed plans to match the 'meticulously prepared' proposals of the institutions. The mammoth gap between their reports and reality convinced me that we were sleepwalking to our doom. Urgent action was necessary. It was time either to surrender or to fight. It was time to fold or to default.

As a first step we needed to announce that we did not intend to continue repaying the IMF, and later the ECB, as long as the Eurogroup and the institutions refused to talk business. On 3 April an informal inner cabinet meeting was convened at the prime minister's office. I arrived at Maximos early in order to confront Alexis and convince him that a decision was overdue: he must either announce an imminent default to the IMF or call Merkel with a request for the terms of our surrender. 'You have no other option, Alexi,' I insisted. 'Prolonging the present stasis only helps Wolfgang and his satellites, who are edging us out of the eurozone through a process of attrition.'

Alexis was unenthusiastic. Evidently downhearted he gave me his usual line: we would default but not yet. 'We must not lose the blame game . . . Let me talk to Angela again . . . The time is not right.'

I retorted that we had already lost the blame game. 'Read the press, Alexi,' I said. 'Every day that passes is reported as another day when we have failed to put forward proposals that add up.' We had waited long enough, demonstrated our readiness to compromise and given the other side a chance to compromise too. On 20 February we had alienated many of our own people in order to do so. And what had been the response? They had reneged on the agreement within days. 'That was a month ago, Alexi. Since then they have been upping the ante while Angela has, despite her kind words and promises to you, failed to intervene. If not now, when are we going to default?'

The ensuing conversation lasted a while. Tenaciously, though with little enthusiasm, he followed his usual practice of agreeing with everything I said but drawing the opposite conclusion. He spoke slowly and lethargically, looking ever more downhearted. Eventually we ran out of time: the ministers were gathering in the conference room opposite his office. I left his office to join them, giving Alexis the opportunity to freshen up a little before chairing a meeting whose purpose was not just to brief key ministers but also to raise their spirits.

Shortly after I had taken my seat at the table, Alexis entered looking a little better. As usual, he kicked off the meeting with a briefing on the state of play, but with no good news to report nor any announcements of valiant initiatives, he soon flagged. Confined to a grim assessment of a process that was evidently going nowhere, the more he talked the greater the gloom in the room. By the time he had concluded, there was a leaden atmosphere of resignation. Every minister who contributed to the ensuing discussion spoke in a distinct tone of melancholy. Once everyone who wanted to had spoken, Alexis took the floor again to wrap up the meeting. He began much as he had ended his introductory speech – slow, subdued, almost depressed – recounting how difficult the situation was and the dangers involved, but gradually he picked up a little in speed and buoyancy.

> Before you all came in, I was talking with Varoufakis in my office. He was trying to convince me that it is time to default to the IMF. He was telling me that they are showing no signs of wanting to compromise so that a difficult but decent agreement, one that is economically viable and politically manageable for us, can be reached. I explained to him that this is not the right time to default. That we will lose the blame game when there are still three months

left in the extension we secured on 20 February. That defaulting to the IMF will trigger the cross-defaults thus giving Draghi the right to close down our banks.[2]

Here we go, I thought. *He is having it out with me in cabinet without my having said a word!*

Except that I was badly mistaken. After a short but theatrical pause he continued, his voice suddenly growing in confidence – and not just his voice; his whole body began gradually to resonate with energy. To my astonishment I heard him say, 'But you know what, comrades? I think he is right. Enough is enough. We have been playing by their rules. We accepted their process. We bent over backwards to show them that we are willing to compromise. And all they did was to delay us and then blame us for the delay. Greece is still a sovereign country and we, the cabinet, have the duty to say, "Enough!"' Then, rising from his chair and with his voice growing louder, he pointed at me and bellowed, 'Not only are we going to default but you are going to get on a plane, go to Washington and tell the lady in person that we shall default on the IMF!'

The room erupted with cheers. Colleagues looked to one another for confirmation of what they had heard, fully recognizing its historic nature. The gloom and darkness vanished as if a curtain had been ripped back on a sunny day. Like everyone else but perhaps more, much more, I allowed myself a moment of elation. At that moment it felt like the nearest thing to a sublime Eucharist a bunch of atheists can experience.

As I headed out of Maximos, Alexis and I hugged silently. Euclid walked out with me, looking just as chuffed. As we were going in the same direction, I gave him a lift on my motorcycle. The photo of two Greek ministers on a Yamaha XJR went around the world. That night Euclid sent me a text message: 'My daughters are jealous. They also want a ride on your bike.' It was a rare happy day.

That night I worked for hours with Spyros Sagias, preparing the legal argument that I would present to Christine Lagarde. Spyros was scribbling in Greek in a legal notebook; I was typing into my laptop, the two of us managing little by little to produce Greek- and English-language versions of our official letter to the IMF managing director. Its gist was that, in the Greek government's opinion, the IMF could not expect us to pay up while, first, the troika had suspended disbursements to Greece even of its own money and, second, the ECB was reducing our liquidity.[3]

Meanwhile, my secretary was trying to get hold of Christine Lagarde's office. It took some time because it was Good Friday.[4] Alexis wanted me to leave immediately for Washington, DC, which meant arriving there on Easter Sunday. Once we had got through to Christine's office and explained that there were special circumstances that demanded a meeting, we were told that she would cut short her Easter break and meet me at her office in the late afternoon of Easter Sunday.

On the long flight to Washington via Munich I was accompanied by Takis Roumeliotis, a former representative of Greece at the IMF who had distinguished himself as an early critic of the IMF's Greek programme.[5] In my bags I carried the official letter that would accompany my verbal announcement that my ministry would not be making the next payment to the IMF of €462.5 million, due on 9 April 2015, while in my mind I was planning the best way to use our impending default as a way of extricating Greece from its doom loop. The long flight at least offered me a few hours of isolation in which to rewrite the document that was, with the help of Jeff Sachs and others, to become my ministry's constructive substitute for the *MoU*. First default, then return immediately with a moderate, sensible plan for Greece – that was the only way of shaking up the creditors and ending the vicious circle.

Upon arriving at Ronald Reagan Washington National Airport I discovered that my US visa was no longer valid, despite having another year to run, since I had resigned from the University of Texas to contest the parliamentary election in Greece. Of course, the fact that I was a minister of state expected by the head of the IMF within two hours and had appointments the next day at the US Treasury and the White House meant nothing to the US immigration officers. Like any other foreigner I had to go through the process of making an official application online, which I proceeded to do at the immigration checkpoint. Even though it was an inconvenience, there was something pleasing about the egalitarianism of US immigration.

The extra time it took to clear the border delayed the turning on of my mobile phone. In retrospect, this gave me another hour or so of mental peace, for when I did switch it on, I found a terse text message from Alexis: 'Call me.' Naturally, I did so immediately.

'Look, Yani,' he said, 'we've decided that we're not going to default, not yet.'

Flabbergasted, I asked, 'Who's "we"? Who decided that "we" won't default?'

Alexis, sounding coy, said, 'Me, Sagias, Dragasakis . . . we decided that it's not the right move just before Easter.'

'Thanks for telling me,' I replied, fuming and dejected. Adopting as cool and dispassionate a tone as I could, I asked, 'So what do I do now? Get on the same plane and return? What's the point of seeing Lagarde now?'

'No, you must hold the meeting. You must go ahead as we agreed. Go in there and tell the lady that we'll default.'

It was the most absurd thing I have probably ever heard. *I cannot be hearing this right*, I told myself. I needed clarification. 'What do you mean? Tell her that we'll default even though you've decided that we won't be defaulting?'

'Yes,' said Alexis. 'Threaten her so that she gets anxious enough to call Draghi and push him to stop the liquidity squeeze. Then we'll reciprocate by announcing that we're not defaulting to the IMF.'

The adrenalin racing through me dissolved all traces of fatigue or jet lag. Keeping my indignation in check, I asked, 'And what if Draghi doesn't relax the liquidity squeeze upon hearing from Lagarde that I threatened to default on the IMF? What then, Alexi?'

'They will give in, Yani, they will!' came back his baselessly optimistic prediction.

'And what if they don't? Don't you see that when David's facing down Goliath with only a small catapult as a weapon, it's silly to put the catapult in jeopardy? Our catapult is the threat of default. You should only take it out if you intend to use it. For if you threaten to use it and then blink when the enemy calls your bluff, we're finished. Then they'll never fear your threats. We are too weak to bluff, Alexi. And, as your finance minister, I cannot let you waste our only weapon. I cannot tell Lagarde we'll default after you have just made it clear to me you don't intend to let me default.'

'You *will* tell her we'll default. Consider this an order from the prime minister.'

It was the first time Alexis had pulled rank on me. And he did so to waste our only trump card. As I was switching off my mobile phone it suddenly felt unbearably hot and heavy. Watching Takis walk ahead of me towards the terminal exit and the waiting car, escorted by embassy staff, I felt separated from him by a haze of grief. I envied him for not knowing and for his freedom from the questions ricocheting through my mind. Had Dragasakis and Sagias changed Alexis's mind while I was in mid-air? Had Alexis's rousing speech in Maximos during which he had embraced my proposal to default merely been a ruse to lift the spirits of his cabinet before cynically calling off the default? How could I serve a prime minister who so casually embraced an empty threat against the world's most powerful financial institution?

As the car pulled away from the kerb I knew I had to find a way of silencing the cacophony in my head. The unanswerable questions about what was going on in Maximos had to wait. Christine Lagarde was expecting me in her office at an otherwise empty IMF headquarters. And I was under orders from my prime minister to walk in and threaten her with something I believed we should do but which he had said he would not.

There's a lady who knows . . .

Of the many offices I visited during my brief ministerial stint, Christine Lagarde's at the IMF was the only one bordering on the aesthetically pleasing. She herself was relaxed and warm. But the absurd instructions I had been given overrode all else. It was as if I had a thorn lodged deeply in my foot: every step into that room was painful. There was a chance, I believed, that Christine and I might reach some kind of consensus, but the appearance of Poul Thomsen at her side eradicated any remaining hope of that.

I apologized for spoiling her Easter Sunday while agonising about how I could possibly carry out Alexis's diktat without damaging our credibility. 'None of us wants to write history in a negative way,' was how I broached the issue. I then tried to impress upon her what a difficult spot they, our creditors, had put us in. I was armed with an impressive number: 14.21 per cent, the proportion of Greece's puny national income that my ministry had had to find during our government's first three months just to repay the IMF.[6] I told Christine that, given our superhuman repayments in March and the ECB's stubbornness, 'as of 9 April we are in the danger zone. To put it bluntly, the government will be pushed into the hideous dilemma of having to choose between defaulting to the IMF or to pensioners and civil servants. As you understand whenever a government has this dilemma—'

Christine interrupted me helpfully to say, 'Yes, it is a no-brainer.'

To her immense credit, the IMF managing director's view of how to deal with this dilemma was precisely the opposite of that of Klaus Regling when Jeff and I had met him after the Eurogroup meeting of 9 March. Of course, when I pushed a little harder and asked her what she would do as a finance minister faced with this conundrum, Christine wriggled out of it by saying that she would have tried not to be faced with this conundrum.

The time had come to deliver my message from Athens. 'Let me convey to you an argument that has been gaining ground in Athens under legal advice,' I said, gearing up to read out the letter that I had scripted with Sagias. The gist of our case was simple, I explained. Greece and its creditors were bound by a loan agreement. The loan agreement specified, first, a schedule of repayments (from Greece to the creditors), second, a schedule of disbursements (from the creditors to Greece) and, third, a set of conditionalities (the *MoU*) under which the disbursements would be made. Since the general election three major developments had occurred: first, the disbursements had ceased, second, Greece's liquidity had been curtailed by the ECB and, third, the conditionalities were under renegotiation in the context of the 20 February Eurogroup agreement. Ergo, until this renegotiation delivered a new set of conditionalities, our repayments should be suspended alongside the disbursements – at least for as long as the ECB exercised its power to reduce our liquidity.[7]

Christine answered quickly, shrewdly, albeit in a manner that violated the spirit of the 20 February agreement. If Athens insisted on a moratorium of repayments based on the argument that the conditionalities were under renegotiation, her rejoinder would be that there were no negotiations over the conditionalities.[8] Smiling, I asked her what on earth we were negotiating about if not the conditionalities? Naturally I got a nebulous reply: 'It is about matching the *MoU* with your commitments.'

Since we were not in a court of law competent to settle the issue, there was nothing more for me to do at that moment other than to say what Alexis had ordered me to say: 'I am not authorized to enter into a war of words with you. But I am authorized to inform you that in four days' time we shall default on our scheduled repayment to the IMF, as long as our creditors continue to stall the negotiations and the ECB continues to limit our liquidity.' And I would have said these words proudly, but only if they were backed by the intention to act on them. In the absence of that intention, I went about things differently: I tried to win the IMF managing director over with an honest account of the situation.

Our conversation lasted a long time and covered a broad range of issues. It was friendly, constructive and pleasant because both of us made an effort to see the other's point of view. Keen to avoid the usual subterfuges, I explained to her my greatest worry: that all the Eurogroup discussions, including the Brussels Group negotiations, were taking place under false pretences. That Greece's recovery and sustainability within the eurozone was not what those running the show cared for. To drive the point home I shared with Christine my conversations with Wolfgang Schäuble, my offer to him of three or four major reform bills that we would draft collaboratively, and how he had dismissed this idea because, in his view, no Greek government could keep Greece inside the eurozone.

'So, do you see Christine,' I beseeched her, 'why we need some evidence that we are all on the same page? That we all want a comprehensive solution for Greece within the eurozone? We are not confident that we are all on the same page.'

'Do you mean politically?' she asked with concern evident on her face.

'Yes, politically,' I answered. 'We crave evidence that everyone around the Eurogroup table wants to avoid an "accident". I hope I am wrong, but my view is that this is not at all evident. A majority are craving the accident. We will compromise, but we do not intend to end up compromised in the sense of signing up to an *MoU* which we think is unenforceable and not helpful even if it is enforced.'

'What do you mean not enforceable?'

I explained how destructive further austerity would be for a country that had already broken the world austerity record: it would lead to a world-record rise in the rate of our debt-to-income ratio. More austerity and the continued denial of the need to restructure Greece's debt would lead with mathematical certainty to the country eventually being evicted from, or falling out of, the eurozone.

From the corner of my eye I could see that Poul Thomsen's gaze was fixed on the floor and recalled how he had enthusiastically endorsed every word I had just uttered on our first meeting in Paris.[9] Recalling also that Poul and other troika operatives had repeatedly accused us of 'ideological fixations', I talked about the troika's ideological fixations using examples: 'Only 9 per cent of the unemployed ever receive unemployment benefits. Greece is a libertarian's wet dream. We have five hundred thousand people who have not been paid for six months. One-third of paid labour is undeclared. The template with which the IMF comes to every country is irrelevant in Greece. Our major problem is not labour market inflexibility. It is undeclared labour, the worst case of informal flexibility. Even a boost in tourism does not create the increase in aggregate demand necessary. You have people in their early sixties who are unemployed and unemployable and with no access to social security, leading to pressure to put them into the pension system. These are the issues I want to talk about.'

'We want to talk about these issues too,' said Christine in a thoroughly conciliatory manner. Except that Poul intervened just at that point to make sure that we didn't. Instead he turned the conversation towards the 'process' of the ongoing negotiations.

'The issue is the process,' he said predictably. 'Bringing it to conclusion is possible. If you engage with us, I can see light at the end of the tunnel. Tell us what you do not like about the programme.'

I related how Chancellor Merkel had already asked Alexis for precisely such a document. I explained how I had produced a twenty-seven-page document with areas of agreement and disagreement and our counter-proposals coded by colour. I also told them about the late-night meeting during which Alexis and Angela sweated over the document.

'She is very impressive,' I said.

'The chancellor?' asked Christine

'Yes, the chancellor,' I confirmed.

'We all love her,' was Christine's reaction.

To which I replied, 'Now that's taking matters a little too far!'

I then handed over the document. Thomsen seemed very pleased with it. Going through, he said, 'This is very helpful,' adding that the IMF 'need agreement on comprehensive measures'.

That would be fine, I retorted. I wanted nothing more than to sit down and produce a fully comprehensive plan for the long term, I told them. We did not want to postpone these discussions for one second. 'But let's overcome the liquidity cliff,' I said, 'while showing our people and the institutions that we mean business . . . Let's come up with three bills that go through parliament in two weeks and generate reformist momentum. And of course let's talk simultaneously about the debt restructuring without which no agreement can be comprehensive.'

Christine stepped in. 'Maybe your approach is the right one, but I'm sceptical . . . I don't think that they [the 'Europeans'] will like the idea of working on three or four bills. You will get the Wolfgang reaction. I think it is better to "go comprehensive" [accept the process of a comprehensive review] and demonstrate that you are determined.'

Sensing that I had convinced her, though not Poul, I ploughed on: 'Christine, the idea that first we agree on everything and then we can do something tangible on pressing reforms, on the liquidity crunch, sounds to us like there is a lack of interest in finding a solution . . . I'm convinced that there are good intentions on both sides – us and the IMF. But I'm not convinced about the others. I want to have my mind changed on this. Wolfgang's position is immovable and disappointing. It is him that you should be arguing with. Not me. This is why we went to Merkel. Because we need clarity on intentions.'

Indicating that I was indeed getting through to her, Christine turned to Poul to ask him, 'Can you describe the [Greek] government's priorities regarding these three, four or five bills that they want to push through? How can this be made agreeable with the comprehensive process?'

Poul was not happy that Christine was warming to my proposal and tried to kick the ball off the pitch. 'What we need is to get started in Athens to build on what I agree has been a better technical process,' he said dragging us onto his favourite subject: the troika's return to Athens.

It was my turn to frustrate him. 'I am afraid, Poul,' I said, 'that your people in Athens behaved appallingly, trying to build up [their] career[s] by emulating what you had been doing there as the IMF's Greek mission chief since 2010.'

Christine intervened, laughing, 'Oh no, no, no . . . I cannot agree with this,' she said unable to contain her amusement. 'I have to support my team!'

'Of course you have to support your team,' I acknowledged, laughing too, 'like I have to support mine!'

Poul interrupted the laughter in his customary humourless style: 'I think . . . to get back to work—'

Only this time he was interrupted by Christine, who added, 'On an accelerated way.' (Meaning a faster negotiation process.)

I then cut in with my own challenge: 'Poul, you talk about getting to work on a comprehensive programme, but let me put to you the awful truth: nobody wants to talk with us about Greece's sustainability and get down to work to make it happen.'

'We want to talk about it,' said Christine.

'Your people in Athens and your people at the Brussels Group are not interested in a serious discussion,' I said.

'You speak like Keynes now,' she replied.

I could not help laughing again. Choosing not to respond to her comment, I continued: 'The way your people are conducting the conversation is as if they are either pushing us out of the eurozone or wishing to keep us in as a zombie. Angela Merkel's position is clear. She wants a pseudo-solution that muddles through, does nothing to resolve our insolvency but keeps Greece in the eurozone. Wolfgang Schäuble's is even clearer. He does not want a solution within the eurozone. He wants Greece out of the eurozone. We are merely collateral damage of his attempt to discipline the rest of the eurozone. And this is a grave danger to Europe.'

After another minute or so of disagreement, Christine eventually conceded the point. 'Making an example of Greece is not smart,' she admitted, justifying my hunch that, unencumbered by Thomsen, Schäuble and others, she and I could have found common ground.

In a bid to show my appreciation, I then said something that triggered the following exchange.

> VAROUFAKIS: I am happy to accelerate but we need to find a solution to the liquidity problem . . . When I do not know whether I shall be in default in a fortnight it is very hard to sit around the table with a clear mind to plan for 2025. The idea that we will complete this review before the last drop of liquidity runs out is absurd. Consider this: we would not be here today if our monies from the ECB's SMP profits were passed on to you on our behalf, as I have proposed. No liquidity, no progress. It's that simple.[10]

LAGARDE: You must press Mario Draghi on this. He appreci-
ates the speeding-up over the past ten days of the discussions. Press him on this.

VAROUFAKIS: The IMF can press him too. You cannot expect
your money back while Mario is drying us up.

LAGARDE: We talk all the time. But this is a resolution that
he needs to reach by himself, after hearing his own team.

VAROUFAKIS: I think you need to pressurize him, Christine,
too. We are doing our bit. But given that we have an IMF
redemption coming up which we cannot meet without
defaulting to our people, the IMF must decide: do you
think a post-mortem is more desirable than a moratorium?
Isn't it better to prevail upon the ECB to do its job? There
is a dereliction of duty here by the ECB.

LAGARDE: But they are not lenders of last resort, as they will
tell you.

VAROUFAKIS: They were to the Samaras government in July
2012. If Mario does not want to be tainted as a politicized
ECB president then he must apply the same rules. We are
not asking for special treatment.

A fascinating debate on what had to be done to take our default
to the IMF off the table was reaching its natural conclusion. I had to
exploit that unique opportunity to present the crux of the problem
to the only interlocutor that I could communicate with properly.

VAROUFAKIS: Let's get serious here. You folks – Mario, Angela
and you – have to give us a road map. I am leaving
Wolfgang out because we know where his map would
take us. We cannot just drift into the unknown on the
basis of hearsay that something may happen one day to
render Greece viable. We need to have an adult conversation with clear markers on dates so that on 13 April or
thereabouts the liquidity tap is turned back on. I cannot
go back to Athens to say to my cabinet that we agreed
that something magical might happen at some point
before we reach the cliff's edge. I cannot energize my
colleagues without someone picking up the phone and
giving us some assurances that we have a process that

comes with [the] liquidity provisions necessary to salvage
the negotiation process.

LAGARDE: But there is a clear link between the two.

VAROUFAKIS: Yes, but we need more than that. We need an
indication that the process will be timely.

Poul stepped in to put me back in the dock, unwittingly I hope,
unless he had eavesdropped on my last conversation with Alexis. 'Not
paying on the ninth is not the solution,' he said, 'if that is what you
will tell your colleagues in Europe.'

'I never said that,' I protested.

Christine intervened in my favour. 'He did not say that,' she
confirmed.

'What I *did* say,' I clarified, 'was that if we do not get any liquidity
provisioning then we will be forced to default independently of our will.'

Returning to my request for an 'adult conversation', Christine
counter-proposed: 'But it must be a grown-up conversation without
drama, without journalists chasing me, no game[s], no improvisation –
we are very boring people. It has to be very technical, boring. We
have not been able to have that conversation. It is just beginning now.
We are prepared to do it day, night, on the weekend, no matter where.
We would prefer to do everything in Athens. But from an optics point
of view [from the perspective of public perception in Greece] we can
have some of it in Brussels. What you are proposing, a little less
shallow than your list of reforms [meaning if they were fleshed out
further], is actually to meet the objectives of the initial proposal.'

We were on the right path. To broaden that path as far as possible,
I suggested that we start our new collaboration with a small step:
both in Athens and at the Brussels Group, from now on we should
divide our discussions thematically, so that a deadlock over one issue
did not prevent progress elsewhere. Christine very much liked the
idea, and Poul seemed happy too. It was progress. We had established
the basis for a common understanding of the questions if not the
answers.

For the first time we were faced with the opportunity of having a
serious discussion about what reforms each of us thought were
pressing. I invited Christine to have a first stab.

'Can I? Can I?' she asked excitedly. 'I know that this is anecdotal,
and you might find this trivial—'

'Not the pharmacists, please!' I interrupted. 'Is this what you were going to say?'

'Why not?' she replied. 'I find it just amazing that in the *Wall Street Journal* you defended the pharmacists. I thought, *Not Yanis!* I found it amazing that you support their monopoly of baby foods and cosmetics – which I know causes problems, from when I was finance minister. And I had my fights.'

I knew of the IMF's obsession with Greek pharmacies. These invariably small family-owned businesses were protected by a law that permitted only pharmacy school graduates to own one and prohibited the sale of non-prescription drugs by supermarkets. But that, of all possible subjects that needed tackling, the managing director of the IMF, faced with a European country on the brink of default, wanted to discuss this one? I had to pinch myself. I explained that the pharmacies' monopoly over the sale of baby foods and cosmetics had already ended, and that what I opposed was not the end of their monopoly over certain other commodities but the proletarianization of thousands of owner-pharmacists via the takeover of the pharmacy sector by one or two multinational chains.

Giving me the benefit of the doubt on this matter, Christine then took me to task for our tax arrears instalments measure – part of my Humanitarian Crisis Bill aimed at bringing the 40 per cent of Greek citizens back into the tax system by allowing them to pay even very small instalments each month – which she 'found shocking':[11]

> LAGARDE: I cannot believe that you would introduce this rescheduling of tax payments without discriminating between those who cannot pay and those who organize themselves so as not to pay.
>
> VAROUFAKIS: Let me explain the practices of rich defaulters. When charged they take the tax office to court and get a court hearing for 2022. In the meantime we cannot touch them. So what we are doing is giving them the opportunity to start repaying little by little while organizing out-of-court settlement procedures. At that point we can force things to a head and confiscate available funds of strategic defaulters.
>
> LAGARDE: That's fine.

VAROUFAKIS: But to be told that what we did is a unilateral move and [be] ordered to take it back, when we have 3.6 million people owing less than €3000 to the state that they can't pay – who are dying to become part of the formal economy again by starting to pay small sums little by little—

LAGARDE: But you could have checked their capacity—

VAROUFAKIS: Our tax authorities do not have the resources to check three to four million people in a short time. So, what we plan to do is to let them get into the instalment plan – start repaying – and then go after the strategic defaulters.

It was now my turn to tell Christine which reforms I thought truly mattered. These were not even on her radar screen, and, as I would go on to explain, the fact that she did not know of them was intimately linked to the liquidity crunch our government was facing. It all related to Greece's corrupt bankers. 'I'm sure you're not privy to this but the word "reform" becomes a dirty one the moment the troika pats on the back our corrupt bankers while targeting the pharmacists and the pensioners. Even worse, when the ECB collaborates with the same bankers to deny liquidity from the government that the people just elected, in order to force us to accept cuts in the lowest of pensions, the whole population turns against the ECB, you, everyone in authority.'

Christine seemed fascinated. I proceeded to tell her of the trick pulled by the Greek bankers (recall Aris, Zorba and their ilk) which kept them in control of the banks that they had bankrupted, all with the active support of the Eurogroup Working Group, which dominated the HFSF, whose funds kept the banks going and the bankers unaccountable. As I talked, Poul looked like a man about to have a stroke. But there was more. The bankers, I explained, then used the liquidity provided by the ECB and the capital channelled to them by the creditors, which of course burdened the weakest taxpayers, to fund media outlets and spread propaganda in favour of those politicians who were in the bankers' pockets: the triangle of sin.

'When the ECB gets into bed with corrupt and corrupting bankers, who are actively sabotaging democracy, we consider this enemy action,' I said. 'I am not telling you that Mario knows this.

But someone in Frankfurt must know it if I do. Your people in Athens are smart enough to have picked it up, even though I do not doubt that they keep it from you. When our people see the same figures, aided and abetted by the troika, retain control of bankrupt banks and bankrupt media with new debt burdening the little people against whose interests the banks and the media labour, you cannot expect them to take you seriously. Or take us seriously if we do as you tell us.

'We cannot go on like this, Christine. This is very hard for us. We want to talk about reforms. But in this state of warfare, and with Wolfgang Schäuble telling me, "I am not going to talk to you," I am sounding an alarm bell that this is not the Europe that we signed up to. We are mightily pro-European. We want to keep Greece in the euro. I think it would be excellent for official Europe to demonstrate that Europe can do business not only with the establishment political parties it is affiliated to but with pro-European political parties who have a different – weird for you – view of the world. And to show the Greek people that they can be part of this process. Alas, all the people of Greece now see is your functionaries in bed with our oligarchy's triangle of sin: bankrupt banks, toxic television channels, corrupt procurement . . .'

Christine looked concerned and I believe she genuinely was.

LAGARDE: But why don't you go after them, if you have evidence that they—

VAROUFAKIS: They have all the cards. The press are their agents. The judiciary is ineffectual and in some cases corrupt. Of course we will go after them even if it means falling. But that is why we need breathing space . . . The TV stations are lambasting us for throwing the country onto the rocks by resisting the troika while at the same time criticizing me for coming here to negotiate pension cuts with you. We will prevail because we are doing very well with the people and because we have managed to create a disconnect between the majority of Greeks and the TV channels, which is a remarkable achievement – they are not influenced by them any more. For how long I do not know. What we need is a little peace and quiet. What we are asking for is ninety days—

LAGARDE: You can create that—

VAROUFAKIS: I hope so.

LAGARDE: To demonstrate that you have the will to do it, we
will go out of our way. Working with you.

Poul then made a point of saying that Christine and he spoke with
one voice, something that I had just witnessed was untrue. 'Anything
you hear from me, or from our mission in Athens,' he claimed, 'be
assured that everyone at the IMF speaks as one.'

Incapable of resisting, I said, 'Yes, I know. You are like the Catholic
Church!'

Christine took the joke with good humour, insisting the IMF was
the better institution.

By now night had fallen. As we were wrapping up, Christine was
keen to know that I would not now be heading to the press to announce
an imminent default. And I was eager to get her to commit to doing
something to ease the waterboarding. We had understood each other
but we were obliged to finish with a last rendition of our tussle, one
that was performed with the greatest courtesy.

LAGARDE: A default would be terrible for Greece.

VAROUFAKIS: Of course, but it would be terrible for the IMF
and for Europe too.

Lagarde: Yes, yes.

VAROUFAKIS: Defaulting to you, to the IMF, would trigger the
cross-defaults, and then Mario would refuse to lift ELA
with the result that the banks would run out.

LAGARDE: Then capital controls—

VAROUFAKIS: We would not accept that, Christine. This is
a political decision. It is a nightmare of course. We do
not sleep at night. But we cannot accept capital controls
in a monetary union. And we are preparing as we
should.

LAGARDE: That would be terrible for Greece. Think about
inflation.

VAROUFAKIS: Why? Do you think that having capital controls
imposed and turning into a kind of protectorate without
any access to liquidity would be better?

We had said all there was to say, but as we got up to leave Christine asked me to stay back for a word in private. She was 'flabbergasted' she said by what I had told her about the triangle of sin and in particular about our bankers. 'I'm a lawyer, and I would love to understand . . . I know it is hot sensitive but I would love to understand what is happening.' I shared with her my plan for cleansing the banks, by which Takis, my companion that day, would be appointed chair of the HFSF and new CEOs would be brought in to the key banks.[12] She nodded, if not in agreement then at least to show she had a clear understanding of what I was up to and what I was proposing. In a low voice, she then said, 'I will speak to Mario. I cannot guarantee the outcome.' It was the best I could get, given the position I had arrived in.

As if to offer me some solace, Christine's parting gift was a promise to do some 'digging' into the background and activities of Greek individuals who might jeopardize my work and to get back to me about them. Even though she never did get back, which I never expected her to, it was the thought that counted.

'Thanks once more for sacrificing your Easter Sunday,' were my last words as I made my way out.

14

The cruellest month

The next day I flew back to Greece knowing that I would be returning to Washington a week later to try to win President Obama's people over to our side.[1] A week earlier I would have been over the moon with excitement at the prospect. Alas, as my trust in my comrades had withered, any such excitement had died with it.

So I felt none of the excitement I had previously felt on other returns home at the thought of going to Maximos to brief Alexis. I could picture in my mind how he would agree with everything I said but act on nothing. Yet the volume, substance and urgency of what I had to tell him were such that I decided it was my duty to put my brief in writing in the form of a comprehensive policy proposal for recovering control of our fate. By the time I got off the plane, it was almost complete. I called it the N+1 Plan, the 'N' referring to the large number of reforms that would be required but whose number was flexible, and the '1' to the debt restructuring without which nothing else mattered.

When I saw Alexis I was blunt. 'Time has run out. We have a fortnight until Riga [where the next Eurogroup meeting was to be held on 24 April]. My trip to Washington is crucial. Either we take the initiative with a comprehensive policy proposal of our own,' I said while handing over my brief, 'or we are dead meat.' Alexis's eyes glazed over as he glanced at the document, which contained a day-by-day action plan for the fortnight ahead.[2] It was clear that he was either unwilling or unable to engage with it.

Sad but unfazed, I returned to the ministry to work with my team on our latest debt sustainability analysis and debt swap proposals. Four days of unrelenting toil later, the improved N+1 Plan was ready to be presented to the cabinet at a meeting convened on 14 April, the day before I flew back to Washington. At the meeting I warned my fellow ministers that we were out of time and that the N+1 Plan in front of them was our last chance.

> If we do not want to surrender, we must tell the creditors that this plan is, from now on, the sole basis of our discussions. To back this demand, we must issue two promises: first, tell Draghi that if he moves to impose capital controls, we shall haircut unilaterally his SMP bonds and activate our parallel payments system; second, tell Merkel that if she succumbs to Schäuble's plan to eject us from the euro, we shall not go begging to her, ready to sign anything she gives us – we shall reluctantly fall back on our Plan X, which is being completed as I speak. The only alternative to this strategy is surrender.

The next day I flew back to Washington. Perhaps the most telling sign of the complete breakdown in our government's discipline was that Chouliarakis called me to say he would rather go to Brussels to spend time with Thomas Wieser and Co. I insisted that, as chair of my Council of Economic Advisers, he should accompany me, not least in order to attend the IMF spring meetings that were taking place. He insisted that he was going to Brussels. I gave up. It was hopeless arguing. Besides, if I could salvage anything in Washington it would be in spite of Chouliarakis and Wieser, not because of them.

My first day in DC could not have been fuller. It began with a heart-warming visit to the offices of the American Federation of Labor and Congress of Industrial Organizations, the country's centre for trade unions. Rich Trumka, its president, told me that our success would strengthen labour's voice within the Democratic Party, while Damon Silvers, the policy director, encouraged me with some wise advice: 'They complain you are unreasonable until they realize they can't buy you or bluff you or intimidate you. Then they really negotiate, often late at night.' Rich showed me a sign over his desk that read, NOTHING WAS EVER ACCOMPLISHED BY A REASONABLE PERSON.

Next I met a bunch of friendly journalists to deliver a grim message: the Greek government was losing the propaganda war. The troika had invested incredible resources in blackening our image, mine in particular, so we needed a professional lobbyist and PR firm in Brussels.

But I can't even afford a proper press office in Athens, I thought to myself as I made my way to the IMF building for my next meeting – with Christine Lagarde and Poul Thomsen.

In Christine's office I felt embarrassed when she complained that our side had not moved with the speed that we had agreed a week earlier. She was right, but how could I admit to the exasperation that I was feeling at the state of paralysis in Maximos? It was a short meeting but in it she conveyed an important message: unlike many in Berlin and elsewhere, she agreed with me that Europe could not manage Grexit smoothly. And she had spoken to Draghi about this and about our liquidity. But, once more, she implored us to speed up whatever it was we were doing. I only wished it was up to me.

My next stop was the venerable Brookings Institution, where I delivered a high-profile speech on the causes of the Greek crisis and my proposals for ending it. It so happened that a couple of hours earlier Wolfgang Schäuble had delivered a policy speech of his own there. After the event my hosts were bold enough to compare and contrast the two: whereas my economic analysis held water and contained tangible proposals, they told me, Wolfgang's speech was an hour-long exercise in denial, offering not one idea on how to rebalance Europe. Perhaps, as good hosts, they were exaggerating, but they made it clear that they had given Wolfgang a tough reception and openly disagreed with him.

Not in our case, Mr President!

From Brookings my minders rushed me to the White House, where I would have the chance of a brief chat with President Obama. That day, 15 April, Obama had invited members of the Greek-American community to celebrate, belatedly, Greece's national day (25 March). I had been told that if I attended the reception the president would want to talk with me informally.

'We have the Greek finance minister in our midst,' said the president in his welcoming speech at the reception. 'I might as well walk up to him and ask to borrow some money.' Despite the under-whelming joke and the circumstances, which were far from ideal, our brief discussion, as we stood among all the other guests, turned out to be more substantial than many I have had with officials in secluded rooms.

> OBAMA: I don't envy you at all. You have a difficult task under trying circumstances. We shall try to help the best way we can.
>
> VAROUFAKIS: Thank you, Mr President. From your first supportive statement after our election you have been a breath of fresh air for our people, and for us.
>
> OBAMA: I know what it means to inherit a gigantic crisis upon winning office. I had to deal with it in 2009.
>
> VAROUFAKIS: The greatest since 1929, we all recall. However, the main difference, Mr President, is that you had a central bank backing you every step of the way. We have a central bank stabbing us in the back every step of the way – because we are trying to do things similar to what you did in 2009!
>
> OBAMA: I understand. But you must know that I was forced to do things that were very hard for me. Things that I did not want to do. Things that amounted to political poison. I had to go against my policy to save Wall Street. To collaborate with people that had created the problem.
>
> VAROUFAKIS: We appreciate this well, Mr President. Believe me, we too are ready to collaborate even with those who caused our crisis. To take the political cost of doing so. As long as the balance sheet is in the black, as long as the benefits outweigh the losses. I'm sure you know that the combination of unpayable debt and austerity have generated a humanitarian crisis.
>
> OBAMA: I know, I know. Austerity sucks! But you must compromise in your dealing with the institutions so that an agreement can be locked in.
>
> VAROUFAKIS: Mr President, we are ready to compromise, compromise and compromise some more. But we are not ready to end up compromised.

Obama smiled at that point and placed his right hand sympathetically on my left arm. His minders were trying to get his attention, indicating that he was late for his next meeting. He shook my hand

and began to walk away. But then he changed his mind and turned back – to the poorly hidden annoyance of a bodyguard.

> OBAMA: We will help by keeping the pressure on the Europeans. But you must meet them halfway.
>
> VAROUFAKIS: More than halfway, Mr President. We have *already* walked four-fifths of the way towards them but they are not budging at all.
>
> OBAMA: You have no other alternative but to keep trying. And we will help.
>
> VAROUFAKIS: I hope that this applies to your Treasury too. I must tell you that we are disappointed that Jack Lew is not toeing the Obama line on this. In his official statements he blames the lack of progress on our side.
>
> OBAMA: [*laughing*] You know how it is. Finance ministers are more conservative than their leaders.
>
> VAROUFAKIS: [*almost laughing*] Not in our case, Mr President . . . But still, we would appreciate it if your Treasury was closer to your wavelength.

Another warm handshake, another friendly smile and he was gone.

I too had to leave. Nearby, at the legendary Cosmos Club, around fifteen Greek-American politicians had gathered to have dinner with me. It had been organized by Jamie Galbraith and Phil Angelides, former California state treasurer and chair of the Financial Crisis Inquiry Commission charged by President Obama with investigating Wall Street's collapse in 2008.[3] It took less than an hour to dispel the distortions of my policy objectives and practices the press had been feeding them and thus win them over. So enthusiastic were they by the end that, before we called it a night, they formed a five-member committee to coordinate support for our government in Congress.[4]

By the time I left it was already late, but the long day was nowhere near over. A call summoned me to the IMF offices for a brief discussion in order to pave the way for the following day's meetings. From there I walked alone to the hotel bar where I met Larry Summers for a drink and the long, illuminating conversation with which this book began.

Improbable American friends

Trade union officials and Greek-American politicians were always going to be supportive, but it took two Americans few would consider Greece's friends to restore my depleted energies. One of them was Lee Buchheit, a high-flying Washington bankruptcy lawyer; the other was David Lipton, number two at the IMF. I met both the following day, between countless other insubstantial meetings with far more celebrated folk.

I visited Lee at his firm's offices, accompanied by Jamie Galbraith. I went incognito because Lee Buchheit is renowned as the fairy godmother of finance ministers seeking debt restructuring. If the press got word of our meeting it would be portrayed as a unilateral move to renege on our debt. Even if this is what we should have done, the time had not come for such headlines. Jamie and I walked there and entered through a side entrance. Along the way I told Jamie what Mario Draghi had just told me over the course of an hour-long conversation. Mario had gone out of his way to convince me that he was not part of any conspiracy to overthrow the Syriza government but that his 'hands were tied'. I believed him. Despite his protestations of independence, no Western central banker is more affected by discreet political machinations than the ECB's president. 'The one, fascinating thing I got out of Mario just now,' I told Jamie, 'is his advice that I should seek an agreement with the IMF. He concurred on the importance of debt relief. Ergo, only an agreement and a close working relationship with the IMF would work for Greece.'

Lee Buchheit is an intensely clever, gentlemanly figure seemingly from a bygone era. Before talking about the present, he wanted to come clean about his past association with Greece's governments, which in his view had employed his skills in a manner that squandered a fantastic opportunity to liberate Greece from its debtors' prison.[5] He made no bones about it: he saw in our meeting a chance for redemption. As for the present, his assessment was bleak. 'They are determined to demolish you with threats that may well be empty.' His advice was sharp and clear: we needed to signal to Angela Merkel that we were not going to be cowed into submission by the threat of Grexit. It was our only chance for a decent agreement within the euro. It was like hearing myself speak.

Lee suggested two practical moves. First, within the next week, Alexis should pre-empt the threat of Grexit by relaying to Angela Merkel that the institutions were dragging their feet to an extent that an accident seemed increasingly unavoidable and that, as responsible leaders, they needed to prepare for this. Alexis should then propose that Merkel dispatch to a Greek island three or four technicians whose competence and discretion she trusted. There they could work alongside our team of technicians on how to deal with the accident, quietly, professionally and far away from publicity. They should report only to Merkel and Alexis. To prevent any leaks, but also for its symbolic value, Lee suggested that this message be conveyed by an envoy to Berlin and spoken aloud to the chancellor without handing over anything on paper. We would soon find out whether Merkel was prepared to go along with Wolfgang's push for Grexit or whether she would step in to offer us the minimum debt restructuring that we could not live without.

Lee's second recommendation concerned the central bank of Greece and our gold deposits.

> Make sure that the property rights over Greece's gold do not belong to the Central Bank of Greece but are transferred to the Greek government. For if there is a clash with the ECB, Mario Draghi will try to seize your gold and all the assets of the Central Bank of Greece in lieu of the latter's liabilities within the European system of central banks. If you are forced to start a new currency, create a new central bank to do it and let the existing one fail, so that all of Frankfurt's claims upon it die with it.[6]

My head spinning with Lee's advice, I headed for the US Treasury to meet Jack Lew. For the reasons I had explained to President Obama, I took with me little expectation of any useful outcome to the discussion. Predictably enough, he pressurized me to submit to Berlin, making it clear that, even though my analysis was right, the United States considered Greece to be within Berlin's sphere of economic influence. The only positive thing I got out of our tedious encounter was an admission, similar to Lagarde's, that 'the Europeans' were deluded to think that they could manage a Grexit.[7]

After a long and similarly tedious session at the IMF, at which the world's finance ministers and their minders congregated for a succession of pointless speeches, I met Jeff Sachs, who was bearing bad news: Wolfgang had managed to turn most of Washington's establishment against us, he told me. Jeff was particularly worried by the animosity that David Lipton harboured against us. 'You must see him tonight,' he insisted. Jeff judged that only an alliance with Lipton, the IMF's link with the White House, could bring in Mario Draghi and ultimately persuade Angela Merkel to get off the fence on our side rather than Schäuble's. 'I have arranged for you to see David tonight at his office.'

That night, accompanied by Elena Panariti, who knew Lipton from her Washington days, I returned once more to the IMF to meet him. A stocky, prickly man, Lipton did not try to hide the hostility that Jeff had warned me about. It took an hour of extreme reasonableness on my part before Lipton began to mellow. He then mentioned his conversations with Jeff Sachs, telling me that he was his former student and so quite impressed by the kind words Jeff had for me. But despite the warmer atmosphere, our conversation stalled, with Lipton repeating ad nauseam the IMF's standard line that they needed a comprehensive review based on the *MoU* and with me repeating ad nauseam why that was a recipe for an unwanted accident. Suddenly, Lipton surprised me, breaking off from his mantra and looking at me as if he had had a eureka moment, saying, 'Unless . . .' followed by a long pause.

'Unless?' I asked.

'Unless you adopt the Polish strategy,' he said thoughtfully.

I have no idea if this was spontaneous or if he had planned it in advance. It didn't matter. It was a major breakthrough. The Polish strategy, as he explained, was simple. In the 1990s, when Poland was burdened by huge communist-era debts and the IMF had been called in to impose austerity, reform and a debt-restructuring programme, the Warsaw government had refused to accept the IMF's *MoU*-based process. 'Just like you're refusing,' he said. What the Poles did was to put together their own plan covering debt, fiscal policy and reforms, which they presented to the IMF as the basis of the negotiations. 'It was the only occasion I know of when the IMF was forced to abandon its own programme and to accept as the basis of negotiations that of the government.' Glancing at the ceiling, Lipton asked, 'Why don't you try the Polish strategy? After all, Jeff had helped them put it together.'

It was one thing to insist, as I had on 20 February, that we replace the *MoU* with a new contract of which we were at the very least the co-authors. But to have America's man at the IMF, Christine Lagarde's second in command and Jeff's former student, tell me not only that we should write our own plan from scratch but that there was a precedent in Poland for this being adopted by the IMF was something altogether different. This was the most encouraging breakthrough I had had since 20 February. Together with Lee Buccheit's advice, it seemed the foundation of a winning strategy. 'This is the best advice I have had, David,' I told him while shaking his hand on the way out. 'Jeff is waiting at my hotel as we speak,' I added. 'We shall get down to work immediately.' Smiling for the first time during our encounter, Lipton wished me luck.

Back at my hotel bar, I met Jeff. We hugged and I told him what Lipton had suggested. Jeff was pleased and ready to stop everything he was doing to work with me on our own Polish strategy, but he warned me, 'You must still be prepared for the clash. I am pleading with you to get your prime minister on board, to allow you to prepare for the bank closures that they will try out to intimidate you. Even if you manage to forge an alliance with Lipton and Draghi, Schäuble has the Eurogroup stitched up and is determined to drag you through negotiations with your banks closed.'

It was exactly what I had been thinking: to utilize David Lipton's advice we would have to combine it with Lee Buccheit's. We had to work on two fronts: compile our own comprehensive anti-*MoU* Plan for Greece while convincing Alexis to send an envoy to Berlin with the message Lee had scripted for us. It was the only way. But was it one that my exhausted comrade at Maximos would countenance?

The troika in Paris

The following day, 16 April, was spent entirely at the IMF in meetings. My experience of the morning's plenary session resembled that of a soldier: prolonged boredom punctuated by sudden moments of intense agitation. For much of the meeting I was sitting next to Benoît Cœuré, second in command at the ECB. While the interminable lectures dragged on, the two of us chatted like naughty schoolchildren. Always friendly, ever eager to present himself as our friend at the ECB, Benoît's apparent concern could not disguise the threat implicit in his words when, at one point in our conversation, he said, 'We must prepare now for an accident.' His advice was that I request the imposition of capital controls.

'Are you referring to the "accident" the ECB has been working towards since December?' I asked sarcastically.

He was unashamed: 'If there is a bank run and if the ECB do not increase ELA liquidity then maybe we shall have to close the banks down while the negotiations continue.'

Just as I was telling him that it would be unreasonable to expect us to cooperate in blackmailing ourselves by asking for capital controls and that they were fundamentally at odds with the principles of monetary union, Michel Sapin, the French finance minister, approached to ask me if I had news from the Brussels Group and our negotiations with the institutions. A brief chat ensued, after which Michel resumed his seat on the other side of the hall next to Wolfgang Schäuble. Benoît and I had resumed our whispered conversation when suddenly I heard shouting. Benoît looked concerned.

'What happened?' I asked him. Concentrating as I had been on my discussion with Benoît, I had failed to notice the drama unfolding behind me.

'Michel shouted at Wolfgang,' he replied.

'Why?' I had been aware only of raised voices, whereas Benoît, who was facing me, had seen everything and might also have actually heard what was said.

'Because Wolfgang said that he wants the troika in Paris,' said Benoît with a bitter grin.

It all made perfect sense. The troika that had been born and raised in Athens was now Paris-bound because its ultimate mission was to control the French national budget. The harsh and failed policies imposed upon Greece had nothing to do with our country. The threat to close down Greece's banks that Benoît had been relaying to me at the very moment Michel yelled at Wolfgang had nothing to do with our banks. They were Wolfgang's signal to Paris: if France wanted the euro, it must forfeit sovereignty over its budget deficits. There was a logic to all this – a twisted logic perhaps, a logic of the type that would end up damaging the European Union irreversibly, but a logic nevertheless. One thing remained puzzling, though: the manner in which Michel and Benoît were colluding in the French government's subjugation by playing their part in ours.

On my way back to Athens I bumped into another Frenchman, Pierre Moscovici, at Washington airport. With half an hour to spare before boarding our respective planes, we struck up a conversation. 'Germany is a problem, and not only for you,' he suggested. But he added that an agreement between us and our creditors was possible 'despite Schäuble'. I retorted that the news I was taking home with me from the IMF and the US administration was that an agreement could only be sealed with the joint consent of Washington, the ECB and the European Commission. He agreed. I mentioned my exchange with Benoît and the threat of bank closures during the negotiations.

'Such loose talk can easily be interpreted in Athens as an existential threat,' I told Pierre.

'Don't worry,' Commissioner Moscovici replied. 'Benoît is prone to angst and, as a central banker, feels the need to have contingency plans over everything. I shall speak to him on your behalf.'

We agreed to meet the following week. Unconvinced by his reassurances, I bade him farewell.

Back in Athens, Benoît called me to complete the conversation interrupted by Michel's spat with Wolfgang. Possibly because Pierre had called him in the meantime, Benoît was far more reassuring. I then took him to task on the veiled threat of bank closures, reminding him that the banks would be closed not by natural causes or because of some accident but as a result of a purely political decision by his ECB.

> CŒURÉ: Don't say that. The banks may close because they have run out of eligible collateral.
>
> VAROUFAKIS: This is impossible. In my capacity as finance minister, every other week I guarantee worthless IOUs issued by the banks to the tune of tens of billions of euros which they then post for collateral with the Bank of Greece. The only way they will run out of eligible collateral is if you guys at the ECB ban the Bank of Greece from accepting my guarantees. And this is 100 per cent a political decision, since we all know that the Greek government never had the capacity to honour these guarantees.
>
> CŒURÉ: You are right. But as a central banker I must be ready for such a decision by two-thirds of the governing council.[8]
>
> VAROUFAKIS: I understand this. Just know that, if this happens, our government will not stay passive and simply await the Cyprus-style 'solution' that some are planning for us.

We shall not budge. Instead we shall, even if you close down our banks, create our own euro-denominated liquidity based on electronic tax-backed IOUs. Of course if you push us down that road, with defaults on the IMF and the ECB, you will be pushing us, against our will, to the point of no return.

CŒURÉ: Thank you for telling me all this. It is good that I know it. Now let me make my own commitment to you: if I sense that events are moving in that direction, against our will, I promise to let you know in advance so that you can call for an extraordinary EU Council summit to demand a political decision at the highest level.

VAROUFAKIS: I am happy to hear this, Benoît. These matters are above our pay grade.

And so they were. The decision would rest with Alexis.

Ambushed in Riga

Two days. That's all the time I had in Athens in which to convince Alexis to adopt the strategy that my Washington trip had produced – the Plan for Greece along the lines of the Polish strategy which David Lipton had suggested and the missive to Merkel proposed by Lee Buchheit – before flying to Riga, Latvia, for a Eurogroup meeting on 24 April that would surely be the beginning of the endgame. I put my proposal in writing, taking care to ensure that no copy could escape online and that the only copy Alexis received was the printout that I handed him myself.

My meeting with Alexis went exactly as I had feared. 'They will consider it a *casus belli*,' he said with his familiar expression of melancholy in response to the idea that we put forward our own Plan for Greece. As for Buchheit's idea, Alexis barely gave it a second thought. Having skimmed my written proposal for a few seconds, he set it aside and said, 'Merkel promised me that she will step in. Let's not cross her now.'

'She will give you nothing,' I replied, 'unless we present our own credible agenda and back it up without our own pre-emptive strike.'

'Now is not the time. You go to Riga tomorrow and yield on nothing. Don't be intimidated. Just hold the fort there. I shall be talking to Merkel again tomorrow night to get to an agreement at our level.'

It was clear that Merkel's spell had taken hold. All I could do was hope that somehow Alexis would convince her to do something she neither wanted nor had a compelling reason to do.

The Eurogroup of 24 April had been convened primarily as part of the celebrations for Latvia's presidency of the EU. In theory it would be relatively informal, and the whole meeting had been scheduled to last no more than two hours. The day Nicholas Theocarakis and I flew to Riga, Alexis contacted us with words of encouragement: 'It will be an easy Eurogroup, as it is largely ceremonial and nothing much will be said about Greece. Whatever you do be cool and do not yield an inch to them.' Alexis's capacity to lift my spirits with a few well chosen words was undiminished. Despite the qualms weighing me down, his heartening message would serve me well in the hell of Riga.

Fotini, my secretary, alerted me to the first sign that something was amiss the moment we arrived in the Latvian capital: my team was booked into a hotel a fair distance away from where I was staying, making it hard for us to meet for essential consultations. Unwilling to succumb to conspiracy theories, I decided to interpret it as a logistical cock-up.

On that first night, after a gala dinner of no consequence, I returned to my hotel. Unable to relax, I summoned Nicholas from his distant hotel to brainstorm the next morning's Eurogroup. With half an hour to kill before Nicholas arrived, I went downstairs to wait for him in the lobby. There I saw them.

All the troika players were at the bar: Poul Thomsen, Benoît Cœuré, Thomas Wieser, Jeroen Dijsselbloem, Pierre Moscovici and some others I cannot recall. I decided to say a collegiate hello. They were tongue-tied and manifestly uncomfortable. To break the ice, I asked playfully, 'So, what have we here? Have I caught you in the act?' My light-hearted remark was not reciprocated; instead I was told that they were having a meeting but I would be welcome to join them a little later. I smiled, wished them a good night and left.

Next morning, Nicholas and I were walking towards the room where the Eurogroup was to be held. Behind me I heard Pierre Moscovici greet me convivially. So we walked together and chatted.

'I am proud we did this,' he said, referring to the Brussels Group. 'It is only right that these negotiations take place in Brussels with ministers talking only to ministers and technocrats talking with technocrats.' Some of the lost honour of the Commission had been recovered, I told him as we arrived.

The room was eerily half-empty. Where was everybody? Apart from Pierre, Nicholas and me, only Jeroen Dijsselbloem, Thomas Wieser and four or five other delegations were present. Wolfgang Schäuble, Mario Draghi, Poul Thomsen, Michel Sapin and other key ministers were missing. As the meeting began, Nicholas and I looked at each other, convinced that something distinctly unpleasant was brewing nearby. The first item on the agenda was a procedural issue that required no debate. Once that had been dealt with, Jeroen said, 'OK, colleagues, let us now move on to the second item on the agenda, Greece.' Suddenly the doors opened, and Wolfgang, Mario, Poul, Michel and the other missing ministers flooded in.

First blood was drawn by Jeroen. In his introductory statement he demanded the troika's return to Athens in order to end the 'inefficiency' of the Brussels Group. I looked at Pierre. Would he defend the process he had so recently been praising? It was as if the Eurogroup's president had planned to humiliate the commissioner once more by making him eat his words, just as he had before the second Eurogroup meeting in February.[9] And eat them he did. 'Technical discussions and political ones,' Pierre conceded in the last sentence of his statement, 'must be combined and held at the same place, together.' In case anyone was in any doubt, Poul Thomsen hastened to clarify that the place he was referring to was Athens.

Poul then performed a volte-face of his own to rival Pierre's. The same man who had confessed to me on 1 February during our first encounter in Paris that Greece's debt was unsustainable and that tens of billions of euros of debt relief should have been granted well before 2015 now sang a radically different tune. Until the Syriza government was elected, Poul argued, Greece's debt had been sustainable; it was only after we had come to power that it had become unsustainable; neither debt relief nor extra money would now be necessary were it not for our government.[10]

The ground for the next blow was prepared by Mario Draghi, who presented his view that, unlike previous bank runs, the current one in Greece was not infecting the rest of the eurozone. In other words,

Grexit would hurt the Greeks but not the other countries who shared its currency. This was the cue for Schäuble's cheerleading brigade of finance ministers to go on the offensive with the threat of Grexit. In response to Thomsen's absurd report that our backtracking and delays had pushed us once more into the red, the Slovak minister exclaimed, 'Unbelievable!' and went on to make a speech that ended, 'We are ready to help Greece. But if Greece does not need help, maybe the time has come to talk consequences.' Soon after, Wolfgang Schäuble lent his support to the Slovak's tough talk: 'We have moved fast in the wrong direction . . . [Laughing. More exclamations of 'Unbelievable! Unbelievable!'] . . . I cannot imagine how we shall have a solution.' The task of speaking the unmentionable words fell to the Slovenian minister: 'There is no way Slovenians can be persuaded, who are most exposed to Greece, that they put additional effort to help Greece get out of the situation. So, I think we should talk about Plan B . . . I know that we did not want to talk about Plan B. We wanted, including Slovenia, to resolve this. But now I don't see this.'

I began my response by coolly and moderately addressing every point that had been raised and putting to bed every inaccuracy before coming to the crux: 'Plan B should not [even] be mentioned. It is highly and immoderately anti-European even to bring about this discussion. My dear colleague from Slovenia should know that it is not in the interest of his citizens that we even discuss this at the moment. I reject such a discussion. Our government intends to do whatever it takes to remain sustainably within the eurozone.'

From that point on, every time I opened my mouth to speak it was to present constructive proposals for reaching an agreement quickly. Each time I did so, Jeroen reacted with aggression, demanding that I consent to the troika's return to Athens, agree not to legislate without the troika's consent and acquiesce to the troika's all-or-nothing approach, which meant ditching my proposal for an interim agreement based on three or four reform bills and a viable fiscal plan. Faithful to Alexis's directive not to 'yield an inch', I stood my ground.

Character assassination

The troika's assault in Riga was accompanied by a well-prepared propaganda drive. During the tense Eurogroup meeting the media had reported falsely that my fellow ministers had reproached me personally. According to a Bloomberg report, 'Euro-area finance chiefs said Varoufakis's handling of the talks was irresponsible and accused him of being a time-waster, a gambler and an amateur, a person familiar with the conversations said, asking not to be named because the discussions were private.'[11] At the press conference that followed, Jeroen was asked explicitly whether I had been called these names. Instead of simply saying no, the Eurogroup president gave the fake news credence by not denying it and instead, smiling meaningfully, replied, 'It was a very critical discussion and it showed a great sense of urgency around the room.'

That night, after my own press conference was over and my official business for the day was done, I was told that finance ministers were invited to an informal dinner in the nearby countryside, a forty-five-minute coach ride away. Exhausted and wishing to prepare my speech for the following morning's Ecofin meeting, I decided to give it a miss. Instead, I arranged to have dinner with Nicholas, Fotini and another member of my team in downtown Riga so that we could take stock of the day's events and plan ahead. Walking by myself across town through the cold to meet them promised to revive me sufficiently for the long night's work that awaited me on my return.

How invigorating it was! I walked for about half an hour, taking in the old buildings bathed in the orange rays of the street lights which pierced the freezing haze, breathing in the crisp air, feeling human again. Dinner with my colleagues at a German-themed beer-and-sausage restaurant was just as restorative as I had hoped it would be and reminded me what it was like to have a normal life. The next morning Reuters carried the following report.

> As the buses carrying European finance ministers left for a gala dinner in the Latvian capital on Friday night, one of the party hung back at the hotel and then wandered off alone into the dusk. Greece's Yanis Varoufakis had other dinner plans, he said, after a bruising first day of meetings in Riga that underlined his isolation as he tries to avert national bankruptcy. While other ministers were feted by their entourages with food and warm clothing during the meeting in Riga, Varoufakis was seen alone at almost every

turn, eschewing aides or any security detail. 'He is completely isolated,' a senior eurozone official told Reuters on condition of anonymity. 'He didn't even come to the dinner to represent his country.'[12]

'Gambler', 'amateur', 'time-waster' and now 'alone at almost every turn', 'isolated', disrespectful of other ministers and unwilling to represent his country. It was almost precisely as that friendly official at the US Treasury had warned me: that I would face a character assassination campaign within a week. He was out by only one day.

Of course it was the worst-kept secret in Brussels and beyond that I was to be targeted in this way. In early February 2015, around the time of my first two Eurogroup meetings, some Greek journalists were told as much by a reporter with first-hand knowledge of the campaign. One of those Greek journalists later reported the conversation.

> 'Will Mr Varoufakis be able to survive the pressure?' asked the reporter.
>
> 'At least Mr Tsipras still trusts him,' we [the Greek journalists] replied.
>
> 'Then inform them in Greece, both the government and the people, that they can expect even more of these attacks,' he said.[13]

The bond of trust between Alexis and me was the troika's greatest obstacle. I knew it. Evidently they knew it too. And as I was about to discover, Alexis knew it also.

The jumper's thread

On the flight from Riga back to Athens I was informed that Alexis's conversation with Angela Merkel, on which he had pinned so much, had gone badly. To make things worse, the Chancellery had leaked to the media that the German leader not only gave Alexis the cold shoulder but that she was unhappy with his attempt to bypass the Eurogroup. It was an extraordinary if unsurprising act of bad faith.

Having promised Alexis that the two of them would find a solution behind the scenes while Varoufakis and Schäuble cancelled each other out, she was now hanging him out to dry.

Arriving at Athens airport I asked to be driven directly to Maximos. Once in Alexis's office I realized what a beautiful spring afternoon it was. Attica's gentle sunlight streamed through the large bay window. Alexis and I hugged and sat down in two armchairs by the bay window, away from his desk and from the conference table where the war cabinet met, directly in the sunlight. I spoke first, describing what had happened in the Eurogroup, and gave my opinion that the three major developments – Merkel reneging on him, the troika's ambush at Riga and Benoît's pressure that we request the capital controls with which they were threatening us – were combining to form a formidable onslaught.[14]

Before Alexis had a chance to respond, I spoke to him from the heart: 'Alexi, allow me to remind you why I am here. I did not leave my job in Texas because I wanted to be minister. I came over to help you personally. And I did this because you told me you agreed with my plan for ending the doom loop. But now we are at a crossroads. I have attracted the creditors' arrows, bullets and missiles. I do not mind this at all as I fully expected to be the lightning rod that shields you. However, you seem to have developed different ideas to the ones we agreed on. Maybe I am now in your way. Maybe you feel that another finance minister would suit your plans better, given that I still think our original plan offers the only chance. If so, you should replace me with my full public support. Remember why I am here? To help you.'

Alexis gave me a long warm comradely look and, after a pause, said, 'Yani, listen. You and I are like a woollen jumper. If we let them get hold of a thread and start pulling it, eventually the jumper will be undone. This is their strategy. They are aiming at your undoing to undo me. They want to get you to get at me. We are not going to let them, right? We are going to stand together. I do not want to hear again about this nonsense. Stay strong. We have a war to win.'

Once more it took only a few words from Alexis to make me forget and forgive. Combined with my deep desire to believe what he said and the genuine opportunity we had to extract our country from its vicious cycle, they revived my hopes and steeled my nerves.

A few minutes later that sense of purpose received another boost when Nikos Pappas walked in. He smiled widely upon seeing me and congratulated me for having stood up to the troika in Riga, briefly reviving the spirit of our earlier meetings in Psyrri. Pappas had some news: apparently, Jeroen Dijsselbloem had just emailed Alexis's office to demand that I be replaced.

'See?' Alexis said, looking at me. 'They're at it! Trying to divide us.' Turning to Pappas, he said, 'Niko, tell him to go jump off a cliff.'

But Pappas responded aggressively: 'It is all *your* fault, Alexi,' he said, adding a number of adjectives that I would rather not repeat. 'By talking to him directly, instead of referring him to Yanis, you gave Jeroen the impression that he can have direct access to the prime minister and bypass the finance minister that stands up to him. You have no one to blame but yourself,' he concluded at the top of his voice.

Alexis acknowledged his 'mistake' and said, 'I shall email him tonight, making it clear that anything he wants to say to us he must say via Varoufakis.'

That night I went home feeling hopeful again. 'The jumper seems intact,' I told Danae cryptically before explaining myself.

The following day, after a meeting of the war cabinet, I asked Alexis whether he had sent the email to Jeroen. 'No, I decided not to, Yani,' he said. 'Why antagonize him needlessly? Let him find out the hard way that he will have to deal with you.' Alarmed at this decision, I nevertheless failed to recognize the bitter truth: the jumper was already unravelling.

The cruellest April day

'April is the cruellest month,' wrote T.S. Eliot in the opening of *The Waste Land*. In the April of 2015, Monday 27 was its cruellest day. Our war cabinet lasted six hours and fifteen minutes. It began with Alexis announcing his decision to give the troika something as an expression of goodwill. That 'something' was the head of my deputy, Nicholas Theocarakis, the man who, on the orders of our prime minister, had put the phone down on Thomas Wieser and the Eurogroup Working Group.

Alexis sounded almost reasonable when he explained his decision. 'I talked to Dijsselbloem twice. He demanded Varoufakis's head. He also wanted Chouliarakis to represent us at the Eurogroup Working Group. I can't let him choose for us, but at the same time we cannot say no to everything. So I decided to burn Theocarakis and restore Chouliarakis.'

Spyros Sagias, the cabinet secretary, was first to respond. He spoke of a 'faulty negotiation', that we had been pursuing the 'wrong process', of the need to wrap up a deal quickly. It was a drawn-out speech delivered with low intensity, in which I was not mentioned by name but which laid the blame clearly at my door. George Stathakis, the economy minister and a long-standing academic colleague of mine, went further: 'The duo Varoufakis–Theocarakis, I love them both as brothers, but they cannot bring home an agreement. Chouliarakis can.'

If by 'agreement' he meant capitulation to Wieser and Dijsselbloem's demands, then Stathakis was perfectly correct. Chouliarakis was the right man to sign a surrender document. I intervened to say so. My brief statement was greeted with an awkward silence.

Then Euclid took the floor. Surely he would oppose the developing coup? He didn't. Instead, without mentioning either Chouliarakis or me, he pronounced Theocarakis a fine scholar, thinker and comrade but not someone with the organizational skills necessary for such complex negotiations. By implication, he was endorsing Chouliarakis's return.

I never felt the slightest animosity towards Stathakis. His views had been clear from the beginning: we should accept whatever the troika presented us with. It was those of my comrades who had pledged never to surrender who disappointed me bitterly. Euclid's position saddened me immensely. He knew who Chouliarakis was and what he had done. He had talked to me about him in language more scathing than I would ever have used. Why was Euclid now tearing strips off our friend Theocarakis in support of Alexis's horrendous proposition? Why did he not at least stay silent like Pappas, who had swallowed his bravado of two days before, or even Dragasakis, who was no doubt happy at the decision but felt no need to say a single word? The answer arrived minutes later when Alexis announced that Euclid would coordinate the negotiations of the Brussels Group with the technical process in Athens and my struggles at the Eurogroup.

During the remainder of that long, long meeting I kept uncharacteristically silent while the rest plotted a course of complete alignment with the *MoU* process, in stark contrast to the plan that I had brought back from Washington. The reason for my silence was that in my head I was scripting a new resignation letter. The end of the road had arrived. There was no place for me in a cabinet that had wittingly or unwittingly surrendered.

Like blood to a shark

Later that day I visited Alexis at his parliamentary office with my resignation letter in my pocket. I had not spoken to a single person about it, not even to Danae. I wanted to give Alexis one more chance to reconsider, and I would not be satisfied this time with rousing words that masked the unpleasant truth. Thankfully, there were none.

When I arrived, Alexis welcomed me in but asked me to wait for a minute while he went to the bathroom. As I was sitting down on the couch to await his return, I caught sight of a few A4 pages on the adjacent coffee table. I picked them up. When Alexis emerged, my expression no doubt conveyed my indignation at what I had read.

With the pages in my hand, I asked, 'Am I right in presuming that you didn't run these concessions by me because you knew I would veto them?'

'Yes,' he confessed with a guilty smile.

'Do you understand what these numbers are, Alexi? Do you realize what you have done by conceding them? Don't you get it that you have just accepted huge new austerity?'

The main number I had in mind – which had snagged my attention like a rusty nail – was 3.5. The pages were a letter signed by the Greek prime minister and addressed to the troika, committing to a budget with a primary surplus target of 3.5 per cent of national income. Unbelievably, the same number appeared next to the years 2018, 2019 . . . all the way to 2028. With the exceptions of Singapore and oil-rich Norway, no country in the world has ever posted a 3.5 per cent budget primary surplus for ten years in succession. The chance that a depressed economy lacking functional banks and with negative investment could do so was the nearest to the theatre of the absurd that economic policy can produce.

'How did this happen, Alexi?' I demanded.

'Chouliarakis thinks that we need to make this concession to get an agreement,' was his answer. Evidently, this was what Stathakis had meant when he said that Chouliarakis was the only one who could bring home a quick agreement: complete capitulation.

I took a deep breath to compose myself. 'I bet Chouliarakis was also the one who convinced you to send these concessions to Wieser and Dijsselbloem without asking me.'

'No,' replied Alexis, 'that was my idea. Admit it, Yani. You would have objected, for good reasons I am sure. But Yani, when negotiating you must give something to get something back.'

'And what is it that you got back? What did Chouliarakis tell you to expect from the troika in exchange for another lost decade of punishing austerity for a people that elected us to put an end to the worst and longest austerity drive in capitalist history?'

'They'll now have to give us something on debt relief,' he replied.

For a moment I was lost for words. The folly in his argument was choking me. Then for the first time I spoke to him condescendingly.

'Are you serious? Have you gone completely off your rocker? Why would they ever concede on debt restructuring if you offer them 3.5 per cent primary surpluses for ever? Your argument is like trying to fend off a shark by pouring blood into the sea. Think about it: in declaring your readiness to extract from the body of what's left of the Greek economy 3.5 per cent of national income every year in the form of a surplus you're implicitly declaring that you can pay the creditors 3.5 per cent of national income every year for ten years! How difficult is it to see that, in saying this, you are declaring that we don't really need debt relief? That we would like it but that we don't really need it?'

'Chouliarakis believes that we can achieve the 3.5 per cent surplus target if we start growing again.'

This was the inane argument of the regime we had fought so hard to replace.

'If this is so, Alexi, why did we strive to win government? For the glory? Did we not argue strongly against the Samaras government that our economy will *never* recover unless we end austerity, which means tearing up ridiculous surplus targets and replacing them with one of at most 1.5 per cent?'

Alexis looked troubled and tried to mollify me. 'Nothing is final, Yani. Until there's a comprehensive agreement no concession I have made is cast in stone – I can always take it back.'

'*What?*' I exploded. 'Do you *really* think that you can take back the massive austerity you just gave them? You gave the shark a taste of your blood, its jaws grabbed your arm, and now you think you can pull it back because there is no deal until there is a final deal? Are you confusing us with the powerful side in this negotiation?'

By that stage my blood was boiling. In fact I was so enraged during most of this exchange that I almost forgot I had visited him to offer my resignation. When I did remember, towards the end, I decided not to make a hasty move in anger. I needed to leave, calm down and think things over before making a final decision.

When I returned to my office, I called my friend Wassily and told him what had happened. He breathed in deeply and emitted a sound expressing deep discontent before telling me to forget about resigning. 'Remember the one hundred and forty thousand people who voted for you. They don't want you to resign. They want to see you stay in the mix and give those bastards hell.'

Back at home, without knowing what Wassily had said to me, Danae made the same point. 'Think of the one hundred and forty thousand people who put their trust in you,' she said. I then spent a heart-wrenching hour on the phone explaining to Nicholas Theocarakis that the prime minister had 'burned' him in favour of Chouliarakis.

I faced a merciless dilemma. The *Financial Times*, as Nicholas informed me, was already reporting that I had been replaced as chief negotiator by Euclid even though in reality the negotiations were clearly being handled by George Chouliarakis. The war cabinet, meanwhile, had been turned, with a large majority now favouring wholesale capitulation and seeing me as the main impediment. Dignity demanded that I resign. But that night, once I had calmed down and thought things through, I realized that it was not just duty that obliged me to stay on.

Beneath Alexis's political, economic and moral error in surrendering to austerity lay another, larger error: his belief that the troika would give him a speedy agreement and a third bailout in return. Undoubtedly, Merkel and Wieser had encouraged Alexis and Chouliarakis to believe this. But setting aside the fact that we had no mandate from our voters for such an agreement, there were two reasons why not even this was on the cards. First, the creditors would surely want to make an example of Alexis – who had spent years in opposition, and some months in government, lambasting them – as a deterrent to any other politician in Spain, Italy, Portugal or indeed France who might be tempted to confront them. For this they would need not just his capitulation but his very public humiliation too. Second, the troika had been denying for years that either a third bailout loan or significant debt relief were necessary. The only way they could explain a third bailout loan now was by claiming, as Poul Thomsen had done during the Riga Eurogroup, that the Greek debt had in fact been sustainable until Syriza won government, and to prove their charge it would be necessary to close down Greece's banks, cause massive new losses and bankruptcies and then blame the costs on Alexis's government.

Just before dawn I arrived at the conclusion that the more concessions Alexis made, the more they would ask for, that there would be no agreement until after the banks had been shut down and that then he would be forced into an agreement so degrading that the Eurogroup could hold it up to the cameras and say to all Europeans, 'This is what you get if you cross us!' This realization invited the question of how Alexis would react. He was only forty-two years old, I thought to myself. Surely he could not contemplate hiding for decades after acquiescing in such disgrace? When he finally saw what the troika and Angela Merkel were demanding – his ignominy and the crushing of our people – there must be a strong chance that he would refuse. And as long as there was a significant chance of that I had a duty to be there, ready to assist by putting forward our Plan for Greece and activating the payments system that would allow us to continue to function until Merkel made her mind up: side with Wolfgang Schäuble in kick-starting the eurozone's disintegration beginning with Grexit, or accept our plan as the basis for an agreement.

So I decided to stay on. I would dedicate myself to keeping our deterrent alive for the moment Alexis might need it and to finishing our Plan for Greece together with Jeff Sachs and Nicholas Theocarakis – whom I also dissuaded that night from resigning – and aided by supporters including Norman Lamont, Larry Summers, Thomas Mayer as well as my immediate team. It was a hard, thankless path. I had known all along that the troika saw me as its primary obstacle, but now I knew that our own war cabinet felt the same. The single thread of hope that kept me going was that Alexis would, at the moment of his impending humiliation, come to me and finally say, 'Let's do it!'

Tapped

Friends chastise me for my forbearance. They think I was naive to maintain faith, despite all the evidence, that Alexis might bounce back. Hopefully, the following two episodes will help convey something of the pressure we laboured under and the scale of what we faced.

When I arrived home from Maximos that evening, Danae bombarded me with questions, videoing my replies with her phone. As she was doing so, my mobile rang. It was Jeff Sachs. Reluctant to convey my desperation over an unsecured line, I chose to share with him the only good news of the day: almost a month too late we were at last ready to default to the IMF. While Sagias, Dragasakis and Chouliarakis had objected, Alexis, Pappas and Euclid had sided with me on this. The coffers were bare. If the IMF wanted its money, it was time for the rest of the troika to release some liquidity. 'The die has been cast,' I told Jeff. 'I think Alexis means it this time. The next payment to the IMF will not be made.'

Jeff was ecstatic. 'It was about time,' he remarked before offering advice on how to handle the fallout of a default.

Half an hour later my phone rang again. It was Jeff, laughing uncontrollably. 'You will not believe this, Yanis,' he said. 'Five minutes after we hung up, I received a call from the [US] National Security Council. They asked me if I thought you meant what you'd said! I told them that you did mean it and that, if they want to avert a default to the IMF, they'd better knock some sense into the Europeans.'

I had fully expected my phone to be tapped, but two things made Jeff's news remarkable. First, the eavesdroppers not only had the capacity to recognize that what I had said was of real significance but they must also have had an open line to the NSC. Second, they had no compunction whatsoever about revealing they were tapping my phone!

It was around three in the morning, but I called Alexis to inform him. Despite the collapse of our united front, despite our shattered bond, such moments reminded me that we were, ultimately, fighting a common enemy.

Danae's feat

The other episode came the following evening, when I was in for a rare treat: dinner with Danae and a friend visiting from Australia at our favourite restaurant in Exarcheia.

Exarcheia is where I lived when I first met Danae. It was at my flat there that my daughter Xenia took her first steps; in fact, the inner-city suburb was where I had taken my first steps as a teenager in the 1970s. A neighbourhood on the wilder side of Athens, it is known for its off-beat record stores, bookshops, bars and, last but not least, for the powerful presence there of Greece's multifarious anarchist groups. In short, Exarcheia was, and to some extent remains, my neighbourhood, even though I have not lived there since 2005.

Danae and our friend arrived first. I came straight from a meeting with Dragasakis and his team, parked my motorcycle outside the restaurant and joined them at a table in a corner of its lovely walled garden on Valtetsiou Street. It was almost May, and the jasmine bushes were spreading their hypnotic scent through the warm spring evening. After an emotionally draining day it was a much-needed tonic to sit in that garden, sipping wine and relaxing with close companions.

I heard them before I saw them. An hour or so later, as we were about to order dessert, three hooded men entered the garden shouting abuse. At first I did not realize that I was their target, but then they threw some bottles which smashed on the brick floor just in front of our table, shards of glass hitting my feet. Telling the other patrons to leave, the attackers approached our table, wielding broken beer bottles and continuing to shout abuse. I sprang up and walked towards them in order to screen my companions from the men but I had not factored in Danae's determination and speed.

Danae jumped between the attackers and me, hugging me, her back towards them, her hands covering the top of my head. She literally turned herself into a human shield. I tried to push her away towards safety but her hold was so strong I realized that I would not be able to get her off without hurting her. Meanwhile, with the side of her head pressed firmly into my face to shield it, she yelled at them, 'You'll have to get through me first!'

The hooded men tried to get at me with the jagged bottles, but Danae's embrace was too powerful and her body covered me so fully that they couldn't without hitting her. Frustrated, they dropped the bottles and landed a few blows with their hands and fists on us both. As Danae received more of the blows than I did, they relented, no doubt reluctant to hit a woman, and left the way they had come, bellowing curses and threats. Stunned, we sat down at our table again, our Australian friend shaking.

However, the night was still young. Our attackers must have called for reinforcements, for within half an hour more than sixty of them were lined up outside the restaurant, which was now empty except for us, the patrons of one other table who seemed unperturbed, and the staff, who were concerned and apologetic. I insisted that they not call the police: were they to arrive in large numbers, there would most definitely be bloodshed. In fact, it was just as well perhaps that I did not have a police escort with me already.[15]

'What will you do?' asked our friend. The restaurant owner offered to put us up for the night in the restaurant.

'I shall just walk out and engage them in dialogue. If they want to hit me, then they will hit me.' Our friend thought I was crazy.

Danae said, 'OK, let's do it.' We told our friend to stay put until the gang had left, and then the two of us, Danae and I, stepped out onto the pavement.

Sixty hooded youngsters shouting and swearing on a narrow Athenian street is a sight to behold. My heart was beating fast but I did not expect them to hit us again. Danae had impressed them, and I was sure they would appreciate the fact that we had neither called the cops nor hidden in the restaurant. I was also encouraged by the fact that they had not damaged my motorcycle, as they easily could have, but instead remained ten metres or so away. If they had been planning to attack us again, I thought, they would have been all over the bike.

So Danae and I walked straight towards my motorcycle, holding our helmets but not wearing them. The mob continued to shout abuse at us but did not make a move. After I had unlocked the bike, Danae sat on it and slowly began to put her helmet on, but I decided I was not going to be chased out of Exarcheia, my own neighbourhood. So I left my helmet on the bike and walked towards them. 'I'm here. Tell me why you want to hit me. I'm all ears,' I said.

The ringleader warned me off: 'If you come closer you'll regret it.'

'I want to know what I've done to anger you. If this means I'll be hit, so be it,' I said, taking courage from the fact that they had still not attacked.

Thus an improbable, boisterous dialogue began. At first they were reluctant to explain their anger but simply continued swearing and threatening. Eventually, after a lot of prompting, they accused the police in Exarcheia of being in cahoots with heroin dealers. I told them that I would not be surprised if that were the case. 'But why so much anger at me?' I asked.

'Don't be stupid,' one told me. It was not me, personally, they were angry with, but 'state terror and its representatives. You are one of them. A minister. Fuck off out of here. Exarcheia is our liberated zone. Go anywhere else you like. Just not here. Leave us in peace.'

Fresh from my clash with Alexis and the war cabinet and all too aware that Greece and Europe's deep establishment were trying to pulverize me, I decided to let them into a secret.

'I see your point,' I said. 'I can accept that you hate me because I represent state power. But know this: the same establishment that you loathe, loathes me. I am a thorn in their backside and, believe me, they are about to discard me. To vomit me out. Just so that you know . . .'

Miraculously their anger dissipated. A pause ensued, after which their leader spoke for the first time in a calm, almost friendly, voice: 'Enough now. Get on your motorcycle and go home.'

I made my way back towards the motorcycle and to Danae, but before putting on my helmet and getting on the bike, I turned round and said, 'I was roaming around Exarcheia decades before you were born. Are you now telling me that I cannot come back here? Are you banning me from my neighbourhood?'

He thought about it for a couple of seconds before responding: 'You're welcome to return when you're no longer a minister.'

'See you soon then,' I replied.

As we set off on the motorcycle, I looked in my mirrors. The sixty or so suddenly looked more like guards ensuring our safe departure than attackers. When we arrived home and I was putting the motorcycle on its stand, Danae hugged me. I hugged her back, both of us trembling a little. The next morning a journalist who was usually critical of me wrote, 'Last night, the anarcho-fascist hoodlums of Exarcheia were dealt their greatest defeat in thirty years by a woman: Danae Stratou.'

But now a more sinister kind of violence was coming our way.

PART THREE
Endgame

15

Countdown to perdition

After that night in Exarcheia, it took sixty-six days for the endgame to unfold. A political cartoon by the artist Yannis Ioannou sums them up vividly. In it Greece appears on her knees, her arms bound behind her back, struggling to escape. A menacing figure representing the EU, wielding an executioner's axe, castigates her for refusing to stay still and place her head obediently on the block: 'Will you *at last* show a modicum of responsibility?'

My own experience of those days is better encapsulated by a different cultural reference: Samuel Beckett's play *Endgame* – which might also serve as the leitmotif of Europe's establishment since the financial calamity of 2008 left it bereft of ideas as to how to sustain our societies yet unable to relinquish its grip on them – depicts a blind authoritarian barking orders at his servant, Clov, whom he took in as a child, in a grinding repetition of pointless behaviour, moving ever closer to an end that is both inevitable but elusive, simultaneously cursed and desired. For throughout May and June I was under no illusion that the game that Alexis and the war cabinet had chosen to play was already lost. We were merely going through the motions leading to an inescapable checkmate. The one illusion that did remain was my faint belief that Alexis would ultimately baulk at the humiliation the troika were planning for him and at the last moment choose to play another game – the one we had planned all along. That belief faded with every day that passed, but as long as it endured, however faintly, I would stay put. If nothing else I was not going to make it any easier for the creditors to replace the finance minister whose signature they required in order to renew Greece's indefinite jail sentence.

I dedicated my remaining energy to four tasks: the campaign against tax cheats and gambling machines, preparing my presentations for the Eurogroup so that they were as immaculate as possible, developing the parallel payments system, including Plan X, and, top of the agenda, compiling our Plan for Greece. Jeff Sachs and I were already working on the last of these, and in addition to contributions from Norman Lamont, Larry Summers and Thomas Mayer, we had the help of Jamie Galbraith and fellow economist Mariana Mazzucato.

On 7 May I would be delivering a keynote speech in Brussels. It would be an opportunity to test the water with an early draft of the plan before presenting it at the next Eurogroup, which was scheduled for 11 May, at which point Jeff would start canvassing support for it at the IMF and elsewhere in Washington. I did not imagine for a moment that it would be welcomed with open arms by Wolfgang and his people, whatever its calibre, but there was a chance that a convincing plan would prompt other, less hostile, ministers to break ranks in its support. Before the speech in Brussels, I decided to fly to Paris and Rome, and then after the speech to Madrid, to see if my plan cut any ice there.

With foes like these who needs friends?

Having little to lose and knowing that the current impasse worried the French, Italians and Spanish too, I resolved to be frank and ask them directly to respond to a bold suggestion. I proposed that the Greek prime minister persuade the German chancellor that the only way forward was for them to take a joint Graeco-German proposal to the institutions. This would comprise, first, a package of reforms to be passed through Greece's parliament by the end of May (including a revised fiscal plan, a simplification of VAT, major reorganization of the tax administration, severe limitations on early retirement, etc.), which would become the new 'common conditionalities' for completion of Greece's current programme; and, second, a long-term Greek recovery contract between the EU and Greece (our Plan for Greece), which would itself comprise the debt swaps I had been proposing, a major investment initiative, a public bad bank to deal with the banks' non-performing loans, many much-needed reforms in public administration and product markets and a programme for combating the humanitarian crisis.[1]

I argued that approaching Merkel with this plan was our only chance. It was a moderate proposal, containing everything that Greece needed immediately and in the longer run while maximizing the creditors' chances of getting their money back, but above all this strategy would allow the chancellor to present it as her own idea. If she refused it, I argued, then no sustainable solution was possible. In that case, I said, let the chips fall where they may.

In Paris, on 5 May, I met Michel Sapin and Pierre Moscovici. They talked at cross-purposes, offering the usual empty promises of support and no ideas of their own, and when it came to the strategic question – of whether to approach Merkel in this way – they were neither in favour nor against. But there was another French politician I met that day who truly engaged with the plan, who told me it was a good one and who encouraged me to proceed with it: Emmanuel Macron.

In Rome, on 6 May, Pier Carlo Padoan had a major surprise in store for me. In the Eurogroup he was reliably conformist with one eye firmly trained on Wolfgang for his approval. In his own office, however, he revealed what I supposed were his true colours. 'You must most certainly go ahead with this,' he told me. 'There is no time to waste. Your prime minister must call Merkel now, or at most by tomorrow, and press her on this. Do *not* wait until Monday [11 May, the day of the Eurogroup]. By then, if there is no action by Angela, Wolfgang will have the upper hand.'

I was astounded. But that was not all. To strengthen our argument that there should not be two sets of conditions for us to adhere to – which would have meant being unable to embark on our new agreement until we had satisfied the conditions of the current programme – but common conditionalities that covered them both, Pier Carlo advised us to make the case that the previous two troika programmes – those rejected by the Greek people when they elected us – were based on the logic of the IMF, whereas any new arrangement should depart from the IMF's logic and come closer to the developmental logic of the World Bank. Pier Carlo's only piece of criticism was that it was a mistake to refer to a 'humanitarian crisis'. 'They don't like being criticized for having caused such a thing,' he told me. He suggested using the term 'anti-poverty campaign' instead, advice that I adopted instantly. As I left his office for Fiumicino Airport, I was both pleased and aghast: pleased that there was intellectual life and honesty in at least one of Europe's seats of power; aghast that

Europe had conspired to ensure that neither ever showed its face in our common institutions, especially in the Eurogroup.

Having delivered my speech in Brussels on 7 May, I arrived in Madrid on 8 May to be received by my next-door neighbour at the Eurogroup table, Luis de Guindos. As the finance minister of a conservative Spanish government that was the sworn enemy of Syriza's sister party in Spain, Podemos, Luis had never missed an opportunity in the Eurogroup to side with Wolfgang against me, but I had already gathered that this might well be due to tactical expediency rather than out of conviction. That day in his office he confirmed my suspicion. Over a simple but fabulous dish of paella, with a glass of excellent red wine to complement it, a disarmingly friendly conversation ensued. Not only was Luis quick to endorse my idea for breaking the deadlock, but when I told him of Pier Carlo's similar reaction he shook his head appreciatively and said, 'You, the Italians and we must band together.'

Intrigued, I encouraged him to come clean. 'Are you telling me, Luis, that you are no longer interested in overthrowing our government? Was that not your not-so-secret desire?'

Luis thought about that for a moment. 'Not any more,' he said with a wicked smile.

'What changed?' I asked. 'I was under the impression you had joined Wolfgang in seeking Grexit.'

'What changed,' Luis replied thoughtfully, 'is that Podemos are no longer posing a threat to us the way they had been a few months ago. And, also, I now fear Grexit more than I did. I am not sure any more that we can contain it.'

Spain's credit-fuelled mini-recovery was indeed fragile and incapable of surviving the shocks that Grexit would cause, and it was true that Podemos's rise had stalled owing to internal divisions. Even though he would never come out and say so in public, a pact between Greece, Italy and Spain that averted Grexit and calmed the markets made sense from his perspective.[2]

On the flight home from Madrid I was plagued by the thought of missing the opportunity we now had before us. The French economy minister and the finance ministers of Italy and Spain had agreed wholeheartedly that Alexis should immediately call the German chancellor with my proposition. They would never take the lead themselves of course, but if Alexis did, they would support us, at least from behind the scenes.

By the time I landed in Athens, the Plan of Greece had been finalized. Jeff Sachs had beautifully edited the draft I had sent him a couple of days before; Norman Lamont had added some important vignettes; the people from Lazard had refined the debt-swap proposal, and Larry Summers had provided his endorsement. There were other contributions too, including sterling work on a debt sustainability analysis and a bad bank policy. Jeff suggested that the title of the paper should make it sound boring and modest, the way the IMF liked it, and it accordingly became *A Policy Framework for Greece's Fiscal Consolidation, Recovery and Growth*. Co-signed by policymakers who combined exceptional pedigrees with experience of the highest levels of governance from across the political spectrum, it was a powerful weapon.[3]

That Saturday morning, two days before flying back to Brussels for the 11 May Eurogroup, I had my office print out copies of the *Policy Framework*, placed a few in my rucksack, got on my bike and headed over to Maximos to see Alexis. There I told him of the encouraging reception of my proposition in Paris, Rome and Madrid and handed him copies of the *Policy Framework* with firm advice that it was his only remaining weapon if not to win the war, at least to prevent annihilation.

Without even pretending that he wanted to read it, Alexis pushed the *Policy Framework* aside. 'This is not the time to antagonize her,' he said, referring to Merkel.

Words eluded me. In refusing the opportunity to adopt this document and proclaim it our government's anti-*MoU*, he was wasting the chance to table a plan for Greece's recovery devised by the Greek government for the Greek people with the able assistance of some of the world's brightest and most experienced policymakers. Denied the prime minister's stamp of approval, the *Policy Framework* was from then on nothing more than a Ministry of Finance green paper, handing the creditors a licence to ignore it altogether.

Alexis's one act of resistance remained his threat to default to the IMF (while signalling behind the scenes to Merkel his readiness to roll over). The next IMF payment, totalling €765 million, was due on Tuesday, 12 May, the day after the Eurogroup meeting. But on Sunday, 10 May, just before another war cabinet gathering, Yannis Stournaras, governor of the Greek central bank, called to relate that €650 million had miraculously been discovered idling around in some forgotten account that happened to be stuffed with funds that we were allowed to repay the IMF. There was no way we could justify defaulting over the remaining €115 million. 'Bastards! They have resorted to paying themselves to stop our default,' was how Alexis put it.

'The fact that they're paying themselves rather than announcing a default by Greece should give you strength and courage, Alexi,' I told him. 'It shows the kind of power you have.'

My attempt to revive his spirits went unnoticed, and over the next few hours, as the war cabinet discussed new ways to succumb to the old programme, I remained quiet. Only towards the end of the meeting did I ask, 'Tomorrow I have to fly to Brussels to attend another Eurogroup. What are my instructions?' The answer I received was to fend off Wolfgang and his troops in the hope that Merkel would come to our rescue.

Wolfgang's move

Keeping my friends close but my enemies even closer, I arranged to visit Wolfgang, along with Theocarakis and Chouliarakis, at the German delegation's Brussels office an hour before the Eurogroup began.[4] He received us with his two deputies by his side. Setting aside the usual preliminaries, he got straight to the point. 'Look,' he said, 'it's a mistake to believe anything the commission tell you. What can they offer you? They talk and talk and talk but it is all just talk. Pay no attention to them.'

On past experience he was right. What I had not expected, and what I now discovered, was that his advice to ignore the European Commission applied equally to his own chancellor. 'I know that your prime minister talks to her all the time,' he said. Growing visibly agitated, he asked, '*Why* is he talking to her all the time? What for? What does he expect from her? There is *nothing* she can give him!' Perhaps realizing that he had exceeded the limits of propriety, he took a step back: 'I was very pleased to have heard your prime minister mention the possibility of a referendum because that would be *fantastic*! But you must be very careful. You must make it very clear – *very, very* clear – to the Greek people what their choice is. Opinion polls say that they want the euro. You must tell them that if they want the euro they must have the *MoU*. If they don't want the *MoU* then that's fine, move on. Just move on.'

I retorted that membership of the eurozone could hardly be made conditional on consenting to failed policies that made one's country unsustainable within that same eurozone.

He dismissed my argument immediately: 'The *MoU*, the *MoU* as it is, with no changes. Or the drachma. You have to take the *MoU* if you want the euro. If you don't want the euro, that's another matter. The people of Greece must decide that question. That's why I was happy to hear your prime minister speak of a referendum. You should set up this referendum. And, you know, if it takes six months for the Greek people to have plenty of time in order to make up their minds, that's fine. We will fund you *completely* for six months.'

So there I had it. All the talk about the ECB merely following its rules in denying us liquidity was claptrap. If they wanted to, for political purposes they would fund Greece's debt obligations 'completely'. And not just for the two or three weeks that we had been requesting but for six whole months – which would amount to €11 billion!

'But Wolfgang,' I replied, still reeling at his words, 'as responsible leaders and Europeans, we should do all we can to prevent Grexit and to offer our peoples a clear vision of a decent life within the eurozone. Pushing them to make a choice between a catastrophic fiscal policy *within* the eurozone and a catastrophic exit *from* the eurozone is not the mark of an enlightened political leadership. Don't you see that the problem with the *MoU* is that it offers no hope whatsoever for a decent future?'

Of course he could see it, he admitted. 'The *MoU* is bad for your people. It will not allow you to recover. It is not good for growth. That's why you need the referendum. To make this *clear*.'

Shocked at the ease with which he appeared willing to endorse the disintegration of the eurozone, I said, 'Leaving aside Greece for a moment, do you really think that you can control the demonic forces that a Grexit would unleash? This is pure folly. No one can control them. It would be an error of historic proportions.'

'Don't call it a Grexit then,' Wolfgang said. 'You don't have to think of it as Grexit. Think of it as a time out. The way I understand it, you get out for a while, you rebound very quickly, so you gain your competitiveness again through the devaluation. And then a year later or so, when you have recovered a large part of your lost competitiveness, you can come back in.'

I hardly knew where to begin. 'Wolfgang, I cannot condone Greece's exit from a currency that admittedly we should never have entered. Since it takes up to a year to create a new currency before devaluing it, it is equivalent to announcing a currency devaluation a year in advance. The short-to-medium-term costs would be immense. While I fear these costs less than the costs of staying ad infinitum in the euro under a destructive *MoU*, I insist that putting us in the *MoU*-or-drachma dilemma is not consistent with the interests of Europe. Even if you don't care about Greece, Grexit – or a Greek time out, or however you want to spin it – will end the euro's aura of inevitability. This will hit Italy and Spain badly and immediately, before the secondary effects reach Paris. And there is nothing that Mario Draghi can do to ameliorate this damage even if he prints pyramids of euros. The monetary union will be unstitched everywhere by forces that you will not be able to control.'

Wolfgang disagreed, but expressed his disagreement via a curious overlap in our opinions. 'In the Eurogroup you are probably the one who understands that the eurozone is unsustainable,' he said. 'The eurozone is constructed wrongly. We should have a political union, there is no doubt about it.'

'I always knew you to be a dedicated federalist,' I interrupted. 'I recall your disagreement with your colleagues back in the early 1990s. I am sure Mrs Merkel could not see as well as you did the importance of a federal political structure to go along with the monetary union.'

He seemed pleased for a moment. 'And the French too,' he added. 'They opposed me.'

'I know,' I said. 'They wanted to use your Deutschmark but without sharing sovereignty!'

Wolfgang agreed heartily. 'Yes, this is so. And I won't accept it. So, you see,' he continued, 'the only way I can keep this thing together, the only way I can hold this thing together, is by greater discipline. Anyone who wants the euro must accept discipline. And it will be a much stronger eurozone if it is disciplined by Grexit.'

From the corner of my eye I could see Chouliarakis going pale. Theocarakis, on the other hand, looked impressed but unsurprised by the sight of the German finance minister firing on all cylinders. Taking my chance, I said, 'You will *not* be able to control the chaotic process that a Grexit would trigger. Forget about a temporary time out. Once one is out, one is out, and the rest will begin to fall out too. You are planning for a dynamic that you will *not* be able to control.'

'I don't agree with you,' he replied, shaking his head and looking at the floor. 'We can safeguard the euro much better after you leave, with *huge* help from us, and then you can come back in.'

It was evidently pointless to challenge his faith in his ability to control a vicious force of nature, and when the German finance minister offers your battered country 'huge help', you have a duty, as its finance minister, to ask for clarification. So I asked him, 'OK, when you say "with huge help", what do you mean by "huge"? By the way, Wolfgang, have you briefed the chancellor on this?'

Looking at me intensely and with a meaningful smile he said, 'If I answer this question and you leak this, I'm going to kill you with my own hands!'

'Wolfgang,' I said, 'have I ever leaked anything we have talked about in our meetings? You have, but, as you know, I have not!'

He laughed and said, 'Yes, you are right, you are right. She knows and I will convince her that it's a good idea.'

As I had suspected, the chancellor knew of Wolfgang's plan but had not approved it. At that point it hit me: he and I had something important in common. We disagreed on everything, Grexit included, but there was one thing we shared: a leader who was muddling through.

'From what you are telling me,' I probed, 'this is a conversation that you do not have a mandate to have with me.'

'Yes, you need a mandate from your prime minister for us to have this conversation and I need a mandate from the chancellor.'

'OK,' I said. 'I'll call you later.' We exchanged telephone numbers and agreed to talk again later.

Meanwhile, we had the Eurogroup meeting to attend. From within the Eurogroup I texted Alexis with Wolfgang's news. The following rapid exchange ensued.

VAROUFAKIS: [16.21] Wolfgang pirouetted amazingly today during our meeting.

TSIPRAS: [16.22] Meaning?

VAROUFAKIS: [16.25] He is sending you a message about a time out . . .

TSIPRAS: [16.26] Is he proposing exit or adopting a parallel currency?

VAROUFAKIS: [16.27] The former by means of the latter; in the full knowledge that the *MoU* is throttling us.

TSIPRAS: [16.30] In that case tell him that, if he means it, let's discuss how it could happen under the best terms. Funding, consensus and mutual assistance without default.

VAROUFAKIS: [16.35] He is offering huge help for the transition.

At that point Jeroen called on me to respond to the usual charges against the Greek government: causing delays, being unwilling to offer credible proposals and so on. After delivering my by then standard rejoinder and an urgent plea for a balanced communiqué, I resumed my exchange with Alexis.

TSIPRAS: [17.50] I am curious to find out what on earth he has in mind. Tell him also about that other proposal to see how he sees it.[5]

VAROUFAKIS: [17.51] OK. Do I have your green light to talk with him in strict confidentiality about all these matters?

TSIPRAS: [17.53] Yes, but make sure that you do not give him the impression that you agree. And be careful that he does not leak it.

VAROUFAKIS: [17.53] OK. Our line is: 1. That I am simply speaking with him to explore his proposal without any commitment to it. 2. If he leaks it we shall deny it.

As the Eurogroup moved on from discussion of Greece to other topics, Wolfgang beckoned me over to his side of the enormous conference table. I walked over and knelt down next to him.

SCHÄUBLE: I have been thinking about what we were saying.

VAROUFAKIS: Me too. And I am glad to report that I have my mandate from my prime minister to discuss your idea, without any agreement or commitment to it.

SCHÄUBLE: Listen, it is not enough for us to have the mandate to talk. It is important that *they* talk about it first.

I could see his point: it would be very easy for both of us to land in hot water, accused of going rogue on such a crucial matter.

VAROUFAKIS: I see. How should we then go about it? In any case, did you get your mandate from the chancellor since we spoke?

SCHÄUBLE: I shall talk with her tomorrow morning. But it's not enough for her to agree. She and Tsipras must have this discussion first. Why doesn't your prime minister, in one of their many talks, mention it?

VAROUFAKIS: [*smiling*] Come, come, Wolfgang. You do not expect him to make such a mistake? If he does mention it, the next moment the *Financial Times* or *Der Spiegel* will be reporting that the Greek government is putting Grexit on the table! I have a better idea: why does the chancellor not mention this idea to Tsipras instead?

SCHÄUBLE: [*smiling*] Because then you will leak that the chancellor is pushing Greece out of the eurozone.

VAROUFAKIS: This sounds like a stalemate, Wolfgang, doesn't it?

Wolfgang screwed up his face in deep thought and then, a few seconds later, shared a fresh idea with me: 'Why doesn't Tsipras, whenever they talk, ask her aggressively, "What's this idea that Schäuble is pushing on Varoufakis for a time out?" If he says this as an accusation, no one will be able to leak this as either Tsipras or you having endorsed my proposal. But, at the same time, the chancellor will have the chance to say, "It may not be a bad idea, let's discuss it." If they do, then you and I can have our discussion about what "huge help" means.'

I agreed and upon my return to Athens related faithfully the whole exchange to Alexis. Somewhat bemused, he nevertheless promised to put to Merkel the aggressive question Wolfgang had devised.

Melted euros, sunken hearts

Almost a month later, on 8 June 2015, I was in Berlin. Accompanied by Jamie Galbraith, I met Wolfgang in his office for the last time. Schäuble received me warmly, even though he could not resist a barbed joke. Once we had sat down, he produced a pile of euro coins made of milk chocolate. 'They were given to me by German schoolchildren, but I told them I was going to deliver them to my Greek colleague because he would need them to calm his nerves.' I took them with a smile, offered him one (which he rejected), peeled the aluminium foil off another and ate it.

'Pretty good for the nerves,' I confirmed before unnerving him with bad news. 'Wolfgang, it seems that you most definitely do *not* have a mandate for that conversation that you started a month ago in Brussels.'

Genuinely puzzled, he asked to know more, so I told him what Alexis had relayed to me. He had spoken to Angela Merkel. As advised, he had confronted her with the question: 'What on earth is Schäuble telling Varoufakis about a time out?' She was annoyed and told Alexis that this was not something she wished to contemplate, adding portentously, 'If he [Schäuble] approaches you with this again, let me know!'[6]

Wolfgang looked as if he had had the wind knocked out of him. That he did not even try to contest Alexis's account suggested it was in tune with his understanding of Merkel's attitude. His smile disappeared, his shoulders drooped, his cheerfulness vanished. He shrugged repeatedly and told me that, given this development, he was out of ideas. He seemed lost for words. Again and again he said he had 'no idea' about how to resolve the impasse, that he had 'no authority' to discuss an agreement within the eurozone behind the institutions' backs. For the first time I recognized not a lack of interest or some cynical stratagem but genuine helplessness, so, I tried to revive his spirits a little.

'The people out there, Wolfgang,' I said, pointing out of the window, 'do not look to Mario [Draghi] or to Christine [Lagarde] to do what is right, avert disaster and find solutions. They never voted for those people. They voted for you and for me to get together and hammer out an agreement. They mandated us to find a solution and will blame us if we do not.'

He refused to look me in the eye. In fact, he did not look well.

'Our conundrum,' I continued, 'our task is to find a solution that minimizes pain under the twin constraints that you and I have agreed are binding: first, the *MoU* does not offer a viable solution for Greece and, second, neither you nor I have a mandate to discuss Grexit, time outs and the like. So let's find the best solution within our current set of constraints. This is what elected politicians must do.'

'What could that solution be?' he asked, leaving the door ajar for me to propose an alternative. It was my chance to connect with him over a practical resolution.

I explained how debt could be swapped in a manner that he could sell to the Bundestag, how Greece would need no new money, how we could guarantee that Athens would never fall into the ignominy of a primary deficit again, how we could institute far-reaching reforms that he and I could agree upon and a development bank along the lines of proposals I had developed in conjunction with German consultants close both to the Chancellery and to his own ministry. In short, I gave a summary of the revamped version of my *Policy Framework* paper, which we had been working on that past month and which now featured new ideas and a new title: *Ending the Greek Crisis: Structural reforms, investment-led growth & debt management*.[7]

My recollection is that Wolfgang found nothing to fault in my proposition. Later, seeking a second opinion on his response, I asked Jamie Galbraith to write down his impressions. Here is how he described Wolfgang's reaction.

> Schäuble listened to the presentation at length with close attention and body language that suggested no disagreement on any point of the argument. Varoufakis stated repeatedly that a solution should be definitive and not a predicate for further failure and ongoing bailouts . . . The most important fact about Schäuble's response was that he said, repeatedly and with a shrug, that he has 'no idea' about how to resolve this matter.

I pressurized him for some kind of response. 'Here I am, asking you, the finance minister of the richest and most powerful country in Europe, to tell me what I should do. You reject my ideas; your own proposal was rejected by your chancellor, and meanwhile the negotiations between my prime minister's team and the troika in the Brussels Group are heading in a direction that is the opposite of a solution. What should I do, Wolfgang?'

He looked up for the first time in a while and said without any enthusiasm, 'Sign the *MoU*.' We had come full circle.

'OK,' I said. 'Let's suppose I do it. Let's assume that I sign the damned thing. Tell me this: are we not going to be in the same situation again in six or twelve months? With another funding crunch feeding GREECE ON THE VERGE AGAIN headlines, more recession, and a political backlash in the Eurogroup?'

Perking up a little, Wolfgang agreed and said, 'This is why I told you to convince your prime minister to consider a time out.'

'Except that your chancellor put an end to that discussion.'

'Well, that leaves you with the *MoU*,' he said, falling back once more on the same non-solution.

Only a move beyond reasoning and rhetoric could break the vicious cycle, I thought, a human gesture. 'Will you do me a favour, Wolfgang?' I asked humbly. He nodded warmly. 'You have been doing this for forty years,' I said; 'I have only been doing it for five months. You know from our earlier meetings that I have followed with interest your articles and speeches since the late 1980s. I need to ask you to forget for a few minutes that we are ministers. I want to ask you for your *advice*. Not to tell me what to do. To advise me instead. Will you do this for me?'

Under the watchful eye of his deputies, he nodded again. Taking heart, I thanked him and sought his answer as an elder statesman, not an enforcer. 'Would you sign the *MoU* if you were in my place?' I was expecting him to give me the predictable answer – that, under the circumstances, there was no alternative – along with all the usual, senseless arguments. He didn't. Instead he looked out of the window. By Berlin standards, it was a hot and sunny day. Then he turned and stunned me with his answer. 'As a patriot, no. It's bad for your people.'

A chink had appeared. Naturally, I tried to prise it open. I said that since we now agreed that the *MoU* was 'bad' and Grexit was off the table, an agreement like the one I was proposing was the only solution consistent with our mandate and duty to our people – the Germans as well as the Greeks. But by that stage Wolfgang looked like a broken man.

The cynic would say that Dr Schäuble was playing a larger game – that, as he had said at the IMF conference, causing Michel Sapin's outburst, and as he had said to me before the Eurogroup on 11 May, Grexit to him was an instrument with which to pursue his vision of a smaller, more disciplined eurozone, with the troika firmly entrenched in Paris. The cynic would be almost right.[8] Except it would not be the whole story. As I departed that day, I was not leaving behind me a Machiavellian dictator; I was leaving behind a sunken heart, a man ostensibly more powerful than almost anyone in Europe who nevertheless felt utterly powerless to do what he knew was right. As the great tragedians have taught us, nothing causes greater wretchedness than the combination of supreme authority and wholesale powerlessness.

Before leaving his office, I took the chocolate euros and put them in the inside pocket of my jacket. We said our goodbyes. I took the lift to the ground floor and walked out into the sunniest of days. As I got into the car that awaited us, I looked up in the direction of Wolfgang's office surprised to feel a strange sadness at the memory of his sunken spirits. Later I would be making a speech at Berlin cathedral. Who among the enthusiastic crowd that received me that night would have believed I had felt this way?[9] By the time I arrived at the cathedral, the heat had melted the euro coins. The undated resignation letter that I made a point of keeping in the same pocket was smudged with chocolate.

The war of the models

'A Taste of Armageddon', episode twenty-three of the very first *Star Trek* television series, first aired in 1967, tells the story of a five-century-old war between two planets, Eminiar and Vendikar. In order to reduce the war's economic costs, the combatants have come to an interesting arrangement. Instead of firing real missiles at one another, they have agreed to continue their conflict in the purely digital environment of a computer model where their attacks on one another are simulated, with model-based missiles unleashed against each other's model-based cities. But while no material damage is done, the casualties are very real. For the agreement also compels each side to send to specially made 'disintegration chambers' the number of people who, according to the model, would have died had the attacks been real.

During the negotiations with the troika a similar 'war of the models' took place, with real casualties among the Greek people. For example, whenever I argued that in a struggling economy marred by poverty and tax evasion the best way to increase the state's revenues from VAT or from corporate tax was to *reduce* VAT and corporate tax rates, the troika would retort that their computer models showed the opposite: only by *increasing* the rate of VAT and corporate tax would tax revenue rise. And my ministry's Council of Economic Advisers, under George Chouliarakis, was using the same models to produce the same arguments in favour of austerity. One day, incensed and incredulous, I asked to be allowed a glimpse inside the models. I was told that such models were complex, the implication being I would not understand, but I insisted: in a previous life I had been an econometrician, I replied.

When they showed me their models, I realized why they had been reluctant to do so. Inside there lay a scrupulous economist's nightmare: an inbuilt and frankly ridiculous assumption that price increases such as those produced by VAT increases *never* reduce sales, and that rises in corporate tax rates *always* lead to more tax paid by business. They had omitted to include any 'price elasticities' in their models – to use the technical term for this blunder. To my knowledge, no economist ever assumes that a price increase, *however steep*, will leave sales unaffected. Or, conversely, that a price drop will *never* stimulate sales. Or that increasing corporate tax rates will *always* lead to corporations paying more taxes to the state. And yet the troika, my Council of Economic Advisers and the respected financial press – even those among them who refused to endorse higher tax rates for Greece – implicitly endorsed precisely this economic idiocy every time they defended these models against my arguments.

To demonstrate the flaw, I performed a simple exercise: I asked the troika's model to simulate the impact on the government's revenues of raising the VAT rate from 23 per cent to 223 per cent. We all know what would happen in reality after such a ludicrous tax hike: sales would collapse and so would the government's revenues. But not in the troika's model, which produced a massive increase in revenues. Like all models, garbage assumptions beget garbage predictions. Even so, just as in 'A Taste of Armageddon', the casualties would be real enough: poor pensioners further impoverished, businesses pushed over the precipice, a whole social economy on the edge.

To counter the troika's models I urgently needed our own, one scientifically superior and socially humane. Normally, this would fall to the Council of Economic Advisers to provide, except that Chouliarakis lacked the expertise and, more importantly, the will. He seemed perfectly satisfied to defer to the troika's models, whose results strengthened Wieser and Costello's hand. But as he now had the full support of Maximos, there was no point arguing with him. Instead, I asked my own team, under Elena Panaritis, to create a decent model from scratch.

Without the resources of the seventy-strong Council of Economic Advisers, without even a proper office to work in, this tiny team did magnificently. Together we worked out the econometrics, built in decent estimates of the responsiveness of different markets to price and tax changes and completed the coding. Within a fortnight even the troika's technicians in Athens admitted that our model was superior to theirs. The trouble, of course, was that this was no academic game in which the most accurate model won; it was a war of the models in which the most powerful side won. This can be illustrated by an episode involving the IMF's Poul Thomsen.

One evening in Brussels Poul was wearying me with his standard tirade about our VAT system and how it ought to be simplified: 'It is ridiculous to have six rates of VAT,' he thundered. 'It makes the system susceptible to arbitrage and fraud.'[10]

My response was that the real problem with VAT in Greece was not its complexity but the fact that 23 per cent was too high a rate for an economy in a slump and a society so mired in poverty that millions could not afford to pay it. We needed to offer the Greek people a new social contract: the government would reduce the rates and in return the people would actually pay the tax. Additionally, I argued, we needed to digitize transactions to discourage tax evasion.

Poul was adamant: too many rates is the problem, he kept saying over and over again. 'You need to go to just two rates,' he insisted.

It had been a long day, and I was tired so I decided to cut to the chase: 'OK, Poul. Here's the deal. I shall adopt your idea of just two VAT rates nationwide on condition that you agree that they're 6 per cent and 15 per cent, plus a 3 per cent increase for transactions using cash instead of debit cards. What do you say?'

Poul looked at me. 'Do you mean it?' he asked, evidently pleased at my suggestion.

'Yes, I do,' I replied. 'Let's shake on it.' He gave me his hand and we shook.

Back in Athens it took a vast effort to convince Alexis's people and the cabinet to endorse the new policy. My argument was that it would give people and businesses a huge breathing space, it would help establish a new rapport between the population and its government, and it would be the first time we had seen eye to eye with the IMF on a major reform. While I got the green light, it was clear that many were not happy. Chouliarakis was upset that his troika-sourced model had been set aside, as were others for whom the very existence of my team was the real problem.

On 18 May I was to be interviewed live on Greek television. Beforehand, I asked Alexis for permission to mention the new VAT policy as a sign of progress in the negotiations and of our plans to provide relief from excessive taxation. He agreed, and so I did. The day after the interview parts of the press attacked the VAT proposal as 'unfeasible' and 'a figment of Varoufakis's imagination'. My press officer and Wassily reported that the deputy prime minister's office and Chouliarakis were briefing journalists against the announced policy. I told them that I could not be bothered any more with my comrades' backstabbing: 'I have an agreement with Thomsen and Alexis, and that's good enough for me.'

Two days later I received a call from one of our Brussels Group representatives. He had been very happy with the deal Poul and I had struck and had been eager to seal it at the level of the Brussels Group. He sounded incensed. 'The IMF has gone back on your deal. Their mission chief did mention that Thomsen and you agreed on two rates, but he claims that the top one should go from the current 23 per cent not to 15 but to 24 per cent. This is what their model says.' The words of caution that Jeff Sachs had once shared with me rang true: 'These people lie. Don't trust them.' Still I could hardly believe that Poul could have been so blatant.

The next time I saw him, we were passing one another in a corridor in Brussels. He had his eyes fixed on the floor, clearly keen to avoid a conversation. I stopped him. 'Poul,' I said, 'what happened to our agreement on two VAT rates, one at 6 per cent the other at 15 per cent, plus a surcharge for cash? What's this about a top rate of 24 per cent that my people report?' He mumbled something incomprehensible about the revenues not being high enough. 'We had a deal, Poul,' I insisted.

Grinning mischievously, he said, 'Will you give me the labour reforms?'[11]

This was no way to negotiate, I thought. Saying nothing, I walked away.

Despite the ridicule of the Greek press, I did not give in. For the whole of June my team and I repeatedly demonstrated the superior accuracy of our model and persevered in our arguments. The situation was truly absurd: a left-wing finance minister representing Syriza, the Alliance of the Radical Left, was arguing like a Reaganite Republican in favour of lower tax rates, including for business, against supposedly neoliberal functionaries insisting on increasing them. It was a sure sign that this negotiation had no basis in economics.

One day at Maximos Alexis congratulated me. 'Your model has won,' he said approvingly. 'Brussels conceded that it is better than theirs.' And then he added, 'But, Yanis, they still insist on the same parametric reforms [in tax rates], and we decided to let them have them.'[12] He reminded me of Anan 7, the leader of Eminiar in 'Taste of Armageddon', who demanded that his own people voluntarily enter the disintegration chambers because this is what the model he had agreed with the enemy required.

Clean break

Of the many disgraceful acts the previous government had perpetrated, two concerned the arts and our broader cultural milieu. One was the closure of ERT, the state radio and television broadcaster – our equivalent of the BBC. The other was the illegal removal from the directorship of the National Museum for the Contemporary Arts (EMST) of Anna Kafetsi, a curator who had made its establishment, completion and success her life's work.[13] When in opposition Syriza had pledged to reverse these outrages.

Despite their differing backgrounds, Sagias, a product of the *ancien régime*, and Pappas, who liked to present himself as Alexis's radical alter ego and the guarantor of our defiance, were a crucial component of the majority in the war cabinet that defended our original covenant. The first time I got a whiff that Pappas and Sagias were going over to the other side was when they backed away from our commitments regarding ERT and EMST. During that cruel April Sagias dropped a bomb. In reply to an idle question regarding who would be appointed CEO of the reopened ERT, he mentioned Labis Tagmatarchis, the former CEO who had overseen my blacklisting from ERT in 2011.[14]

'Is this the new era we're planning for ERT?' I asked. 'Did we fight to reopen it only to restore Labis? Are we keen to return to the bad old days of direct government control over a lowbrow public broadcaster?'

Sagias shrugged his shoulders. 'That's what I heard,' he said. 'Don't chastise me. Talk to Pappas.'

The next day, on the sidelines of a regular war cabinet meeting, I confronted Pappas, who was the minister of state with responsibility for the media. 'Are you seriously considering restoring Labis to the ERT throne?'

'Don't be absurd,' he replied. 'As if I would go for him!'

Reassured, I asked him whom he was thinking of instead. Pappas mentioned George Avgeropoulos, a brilliant young documentary maker and former war correspondent. He struck me as being an excellent choice. That night I told Danae I felt bad about doubting Pappas – a mistaken regret, as it turned out.

Meanwhile, every time I bumped into our minister of culture I would enquire about Ana Kafetsi's return to EMST. 'When do you think we can have her back?' I would ask.

'As soon as possible,' was his standard reply, occasionally peppered with encouraging statements such as 'She's the only one who can open the museum properly and who has what it takes to make it globally significant.' Precisely my thinking, I thought.

In short order two announcements wrecked my illusions: Pappas issued a press release that Labis Tagmatarchis was to become CEO of the reopened ERT, and the Ministry of Culture announced that the acting director of EMST, who had replaced Anna Kafetsi by a Samaras government decree, would continue in her position indefinitely. Countless people contacted me, incensed that we had reneged on two commitments to the thousands who had gone to the barricades to demand a different ERT and to those around the world who had protested against Anna's removal.

I was even more incensed than the public because I was aware of things that might not have been widely known. The acting director of EMST was Labis's life partner, while Sagias himself had told me of his long-term friendship with Labis. Pappas was getting closer and closer to Sagias when he reappointed Labis ERT's CEO and was known by all ministers to have the ear of the prime minister – including the minister of culture. Even if these appointments had been on merit, they seemed to me to be a warning of nepotism creeping into our ranks and of a cosying up to the regime we had sworn to replace.

It was no coincidence either, I thought, that they came at the same time as a crucial shift within the war cabinet, with Pappas and Sagias clearly drifting away from our covenant. And as Pappas and Sagias drifted away, the four-to-two majority that had backed the original battle plan – with Alexis providing the fifth vote in its favour at the end of each meeting – became a four-to-two minority, with myself and Euclid increasingly isolated.

Fake intelligence

Pappas and Sagias were not the only colleagues whose shift towards the troika was signalled by seemingly inconsequential choices over personnel. One afternoon in March, Yannis Roubatis, the chief of Greece's national intelligence agency, approached me at Maximos with a request. He wanted, he explained, to put in a good word for the man who had been presiding over the Hellenic Gaming Commission, the regulatory authority overseeing gambling. 'He is very close to the previous regime,' Roubatis admitted, 'but I believe he has found a way to keep that dodgy sector relatively clean. It would be a mistake to remove him just because he is not one of our own.' I was determined to maintain continuity wherever possible, and Roubatis's word would normally have sufficed, especially given our good relationship and the significant esteem I held him in.

However, at the ministry my team would not hear of it. 'If there is *one* person you must remove, he is it,' they said about the man whose services Roubatis wanted me to retain. After researching their claims and assessing the situation, I did remove him. This kick-started a personal campaign by the privatized national lottery corporation against me and the people I appointed to the new Hellenic Gaming Commission.[15] It also coincided, perhaps accidentally, with the cessation of the helpful briefings that Roubatis had been giving me until then.

Meanwhile Pappas and Sagias's behaviour towards me deteriorated markedly. Alexis's decision on 27 April to accede to Dijsselbloem's demands by dismissing Theocarakis marked a significant downturn, and they became increasingly impolite. Within a month their manner towards me had evolved into downright rudeness and aggression. One day on the sidelines of a war cabinet meeting I asked Alexis whether he had noticed it. Nonchalantly he said he had. And when I enquired if he knew why, he shocked me with his answer.

> TSIPRAS: Sagias is convinced that you are in cahoots with
>   Schäuble to take us out of the euro. And I think that he
>   has convinced Pappas too.

VAROUFAKIS: Do you believe this to be so, Alexi?

TSIPRAS: No, but *they* are convinced.

VAROUFAKIS: Why? How? On what basis? If I have succeeded
 in anything it is at blocking Schäuble's Grexit efforts on
 your behalf.

TSIPRAS: Roubatis has fed them information to the contrary.

While the rest of the war cabinet continued their discussion, I tried
to make sense in my head of this astounding information. *Roubatis is
telling them I'm in cahoots with Schäuble? If so, our chief spook is peddling
outright lies,* I thought. *Evidently, someone has influenced two of my war
cabinet colleagues, who have in turn influenced Alexis. But I'm getting all this
from Alexis. How can that be? If Alexis believes I'm Schäuble's stooge, why is
he telling me? Surely he would use this information to bait me before getting rid
of me? Then again, if Alexis does not believe this, why doesn't he side with me
against Sagias and Pappas? Could it be that Alexis is lying and Roubatis did
not accuse me of collaborating with Schäuble?* I needed to find out the truth.

I got my chance the night before the Eurogroup meeting of 11 May.
The war cabinet had decided the strategy that I should take with me
to the meeting and was in the process of adjourning. Roubatis
happened to have joined us for the last quarter of an hour of discussions. As we were getting up to leave, Alexis turned to me and said
in front of everyone, 'Be calm tomorrow. Don't lose your cool.'

I smiled and in a calm voice said, 'I am *always* ultra-cool during
Eurogroup meetings.' Looking at Roubatis, I asked Alexis, 'Have you
been told otherwise Alexi?'

Alexis glanced at Roubatis but said nothing.

'You *did* lose your cool at Riga, Yani,' Roubatis said.

'No, I did not. Not for one moment did I lose my cool. If you have
been telling my colleagues otherwise,' I said to Roubatis, pointing at
the others in the room, 'either you have been misinformed by your
agents or you are lying.'

Back at my office I downloaded from my phone onto my computer
my recording of the Riga Eurogroup. I copied it onto a USB stick and
gave it to my secretary with instructions that the stick be reproduced
and delivered personally to the members of the war cabinet, with a
note from me: 'Here is what really happened.' Interestingly, none of
them ever mentioned it to me. To this day I do not know whether
they even bothered to listen to it.

Countdown to perdition

With little support from my ministry's key departments, such as the tax office and the Council of Economic Advisers, I was now wholly reliant on a small team of advisers. The strength of their models and their tenacity were nonetheless a great source of annoyance to those who had worked harmoniously with the troika from the start as well as to those who had now chosen, mid-course, the path to surrender. One of those advisers was Elena Panaritis.

In early May I informed the IMF that Elena would be taking on the role of Greece's representative to the IMF. I did so with Alexis's permission and with the full support of Takis Roumeliotis, our former IMF representative, as well as that of our economy minister, George Stathakis. Her appointment was approved a few days later. In mid-May, however, Alexis asked me to dump her because 'the party cannot tolerate someone who had signed an *MoU*'. Truth be told, Elena had a conspicuously neoliberal background, attended gatherings of neoliberal politicians and economists and addressed the media in the manner of a former member of parliament, which she was, rather than in the more deferential style expected of a minister's adviser – that Greek was not her first language may not have helped either. But the only thing that mattered to me was that she represented me and our government brilliantly at international forums and was absolutely committed to the task of getting Greece off the hook. She was by far the best person for the job.

In response to Alexis, I explained that it was precisely because of the intellectual and moral courage with which she had turned against the logic of the *MoU* that I trusted her, certainly more than I trusted unschooled Syriza militants who did not know what they were up against. Alexis smiled at my reasoning but repeated that we had a problem. I put my foot down. This appointment was for the finance minister to make. Full stop. However, in order to help him fend off pressure from the party ranks, I proposed we go through an open recruitment process, with Dragasakis, Stathakis, Euclid and myself on the deciding committee, to assess Elena's suitability in the context of other candidates. Alexis agreed. Once again Elena was judged the right candidate and appointed.[16] A fresh letter to the IMF reconfirming her appointment was dispatched.

Four days later a newspaper reported that Sagias could not stomach her appointment, calling Elena an 'MoU choice'. The fact that he was at that very moment striving to drag Alexis down a path that led back to the MoU was ironic to say the least. But by 1 June, under immense new pressure from Alexis, Elena had resigned.

It would be a mistake to think that such episodes were unimportant. The troika had made it clear that a deal would be possible only if we were to postpone debt relief and increase tax rates, so the Plan for Greece had to be shot down because debt relief was at its heart, and the taxation models my team and I had been working on had to vanish. Elena's removal was a great help to Sagias and Chouliarakis's campaign, supported by Pappas and Dragasakis, to steer the Syriza government away from seeking debt relief.

During a war cabinet meeting, Pappas – who had approached me in 2012 because of my dedication to debt restructuring and had insisted that I become finance minister in 2015 – accused me contemptuously of being 'fixated' on Greece's debt.

'You bet I am,' I replied. 'When in a prison camp one has a duty to be fixated on escaping.'

Sagias rushed to Pappas's aid, making the incredible argument that the debt was not a problem as long as the troika funded its repayment. Watching Alexis fail to respond to this disavowal of literally everything we had been saying since 2010 was mortifying. Submitting to the troika's MoU process and remaking our government into a softer version of the Samaras administration was now their goal. I remember hanging around with Euclid at Maximos as we waited for the war cabinet to begin while in an adjacent room Sagias and Chouliarakis, with Dragasakis hovering to lend them support, wrote and rewrote the troika's so-called Staff Level Agreement (SLA). This was effectively a new MoU, identical to the old except but for a few fig leaves and a great deal *less* fiscal sustainability. The awfulness of it all was excruciating.

One day I told Alexis that he would not be able to sell Sagias's SLA to himself, let alone to our parliamentary party. Disarmingly, he agreed and looked even more depressed. Meanwhile, Jeff Sachs was sending me urgent warnings: 'They demand an SLA first, promising talks about debt relief and the like later. But they lie! Once you give them the SLA they will deny they ever promised you anything. Don't fall for it!' How could I tell Jeff that I no longer had Alexis's ear? That he seemed compelled to go inexorably down that path?

By the end of May, Alexis seemed too depressed to control war cabinet meetings. They were now dominated by Sagias, who with the consent of Dragasakis and Pappas was intent on our adoption of the language and content of the troika's SLA. We were conceding every-thing – fiscal targets that required austerity, the creditors' tax models and rate hikes, privatizations without limit – and getting nothing in return. Whenever I pointed out that we were making commitments that were impossible to meet, I met with responses that were more or less a reprise of the Samaras government's arguments: that future commitments were immaterial as long as we got new loans in the meantime; that debt was not an issue because, sooner or later, it would be restructured.

In a desperate attempt to refocus Alexis's attention, with Glenn Kim's help I compiled yet another, even milder and more moderate version of our debt swap proposals and suggested that Alexis present it at his forthcoming informal tripartite meeting with the German chancellor and President Hollande, arguing that any agreement based on Sagias's SLA would be political poison in Greece if it didn't include at least some kind of debt restructuring. Alexis did as I suggested and called me up later with the 'good news'. The meeting had gone quite well, he told me. 'Angela said she was prepared to have our debt proposals studied and asked me to send someone to discuss them with Wieser.'

But Euclid's separate report from Brussels told a different story: 'The tripartite went badly so we will give them more!'

'Alexi,' I said, 'she referred you to our gravedigger, Thomas Wieser, who clearly has no mandate to discuss debt relief with us, and you are telling me this is good news?'

Nevertheless, I was happy to send Glenn Kim to Brussels to meet Wieser, just in case. Glenn was as brilliant as ever in demonstrating to Wieser how simple and effective the debt swaps we were proposing would be and that they would come at minimal political cost to the chancellor. Wieser was forced to concede that our proposals had merit, but the fact that there was no credible threat from our side any more meant that Glenn's success led to nothing.

At a meeting of the war cabinet on 30 May, when Sagias and Chouliarakis suggested to Alexis that another meeting with Wieser should be arranged, I interjected, weighing my words carefully, 'I don't mind us talking to Wieser again, if you wish, but know that nothing will come of it. Our only chance of regaining control of our fate is if our prime minister, at most by Wednesday or Thursday, tables for public scrutiny and debate our own anti-*MoU* – our final proposal both for ending the current programme and for a new contract with the EU. Instead of speaking on the basis of their SLA, to discuss on the basis of our Plan for Greece. I have been saying this for two months now and I have been working on a text fit for that purpose . . .'

Sagias, who was sitting next to me, was repeating sarcastically, 'A rupture proposal, a rupture proposal, a rupture proposal . . . That's what you are doing. Proposing a falling-out.'

I had reached the limits of my patience. I banged my hand on the table and said, 'Look here! You will not interrupt me again. Nor will you put words in my mouth to distort my meaning. The troika and its media are doing a perfect job of that. But not in here. If you disagree, you will wait until your turn comes to put forward your views.'

'Now you've scared me!' Sagias said with aggressive condescension.

'Spyro, careful now. You are descending into the realm of political hooliganism.'

Sagias shouted at me, 'I have forty years of struggling in this country unlike some who saw their chance to return from abroad to make a career here.'

'I am glad the masks are off so that we can all see clearly who has been undermining the finance minister from within,' I replied.

Afterwards, talking to Elena Panaritis in Danae's presence, I described the unpleasantness and the havoc that followed this angry exchange: 'Once again I was inches from resigning today. But I am not going to do them the favour. Alexis tried to defend me but did so clumsily.'

'They have enchanted him,' said Elena.

'No, it's not that,' I said. 'He has surrendered internally. He is tired and has lost his spirit. But he is our last hope. I shall stay until that hope disappears totally.'

16

Adults in the room

Hope continued to dissipate over the next month as the newsreel of our decline went into fast-forward.

On 1 June George Soros tries to contact Alexis via my channels. For years I have been falsely portrayed by the pro-troika establishment and the anti-Semitic Right as Soros's stooge in Greece, so his message to the prime minister comes as a perverse vindication. 'Fire Varoufakis! Europe cannot afford to have two open wounds at once – Greece and the Ukraine [where fierce fighting was taking place]. Athens must capitulate to Germany now so that Europe can dedicate itself to resolving Ukraine. For this Varoufakis must be removed.' Months later, a further, bitter vindication arrives when the EU and the IMF announce that the same debt swaps and nominal income indexed bonds that I had been proposing for Greece would be used to restructure Ukraine's public debt.

On 2 June Euclid texts me from Brussels: 'We are being defeated on all fronts!'

On 3 June the troika announces that, for the first time ever, they will present us with their proposals. Fearful that we will leak them, they summon Chouliarakis to a seminar room at a godforsaken hour to present their demands by PowerPoint, with George taking notes. Having read his notes, I send Alexis my interpretation: 'This proposal was written by the IMF with the intention of forcing you to reject it. Their strategy is clear: demand so much austerity and loss of sovereignty that either Berlin will yield on debt relief or Greece will break.'

On 4 June I ask Euclid, 'Did we present our plan to the troika? Or did we let them beat us about the head with their SLA?' Euclid texts back: 'No prizes for guessing!'

On 5 June our attempts to default on the IMF fail again. This time, instead of discovering a hidden stash of money, the IMF defers our payment to the end of the month, to be bundled up with later tranches, something which Christine Lagarde told me in her Washington office two months earlier was impossible.[1]

On 6 June I inform Alexis of curious meetings taking place between a member of our war cabinet and a functionary within my ministry who has been undermining my algorithmic method for identifying tax evaders. That same day Pappas explains to journalists via text that I have to be removed because I am the 'anchor' that has been holding us back from an agreement with the troika.

Between 7 and 9 June I am in Berlin, where I have the meeting with Wolfgang Schäuble at which he stuns me with his helplessness. I also meet Green and SPD parliamentarians and deliver my speech at Berlin cathedral. In it, I recount US Secretary of State James F. Byrnes's 1946 Speech of Hope, which triggered Germany's rehabilitation and reindustrialisation, and invite Angela Merkel to deliver her own Speech of Hope for Greece.

In response, between 10 and 15 June, Gesine Schwan, twice the SPD's candidate for the German federal presidency, impressed by my speech in Berlin and by the Plan for Greece that I shared with her, tries to convince Germany's vice chancellor, Sigmar Gabriel, to do business with me. His office responds positively to the latest version of my plan, signalling that it is a good basis for an agreement. A promising dialogue evolves until 15 June, when Gabriel tells the German tabloid *Bild*, 'The game theorists of the Greek government are in the process of gambling away the future of their country . . . Europe and Germany will not let themselves be blackmailed. And we will not let the exaggerated electoral pledges of a partly communist government be paid for by German workers and their families.' Gesine is appalled. She emails me to say she feels ashamed for Gabriel. That same afternoon I travel to Herakleion, the capital of Crete, where I address thousands of people in the main square.

On 16 June a meeting of Syriza MPs takes place in the old Senate Room at Parliament House. All seats in the auditorium are taken by the time I arrive, but instead of accepting an invitation to take a ministerial seat next to the podium I choose to sit on a step in the stalls next to a friend and former academic colleague I have not seen for a while.

On 17 June the newspapers print an image of me sitting on the step under the headline FLOORED! and accuse me of a lack of respect for parliament. Upon seeing a photo of me on the front page of the *Financial Times*, Norman Lamont emails me: 'Dear Yanis, I see you remain bloodied but unbowed. You looked tired but absolutely determined . . . And rightly so, let's hope for some light and reasonableness soon.' That same day I contact Ángel Gurría, secretary general of the OECD, seeking more help with my version of the reform agenda. Ángel replies that the OECD and his team are at my disposal.

The next day, 18 June, the Eurogroup meets. It is the troika's final onslaught.

Adults behaving badly

Christine Lagarde arrived at the Eurogroup meeting of 18 June fuming. At the meeting of our parliamentary party on 16 June, where I had sat on the floor, Alexis had claimed that the IMF bore 'criminal responsibility' for the situation in Greece. 'Hi, the criminal-in-chief is here,' said Christine sarcastically by way of greeting. My expression seemed to calm her down. 'I am not holding you responsible,' she said graciously.

The free-for-all against us was led by Mario Draghi. His was less a speech and more a recital of the numbers of euros that Greek depositors had withdrawn from their accounts during the past week: 'Monday, 358 million. Tuesday, 563 million. Wednesday, 856 million. Thursday, 1,080 million.'

Luis de Guindos later asked, 'Will the banks open tomorrow?'

The answer from Benoît Cœuré, Draghi's deputy, was, 'Yes, they will open tomorrow. But Monday?'

Nothing speeds up a bank run more effectively than a central banker reciting its progress while his deputy signals their intention not to intervene except perhaps by closing the banks in three days' time.

Months later, a whistle-blower from within the ECB let it be known that on 18 June, the very same day as the Eurogroup meeting, Mario Draghi commissioned an independent legal opinion from an outside law firm. The question he asked was whether the closure of Greece's banks was legal or not. The ECB has a large, competent and expensive legal department of its own. That Mario should choose to bypass it and go to a private firm suggests a certain queasiness about what he was about to do – shut Greece's banks.[2]

Meanwhile, Wolfgang's Eurogroup cheerleaders were taking pot shots not at Greece this time but at the troika – for being too lenient on us. Slovenia's finance minister chastised Lagarde and Moscovici for having watered down the original *MoU*, a criticism Christine and Pierre no doubt welcomed as evidence of their even-handedness towards us. Meanwhile Wolfgang reprised one of his favourite routines, demanding that no one şend him any amendments to the *MoU* in writing because he would then be obliged to take them to the Bundestag.

When my turn came, in addition to my usual review of the burning issues – reforms, debt swaps, the need for credible targets, a management plan for investment and non-performing loans, the reasons why the institutions' PowerPoint proposals made no financial, economic or political sense – I put forward one new proposal. Instead of quarrelling about the details of tax rates on the basis of unsafe models, I said, how about 'a deeper, more comprehensive, permanent reform? An automated hard deficit brake that is legislated and monitored by the independent fiscal council that we and the institutions have already agreed upon . . . Consider this to be a firm proposal that our government will implement immediately after an agreement.'[3]

If they had *any* interest in reaching an agreement with us, they ought to have jumped at my proposal. Michel Sapin made some encouraging noises. 'The institutions must take Yanis's proposal seriously. Yanis is right on this. He was right on investment too . . . Experts cannot resolve everything. The Eurogroup is a political forum. It should make its political contribution – even if the matter is elevated to a higher political level.' But from everyone else, I received the Swedish national anthem treatment.

When, later in the meeting, I expressed my astonishment that such a momentous proposal had been ignored, Jeroen killed the discussion with majestic authority: '[A]ny new proposals brought today must be looked at by the institutions. It is not for the Eurogroup to assess them.' In due course, my debt brake proposal was dropped by Chouliarakis and Sagias so as to appease Wieser and the Eurogroup Working Group.

At the post-Eurogroup press conference a Greek journalist asked Christine Lagarde whether she was happy that the rest of the Eurogroup had quashed the IMF's support for Greek debt relief. Christine pointedly ignored the question's substance and chose to vent her anger instead: 'For the moment we are short of a dialogue; the key emergency is to restore the dialogue with adults in the room.'

She was of course right. We needed adults in the Eurogroup, adults in Berlin and adults in Maximos. The problem was that there was a scarcity of adults in all three. However, the media reported Lagarde's words as an attack on me, providing an addition to the long list of epithets they had used to describe me thus far – 'adolescent'. The next time I saw Christine, I said, 'The press report that your we-need-adults-in-the-room comment referred to me.'

'Nonsense,' she replied amicably.

The next day, 19 June, I received a message from Gesine Schwan: 'I was moved by your speech at the Eurogroup.' By that stage I had learned my lesson: to get round the media's distortions and fend off future misreporting of my Eurogroup contributions, I was now posting my speeches on my website verbatim. 'Gabriel and the SPD must be mad not to see the merit in what you proposed,' she said. In my diary I wrote, 'If only Alexis had been moved too.' On Gabriel and the SPD, recalling my not-so-secret dinner with Jörg Asmussen and Jeromin Zettelmeyer in early February in Berlin, I scribbled, 'They are not mad. They simply seem to share Mrs Merkel's strategy not to touch the issue of debt restructuring.'

That night, back in Athens, Danae and I took a break to have dinner with a friend and his wife. Olga said something that hit a nerve: 'You seem to have lost this battle. From what you are telling me, Alexis wants to surrender. Encourage him to do so with some dignity. Tell the people that this battle has been lost.'

On 20 June, as Sagias and Chouliarakis continued their comical attempts to write the final SLA on the troika's behalf, I met Alexis in Maximos and offered him a piece of advice that was very different to anything I had ventured before. I told him that it was now clear to me that his mind was made up – that he wanted to surrender – and that while I disagreed with his decision with every sinew, as he knew, he was prime minister and must be the one to decide. 'However, whatever you decide, don't for goodness' sake mislead our people. Do not get them out onto the street, fire them up, only to deceive them afterwards. I hear you occasionally speak of a referendum. Don't do it unless you want to revive our original battle plan. If you want to surrender, surrender. But do it this way . . .' I handed him a single page with a draft of a short speech, an address to the nation to be read out on television

> Fellow Greeks. We have fought valiantly against an ironclad troika of creditors. We gave it our all. Alas, it is hard to argue with creditors who do not want their money back. We faced down the world's strongest institutions, the local oligarchy, powers much greater than ours. We have received no help from anyone. Some, like President Obama, had kind words for us. Others, like China, looked sympathetically towards us. But no one came forward to offer any tangible assistance against those who are determined to crush us. We are not giving up. Today I am signalling to you that we choose to live to fight another day. Tomorrow morning I shall accede to the troika's demands. But only because this war has many battles ahead. As of tomorrow, and after I yield to the troika's terms, my ministers and I will embark upon a pan-European tour to inform the peoples of Europe about what happened, to energize them and to invite them into a common struggle to end the rot and to reclaim Europe's democratic principles and traditions.

After reading it Alexis said in his now familiar dejected manner, 'I cannot admit to our people that I'm going to surrender.' His meaning was clear: he had indeed decided to surrender; he just could not bring himself to tell the people.

A special eurozone summit had been scheduled for Monday, 22 June in Brussels. At our cabinet meeting the day before I told my colleagues that we faced an historic choice between two clear options. One was to surrender, and I told them about the speech I had suggested Alexis make to the nation. The other option was to fight on. But if we did so, I warned them,

> As of Tuesday the ECB will attempt to close the banks and put in place capital controls. It only makes sense to go down that road if we mean to respond to their threat with ones of our own: that we shall respond to the ECB's aggressive move by deferring unilaterally the redemption of the

€27 billion of the ECB's SMP-era Greek government bonds to some distant future date; and that we shall activate the parallel payments system that I first introduced to you last February. If we are *not* prepared to respond this way, we should surrender tomorrow.

Before the eurozone summit, a Eurogroup meeting was held in preparation. In my speech I reviewed and defended the concessions Alexis had made without mentioning my strong disagreement with them and added a concrete proposal that would help reduce the new loans that would be required from the Eurogroup in the event that they were accepted.[4] Looking back, I am amazed at my loyalty to a cause I considered both lost and wrong. But I suppose I remained loyal not only because I had a duty to do so but because I knew that the troika was not interested in Alexis's concessions. They were determined to shut down the banks to make an example of him – at which point there was a slight chance, I thought, that he might shake off his acquiescence and bounce back.

The otherwise pointless Eurogroup meeting featured two interesting exchanges. At one point Wolfgang Schäuble attacked Pierre Moscovici for daring to make positive comments about Alexis's concessions before he had been given the green light to do so by the IMF or, indeed, by Berlin. When Pierre attempted to deny this, suggesting that the IMF had been tardy in giving its consent, Wolfgang blew his top. 'There have been positive comments by the commission . . . We are not idiots! You can play any game to blame the IMF. Without the full involvement of the IMF there is no way . . .'

Browbeaten, Pierre begged for mercy. 'It was never, never, never in the mind of the commission to blame the IMF,' he pleaded. 'Maybe we reacted faster but we work together.'

The second exchange was between Schäuble and Mario Draghi. Wolfgang demanded to know how much longer the ECB would provide emergency liquidity assistance to Greece's banks. Visibly angered, Mario responded, 'I understand that there is an interest in how long we provide ELA. I appreciate the interest in knowing how long we shall continue providing ELA. But you will want to appreciate that our independence is even more important. So, like I am asking you questions about fiscal policy, and I have to restrain myself from doing so, I would expect the same restraint from yourself.' For the rest of the meeting Wolfgang and Mario were clearly angry with one another.

Afterwards, Alexis and I met Donald Tusk, the Polish president of the EU Council. His message was stark: there should be no mention of debt relief in any meeting from then on. As we were leaving, I said to Alexis, 'Your duty is to mention nothing else, unless you want to fold – in which case do it quickly to end the agony.' His expression made it clear that he wanted to.

According to Euclid, who accompanied him to the eurozone summit that night, Alexis did everything in his power to surrender, but, as I had feared, Merkel would not allow him to. His concessions were dismissed as insufficient and he was told to return to the troika, conclude a further agreement with them and then pass that through another Eurogroup in two days' time.

On 23 June Sagias and Chouliarakis continued their pitiable redrafting of the troika's SLA, convinced that greater concessions would secure them a deal with the troika the following morning, which would be formally agreed in the Eurogroup meeting that afternoon. It was as if Faust were preparing to sell his soul to Mephistopheles, not realizing that Mephistopheles had no interest in buying. In the event there was no deal. All that these concessions bought Alexis was a proposal from the troika for a three-month extension of Greece's loan agreement, after which the creditors would come back for more – much more.

At the ensuing Eurogroup the gathered finance ministers were justifiably annoyed that they had been convened to no purpose. Jeroen Dijsselbloem undershot his own low standards by refusing to distribute the revised SLA that Alexis had tabled, distributing only the troika's proposed SLA instead. Taking advantage of everyone's fatigue, I suggested that the Eurogroup as a whole deserved a break from Greece, and that the proposed extension be increased by a further six months at least, until March 2016, so as to spare those involved these incessant meetings. Almost everyone seemed sympathetic to the proposal, which was a rare experience for me, but ultimately no one dared to support it. Two hours later we adjourned until the following day in the hope, which I did not harbour, that Alexis's team and the troika would reach an agreement overnight.

Back at the hotel, Alexis, Sagias, Dragasakis, Euclid, Pappas, Chouliarakis with some of his team and I gathered in a meeting room.

I had nothing to say. They all knew where I stood. Those who had been confident that significant concessions would lead to some kind of agreement were deflated. Instead, the Eurogroup had ended with an agreement that we would all meet up at 6 a.m. to resume work on our concessions. Leadership was needed. It was time for Alexis to show his strength, but he went to ground, announcing that he was tired and would be dining with Kammenos, our right-wing minister of defence.

As he left the room, Euclid and Dragasakis erupted into a huge row for reasons I did not catch, which ended with Euclid storming out. Dragasakis and Sagias then disappeared, leaving me behind with Chouliarakis and two of his aides. Perhaps it was sheer inertia that impelled them to continue work on the SLA. Whatever the reason, they were busily writing in yet more concessions. I took a look at what they were doing. 'There's no way that our MPs will vote for the elimination of the tiny "solidarity" benefit to pensioners on less than €200 a month,' I told them.

'There are MPs from other parties that will,' one of them replied.

There I had it: we were already counting on enlisting pro-troika opposition MPs. Operation Split Syriza was under way.

Euclid would not answer his phone or open his door. An hour later he texted me with apologies and a message that he could no longer stand 'their frivolity' and had needed to vent his frustration. Just after midnight, he texted me again: 'And needless to say the frivolity does not hold for us two.'

In my reply I said, 'I think that the best service we can offer Alexis now is to abstain. To stay in our hotel. Maybe he will realize that he needs to rethink his modus operandi.'

Obviously embarrassed, Euclid replied that they were all currently at the European Commission, being pressurized by the troika. 'I assumed you were in another car,' he texted. I told him that the finance minister had not been invited. Euclid said, 'I will insist they bring you in,' to which I replied, 'No need, Euclid. Not coming. It is clear that I am decorative. Can't legitimize that or them any more.'

Early next morning Euclid called me to say that the late-night talks had been another disaster but that we were about to meet them again. 'It's important that you come. Our side is very weak.' That night I had written what was, I think, a sixth draft of my resignation letter. I was planning to represent Greece at that day's Eurogroup meeting and then resign at the end of the press conference, citing my government's abandonment of debt restructuring, which to me was the A and the Z of our mandate, as the reason for stepping down. But for as long as I remained finance minister, I thought I might as well attend the pre-Eurogroup meeting as Euclid had suggested.

When we arrived at the commission, I was not invited to join Alexis, Dragasakis, Pappas and Chouliarakis in the meeting with Lagarde, Draghi, Juncker, Wieser and Dijsselbloem, but a few minutes later Alexis emerged to fetch me. As we were walking to the conference room, he told me, 'Euclid insisted you should come. I agreed even though Dijsselbloem will be annoyed to see you.' It appeared that Jeroen had been the one to veto my presence.

I was horrified by the dynamic in the room. The latest SLA the troika was proposing seemed designed to ensure that Alexis would be lynched on arrival back in Athens were he to accept it. It demanded, for example, that VAT on hotels should jump from 4 to 23 per cent; in the Turkish resorts on the coast opposite the holiday islands of Lesbos, Kos and Rhodes it was 7 per cent. Chouliarakis spoke little. When he did, he sounded uncannily like Wieser. Dragasakis was silent. Pappas, on the other hand, was spouting adolescent inanities. It was left to Alexis to address the troika like a supplicant.

Christine and Mario, meanwhile, were being allowed to get away with statements that held little water while Jeroen steered the meeting skilfully to another impasse. I made two interventions that exposed the incoherence of the troika's funding formula, but while Christine and Mario took some notice, it had become apparent to everyone that my role was indeed decorative. A few months later Alexis told a journalist in reference to this particular meeting, 'Yanis was good and said useful things but it was clear that he had no credibility in the room.'

Rekindled

Now that the Greek finance minister had been vanquished, my colleagues at the Eurogroup meeting of 25 June ought to have felt invincible, but it did not pan out that way. That afternoon I entered the meeting convinced it was my last, with my revised resignation letter ready in my pocket. Maybe the sense of relief it imparted, or maybe because I had nothing left to lose (Janice Joplin and Nikos Kazantzakis's definition of freedom), I gave what turned out to be quite an effective performance, driving a wedge between the troika institutions.[5]

The proceedings began with Jeroen informing us that no agreement had been reached. He then distributed the troika's final offer in the form of three documents: a full Staff Level Agreement (SLA) comprising the harshest austerity imaginable, full-on fire-sale privatizations and further losses of national sovereignty over key areas of public policy and property; a funding proposal that would take us only to November 2015, meaning that a fresh round of Eurogroup meetings would soon be required to extend it further; and a debt sustainability analysis. Remarkably, the IMF was refusing to endorse this last document. Moreover, for the first time ever Mario Draghi refrained from saying a word about funding. I sensed there was discord between and possibly within the institutions. And no wonder: the latter two documents were clearly built on sand and ready to be toppled by the slightest of touches.

For the first time in my Eurogroup career I decided to focus my attention not on the reforms being proposed but on questions of funding and debt sustainability.

I take it that the institutions want us to pass the austerity and reform measures. These are difficult decisions for an economy in recession. What are you offering us in return? Do you envisage that your reforms and funding proposals open up a clear path out of the debt–recessionary cycle? Is there a credible path for coming out of the woods? I cannot table at my parliament prior actions, like you can't, Wolfgang, table them at the Bundestag, without being able to answer the question: is this sustainable? Colleagues, no one in this room has had the courage to stand up and say that what the institutions are proposing is rendering Greece sustainable in the medium term. This should be of great concern to all of us – as Europeans. Here we have, after many meetings and months of negotiations, a proposal from the institutions that raises major concerns about the way we are running our monetary union. We should not be in a position where we throw our hands up in the air and we declare that we do not know how to stabilize a country like Greece for the medium term.

Christine Lagarde and Mario Draghi were not looking happy. Wolfgang Schäuble seemed livid. But I had only just got started. I now pointed out two technical problems. The first was that the troika's funding proposal went only as far as November 2015, 'But the IMF's programme continues until March 2016. Which means it is illegal for the IMF to continue with its programme since there is a funding gap between November 2015 and March 2016.' The IMF's rules are clear on this: it cannot lend to and participate in the reform of a country whose funding needs are not fully covered during the period of its contract with the IMF.

The second technical error also related to the funding proposal: 'From what I see here, it is proposed that the SMP bond redemptions in July and August, amounting to a total of €6.7 billion, will be taken out of the HFSF [Hellenic Financial Stability Facility] kitty of €10.9 billion . . . I submit to you, colleagues, that this is not something Wolfgang can pass through the Bundesbank.' Sensing the tension in the room, I proceeded to explain why.

I remind you that the €10.9 billion kitty of the HFSF was approved as part of the second bailout agreement for the purpose of recapitalizing Greece's weak banks. Suppose that we all turned a blind eye to this and agreed to cannibalize this kitty to repay the ECB this summer, as the institutions propose. What happens tomorrow or in the next few months if the ECB, in its role of our banks' supervisor, deems that Greece's banks need more capital? With the HFSF kitty gone, there will be no money to do it. When I asked Benoît Cœuré about this he replied that, if it came to this, then the HFSF kitty will be replenished by new loans from the ESM [European Stability Mechanism] – from your taxpayers, that is. And here lies the problem: for this to happen, Wolfgang's parliament, and other parliaments, will need to approve a third bailout, a third programme for Greece. But the whole point of the institutions' proposal was to extend the second bailout, a second programme, in order to *avoid* a third bailout, a third programme. But by cannibalizing the HFSF kitty to pay the ECB you are embedding a third into the second programme. This is both illegal and illogical. And the only alternative is to repay the ECB by allowing the Greek banks to buy €7 billion more of Greek government T-bills. I cannot propose this to my parliament. Can you, Wolfgang? And remember, colleagues, that we must answer these questions now. We do not have a right not to reach an agreement today.

After the previous night's discovery that Chouliarakis's team was plotting an alliance with the opposition, I had refused to have him at my side in the Eurogroup. Euclid, who had stepped in to replace him, now whispered in my ear, 'Impeccable!'

Wolfgang's intervention in response was a gift to me and a blow to the troika.

Are we being asked to agree that Greece will finance its obligations by the issue of T-bills in November to replace the monies from the EFSF buffer? Is this a joke? To replace the EFSF buffer by T-bills? Come on! . . . Looking at the debt sustainability analysis, you can see no hard analysis for a three-year programme. I must repeat myself: I cannot see a way out of the SMP problem in 2015 . . . And I would have to ask for all of those changes to be approved by parliament. Do you imagine that that would work? . . . I cannot imagine that I can convince my parliament.

As Wolfgang told the troika that its final offer to us was worthless, one that he could not take to his parliament, I whispered to Euclid, 'This is why I like this guy,' fully aware as I did so that our intelligence service would probably relay this back to Maximos as further evidence that I was Wolfgang's stooge.

The Slovenian minister, having missed the significance of Wolfgang's intervention, continued as if nothing had happened: 'The only thing we could do today,' he asserted, 'is to say to Greece, "Take it or leave it."' Malta's representative shared his concern that the concessions the troika was offering Greece were so lenient as to bring into doubt the

Eurogroup's credibility. A few others spoke too, but with Wolfgang opposing the commission and with Jeroen and Draghi silent, our opponents were backed into a corner.

Having requested the floor again, I turned to Christine Lagarde and asked, 'Is it the view of the IMF that Greece's debt is sustainable under the proposed agreement?' When her turn came to speak, Christine tried to avoid the issue but in the end conceded that Greece's public debt 'had to be looked at again'. I interjected that to my mind this meant that the SLA I was being pressured to accept lacked the IMF's seal of approval. Not only was it insufficiently comprehensive, it was unsustainable. Not only would it be impossible for Wolfgang to push it through the Bundestag, it was also in contravention of the IMF's internal guidelines.

Christine looked off-colour. It later transpired that the previous night the IMF had been pressured into withholding its latest sustainability analysis of Greece's debt. No doubt the reason was that, as the *New York Times* reported, 'having run the numbers, the fund now accepted the central argument being made by Mr Varoufakis: Greece was bankrupt and needed debt relief from Europe to survive.'[6] As I discovered a little later, the silencing of the IMF during the Eurogroup of 25 June had caused a rebellion at its Washington headquarters. People I know who work at the fund confirmed that 'things reached breaking point', and Christine's leadership was looking shaky.

Before Christine had a chance to respond, Wolfgang dived in once more. 'The institutions' paper is not acceptable to us,' he said. 'There can be no new money . . . We do not want to extend even by a month . . . There can be no new financing so they must rely on more growth.'

Despite Wolfgang's clear position, Jeroen continued to put pressure on me to accept the institutions' proposals. It was as if he had not heard Wolfgang at all. I admit that I was almost enjoying myself when I asked Jeroen, 'Does it mean that either we accept the institutions' document or else? Is it, as a colleague said, a "take-it-or-leave-it"? I'm asking because I need to convey this to my government.'

Looking frazzled, Jeroen replied in typical fashion: 'There needs to be an agreement. And if you want a take-it-or-leave-it approach, that's also possible. You can simply say yes. That is also an option. Seriously.' Perhaps seeing that he was not getting anywhere, Jeroen called for a short break.

'He will use it to concoct something against us,' I told Euclid, who nodded.

During the break, when I came back into the room Wolfgang gestured for me to join him. 'Sit down,' he said, offering me his deputy's chair. Our conversation lasted twenty-five minutes. Jeroen, who wanted to restart the meeting, did not dare to while Wolfgang was talking to me. Our chat was a direct extension of our earlier conversations.

SCHÄUBLE: I am very worried.

VAROUFAKIS: Me too.

SCHÄUBLE: I know. Europe is not going well.

VAROUFAKIS: Evidently.

SCHÄUBLE: I cannot see an agreement emerging here.

VAROUFAKIS: Nor do I. But is this not what you want?

SCHÄUBLE: No, I want a solution. I do not want an agreement that makes things worse in the future.

VAROUFAKIS: This is why we were elected, because that's what these *MoUs* and loans did. They extended the crisis into the future pretending to have resolved it.

SCHÄUBLE: I know, yes.

VAROUFAKIS: Tell me, Wolfgang, something: if you were me, would you take to your parliament what the institutions are pushing for? To raise VAT on hotels in Samos, Lesbos, Kos and Chios to 23 per cent when the Turkish rate, a stone's throw over the sea, is 7 per cent? Tourism is our only industry left standing. Would *you* do it?

SCHÄUBLE: If you do it you will have to answer to your people!

VAROUFAKIS: That's why I'm not doing it.

SCHÄUBLE: You are doing the right thing. You have to convince your prime minister about the things we talked about last time.

VAROUFAKIS: We've been through this, Wolfgang. You cannot ask me to say this. Not just because I do not think it is the best solution but primarily because of a certain lack of mandate on your part.

I was referring of course to the fact that Chancellor Merkel had explicitly quashed Wolfgang's idea of Greece taking a 'time out' from the eurozone.

Whatever Jeroen might have been planning during the break, watching Wolfgang and me talk amicably for so long must have put paid to it. After a neutral wrapping-up, the meeting was declared closed. Afterwards, the communiqué Jeroen put out ended with the sentence: 'Ministers invited the Greek authorities to accept the proposal by the institutions.' Nothing could have been further from the truth. The only way Jeroen could have got away with so false a statement was if it had the backing of someone more powerful than Schäuble, Draghi and Lagarde. The only person that could be was Chancellor Merkel.

Emergency exit

Early next morning, Friday, 26 June, Alexis gathered us all on the top floor of our hotel, which overlooked the centre of Brussels. Along with me were Dragasakis, Sagias, Euclid, Pappas, Stathakis, Chouliarakis and maybe one or two aides. Greater precautions than usual were taken to prevent eavesdropping before Alexis explained what would now happen. With no scope to reach an agreement, everyone apart from me and Euclid, who were required at another Eurogroup the following day, and Chouliarakis, who might be required for a Eurogroup Working Group, would go back to Athens. That night Alexis would convene the cabinet, where he would propose that the institutions' ultimatum be put to a referendum, to take place just over a week later, on Sunday, 5 July, in which we would advise our people to vote no.

'I want to make this very clear to all of you,' he said. 'I demand complete radio silence. It is crucial that no one finds out until we announce the referendum formally in Athens after the cabinet meeting. Do not talk to anyone – journalists, your wives on the phone and especially not to any troika people. OK?'

There was little discussion. We all recognized the enormity of what had been decided. I asked only one question: 'Are we calling this referendum to win it or to lose it?'

The only answer I got, and I believe it was an honest one, came from Dragasakis: 'We need an emergency exit.'

Like him, I was convinced that we would lose the referendum. In January the combined pro-government vote had only been 40 per cent, and we were now facing a whole week of closed banks and scare stories in the media before 5 July. But unlike me, Dragasakis wanted to lose so as to legitimize our acceptance of the troika's terms.

As everyone was leaving, I approached Chouliarakis to deliver a blunt message: 'You heard what the prime minister said. I know that you find it hard to keep away from your troika friends. If I find out that you have been talking to Wieser or Costello, I shall deal with you personally. OK?' Chouliarakis signalled he understood.

When I got back to my room, I took the resignation letter I had been planning to submit to Alexis that day, tore it up and put the pieces in the bin. Now we had a referendum to fight. If necessary, I would draft another letter in a little over a week's time. I then set about preparing my speech for the following day's Eurogroup meeting and drafting an official letter requesting a one-month extension of our loan agreement to allow the referendum to take place.

After several hours, I looked out of the window and realized it had got dark. I decided to step outside for some fresh air and something to eat. In the hotel lobby I bumped into Glenn Kim, slightly surprised that he was still in Brussels. Always happy to see Glenn, I invited him to join me. Immediately I sensed reluctance. 'I have a meeting to attend,' he said.

'Really?' I replied. 'Who with?'

'With Chouliarakis, Wieser and Costello.'

Over the past weeks, despite initial resistance from some within Syriza to Glenn's involvement in my team, Sagias had recognized his skills and enlisted his help in drafting their concessions to the troika. Embarrassing as Glenn's reply was for both of us, it was the presence of Wieser and Costello at this meeting that really disturbed me. I bade him goodnight, said nothing else and walked out into the street.

I then called Chouliarakis and calmly asked him what the meeting was about and whether I had failed to make myself clear earlier that day.

'It's no big deal,' he said. 'We're just meeting to exchange ideas.'

Without another word, I hung up and dialled Alexis's number. His secretary answered and told me that he was about to start the cabinet meeting. 'It is imperative that I speak to him,' I persisted. When Alexis came to the phone, I told him how Chouliarakis was disregarding his explicit instruction to avoid any contact with the troika.

For the first time ever, Alexis raised his voice at me. 'I've had enough of your animosity towards Chouliarakis,' he said. 'If you continue I shall have to put the phone down on you.'

Fed up and exasperated, I said, 'Go ahead! Put the phone down on me, Alexi!'

He did. Two minutes later he called me back to apologize, blaming his outburst on stress. 'As for Chouliarakis, it doesn't matter any more,' he added. 'Soon I shall be announcing the referendum.'

Over my solitary dinner I thought things over. However much I wanted to escape this cesspit, I had two jobs to do: first, see through the next day's Eurogroup and, second, return to Athens to ensure that the no campaign got the best possible support in the referendum. Alexis was issuing a call to arms. For the first time the Greek people would be given the opportunity to express their will. This was no time for introversion or squabbling.

On the morning of Saturday, 27 June, just before the Eurogroup, Euclid and I met Dijsselbloem, Wieser and Michel Sapin. Unsettled by the announcement of the referendum, they pushed me to have it cancelled. I explained the rationale that lay behind the decision: we did not feel we had a mandate from the people of Greece either to clash with our European partners or to sign an agreement that made no sense, not just to us but to the German finance minister, to another five finance ministers and indeed to the staff of the IMF. Jeroen then took me to task for the recommendation we were making to the Greek people when they came to cast their votes.

DIJSSELBLOEM: You recommend they say no.

VAROUFAKIS: The sovereign power is the electorate. It is not the government, not the minister. We get our marching orders from the electorate.

DIJSSELBLOEM: Political parties campaign . . .

VAROUFAKIS: Of course. And that is not the subject of this discussion. What we are going to campaign for is our business. What you need to know—

DIJSSELBLOEM: But it shows your intentions.

VAROUFAKIS: Your view of our intentions as politicians, Jeroen, is neither here nor there. Just like my views about your intentions as a politician are neither here nor there. It is between yourself and your electorate.

At that point Sapin objected that we would be asking the Greeks to vote against the tough parts of the deal, such as austerity, without acknowledging its advantages. I asked what advantages he was referring to. 'The debt measures, investment help and so on,' Sapin replied. Euclid pointed out that these had never been on the table, as our creditors had refused doggedly to put them there, and Jeroen stepped in again.

> DIJSSELBLOEM: Let us look at political feasibility. Build trust, and then even the toughest ministers after the summer will be prepared to discuss this. If they have gained some confidence that the programme will be back on track.
>
> VAROUFAKIS: I accept that. I understand that. But do you understand that confidence is a two-way process? That the Greek population does not have confidence in the Eurogroup to deliver this? The Eurogroup does not have confidence in Greek governments, but trust has broken down on both sides of the equation, Jeroen. You need something binding on the table and so do we.

The ensuing conversation did not get us much further, so I suggested we leave it for the time being and resume our discussions in the Eurogroup a few minutes later, with everyone present.

The Eurogroup does not exist!

The Eurogroup Meeting of Saturday, 27 June 2015 will not go down as a proud moment in European history. Our request that the Greek people be granted a brief window in which to decide whether to accept or reject the institutions' proposals was denied. As the extension of the loan agreement, which I had secured on 20 February, expired on 30 June, the rejection of our request for another extension meant that the ECB would be within its rights to refuse the Greek banks more liquidity via the Central Bank of Greece's ELA facility. In other words, the Greek banks would not reopen on Monday.

Interestingly, the idea that a government should consult its people on a problematic proposal put to it by the institutions met with incomprehension and was treated with a disdain that bordered on contempt. How could we expect normal people to understand such complex issues? I was asked by Italy's Pier Carlo Padoan.

'We are strong believers in the capacity of the people, of voters, to be active citizens,' I replied. 'And to make a considered analysis and take decisions responsibly concerning the future of their country. This is what democracy is all about.'

The fact that I had to make this point and the negative reaction to it from almost everyone in the room reflected badly on European democracy and its institutions.

After our request had been rejected, the Eurogroup president broke with EU tradition to make two extraordinary announcements. The first was that he would issue a communiqué without Greece's consent, violating the Eurogroup (and EU) convention that unanimity was required. The second was that, later that day, he would reconvene the Eurogroup without inviting Greece's representative in order to discuss the 'next steps'.

At that point I asked the secretariat, which sat at a table behind Dijsselbloem and Wieser, 'Is the Eurogroup president at liberty to issue communiqués when there is no unanimity and also to exclude finance ministers at will from Eurogroup meetings?' There was a short adjournment while some of them made phone calls and others consulted thick volumes.

After a while, Jeroen called us back to order and a member of the secretariat addressed me: 'Minister, the Eurogroup does not exist in law, as it is not part of any of the EU treaties. It is an informal group of the finance ministers of the eurozone member states. Thus there are no written rules about the way it conducts its business, and therefore its president is not legally bound.'

On my way out, as I was waiting for the lift I bumped into a worried-looking and unexpectedly friendly Mario Draghi. 'What on earth is Jeroen doing?' he said.

'Damaging Europe, Mario. Damaging Europe,' I replied.

He nodded, looking even more concerned. We took the lift down and then parted silently.

17

Lions led by donkeys

Back in Maximos that night, the war cabinet convened. As soon as Euclid and I entered the room, I reminded them of the agreement which they had repeatedly sworn to uphold: if the ECB were to close down our banks, we would respond by haircutting the SMP bonds owned by the ECB, activating the euro-denominated parallel payments system and announcing our intention to return the Central Bank of Greece to the full control of the Greek parliament. I told Alexis that the moment had now come; on Monday the banks would be closed. Would we now implement the countermeasures that we always said we would?

'We don't have to rush into them,' I said. 'Just signal them today. My proposal is that we announce today that we shall defer Draghi's SMP July and August repayments by a couple of years. Also, we can announce the activation of the parallel payments system for the week after the referendum. And the change in the law regarding our central bank for next month. That way we signal that we are not rolling over but also that we want to leave them an opening to come back to us with a decent proposal soon.'

Dragasakis spoke against my proposal with uncharacteristic energy and speed. He dismissed it as dangerous bluster, using a Greek word that denotes a lion's roar. 'I veto this,' he said 'I propose that we do not antagonize Draghi but proceed consensually with him.'

No one else spoke. Everyone was looking at Alexis. He walked over to the bay window; he was smoking a cigar – a relatively recent habit. After a few moments he turned towards me, took another moment and said, 'We will go with Dragasakis, Yani.'

I looked around the room to see that only Euclid was on my side. I was in a minority of two.

The discussion then moved on to the management of the greatest nightmare a finance minister can face in peacetime: the indefinite closure of the country's banks. It was essential, I argued, that we make clear who was responsible for this calamity. Ever since our election, we had bent over backwards, even accepting concessions that we knew to be impossible to implement, in order to keep the banks open; Stournaras and Draghi, in contrast, had done everything in their power to create and fuel the bank run that had precipitated the closure. We should not do them the favour, I argued, of letting ourselves be portrayed as the government that chose to deny its citizens access to their deposits. I therefore proposed that we let the banks open on Monday morning as usual, so that when the counters ran out of cash the managers would be forced to close down their branches themselves. At that point we should be outside, protesting with the people against the troika.

Naively, I had anticipated agreement. This time not even Euclid was on my side. If banks opened only then to run out of cash, it was argued, we risked civil disorder inside and outside the branches. There was something in this argument, but the risk, I thought, was grossly exaggerated and various measures could be taken to mitigate it, whereas failing to protest publicly against the bank closures and instead allowing them to be presented as our idea was a catastrophic political error. I told them that to close the banks by government decree would mean losing the blame game domestically, which meant defeat at the referendum.

It was as we were leaving Maximos that the realization hit me hard: this was, in fact, their intention. But it was not they who would take the blame; it would be me.

As we made our way out, Dragasakis approached me looking surprisingly friendly. 'Tomorrow you must convene the Council for Systemic Stability,' he said. 'I will not be able to come but I am sure you can handle it well.' The Council for Systemic Stability is a body that no finance minister ever wishes to convene. It only meets when the banks must be closed down in an emergency. From day one of our government, Dragasakis's office had issued a series of decrees that removed all powers over regulation of the banks from the finance ministry and placed them instead under his control as deputy prime minister. Now that the war cabinet had decided, at his behest and against my express opinion, that the government should convene the Council for Systemic Stability in order to shut down the banks, he would not even attend the meeting, let alone chair it. He was confident

I would swallow the poison he had handed me because my only alternative, being in a minority of one within the War Cabinet, would have been to resign as finance minister, and he knew that I would not contemplate doing so for fear of causing a rift among those who supported the no campaign. Unspeakably cowardly as it was, the strategy of making me convene the Council despite my passionate opposition to the idea worked. To this day sections of the Greece press refer to me as the man who closed the banks.

Alongside my own deputies, the members of the Council for Systemic Stability included Stournaras, his deputy at the Bank of Greece and the CEOs of Greece's commercial banks. I began the meeting with an explanation of how we had come to our current predicament. In my speech I made it clear that Stournaras was one of the driving forces behind the calamity. Stournaras did not seem to mind at all. In fact, he radiated happiness and was extremely friendly towards me.

That night, once the meeting was over, my team and I embarked on the gigantic job of devising a formula to determine how much cash the ATMs should release, working out what to do for the 85 per cent of pensioners who did not possess debit or ATM cards and deciding which imports to finance with the little liquidity that was left in our central bank. Like the Hydra's heads, new problems sprang up wherever one was dispatched. At 1.40 a.m. that Monday I received a text message from Stournaras: 'Dear Yani, thank you for the exquisite collaboration.' Knowing him well, I think the appreciation he conveyed was just as genuine as his evident glee at the success of his project to undermine our government, ever since Samaras appointed him to the governorship of the bank twelve months earlier.

For my part, the adrenalin coursing through my blood helped me fend off despair and work ceaselessly with my team until 9 a.m. Normally, this was when the banks opened; instead, our television screens were filled with scenes of endless queues at ATMs as the Greek people attempted to withdraw the sixty euros we had calculated was the most each account holder was allowed if we were to survive until the morning after the referendum on 5 July. It was at this point that I was informed that over the weekend, before the decree imposing limits on withdrawals had been announced, MPs had emptied the ATMs located in Parliament House five times over. I was scandalized that the people's representatives should abuse their access to Parliament

House's ATMs, which were evidently re-stocked more diligently than all others were. So when a Bloomberg correspondent asked me if I had lined up to withdraw some cash at an ATM, I replied that I had not had time but that in any case I did not think it appropriate. It was soon reported in the press that I, the man who had closed the banks, thought myself too important to queue up with the rest of the population.

Later that week I was interviewed for the *New Yorker* by a journalist to whom I had granted special access, including to our apartment and members of my family. During dinner with friends at which the journalist was present, I described the irony and the sheer pain of having to shut down the banks on behalf of a war cabinet that had turned against my strategy for keeping them open. 'I don't wish this fate on my worst enemy,' I said. Realizing that I had cast a depressing cloud over the party, I tried to brighten the mood a little and joked, with light-hearted self-pity, that a cruel screenwriter dramatizing these events would have had me say to Danae, 'Honey, I shut the banks' – a reference to the Hollywood film *Honey, I Shrunk the Kids*. The *New Yorker* piece featured that reference, to which the Greek media gave their own special spin: 'Varoufakis celebrated as he closed the banks, telling Danae, "Honey, I shut the banks!"'

My image and the distortions that were meant to destroy it are unimportant in themselves, except that, in tarnishing me, my enemies were damaging the no campaign and the brave people who took it upon themselves to save our collective dignity by supporting it. They were indeed lions led by donkeys. And the donkeys came in a variety of colours. I recall being approached in parliament by a Syriza MP, a member of the pro-Grexit Left Platform, who was displeased with me. This was hardly surprising given that he had spent months criticizing me for not implementing capital controls and not getting us out of the eurozone. What was surprising was the reason for his anger now that capital controls were in place: owing to the restrictions on wiring money abroad, he was now unable to pay the mortgage on his house in London. 'But you were in favour of the drachma and of capital controls,' I exclaimed. 'If I had done what you were imploring me to do, how would you be paying your London mortgage? In drachmas?' This was not the kind of leadership our people deserved.

Back at Maximos, I suggested that ministers should travel to all of Greece's major cities and islands to campaign for a no vote. Despite assurances that it would be done, nothing transpired. Instead, Pappas and Dragasakis's office were leaking fake stories about me to the press, while Wassily showed me evidence that my own ministry's Council of Economic Advisers, still chaired by Chouliarakis, was campaigning openly for yes. My greatest concern, though, was that the stance of the war cabinet prohibited me from explaining to the electorate what a no vote actually meant. It was essential, I thought, to make clear that a no vote would be an instruction to the government not to leave the eurozone but to hold firm in order to broker a new agreement within it – one that freed us from debtors' prison, recovered our dignity and ended the downward spiral. If Mario Draghi and Angela Merkel refused us this, a no vote meant haircutting the ECB's Greek bonds and starting a euro-denominated parallel payments system that would buy us and the creditors space and time to return from the brink of Grexit. And if Wolfgang's Grexit strategy were to prevail, the euro-denominated parallel payments system could potentially turn into the foundation of a new national currency.

If we spoke openly to voters and explained the strategy in full, I felt certain our hand would be strengthened because Draghi and Merkel would be forced to take notice and a proper compromise would surely be found. For as ECB Vice President Vítor Constâncio confessed in the autumn of 2015, the ECB would *never* carry through the threat of Grexit. But the majority view in the war cabinet prohibited me from saying any of this. The best I could do was to proclaim our determination not to play with Grexit but also not to fear it or buckle when threatened with it, and leave the rest for the voters to infer.

Occasional boosts to my spirits came from abroad. On the day the banks closed a good American friend sent yet another letter to Christine Lagarde, which his office copied to me. 'In my view,' wrote Bernie Sanders, 'the Greeks have every right to vote no in the referendum. By threatening to force Greece out of the euro, German Chancellor Angela Merkel, French President François Hollande and Italian Prime Minister Mateo Renzi are playing a dangerous game with the stability of the global financial system as well as the very fabric of European democracy.'

That same day, at a meeting in Maximos to discuss the plight of Greek pensioners, many of whom were distrustful of technology and preferred to visit the – now closed – banks in person to withdraw their pensions, Alexis looked at me happily. 'Juncker called to say that he accepts your debt swap proposals. You scoundrel, you got what you have been going on and on about for years. You got your debt restructuring. But the price Juncker is asking is that they crush us on social issues: VAT, islands, pharmacies, labour relations, privatization – they're demanding everything.' He showed me Juncker's non-paper and asked, 'Is this a basis for reopening the negotiations?'

I read it quickly. 'Yes, it is,' I said. 'It opens a new window to a sustainable future and puts the second bailout behind us.'

That was the last I heard of Juncker's proposal. Whether it was killed off directly by Merkel, who could now see that we had capitulated, or indirectly by Dragasakis, Sagias and Chouliarakis, who had given up on debt restructuring long before, I shall never know. What I did know was that, had we stuck to the strategy we had originally agreed, Brussels would have met us halfway.

But of all the moves made by politicians seeking to salvage Europe's honour during that week, the most interesting and genuine arrived as a text message on Black Sunday, the day before the banks shut down.

Macron's gesture

Emmanuel Macron, economy minister of France, texted me at around 6 p.m. on Sunday, 28 June to inform me that he was attempting to convince President Hollande and Sigmar Gabriel, Germany's social democratic vice chancellor, to find a solution. 'I do not want my generation to be the one responsible for Greece exiting Europe,' he said.

Less than a minute later I replied, 'But of course. Just know that we need an agreement that offers respite for the long run and a prospect that this situation will not be repeated in a few months.'

Emmanuel agreed. He would talk to his president and get back to me. 'Sustainable solution is key, I agree with you,' he said, proposing that he travel to Athens the next day, incognito, to have dinner with me and Alexis and to hammer out a deal between Athens, Berlin and Paris.

After midnight, while we were in the thick of preparations for the bank closures, Emmanuel wrote again to inform me that President Hollande was planning to issue a statement in the morning announcing the reopening of negotiations. 'Would Alexis agree to go to Paris on

Monday evening or Tuesday morning?' he asked. I implored him to come to Athens himself instead. With the situation in Greece so volatile, Alexis could not leave the country for open-ended talks.

'OK,' Emmanuel said. 'I am ready, and I am sure that Alexis, you and me could find a deal . . . I will convince the president tomorrow. We have to succeed!'

Deeply appreciative, I texted him: 'I always felt that you and I could see eye to eye. The difficulty will be to find a solution that is viable for us and acceptable to Wolfgang.'

On Monday, 29 June, the day he was meant to come to Athens, Emmanuel called, asking for a favour: could Alexis contact President Hollande to let him know that he was ready and willing to receive Emmanuel in Athens as the French president's emissary? I called Alexis, explained the opportunity that was being presented to us, and he agreed. An hour later, however, Alexis called me back, understandably cross. 'What's going on? Hollande's office replied that they have no idea about a possible mission by Macron to Athens. They referred us to Michel Sapin. Is he pulling your leg?'

When I relayed this exchange to Emmanuel, his explanation shocked me. 'The people around Hollande do not want me to come to Athens. They are closer to the Berlin Chancellery than to our government. They clearly blocked Alexis's approach. But let me have his personal mobile phone number. I shall go to the Élysée personally in an hour to speak with him [Hollande] and ask him to call Alexis directly.'

Some hours passed, but Hollande never called Alexis. So I texted Emmanuel: 'Do I take it there has been no progress? And that your trip has been cancelled?'

A dejected Macron confirmed that he had been blocked by his president and the president's entourage. 'I will push again to help you, Yanis, believe me,' he promised. I believed him, and of course I understood exactly how he felt.

Three months after my resignation, in October, Emmanuel invited me to visit him at his ministerial office even though I was not in government any more. He told me that at a summit meeting before his failed attempt to mediate with Alexis he had used my line that the troika's deal for Greece was a modern-day version of the Versailles Treaty. Merkel had heard him and, according to Emmanuel, ordered Hollande to keep Macron out of the Greek negotiations. Merkel's spell was every bit as powerful as I had imagined.

A very Greek farce

It is both absurd and lethal for a finance ministry to lack the support of its central bank. One of the absurdities during that awful week, as we struggled to make very little liquidity last as long as possible, was that I did not even know how much liquidity there was in the system. But the fact that the Bank of Greece was headed by the governor who had started the bank run and who was plainly ecstatic the night the banks closed made me suspect it was under-reporting the amount of available cash.

After performing some research, to which Jeff Sachs contributed, I discovered an interesting if unusable piece of information: not only was there more liquidity in the system than the Bank of Greece was reporting, there was also €16 billion of ECB-owned cash stashed in the vaults of its branches around the country. It was there as a consequence of the previous cash crisis, which had taken place in the summer of 2012, when the ECB had organized hundreds of cargo flights into Athens from Frankfurt in order to keep Greece's ATMs stocked with banknotes. To prevent the need for another airlift, the ECB had been building up cash reserves in Greece, just in case.

That day, on my daily visit to Maximos, I found Alexis in his office entertaining Alekos Flabouraris, a minister without portfolio in the government and something of a father figure to him. As usual, I briefed the prime minister on everything of consequence that day, primarily the rate at which cash was leaking out of the ATMs. I also mentioned the €16 billion stash.

Alexis's eyes lit up. 'What? There is €16 billion in cash lying around and we are not using it to stuff the ATMs and make them function normally?'

I explained that we could not touch the money. Confiscating it would be theft. 'But, Yani,' protested Alexis, 'if my child is starving, and I have no money, I have a moral right to steal a milk carton. Is this not similar here?'

'Since when did theft become part of the Left's arsenal?' I asked.

Flabouraris leaped to his protégé's defence. 'We have *every* right,' he bellowed, 'to get that money to stop the people's suffering.'

As the conversation unfolded, another minister joined us, Panagiotis Lafazanis, the leader of the Left Platform, a declared enemy of the eurozone and a passionate Grexiteer. He asked what was going on.

Alexis and Flabouraris informed him that I had discovered €16 billion in cash. Flabouraris told Lafazanis that he and Alexis, unlike me, believed the situation justified our tapping into this cash, currently languishing in state-owned vaults. I tried to calm them down and, in view of Lafazanis's pro-Grexit position, to explain what our real options were.

If we wanted to stay in the eurozone, I told them, we could not possibly confiscate the ECB's money. If, on the other hand, we wanted Grexit, then there was something useful we could do with the cash without being branded thieves: we could nationalize the €16 billion, stamp the notes with special ink to invalidate them as euros and rebrand them as new drachmas, put them in the ATMs and use them as a new currency. We would have to apologize to Mario Draghi, explain that we were in a national emergency and ask him to tell us what the paper value of his €16 billion cash was so that we could compensate him.

I also reiterated my own view, which was that we should do none of this but instead activate the electronic parallel payments system that I had been preparing. This would extend our fiscal space within the euro even if we did ultimately reach a good agreement with the troika, and if there was no agreement, it would buy us time or, in the most extreme scenario of Grexit, serve as the foundation of a new digital national currency.

Naturally Lafazanis liked the idea of using Draghi's €16 billion as the foundation for a new drachma and agreed, were we to do so, that the ECB should be compensated for the production costs of the bills. But as he lacked the power to persuade Alexis to pursue Grexit, the idea was academic. As for Alexis, he soon forgot about the €16 billion but continued to block the activation of my parallel payments system, holding to Dragasakis's veto of a few days before.

Months later, a conservative pro-troika newspaper published as fact the false and libellous rumour that Lafazanis had planned to storm the Bank of Greece's vaults, arrest Stournaras and steal the cash. Some of the reports even portrayed me as a party to this conspiracy. Its purpose was clear: vilify anyone who had sincerely supported the no campaign in order to present Alexis, by contrast, as a sensible man who at the last moment saw the light and saved Greece from rogues in his own party. The fact that it was Alexis and Flabouraris who had momentarily toyed with the idea of storming the Bank of Greece's vaults never reached the public's attention.

Gazing into an abyss: comrades in retrospect

'If thou gaze long into an abyss, the abyss will also gaze into thee.' Nietzsche's disturbing dictum captures what it was like to peer into my comrades' souls. After an academic career in which success largely depended on my own efforts, I had found myself on the front line of a war, depending on comrades to guard my flanks and rear. Deciphering their thinking in order to gauge whether they had my back or not was the hardest thing I had to do.

Friends and critics criticize me for having seen things in Alexis that were not there. I think they are wrong. His desire to liberate Greece from its vicious cycle was there. His intelligence and capacity to learn quickly were self-evident. His enthusiasm for the deterrent I had proposed and the debt relief I was prioritizing was real. His appreciation of what I brought to his team was genuine. When he had instructed me, in front of our cabinet, to fly to Washington to tell Christine Lagarde we were going to default, the enthusiasm had been authentic. The reason I had seen all these things in him was that they were there. My mistake was to miss other things that were bundled up with them: his back-up plan, which would inevitably annul my work; his frivolity; his tendency to melancholy; and lastly his intense desire to prove to a sceptical world that he was no shooting star. When he instructed me, on our first day in office, to remain ready to hand over the keys of our offices to the opposition rather than capitulate, he was not lying. The part of him telling me that was speaking the truth. This is why I was brought to tears by his words. This is why I believed him.

I believed him also, despite his distressing U-turns, because of the inhuman pressure he was under. During that first week of July, with the banks closed and while I was giving everything I had in the campaign for a no vote, I presented him with the final version of Plan X – the contingency plan that he had asked me to compile in case Grexit was forced upon us. As I was handing it over, he asked me, 'Is it doable?'

I answered him honestly: 'Read it and weep.' The transition to a new drachma would be so painful as to be debilitating. Plan X outlined the pain, blow by blow. As he sank into his seat, I reminded him that Plan X was there to have but not to use, unless Schäuble got his way with Merkel. But I did recommend that we activate immediately the euro-denominated parallel payments system, which was the opposite of Plan X: a system that would allow us, in the event of a no vote at the referendum, to stay in the eurozone long enough for Merkel and Draghi to have the chance to come back to us – as Juncker had done already – with an agreement that included our minimum demands of debt relief and an end to self-reinforcing austerity.

Alexis looked at me serenely and asked, 'What are the chances that they will come back to us with something decent, Yani?'

At that critical juncture in our country's history I was obliged to answer with the greatest possible precision. I told him that the probability they would do so was 100 per cent *if they acted rationally*. But, I warned, as Dan Ellsberg, the great American economist and Pentagon strategist turned pacifist whistle-blower, had emailed me a few weeks before, 'Keep in mind that the ruling class can be self-destructively mad; not just pretending!'

'Powerful European leaders have a track record of being bad at serving their interests, of falling prey to irrational urges,' I said. And given that irrationality breeds unpredictability, I estimated that a more sensible probability – that Chancellor Merkel would opt for the mutually assured damage of Grexit rather than a mutually advantageous deal – was around fifty-fifty.[1]

Watching him buckle under the pressure of that probability made me want to forgive, legitimize and rationalize his unforgivable, unethical and irrational slip-ups. There were many of these, but two above all: his retreat from our firm agreement, on which we had based our original strategy, that a continuation of the nation's insolvency through a new bailout would be worse than Grexit, however painful Grexit might be; and his rejection of my plea to address the nation with the dignified surrender speech I had prepared for him, instead of organizing a referendum that he secretly hoped to lose.

During the referendum campaign I issued a statement to the press that if yes were to win I would resign. 'As a democrat,' I said, 'I shall respect the people's choice to have their government accept the creditors' terms. But, at the same time, I have no obligation to sign and implement that agreement myself. If yes wins, I shall resign and let my successor do it.' The fact that none of my government colleagues, Alexis and Euclid included, committed themselves to doing the same told me everything I needed to know. In essence, the difference between my Syriza comrades and me was that I concentrated all my strategizing against the troika. In contrast, after that cruel day, 27 April, when Alexis decided to burn Theocarakis and sideline me, even as I was attempting to persuade him that neutralizing his finance minister in the face of the ruthless Eurogroup and the formidable forces of Merkel–Schäuble was self-defeating, he was busily strategizing how best to sacrifice me.

If there was callousness in Alexis, I did not discern it. I think its apparent absence was due to his capacity to do something that I believe the rest of his entourage could not: reflect upon himself. I remember one May afternoon when we were in his office at Parliament House, well after he and I had clashed over the concessions he was making to the troika. Before I had the chance to challenge him on whatever doomed tactic he was currently proposing, he told me, 'I was reading an article by Stavros Lygeros [a political commentator] just now. The rascal has me all sized up. He likened my situation to swordfish fishing. I have taken the hook but I am too strong for them to pull me out of the water. So they bide their time. They pull me in for a while and then give me more line. Then they pull me back in. And they will carry on doing this until I am exhausted. Once they sense my weakness, they will they pull me out in one violent move.'

The others, like Dragasakis and Chouliarakis, could never have fooled me. I would never have believed their subterfuges nor joined any cause they espoused. With Alexis it was different. He had to talk himself into crossing his own red lines, which is the opposite of never having the intention of keeping to them. I can imagine Alexis saying to himself, like Shakespeare's Richard III, 'And therefore, since I cannot prove a lover, / To entertain these fair well-spoken days, / I am determined to prove a villain', except instead of 'lover' it would be 'insurgent', and instead of 'villain' it would be 'insider'. Alexis's actions were not banal, to adopt Hannah Arendt's sense of the word; he struggled hard to reconcile himself to them and to find peace. It was, I am convinced, that inner voice of his that was both his strength and his downfall, both the usurper of our common project and the reason why I believed him almost to the bitter end.

The puzzlement Alexis's inner voice caused me was compounded by my friend Euclid – a rare hybrid: an academic from a milieu close to mine but also a party apparatchik. Euclid and I met in the English language, to borrow another of Arendt's phrases.[2] We shared the same jokes, the same cultural references, the same radical Europeanism, the same understanding of 'Blighty'. He liked to pretend that he was politically to my left, acting as my left-wing conscience whose job was to pull me into line and prevent me from drifting into bourgeois tendencies and suspect friendships, such as with Norman Lamont, something I enjoyed letting him do. His dislike and scorn for Alexis and Pappas, which were reciprocated by them, coupled with the fact that I had had to fight hard to have him included in the cabinet, made me feel safe in his company.

When Alexis broke with me on 27 April under Merkel and Dijsselbloem's pressure, he told the world that Euclid was the newly appointed coordinator of our negotiating team. The media relayed the news around the globe and heralded Euclid as our chief negotiator. Of course, neither he nor I had any real influence over the timeline of concessions Alexis was making. When Euclid found out about Alexis's surrender to new austerity – the acceptance of a decade of 3.5 per cent budget surplus targets – he was just as shocked and livid as I had been. Until the end we frequently found ourselves at Maximos or in some Brussels room, staring at each other in bewilderment while Sagias and Chouliarakis edited drafts of the SLA, wondering what our role was. A sort of gallows humour developed between us: I would ask him what on earth was going on, and he would answer, 'Are you confusing me with someone in the know?'

However, we differed in a crucial respect: Euclid was a Syriza functionary, and I was not. By appearing to perform his allotted role as chief negotiator and thereby allowing the world to think that any kind of negotiation was actually taking place, he lent the hideous negotiation process legitimacy. I clung on in the hope that after a rupture Alexis would require my expertise with the parallel payments system and debt restructuring while determined to resign the moment it became clear that I would be asked to sign an unsustainable agreement. Lulled by the assumption that Euclid and I were of one mind, that we were somehow interchangeable, I failed to foresee quite what being interchangeable would lead to – that Euclid would ultimately become the person used by the establishment to sign the loan agreement, which they knew I never would sign.

Until the referendum I did not see that this could happen, even though I had noticed two incongruities which should have alerted me. The first was that when just the two of us were talking, Euclid would be magnificently witty and accurate in his disparagement of the rest of the war cabinet, Chouliarakis and Alexis in particular, but during war cabinet meetings his interventions were meek, verbose and unrecognizable as views that supported mine. Frequently he would not back me up at all. The second was that in our private exchanges he would habitually agree with my assessment of the day's events, but when I proposed that we react before it was too late, he would advise me to bide my time and warn against developing a bunker mentality. One day I had had enough. 'When in a bunker,' I said emphatically, 'a bunker mentality may be helpful. Given that they *are* trying to get me, it is *not* paranoia to think that they are trying to get me!'

After it was all over it took me some time to diagnose the cause of my failure to read my two comrades: Alexis's inner dialogue and Euclid's hybridity had blocked my sensors very effectively. It took the referendum outcome and their sudden metamorphosis to unblock them. It was a transformation portrayed by Syriza's ideologues as true radicals behaving truly responsibly, but to me it is best summed up by the ending of George Orwell's *Nineteen Eighty-Four*.

> He was not running or cheering any longer . . . He was in the public dock, confessing everything, implicating everybody . . . The long-hoped-for bullet was entering his brain . . . O cruel, needless misunderstanding! O stubborn, self-willed exile from the loving breast! Two gin-scented tears trickled down from the sides of his nose. But it was all right, everything was all right, the struggle was finished. He won the victory over himself. He loved Big Brother.

Square of hope and glory

On the afternoon of Friday, 3 June, as the working day drew to a close, I breathed a sigh of relief. A week of closed banks was almost over. Despite the long queues at ATMs and the uncertainty of what awaited us the following Monday, there had been no violence, no panic, no civil unrest. The Greeks had proved themselves a sensible people.

The media, however, had managed to fall below their already absurdly debased standards, competing with one another to find the most innovative ways to frighten the public away from voting no. Much of the reporting of the no sponsors and supporters would in other countries have been deemed incitement to violence. The opinion polls consistently predicted that yes would win with more than 60 per cent of the vote, while comment writers foamed at the mouth at the government's audacity in holding a referendum against the creditors' wishes. Meanwhile, the parliamentary opposition had managed to persuade its supporters to take to the streets in some numbers, waving EU flags and placards proclaiming, WE ARE STAYING IN EUROPE![3]

Later that Friday afternoon I received an email from Klaus Regling, the managing director of the European Stability Mechanism, the eurozone's bailout fund. It was a reminder that he had the legal right to demand from me full and immediate repayment of the €146.3 billion lent to Greece as part of the first two bailouts. It was phrased in such a way as to suggest that I was personally liable, not least because as finance minister my name was on the loan agreement. It was too good an opportunity to pass up. I instructed my office to reply to our main creditor – to the man who had advised me to default to my pensioners instead of the IMF – with two ancient words. These were the defiant response of the king of Sparta, leader of the three hundred men who attempted to resist the entire Persian army at the legendary battle of Thermopylae in 480 BC, when instructed by the enemy to throw down their weapons: 'Μολών λαβέ' – 'Come and get them!'

That evening two rallies took place, one in favour of yes, outside the ancient Olympic stadium where the first modern Olympics were staged in 1896, and one at Syntagma Square for the no campaign. The yes rally was held in the late afternoon, and was large and good-natured, but the no rally at Syntagma was one for the ages. Since I was a boy, I had attended some magnificent, life-changing rallies at Syntagma Square, but what Danae and I participated in that night was unprecedented.

We walked to Syntagma from Maximos with Alexis and other members of the cabinet, their partners and aides. On the way we were mobbed by rapturous supporters. As we approached the square, the crowd's energy exploded. A sea of five hundred thousand bodies consumed us. We were pulled into its depths by a forest of arms: tough-looking men with moist eyes, middle-aged women with determination written all over their faces, young boys and girls with boundless energy, older people eager to hug us and shower us with good wishes. For two hours, struggling to hold hands so as not to be separated, Danae and I were absorbed by a single body of people who had simply had enough.

People from different generations saw their distinct struggles coalesce on that night into one gigantic celebration of freedom from fear. An elderly partisan from the Second World War pushed into my pocket a carnation and a piece of paper bearing the phrase 'Resistance is NEVER futile!' Students forced to emigrate by the crisis who had returned to cast their votes begged me not to give up. A pensioner promised me that he and his sick wife did not mind losing their pensions as long as they recovered their dignity. And everybody, without a single exception, shouted at me, 'No surrender, whatever the cost!'

I believed they meant it. The banks had already been closed for a week. The hardship imposed by the creditors was plainly visible. And yet, here they were, these magnificent people saying in one word everything that had to be said: 'No!' Not because they were recalcitrant or Eurosceptic. They craved the opportunity to say a big fat yes to Europe. But yes to a Europe *for* its people, as opposed to a Europe hell-bent on crushing them.

That night, as Danae and I eventually found ourselves walking up the marble steps leading to parliament, the phrase I had been looking for to describe what all this was about finally came to me: constructive disobedience. This was what I had been trying to practise in the Eurogroup all along: putting forward mild, moderate, sensible proposals, but when the deep establishment refused even to engage in negotiation, to disobey their commands and say no. The war cabinet had never understood this, but the body of humanity that filled Syntagma Square that night surely did.

One for true believers

That night the months of frustration, each terrible moment in Maximos, every disappointment along the way, all the nastiness and the stress had been wiped away, leaving nothing but contentment, and yet I was still not convinced that the no campaign would win the referendum. The demonstration suggested support for the cause had risen, but with the banks closed and the media screaming blue murder at anyone who even contemplated voting no, success looked unlikely.

Over dinner with Danae, Jamie and some other friends at an outdoor restaurant in the neighbourhood of Plaka, I was asked if Alexis and Euclid would resign were yes to win. 'Alexis will form a coalition government with the opposition,' I predicted, 'after most of the true believers resign or are pushed.' And I would be long gone by then, I said. But Jamie insisted I was wrong. No would win, he believed, and my leverage with Alexis would skyrocket, as I would have played a large part in delivering the result. Unconvinced, I nonetheless raised my glass to toast Jamie's optimism. '¡Hasta la victoria siempre!' he said with an intense and committed look – 'To victory, always!'

On the day of the referendum I drove to Palaio Phaliro, the southern Athenian suburb where I grew up and where my father still lives. Together we made our way to the polling station. Inside, the majority of voters were ebullient when they saw me, except for one or two who remonstrated angrily with me that I had closed down the banks. With the television cameras rolling, I told one angry man that the troika had given us an ultimatum and that accepting it would shape his and his children's future. What we had done was to give him the opportunity to vote for or against it. 'Vote yes if you think it is a manageable deal. We are the only government that have respected your right to decide. The fact that the troika decided to close the banks down before you got the chance to express yourself is something that only you can interpret.'

After voting, as I was helping my father back to the car, an elderly woman approached me, surrounded by the usual television cameras. She asked me sternly if I knew where she lived. I admitted I didn't. 'I sleep in an orphanage here in Palaio Phaliro. And do you know why they let me? Because your mother worked tirelessly to let vagrants like me have a permanent shelter.' I thanked her for her spontaneous and wonderful memory of my mother.[4] But she was not finished. 'I bless her every day. But do these bastards know this?' she said pointing at the cameras and the TV crews. 'I bet they don't and they don't even care.'

'It doesn't matter,' I assured her. Even if they didn't, it was enough that she knew. Nonetheless, I was upset when on the evening news our heart-warming encounter was presented as me being accosted by a homeless woman blaming me for her destitution.

It was not until late that afternoon that I began to sense an historic victory might be on the cards. At my office I composed a piece, in English, for my blog. 'In 1967,' I wrote, 'foreign powers, in cahoots with local stooges, used tanks to overthrow Greek democracy. In 2015 foreign powers tried to do the same by using the banks. But they came up against an insanely brave people who refused to submit to fear. For five months, our government raged against the dying of the light. Today, we are calling upon all Europeans to rage with us so that the flickering light does not dim anywhere, from Athens to Dublin, from Helsinki to Lisbon.'

By 8 p.m. I could see from the drooping shoulders and morose expressions of TV presenters that we had won. What I did not yet know was the extent of our victory. My fear was that a close shave would give Alexis the excuse to say we had a divided nation and thus insufficient support for a rupture with the troika. I told my team that the magic number was 55 per cent. If the votes for no were any greater, Alexis would have to honour the result. I thought carefully of what I would say to the journalists gathered in my ministry's press room in order to give him the necessary impetus to do so. By 9 p.m. I had written my speech. Traditionally, ministers wait for the prime minister to make his statement before issuing their own, so I waited in my office for Alexis to address the press at Maximos.

At 9.30 I began to feel something was wrong. The results were more or less final, indicating that the 55 per cent mark had been reached, but Alexis was still holed up in his office. My chief of staff was pressurizing me to go to our press room as the journalists were getting agitated and were beginning to tweet that something sinister was afoot. I waited until after 10.00 p.m. I called Alexis. He did not pick up, and nor did a secretary. Wassily walked in to inform me that other ministers were beginning to speak to the media, issuing luke-warm statements in response to what was in reality an earth-shattering outcome. I could not allow this to continue. Our voters deserved a proper response.

So at around 10.30 I headed for the press room to make my state-ment, intending to go to Maximos straight afterwards to discover what was going on there. As I read out my prepared statement I had the very strong feeling that it would be my last as a minister. That feeling, combined with the memory of Syntagma Square two nights earlier, made me read it defiantly, brazenly even.

On 25 January dignity was restored to the people of Greece. In the five months that has intervened since then, we became the first government that dared raise its voice, speaking on behalf of the people, saying no to the damaging irrationality of our extend-and-pretend bailout programme. We confined the troika to its Brussels lair; articulated, for the first time in the Eurogroup, a sophisticated economic argument to which there was no credible response; internationalized Greece's humanitarian crisis and its roots in intentionally recessionary policies; spread hope beyond Greece's borders that democracy can breathe within a monetary union hitherto dominated by fear.

Ending interminable self-defeating austerity and restructuring Greece's public debt were our two targets. But these two were also our creditors' targets. From the moment our election seemed likely, the powers that be started a bank run and planned, eventually, to shut Greece's banks down. Their purpose? To humiliate our government by forcing us to succumb to stringent austerity. And to drag us into an agreement that offers no firm commitments to a sensible, well-defined debt restructure.

The ultimatum of 25 June was the means by which they planned to achieve these aims. The people of Greece today returned this ultimatum to its senders, despite the fear-mongering that the domestic oligarchic media transmitted night and day into their homes.

Our no is a majestic, big yes to a democratic Europe. It is a no to the dystopic vision of a eurozone that functions like an iron cage for its peoples. But it is a loud yes to the vision of a eurozone offering the prospect of social justice with shared prosperity for all Europeans.

As I stepped out into Syntagma Square I saw delight in the faces around me. A proud people had been vindicated and were justly celebrating. The night air was full of anticipation and confidence. Alexis's silence filled me with apprehension, but I refused to believe that Maximos was sealed off from that intoxicating air of defiance. Surely, I thought, it had found its way in through some crack in the walls or through the hearts of the people working there who had also learned their politics at Syntagma Square. And yet, as I walked in, Maximos felt as cold as a morgue, as joyful as a cemetery.

The overthrowing of a people

In Maximos the ministers and functionaries I encountered looked numb, uncomfortable in my presence, as if they had just suffered a major electoral defeat. Alexis was with the president in the adjacent presidential palace and would see me later, his secretary informed me, so I waited in the conference room with other ministers, watching as the last results were declared on television. When the final number flashed up on the screen, 61.31 per cent for no in a turnout of 62.5 per cent, I jumped up and punched the air, only to realize that I was the only one in the room celebrating.[5]

As I sat waiting for Alexis, I found a message on my phone from Norman Lamont: 'Dear Yanis, congratulations. A famous victory. Surely they will listen now. Good luck!' They would listen, I thought, but only if we were prepared to speak up. Sitting there, I began noticing things about the people around me that had previously escaped me. The men had shed the rough Syriza look and resembled accountants. The women were dressed as if for a state gala. When Danae joined me, I realized that not only were we the only happy people in the place but the only ones in jeans and T-shirts. It felt a little like being in one of those sci-fi movies in which body-snatching aliens have quietly taken over.

Eventually Alexis arrived and, half an hour later, addressed the nation on television. Two key phrases in his speech unlocked the vault of his intentions. One ruled out a rupture with the troika; the other was his announcement that he had just asked the president to convene immediately a council of political leaders. On the morning after their decisive defeat, the pro-troika leaders of the *ancien régime* were being summoned to join him at the discussion table. 'He is splitting Syriza and preparing a coalition with the opposition to push the troika's new bailout through,' I told Danae. I waited another hour and a half as he held separate meetings with Sagias and Roubatis before he would receive me.

It was after 1.30 a.m. when I entered his office. Alexis stared at me and said we had messed up badly.[6]

'I don't see it that way,' I replied flatly. 'There were plenty of mistakes, but on the night of such a triumph we have a duty to rejoice and honour the result.'

Alexis asked me if I minded Dimitris Tzanakopoulos, the Maximos legal adviser, sitting in on our meeting.

'Sure,' I replied. 'In fact I want him here as a witness.' This was not going to be just another chat.

Alexis asked if the banks would open soon. It was a trick question. He was looking to justify his decision to capitulate. I pretended not to understand, saying that to honour the no vote we had immediately to start issuing electronic IOUs backed by future taxes and to haircut Draghi's SMP bonds. 'Without these moves to bolster your bargaining power,' I said, 'the 61.3 per cent will be scattered in the winds. But if we announce this tonight, with 61.3 per cent of voters backing us, I can assure you that Draghi and Merkel will come to the table very quickly with a decent deal. Then the banks will open the next day. If you *don't* make this announcement, they will steamroller you.' I explained that I needed only a couple of days to activate this system using the tax office's website.

He pretended to be impressed, so I continued.

'This 61.3 per cent result is a capital asset that you must use well. You must manage it with greater respect to the people out there than you showed before the referendum. You must respect yourself more too. After tonight you have a simple choice. Either you reactivate our plan, giving me the tools I need, or you surrender.'

We talked for a long time. We reviewed the previous months, weeks and days. I took no prisoners, giving a litany of his errors, pointing out the ways in which members of the war cabinet had jeopardized our struggle, often in collaboration with the troika and its operatives. I shared with him evidence of one of them behaving in a way that bordered on corruption.

Looking surprised, Alexis asked Dimitris: was the person I referred to such a problem? Dimitris answered, 'Yes, even more so.'

The conversation was meandering, so I decided to put it to him straight: would he honour the no vote, I asked, by going back to our original covenant, or was he about to throw in the towel?

His answer was elliptical, but there was no mistaking the direction in which it headed: towards unconditional surrender. The first time in that conversation that he spoke decisively was when he said, 'Look, Yani, you are the only one whose predictions were confirmed. But here is the problem: if any other government had given them what I did, the troika would have sealed the deal by now. I gave them more than Samaras ever would, and they still wanted to punish me, as you had said they would. But – let's face it – they do not want to give an agreement either to you or to me. Let's be honest. They want to overthrow us. However, with the 61.3 per cent they cannot touch me now. But they can destroy you.'

'Don't worry about me, Alexi,' I said. 'Worry about honouring the people out there celebrating tonight while you're planning to give in. If we stick together, activate our deterrent and show them we're united, they will touch neither you nor me. We could propose to them a deal that they could package credibly as their own idea, their own triumph.'

At that point Alexis confessed to something I had not anticipated. He told me that he feared a 'Goudi' fate awaited us if we persevered – a reference to the execution of six politicians and military leaders in 1922.[7] I laughed this off, saying that if they executed us after we had won 61.3 per cent of the vote, our place in history would be guaranteed. Alexis then began to insinuate that something like a coup might take place, telling me that the president of the republic, Stournaras, the intelligence services and members of our government were in a 'readied state'. Again I fended him off: 'Let them do their worst! Do you realize what 61.3 per cent means?'

Alexis told me that Dragasakis had been trying to persuade him to get rid of me, everyone from the Left Platform and Kammenos's Independent Greeks and instead forge a coalition government with New Democracy, PASOK and Potami. Dragasakis had assured him that once the agreement with the troika had been signed, Alexis could then get rid of New Democracy, PASOK and Potami and bring me back. I told him it was the stupidest idea I had ever heard.

He smiled, seeming to agree, and used an expression for Dragasakis that is not reproducible here.'But there is something to the idea of proceeding in two ways, one public, one hidden. Publicly, we can approach the creditors in a right-wing manner, involving a reshuffle that says, "We're good kids now," but at the same time, hidden from public view, we can prepare a counterstroke.'

'This is bad thinking, Alexi,' I told him. 'Look, tonight the people voted. They didn't vote no for you to turn it into a yes.' I told him he had to come out and say what I had said in my press statement earlier: that the no vote had given him the mandate he required to bring about a solution in cooperation with our European partners. 'Add some complimentary words for the commission, the IMF, even for the ECB, to illustrate that we mean it when we say we want a cooperative solution, but simultaneously project strength. None of this nonsense about preparing for an underground war in the catacombs.' I told him that whatever we did now, we had to do it out in the open. We had to state clearly that we were preparing our own liquidity, as we had a duty to do when the ECB was keeping our banks closed. And we had to state clearly that the ECB's SMP bonds would be restructured according to Greek law, the law under which they were created.

'It will be very difficult for them to give us a solution, Yani,' he said.

'You keep making the mistake of thinking of a solution as something they give us,' I replied. 'That's not the right way to think about it. They need a solution as much as we do. It's not something that they hand out. We must extract it from them. But this requires that we have a credible threat. The SMP haircut and our own liquidity is exactly that!'

We were going round in circles, our bodies and minds wrecked by fatigue, so I told him that, since he had made his mind up to surrender one way or another, he had better just tell me what he had decided to do now. He said he was thinking of reshuffling the cabinet so as to stop the troika, the creditors and the media from targeting me. He asked me who I thought should replace me at the finance ministry. He had clearly decided who it would be already, but I decided to play along, suggesting the person who I was certain had agreed to take over from me already – my good friend Euclid. I even offered to try to convince Euclid to accept. (And when I did, Euclid pretended he needed to think about it.)

'I would like to ask you to take over the economy ministry, so as to team up again with Euclid,' Alexis said.

'What about Stathakis?' I asked.

'I'll be happy not to see him in front of me again. Let him vanish to the backbenches.'

'No, Alexi, I'm not interested.' I told him. 'You met me years ago because I turned Greece's debt into the dragon to be slain, and because of my proposals for how to slay it. I live, breathe, think and dream of debt restructuring, of a reduction in surplus targets, an end to austerity, tax rate reductions and the redistribution of wealth and income. Nothing else interests me. To take on the economy ministry to manage the EU's structural fund handouts, just so as to remain minister, is not something I want to do. Do you recall why I moved from America? Because you asked me to help you to liberate Greece financially. I ran for parliament not because I was dying to be an MP but because I did not want to be a technocrat, an unelected finance minister. I thought that that way I would be more useful to the cause. Now, given your abandonment of that cause, I have no reason to be a minister. It's OK. Let someone else do it. I shall be in parliament, where I will help to the best of my ability.'

'You can have some other ministry – maybe culture, which you and Danae know so much about?' he said laughing. 'In any case, there will be many posts in the future where you can help.'

'You're again confusing me with someone who cares about positions, Alexi. There's only one thing I care about, and you know what it is!'

'Let's sleep on it, let's think about it.'

'There's nothing to think about,' I said. 'There's no time. You have a lot to do.'

When I saw Danae afterwards, she asked me what had happened. 'Tonight we had the curious phenomenon of a government over-throwing its people,' I said.

Minister no more

Back at the flat, I narrated my discussion with Alexis for Danae and her camera and slept for a couple of hours before writing my seventh and final resignation letter. After proofreading it a few times, I posted it on my blog under the title 'Minister No More'. It was one of the hardest pieces of prose I had ever had to compose.

On the one hand, I had a duty to warn the people, the Greek *demos*, that their mandate was about to be trashed. On the other hand, I felt an obligation to preserve whatever progressive momentum there was within our government and within Syriza. At that stage I still believed strongly that comrades like Euclid, with clout in the party that I lacked, would not sign up to the surrender document Alexis and Dragasakis were preparing. Losing a second finance minister in a month or two, if Euclid refused to become complicit in another harsh and hopeless bailout, might cause a rupture within the government and the party. This in turn might lead to new elections, which could further undermine the chances of our honouring the wishes of the 61.3 per cent. I needed to signal both my defiant commitment to the no vote but also to issue a call for unity. The result was the following text.

> Like all struggles for democratic rights, so too this historic rejection of the Eurogroup's 25 June ultimatum comes with a large price tag attached. It is therefore essential that the great capital bestowed upon our government by the splendid no vote be invested immediately into a yes to a proper resolution – to an agreement that involves debt restructuring, less austerity, redistribution in favour of the needy and real reforms.
>
> Soon after the announcement of the referendum results, I was made aware of a certain preference by some Eurogroup participants, and assorted 'partners', for my . . . 'absence' from its meetings; an idea that the prime minister judged to be potentially helpful to him in reaching an agreement. For this reason I am leaving the Ministry of Finance today.
>
> I consider it my duty to help Alexis Tsipras exploit, as he sees fit, the capital that the Greek people granted us through yesterday's referendum.
>
> And I shall wear the creditors' loathing with pride.
>
> We of the Left know how to act collectively with no care for the privileges of office. I shall support fully Prime Minister Tsipras, the new minister of finance and our government.
>
> The superhuman effort to honour the brave people of Greece, and the famous no that they granted to democrats the world over, is just beginning.

In hindsight, I should have sounded a much louder alarm bell about Alexis's intentions. That I did not reflects my misplaced trust in many people in the government – Euclid primarily – to carry out the task of preventing a recapitulation of the Samaras government. But I am not sure that a clearer warning would have made much difference. Everyone I have spoken to since that morning understood very well what had happened the moment they heard I had resigned on the night of our triumph.

As well as the creditors and their groupies, there was one other person who was unconditionally happy at my decision. On hearing the news that I had resigned, my daughter Xenia, who had come from Australia to see me two weeks before but had hardly laid eyes on me, gave me a sleepy early-morning look and said, 'Thank goodness, Dad. What took you so long?'

You did that, didn't you?

Over the days that followed I watched Alexis's surrender evolve at breathtaking pace. Unwilling to be a dividing force within a party and a government that might still rebel against its own annulment, I kept quiet for a couple of weeks, but there was no rebellion. Paving the way for the third bailout, at a eurozone summit meeting on 13 July Alexis acceded to the troika's demands by signing his own version of the Treaty of Versailles, which he condemned as a coup against democracy while promising to honour it. During the ensuing days, the more he demonstrated his determination to do as the creditors prescribed, the harsher the attacks against me became.

For weeks I was ridiculed for clashing with the troika without a credible deterrent, but when, as I described in Chapter 4, 'A parallel payments system', I eventually let it be known that I did in fact have a well-planned deterrent, which Alexis had prevented me from activating, suddenly those who had laughed at my foolishness accused me instead of treachery.[8] The charge of national traitor, first laid against me in 2010, turned into a fully fledged campaign to convene a special court to try me for high treason.[9]

At the time of writing I still stand accused of having intentionally delayed an agreement with the troika in order to bring about bank closures, so that, in cahoots with Wolfgang Schäuble, I might engineer a parallel currency leading to Greece's exit from the euro. Imagine if the soldiers who returned from Dunkirk in June 1940 had been met in Britain with the accusation that they were responsible for the Second World War, while Berlin was celebrated for its rational restoration of order.[10] It was a comical turnaround: treason charges for me, adulation and respect for those who had done their best to shut down Greece's banks and push us to the brink of Grexit.

The motives of the troika and Greece's domestic oligarchy are obvious. Debt is creditor power, and unsustainable debt gives creditors exorbitant power. The Greek Spring challenged the right of creditors and their domestic agents to govern a debtor nation. The 61.3 per cent who voted no had to be discredited as a people led astray by opportunists, and since Alexis had now repented, that left me in the troika's sights.

Troika functionaries like Klaus Regling and Yannis Stournaras argue seriously that I cost the Greek economy around €100 billion. These are the same people responsible for piling so much debt on bankrupt Greece with the bailout loans of 2010 and 2012 that by 2015 the only solution was to haircut our debt by €100 billion. I told the Greek people this explicitly, and they elected us to do just that. But the troika was unwilling to admit its culpability, so they crushed our government in order to roll the debt over instead. It was the same story within Greece. The very political parties, bankers and media owners who had demanded that I sign the troika's agreement protested at the tax increases the agreement entailed. The same people who had orchestrated the bank run blamed me for the bank run. The journalists who had ridiculed me for being removed from the negotiations in April blamed me for the stalling of negotiations in May and June. The same people who want to see me in the dock on charges of high treason for gambling with Greece's place in the eurozone are full of admiration for Mario Draghi and Wolfgang Schäuble, the two men who jeopardized the integrity of the entire eurozone by closing down Greece's banks. Friends ask Danae and me how we cope with the opprobrium, especially from within Greece. My answer is that I can only consider it an honour to have the antipathy of such people.

Having said all that, it is time for a confession. Although I am immune to the slings and arrows of the troika, which I fully expected, having former colleagues – my parliamentary comrades who stayed in government and assented to the third bailout – do the same is hurtful.

It began with silence. When opposition MPs delivered fiery speeches condemning me for having brought the country to its knees, Syriza

MPs would stare at the ceiling and say nothing. Then some of them began to join in, confessing it had been a great error to have entrusted the finance ministry to me. Then former cabinet colleagues began to tell tall stories that contradicted one another. In one account I was eager to push Alexis into surrendering to the troika in February 2015, while in another I was responsible for a futile clash with the creditors that same month. Then some even went so far as to endorse the call for me to be tried in a special court. For the most part Alexis and Euclid would let these allegations run for a while, before intervening, suspiciously belatedly, to rule out charges against me by damning me with faint praise. Whatever I had done, they would say, at least I was not a crook; it would absurd to blame everything on Varoufakis, they would insist.

One explanation for this behaviour is that those same MPs and ministers were voting in favour of bills they knew to be calamitous and whose passage annulled everything they had stood for since entering politics. When a person believes one thing but chooses or is forced to advocate its opposite, the result is cognitive dissonance. Eventually, in order to endure the internal conflict, one is forced, like Orwell's Winston Smith, to change one's mind. But the emotional fallout from such stress must somehow be vented; someone else must take the blame. Since I had been chosen to perform the role of scapegoat by the victorious trinka, I was the obvious choice for my defeated comrades too.

But of course this is not the whole story. I recall something my father said to me when he realized that, at a young age, I was becoming enthusiastic about left-wing politics. 'When I was in the concentration camp as a communist,' he said, 'I knew that, had our side won the civil war, I would be in the same camp only with different guards.' Since my resignation, when witnessing the nastiness and blatant untruths of my former comrades, I have been reminded of my father's prescience.

Drawing up a final balance sheet for the Greek Spring of 2015 may seem like a tall order. It is not. On Thursday, 23 July 2015 I had two experiences that place this book's story in its rightful context.

That day I had two appointments to keep in the late morning with the international media. The first, around mid-morning, took place at an office in a dilapidated old arcade near Syntagma Square. When I left, there were cameras waiting downstairs in the arcade and journalists asking for a statement. As I was speaking, a middle-aged man began to abuse me, accusing me of having destroyed his business by shutting down the banks. I tried to enter into a conversation with him but he was only interested in shouting abuse, so I said my goodbyes and headed towards the exit of the arcade, where my motorcycle was parked. The man followed me to my bike, continuing to abuse me. The news bulletins that night were full of the story: 'Varoufakis hounded by irate businessman whose living the former minister destroyed'.

A little later I had a second appointment inside the National Gardens, just behind parliament – for a photo shoot with a German magazine about to publish a major interview with me on the Eurogroup and the state of Europe. A little way from where the shoot was taking place, a couple of young boys were playing. I noticed their modest clothes and the fact that they were unsupervised. The younger boy, who looked about five years old, remembered having seen me on television but could not put a name to me. He called to his older brother, who seemed around eight, to ask who I was. The older boy recognized me at once and approached. Surprisingly, it was to thank me. 'Do you know who this guy is?' he asked his brother while pointing at me. 'He is the guy who gave our mother her plastic card. It lets her buy stuff from the supermarket. Two hundred euros a month!' he said, proud to have remembered the number. Turning to me again he asked, 'You did that, didn't you? Did you really?'

'We tried our best,' I replied and hugged the boy. No one was there to witness this scene except the German photographer, who didn't understand our exchange in Greek, which made the whole thing so much more satisfying.

That same night I was at home chatting with Danae and a journalist friend, with the TV on in the background. When the footage of the stricken businessman accosting me was replayed, our friend pointed out something interesting. 'Did you notice that while the camera filming the scene is stationary, and the two of you are moving away from it, your voice fades but the businessman's doesn't?' I said that it seemed so. 'Can't you see? The businessman was wired for sound. You were set up!'

'Not for the first time,' I replied, somehow relieved.

Once our friend had left and Danae had gone to bed, I checked my emails and stumbled upon one sent by the Spanish journalist who had brought Lambros, the homeless translator, into our flat just before my election in January 2015. In it she said that Lambros had used the bill I had passed to get assistance with his rent. This was the same bill that had provided the boys' mother with her card and the very same bill that Declan Costello and his troika cohorts were so upset by and so eager to kill off. The Spanish journalist's email finished: 'Lambros wants me to tell you that he is moving into his new apartment tomorrow, and that he is very proud of you, and that you have his support more than ever.'

When all was said and done, how could I consider myself anything other than undeservedly privileged?

Epilogue

In mid-August 2015 Alexis and Euclid brought the third bailout loan agreement and its accompanying *MoU* to parliament. Convening at 9 p.m, we received more than a thousand pages – which read as if translated from troika-English into Greek by something like Google Translate – to sift through overnight before the vote scheduled for early the following morning. Sitting in parliament that long night – a night that resembled a wake more than a debate – I studied the *MoU*.

The full horror was evident from its first page, in which the Greek authorities committed to agree to everything the creditors demanded, with no reciprocal commitment from the troika to agree on anything in return – a pledge of utter subservience that no court of law would ever recognize as binding. Incensed, I worked through the night to produce an annotated version of the *MoU*.[1] By 9 a.m. 118 Syriza MPs and 114 pro-troika opposition MPs had accepted our new sentence to debtors' prison. I was one of 32 Syriza MPs who voted no, while another 11 abstained.

Predictably, the repercussions were devastating. All taxes soared. VAT rose on everything: food, hotels, books, pharmaceuticals, utility bills. Businesses tiny, medium and large saw their taxes and social security contributions increase and, staggeringly, were forced to prepay immediately 100 per cent of the following year's estimated taxes. The small sum paid to pensioners receiving less than the standard €300 per month was cut, while the majority of pensions were curtailed. All the state's remaining assets were put up for sale as part of a new fund to be controlled directly by the troika. The catalogue of horrors was endless. They were the kind of measures you impose on a weak economy if you want to crush it.

A few months later, at a conference in Italy, Jens Spahn, Wolfgang Schäuble's deputy, reprimanded me for saying that the third bailout was an example of latter-day gunboat diplomacy. 'But your parliament voted in favour of it with a large majority, didn't it?' he pointed out. Sure it did, I replied. Except that consent without the freedom to say no is a form of slavery, as feminists and civil right campaigners taught us long ago.

Shortly after my resignation I received two dismaying phone calls. One came from Panagiotis Danis, with whom we had set up the finance ministry's team of untouchables charged with the algorithmic hunt for tax cheats. 'They are about to pull the plug,' he told me, 'just when we were about to catch hundreds of thousands of large-scale evaders, raking in billions for the state.' I looked at the *MoU*. Buried in its verbiage there it was: a provision for the troika-dominated tax office to absorb Danis's team and thus defang it. Exercising my prerogative as a member of parliament, I made a speech warning against this travesty. 'We created a fantastic opportunity to strike at the heart of tax evasion, to collect very large sums and to give our people a sense of justice. Do not sacrifice it on the altar of the *MoU*,' I said. Euclid listened in silence from the ministerial benches. My fellow Syriza MPs looked at me as if I were the village idiot, incapable of shutting up about inconvenient truths. Nothing was reported in the press. By the autumn Danis had resigned, after submitting his report to Alexis. The tax-evading oligarchy, aided by its best friend the troika, had got away scot-free.

The other phone call came from Antonis Stergiotis, my appointee to the regulatory body overseeing the gaming industry – whose appointment had coincided with my estrangement from Roubatis. He told a similar story: the industry lobby, in collaboration with the deputy prime minister's office and with the acquiescence of the finance ministry, was pushing him out in order to rescind the measures we had put in place to halt the spread of thousands of video lottery terminals. By the end of the year Stergiotis was gone and so were the constraints we had imposed upon those trying to profit from the desperation of our impoverished population.

Liberal establishment?

Despite the pride I retain in having played a part in the Greek Spring and the real, albeit brief, scare it gave Greece's irresponsible and inhumane creditors, our defeat came at a great cost. The economic bill for that defeat was footed, of course, by Greece's weakest and neediest. Its political price, meanwhile, was paid by progressives around the world, whose hearts sank when they saw Syriza succumb to the dogma of TINA – There Is No Alternative – with the same enthusiasm that Orwell's Winston Smith realizes he loves Big Brother. But a defeat is always easier to bear if one can recognize it as but one episode in a larger struggle.

'Observing the European Union's attempts to deal with the crisis is a bit like watching *Othello* – one wonders how our rulers can be so deluded . . . In this titanic battle for Europe's integrity and soul, the forces of reason and humanism will have to face down the growing authoritarianism.' I spoke these words in 2013 in a speech entitled The Dirty War for Europe's Integrity and Soul.[2] A little less than a year after my resignation the people of Britain voted to leave the European Union. Then in November 2016 Donald Trump romped into the White House. Xenophobic Eurosceptics were appearing everywhere – in France, Germany, the Netherlands, Italy, Hungary, Poland. The scandalous treatment of the refugees landing on Greece's shores was a symptom of the same change. Meanwhile, commentators and those in authority began to fret about this unexpected challenge to the liberal establishment.

Having just emerged from an intense engagement with that very establishment, 'liberal' is the last adjective I would use to describe it. Once upon a time the liberal project was about the readiness to 'pay any price, bear any burden, meet any hardship, support any friend, oppose any foe, in order to assure the survival and the success of liberty with hope and justice', to use JFK's stirring words. An establishment that used truth-reversal so casually to annul a democratic mandate and to impose policies that its functionaries knew would fail cannot be described as liberal. Impoverishing Jill to keep Jack in his place is the opposite of liberalism. Something other than liberalism, or even neoliberalism, had taken over the establishment without anyone noticing.

The third *MoU* that I read and annotated that night in parliament begins with the words 'Greece has requested support from its European partners, to restore sustainable growth, create jobs, reduce inequalities, and address the risks to its own financial stability and to that of the euro area. This Memorandum of Understanding (MoU) has been prepared in response to a request of 8 July 2015 from the Hellenic Republic . . .'

The victim was being forced to pretend that it had requested its punishment and that the creditors were only responding generously to that request. Just as an unnamed US officer in the Vietnam War had claimed that a particular town had to be destroyed in order to be saved from the Vietcong, our country's fiscal waterboarding was celebrated as a sensible way of bringing a lost people back into the fold. In a sense, Greece experienced collectively the same treatment that Britain's poor receive when they go to claim their benefits at Jobcentres, where they must consent to their humiliation by espousing 'affirmation' phrases such as 'My only limitations are the ones I set for myself.'[3]

In the bonfire of its illusions that followed the financial crash of 2008 and the subsequent euro crisis, Europe's deep establishment lost all sense of self-restraint. I witnessed first hand what I can only describe as a naked class war that targeted the weak and scandalously favoured the ruling class. It came to my attention, for example, that some of the employees in my ministry, specifically the chair, CEO and members of the board of the Hellenic Financial Stability Facility (HFSF), were collecting what I considered to be outrageously high salaries. To economize but also to restore fairness, I used the powers vested in me by law to announce a salary cut of 40 per cent for these posts, reflecting the average reduction in wages throughout Greece since the crisis had begun in 2010. The CEO, who had been paid €180,000 in a country where a high court judge earns not more than €60,000 and the prime minister €105,000, would now receive €129,000 – still a large sum by crisis-ridden Greece's standards. Did our creditors, usually so keen to shrink my ministry's outlays on wages and pensions, embrace my decision enthusiastically? No, they did not. Instead, Thomas Wieser wrote to me repeatedly on behalf of the troika to demand that I reverse the decision. Why? Because these salaries went to functionaries that the troika considered their own. After I had left the ministry, those salaries were raised by up to 71 per cent, the CEO's salary being bumped up to €220,000.

This is what happens when those with unwarranted power lose legitimacy and self-confidence: they turn ugly. No longer interested in winning the intellectual or ideological argument, the establishment resorted instead to character assassination and punitive measures that it knew would result in less prosperity and less freedom. It employed brute force to impose policies that not even Ronald Reagan and Margaret Thatcher would have endorsed. And once it had throttled the rebellion against itself, it imposed performative incantations such as our *MoU* upon the defeated and went about shutting off any space where debate or critical inquiry might take place. In short, it became a highly illiberal establishment.

During my discussions with the creditors I often warned them that crushing us was not in their interests. If our democratic, Europeanist, progressive challenge was strangled, the deepening crisis would produce a xenophobic, illiberal, anti-Europeanist nationalist international. This is exactly what transpired after the crushing of the Greek Spring. How did the so-called liberal establishment respond to the nationalist, bigoted backlash that its dark and dangerous illiberalism brought about? A little like the parricide who throws himself on the court's mercy, demanding lenience because he is now an orphan.

Unwelcome vindication

Before the crisis, as an academic writing obscure scholarly articles and loving every minute of it, I was keen to avoid two kinds of people: followers and enemies. After my stint in government I now have plenty of both but not enough people willing to hear me out critically before either agreeing or disagreeing. This I regret. But I do not regret the decision to enter government to oppose continental-scale irrationality. But, 'Isn't it idiotic to put your job on the line to eradicate idiocy?' an American journalist once asked me. 'Not if you don't care for the job except as a lever against idiocy,' I replied.

Accusations such as 'You gambled with your country and lost' hold no water. It was my basic tenet that, as the finance minister of a bankrupt country, I had no right to gamble with its future. And I didn't. It is not a gamble to adopt a stance that is optimal irrespective of how your opponent chooses to respond. To resist the third bailout was the right thing to do whether the creditors agreed to a sustainable set of policies or opted to evict us from the eurozone. While we had a strong preference for the former, the latter was better than capitulation. Denunciations for having resisted the creditors for too long cut no ice either, given that even Wolfgang Schäuble told me he would have refused to sign the third bailout agreement were he in my shoes.

One night in March 2016 I spent a few hours in Ecuador's London embassy with Julian Assange listening to a recording of a telephone conversation between the IMF's Poul Thomsen and his Greek mission chief. With bitter satisfaction I heard Poul confirm everything I had been saying about the unsustainability of the third bailout agreement. I also heard him insist passionately that the correct fiscal targets were the ones I had been proposing – and which he was, interestingly, rejecting in the Eurogroup.[4] Vindication in defeat may be hollow, but at least it steels one's nerves in the face of the ensuing witch-hunt, whose purpose has been to shield from blame those who abandoned our plan midway and to absolve the illiberal establishment of responsibility for forcing such a plan on us in the first place.

No country is an island

> No man is an Island, entire of itself; every man is a piece
> of the Continent, a part of the main; if a clod be washed
> away by the sea, Europe is the less . . .
>   John Donne, *Devotions upon Emergent Occasions*, 'Med-
> itation XVII'

In the summer of 2015, with our people defeated yet unbowed, I was under pressure to start a new political party to keep the Greek Spring alive. The idea failed to light a fire in me. Then, one day in August, Danae and I found ourselves at a political meeting out in rural France. I was to speak. To my considerable surprise, a large crowd had gathered. I suspected they were there less to show solidarity with me or to my defeated country than for another reason, and I tested my suspicion by telling them this.

> I am here because our Athens Spring was crushed, just like
> the Prague Spring before it. But I am not here today to
> drum up support for Greece's crushed democracy. I am
> here to lend the Greek people's support and solidarity to
> France's democracy. For this is what is at stake. French
> democracy. Spanish democracy. British democracy. Italian
> democracy. Democracy throughout Europe. Greece was,
> and unfortunately remains, a laboratory where the destruc-
> tive powers of extend-and-pretend loans plus self-defeating

austerity were tried and tested. Greece is a battleground on which a war against European democracy, against French democracy, is tried and tested. Greece was never the issue for the troika and its minions. *You are!* This is why I am here. I am here because what happened to us is beginning to happen to you.

Judging from the roar of approval this received, I knew I had hit a nerve. They had gathered because they could sense that what had been done to Greece was coming their way. They were fully alive to Wolfgang Schäuble's desire to see the troika in Paris. In that field in France I saw what had to be done. Similar experiences at meetings in German town halls reinforced my conviction: we needed to band together regardless of nationality and transcend the divide between debtor and creditor countries. The only practical way to oppose both the deep establishment and the nationalist international it had spawned was to form a pan-European, democratic, humanist movement whose purpose is to succeed where the generation of 1929 failed: to reach out across borders and political divisions to stem the descent into a post-modern 1930s.

A few months later, on 9 February 2016, that movement was born. We chose Berlin's famous Volksbühne theatre to inaugurate DiEM25, the Democracy in Europe Movement. The energy that had failed to rise within me at the thought of starting a new party in Greece overflowed in response to the hunger across Europe for the spirit of the Greek Spring. One day, soon I hope, that transplanted spirit may be strong enough to return home to fire up our inordinately brave and virtuous people again. When that day comes, the Greeks may be able to address the rest of Europe by paraphrasing poet George Seferis: 'We who had nothing taught you tranquillity.'[5]

Over the winter and spring of 2016 I puzzled many friends in the UK with my campaign against Brexit. 'How can you tell us to stay in the EU after the way Greece has been treated?' they would protest. 'We want our country back!' was their wholly legitimate demand. 'So do we,' I would respond. But to take back our countries, I would explain, we need to reclaim common decency and restore common sense across Europe. Just as no one country can tackle climate change by itself, the task we face cannot be achieved by solitary nations.

'Would the weak in Britain suffer less after Brexit?' I would ask. 'Would the weak in Europe be better off?' Or would reinforced borders and Europe's disintegration favour the deep establishment and the political monsters its failures have spawned?

Some were convinced, others remained sceptical. The idea of Europe has been wounded so deeply, and mainly by the events of 2015, that good people are turning away from it. Even some who sympathize with DiEM25's pan-Europeanism dismiss it as utopian. But allow me, dear reader, to share a strongly held belief as my parting shot: our movement may be utopian, but its policy of *constructive disobedience* within the EU, of being both *in* and *against* this illiberal and anti-democratic Europe, is the only practical alternative to the dystopia unfolding as Europe disintegrates. That was my stance as Greece's finance minister. It remains my stance today.

Of course I may be wrong. Even so, I believe it is a cause worth pursuing. The danger is not that we shall aim too high and miss; the real danger is that we train our eyes on the floor and end up there. Minutes after the inauguration of DiEM25 in Berlin, filled with adren-alin and hope, my colleagues and I came across an older German activist who looked unimpressed. 'This movement is doomed,' he told us gloomily.

'So what the hell are you doing here?' my slightly peeved colleague asked him.

'I want to be around the people who will have to pick up the pieces when the whole edifice comes tumbling down,' he replied.

That's a good enough reason to keep alive, across Europe, the small flame lit by the people of Greece during the spring of 2015.

Acknowledgements

To thank all those who deserve gratitude for a book of this nature would require even more pages than this hefty volume already contains. Trusting that they know the extent of my gratitude, I shall confine myself to thanking just two persons: Will Hammond, my editor, whose perseverance, skills and tolerance I have exploited shamelessly, and Christine Lagarde, to whom I owe the book's title.

APPENDICES

Appendix 1: False dawns in deflationary times

There is a data series that supports the establishment's view that 2014 did see a rise in Greece's national income. It is derived from so-called real national income, or real GDP (gross domestic product) data – except that during periods of deflation (negative inflation) the economic term 'real' means precisely its opposite. This fascinating statistical mirage, in which a depression looks desirable, works as follows.

Asked whether you are better off today compared to a year ago, you would answer in the affirmative if your money income (its dollar, pound, euro or yen value) had risen during the last twelve months. But you might accompany your response with the reasonable proviso that the cost of living had gone up too. To account for the gap between your money income and its capacity to buy you things, economists focus on your money income's purchasing power – also known as real income – which is money income adjusted for average prices.

So too with the measurement of a nation's aggregate income. Economists begin by totalling everyone's money incomes to derive nominal gross domestic product – or, for simplicity, the nation's total money income (N). Then they adjust this number N for changes in average prices (P) by dividing N by P. The resulting ratio (R) is used as the measure of the nation's real income ($R = N/P$).

During inflationary times the utility of the real national income number is that it stops us from getting overexcited when we hear that money income has risen substantially. For example, at a time when prices are rising by, say, 8 per cent, a 9 per cent increase in money incomes translated into a mere 1 per cent growth in real income. So, clearly, in inflationary times the real national income number is the one to look at before rejoicing that the economy is growing. Only when R rises strongly do we have good cause to believe that economic activity is rising.

However, in periods of deflation (when prices are falling) R can be very, very misleading. Consider the fictitious example in the table below depicting a deflationary economy.

	Year 1	Year 2	Year 3
Money National Income (N)	100	98	96
Average Price Index (P)	100	99	93
Real National Income (R = N/P)	1	98/99	96/93
Growth of N		−2%	−2.04
Inflation Rate		−1%	−6.06%
Growth of R		−1.01%	+4.28%

From Year 1 to Year 2 the nation's money income (N) shrank by 2 per cent (from 100 to 98) while the index of average prices fell by 1 per cent (from 100 to 99). In the following year (Year 3), the recession deepened, with a further 2.04 per cent drop in money national income (from 98 to 96) and an even larger fall in prices as deflation hit 6.06 per cent. This is what an economy sliding from recession towards something reminiscent of depression looks like: falling incomes but an even faster decline in prices.

But look at the last row: real national income seems to have bounced back emphatically in Year 3, up from Year 2 by a healthy 4.28 per cent. How could that be? Well, this is a mirage caused by falling prices. Put simply, in deflationary economies where people and the state bear significant debts, only rises in money (as opposed to so-called real) income are a cause for celebration.

One may retort that the rising 'real' number is always good news even if money incomes are falling. For if prices are falling faster than money incomes, surely this means that we can afford to buy more for less? Is this not a good thing? It is in the absence of the usual spanner in the works: debt. For when people and governments are deep in debt, and as long as they pay positive interest on that debt, declining national income is a recipe for collective insolvency.

Lastly, and for the record, in 2014 Greek nominal national income was down by €2.8 billion or −1.569 per cent when inflation was −2.21

per cent. If you *subtract* −2.21 per cent from −1.569 you get a positive real growth number – a statistical mirage covering up for a depression (falling income, falling prices, rising debt-to-income ratios). By contrast, that was not the case in 2013, when nominal GDP fell −5.66 per cent and prices by −2.54 per cent: subtract −2.54 from −5.66 and the result is still a negative number.

Appendix 2: The IMF's motivated error

The IMF's miscalculation of the impact that the bailout programme would have on Greece's economy surely qualifies as the worst but also the most lucrative in the history of economic forecasting. At the time of the first bailout the IMF predicted that in 2011 it would depress investment by 11.8 per cent. The actual drop in the investment level in 2011 was 19.4 per cent. For 2012 the IMF predicted a boost of 0.8 per cent, but it in fact fell again by 19.4 per cent. And for 2013 the IMF had predicted investment growth of 4.8 per cent, but it fell once more, this time by 13.2 per cent. Turning to price inflation, the IMF was predicting −0.5 per cent for 2011, 1 per cent for 2012, 0.7 per cent for 2013, 1 per cent for 2014 and 1.1 per cent for 2015. Actual price inflation was 1 per cent in 2011, −0.3 per cent in 2012, −2.1 per cent in 2013 and −2.6 per cent in 2014.

At the heart of the IMF's calculations was a serious error. In order to pretend that by 2022 Greece's debt would be curtailed, to end the country's bankruptcy, the authors of the Greek programme had calculated:

- How much surplus the state should generate over the period 2015–22 so as to repay its creditors. Let's call this S (surplus).
- How much national income, or GDP, had to grow by in order for that surplus to be possible, given the taxes. Let's call this G (growth).
- The level of overall taxes the government should milk from the economy to pay its creditors and run the state. Let's call this T (taxes).

Once they had these numbers, they announced them as targets. They made the Greek finance ministers and prime ministers sign affidavits (also called memoranda of understanding) which said things like, 'The Greek authorities commit to striving for a growth rate of G that will allow for taxes T to be collected and leave at the end of each year a surplus equal to S. As S will suffice to meet Greece's debt repayments to creditors, Greece's debt is sustainable.'

It all sounded great except for one little problem: the three numbers (S,G and T) were calculated backwards, starting from what was needed in 2022 to repay Greece's debt (in terms of cumulative surplus S) and ending up with the growth rate G that should come into play at the beginning – from 2015. But the announcement that the government would be taxing business and families to the tune of T (the extraordinary sum necessary to generate S) was enough to stop business investing and families consuming in 2015. Put simply, the T and S numbers necessary to make the programme work, to make the 'numbers add up' (as IMF officials always say), were not just inconsistent but fundamentally at odds with the growth rate G that was necessary to bring them about.

Despite its spectacular predictive blunder Greece proved a nice little earner for the IMF. By the time I resigned, the bankrupt state had paid over €3.5 billion in interest and fees to the IMF, averaging 37 per cent of IMF total net income, and covering 79 per cent of its total internal expenses. Ever since Greece entered debtors' prison, the IMF has had an average operating profit of 63 per cent, much larger than that of Goldman Sachs or J.P. Morgan. And where have the IMF's profits come from? Europe's taxpayers, of course. In a sense, Brussels- and Berlin-based officials who look discomfited every time the IMF calls upon them to grant Athens debt relief do have a point: the International Monetary Fund wants Greece's European creditors, who have provided the IMF with immense profits, to haircut the country's debt to them but not to itself. And thus Greece is caught between the IMF, which correctly proposes debt relief despite having profited from Greece's being denied it, and the EU, which has used the IMF to deny Greece debt relief.

Appendix 3: Why I had ruled out bluffing

One of the courses I taught during 2012–14 at the Lyndon B. Johnson School of Public Affairs of the University of Texas was on Europe's financial and economic crisis. As part of the course, I devised a game to demonstrate to students how simple game-theory analysis can elucidate a complex strategic interaction. The following is copied from my notes to students.

The day after a Syriza government wins office on a mandate to challenge the logic of the bailout agreement keeping Greece in a permanent state of disrepair, the official creditors of the EU and the IMF (let's call them the troika) will face a choice:

The troika's first choice

1. Be accommodating to the new government, leading to a viable agreement (Outcome 1). (Game over)
2. Adopt an aggressive stance towards the new government, including fomenting a bank run, preparing bank closures and threatening Greece with Grexit if Syriza do not sign up to their fresh bailout. (Syriza's turn to move)

In the case of 2 above, Syriza has two options:

Syriza's choice

3. Surrender and accept third bailout (Outcome 2). (Game over)
4. Fight back. (The Troika's turn to move)

In the case of 4 above, the troika has two options:

The troika's second choice

5. Acquiesce to a viable agreement (Outcome 3). (Game over)
6. Push Greece out of the eurozone (Outcome 4). (Game over)

How will this confrontation play out? The answer depends on the two sides' preference orderings. Figure 3 examines what will happen if the two sides are rational in the neoclassical sense of behaving in a manner that satisfies their preferences best, given logically defensible beliefs of what the other side will do, assuming its known preferences.

The following is common knowledge. The troika prefers Outcome 2 to 1 and Outcome 1 to 3 – in symbols {2,1} & {1,3}. In plain words, the troika prefers a Syriza surrender to offering Syriza a fair deal at the outset, but it also prefers offering Syriza a fair deal at the outset to doing so after a fight with Syriza. The Syriza government prefers a quick compromise on a fair deal, Outcome 1, to a fair deal after a fight – {1,3} & {3,2}.

What will determine the outcome hinges on Syriza's ranking of Grexit (Outcome 4) in relation to surrender (Outcome 2) and the troika's ranking of Grexit (Outcome 4) in relation to a fair deal once a fight has begun (Outcome 3). There are four possible cases, depicted in Figure 3 below.

1. Syriza prefers surrender and a third bailout (Outcome 2) to Grexit (Outcome 4), while the troika prefers Grexit to any compromise. In that case the troika will be aggressive, predicting that Syriza will surrender, a prediction that will be confirmed. Thus, Outcome 2.
2. Syriza prefers Grexit (Outcome 4) to surrender (Outcome 2), while the troika also prefers Grexit (Outcome 4) to acquiescing after Syriza has fought (Outcome 3). In this case Grexit is guaranteed, even if both the troika and Syriza prefer a quick fair deal. Thus, Outcome 4.

3. Syriza prefers surrender and a third bailout (Outcome 2) to Grexit (Outcome 4), but the troika too is Grexit-averse, preferring Outcome 3 to Outcome 4. Thus, Outcome 1.

4. Syriza prefers Grexit (Outcome 4) to surrender (Outcome 2), but the troika is Grexit-averse, preferring Outcome 3 to Grexit (Outcome 4). In this case the troika will predict that Syriza will fight if provoked and so settle immediately – opt for Outcome 1 by choosing non-aggression. Thus, Outcome 1.

The above of course presupposes that each side knows the preferences of the other. If they do not, a Grexit-averse troika may test the Syriza government with initial aggression or, equivalently, a Grexit-averse Syriza may test the troika by fighting after the troika's initial aggression.

Reading these lecture notes years later, after the events narrated in this book, should explain clearly why at the time I ruled out bluffing and instead concentrated all my energies on convincing my colleagues that, unless we feared Grexit less than we feared surrender, there was no point in being elected; indeed, the only way of keeping Greece within the eurozone sustainably was to fear Grexit less than we feared a third bailout.

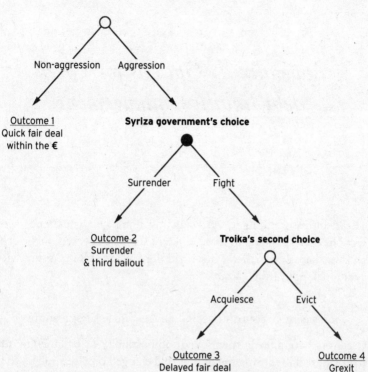

Outcomes of a rational negotiation		
Fixed rankings Troika: {2,1} & {1,3} Syriza government: {1,3} & {3,2}	**Syriza government rankings**	
	Grexit-averse {2,4}	Surrender-averse {4,2}
Troika rankings — Compromise-averse {4,3}	(i) Outcome 2 Surrender and third bailout	(ii) Outcome 4 Fight and Grexit
Troika rankings — Grexit-averse {3,4}	(iii) Outcome 1 Non-aggression and viable agreement within the €	(iv) Outcome 1 Non-aggression and viable agreement within the €

Figure 3: Outcomes depending on the preference ordering of the troika and Syriza. NB {X,Y} denotes a preference of Outcome X over Outcome Y.

Appendix 4: Options for Greek debt liability management

The debt-restructuring proposal in my non-paper contained three sections corresponding to three different slices of Greece's public debt and was based on earlier work I had done when still in Austin, with additional input from Lazard.

1. PERPETUAL BONDS IN EXCHANGE FOR THE ECB'S SMP BONDS

Creditors have already mentioned the possibility of lengthening the maturities and reducing the interest bill charged on Greece. This idea should be taken to its logical limit in the case of the SMP bonds that are held by the ECB and which would have been haircut massively had the ECB not purchased them. Our proposal is that this slice of Greece's debt, which presently comes to €27 billion, should be swapped for a new perpetual bond, so as to avoid any amortization. The proposed swap of the SMP bonds for a new perpetual bond will not reduce the nominal debt, but this is a secondary issue compared to the benefits of foregoing amortization.

2. GDP-INDEXED BONDS TO BE SWAPPED FOR THE FIRST GREEK LOAN DEBT

The outstanding first Greek programme debt (also known as the Greek loan facility) can be swapped against *GDP indexed bonds* and/or *asset-backed securities*. That way, Greece could share with its official creditors the benefits of the recovery. As pointed out in a note by the German institute DWI, the merit of GDP-indexed bonds is to introduce counter-cyclicality by linking the debt service to the country growth performance.

However, given the high level of interest concessionality already granted on the debt, the indexation could rather focus on the amount of principal debt redemption. Asset-backed securities could also be swapped in exchange for the EFSF debt. In the specific case of banks shares currently held by the EFSF's Greek branch, Greece could swap these assets for EFSF bonds, thus benefiting from the new capacity granted to the European Stability Mechanism directly to hold banking assets.

3. SPLITTING THE SECOND GREEK LOAN EFSF DEBT INTO TWO PARTS

The outstanding second Greek programme debt to the EFSF can also be swapped for *GDP-indexed bonds* and/or *asset-backed securities*. Additionally, a splitting operation could help too: Greece's debt obligations vis-à-vis the EFSF into two instruments; half of it turning into a 5 per cent interest-bearing instrument, and the other half into a series of non-interest-bearing instruments (zero coupon bonds), repaying the other 50 per cent principal at maturity. This idea follows the comment made by Klaus Regling, European Stability Mechanism director general, in 2013 stating that the true economic burden of the debt is not correctly captured by the DSA analyses undertaken by the IMF. The debt parameters are as important to assess debt sustainability as the debt nominal level itself: EFSF loans are very long term, with very concessional interest rate reduced to EFSF funding cost. The merit of making explicit the concessionality of the debt is to allow for a wider range of options. The liability management exercise would then focus on the non-interest-bearing asset. In the simpler option the creditors could cancel the part that carries no coupon. In real economic terms they would lose little, only the market value of the non-interest-bearing bonds, and would still cash the amount of interest originally due. However, the impact of debt cancellation of half of the EFSF's claim would have direct negative consequences on the EFSF itself and, subsequently, on member states' fiscal accounts. One key objective of the forthcoming discussion with European creditors, and possibly the ECB, could be to structure a mechanism that would bring to Greece the benefits of debt cancellation while spreading over time, in a phased fashion, the direct financial impact on creditors' public accounts. In another option, Greece could offer to swap the non-interest-bearing asset against other instruments such as asset-backed securities or the GDP-indexed bond previously mentioned. In a third option, the government could directly sell some of its assets to extinguish at market price the non-interest-bearing instrument held by the EFSF. The EFSF could then use these resources to purchase in the market zero-coupon instruments to match its balance sheet. The debt owed by Greece would be nominally reduced by half in such a scheme.

Notes

Chapter 1: Introduction

1. A few months after I had resigned the ministry, my good friend and academic colleague Tony Aspromourgos, upon hearing about my exchanges with Larry Summers, confirmed my suspicion when he sent me this quotation from Senator Elizabeth Warren, documented in 2014:

> Late in the evening, Larry leaned back in his chair and offered me some advice . . . He teed it up this way: I had a choice. I could be an insider or I could be an outsider. Outsiders can say whatever they want. But people on the inside don't listen to them. Insiders, however, get lots of access and a chance to push their ideas. People – powerful people – listen to what they have to say. But insiders also understand one unbreakable rule: they don't criticize other insiders. I had been warned.
>
> John Cassidy (2014), 'Elizabeth Warren's Moment', *New York Review of Books*, Vol. 61 (no. 9), 22/5–4/6/14, pp. 4–8.

2. Quotations from catalogue entry for Danae Stratou's 2012 exhibition *It is time to open the black boxes!*

Chapter 2: Bailoutistan

1. One-third of the €110 billion came from the IMF, which means from the taxpayers of the IMF's member states, which is more or less the whole world. The remainder came from the EU's taxpayers.

2. 'Programme' is shorthand for the troika's enforced measures of fiscal consolidation and reform – the so-called conditionalities of the bailout loan – whose purpose was the recovery of Greece's economy and its government's capacity to borrow from private investors. In reality, it meant cutting wages

and benefits savagely, raising taxes and selling off the family silver on behalf of the creditors. Note also Lagarde's use of 'they' instead of 'we'. This reflects the fact that the IMF has consistently disagreed with important aspects of the conditions placed upon Greece by the European members of the troika. Still, these disagreements never triggered the IMF's veto. In the final analysis, after IMF officials expressed their reservations, even their apologies to Greece, the IMF consistently backed the European powers' absurd decisions.

3. Greek government bonds were trading at 19 per cent of their face value, meaning that German banks wanting to offload Greek debt by selling it to investors would have to take an 81 per cent loss.

4. http://www.telegraph.co.uk/news/worldnews/europe/eu/10874230/Jean -Claude-Juncker-profile-When-it-becomes-serious-you-have-to-lie.html

5. These numbers reflect the fact that Germany represented around 27 per cent of the eurozone's total income, France's around 20 per cent, and so on.

6. The IMF was in a slightly different position, in that Christine Lagarde felt immense pressure from non-European members of the fund to retrieve every penny loaned to Athens. These members, such as Brazil, were immensely annoyed with the European leadership of the IMF for having embroiled them in a melee that was none of their business, through bending the IMF's sacred rule and jeopardizing their money.

7. This is a statement that Mrs Thatcher made often and in a variety of ways. For example, in an interview for Thames TV (*This Week*, 5 February 1976) she said '. . . and socialist governments traditionally do make a financial mess. They [socialists] always run out of other people's money. It's quite a characteristic of them.'

8. As if that were not enough, for every dollar, pound or euro that Europe's banks had access to, they had lent, or wagered, a cool forty. Given this so-called leverage ratio of 40:1, a back-of-an-envelope calculation reveals that if a mere 10 per cent of these bets or loans were to go bad, someone would have to pump $2.25 trillion into the banks, or else the ATMs would dry up and the banks' shutters would come down permanently.

9. One of them in fact was Yannis Dragasakis, who would become deputy prime minister in the Syriza government in which I served as finance minister.

10. To illustrate the point, in 2015 the British Treasury repaid a bond issued during the South Sea Bubble crisis of the 1720s.

11. As late as early 2008 its income mountain was rising at a healthy rate of 5.8 per cent while its debt hole was increasing by a mere 4.4 per cent.

12. The state would frequently borrow from foreign banks and pass the money on to developers to build motorways and the like.

13. From its 5.8 per cent growth a year before it subsided by 4.5 per cent. Meanwhile, the debt hole deepened at a rate of 5.7 per cent, up from 4.4 per cent year on year.

14. It is fun to look at what a fully fledged austerity drive would have done to Britain's economy. Around 2010 the UK's public debt came to almost 80 per cent, or four-fifths, of national income. At the same time the UK government's total expenditure was about half of national income. Now, suppose Chancellor Osborne had given his pro-austerity instincts free rein and gone into a frenzy, slashing government spending by half, a cutback equal to a quarter of national income. Cutting this much government spending would reduce national income by at least a fifth. Suddenly public debt would go from four-fifths to four-quarters, or 100 per cent, of national income, without even counting all the public money that 'had' to be given to the City's bankers. This is why austerity, in times of private-sector consolidation, fails by its own criteria – the consolidation of public debt.

15. Indeed the numbers are telling. During his first two years in the Treasury (2010–12) Osborne actually increased government expenditure by 6.9 per cent. In this sense no actual austerity was practised by the Cameron–Osborne government at all. Austerity *was* utilized by them as a cover for a substantial redistribution of spending and tax cuts that favoured the rich and disadvantaged the poor. In simple terms, the top 20 per cent benefited greatly while the bottom 20 per cent suffered even more.

16. The order was not issued immediately. It happened a few days later, in my presence, when I shared a panel with the said minister. When the show finished, aggrieved by my criticisms, he turned to the producer angrily. 'We pay your salaries and you keep inviting him here to undermine us? Never again!' After that the invitations ceased. However, to my great surprise an ERT producer did call me a few weeks later with an invitation to appear the following day. I told her that, while perfectly happy to accept her kind invitation, perhaps she should look into the matter once more, mentioning my blacklisting. Her reaction was one of healthy incredulity. 'The days of fascism at ERT are well and truly over,' she pronounced. 'Be that as it may,' I said, 'ask around and if you still want me to appear on your programme tomorrow, give me a call and I shall be there.' Two hours later my phone rang again. In a subdued voice came the sad admission: 'I had been away on maternity leave and, as the order was never written down, I did not know. I am ever so sorry. For us more than for you. Thank you for protecting me.'

17. I was to find this out during one of my ministerial visits to Washington, DC.

18. Greek pension funds, like in most countries, were forced by law to hold much of their reserves in Greek government bonds. In effect, pensioners were made to lend their fund reserves to the state. The charters of professional bodies, like the lawyers' association, also compelled their fund managers to invest in government bonds. Greece's bankers would be hit too, but unlike pensioners and private investors they would be compensated fully with the European taxpayers' money that the Greek state would borrow as part of the second bailout loan and return to the bankers – in the interests of financial stability, of course.

19. The interim government was formed in the autumn of 2011; the second bailout legislation was approved in the spring of 2012, and the new elections were called in May 2012. Having produced a hung parliament, they were repeated a month later, in June, at which point Mr Samaras managed to form, under his premiership, a coalition government with the massively depleted PASOK and a tiny pro-establishment party of the Left.

20. Unlike Greek pension funds, professional organizations and small bond-holders, who lost up to 90 per cent of the money they had lent to the Greek state, very few foreign owners of Greek government bonds suffered a loss. The reason is that, by the time the haircut kicked in, in 2012, foreign banks and other institutional investors had already sold, at a discount, their Greek government bonds either to the European Central Bank or to risk-loving hedge funds. By 2012 the foreign institutions holding Greek government bonds were paying less than 30 per cent of their face value for them. So, they even made money from the 2012 official haircut, taking into consideration the 'incentives' they were offered to accept the terms of the haircut.

21. When I became finance minister, the fine lady in charge of the tax office had no obligation even to brief me on what she was doing. But while neither I nor parliament could fire her without the troika's consent, I nonetheless was answerable to parliament for any scandal, misdemeanour or failure to meet targets by her office.

22. Margaret Thatcher, the politician who made privatization her political legacy, would have been appalled. Her arguments in favour of selling public assets were the enhancement of competition and the reduction of tax rates made possible by the injection of income and lower running costs. In Bailoutistan 2.0 privatizations meant something else: selling public assets for small change, as the economic depression had sent prices through the floor, with the proceeds thrown into the bottomless pit of Greece's unpayable public debt.

Chapter 3: They bend their tongues like their bows

1. An even more outrageous trick was employed: in addition to the millions from Zorba's bank, the Aris family's offshore companies also borrowed millions from Aris's own bank. These loans were also written off as unserviceable or non-performing, or were used to buy office space that was then resold to other parties only to be leased back to the bank or sold to it at inflated prices. The newly conjured-up funds or 'profits' would also be used to buy new shares in the same bank, keeping up the pretence that investors were injecting private capital into them.

2. My constituency being Greater Athens (or Athens B, as it is known), I did not have the opportunity to vote for Alexis in that mayoral election. But in any case I would not have done so, as I was sceptical of Syriza.

3. To be precise, the party was not yet known as Syriza. Prior to 2013 it was called Synaspismos, meaning 'Alliance'. In the 2009 election Synaspismos formed a broader coalition with many quasi-independent parties and movements. In the 2012 twin elections (May and June) it stood under the name Syriza (Alliance of the Radical Left) as one party in order to become eligible for privileges not afforded to coalitions of parties. It was only in July 2013 that a congress was held that turned Syriza into a unitary party.

4. Yanis Varoufakis, *Foundations of Economics: A Beginner's Companion* (1998), Routledge, London.

5. A summary of the *Modest Proposal*, which in 2013 received a makeover with the help of a new co-author, Jamie Galbraith, can be found as an appendix to Yanis Varoufakis, *And the Weak Suffer What They Must? Europe, Austerity and the Threat to Global Stability* (2016), The Bodley Head, London.

6. Argentina, like Mexico and other Latin American countries, had pegged its currency at one peso to one dollar, but this made Argentinian exports prohibitively expensive and flooded Argentina with imports. As the country's trade deficit burgeoned and dollar debts accumulated within Argentina, it eventually became clear to everyone that something had to give. The exodus of capital from the country and the collapse of its domestic economy was cured, eventually, by ending the one-peso-for-one-dollar rate. Technically this was a simple operation, even though it left many Argentinians with dollar debts they could not service once their pesos lost value. All it took was a government decision on a Friday afternoon that the peso would no longer be worth one US dollar.

7. To my genuine surprise, we discussed in depth the *Modest Proposal*'s remedies for Europe's sub-crises of public debt, insolvent banks and ultra low investment.

8. Yanis Varoufakis, *The Global Minotaur: America, the True Causes of the Financial Crisis, and the Future of the World Economy* (2011), Zed Books, London. Since then there have been two new editions, in 2013 and in 2015, with the subtitle: *America, Europe and the Future of the World Economy*.

9. My first experience of moving countries came at the age of seventeen, when along with thousands of other Greeks my age I moved to Britain to study. Then, in 1988, asphyxiating in Margaret Thatcher's Britain, I migrated to Australia, where I took up a lectureship at the University of Sydney. My next migratory flight occurred when, at the age of forty, I decided to resign from Sydney and return to Greece, accepting a professorship at the University of Athens. Our 2012 move to the United States was my penultimate shift, the final one (I hope and trust) being the passage in 2015 into the arena of politics.

10. Angela Merkel was of course Germany's chancellor, and Mario Monti the unelected economist who had replaced the ghastly, but elected, Sylvio Berlusconi as prime minister of Italy. Monti, despite his reputation as Merkel's man, did his country a major service by pressing Merkel to accept debt sharing across the eurozone (not to be confused with loans) as well as the creation of a proper banking union. That he failed is not due to his lack of effort (see Varoufakis,

2016, Chapter 6) but rather to a combination of Merkel's unwillingness to come to the aid of the man she had backed and to Monti's lack of domestic support.

11. A video game company whose multi-million-strong player / customer community had spontaneously generated a substantial macroeconomy, including an evolved monetary system, which I was keen to study.

12. See Varoufakis, 2016.

13. The coalition also included a small, openly racist, ultra-nationalist, Christian fundamentalist party called LAOS, which was later absorbed partly by New Democracy but mainly by the emergent Nazis of Golden Dawn.

14. PASOK had lost the bulk of its support in 2009 after shepherding through the first bailout (down from 44 to a mere 13.2 per cent) while New Democracy, which had lent a hand in the second bailout, saw its electoral base shrink from 33.5 per cent in 2009 to 18.8 in May 2012.

15. Technically this would be simple. The second bailout money, from which Greece's bankers would receive up to €50 billion, came from the European Financial Stability Facility. The EFSF (effectively Europe's bailout fund) belongs to all eurozone member states and borrows on behalf of European taxpayers in order to pass the money on to Greek banks, Spanish banks, the Portuguese state, etc. My proposal was that, as the EFSF was pumping money into the Greek banks on behalf of Europe's taxpayers, the EFSF should own their shares, becoming their owner on behalf of all Europeans. The banks' directors would then be replaced by appointees of the EFSF (and possibly the European Central Bank) with the remit to cleanse and 'europeanize' Greece's banks.

16. The technical term for this is 'nominal GDP-indexing'. It means that repayments would be suspended until Greece's national income, in euros, exceeded a certain level (for example the pre-crisis level of GDP or some agreed percentage of it) and its growth rate was above some annual percentage threshold.

17. In his speech, echoing the views of Syriza's inner circle, Alexis called for taxing capital transfers out of Greece (not permissible within the eurozone), a home-grown investment programme (when domestic investment funding was totally absent), a tax on shipowners (who are domiciled mostly in London and therefore cannot be touched by the Greek tax office), legislating to force Greeks to repatriate their foreign bank deposits (legally impossible within the EU) and, last but not least, the nationalization of the banks (ignoring my briefing that the Greek state could not afford to capitalize the banks within the eurozone). Most of these pronouncements required Greece to exit the eurozone, but in the same speech Alexis proclaimed that Syriza's policy was to stay within it.

18. Syriza did make further large gains between the May and June 2012 general elections: up from 16.8 per cent in May to 26.9 per cent in June. But New Democracy made similar gains, from 18.8 to 29.7 per cent, cannibalizing the PASOK socialists, who fell yet again from 12.3 to 4.68 per cent.

19. The new coalition government was an interesting twist on the previous one, that led by Lucas Papademos, the former ECB vice president. At its core were still New Democracy and PASOK, but the third party changed dramatically: LAOS, now absorbed into Golden Dawn and New Democracy, was replaced by a small splinter of Syriza called Democratic Left – moderate left-wingers who had accepted the basic logic of the troika's Greek programme. The other difference was that the new coalition was dominated by New Democracy, given PASOK's implosion.

20. Rumours spread by Peter Spiegel of the *Financial Times* and others that Stournaras had played a role in my appointment are false. He and I first met after my appointment, which was the result of a rare unanimous vote by the Economics Faculty Board. In fact, the original invitation to return to Athens and consider taking up a post there came in the early 1990s from a German-trained left-wing growth theorist, a professor of the old school who graced the university with his erudition and virtue.

21. Stournaras told me an amusing story about the famed 'Greek statistics', which have been blamed for letting a thoroughly unprepared Greece into the quicksands of the eurozone. All he and his colleagues had to do to convince official Europe to let Greece in was to copy the tricks that others – primarily the Italians but also the German Finance Ministry – had used to massage their statistics so as to present them as consistent with the eurozone's rules. Given that Athens was not using any trickery not used by Rome, or indeed Berlin, Stournaras's subtle strategy was to let it be known that, were Greece to be left out, the world might come to know what Rome and Berlin had been up to. In other words, it was not Greek statistics that got Greece into the eurozone; it was European statistics coupled with a large dose of hypocrisy.

22. The bank was later renamed the Emporiki Bank. In 2004, after Stournaras was fired by the new conservative government, the Emporiki Bank was sold to Crédit Agricole. Following the 2010 crisis the Emporiki bank was wound down.

23. For example, the international PhD in economics programme we introduced required candidates to spend two years taking full-time courses. Previously, some professors would have candidates work for a pittance on their own lucrative projects (or in their business) in exchange for a promise that, one day, four or five years later, they would be awarded a doctorate. Naturally, the dissertations that resulted from this system were worthless, as the students neither received any proper education nor had the time to study on their own. The new programme put an end to the practice and made me very, very unpopular among those colleagues.

24. Stournaras had been a party functionary or, as he preferred to think of himself, a PASOK technocrat. But he was close to, and had worked with, Papandreou's predecessor, whose legacy Papandreou had been trying to expunge since 2004. Thus Stournaras was sidelined, making him feel bitter and distant from the party that he identified with. In contrast, I was close to the Papandreou family but not to the party, which I could not bring myself to vote for. Even though I did respond to Papandreou's request to help him and his team (with speech writing, economic analyses, proposals for encouraging a cooperative enterprise sector, etc.), I did so as an outsider and as a personal favour to Papandreou. Nevertheless, by 2006 I could not work with his economic team and I resigned even my informal advising role. This, quite accidentally, brought Stournaras and me closer, as we now shared a distance from Papandreou.

25. The government's primary budget surplus is the difference between its revenues (taxes, customs duties, returns on public investments, etc.) and its expenditures, not counting the money the government pays to its creditors in the form of debt instalments (interest and principal).

26. This story was relayed on 9 January 2014 in a report in the *Financial Times* by Peter Spiegel and Kerin Hope. They quote Stournaras: "'Poul [Thomsen, the IMF's point man in Athens] and Lagarde said I had to [stand] by their side," he recalled. "I said: 'OK, but if I come by your side, it is what would really help Greece, but it's something which is totally out of the question.' Schäuble told me: 'Stournaras, forget it.' So it cannot be done, so what can I do?'"

27. The chancellor had visited Beijing with a number of requests, one of which was that China use a small part of its foreign currency reserves to fund the eurozone's bailout fund (by buying the bonds it issued). A high-ranking Chinese official confirmed to me that Beijing agreed to do this on condition that Angela Merkel took Grexit 'off the table'. The Chinese were right: they could not be asked to fund the eurozone's bailout fund when most of the loans it had handed out were likely to be written off – which is precisely what would happen if Greece, the main recipient, no longer had access to euros.

28. After the summer of 2012, markets had received a signal from the European Central Bank that it would buy unlimited amounts of Irish, Italian, Portuguese and Spanish government bonds to stem the euro's deconstruction. Indeed, it took Mario Draghi almost a year to make this signal possible, winning over to his cause Angela Merkel against the Bundesbank's severe opposition. Greece was never offered a place under the ECB's protective umbrella.

29. The precise condition was that the government achieved a positive primary surplus – its revenues exceeded all government expenditures, excluding the mind-boggling debt repayments.

30. The reason why early 2015 was the focal point is that the president of Greece's term expired in March 2015. Greek presidents are elected indirectly, by parliament, and if no candidate musters the required figure, parliament is dissolved. Prime Minister Samaras could only therefore avoid a new election in March 2015 by securing the votes of smaller parties and independents in the presidential election. He liked neither the prospect of doing that nor his chances of succeeding even if he tried.

31. An extract from the speech:

The fear-mongers will tell you that our party will, if it comes to government, tear up the loan agreement with the European Union and the IMF, that it will take the country out of the eurozone, that it will sever Greece's links with the civilized West, that Greece will become a new North Korea. This is fear-mongering at its worst. Syriza, my party, wants none of that. We have always been, and always will remain, a pro-European party. That we now think that Europe has lost its way and that it is imposing misanthropic policies on its own peoples is not to be anti-European. It is to be loyal to the people of Europe. To the idea that Europe is our home and we need to defend it from the great depression that is spreading and which is threatening not only us Europeans but also the whole global economy. We want to stop the fragmentation of Europe. And this means opposing Europe's current policies . . . Does this mean that a Syriza-led government will tear up its loan agreement with the troika? No. What we are saying is far more basic. We are saying that this agreement is being violated daily by reality. The IMF itself is warning Brussels, Frankfurt and Berlin that this agreement has been overtaken by reality. That it is impossible to implement successfully even if Syriza convinces every Greek man, woman and child to wake up every day and go to sleep every night intent on implementing it . . . So, if Syriza's radical Left politics is not about getting Greece out of the eurozone. And if it is not about tearing up our agreements with the European Union. What does our radical Left label signify?

It signifies that we will not be party to depression-era economic policies.

It signifies that we will keep insisting that the Eurozone is redesigned rationally, instead of having its peoples waterboarded every day of the week.

It signifies that we shall not accept Herbert Hoover's European reincarnation to haunt Europe's peoples.

It signifies that we will demand a new deal for Europe that mobilizes our continent's productive capacities against want, against poverty and against hopelessness.

Last but not least, my message to this audience, here at Brookings, is that our party wants to establish a mutually profitable dialogue with well-meaning, progressive thinkers on your side of the Atlantic. I want to tell you that the people of Greece, even its radical Left, think of you as partners in the complex but important enterprise of restoring prosperity and hope on both sides of the Atlantic. The rest

of the world, having made huge progress over the past decades, is
watching us Europeans and Americans with anxiety. We must not fail
them just as we must not fail our own people.

32. 'Only Syriza Can Save Greece', 23 June 2013:

> Greece's problem today is with Europe, and Mr Tsipras doesn't want to
> pick a fight with Washington. The global financial sector would view a
> Syriza victory with horror. But banks and hedge funds know that most
> Greek debt is held by European taxpayers and by the European Central
> Bank, and what's left is being snapped up by investors because they know
> it will be paid. Big Finance is worried about what may happen elsewhere
> if a left-wing party wins in Greece. This instinct is natural for bankers.
> But for the American government to adopt the same fear-driven stance
> would be strategically shortsighted. Indeed, right now, Syriza may be
> Europe's best hope. Greeks neither want to leave the euro nor see the
> eurozone disintegrate, an eventuality likely to bring down the European
> Union. They also know that Europe's approach to the crisis, involving
> increasingly harsh austerity and larger loans, has failed miserably.

33. The full background to this is as follows. At the time of the first bailout,
under a lesser president than Mario Draghi, the ECB had purchased a lot of
Greek government debt (bonds) in a desperate and ill-fated bid to keep it solvent.
This doomed operation was the so-called Securities Market Programme (SMP).
By buying Greek, Portuguese, Irish, Spanish and Italian government bonds, the
ECB hoped to quell the panic-selling of those bonds by investors. Incredibly,
though, the ECB had also signalled to investors that it would not be spending
more than €200 billion – a clear invitation to speculators to wager that the SMP
purchases would fail to prevent the drop in the value of these bonds. When the
SMPs failed, the ECB was left holding tens of billions of unpayable Greek debt.
In 2012, when the Greek debt was haircut by imposing large losses on private
owners of government bonds as part of the second bailout, the ECB-owned SMP
bonds were exempted. This meant that the bankrupt Greek government had to
repay the ECB in full for bonds that would have been haircut by up to 90 per
cent if it were not for the folly of the ECB's previous president in purchasing
them. In short, the ECB, our nation's central bank, was behaving like a hedge
fund hold-out against a bankrupt state. Hedge funds often buy distressed debt
(bonds) of countries in trouble at ludicrously low prices, wait for other creditors
to agree a haircut (or debt restructuring) with the government and then refuse
to participate in this deal, holding out for full payment – hence the term 'hold-
out' or the more emotive 'vulture fund'. Only in Europe could such a travesty
be perpetuated and defended as sensible policy.

34. The Bundesbank had a long history of clashing with Germany's federal government (see Varoufakis, 2016). Jens Weidmann, the Bundesbank's president, was so opposed to the ECB purchasing the potentially bad debts of the Graeco-Roman states and banks that he sued Draghi and the ECB (of which the Bundesbank is an integral part!) in Germany's constitutional court, tabling a fiery 120-page deposition. The luckless German judges, unwilling to rule over this most peculiar dispute, which went totally over their heads and expertise, decided to . . . not decide.

35. The ECB's desperate need to keep up the pretence that Greece was redeeming the Greek government bonds that the ECB owned was the deeper cause of the remarkable trickery described earlier under 'Success story'.

36. Syriza was built as a loose alliance of socialists, ecologists, social democrats and communists. The Left Platform was one of its larger factions with historical links to the old pro-Soviet communist party, prior to its split in 1991. The Left Platform was traditionally, as the communists remain to this day, in favour of Greece pulling out of the eurozone. Once the euro crisis erupted and the Greek economy went into sharp recession, Left Platform Syriza members began campaigning strongly for Grexit.

37. The European System of Central Banks, built around the ECB, is a strange confederacy of the national central banks that make up the eurozone. While the national central banks have no right to issue currency or the ability to set interest rates, they retain some important functions. The most significant is that of providing the banks domiciled in their country with emergency liquidity assistance (ELA). The idea is this: under normal circumstances, the banks of a country such as Greece or Italy tap directly into the Frankfurt-based ECB for cash. They post collateral with the ECB (government bonds, mortgages and other paper assets that they own) and receive cash in return, but if the collateral is considered to be of poor quality, the ECB can refuse it. If matters were allowed to rest there, these banks would have to close down immediately, as they would not be able to give out cash to their depositors, triggering a run. This is when ELA kicks in. Effectively, the ECB tells the bank, 'No cash for you from us in Frankfurt but do try your friendly national central bank; it may accept your poor collateral.' So the distressed banker takes his poor collateral to his national central bank, which is essentially a branch of the ECB, and pleads for cash in return. The national central bank is unlikely to turn the banker down because otherwise a domestic banking crisis would erupt. There are two reasons why bankers do not like to be diverted from the ECB to their national central bank: it is bad for their reputation (revealing that the ECB has deemed their collateral to be poor) and it is bad for their bottom line (as ELA cash costs the banks more than ECB cash in terms of the interest rate charged). Finally, and importantly, the right and capacity of a national central bank to provide ELA cash to bankers can be curtailed by the ECB. All it takes is for two-thirds of the ECB Governing Council (thirteen of the nineteen governors of the eurozone's central banks) to vote in favour of shutting down a member state's national central bank's ELA. Then the banks of the said member state run out of cash within hours and its whole banking system collapses.

Chapter 4: Treading water

1. 'Blood, sweat and tears', 15 September 2014, protagon.gr.
2. For a concise version of the *Modest Proposal for Resolving the Euro Crisis*, co-authored by myself, Stuart Holland and Jamie Galbraith, see Appendix in Varoufakis, 2016. To this day I remain convinced that had those proposals been implemented they would have prevented the European Union's slide into ignominy and deconstruction, including Brexit.
3. Elections in Greece are always held on a Sunday.
4. 2015 was a minefield of repayments for any incoming government, with the IMF and the ECB alone demanding from the Greek government a sum equal to almost half of its tax revenues. Looking at the repayment schedule was enough to give the incoming finance minister a migraine.

6 March	€301.8 million – IMF	6 August	€189.5 million – IMF
13 March	€339.6 million – IMF	4 September	€301.8 million – IMF
16 March	€565.9 million – IMF	14 September	€339.5 million – IMF
20 March	€339.6 million – IMF	16 September	€565.9 million – IMF
13 April	€452.7 million – IMF	21 September	€339.5 million – IMF
12 May	€969.1 million – IMF	13 October	€452.7 million – IMF
5 June	€301.8 million – IMF	6 November	€166.5 million – IMF
12 June	€339.5 million – IMF	7 December	€301.8 million – IMF
16 June	€565.9 million – IMF	16 December	€565.9 million – IMF
19 June	€339.5 million – IMF	21 December	€339.5 million – IMF
13 July	€452.7 million – IMF	**Subtotal**	**€8.53 billion – IMF**
July	*€3,490 million – ECB*	*Subtotal*	*€6.66 billion – ECB*
August	*€3,170 million – ECB*	**Total**	**€15.19 billion**

5. My information that top ECB officials were worried about the effects of a haircut of the ECB's Greek government bonds on their freedom to embark fully in March 2015 on quantitative easing (the usual term for massive debt purchases) had come from a source high up the ECB hierarchy. More recently, in June 2016, that insider information was confirmed by a press release of the German Constitutional Court (Bundesverfassungsgericht) concerning an interpretation of the European Court

of Justice decision on the ECB's debt-purchasing activities, in particular on the so-called outright monetary transactions programme that Draghi had introduced as a preamble to his fully fledged quantitative easing programme. In it the German judges ruled that 'although the European Court of Justice considers the policy decision to be permissible even without further specifications, its implementation must fulfil *further conditions* in order for the purchase programme to not violate Union law' [emphasis added]. Which conditions? One was that all purchases of government debt, presumably extending to past ones, 'do not manifestly violate the prohibition of monetary financing of the budget'. As Draghi once told me in person, any delay in redeeming the Greek government bonds owned by the ECB would be considered 'monetary financing', thus giving the German constitutional court a trigger to stop the ECB's crucial debt-purchasing programme. Furthermore, the German judges also stipulated that 'purchased bonds are only in exceptional cases' to be 'held until maturity'. If the Greek government were to legislate the prolongation of repayment two decades beyond maturity (as I was proposing), Draghi and the ECB would have fallen foul of the German Constitutional Court. Even if the latter did not act against Draghi upon such a Greek government move, the markets would panic, interpreting the Greek action as a significant boost to the probability that the ECB's trillion-euro debt purchases were in jeopardy. See Bundesverfassungsgericht press release no. 34/2016, 21 June 2016, 'Constitutional Complaints and Organstreit Proceedings Against the OMT Programme of the European Central Bank Unsuccessful', http://www.bundesverfassungsgericht.de /SharedDocs/Pressemitteilungen/EN/2016/bvg16-034.html, last accessed 11 November 2016.

6. A former PASOK finance minister reported in 2011 that Wolfgang Schäuble had expressed his preference for Greece to exit the euro and return to the drachma. My conversations with Dr Schäuble, described fully in following chapters, confirmed this.

7. The president of the Hellenic Republic is voted in by parliament. Three ballots are allowed. In the first one the winning candidate must be voted in by a minimum of 200 of the 300 members of parliament. If no candidate secures this two-thirds majority, a second ballot takes place under the same rule. If again no candidate succeeds, then there is a final ballot in which the required number of votes falls from 200 to 180. If no candidate secures 180 votes, parliament is automatically dissolved and the next parliament elects the president with a simple majority (151 members out of 300). In December 2014 the Samaras government could count on only 153 members and would have to secure the support of a smaller centre-Left party plus a handful of independents to achieve the necessary 180 votes.

8. The Ministry of the Economy includes trade, industry, shipping, tourism and the crucial portfolio of managing the EU's structural funds. The new Ministry of Productive Reconstruction would include public works, energy and the environment.

9. When I asked Alexis in private why Syriza had ditched my *Five-Pronged Strategy*, his masterful response was that the party was not sufficiently mature. He said the leadership lacked the determination to win the June 2012 election and admitted they were not prepared for government.

10. I also said that our proposals must correspond to substantial debt relief but be of the sort that Merkel could present to her people as her own idea. This could be achieved without an outright haircut by utilizing financial 'engineering' or debt swaps – of the type I ended up proposing to Berlin and to the Eurogroup in February 2015 (see Chapters 5 and 6).

11. Unlike Britain, where ministers must be members of parliament, the Greek prime minister can appoint extra-parliamentarian ministers, as long as the government wins a general vote of confidence in parliament.

12. Greek electoral law specifies that a small number of members of parliament are drawn from a ranked party list. If Syriza, for instance, wins four such positions, the first four candidates on the Syriza list become members of parliament. Each party's quota for these seats is based on its nationwide percentage of the vote.

13. Voters first choose which party they prefer by picking the party's ballot paper and then indicate which of the party's candidates they want to send to parliament.

14. Plan Z, the troika's plan for ejecting Greece from the eurozone and managing Grexit's repercussions, was devised within the ECB but in collaboration with the German government and the European Commission. It involved a very small number of officials who worked in secret. See 'Inside the ECB's Plan Z' by Peter Spiegel in the *Financial Times*, 14 May 2014. https://www.ft.com/content/0ac1306e -d508-11e3-9187-00144feabdc0

15. The first two ballots for the election of Greece's president are ritualistic unless the two larger parties have agreed on a common candidate (see Chapter 4, Note 7).

16. 'Xenophon Zolotas: Parallels and Lessons from back then for today', Speech by Bank of Greece Governor, Mr Yannis Stournaras, Bank of Greece, 15 December 2014.

17. See Appendix 3 for a more analytical presentation of this argument.

18. Not content with the accusations of idiocy and irresponsibility I faced from establishment opinion makers, I invented tough questions of my own. Here is a Q&A that I published online around the same time.

> Q: What will you do if Berlin and Frankfurt respond to your overtures for a renegotiated deal with a fat *Nein*, deciding to punish you with a liquidity switch-off?
>
> A: This is a pertinent question, as such a development would be seriously unpleasant for Greece. But allow me to answer with a question of my own: is there any demand by the creditors to

which you would say no, incurring a similar threat from them? Do you possess no thin red line of your own? If you don't, does this not mean that you are relying on the kindness, and wisdom, of the creditors? Does it not also rely on them caring about Greece, rather than using Greece's crisis as collateral damage in their tussle against Paris, Rome and Madrid. Please tell the voters and let them decide which policy is most dangerous and least dignified. Yours or ours?

19. I met Thomas Mayer at the conference in Florence that I attended in November 2014, the day before flying to Athens for the pivotal meeting with Alexis, Pappas and Dragasakis. We had a long, interesting conversation about the eurozone and exchanged details. He called his parallel currency solution the G-euro. Other advocates of a parallel currency included Dimitri Papadimitriou, who led the Levy Institute at Bard College.

20. See Chapter 3, Note 32.

21. To give it its proper name, the bailout fund was the temporary European Financial Stability Facility (EFSF), based in Luxembourg and subsequently merged with the permanent European Stability Mechanism (ESM).

22. Even astute private-sector operatives cottoned on. A day after that BBC interview (broadcast 13 January 2015), I know not whether as a result of it or independently, Mohamed El-Erian, then Allianz's chief economic adviser and Pimco's CEO, wrote the following in his Bloomberg column.

As it prepares for a possible role in government, Syriza should be supplementing its emphasis on orderly economic management within the eurozone with behind-closed-doors work on the mechanics of an exit, should such an event prove inevitable. In addition to careful and detailed internal preparations for a Plan B for alternative exchange and payments regimes, this would require clear communication of an alternative economic vision for the country.

Keen to signal that our government was neither planning for nor trembling at the knees when threatened with Grexit, I replied to El-Erian on my blog with a clarification: our alternative 'payments regime' did *not* involve a parallel currency but a parallel payments system that would allow us more room to negotiate a decent deal within the eurozone. And yes, we were ready to present an alternative economic vision based on an end to austerity, a permanent end to government deficits and a combination of lower tax rates for businesses and citizens coupled with a development bank to generate new investments, a public bad bank to deal with non-performing loans and a reinforced system of addressing destitution and despair.

Chapter 5: Raging against the dying of the light

1. Alekos Papadopoulos had been close to my mother, a PASOK stalwart herself and one-time deputy mayor of our south Athens municipality. She had used her remarkable capacity to deliver votes in parliamentary elections to support Alekos over many elections, something that he remembered appreciatively. Mum liked and trusted Alekos well before I got to know and work with him. Our relationship solidified when, holed up in the foreign affairs ministry over three days and nights, we worked feverishly to put together PASOK's platform for the April 2004 election campaign in a futile bid to help George Papandreou develop a half-decent economic plan. Neither of us truly believed that it was possible but saw it as an important exercise.

Unfortunately, as it turned out, I ended up regretting his recommendation for a deputy minister in charge of the Treasury. Within a month or so of his appointment I realized he had no capacity to see through the subterfuge of the Treasury officials he was meant to oversee and was concerned at his apparent interest in influencing the appointment of high-powered positions in state-owned or -controlled organizations.

2. See Chapter 3, 'A friendship's last gasp'. The other was the German-trained growth theorist who had approached me in the early 1990s about moving from Sydney to Athens University.

3. This was around the time I was blacklisted from state radio and TV, so I was not surprised to see the video of her performance speedily removed from parliament's website.

4. These institutions were the EFSF and its successor the ESM, whose charter and rulebook Glenn had a hand in authoring.

5. Racism is very thinly veiled in Greek establishment circles. Glenn is as Korean as Barack Obama is Kenyan.

6. When gross fixed capital formation (investment in physical infrastructure such as machinery) is zero, this means that it is not even enough to cover the replacement of broken machinery or depreciation in its value.

7. If ever proof were needed that wage cuts in the midst of a harsh multi-dimensional recession fail to instil confidence in employers, Greece has provided it. Anecdotally, meanwhile, I asked a business acquaintance whose factory made bathroom furniture why he did not employ more people now that labour was dirt cheap. His answer: 'Who will buy my toilet bowls now that wages are so low everywhere that no one can afford to refurbish their bathrooms?'

8. The standard troika response to this observation is: exports did not rise because Greece did not reform sufficiently. But this is to shift the goalposts. Neoliberalism predicts that, all other things being equal, a reduction in average wages in a eurozone country should boost exports, so exports should have increased after wages fell, even if no reform had taken place. They didn't.

9. On 19 May 2014 the IMF's debt sustainability analysis was made public. In it the fund stated,

> more fiscal adjustment is needed to restore debt sustainability. And once there, the primary surplus will have to be maintained at above four per cent of GDP over the full political cycle for many years to come. The adjustment fatigue now evident and the 'social dividends' and 'no new measures' promised by political leaders suggest that the political commitment to the debt strategy will be severely tested going forward. This strategy leaves no scope for any notable increases in wages and pensions from current levels in the run-up to national elections in 2015 and 2016. On the contrary, with tax rates already high and discretionary spending compressed, achieving the necessary additional fiscal adjustment without further cuts in wages and social transfers, not least pensions, which remain high relative to GDP, will only be possible with a dramatic improvement in the efficiency of the public sector . . . Debt sustainability remains a serious concern. Debt to GDP is yet to peak, and the extraordinary levels projected well into the next decade suggest that sustainability concerns will remain an obstacle for the recent improvement in investor sentiments to translate into a durable recovery, especially if doubts resurface about the political resolve.

10. Austerity is measured here in terms of the reduction in the government's budget structural deficit (or increase in its surplus) as a percentage of nominal national income.

11. Britain is an interesting outlier, the reason being that it is the only country on this chart with its own central bank, which under George Osborne's 'expansionary contraction' policy pumped oodles of cash into the British economy while the chancellor practised his contractionary austerity.

12. See Chapter 2, 'Prisoners of their own device'.

13. Chapter 6, Note 2 describes an email from my immediate predecessor to the troika, which I saw on taking office, that illustrates the Catch-22 beautifully.

14. In March alone €1.1 billion would be needed to repay four debt instalments to the IMF.

15. Wieser's actual words were: 'Based on current cash-flow projections, which assume no further IMF or EFSF disbursement and no transfer of European Central Bank profits on Greek bonds held as part of the SMP programme . . .' The EFSF was the source of the second bailout loans extended to Greece in 2012. The origin of the ECB profits on Greece's SMP bonds was as follows: in 2010–11 the ECB had bought these bonds from French and German banks at less than 70 per cent of their face value, when their market price was languishing at around 10 per cent of face value (see Chapter 3, Note 32). This was a major boost for Northern

European banks disguised as a move to help Greece's debt retain its value – more fake solidarity with Greece. Every time one of these bonds matured, the bankrupt Greek government was forced to borrow from Europe's taxpayers (the EFSF) in order to repay – at *face value* – the ECB, which now owned those bonds. In other words, the ECB was making a hefty profit at the expense of the bankrupt Greek state and Europe's taxpayers. Some time in 2012 the Eurogroup decided that some of these profits would be returned to the Greek government, not because the Eurogroup had seen the error of its ways but because it was keen to reduce the headline figure of how much more of Europe's taxpayers' money it would be giving Athens to continue with the extending-and-pretending of its insolvency. The meaning of Wieser's sentence, then, is this: You will be getting none of the loan instalments we had agreed with the previous government. You will not even receive any of the profits the ECB made from Greek bonds – your money – that we had agreed to return to you. But you will be expected to make all the debt repayments the previous government was committed to.

16. Note that both Athens's repayments to the troika and the troika's disbursements to Athens were fully specified in the time schedule of the second bailout loan agreement.

17. To quote Wieser: 'To avoid defaulting on Greece's debt obligations a further extension of the current "programme" must be sought . . . [a] measure to fill the financing gap, already used in the midst of the crisis in August 2012, would be an extra issuance of T-bills [but this] requires approval by the troika, which would only happen in the context of a cooperative approach by the new government.' The T-bills he refers to are short-term Treasury bills, IOUs issued by the state with an expiry period of usually three months. Because T-bills are so short term, they are normally considered safe and attract investors at low interest rates. And because they are safe and liquid, central banks accept them readily as collateral in exchange for cash loans, so commercial banks tend to buy these T-bills, post them with the central bank for cash and collect the interest from the state. The problem emerges when the state has no other way of borrowing except T-bills. To prevent the state from issuing too many of them and thus making them unsafe and less acceptable as collateral by the central bank, the ECB places restrictions on how much outstanding T-bill debt a government can have at any point in time. In the case of Greece, this limit was set at €15 billion. But in the summer of 2012, when the Samaras government had just been elected, the ECB increased the limit to €18.3 billion. The reason was self-serving: in August 2012 the Greek government had to redeem Greek government bonds that the ECB owned. Lacking the money to do so, the ECB allowed Athens to issue an additional €3.3 billion of T-bills so as to repay it. Wieser also informed us that we would need to secure this extension before 10 February as it would need to be approved by various parliaments before the guillotine-deadline of 28 February.

18. See Varoufakis, 2016, pp. 160–1.

19. See Chapter 4, 'Chronicle of an ambush foretold'.

20. This was a withdrawal of 6.7 per cent of total deposits, bringing them down to €152 billion, a total similar to the previous low in June 2012 when a similar panic had reduced them to €150.5 billion.

21. There was no other justification for it. The Greek banks were no more inherently troubled than, say, the Italian banks. Only a few months earlier, in fact, the ECB itself had declared that the Greek banks had passed the stress tests it subjected them too. This is in contrast to the Cypriot banks in 2013 or the Irish ones in 2009, which had well and truly failed.

22. In his email of 21 January 2015, Glenn added,

> An ECB decision is also due to be discussed today post the ELA applications by Eurobank and Alpha Bank and presumably the other two as well. I would have thought that access to ELA is all but certain given the escalation of events even before their Pillar II bonds lose their eligibility as collateral with the ECB funding at the end-February. This drain on liquidity should also be seen in the context of margins calls on Swiss Franc deposits and the potential need for the government to continue tapping investors for short-term Treasury-bill funding. Meanwhile the *New York Times* picked up yesterday on your comments that the ECB's quantitative easing would not in itself solve Greek liquidity issues and your call upon the ECB not to exclude Greece from its bond-buying program.

23. To cut a long story short, Kammenos alleged that George Papandreou had bankrupted Greece on purpose to enrich himself and his family. How? By having his younger brother Andreas (a friend and colleague of mine) purchase credit default swap (CDS) derivatives which were due to pay out to their owner in the event of a Greek government default from the Greek Postbank. (The figures Kammenos mentioned were in the tens of billions of euros.) In my deposition I showed that: the actual payouts from the said CDSs were relatively minuscule; Andreas, if he wanted to conspire in this manner, would never have bought CDSs from the Greek Postbank but in Wall Street or the City directly; and Prime Minister Papandreou's 'crime' was not that he bankrupted Greece to enrich himself but that he did not admit to the state's bankruptcy at all.

24. From Rudyard Kipling's 'If'.

25. Syriza won 149 seats. The Independent Greeks won 13, giving us a parliamentary majority of 12. The official opposition, New Democracy, won 76 (the lowest number in their history), the River (To Potami) won 17, the Golden Dawn won 17, the Greek Communist Party 15, and the depleted PASOK-socialists won 13.

Chapter 6: It begins . . .

1. Foreign Account Tax Compliance Act, a law passed in 2010 that obliges US citizens to report all their foreign transactions.

2. In December 2014, a month before our meeting, my predecessor had sent an email to the troika in which he proposed a series of reforms. His and Antonis Samaras's hope was that the troika would accept these as the last batch of austerity measures and disburse the remaining €7.2 billion that Greece should have received from the troika, mostly to repay the troika. There were three major reasons why that email was ignored: first, the new austerity measures therein were too much for the Samaras government to push through parliament; second, they were too little to satisfy the troika's voracious appetite; third, a third bailout was essential to keep extending-and-pretending the state's bankruptcy, something that the Samaras government was neither willing nor able to pass through parliament given its depleted majority.

3. *The Serpent's Egg* is a film by Swedish director Ingmar Bergman. Its depiction of the genesis of the Nazi mindset among scientists had shaken me up when I first watched it as a young man.

4. Jamie's brother Peter served as a Vermont state senator after retiring from the State Department's diplomatic service. He was the first US ambassador in Croatia and East Timor, while also playing a significant role in Iraqi Kurdistan.

5. See Chapter 4, Note 13.

6. That was perfectly accurate. But what I did not say was that my Syriza friends wanted them out. In particular Deputy Prime Minister Dragasakis was keen to replace them with people from his own burgeoning circle of apparatchiks.

7. In 1990, shortly after moving to Australia, I arranged for Wassily to follow me. He ended up teaching economics at Charles Sturt University while I taught at the University of Sydney. Four or five years later he returned to Greece to join KEPE – the Greek government's Economics and Planning Research Centre.

8. This is the EYP, the government's National Intelligence Agency, though most Greeks still refer to it as the Central Intelligence Agency (KYP), as it was known during the seven-year dictatorship (1967–74), when it was fully controlled by the American CIA.

9. Andreas Papandreou, prime minister 1981–9 and then again from 1993 until his death in 1996, was the father of George Papandreou, who was elected PM in 2009 and jettisoned by Chancellor Merkel, with the help of pretenders within his father's party, in 2011 (see Chapter 2). The original George Papandreou, George Junior's grandfather and Andreas's father, was prime minister in the 1960s. His overthrow set Greece on course for the military *coup d'état* on 21 April 1967 which ushered in the dictatorship during which my generation grew up.

10. When its members were in Greece, rather than in Brussels or elsewhere, the war cabinet met daily. It comprised Alexis, Deputy Prime Minister Dragasakis,

Alexis's alter ego Nikos Pappas, myself, Euclid and Sagias, the cabinet secretary. Often we were joined by Chouliarakis, chair of the Council of Economic Advisers, Stathakis, the economy minister, and Gabriel Sakellaridis, the government's spokesperson. Later on, as the plot thickened in May and June, two Syriza party representatives were added to the group, ostensibly to provide a link with the party faithful.

11. Consider the example of François Hollande. He was elected in 2012 on a combative pledge to oppose Chancellor Merkel's 'fiscal compact' of austerity and to use France's might to drag the EU into a pro-growth, public-investment-led recovery programme. And yet on the day after his election, all that courageous talk was forgotten, never to be recalled again. Why? Sources close to the president told me that immediately after his election he received a phone call from the governor of France's central bank warning him that the French banks were still in serious trouble and that the ECB's indispensable support might not come if he continued to antagonize Berlin.

12. See Chapter 6 in Varoufakis, 2016.

13. In 1953 the US government brokered the so-called London Debt Agreement. In essence, the United States leaned on Britain, France, Greece, Italy, Spain, Sweden, Yugoslavia, Norway, Switzerland and many other countries to write off the greatest part of Germany's pre-war debt to them. The British government protested, arguing that Germany had both the capacity and the moral duty to pay. Washington vetoed London and, to lead by example, immediately wrote off the loans that it had forwarded to Bonn after 1945. Germany's debts to nations and private creditors were haircut by more than 70 per cent. See Varoufakis, 2016.

14. Βάστα Ρόμελ! – from the Greek verb βαστώ or βαστάζω, which translates as 'to bear', 'to hold on', 'to hang on'.

15. I took it for granted that Jeroen would never have issued the ultimatum without Berlin's approval. I also assumed that we could not count on Paris for significant support. Nevertheless, it was incumbent upon me to verify the extent to which Paris had pre-agreed with Berlin our asphyxiation or to what extent I could count on the French finance minister for support in the Eurogroup.

16. SDOE was the Greek acronym, standing for Σώμα Δίωξης Οικονομικού Εγκλήματος.

17. To make it all possible, I appointed Michalis Hatzitheodorou head of the ministry's General Secretariat for Information Systems. Having completed a PhD at Columbia in image processing, he returned to Greece to set up a small IT-service-providing company. With no connections to politics or the oligarchy, and with an adamantine character that I could vouch for personally (we had been friends since school), he was ideal for the job.

18. While she was France's finance minister, Christine Lagarde had sent my predecessors in government a list of names of Greeks with accounts at HSBC Switzerland that a whistle-blower had leaked. Unlike the German, French

and Spanish tax authorities, which used the information to ascertain tax evasion by their citizens and recover significant sums, previous Greek governments had been conspicuous by their refusal to act. This was not the only such list in circulation. But while it was important to look into such lists, I did not trust the tax office's capacity or willingness to delve properly and effectively into them. Additionally, the lists were old (going back to 2004) and were mere snapshots of bank account balances and therefore of little use in uncovering actual income streams. Finally, without the cooperation of the Swiss authorities, which was wholly unforthcoming, it would be difficult to use what information we had to make any prosecution stick. The deal I made with the Swiss finance minister tackled the underlying problem – the holding of untaxed Greek income in Switzerland – while circumventing all these obstacles to doing so.

19. As these agreements take some time to complete, the Swiss finance minister and I shook hands on this deal on 28 April in my office.

20. Επιτροπή Παιγνίων.

21. Stergiotis stood up to OPAP, which went to great lengths to undermine my policies. He paid the price for doing so, with his term cut short once I was out of the ministry.

22. *An Inquiry into the Nature and Causes of the Wealth of Nations*, 1776, Book 1, Chapter 2.

Chapter 7: Auspicious February

1. The notion of 'Bankruptocracy' in Varoufakis, 2011, is relevant: a regime in which bankrupt banks rule based on the principle that the greater one's losses, the greater one's power to extract rents from the rest of society.

2. Collective bargaining was dismantled by the previous New Democracy–PASOK government at the behest of the troika, with the IMF leading the charge.

3. As explained in Chapter 5, 'First contact'. The only difference between the situation of our newly elected government and Samaras's was that our repayment was due not to the ECB but to the IMF.

4. See Varoufakis, 2016 for a historical and economic account of how the French elites' determination to share a currency with Germany put France on a long path towards political and economic decline.

5. Aegina has a rich history going back to the Neolithic age and was the first Greek polis to mint official coins.

6. ELA would provide around €22 billion of liquidity. The people at Morgan Stanley, who for some reason saw fit to send me helpful updates on their views, informed me that in addition to this Greece's four systemic banks had another €30 billion to play with courtesy of structured (or, as they call them in the trade,

ABS/Covered) bonds at their disposal. They added that, in their opinion, the eurozone would not dare to choke us completely as Grexit would cost it dearly.

7. See http://www.bbc.com/news/world-europe-31083574

8. See http://www.cityam.com/208589/adam-smith-institute-calls-osborne-back-varoufakiss-greek-debt-swap-plan

9. Explained more fully in Chapter 3, Note 36, and mentioned crucially in the confrontation with Jeroen Dijsselbloem in Chapter 6, 'Ultimatum'.

10. To get Merkel to agree to the quantitative easing programme in spite of the wishes of the Bundesbank, one of the conditions that Draghi had to impose was that no more than a certain percentage of a government's outstanding bonds/debt could be purchased by the ECB. If the new perpetual bond I was recommending had stayed on the ECB's books, it would have limited the number of new Greek bonds that the ECB could purchase, thus limiting the positive impact of quantitative easing on the Greek government's capacity to borrow again, afresh, from private investors.

11. Glenn's email confirmed that the four Greek banks would be hit badly by Draghi's move. 'From what I see,' Glenn wrote, the waiver removal would

> involve some €27 billion of cash collateral (out of a total €41 billion of pre-waiver withdrawal ECB exposure) which will come at a cost of 1.55 per cent. The most affected would be Eurobank (roughly a 6–7 per cent hit to 2015 net interest income) and Alpha (6 per cent hit), while Piraeus (4 per cent) and National Bank of Greece (2 per cent) would be the least affected. Note, however, that banks have increased exposure to ECB after deposits outflows by I guess about €20 to €21 billion . . . hence the real impact could much higher than that. At this stage, only EFSF bonds will be still eligible for ECB funding.

12. The economic mantra of General Augusto Pinochet's fascist regime in Chile and that of Schäuble's wing of the CDU had many similarities.

13. Of course, when we did go to the institutions with our proposals, the institutions would also refuse to engage with them, demanding reams and reams of data instead. The purpose of this interminable data gathering was to avoid any response, positive or negative, to our proposals. Meanwhile the press would broadcast that I was arriving in Berlin, Brussels and Frankfurt with no proposals.

14. Alexis's wreath-laying had been interpreted in Germany as a hostile gesture. By mentioning it during a speech in which I was praising the Germans for their successful purge of Nazism, I was trying to build a bridge. My point was that Greeks and Germans shared a common experience of Nazism and therefore a common aim: combating its economic underpinning, which was a permanently deflationary economy.

15. Willy Brandt was the SPD's leader 1964–87 and West Germany's chancellor 1969–74. During the latter period he had played an important role in marginalizing Greece's right-wing dictators while at the same time giving sanctuary to fleeing Greek democrats.

Chapter 8: The frenzy before the storm

1. The title of his memoir about that work suggests those words stayed with him. See James K. Galbraith, *Welcome to the Poisoned Chalice: The Destruction of Greece and the Future of Europe*, 2016, Yale.

2. Without this small army of aides I would have been at the mercy of the ministry's Council of Economic Advisers led by George Chouliarakis, who had already demonstrated himself and his team to be utterly unwilling and possibly incapable of doing anything beyond regurgitating the troika's models and projections. With the clock ticking I thought it best to defer a confrontation until after an interim agreement had been reached at the Eurogroup.

3. https://www.nytimes.com/2015/02/17/opinion/yanis-varoufakis-no-time-for-games-in-europe.html?_r=0

4. Oscar Wilde, *The Soul of Man Under Socialism*, 1891.

5. I was paraphrasing John Maynard Keynes, who wrote of the Versailles Treaty: '[the German government's] insincere acceptance . . . of impossible conditions which it was not intended to carry out – an acceptance which made Germany as guilty to accept what she could not fulfil as the Allies to impose what they were not entitled to exact'. See John Maynard Keynes, *Dr Melchior: A Defeated Enemy*, 1920 and Chapter 8 of Varoufakis, 2016.

6. Such evidence included the rehiring of the cleaners who had been dismissed from the Finance Ministry illegally (according to the Greek courts) as well as a few hundred state school janitors, and a pledge not to reduce pensions beyond the twelve separate cuts that had already reduced them by a stupendous 40 per cent.

7. Even though Dombrovskis was senior to Moscovici, he rarely took the lead. I suspect this was because his presentation skills left much to be desired. In any case, his real job was to watch over Pierre, rather than lead anything, let alone a discussion.

8. Recall that, well before our election, the Eurogroup had agreed that the ECB's profits on the Greek government bonds purchased as part of the SMP programme should be returned at regular intervals to Athens, but as Wieser's non-paper, sent to us via email by Thomas Asmussen, had made clear, the troika now intended to withhold that money. See Chapter 5, 'First contact'.

9. Just before I entered the room, Glenn Kim had sent me a warning. According to his sources, Chancellor Merkel, unwilling to get involved herself, was inclined to let the European Commission find a solution to the new Greek drama, but the Spanish government was kicking and screaming. The reason was that they faced elections in which Syriza's equivalent, Podemos, was threatening to do well. Glenn recommended that I keep an eye out for any sabotage Luis de Guindos attempted.

10. The Austrian and Belgian governments were internally divided in that they were headed by social democrats while their finance ministers came from the equivalent of Wolfgang Schäuble's Christian Democrats.

11. Some member states' constitutions or parliamentary rules require any EU decision with a potential impact on the state's finances to be passed through their parliaments. This includes Germany, Austria and Finland. But in most member states, such as Italy or France, there is no need for a parliamentary vote.

Chapter 9: A moment to savour, darkly

1. See Chapter 6 in Varoufakis, 2016.

2. In my introduction I repeated my argument that reforming the troika's programme was essential if we were to persuade the people of Greece to accept it, and that the manner in which the troika had conducted itself in Athens until then had been counterproductive in that regard. 'Our commitment to working with each one of the three institutions is unwavering . . . We consider today's meeting here in Brussels to be a new beginning that will serve the interests both of Greece and the EU . . . We have reviewed the *MoU* in detail and want to discuss it with you.' I was frank about our government's inexperience, and contrasted our team's meagre resources with theirs. But our inexperience was a normal feature of the democratic process, I assured them, was to be expected whenever an electorate voted in a new government, and granting an incoming government a honeymoon period in which to develop its ideas into policy was an essential part of that process. That being the case I suggested that the meeting consider our team's overarching policy framework rather than get bogged down in minutiae. After all, the Eurogroup was waiting for an agreement in principle based on the identification of common ground between the *MoU* and our government's plans. I also mentioned my team of untouchables and our serious attempt to apprehend hundreds of thousands of tax cheats. If the troika was interested in reforms of substance and a large-scale infusion of cash into our state's coffers, I told them I expected them to support this particular effort enthusiastically.

3. Over the course of the first day the leaks got worse. At one point Jamie reported to me that our team was upset at the press's suggestion that they were incapable of putting forward proposals for 'extending the programme' that the troika could accept. Immediately I wrote back,

> We must turn their own narrative against them, simply by saying: thank you for pointing this out. You are right. We are unable to present any policies leading to successful completion of the current programme

for the simple reason that this programme cannot be salvaged. This is why we insisted in the Eurogroup on major amendments. Indeed, our teams are meeting today and tomorrow on a mission not to complete the current programme but to build a bridge to new, viable arrangements. Without amendments on the logic of its financial, debt and reforms agenda, and tranquillity over the time required to reach them, there can be no programme.

4. For example, in my summary of our discussions with the troika I had written, 'On structural reforms, good progress was made to identify a large number of areas where the Greek authorities can support the ongoing reform agenda . . . Time is needed over the coming weeks for the new government to make a more detailed assessment of ongoing reforms. The Greek government is fully committed to continue efforts made in these areas.' Euclid told me to delete 'large' in the first sentence and recommended that I replace the last sentence with: 'The Greek government is committed to continue a reform agenda which takes the best elements of the current programme and its own reform agenda.' Elsewhere I had written, 'The Greek authorities are committed to continued primary surpluses over the next decade to ensure sound public finances.' He advised me to replace 'decade' with 'near future', adding, 'After all we are seeking a debt conference which should make such a promise redundant.' How things would change a few months later when Euclid replaced me.

5. This is also true of paper money if restrictions are in place on its removal from the country.

6. A frequent criticism of my planned parallel payments system was that it would be euro-denominated only in theory, but in reality a euro within the parallel payment system would be worth less than a 'proper' paper euro. This is true, but if the ECB introduced capital controls, then the country would in effect have a dual currency already, so the argument is somewhat academic.

7. At the core of this informal and rather loose war cabinet, which had been convening in the prime minister's office at Maximos to discuss strategy in the previous weeks, were Alexis, Pappas, Tzanakopoulos, Dragasakis, Sagias and Euclid.

8. In an admirable display of restraint, the press made very little of the story of how Jeroen Dijsselbloem's office had retracted a claim it originally made, that he had been awarded a Masters degree by an Irish university. I often wondered how the same journalists would have treated me if my credentials had been subject to similar controversy.

9. Juncker's draft proposed the adoption of a code of civil procedure, changes to the income tax code and the tax procedures code, legislation to broaden the definition of tax fraud and evasion and reform of the gas market. It also asked us whether there were other reforms that could be adopted swiftly – a most collaborative and thus welcome approach.

10. The European Commission is the closest the EU has to a government, and a commissioner has a status equivalent to a minister of state, whereas the Eurogroup, as previously mentioned, has no legal standing in any of the EU treaties. In that sense, Dijsselbloem was, officially and legally, no more than the Dutch finance minister, outranked in law by Moscovici.

11. In our *Modest Proposal* the EIB is hailed as a possible pillar for economic development, to sit alongside the pillar of financial stability that the ECB was meant to be. See Appendix in Varoufakis, 2016.

12. Dimitris Tzanakopoulos was a young lawyer and Syriza activist who was elevated to government spokesperson and given a ministry without portfolio a few months after my resignation.

13. Only George Stathakis, my academic colleague and economy minister, was prepared openly to dispute the strength of this commitment – and he did so from the very first day we were in government. I remember him telling me in private that when the crunch came 'we would accept whatever they gave us'. At the time I was outraged, as was Alexis, who for this reason kept Stathakis at arm's length, which explains why Stathakis was not a regular attendee at the war cabinet during our first months in government. As it turned out, George was the only Syriza insider who was consistently honest with me, and to his further credit, he tried to warn me that the others' militancy was 'impermanent'.

14. The €10.9 billion in question was left over from the second bailout's recapitalization of Greece's banks, worth €50 billion in total – see Chapter 2, 'Bailoutistan 2.0' and Chapter 5, 'Greek-covery'. This left-over capital was insufficient to restore the Greek banks to health, in view of the huge non-performing loans on their books, and the troika was reluctant to let the Greek government pour more good money after bad before some solution had been found for the non-performing loans. The IMF and the ECB wanted this to take the form of foreclosures and auctions of repossessed homes and offices. Politically that would have been exceptionally toxic, so the €10.9 billion simply sat gathering dust on the books of the HFSF, the EFSF's Greek branch, in the form of EFSF bonds. The ECB wanted to repatriate these EFSF bonds from the HFSF to the EFSF. Why? For effect, to demonstrate that they were getting tough on us. But in reality it made no difference since, even when these EFSF bonds were in the bosom of the HFSF, the Greek government had no authority to use them without the authorization of the Eurogroup Working Group and thus of the ECB. Remarkably, the opposition in our parliament portrayed this inconsequential transfer as 'Varoufakis's loss of €11 billion from under his nose'.

Chapter 10: Unmasked

1. Manolis Glezos called the 20 February agreement an exercise in 'rebranding meat as fish' – in Orthodox Christianity consumption of meat is prohibited during Lent, but fish is sometimes deemed acceptable – and apologized to the people of Greece for having supported our government and thus participated in their deception. Mikis Theodorakis described me and Alexis as insects lured by a ruthless spider into its web.

2. It is remarkable that a minister of state had to negotiate for the right to introduce a clause into an agreement with international creditors stating that the courts of the land should be allowed to carry out the duties vested in them by the constitution. From my discussions with judges from Greece's Council of State it was clear that, since the first bailout, they had been leaned upon to make rulings that went against their actual legal opinions – the ultimate humiliation for decent men and women who had dedicated their lives to the rule of law.

3. George Chouliarakis is the only person to have succeeded in my presence in making Euclid Tsakalotos so furious as to swear.

4. The reader may suspect that Wolfgang Schäuble's opposition to the communiqué of the 20 February Eurogroup was mere pretence, designed to lure me into the belief that I had got my way in order to trap me at the meeting of 23 February. I do not believe so. During the Eurogroup of 20 February Wolfgang was visibly agitated. He is neither as duplicitous nor as good an actor as would be required for such an elaborate ploy.

5. The relevant passage stated, 'The Greek authorities have also committed to ensure the appropriate primary fiscal surpluses or financing proceeds required to guarantee debt sustainability in line with the November 2012 Eurogroup statement. The institutions will, for the 2015 primary surplus target, take the economic circumstances in 2015 into account.' The phrase 'appropriate primary fiscal surpluses' signalled that the previous targets had been set aside and were open to negotiation with our government, recognizing our right to negotiate the end of austerity, while the phrase 'guarantee debt sustainability' opened the door to a genuine negotiation on debt restructuring.

Chapter 11: Whittling our spring

1. Syriza members of parliament were split between those who were relieved at the extension of the loan agreement and those, mainly from the Left Platform, who were livid that it had been extended instead of rescinded. Interestingly, almost none objected to the lack of prior parliamentary approval per se, concentrating instead on whether the extension should have been secured at all. (Had they known how between 20 and 25 February our position had been jeopardized by my representative in the Eurogroup Working Group, I am sure they would have reacted differently.) At a specially convened tumultuous parliamentary party meeting I spent a good hour on the podium explaining why the extension had been necessary, taking personal responsibility for the whole affair while Alexis, Pappas and Dragasakis looked on.

2. See Paul Mason, 2016, 'The Inside Story of Syriza's Struggle to Save Greece: Exclusive interviews with the party's top players shed light on the eurozone showdown', *The Nation* http://www.thenation.com/article/the-inside-story-of -syrizas-struggle-to-save-greece/

3. See Alastair Crooke, 2011, 'Permanent temporariness', *London Review of Books*, Vol. 33, no. 5, pp. 24–5.

4. See Chapter 6 of Varoufakis, 2016.

5. For more on T-bills see Chapter 5, Note 17.

6. With the remaining 33 per cent dispersed across multiple investors who would gradually sell their share to Cosco.

7. See Chapter 4, Note 4 for the full repayment schedule. The payments in July included €3.49 billion to the ECB to redeem some of the infamous SMP bonds, and the payments in August were all to the ECB in lieu of more maturing SMP bonds.

8. In January 2016 the creditors proceeded with the transfer of the port of Piraeus to Cosco on the terms that pre-existed our government. Cosco may have ended up with the 67 per cent equity in the third quay it sought, but China lost out on the long-term large-scale investments I had proposed in Greece's railways, which the troika sold to an Italian company incapable of serious investment, a tech park and shipyards, which at the time of writing are close to permanent closure. The privatization took place without the minimum investment or labour protection or safeguards for the local economy that Beijing had committed to in our dealings. Also lost was Beijing's readiness to help the Greek state get back on its feet (by buying government bonds) when one day it regains solvency. In other words, Greece lost a strategic industrial partnership that went far beyond a port deal.

9. See Chapter 7, 'Social democracy's Waterloo'.

10. When I took over the finance ministry, arrears to the state amounted to €76.08 billion. Of this the tax office estimated that only €8.9 billion was potentially collectable. When I pressed them they confessed that of that €8.9 billion, €1.6 billion was owed by 3.5 million citizens who owed less than €2,000 each – the little people who had been squashed by the crisis and the ensuing austerity. It was these little people that the bill aimed to rescue from official insolvency. The troika's retort was that rich Greeks, who had defaulted strategically seeking to have their arrears to the state written down, were let off the hook by our legis- lation – and it was they who owed the bulk of the €76.08 billion. Correct. Except that my ministry and Greece's courts did not have the resources and mechanisms necessary to identify strategic defaulters and separate them from the little people. It would take years for these to be developed, and the little people would perish in the meantime. Besides, as I kept telling the troika, the strategic defaulters were mostly beyond our reach, as they lived in London, New York, Paris and so on. 'Let us release the little people from their debt bondage,' I remember telling Christine Lagarde, 'and then, in a few months, once our algorithmic method for catching the cheats is in place, we will deal with them separately.' But no, the troika knew better. As these lines are being written two years later, arrears to the state have topped €90 billion.

11. Kemal Dervish also advised me to resist fire sales and blanket privatizations. This intrigued me because he had a reputation in the West as a great neoliberal modernizer. But his real story is different. Take for example the case of Turkish Airlines. In 2001 the IMF placed Kemal under immense pressure to privatize loss-making Turkish Airlines, but he chose not to. Instead he identified the cause of the losses: 'stupid price controls, no peak-load pricing and political interference' as he put it to me. Instead of giving the company away to a foreign airline Kemal reformed the aviation law and allowed aggressive peak-load pricing. Today Turkish Airlines is recognized as a leading airline worldwide. Kemal finished his excellent advice to me with: only privatize when you think the price is right.

12. See Yanis Varoufakis, Joseph Halevi and Nicholas Theocarakis, *Modern Political Economics: Making sense of the post-2008 world* (2011), Routledge, London and New York, pp. 125–7.

13. http://www.telegraph.co.uk/news/worldnews/islamic-state/11459675/Greeces-defence-minister-threatens-to-send-migrants-including-jihadists-to-Western-Europe.html

14. Since by early March it was clear that the creditors were leaking falsehoods to the media about what I was telling them, what they were telling me and the level of sophistication of my presentations, I made sure there was an eyewitness present at those meetings. Jeff Sachs's personal acquaintance with most of the major players including Lagarde and Draghi and the respect they had for him made him the ideal candidate.

Chapter 12: Merkel's spell

1. Jeff was referring to the postwar Americans and Europeans who had designed and built the European Union.

2. For example, see my article 'Europe Needs an Hegemonic Germany', 24 July 2013, in the German financial daily *Handelsblatt*.

3. A swap deal between central banks of different countries means that one bank commits to exchange a certain amount of its currency with the currency of the other. A swap deal between the Fed and the Central Bank of Greece was likely to give us access to dollars (after Grexit) at a given exchange rate with Greece's new currency.

4. Jamie wasted a day or two travelling to Wall Street to meet these gentlemen. He reported back to me that they talked a good talk, had booked offices in the building

where the legendary Paul Volcker's offices were and were concocting a mechanism by which a Fed swap line would be combined with Greece providing US companies with oil and gas drilling rights in the Eastern Mediterranean basin. The unfortunate hitch was that no one had talked to the Fed. It was a little like saying that your student newspaper could offer major publicity exposure once Rupert Murdoch had invested massively in it but neglecting to discuss the idea with Rupert.

5. So Alexis reported to me. After an initial trip to Moscow Alexis returned full of smiles, as he had secured an advance of €5 billion from Putin for the construction of a pipeline. Alexis had expected me to be enthused – €5 billion, he thought, would go a long way – but I had disappointed him by replying that, even if the money was available, we should delay receiving it for as long as possible. If we took it, the troika would simply delay negotiations so that the entire sum would go on paying back the IMF and the ECB. Thankfully we were spared this dilemma by the Russians. During his second visit to Russia, this time to St Petersburg, Alexis reported that Putin had withdrawn his offer and told him to go to the Germans instead. I had this confirmed personally when the Russian finance minister called me to say that international sanctions were depleting Moscow's coffers and unfortunately he did not have the capacity to help us. As I had neither expected nor wanted their help, I was not especially disappointed, but I could foresee the negative impact it would have on Alexis.

6. Not being there to witness any of this, I am basing this part of the narrative on the description Alexis gave to me on his return.

7. It was during their late-night meeting in Brussels in the early hours of 21 March that Merkel formally invited Alexis to Berlin, another move by her that gave Alexis the illusion of a special relationship between them.

Chapter 13: The right stuff, foiled

1. The Battle of Crete began on 20 May 1941. Mainland Greece had already fallen to the Nazis when Hitler ordered the first mass airborne invasion in history in order to capture the island. Crete was defended by Greek, British and what were still referred to as ANZAC troops in Crete and Australia, but the civilian population, including women, old men and children, also fought pitched battles against the German invaders using farm tools and kitchen implements. The island was subdued by 1 June 1941 and many civilians were executed by the occupiers. To this day Cretans walk tall as a result of their defiance.

2. His correct point was that Greece's first and second bailout loan agreements specified that defaulting to one of the three creditors could be considered by the other two as grounds for declaring Greece to be in default to them too.

3. The key argument in my letter to Christine Lagarde was, 'The contractual arrangement binding the Greek authorities and the institutions together implies that . . . while we are renegotiating the loan agreement's conditionalities, parties cannot call an event of default, and a moratorium of payment should apply. In this context, and with a view to allowing the necessary "quiet time" for reaching the 24 April Eurogroup meeting without an "event", we are suggesting either a moratorium of repayments by Greece to the IMF until that date or, alternatively, the removal (prior to 8 April) of the ECB's restrictions (i.e. the return of the waiver and/or the end of limits on the Greek banks' constraint to stay within very low limits of T-bill ownership).'

4. In 2015 the Catholic/Protestant Easter fell on 5 April whereas the Greek Orthodox Easter came a week later, on 12 April.

5. Roumeliotis rose to prominence as a PASOK functionary and government minister in the 1980s. In 2010, despite his PASOK background, Roumeliotis soon came out into the open with caustic criticisms of the first bailout. His courageous stance was noticed and appreciated by Alexis and others within Syriza. At the time of my trip to Washington on 5 April, I was in the process of appointing Roumeliotis chair of the board of the Hellenic Financial Stability Facility (at Dragasakis's encouragement) – an appointment that the troika, via Thomas Wieser, eventually blocked. (In the end, Roumeliotis was appointed chair of the board of Athens Eleftherios Venizelos Airport.) Given his knowledge of the IMF, I was glad to have him with me, especially as our IMF representative at the time, an appointee of the previous government, operated as if he worked for the IMF, rather than as our representative promoting Greece's case within the IMF.

6. From our election to that day in April 2015, our repayments to the IMF amounted to 6 per cent of that period's seasonally adjusted national income. In addition, this peak in IMF payments coincided with the period of the year when national income and thus tax receipts are at their lowest – about 0.86 lower than average owing to the drop in sales after Christmas and low tourism income. Add to that the financial shortfall we inherited from the Samaras government of 4.9 per cent of national income, and we are up to 11.76 per cent. Finally, factor in the ECB's liquidity squeeze, which forced us to dig even deeper into state reserves, and the total percentage of national income that we had to plunder to meet the IMF repayments climbs to 14.21 per cent. For a government locked out of the money markets with a humanitarian crisis on its hands, extracting so much cash from its people to wire to a single creditor is unbearable. We had done it, I told Christine, to show our commitment to meeting our obligations and to negotiating in good faith. 'But we cannot carry on doing it when the ECB is squeezing us dry and, to boot, Brussels and Berlin are all refusing to negotiate matters of life and death to us – like a debt restructure.' This last point was intended to touch a raw nerve at the IMF, especially given Poul Thomsen's confession to me in Paris in early February.

7. My precise words were: 'Given that the disbursements the Greek loan agreement had specified have ceased but at the same time, under the 20 February Eurogroup agreement, we are renegotiating the conditionalities of that loan

agreement, there seems to be a case under English and US law for a moratorium on our repayments as well as for refraining from calling a credit event. On this basis, I have been authorized to request that either the ECB will perform its duty or we must discuss the possibility of postponing the April repayment until there is a final agreement by the Eurogroup.'

8. She also said something that history disproved: that there could be no thirty-day delay after a missed payment before Greece was declared to be in default. For when in June we did default on a payment to the IMF, the IMF board unilaterally bundled that payment with future ones, thus delaying by almost a month the declaration of a Greek default. See Chapter 15, 'Countdown to perdition'.

9. See Chapter 7, 'Promising liaisons – 2. The troika man'.

10. Lagarde made the excellent if sad point about these SMP profits that it was not Draghi's fault that I had never received them. It was Wolfgang's. This is why. The ECB's profits from all the bond trading that it does are distributed to the various national central banks in proportion to each country's GDP. As the central bank of the richest country in the eurozone (the country with the 'largest' economy), the Bundesbank gets the largest cut. The national central banks then wire that money to their respective finance ministries to be used in any way they want. In the case of the profits of the Greek bonds that the ECB had bought under the SMP programme, the Eurogroup had agreed that they would be returned to Athens, but Schäuble and the other finance ministers had already banked that money in 2014. Indeed, they had already spent it. This meant that returning it to us was not really possible as it would require them to take the money out of their 2015 tax revenues, something that Schäuble was eager to avoid.

11. See Chapter 11, Note 10.

12. This is how I narrated my bank-cleansing plan. 'The last thing we want our partners to think is that our left-wing government is snatching the banks. At the same time we shall not allow the bankers to rule the land. What I would like to do is to have Takis appointed chairman of the HFSF. I have a good relationship with the CEO of the HFSF, even though she was close to and appointed by the previous government, and I think with her and with Takis we can do good work to cleanse the banks. At the same time we should bring in new CEOs (we are the main shareholders anyway), established bankers with a good reputation from Northern Europe. Something similar to what happened with the Bank of Cyprus, which brought in Ackerman to run it. This is the only way of moving forward. I am not asking you for an opinion; I am simply sharing this with you. I cannot think of any other solution – to end the revolving-door syndrome between the Greek state and the oligarchy. Our party has no connections with the Greek banking community and thus we are well placed to break up this mafia-like group by bringing in reputable well-established bankers from the outside. I was thinking of England, but then I concluded that Germans might be better, signalling to Berlin a determination to do business.'

Chapter 14: The cruellest month

1. Before returning to Athens I had two exploratory meetings: one at the US Treasury with Under Secretary Nathan Steets (as Jack Lew was not in Washington that day), the other at the White House with Caroline Atkinson of the National Security Council. They were like chalk and cheese. Steets was sympathetic, while Atkinson sounded like a cross between a lowly functionary of the German finance ministry and a throwback to the IMF's pre-2008 days. It was my first whiff of how mixed the messages I would receive in Washington would be.

2. My proposed timetable was as follows. On 12 April Theocarakis would present the N+1 Plan to the Brussels Group. Over the next two days, by 14 April, we would amend it in response to feedback. On 15 April I would present it at the Brookings Institution, Washington, DC, where I had been invited to deliver a major policy speech. Meanwhile, Euclid and Pappas would travel to Brussels to present it to Moscovici while Alexis and Dragasakis approached Merkel and Juncker to tell them that, as far as the Greek government was concerned, this would be the basis of further negotiations. On 17 April I would present the N+1 Plan to US Treasury Secretary Jack Lew. On 19 April Pappas should convene the Frankfurt Group and demand acceptance of the N+1 Plan as the basis for drafting the legislation by means of which the final review would be completed. Finally, between 20 and 24 April, when the Riga Eurogroup was scheduled, the drafting of legislation consistent with the N+1 Plan would be completed. 'Only in this manner and by means of such a tight schedule,' I concluded, 'will we be able to strike an agreement with the creditors.'

3. The final report of the Financial Crisis Inquiry Commission was hailed by the *New York Review of Books* as 'the most comprehensive indictment of the American financial failure that has yet been made' and 'the definitive history of this period'. See Jeff Madrick, 'The Wall Street Leviathan', *New York Review of Books*, 28 April 2011.

4. The committee comprised Phil Angelides, Dina Titus (Democrat congress-woman for Nevada), John Sarbanes (Democrat congressman for Maryland), Niki Tsongas (Democrat congresswoman for Massachusetts) and James Bilirakis (Republican congressman for Florida).

5. Lee related the story of his involvement in some detail. In 2011, when the PASOK administration was in denial about Greece's bankruptcy, he was visited by the then finance minister, George Papakonstantinou. It was clear to Lee that Papakonstantinou was not there by choice but rather at the behest of the IMF. The then Greek government did not even want to hear of debt restructuring, indeed went out of its way to vilify people like me for daring to speak the words. But, according to Lee, the IMF was already freaking out at the thought that they had lent to a bankrupt government without first organizing a restructuring of its debts – hence the pressure on Papakonstantinou to see Lee, the world's foremost authority on debt restructuring. 'They leaned on him to come and see me,' Lee told me. 'He was clearly unhappy to be having that conversation with me.' According to Lee, Papakonstantinou delayed a meaningful debt haircut to such an extent that the IMF wanted him out. After Papakonstantinou was replaced by another PASOK politician, Vangelis Venizelos, in the summer of 2011, Lee was approached again. He told me he could not believe that the new minister would not take seriously his warnings against the kind of debt restructuring that Berlin was imposing on Greece: a massive haircut on privately owned debt coupled with a huge new loan from Europe's taxpayers. Lee was pulling his hair out at Athens squandering a wonderful opportunity for debt relief so as not to ruffle feathers in Berlin. In the end, being the professional that Lee is, he delivered the debt restructuring that Berlin demanded. It was to be the largest haircut in history while, remarkably, leaving Greece's debt thoroughly unpayable. 'It was a terrible thing to have done to the people of Greece, and an excellent opportunity to cut your debt that was wasted, with my participation,' he said. 'If there is anything I can do to help now I would do it unreservedly. Greece deserves a break.'

6. This was seriously good advice, despite its alarming content and the sense of dread it instilled. Two years later, in early 2017, when the debate as to whether Italy should leave the eurozone heated up, Mario Draghi signalled to his fellow Italians that, were Italy to leave the euro, the Central Bank of Italy would have to pay hundreds of billions of euros to the ECB. If any Italian policymakers are reading this, I would thoroughly recommend a brief chat with Lee Buccheit.

7. It was while I was leaving this meeting with Jack Lew that I was approached by an official who kindly warned me of the impending character assassination planned against me. See Chapter 1, 'Theseus before the labyrinth'.

8. The decision to close a country's banks (by refusing them more liquidity from their national central bank's ELA) requires a two-thirds majority of the ECB governing council.

9. See Chapter 9, 'The commissioner's humiliation'.

10. Poul Thomsen's precise words were: 'It means that six months ago we thought that Greece could go back to the markets and there would be no need for new money. Now there will be new need for very significant new money. Secondly, until six months ago we thought there would be no need for debt relief. We thought that the targets would be achievable.'

11. See https://www.bloomberg.com/news/articles/2015–04-24/varoufakis-said -to-take-hammering-from-frustrated-euro-ministers

12. See http://www.reuters.com/article/us-eurozone-greece-varoufakis-idUSK BNoNGoEO20150425

13. See Nikos Sverkos, 'Secrets of the Brussels Media Machine', ThePressProject, 2 May 2015, https://www.thepressproject.gr/article/76506/Secrets-of-the-Brussels -media-machine

14. That morning, Saturday, 25 April, before flying to Athens I had attended the Ecofin meeting. Being a rather ceremonial occasion, each member state was represented by not only its finance minister but also its central bank governor. While we were sitting together Stournaras said to me that he thought the time had come to introduce capital controls – just as Benoît Cœuré had told me a week earlier, on 16 April, in Washington. (See this chapter, 'The troika in Paris'.) My reply to Stournaras was the same as my reply to Benoît: our government opposed capital controls as we did not believe they were consistent with a monetary union.

15. In December 2008 a policeman had shot and killed a youth in Exarcheia, claiming he felt threatened. The result was not just the death of a teenager but ten days of fire and violence.

Chapter 15: Countdown to perdition

1. Along with the debt swaps would be an agreement that would allow Greece to enter the ECB's quantitative easing programme, thus reducing our dependence on European taxpayers' money. The investment initiative was to involve the European Investment Bank and the creation of a development bank utilizing the nation's remaining public assets.

2. There was another, more personal, factor that may have been involved. In the summer of 2015 the term of the Eurogroup presidency expired. Luis was ambitious to replace Jeroen and was clearly soliciting votes from finance ministers at this time.

3. The co-signatories, as they appeared on the cover page, were: James K. Galbraith (University of Texas at Austin), Jeff Sachs (Columbia University, special adviser to the UN secretary general), Lord (Norman) Lamont (formerly Britain's chancellor of the exchequer), Mariana Mazzucato (University of Sussex and author of *The Entrepreneurial State*), Thomas Mayer (director of Flossbach von Storch, formerly chief economist at Deutsche Bank), and Larry Summers (Harvard University, formerly US Treasury secretary).

4. Just before this Wolfgang and I had been at a meeting of finance ministers discussing the possibility of imposing a financial transactions tax (FTT) across a subgroup of EU member states. At that meeting the two of us managed to be in agreement for once, voting together against other member states' objections to the FTT. When that meeting ended, Wolfgang retired to his office, where I visited him with my deputies.

5. The 'other proposal' he was referring to was that of a German firm of financial and investment advisers, Goetzpartners, whose proposals were consistent with my idea of a development bank utilizing public assets as collateral. In the weeks that followed I collaborated with the Goetzpartners representatives to improve my *Policy Framework*. See Note 7, below.

6. This is the scene as Alexis had described it to me. Of course I was not present and cannot corroborate Alexis's account of exactly what was said and how.

7. This new document differed from the earlier *Policy Framework* in two major ways. The first was that I had incorporated, despite my misgivings, the fiscal targets that Alexis had accepted. As a loyal member of his government and his finance minister, I had to accept collective responsibility for the woeful concessions he had made while trying to salvage what remained. The second change was a major improvement in the design of the proposed development bank. This would in one stroke stop the fire sales of public assets the troika was insisting upon while putting an end to their underutilization by the Greek state. This policy initiative was developed in association with the German consulting firm Goetzpartners, an outfit with close connections to both with the Chancellery and the federal finance ministry.

8. In fact, months later I put together my interpretation of Schäuble's vision in an article published in *Die Zeit* entitled 'Dr Schäuble's Plan': http://www.zeit .de/2015/29/schuldenkrise-europa-wolfgang-schaeuble-yanis-varoufakis. For an English-language version see https://www.yanisvaroufakis.eu/2015/07/17/dr -schaubles-plan-for-europe-do-europeans-approve-english-version-of-my-article-in -die-zeit/

9. In an op-ed I contributed to the German financial daily *Handelsblatt* on 24 July 2013 ('Europe needs an hegemonic Germany') I had surprised many by arguing in favour of a strong Germany as the best way of leading Europe out of its difficulties. In that context it should not have been surprising that I wanted a robust Schäuble singing in unison with an energised Merkel and doing the right thing. In my mind at least, that wish was perfectly compatible with a determination go to war against them if they insisted on doing the wrong thing by Europe by demanding our surrender.

10. In fact, like many other European countries, Greece had three VAT rates: 6, 11 and 23 per cent. But, dating back to the 1940s, the islands of the Aegean received a discount of 30 per cent on VAT because transport was so difficult and as a result the cost of doing business or living there was higher. Thomsen counted the discounted rates on the islands as an extra three, adding up to six rates nationwide. The fact that other countries such as Spain, which includes the Canary Islands, had similar arrangements was irrelevant to him.

11. The labour reforms Thomsen wanted were a commitment on our side not to reintroduce the right of trade unions to collective bargaining, and to release large businesses, mainly banks and supermarkets, from the legal restraint on mass dismissals.

12. A model's parameters are its constants – its inbuilt assumptions – as opposed to its variables. The tax rate in our models was a constant, whereas the revenue from them was a variable, depending on myriad other factors. A parametric reform would therefore be a change in the model's assumptions – in this case, the tax rate.

13. Kafetsi had been the museum's inaugural director in 2000. For more than a decade she had struggled, mostly alone, to find a dedicated building in the centre of Athens for the museum. Eventually she succeeded in securing an old brewery for the purpose and having it suitably converted, but only weeks before it was due to open the Samaras government removed her from her position. A year later, after we had won the election, EMST remained closed. My sources reported that a banker was blocking its opening in order to prevent a letter of credit he had offered the museum from being cashed in.

14. See Chapter 2, 'Blacklisted'.

15. See Chapter 6, 'Home front'.

16. On 26 May Euclid voted against Elena; Stathakis and I voted for her, and Dragasakis abstained because, as he explained, Elena was clearly the most suitable candidate but, at the same time, the party did not want her.

Chapter 16: Adults in the room

1. See Chapter 13, Note 8.

2. A month after the banks were shut down, a German member of the European parliament, Fabio De Masi, wrote to Mario requesting a copy of that legal opinion. Mario replied that 'confidentiality' did not permit him to share its contents. Later, Fabio and I launched a campaign, Release #TheGreekFiles, involving politicians, academics, law experts and members of the public, to have this legal opinion released.

3. I also said, 'The fiscal council would, under this agreement, monitor the state budget's execution on a weekly basis, issue warnings if a minimum primary surplus target looks like being violated in the foreseeable future and, at some point, trigger automated across-the-board horizontal reductions in all outlays in order to prevent a slide below the pre-agreed threshold. That way a failsafe system will be in place that ensures the solvency of the Greek state and its primary surplus while the Greek government retains the policy space it needs in order to remain sovereign and able to govern within a democratic context.' I proposed the deficit brake as an alternative to pre-emptive austerity. In effect I was saying to the creditors, 'You let me cut tax rates and maintain the minimum pensions, and if I fail to raise incomes and revenues, the automated deficit brake will kick in to increase tax rates and cut minimum pensions.' Having ignored this proposal, a year after my resignation my successor was forced to introduce both new pre-emptive austerity and a deficit break on top of it, i.e. a high surplus target with pension cuts and tax-rate hikes, plus an automated, pre-agreed, further spate of austerity, including even deeper pension cuts and even sharper tax-rate increases, to come into force in the event that their ludicrous targets were not met.

4. I said, 'The conditionalities that we agree upon should be the basis of completing the current – the fifth – review. And at the same time we [should] have a new agreement with the ESM, using the same conditionalit[ies], allowing us to perform an SMP buyback from the ECB, with the SMP profits, which will be around €9 billion, to be disbursed in tranches, with reviews every time so that the implementation of the *MoU* is supervised properly. On top of that, we can have an arrangement that Greece's participation in the ECB's quantitative easing is also subject to the successful completion of these reviews of the new *MoU*. The only reason why I am tiring you with all this is that we need to answer the question: how can we ensure that the *MoU* we are working towards – the set of conditionalities – become[s] not only politically feasible but [is] combined with a financial arrangement that allows it to breathe . . . so that this Eurogroup is not saddled yet again, in a few months' time, with more crunch meetings like this one.'

5. Nikos Kazantzakis' epitaph reads, 'I hope for nothing. I fear nothing. I am free.' See also the first line of Janice Joplin's 'Me and Bobby McGee'.

6. See 'The Greek Debt Deal's Missing Piece', 15 August 2015, by Landon Thomas Junior: https://www.nytimes.com/2015/08/16/business/international/the-greek-debt-deals-missing-piece.html

Chapter 17: Lions led by donkeys

1. Lord Adair Turner, former head of Britain's Financial Services Authority, had also shared with me, at a meeting in Paris, his fear that Berlin was going to go for Grexit even though it would be a catastrophe for Europe. 'They have convinced themselves they can contain it,' he said.

2. Arendt used to say that she met Martin Heidegger in the German language.

3. The first pro-troika rally took place in Syntagma Square on 18 June, while I was in Brussels at one of the many Eurogroup meetings. A good ten to fifteen thousand people gathered, making Alexis and the rest of us feel uneasy.

4. My mother, Eleni Tsaggaraki-Varoufaki, served as a local councillor and deputy mayor of the Palaio Phaliro Municipality for twenty years or so. She had indeed been responsible for the management of the local facilities, including orphanages, that were converted into shelters for young and old people.

5. 62.5 per cent was a very high turnout given that no postal or remote voting was permitted.

6. His precise words were so offensive that I do not reproduce them here.

7. The executed men were held responsible for the rout of the Greek army and the sacking of ethnic Greek cities, villages and communities by the army of Kemal Atatürk and Turkish irregulars, eradicating all Greeks from Asia Minor, where they had lived since Homer's time. Hundreds of thousands died and even more flooded into mainland Greece as refugees. A *coup d'état* ensued in Greece, and a military tribunal was convened at which the political and military leaders of the disastrous campaign were found guilty of high treason.

8. In response to the media frenzy that followed my revelation, I published an explanation of the thinking behind my parallel payments system in the *Financial Times*: 'Something is rotten in the Eurozone kingdom', 28 July 2015: https://www.ft.com/content/27db9c44-3483-11e5-bdbb-35e55cbae175

9. See Chapter 2, '"National traitor" – the origins of a quaint charge'.

10. This is not my comparison. I owe it to someone who appeared on a BBC television discussion programme who said, 'Saying that Varoufakis is responsible for Greece's economic woes is like saying Dunkirk was responsible for World War II.'

Epilogue

1. That annotated version of the August 2015 *MoU* can be found at: https://www.yanisvaroufakis.eu/wp-content/uploads/2015/08/mou-annotated-by-yv.pdf

2. This was the inaugural Europe Lecture of the University of Western Sydney, which I delivered on 23 October 2013 at the New South Wales State Library, Sydney. The entire text can be read at: https://www.yanisvaroufakis.eu/2013/10/25/the-dirty-war-for-europes-integrity-and-soul-europe-inaugural-public-lecture-uws-state-library-of-new/. An audio recording made by ABC Radio's *Big Ideas* programme can be heard at: http://www.abc.net.au/radionational/programs/bigideas/the-dirty-war-for-europee28099s-integrity-and-soul/6261534

3. See 'Positive affect as coercive strategy' by Lynne Friedli and Robert Stearn: http://mh.bmj.com/content/41/1/40

4. The complete transcript is available on the Wikileaks website: https://wikileaks.org/imf-internal-20160319/

5. 'Let the victims' heads turn towards Erebus [the deep darkness]: / We who had nothing will teach them tranquillity. / Let them not forget us.' From a poem entitled 'Mythistorima' in George Seferis, *Poems* (1989), Ikaros, Athens (my translation).

Index